WordPerfect 6 for Windows: The Complete Reference

WordPerfect 6 for Windows: The Complete Reference

Allen L. Wyatt
Steve Dyson
Daniel J. Fingerman
Stephen Cobb
Kristy Clason

Osborne **McGraw-Hill**

Berkeley New York St. Louis San Francisco
Auckland Bogotá Hamburg London Madrid
Mexico City Milan Montreal New Delhi Panama City
Paris São Paulo Singapore Sydney
Tokyo Toronto

Osborne **McGraw-Hill**
2600 Tenth Street
Berkeley, California 94710
U.S.A.

For information on translations or book distributors outside of the U.S.A., please write to Osborne McGraw-Hill at the above address.

WordPerfect 6 for Windows: The Complete Reference

1234567890 DOC 9987654

ISBN 0-07-881926-1

Contents at a Glance

Contents

PART TWO
Exploring More Advanced Features

PART THREE

Command Reference

PART FOUR

Appendixes

Acknowledgments

The difficulty in documenting a program as rich and complex as WordPerfect for Windows cannot be overstated. The diversity of the program and the schedule under which both the program and this book were developed introduced challenges which at times seemed insurmountable.

Much of the completion of this book is owed to Martin Wyatt, my brother, who helped meet the challenges and overcome the obstacles. Throughout the development of this book, he played a key role. I wish to thank him and acknowledge his priceless contributions to this edition.

Thanks also go to the folks at Osborne/McGraw-Hill. Their attention to detail and follow-up helped polish the book into its present form.

Thank you, one and all.

—Allen L. Wyatt

Introduction

You are about to discover an exciting new way to create documents on your computer. For several years, WordPerfect has been the best-selling word processor for all types of computers. Now, this word processing giant is available in a new version for Microsoft Windows. Whether you're new to WordPerfect or a seasoned pro, you'll find WordPerfect 6.0 for Windows provides a raft of new features and improved performance that will significantly improve your productivity.

About This Book

It's very likely that you have purchased, or have considered purchasing, the WordPerfect for Windows software. This software program includes a complete reference manual and workbook, and they are good resource materials. With WordPerfect documentation already in your hands, why should you consider purchasing this book, *WordPerfect 6 for Windows: The Complete Reference*? If you like exploring on your own, perhaps you don't need this book. But if you want to quickly become productive with WordPerfect for Windows, consider taking this book home.

Although the title says "Complete Reference," this book is much more than an alphabetical reference list of command names and features. The book also contains useful examples of common applications, with information organized according to task—not by the order of features on a menu tree. Notes and tips are placed throughout the text to help the novice and expert better use the features of WordPerfect for Windows. With few exceptions, each chapter and section is complete; although references to other chapters are provided, you won't need to look through two or more sections to figure out a specific task or application.

Once you are comfortable with WordPerfect for Windows, this book will continue to serve as an excellent reference for command sequences, feature names, and technical material—much of it beyond what you can find in WordPerfect manuals.

How This Book Is Organized

This book is divided into four parts, with chapters for WordPerfect basics, advanced features, a command reference, and technical appendixes. In Part I, "Getting Started with WordPerfect for Windows," Chapters 1 through 3 cover the basics of using WordPerfect with the Windows program. Whether you are a new or experienced Windows user, here you will find useful information about starting the WordPerfect program, typing text and choosing fonts, performing basic editing tasks, and saving and printing your documents.

In Part II, "Exploring More Advanced Features," you'll find information about the intermediate to advanced features of WordPerfect for Windows. Much of the information is presented with practical applications, rather than as reference material. Chapter 4, "Managing Files with WordPerfect," covers the use of the built-in file management tools which WordPerfect puts at your disposal. In Chapter 5, "Working with Your Printer," you'll find detailed information about setting up and using your printer with WordPerfect; this chapter also includes troubleshooting tips to solve problems with printing. Chapter 6, "Merge Applications," discusses the Merge feature, with practical examples for form letters, mass mailing, and other types of business documents. Also included in Chapter 6 is a discussion of the programmable merge applications and a complete reference of all merge commands.

Chapter 7, "Desktop Publishing with WordPerfect for Windows," explains how to use the graphics and font features to create documents suitable for printing. In Chapter 8, "Applications for Macros," you'll learn how to use the macro features to automate applications and procedures that you perform on a regular basis. Chapter 9, "Spreadsheet and Database Files," explains how to integrate spreadsheet and database files with your WordPerfect documents, using the linking capabilities of WordPerfect and Microsoft Windows. Finally, Chapter 10, "Using WordPerfect for Windows on a Network," provides you with the information you need to effectively use WordPerfect on your office network. This chapter is particularly appropriate for network managers.

Part III, "Command Reference," consists of a single chapter. Chapter 11, "Commands and Features," provides an alphabetical summary list of every menu, command, option, and capability of WordPerfect. Each entry is defined and described, and where appropriate, examples, hints, and warnings regarding use of the option are given. Many commands are cross-referenced to related entries both in Chapter 11 and in other chapters in the book. Note that the entries in this chapter are not only tied to menu choices and functions, but also to common tasks which you may want to perform.

Part IV, "Appendixes," contains five appendixes with additional information about the WordPerfect for Windows program. Appendix A, "Installing Windows and WordPerfect," quickly covers the installation of Microsoft Windows and the WordPerfect program. Appendix B, "WordPerfect Keyboards," serves as a reference of all WordPerfect 6.0 for Windows keystroke commands and the optional keyboard layouts included with WordPerfect. Appendix C, "WordPerfect Codes," contains a complete list of all WordPerfect formatting codes, including the commands required to insert each of the codes into your documents. In Appendix D, "Graphics Programs and Files," you'll find information about the graphics files you can retrieve into your WordPerfect documents, as well as conversion information for the graphics programs that create them. Finally, Appendix E provides a complete icon reference which you can use to quickly understand what each icon in WordPerfect 6.0 for Windows means.

Conventions Used in This Book

In this book, the following symbols and font attributes are used in the text to indicate an action or procedure for the reader.

- **Boldfaced text** indicates text that you should type from the keyboard.

- Keyboard commands, shortcut keys, and function keys are printed in small capital letters, like this: ENTER, BACKSPACE, F12, and ESC.
- When two or more keys should be pressed simultaneously, they are joined by a plus sign. For example, "Press SHIFT+F7" means to hold down the SHIFT key and press F7.
- In WordPerfect 6.0 for Windows, most menu options, commands, and buttons have a mnemonic letter that you can press to select the item. These mnemonics appear in this book as underlined letters in the option names.
- Menu items appear in the text as they do on the screen. When a sequence of menu selections is required, menu items are separated with forward slashes. For example, to save a document, you are instructed to choose File/Save. This indicates that you must first choose File from the menu bar, to display the File menu, and then choose the Save option from the list of menu items.

REFERENCE

PART ONE

Getting Started with WordPerfect for Windows

CHAPTER 1

Windows and WordPerfect

Before you can effectively use WordPerfect 6.0 for Windows, you must know something about Microsoft Windows. This chapter explains how to use the Windows environment, organize the Windows desktop, and start the WordPerfect program. In addition, you will learn the basic parts of the WordPerfect for Windows screen—what they are and how they work. In short, this chapter provides the groundwork you will need to make the best use of the information in the rest of this book.

If you have never used Windows before, this chapter should be considered mandatory reading. You should realize, however, that only the basics are covered here. Several comprehensive reference manuals are available for the Windows program alone, including *The Microsoft Windows User's Guide* that came with your Windows software, and *Windows 3.1: The Complete Reference, Second Edition* by Tom Sheldon (Berkeley: Osborne/McGraw-Hill, 1993).

If you are already familiar with Microsoft Windows, you may want to skip this chapter and proceed directly to Chapter 2, "WordPerfect for Windows Basics," but do read the introduction to WordPerfect for Windows included later in this chapter.

This chapter assumes that you are working with Windows 3.1. If you are using another version instead, you may find minor differences between your version of Windows and the software described here.

What Is Windows?

Microsoft Windows simplifies many computing tasks and provides powerful features to help you use your computer more effectively. With Windows you can manage different applications in a fashion similar to shuffling and stacking physical documents on your desk. In fact, the main Windows screen is called the *desktop*, to reflect how programs and files are managed in the Windows environment.

True to its name, the Windows program displays software applications and files in special frames called *windows*. A window could be compared to a drawer in a filing cabinet, where files and applications are stored together in various groups. As with the filing cabinet, before you can access the files and data contained in the window, you must first open it. Some windows can be *nested* within other windows, which means that when you open one window, there may be other windows inside that can also be opened.

Although some predefined windows and applications are installed with the Windows program, you can add, remove, and organize the windows as you wish. Most software programs written for MS-DOS computers may be added to the Windows desktop, but only those programs designed for Windows can take full advantage of all the features of this environment. Software programs are called *applications*. An application is started by opening the window in which it is found, and then selecting it from the icons contained within that window. *Icons* are pictures that represent software programs and file folders. You can open as many windows as you need to work with different programs and files. You can even exchange text and graphics between applications with the Windows *Clipboard*—an area of memory reserved for storing information. The number of windows you can open depends on whether you have enough memory in your computer to run the applications at the same time.

Each software program written for Windows, including WordPerfect, follows a common Windows design called an *interface.* This means that programs using this interface all use similar keystroke assignments and feature names. Program features are accessed through a clever system of menus, icons, and button controls. Once you understand the basic system, each new program becomes easier to learn.

Perhaps the most obvious advantage of Windows is that it uses a graphical display to show what you'll get on paper. Programs designed for Windows usually display text, fonts, illustrations, and tables on the screen as they will appear in your printed documents. The graphical interface also extends beyond the printed page to make each program easier to use. Instead of keyboard commands and multilevel menus, push buttons and controls appear on the screen to automate most repetitive tasks.

Finally, Windows manages the resources of your computer system, including the system memory; screen display; and communications with attached printers, networks, and other peripherals. This type of control is necessary to integrate the operation of the programs that run under Windows and allows your computer to work with several applications at once.

Getting Started with Windows

Microsoft Windows is an important addition to your system because it offers a standard environment for your programs. If this is your first experience with Windows, the menus, controls, and options may seem a bit overwhelming. Be patient, and give yourself some time to learn about the Windows environment. This is important because many of the keystrokes, commands, and procedures established by Microsoft Windows are also used by WordPerfect. You must install and start the Microsoft Windows program before you can use WordPerfect for Windows.

Starting the Windows Program

If you have not yet installed the Windows program on your hard disk, refer to Appendix A, "Installing Windows and WordPerfect," before continuing here.

During Windows installation, you were asked if you wanted the installation program to modify your CONFIG.SYS and AUTOEXEC.BAT files; if you allowed the program to make the necessary modifications, it added commands to your

AUTOEXEC.BAT file that automatically loads the Windows program whenever you start your computer.

If you chose not to modify your AUTOEXEC.BAT file during Windows installation, you can start the Windows program directly from the DOS prompt. First, change to the directory where the Windows program is stored. If, for example, you accepted the standard directory name when you installed the Windows program, you would type at the DOS prompt,

```
cd\windows
```

and press ENTER. If you installed Windows to a different directory, type **cd** followed by the directory name you used. Then, to start the Windows program, type

```
win
```

and press ENTER at the DOS prompt. You will see the title screen for Microsoft Windows. Then the Windows desktop appears, which will look similar to the screen shown in Figure 1-1.

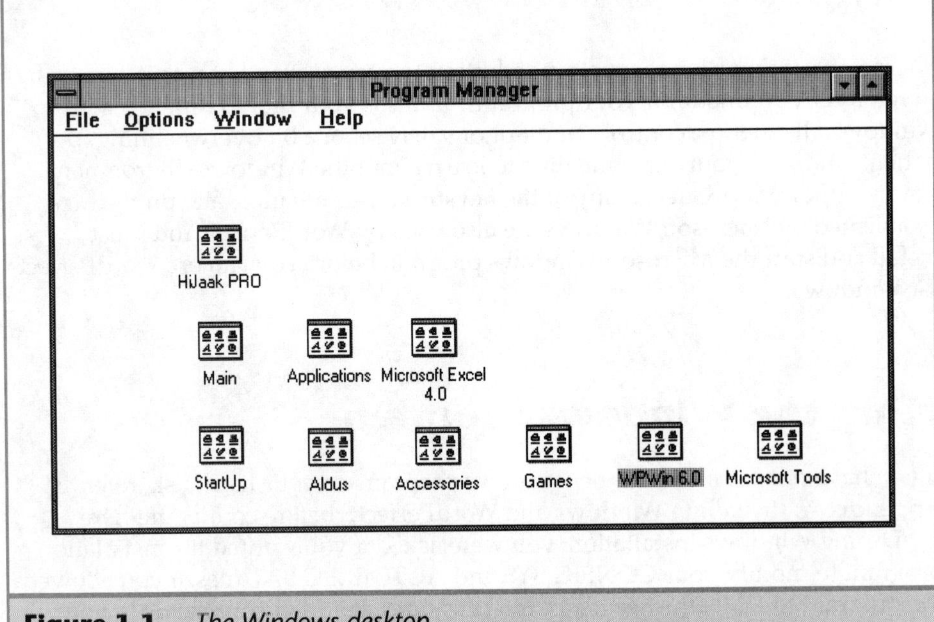

Figure 1-1. *The Windows desktop*

NOTE: If the Windows directory is listed in the PATH command of your AUTOEXEC.BAT file, it is not necessary to change the directory before you start the program. Whenever you attempt to start a program from a directory other than the directory in which the program is stored, your computer will attempt to find the program in the directories listed with the PATH command. You should include the PATH command in your AUTOEXEC.BAT file to specify the directories for all programs running under Windows.

The Windows Desktop

The main screen of the Windows program is called the *desktop*. The first time you start Windows, the Program Manager window appears on the desktop, looking similar to the screen shown in Figure 1-2. The *Program Manager* is the main window from which all other Windows applications are started. Think of it as a circus big top—there may be many things happening at once, but the Program Manager is the main "tent" that surrounds all activity.

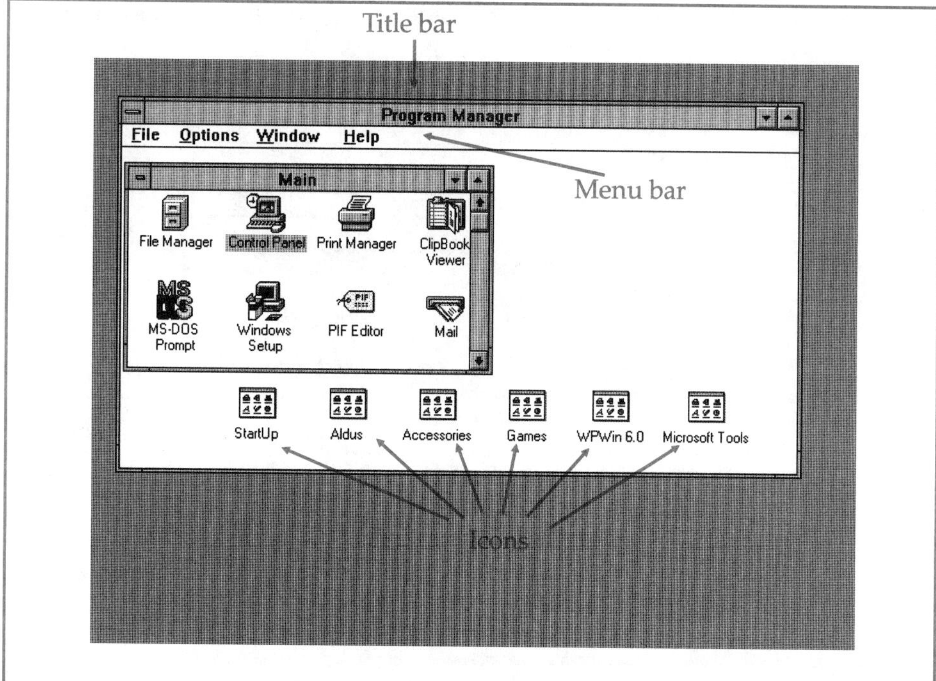

Figure 1-2. *The Program Manager window*

At the top of the Program Manager window, you will see the *title bar*, which identifies the window. Beneath the title bar, you will see the menu bar. The *menu bar* lists features you can choose to manipulate the items inside the Program Manager window. Each application that runs under Windows includes a title bar and a menu bar like those shown on the Program Manager window.

At the bottom of the window, you will see icons that represent groups of programs, which may be started from within the Program Manager. The area inside the window is called the *workspace*, where groups of programs or files may appear.

Types of Windows

As you use Windows, you will discover that there are three different types of windows: group windows, application windows, and document windows. Using the WordPerfect program as an example, Figure 1-3 shows the relationships between the different window types. At the Program Manager, the WordPerfect program files are displayed as icons in a *group window.* When you start or open the WordPerfect program, it is displayed inside an *application window.* Documents

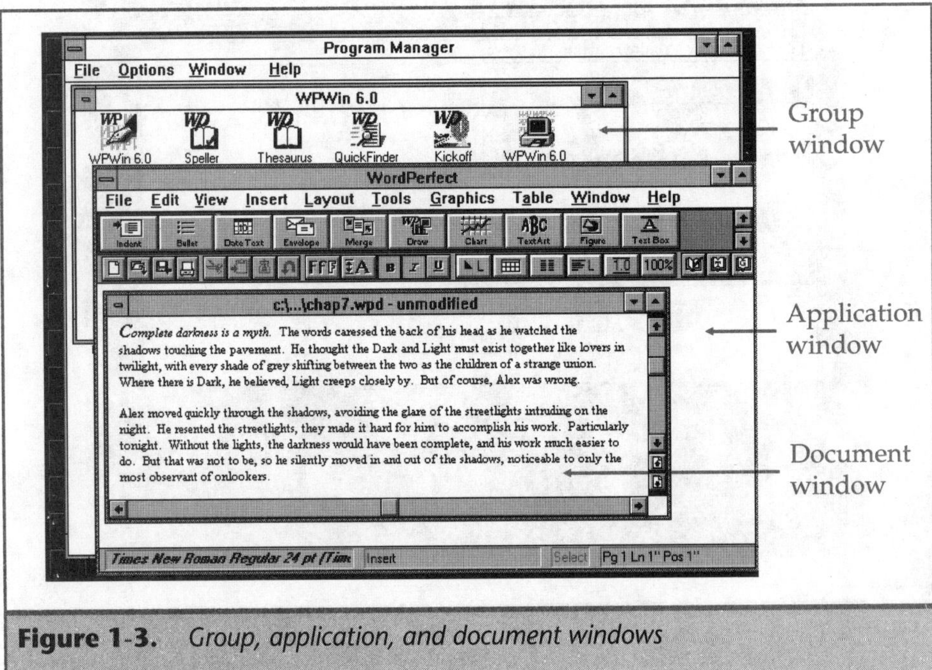

Figure 1-3. *Group, application, and document windows*

that you create or edit with WordPerfect are displayed inside *document windows* within the WordPerfect application window.

Although there are differences between the window types, each can be sized and placed anywhere within the borders of the active workspace.

Group Windows

A group window contains the icons for a group of related programs or files. Initially, each group appears as an icon in the Program Manager window, as shown here:

Choose a group icon, and the window for that group is opened. Figure 1-4 shows the group icon and window for the game programs included with Microsoft Windows. Icons in the window show which programs and files are included in the group. To start a program, simply choose the appropriate icon from the group window.

The concept of group windows is similar to having different directories for various types of programs and files. For example, you might have one group window for the WordPerfect program files, one for your spreadsheet and accounting programs, and another group window for graphics programs and files.

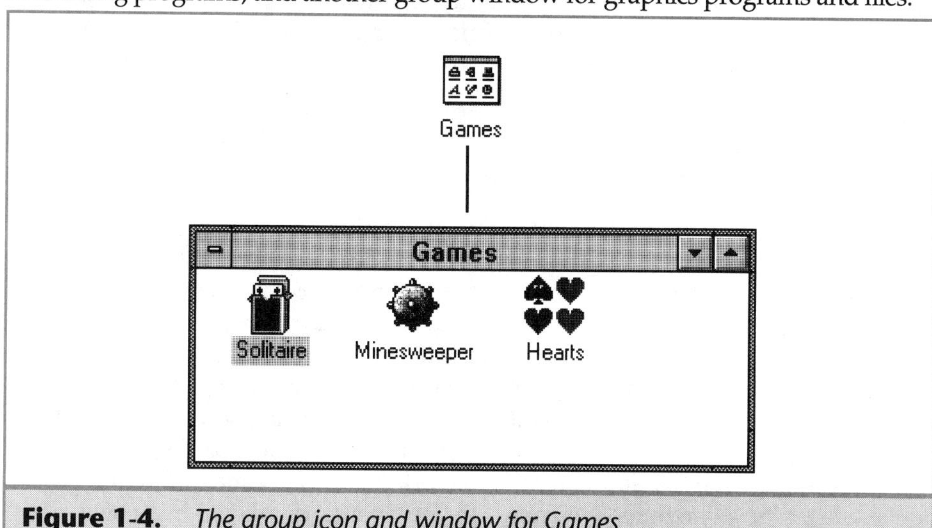

Figure 1-4. *The group icon and window for Games*

Group windows are often defined by the user, but the Windows program has a few that are already created. These include the Main group window, which contains the Windows tools and utility programs, the Accessories group window, which contains the accessory programs that come with Microsoft Windows, and the Startup window, which contains programs you want activated when you first begin Windows. For information about creating your own group windows, see "Organizing Your Desktop" later in this chapter.

Application Windows

Within each group window are application icons, which represent the programs stored in the group. The application window for a program opens when you choose the application icon. Each application window displays the program name in the title bar at the top of the window and a menu bar from which program commands may be selected. For example, the title and menu bars for the Paintbrush program, included with Microsoft Windows, are shown here:

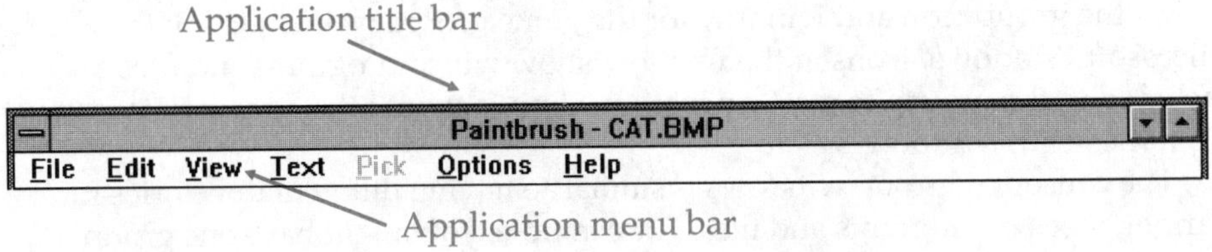

Application windows often fill the entire screen, but you can size and move them anywhere on the desktop. You can also arrange application windows to display two or more different programs and work with several files at once.

Document Windows

Some applications or programs support what is called an MDI, or *multiple document interface.* This means that more than one document can be displayed and edited at once in the program. For programs that support MDI, a new document window is opened for each file you create or retrieve into the program. Figure 1-5 shows the WordPerfect program with a single document window.

The number of document windows you can open at once depends on what the application program allows. WordPerfect 5.1 for DOS lets you work with two documents at once; WordPerfect 6.0 for DOS and WordPerfect 6.0 for Windows take this a step further by allowing you to work with up to nine different documents at the same time. Each new file you open is displayed in its own

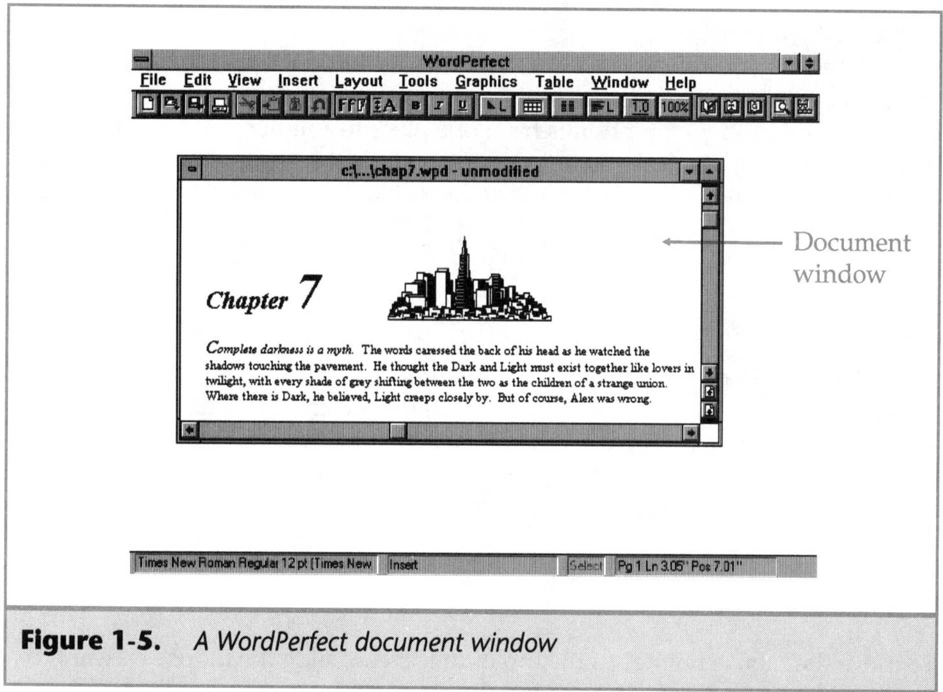

Figure 1-5. *A WordPerfect document window*

document window, inside the WordPerfect application window. In Chapter 3, "Tools and Techniques," you'll see how to open and arrange document windows in WordPerfect.

Using the Mouse

Before you start working with Windows, you need to become familiar with an important accessory called the *mouse*. If you don't already have one for your computer, consider buying one soon. With the mouse, you can easily select and manipulate text, choose menu options, and resize the windows on your screen. These tasks are not easy to perform with the keyboard—and certainly not as much fun as with the mouse.

NOTE: Although it is possible to use only keyboard commands when working with most Windows programs, this is not recommended. However, there are several keystrokes that are useful, regardless of whether or not you are using a mouse. For more information, see "Tips for the Keyboard User" later in this chapter.

The Mouse Pointer

The mouse is a *pointing device*—a tool for placing a cursor on the screen, choosing different items, and moving things from one place to another. When you move the mouse across your desk, the movement controls the position on the screen of a marker, called the *mouse pointer*, which looks like this:

The mouse pointer is used to select something on the desktop, such as a menu item, a filename, or a control button on the screen. If you have never used a mouse before, it might seem a bit awkward at first. This is a common adjustment for die-hard keyboard users.

Moving the Mouse

To move the mouse pointer to the top of the screen, slide the mouse forward, or away from you, on the desk. To move the mouse pointer left or right on the screen, slide the mouse left or right. Slide the mouse backward, or closer to you, and the mouse pointer moves down toward the bottom of the screen. These are just the basic directions, but any movement will work. Try moving the mouse diagonally or in a spiral motion—the mouse pointer will duplicate the mouse's movement exactly. Remember to keep your eyes on the mouse pointer, not on the mouse.

When you run out of desk space, simply pick up the mouse and move it to a free space on the desk; the pointer on the screen will stay in place until you set the mouse down and resume moving it. If this is new to you, don't worry; it will soon become second nature.

Some users might prefer a track ball, which is similar to a mouse except it follows the motion of a ball held in a stationary base.

The I-Beam and Hourglass

As you work within the Windows environment, the mouse pointer will change, depending on its location on the screen and the program function. When the mouse pointer is located within a window where text can be typed, it becomes an *I-beam* (also called the *selection cursor*), which looks like the following:

The I-beam lets you position a text cursor, called the *insertion point*, for typing or inserting text. You will see the I-beam cursor and the insertion point in WordPerfect's document workspace.

Sometimes the active program needs to perform a certain task before you can continue working. In this case, the mouse pointer will change to an hourglass, like this:

When the hourglass appears, this usually means that either Windows or WordPerfect is accessing your hard disk to save or retrieve information. When you see the hourglass, think of it as a "Please Wait" message. After a moment or two, it will change back to the mouse pointer or I-beam, and you can continue working with the program.

When you use graphics programs, the mouse pointer may appear as a cross-hair cursor to make drawing tasks easier to perform. The cross-hair cursor does not appear in WordPerfect, but you will see it in the Paintbrush program included with Microsoft Windows.

Choosing with the Mouse

To select and choose different items on the screen, move the mouse pointer onto a menu item or icon. Then press and release the left button on your mouse.

For example, suppose you want to select and display the File menu from the Program Manager menu bar–simply move the mouse pointer onto the word "File" and use your index finger to quickly press and release the mouse button. When you do so, the File menu is displayed.

This "press and release" action is called a *click*. Generally, a click selects the item indicated by the mouse pointer. In some cases, you can click the mouse button twice, called a *double-click*, to select an item and perform an action.

Throughout this book, the terms "click" and "double-click" are used to indicate how you should select or choose an item on the screen. When you are instructed to click something, move the mouse pointer or I-beam to the item and click the mouse button once. If you are instructed to double-click something, move the pointer to the item and quickly click the mouse button twice.

The Windows program initially recognizes the left mouse button for right-handed users. For left-handed users, you can swap the button assignments at the Windows Control Panel (a program available from Windows' Main group), and use the right mouse button instead. For more information about changing this and other mouse settings, see "Customizing the Windows Program" in Chapter 3, "Tools and Techniques."

Dragging the Mouse Pointer

Sometimes, you will want to move the mouse pointer through a list of menu items until you reach the option you want to choose. This is called *dragging* the mouse pointer and is accomplished by holding down the mouse button while moving the mouse.

For example, you can drag through the items on the menu bar by placing the mouse pointer on one of the menu items: hold down the mouse button—don't release it—and then move the pointer across the menu bar labels. As you drag the mouse pointer across the menu bar, each of the menus is displayed.

While holding down the mouse button, you can move the pointer into any of the menus to highlight, or *select*, the menu options. When the mouse button is released, you choose the item that is currently highlighted. If you do not want to choose an item, move the mouse pointer off the displayed menus until nothing is highlighted; then release the mouse button.

Generally, you drag the mouse to browse through pull-down menus, but this action is also used to move items on the screen.

Starting Programs

The Program Manager is the window from which all programs and applications are started. To start an application, open the group window where the application is stored, and then choose the desired program icon. When working with group windows and applications, you can use options on the Program Manager's File menu to open or close a group window. However, the quickest way to open a window or start an application is by double-clicking the icon that represents the item you want to use. For applications that are not listed on the Windows desktop, you can use the Run command (see "Using the Run Option" later in this chapter) to start programs.

Starting a Windows Application

Before you can start an application, you need to open the group window where the application is found. To open a group window, simply move the mouse pointer onto the corresponding group icon, and double-click the mouse. Then, double-click the icon of the application you want to use.

For example, suppose you want to use the Windows Calculator program; this is stored in the Accessories group window. First, move the mouse pointer onto the Accessories group icon, which is displayed at the bottom of the Program Manager window.

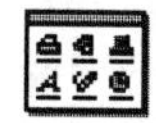

Double-click the mouse button and the Accessories window appears, similar to the screen in Figure 1-6. Then, double-click the icon for the Calculator application, as shown here:

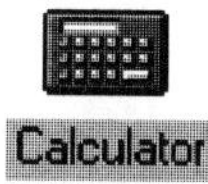

Double-clicking is the easiest way to open a group window or application, but it requires a fast hand. If you click too slowly, Windows recognizes only the first click and the icon is highlighted or selected but not opened. With a single click, a menu pops up next to the group icon; this is the control menu, which provides options for manipulating the group or application.

If you prefer to use the menu bar, you can click an icon once to select it. Then click the File option once from the menu bar and choose Open. This has the same effect as double-clicking to open a group window or application.

Closing an Application

Each window has a *control menu*, which lists options for moving, sizing, and closing the window. The control menu appears as a symbol in the upper-left corner of every window, as shown in the following illustration.

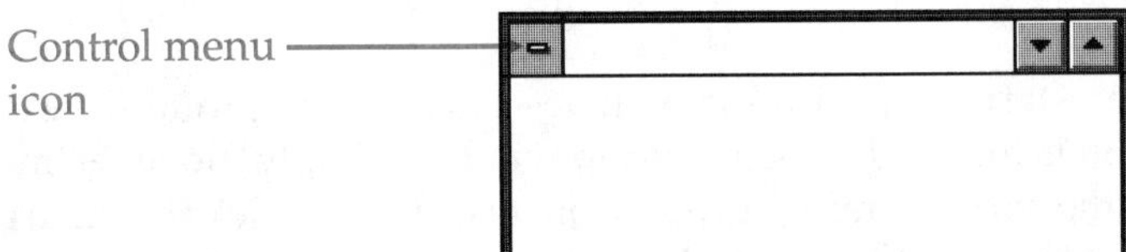

To close an application or group window, simply move the mouse pointer onto the control menu symbol and double-click the mouse button. Again, if you click too slowly, the options for the control menu will appear in a pop-up list.

If you prefer to work with menus, you can close the current window by clicking the control menu symbol once and then clicking Close from the list of options. When you close an application, the Program Manager (or previous window) is redisplayed.

NOTE: The other options on the control menu are explained later in this chapter under the headings "Sizing and Moving Windows" and "Tips for the Keyboard User."

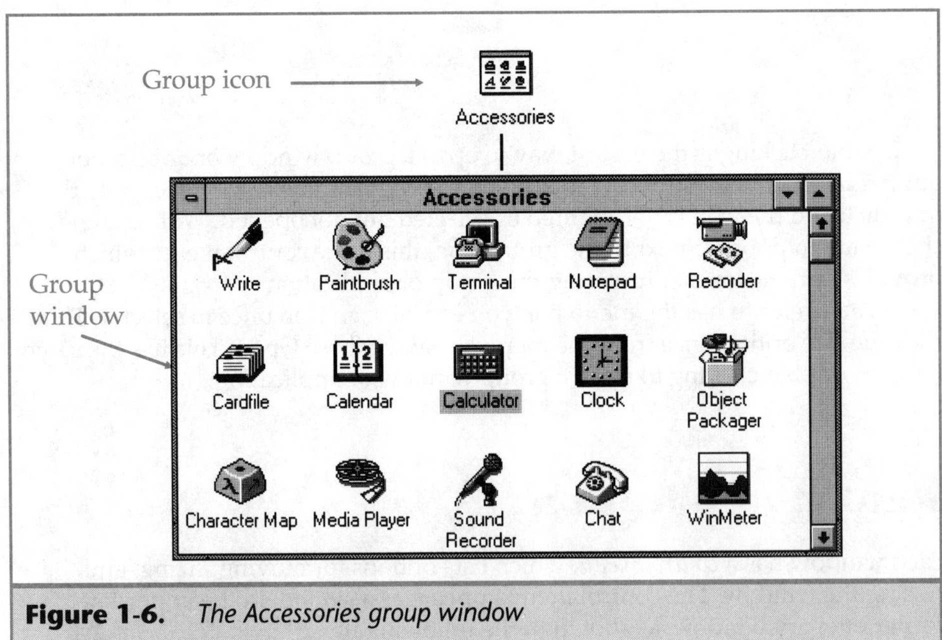

Figure 1-6. *The Accessories group window*

Using the Run Option

From the Program Manager window, you can use the Run command to execute programs that are not shown as icons on the desktop. This command is useful for programs such as DOS batch files and utility programs, which may not be installed as permanent applications. Run also helps you start programs, like installation and utility programs, that set up programs for use with Windows.

To use the Run command, click the File option from the Program Manager menu bar; then click the Run option. This menu, called a *dialog box*, appears:

Run

Command Line:

Run Minimized

OK

Cancel

Browse...

Help

Type the name of the program you want to run, and then click the OK button to start the program. If, for example, you would like to start a batch file called FILELIST.BAT, choose File/Run from the Program Manager menu bar; then type

```
filelist.bat
```

and click the OK button in the dialog box. If the batch file is stored in a directory other than the default directory, precede the filename with the full path name.

When the batch file or program has finished running, the Windows screen is redisplayed with the Program Manager. You can use the Run command to start any program that can be run from the Windows desktop.

Sizing and Moving Windows

Each window displayed on the screen has control points that let you size or move the window. Sizing and moving allow you to rearrange the placement of applications on the screen, which is similar to the way you would move file folders around on your desk.

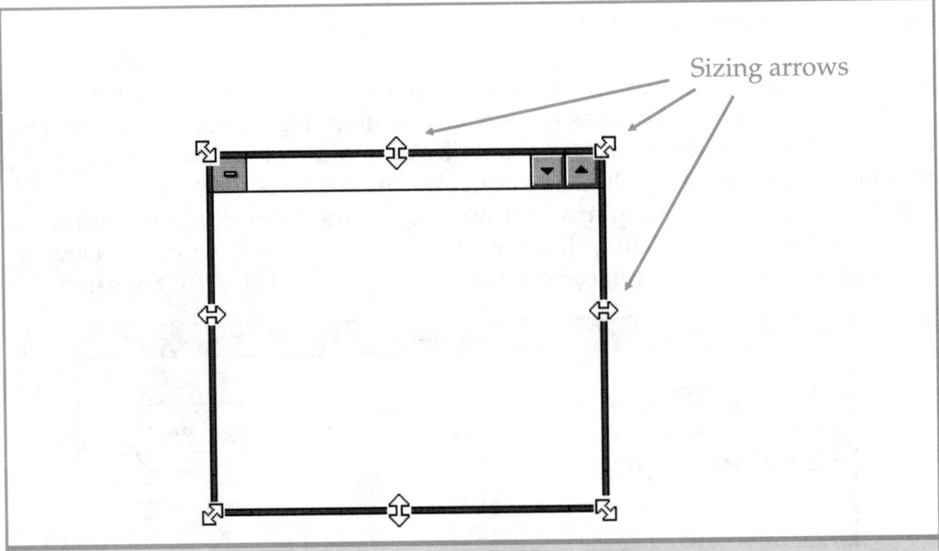

Figure 1-7. *The mouse pointer changes to arrows for sizing*

Changing the Window Size

Windows applications have standard window sizes for each application and group; some windows are small, while others fill the entire screen. For most applications, you can change the size of a window by dragging a side or corner of the window's border. You do this with the mouse pointer.

When you move the mouse pointer over a side or corner of the border, the mouse pointer changes to a sizing arrow. Figure 1-7 shows the sizing arrows that can appear along the edges of the border.

For example, if you move the mouse pointer to the lower-right corner of a window's border, the mouse pointer changes to this:

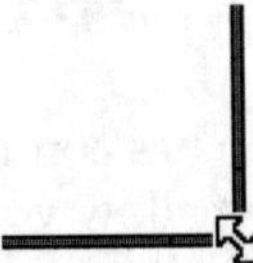

If you move the mouse pointer onto the left or right edge of the border, it changes to the following:

To size a window, move the mouse pointer onto a side or corner of the border until the mouse pointer changes to one of the sizing arrows. Then, hold down the mouse button and drag the side or corner to resize the window border. When you release the mouse button, the contents of the window may shrink or expand to fill the new frame.

Drag the top or bottom border, and you change the window's height; drag the left or right edge, and you change the width of the window. Drag a corner, and you change both the height and the width of the window.

Moving Windows and Icons

You can easily move windows by dragging them to another place on the screen. First, position the mouse pointer on the title bar of the window you want to move; then, hold down the mouse button and move the mouse pointer to the new location. As you move the mouse you will see an outline of the window, which helps you position it correctly on the screen. When the outline is where you want the window to be, release the mouse button, and the window is moved to the new location.

You can also move any of the icons displayed inside the windows. Simply move the mouse pointer onto the icon you want to move, hold down the mouse button, and drag the icon to a new place in the window—or even to a different opened window. When you release the mouse button, the icon is transferred to the new location.

Using the Maximize and Minimize Buttons

At the upper-right corner of each window are two buttons that let you instantly change the size of the window. These are called the *maximize* and *minimize buttons,* which are shown in the following illustration:

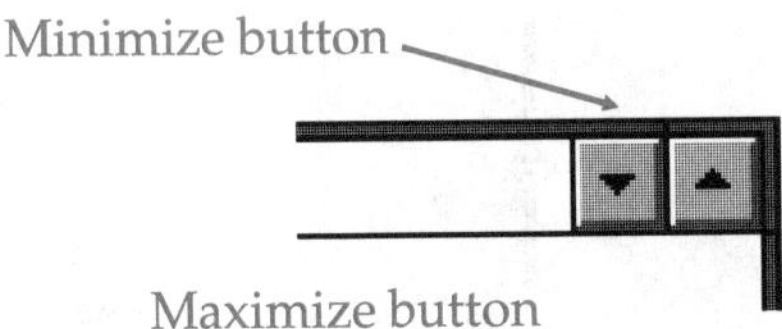

Click on the maximize button, and the active window expands to fill the entire window that surrounds it. If the active window is an application window, the maximize button expands the application to fill the entire screen.

When a window is maximized, the maximize/mimimize buttons change to the restore button, which looks like this:

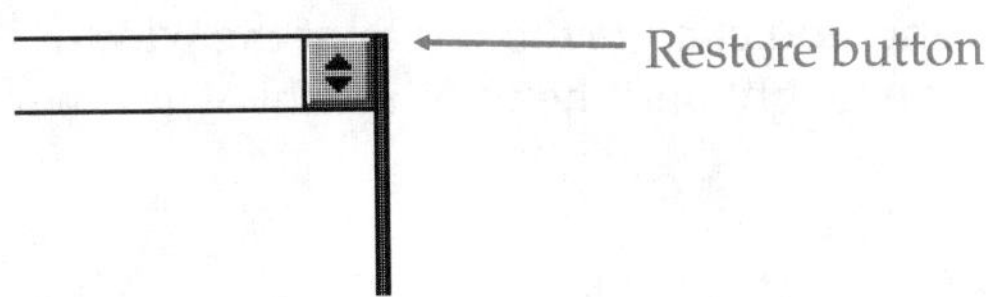

When the restore button appears, it indicates that the window or application is now maximized. Click on the restore button and the window returns to the original size, before it was maximized.

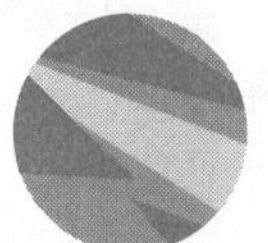

NOTE: When you maximize a WordPerfect window, its border disappears and the window cannot be sized. Use the restore button to restore the window, and the border will reappear.

Click on the minimize button, and the active window or application "shrinks" to an icon at the bottom of the screen. This is called *minimizing* an application. Although this may seem to close the window, it merely reduces the application to an icon to help clear the workspace. The application is still open and active. Double-click the icon, and the application appears as it did before you minimized it.

When an application is minimized, its icon appears outside the borders of the Program Manager, assuming that the Program Manager window does not fill the entire screen. The minimized icon reminds you that the application is still running in the background. A duplicate icon for the application may appear inside the group window within the Program Manager, similar to the screen shown in Figure 1-8. Don't be confused by this. The icons inside the group window show which applications may be started, but the group window provides no clue as to which of these programs are currently running. The program icons displayed outside the Program Manager are applications that are now running but have been minimized. Double-click a minimized program icon, and the program is restored to the screen.

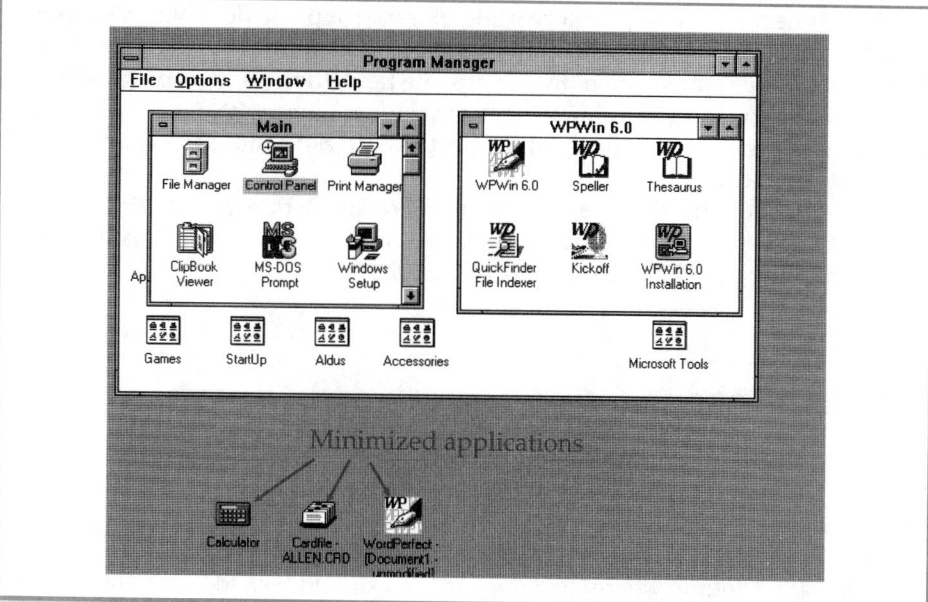

Figure 1-8. *Minimized applications appear as icons outside the Program Manager*

Organizing Your Desktop

The Windows program gives you the power to organize the desktop as you wish. You can arrange applications with the predefined windows, or you can create your own group windows for different applications and files. Once you have the group windows you need, you can easily add or remove programs and even move program items between group windows.

Creating a Group Window

To create a new group window, choose File/New from the Program Manager menu bar. A dialog box appears and prompts you to indicate whether you are creating a new program group or a program item. Click the Program Group option, and then click the OK button. The Program Group Properties dialog box appears. Click the Description field and type the name that should appear in the title bar for the new group window.

It is not necessary to type information in the Group File field; this is simply the name of the file on disk where the group window information will be stored. If you do not type a filename in the Group File field, the Windows program will create one for you by combining the group window name with a .GRP filename extension. Unless you specify a path name, the GRP file is stored in your Windows directory.

Click the OK button to accept the information and a new group window is created. Because it is a new window, it will be empty when it is first displayed, but you can easily add program items to the group.

Adding an Item to the Group Window

Each window includes icons that represent program items (applications) and files. You can add program items to a group window with the File/New option on the Program Manager menu bar.

Before you can add items to a window, the window must be open and active. First, click the window where the program item should be added; this highlights the title bar and activates the window. Then, choose File/New from the Program Manager menu bar. A dialog box appears and prompts you to indicate whether you are creating a new program group or a program item. Click the Program Item option, and then click the OK button. The Program Item Properties dialog box appears. Click the Description field and type the name that should appear below the program icon that will appear in the group window. Click the Command Line field and type the path name and filename of the program that this item will represent. When you are done, click the OK button, and the program you specified is added to the group window. You can start the new program as you would any application displayed in a group window.

When you add a new program item, it should be a program designed to run under Microsoft Windows. If it is a non-Windows program, such as WordPerfect for DOS, you may need to create a *program information file* (PIF). A PIF file contains information that helps Windows work with a non-Windows program. For more information on running non-Windows programs, see *The Microsoft Windows User's Guide*.

Removing a Program Item or Group Window

To remove an icon from a group window, click once to highlight the icon, and then choose File/Delete from the Program Manager menu bar. You are asked to verify that you want to delete the program item. Click the OK button, and the program icon is removed from the group window.

You can also delete a group window from the desktop. First click the title bar of the group window you want to delete. Then, choose File/Delete from the Program Manager menu bar. You are prompted about deleting the window. Click the OK button, and the window is removed from the desktop. When you delete a group window, the corresponding group file is also deleted from your Windows directory.

If you are having difficulties managing your windows or groups, you can always access a program or group from the Windows pull-down menu at the top of the screen.

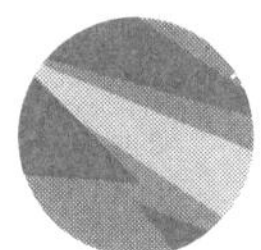

NOTE: *When you remove a program item from Windows, the actual program files on the disk are not deleted. If you want to remove them, you will need to use the File Manager to delete the files from your disk. For more information on this process, see* Windows 3.1: The Complete Reference, Second Edition *by Tom Sheldon (Berkeley: Osborne/McGraw-Hill, 1993).*

Starting WordPerfect for Windows

WordPerfect's Installation program creates a WordPerfect group window within the Program Manager. To start WordPerfect, open the WordPerfect group window and double-click the WordPerfect program icon. The standard icon looks like this:

After you double-click the program icon, the mouse pointer changes to an hourglass, indicating that you must wait while the program is loading into your computer's memory.

If the program icon for WordPerfect is not shown on the Windows desktop, you can start WordPerfect with the Run command. From the Program Manager, choose File/Run from the menu bar, and the Run dialog box appears in the middle of the screen. At this dialog box, you can type the path and filename of the program you want to start. Click the Command Line field and type

```
c:\wpwin60\wpwin
```

If WordPerfect for Windows is installed in a different directory, type the correct path name instead of C:\WPWIN60\. Then click the OK button, and Windows starts the WordPerfect program.

The WordPerfect Display

When you start WordPerfect, your screen display will look similar to the screen in Figure 1-9. Following the design of other Windows programs, the WordPerfect screen includes a *title bar*, menu bar, button bar, and *power bar* at the top of the window, control menus, maximize and minimize buttons, and *scroll bars* for displaying pages of text. At the bottom of the screen is the *status bar*, which displays document information and program messages. The area where you type text and create your documents is called the *document workspace*.

In the document workspace, you will see a blinking vertical bar, called the *insertion point*; this is where new information will be inserted when you type text

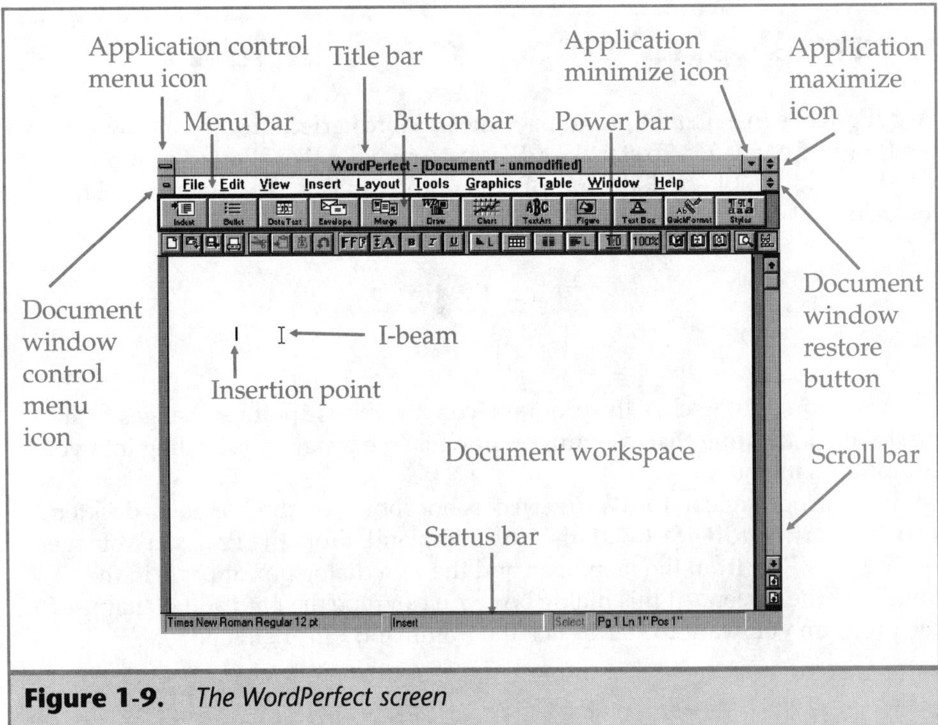

Figure 1-9. *The WordPerfect screen*

or choose formatting commands. (For non-Windows programs, this is commonly known as the *cursor*.)

Title Bar

The title bar displays the name of the WordPerfect program. When two or more windows are open, the title bar of the active window is highlighted. The title bar can also display the name of the current document on your screen.

As described earlier in this chapter, you can size the window that contains WordPerfect and then drag the title bar to move the WordPerfect application window and adjust its position on the screen.

In WordPerfect for Windows, the title bar also does double duty as the quick help area. This comes into play as you move the mouse cursor over the different tools or menus on your screen. As you do this, a one-line help prompt appears where the title bar normally appears. When you move the mouse cursor away from the menus or tools, the regular title bar is again displayed.

Menu Bar

The menu bar lists category names for the WordPerfect commands and features. To display the menu for a category, move the mouse pointer onto one of the names on the menu bar, and click the mouse button once. A menu appears beneath the name. To select a feature, click one of the options displayed in the menu.

Keyboard users can press and release the ALT key and then press the RIGHT ARROW or LEFT ARROW key to highlight a name on the menu bar. Press DOWN ARROW or ENTER, and the menu is displayed for the highlighted name. Use the arrow keys to move through the menu options; press ENTER, and the highlighted feature is selected.

Button Bar

The button bar contains a group of buttons that allows quick access to commands, macros, and other features of WordPerfect. There are 12 predefined button bars that group related commands and features together. These button bars can help you quickly produce professional-looking documents. In addition, the button bar is fully customizeable. This means you can add or remove buttons from existing button bars, or design your own button bars. If your button bar is not visible on your screen, choose Button Bar from the View menu.

Power Bar

The power bar is a new feature with WordPerfect 6.0 for Windows. It consists of a series of buttons that appear just below the menu bar. Each of these buttons is used to perform common tasks within WordPerfect. If you are familiar with any other Windows programs, you may know that this type of feature is often called a toolbar.

If you do not see the power bar on your screen, choose Power Bar from the View menu. The power bar should then appear on your screen. The Power Bar menu option is referred to as a *toggle,* meaning you can turn it on or off by repeatedly selecting the option. When a check mark appears next to the option on the menu, then the option is enabled.

There are many functions you can access by using the power bar. These include options to open or retrieve, save, print, and edit your document. In addition, you can quickly access such features as the spelling checker, thesaurus, or other tools. You will learn more about the power bar as you work with WordPerfect for Windows.

Status Bar

The status bar displays important information about the WordPerfect program and the current document. Program messages and prompts are also displayed on the status bar.

At the left edge of the status bar, WordPerfect displays the current text font and, when necessary, program messages. Along the remainder of the status bar, various labels indicate whether select mode or insert mode is enabled. Near the right edge of the status bar, labels tell you where the insertion point is located in the current document. The "Pg" label shows the page location of the insertion point. The "Ln" and "Pos" labels show the vertical and horizontal locations, respectively, of the insertion point on the page.

NOTE: *The measurements on the status bar show where the insertion point is located in your document, but this may not be the page that is currently displayed on your screen. Because of the nature of the Windows program, it is possible to scroll through an entire document without moving the insertion point.*

When you create columns or tables in WordPerfect, additional labels are added to the status bar to indicate which column or cell contains the insertion point. Table 1-1 lists all the labels that may appear at the right edge of the status bar and what they represent in your document.

You can customize the information displayed on the status bar by choosing File/Preferences/Status Bar. For more information on customizing the status bar, see the entry "Status Bar" in Chapter 11, "Commands and Features."

Scroll Bars

At the side of the screen, you will see the vertical scroll bar. This tool helps you scroll through the text of your document. At each end of the bar, you will see an arrow button. Click an arrow button once, and the displayed document moves up or down one line. To scroll through the document, move the mouse pointer onto an arrow button and hold down the mouse button; the displayed document will scroll continuously in the direction of the arrow, until you release the mouse button.

The length of the scroll bar, between the arrow buttons, represents the entire length of the displayed document. Inside the bar you will see a square button called the *slider button* or *scroll box*. As you scroll through your document, the slider button moves to show you the relative location of the displayed page in your document.

You can quickly move to a general area in the document by dragging the slider button to a certain place on the scroll bar. For example, assume the first page of a document is displayed on the screen. You can quickly "jump" to the middle of the document by dragging the slider button to the center of the scroll bar. To drag, move the mouse pointer onto the slider, hold down the mouse button, and move the slider up or down. When you release the mouse button, a new part of the document is displayed. You can also move the slider button by

Label	Location of Insertion Point
Pg	Page number
Ln	Vertical position on page
Pos	Horizontal position on page
Col	Text column number
Cell	Cell location in table

Table 1-1. *Labels*

clicking inside the empty area of the scroll bar, but it is generally easier to drag the button.

It is important to know that the scroll bar does not change the location of the insertion point in your document; it simply allows you to scroll through your document and view the text. If you begin typing text or select a feature from the menu bar, WordPerfect automatically displays the portion of the document where the insertion point is located. If the insertion point does not appear on the displayed page of text, you can easily move it there by clicking anywhere on the text or by pressing one of the arrow keys on your keyboard.

Choosing from the Menu Bar

The commands and features for the WordPerfect program are found on the menu bar. To select a menu item, move the mouse pointer onto the menu name that you want and click the mouse button. This displays a menu of features for the selected category, like this:

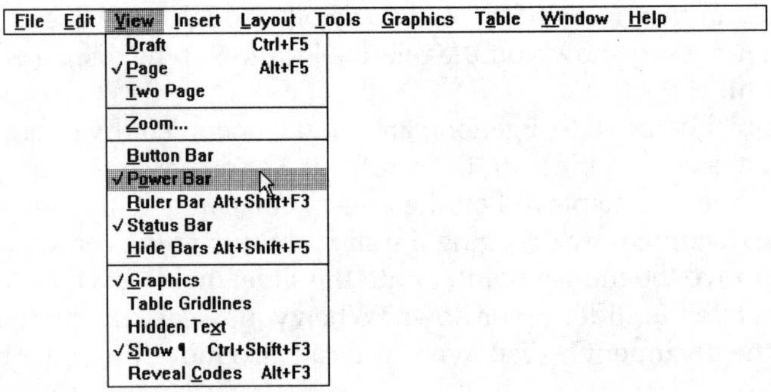

File Edit View Insert Layout Tools Graphics Table Window Help

Draft Ctrl+F5
√ Page Alt+F5
Two Page
Zoom...
Button Bar
√ Power Bar
Ruler Bar Alt+Shift+F3
√ Status Bar
Hide Bars Alt+Shift+F5
√ Graphics
Table Gridlines
Hidden Text
√ Show ¶ Ctrl+Shift+F3
Reveal Codes Alt+F3

From the displayed menu, simply click the feature you want to use. If a feature name on the menu appears grey or shaded, you cannot select this command under the current program situation. For example, the Cut and Copy commands, on the Edit menu, appear grey until you select text to move or copy. After you select a feature, the menu disappears from the screen. If you decide not to make a selection, click or drag the mouse outside of the displayed menu to cancel the operation.

Keyboard users need to perform more steps to select a menu item. First, press and release the ALT key to activate the menu bar. Then, use the arrow keys on the keyboard to highlight the menu name that you want. Press RIGHT ARROW or LEFT

ARROW to highlight the next category on the menu bar; press DOWN ARROW or ENTER to display the menu for a category. Then press DOWN ARROW to highlight one of the features. When the feature you want is highlighted, press ENTER to select it. If you decide not to choose a menu feature, press ESC to cancel the selection, until none of the menu or feature names are highlighted.

For faster access, press ALT to activate the menu bar, and then type the *mnemonic* of the feature you want to choose–this appears as an underlined character in each menu or feature name.

For example, suppose you want to display WordPerfect's File menu with only keystroke commands. First press ALT to activate the menu bar. Press **F** to highlight the File menu, and then press the mnemonic of the feature you want to use. This works for any of the options or features displayed in WordPerfect menus.

Generally, when the insertion point is located at a place where you can type text or enter a formatting measurement, you need to press ALT to activate the menu system for that part of the program. Once the menu is activated, type a mnemonic and you will select a feature.

When a menu is displayed, you will often see other labels or symbols that indicate how the feature is used. Many features listed on the menus have keystrokes assigned to them; you can press the key instead of choosing the feature from the menus. If a feature can be accessed with a keystroke, the keystroke sequence may appear next to the feature name on the menu.

For some menu items, you'll see a triangle displayed next to the item. The triangle means that a submenu will be displayed when you select this item. For example, when you choose Layout/Line from the menu bar, the menu on your screen will look like this:

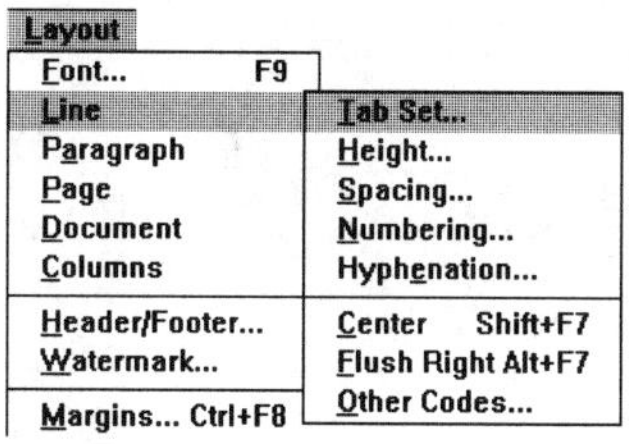

Layout
Font... F9
Line
Paragraph
Page
Document
Columns
Header/Footer...
Watermark...
Margins... Ctrl+F8

Tab Set...
Height...
Spacing...
Numbering...
Hyphenation...
Center Shift+F7
Flush Right Alt+F7
Other Codes...

This is called a *cascading menu,* because it opens a submenu to the right of the main menu. Three dots (ellipses) next to a feature name on the menu means that the menu item displays a dialog box with additional feature options.

Finally, some features like bold text and the formatting ruler are turned either on or off. Earlier in this chapter you learned that these are toggle options. WordPerfect displays a check mark next to the features on the menu that are turned on, like this:

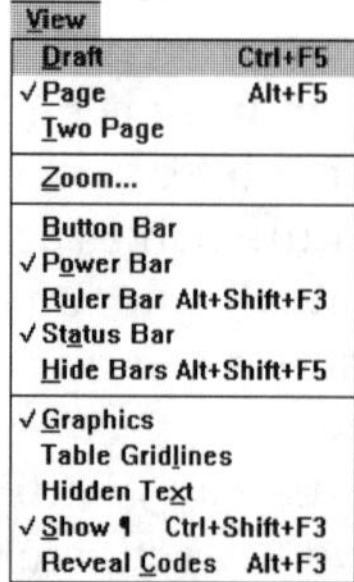

When no check mark appears, it means the feature is turned off. You won't see check marks next to every feature you choose from the menus—only those features that can be turned either on or off will show the check mark to indicate the state of the feature.

Dialog Boxes

When you choose a feature from the menu bar, WordPerfect often displays a dialog box that shows a group of related options. For example, choose Layout/Columns/Define from the menu bar, and this dialog box appears with options for defining text columns:

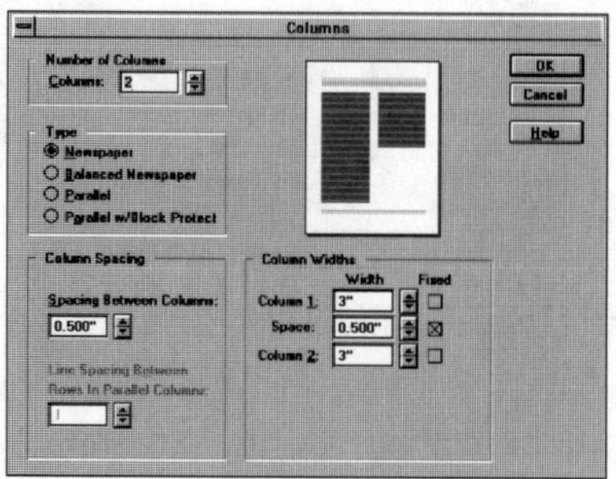

Instead of numbered menu options, the dialog box displays features in different groups, with special controls that let you indicate what you want to do with each feature. These controls include elements called check boxes, radio buttons, text fields, list boxes, pop-up menus, and command buttons. The following sections describe each of the elements that may appear in a dialog box.

NOTE: If you are using the Windows program without a mouse input device, see "Tips for the Keyboard User" later in this chapter for the keystroke commands for dialog boxes.

Check Boxes

Check boxes appear next to certain options to indicate whether features are turned on or off. Here is an example of how check boxes will appear in a dialog box:

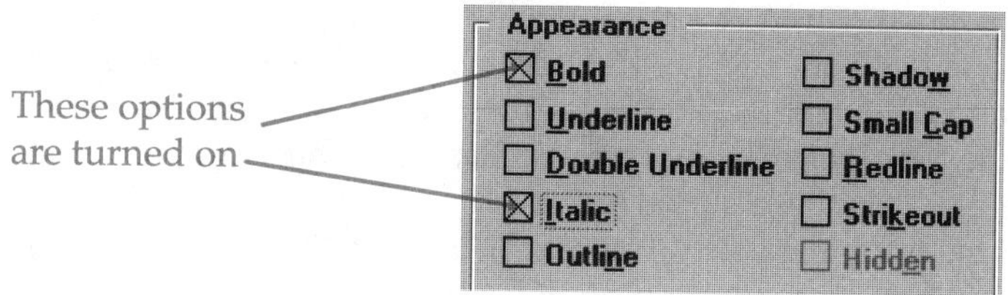

A check box shown with an X means that the feature listed next to the box is active, or turned on. An empty check box indicates that the feature is inactive, or turned off. To turn a feature on or off, click the check box to toggle the current setting. When two or more check box items are shown together in a dialog box, you can turn on one or more of the features at once.

Radio Buttons

Radio buttons appear with a list of features, only one of which can be selected at any given time. For example, when you choose File/Print, the following group box is displayed in a dialog box:

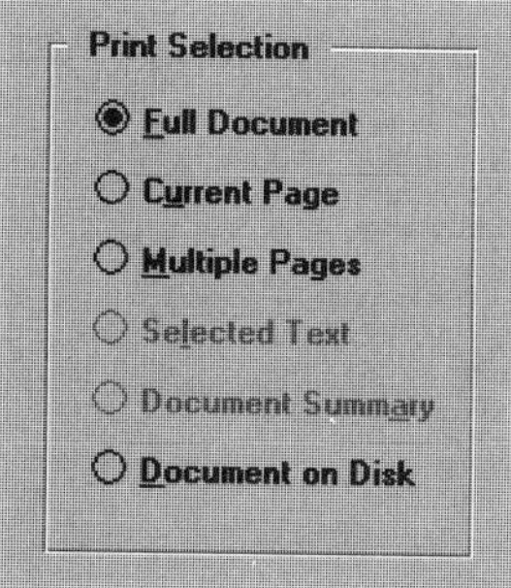

Only one of the radio button options may be selected at a time—just like the tuning buttons on a car radio. The solid circle indicates which of the features on the list is now active. To select a different option, click the button that is next to the feature you want.

Text Fields

In some dialog boxes, you will see blank boxes where you can type measurements for margins, tabs, and other formatting features; or type filenames for saving and retrieving documents. These empty boxes are called *text fields* or *text boxes*.

In this book, the term "text field" describes the place where you type information into a dialog box. This is contrary to the standard Windows term, but because the WordPerfect program also has a graphics feature called Text Box, the new term helps distinguish the two features.

To type something in a dialog box text field, click the field with the mouse. A blinking vertical bar—the insertion point—appears in the text field. Type the text for the field and, if necessary, change other settings in the dialog box. Then, click the OK button to accept what you've typed.

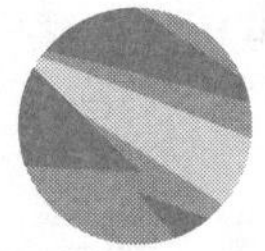

WARNING: *You should not press* ENTER *after typing something in a text field, unless you are finished with the dialog box. In general, pressing* ENTER *accepts what you have typed and closes the dialog box.*

List Boxes

In some dialog boxes, you are required to select an item from a list box. This is how the list box may appear in a dialog box:

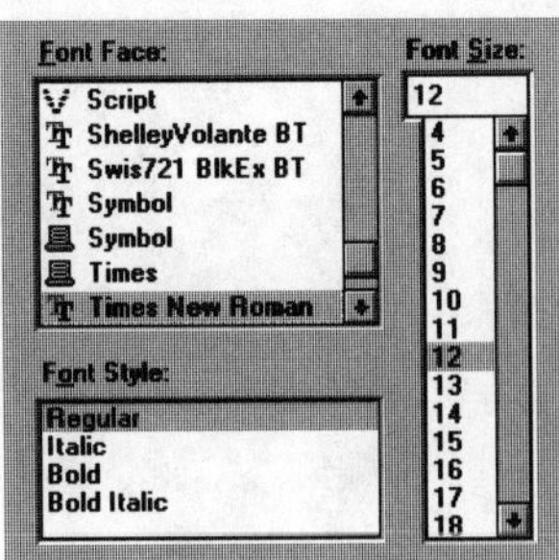

The *list box* displays different items, such as filenames, that you can select. If the number of items is longer than the list box, a scroll bar appears, allowing you to look through the entire list.

To select an item from a list box, click on it with the mouse; if necessary, use the scroll bar to display the desired item. For items such as filenames, you can double-click on the name to open or retrieve it. For other list items, you may need to first click on the desired item, and then choose another command from the dialog box to activate your choice.

Drop-Down Lists and Pop-Up Lists

Drop-down lists and pop-up lists are similar to the list boxes, except that the list of items is "hidden" under a button on the dialog box.

Drop-down list boxes display the down arrow button and show the current selection in a field next to the button, like this:

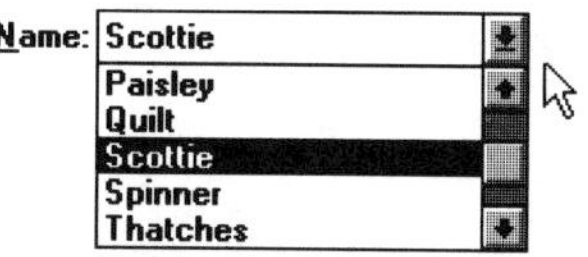

Pop-up list boxes are shown as buttons on the dialog box and show the current selection from the list of available choices. Here is an example of a button that displays a pop-up list:

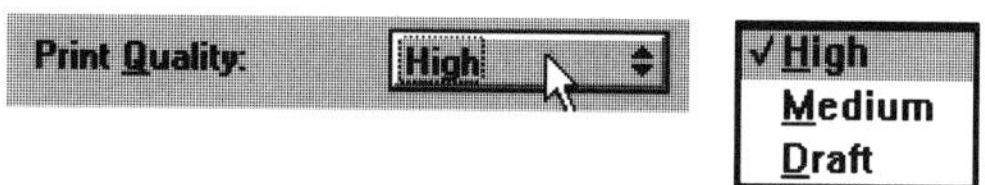

Notice the up/down arrow at the right edge of the button; this tells you that the button displays a pop-up list of items.

Move the mouse pointer onto the pop-up list button and hold down the mouse button; a pop-up list will appear. A check mark appears next to the list item that is currently active. To select a different item, drag the mouse to highlight the option you want. When you release the mouse button, the new option becomes active.

Command Buttons

Command buttons let you accept or reject the changes you've made to the settings in a dialog box. Here are the two command buttons that appear in most dialog boxes:

Click OK, and WordPerfect accepts what you have done in the dialog box. Click Cancel, and the features you have selected are ignored. After you click either button, the dialog box is closed and you can continue working with your document.

NOTE: In Windows programs, the ENTER *key chooses the default command button, which is indicated by a thicker black border around the button. You can press* TAB *or* SHIFT+TAB *to move the black border to a different command button or dialog box option. Then, if you press* ENTER, *WordPerfect performs the action of the button with the thicker border.*

Tips for the Keyboard User

Using the keyboard alone—although possible—is not the best way to access all features of Microsoft Windows. However, in some situations, a keystroke can be more convenient. You can work most effectively by using the mouse and the keyboard together.

Important Keystrokes for Windows

Table 1-2 lists the keystroke assignments for common Windows functions. Although these assignments are standard keystrokes for the Microsoft Windows program, many of the keystrokes are also used by WordPerfect. Keystroke assignments are noted with each WordPerfect feature discussed in this book. For a complete list of all possible keystrokes, see Appendix B, "WordPerfect Keyboards."

Command Description	Keystroke
General Commands	
Cancel dialog box or menu	ESC
Close application	ALT+F4
Close document	CTRL+F4
Help	F1
Undo last action	ALT+BACKSPACE
Menu Commands	
Activate control menu (application)	ALT+SPACEBAR
Activate control menu (document)	ALT+HYPHEN
Acivate menu bar and command buttons	ALT or F10
Deactivate menu bar and command buttons	ESC
Dialog Box Commands	
Accept the default command or select a highlighted list item	ENTER
Select all list box items	CTRL+/
Deselect all list box items	CTRL+\
Move to first item in a list or dialog box	HOME
Move to last item in a list or dialog box	END
Move to next item on menu or dialog box	TAB
Move to previous item on menu or dialog box	SHIFT+TAB
Open a drop-down or pop-up list	ALT+DOWN ARROW
Turn the highlighted check box or radio button on/off	SPACEBAR

Table 1-2. *Function Key Assignments for Windows Programs*

Moving Between Applications and Windows	
Move to next application	ALT+ESC or ALT+TAB
Move to previous application	SHIFT+ALT+ESC or SHIFT+ALT+TAB
Move to next window	ALT+F6
Move to previous window	SHIFT+ALT+F6
Move to next document window	CTRL+F6 or CTRL+TAB
Move to previous document window	SHIFT+CTRL+F6 or SHIFT+CTRL+TAB
Move to next pane (within window)	F6
Move to previous pane (within window)	SHIFT+F6
Display Task dialog box	CTRL+ESC
Clipboard Commands	
Copy active window to Clipboard	ALT+PRINT SCREEN
Copy screen to Clipboard	PRINT SCREEN
Copy selected text or graphics to Clipboard	CTRL+INSERT
Cut and save to Clipboard	SHIFT+DELETE
Paste from Clipboard	SHIFT+INSERT

Table 1-2. *Function Key Assignments for Windows Programs* (continued)

Navigating Through Dialog Boxes

When a dialog box is displayed, a dotted rectangle appears around one of the items in the box. You can press the TAB key to move the dotted rectangle to the next item in the dialog box. Press SHIFT+TAB to move back to the previous item. When the dotted rectangle appears around the item you want to choose, press ENTER to select it.

For radio buttons and check boxes, move the dotted rectangle to the option, and press SPACEBAR to toggle the feature on or off. When items appear in groups within the dialog box, you can press TAB to move the rectangle to the group, and then use the arrow keys on your keyboard to move between the items.

To cancel the dialog box without making changes, you can press TAB to move the rectangle to the Cancel command button and then press ENTER; or simply press ESC.

Most options in dialog boxes have mnemonics—letters you can type to choose each option without using the TAB or arrow keys. In dialog boxes, mnemonics appear as underlined letters within each feature name. Type the mnemonic letter, and the feature is selected. If the insertion point is located at a place in the dialog box where you can type text, you must press the ALT key before typing a mnemonic for another feature in the dialog box.

Using the Control Menus

Each window has a control menu, which lists the options for manipulating the size and location of the window on the screen. Although you can select control menu features with the mouse, buttons and controls on the window perform the same functions and are easier for mouse users to select. The control menu is most helpful for keyboard users, who cannot easily access the window controls without a mouse.

The control menu symbol appears in the upper-left corner of each window, like this:

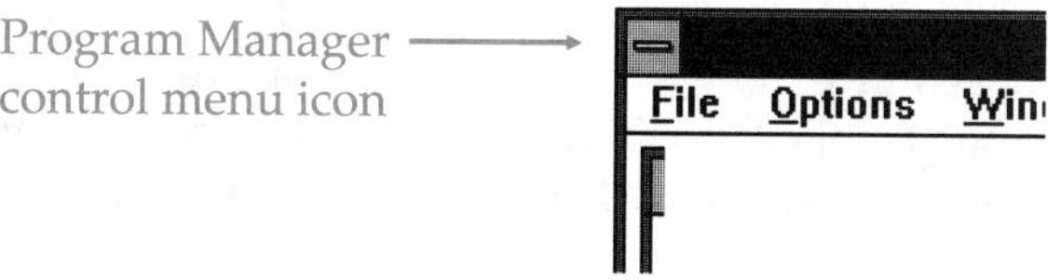

For applications with group or document windows—like WordPerfect for Windows—you may see two control menu icons on the screen at once: one control menu is assigned to the current application that you are using; the other control menu is for the window within the application.

If you are using a mouse, you can click either control menu icon to display the menu. If you are using only the keyboard, you can press ALT+SPACEBAR to display the main control menu. When the screen displays two control menus, press ALT+HYPHEN to display the control menu for the window inside the main application.

If you are using Windows without a mouse, you can move and size a window by using the control menu. First, press ALT+TAB until the window you want to change is highlighted; then, press ALT+SPACEBAR or ALT+HYPHEN to display the control menu for that window. Choose Move or Size and use the cursor arrows on your keyboard to change the position or size of the window. When the window appears as you want it, press ENTER to accept the new position or size.

The Move option also works when you want to move a group icon. Simply press CTRL+F6 until the group icon is highlighted, press ALT+HYPHEN, and choose Move from the control menu. Use the cursor arrows to position the icon, and press ENTER to accept the change.

Although it is easier to size and move things with the mouse, the keyboard techniques described here can be useful when you want to move or size windows with more precision than the mouse allows.

The control menu also displays options for Maximize, Minimize, Restore, and Close. These perform the same functions as the corresponding buttons described earlier in this chapter. On the control menus for application windows, you will see another option called Switch To. This option lets you switch to other applications that are running under Windows; for more information, see "Clipboard" and "Switch to Another Program" in Chapter 11, "Commands and Features."

Exiting WordPerfect and Windows

To exit WordPerfect, choose File/Exit from the menu bar. Another way to exit WordPerfect is with the control menu. You will see at least two control menu icons in WordPerfect: one for the WordPerfect application window, and one for each document window opened within WordPerfect, like this:

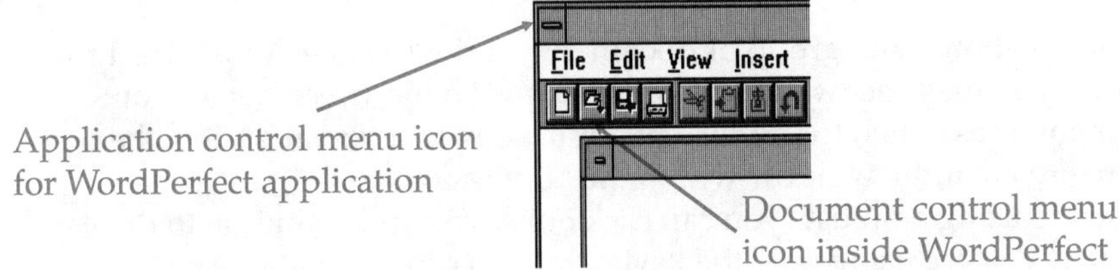

To exit WordPerfect with the control menu, click the application control menu icon once and choose Close from the menu that appears. Or, you can simply double-click the application control menu icon. This closes the WordPerfect program and redisplays the Program Manager.

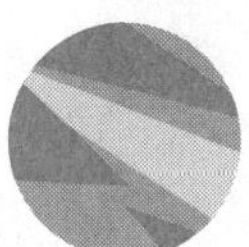

NOTE: *When you have made changes to your document(s) that you have not saved to disk, you are prompted to save the document(s) before the WordPerfect program closes.*

If you are not using a mouse, you can exit WordPerfect by pressing Close (ALT+F4). This is the keystroke equivalent for the Close option on the application control menu.

To exit the Windows program, choose Close from the Program Manager control menu, or double-click the Program Manager control menu. Keyboard users can press Close (ALT+F4) instead. Windows displays a dialog box, which asks you to confirm that you want to exit the Windows program. Click the OK button or press ENTER. The Windows program is closed, and the DOS prompt reappears.

NOTE: *If applications and documents are open when you exit WordPerfect or the Windows environment, and you do not save your documents, you will lose all unsaved changes to the documents or programs.*

CHAPTER 2

WordPerfect for Windows Basics

This chapter explains the basic word processing tasks in WordPerfect for Windows. These include typing and aligning text; enhancing text with fonts; editing, saving, and retrieving document files; and printing. You will also learn how to use WordPerfect's online spelling checker.

If you are an experienced WordPerfect for DOS user, you will find WordPerfect for Windows to be quite different. If you are experienced with previous versions of WordPerfect for Windows, you will still find that WordPerfect for Windows has made subtle changes to the user interface. This chapter will help you make the transition from your current version of WordPerfect.

Using the Keyboard with WordPerfect

Although the mouse is an important tool for WordPerfect and other Windows programs, the keyboard is equally important. Many WordPerfect procedures—such as typing text—are impossible to perform without common keystroke commands. Most users find they are more productive when they use the keyboard in conjunction with the mouse.

The following sections provide information about the use of the keyboard in WordPerfect for Windows. These sections also explain methods for finding the right keystrokes for specific program features.

The WordPerfect Template

A keyboard template, included with your WordPerfect package, lists the keystrokes for the various features. One side of the template shows the WPWin 6.0 or *common user access* (CUA) keystroke assignments, which are the standard keystrokes of WordPerfect for Windows. The other side of the template shows the keystroke assignments of the WordPerfect 5.1-compatible keyboard—an alternate keyboard layout that you can select if you are familiar with WordPerfect 5.1 (DOS) keystrokes.

Place the template over the function keys on your keyboard, and the color-coded feature names will remind you which keys to press. If a feature name is printed in black, it means that you press the function key alone to access the feature. For feature names printed in green, hold down the SHIFT key and press the function key. If a feature name is printed in blue, hold down the ALT key and press the function key to access the feature. If a feature name is printed in red, hold down the CTRL key and press the appropriate function key.

Some features require you to press three keys at the same time: CTRL+SHIFT or ALT+SHIFT and a function key. Features accessed with a CTRL+SHIFT function key combination are shown in red on the template and have a green dot after the feature name. ALT+SHIFT function key combinations are printed in blue with a green dot following the name. In each case, the green dot indicates that the SHIFT key must be pressed with CTRL or ALT before you press the appropriate function key. Once you press one of the function key combinations, WordPerfect displays a dialog box or a special screen where you can use the feature you selected.

Shortcut Keys

You may have already noticed, but when you pull down a menu, many of the menu options include the keystroke you can use to invoke the command or function. These keystrokes, termed *shortcut keys*, are listed to the right of the feature names found on the menus. Often, each letter represents a mnemonic, or the first letter of the word, for the feature you want to access.

The shortcut keys are particularly useful for the common text attributes. Suppose you want to create bold text as you're typing. There are two methods you could use that rely on the mouse:

- Choose Layout/Font and click on the Bold checkbox
- Click on the Bold button on the power bar

Or, you could simply press the shortcut key for bold, CTRL+B. The shortcut keys work the same as if you had selected text attributes using one of the mouse-dependent methods. Press the shortcut key once and you'll turn on the attribute. Press the shortcut key again and the attribute is turned off. Other WordPerfect features represented by shortcut keys also work the same as if you had selected the features from the menus.

Although most menu items have keystrokes assigned to them, not all keystrokes are listed on the pull-down menus. This is often the case when the feature names are too wide to allow the keystroke to fit on the menu. If you see a menu item without a keystroke listed next to it, check the keyboard template to see whether that feature has a keystroke assigned to it.

NOTE: *The displayed keystrokes can change, depending on the keyboard layout you are using. If you use the File/Preferences/Keyboard option to choose or create a keyboard layout, the pull-down menu items will display the new keystrokes you assigned.*

Applying attributes can be done either while typing or to text that you have already typed by first selecting it and then applying an attribute. To see a complete listing of all the shortcut keys in WordPerfect for Windows, refer to Table B-1 in Appendix B.

Keyboard Help

The WordPerfect Help feature can assist you with questions about keystroke assignments. For general keystroke help, choose Help/Contents and click on the green underlined word Keystrokes from the contents list, and a list of keystrokes and their purposes is displayed.

You can also view the keyboard template on-screen to see the assigned keystrokes for a keyboard. To do this, click on the green underlined term "Keystrokes" and then on the green underlined term "CUA Keyboard Template" and a graphic layout of the 12 function keys is displayed showing all assigned keystrokes. When you are finished viewing the help information, choose Close from the menu bar to return to your document.

For more specific keystroke help, use WordPerfect's Help: What Is? feature. Access this by pressing SHIFT+F1. When you do, a question mark appears next to the pointer. Although you can point and click at a menu option or screen area for help, you can also press the desired keystroke to get keystroke help.

NOTE: *Basic help information is explained in the section, "Getting Help," later in this chapter. For complete information about the help feature, see Chapter 11, "Commands and Features."*

Typing and Aligning Text

When you start the WordPerfect program, as described in Chapter 1, a blank document window is open on the screen. Figure 2-1 shows how the WordPerfect screen appears. You can retrieve text into the window or you can type text from the keyboard. Because WordPerfect has predefined margins, line spacing, and other document settings, you do not need to define a document layout before you begin typing.

NOTE: *You can change the predefined document layout with the Layout/Document/Initial Codes Style option. This is explained later in this chapter in the section "Creating a Document Layout."*

Typing Text

When you type text, it is placed in your document at the insertion point. As explained in Chapter 1, the insertion point is the blinking vertical bar, the I-beam,

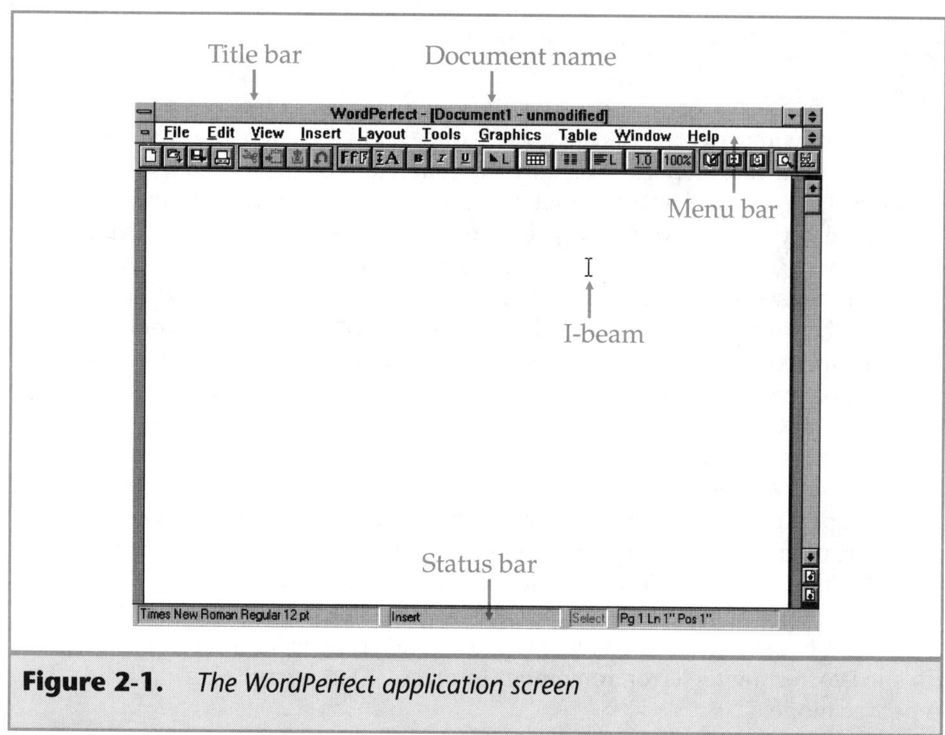

Figure 2-1. *The WordPerfect application screen*

that appears in the document window. In non-Windows applications, the insertion point is commonly known as the *cursor.*

There are two different methods for typing text into your documents. The first method is called *insert mode.* When insert mode is active, you can add new text to your document. As you type, the text is placed into the document at the insertion point. Any existing text is pushed to the right and reformatted to make room for the new text. This is the standard typing mode for WordPerfect.

The second method is called *typeover mode.* Press the INSERT key to turn on typeover mode, and a "Typeover" message appears on the status bar. When typeover mode is active, any text you type replaces the existing text. This is useful when you are editing your document and want to replace a phrase or sentence with something else. Instead of deleting the old text, you can simply "type over" it with the new phrase or sentence. Press INSERT again; typeover mode is turned off, and WordPerfect returns to insert mode.

NOTE: *In typeover mode, the* TAB *key does not insert tab spacing, nor does it replace any text in your document. Instead, the* TAB *key causes the insertion point to skip over the text and move to the next defined tab stop on the line.*

Correcting Typing Errors

As you type the text for your documents, you may make a few typing errors, but these are easy to correct. Press BACKSPACE once and you delete the character at the left of the insertion point—usually the character you just typed. Hold down the BACKSPACE key and you continue to delete characters to the left until you release the key. This is a quick way to delete a few mistyped characters. After the typing error is deleted, simply type the correct characters or text.

You can also remove mistyped characters at the right of the insertion point by pressing the DELETE key. When you hold down the DELETE key, you continue to delete characters at the right until the key is released. After you delete one or more characters, WordPerfect moves the existing text to the left and reformats the paragraph.

WordPerfect's typeover mode also provides a way to quickly delete and correct typing errors with a single step. To correct a typing error, move the insertion point before the first character where the error begins. You can move the insertion point by moving the I-beam onto the character and clicking the mouse button; if you don't have a mouse, use the arrow keys on your keyboard to move the insertion point. Press INSERT to turn on the typeover mode, then type the correct text, which immediately replaces the typing error. When you are finished correcting the error, remember to press INSERT again to turn off the typeover mode.

Typing Paragraph Text

When the text you are typing meets the right margin of the page, WordPerfect automatically moves the insertion point to the next line, where you can continue typing. You do not need to worry about where the margins are defined; just type the text and WordPerfect wraps each line when necessary. This is a standard word processing feature called *word wrap*, and it ensures that your text is formatted correctly to fit the margins in your document.

Using the ENTER Key

Do not press the carriage return key—shown as "Enter" or "Return" on your keboard—at the end of each line. Press ENTER only when you want to end a paragraph, end a single line of text, or insert blank lines in your document.

When you add or delete text, WordPerfect automatically reformats the lines to fit the current margins. If, however, you press ENTER at the end of each line of text, WordPerfect cannot correctly format the paragraphs. This is because WordPerfect inserts a formatting code—called a *hard return code*—into your document each time you press the ENTER key. Although you cannot see it in the document workspace, the hard return code indicates a place where a line of text should be kept separate from the next line in the document. This is usually the case for a title, a headline, or the end of a paragraph.

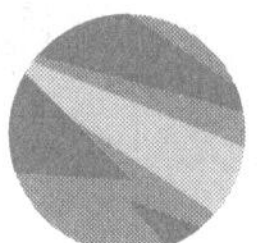

NOTE: WordPerfect's Reveal Codes feature (View/Reveal Codes) lets you display and edit the hidden formatting codes in your document files. This is explained later in this chapter, in the section "Displaying the Codes."

Creating a New Paragraph

When you are finished typing a paragraph, press ENTER once to end the paragraph. Then type the next paragraph. Each time you press ENTER, a hard return code is placed at the insertion point to end the current line or paragraph. If you want a blank line between paragraphs, press ENTER twice at the end of a paragraph, and then type the next paragraph.

Dividing and Combining Paragraphs

Sometimes you will need to divide one paragraph into two or more paragraphs. To divide a paragraph, move the insertion point immediately before the sentence that will begin the new paragraph. Then press the ENTER key to divide the text at that point; press ENTER again if you want a blank line between the two paragraphs. If you change your mind, press the BACKSPACE key to delete the hard return codes that divide the paragraphs, and WordPerfect will reformat the text as one paragraph.

You can use the BACKSPACE key or the DELETE key to remove the hard return codes between two paragraphs and combine them as one. Figure 2-2 shows when you would use BACKSPACE or DELETE. If the insertion point is at the beginning of the second paragraph, press the BACKSPACE key to delete the codes that divide the paragraphs. If the insertion point is at the end of the first paragraph, press the DELETE key. After you delete the codes, WordPerfect reformats the text as one paragraph.

Press DELETE if the insertion point is located here

If you've dreamed about a thick carpet of grass, but can't bear the cost of buying sod, you should consider an economical alternative: hydroseeding. Instead of scattering seeds to the wind, you can contact your local nursery for the nearest hydroseed supplier.

Hydroseeding differs common seeding because the grass seeds soak in a mix of fine mulch and water; fertilizers may also be included in the mix. This is sprayed onto the graded soil where it quickly germinates and sprouts. All you need to do is make sure the soil stays damp until there is a good coverage of grass on your yard. Within three months, you'll see a lawn as thick and green as the sod your neighbors put down— except it cost you about 60% less.

Press BACKSPACE if the insertion point is located here

Figure 2-2. *Using the* BACKSPACE *and* DELETE *keys to combine paragraphs*

NOTE: When combining paragraphs in this manner, you may want to use the Reveal Codes feature to make sure that all hard return codes are removed from the text. Sometimes, it may appear that the two paragraphs are joined, but a hard return code may still be in the text—thus creating a division.

Centering a Text Line

WordPerfect lets you align text precisely between the margins of your page. This is called *centering* text, and it is useful for titles, column labels, and headlines. Figure 2-3 shows an example of centered text.

To create a centered text line, you begin with the insertion point at the left margin of a new line. Choose Layout/Line/Center from the menu bar, or press the shortcut key SHIFT+F7. The insertion point will move to the middle of the page, centered between the left and right margins.

Type the line of text that you want centered. When you are finished, press DOWN ARROW to move the insertion point to the next line. If there is no text after the centered line, press ENTER to start the next line. Text formatted in this manner will remain centered between the left and right margins—even if you change the margin settings. You can also center a line of text that is already in your document. Simply place the insertion point at the beginning of the line you want to center, then use either of the previously mentioned methods to center text, and WordPerfect centers the line between the margins.

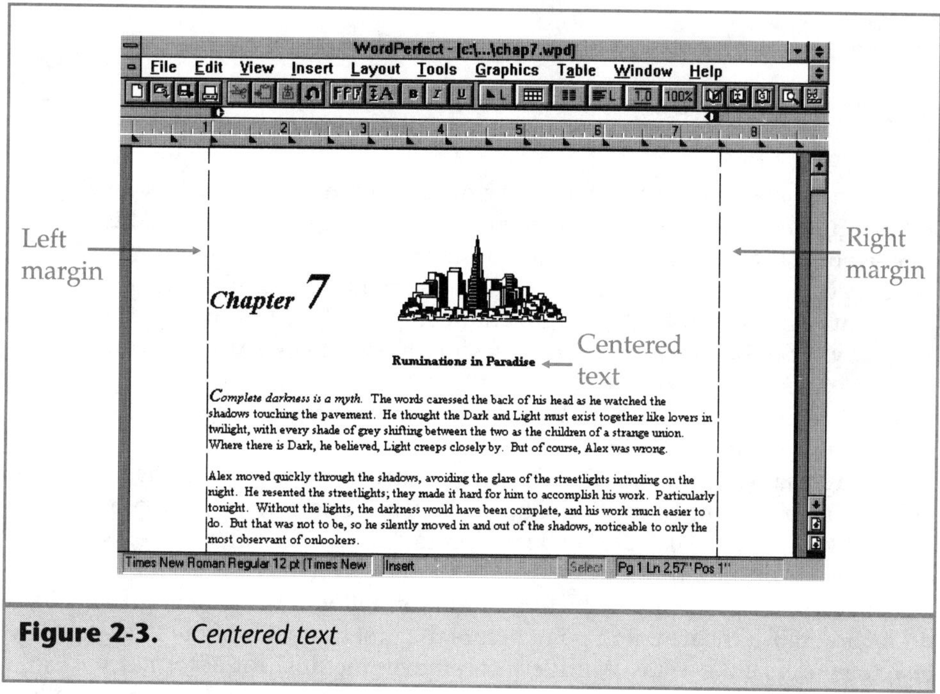

Figure 2-3. *Centered text*

You can cancel or remove the centering with the BACKSPACE key. First make sure the insertion point is at the beginning of the line being centered, like this:

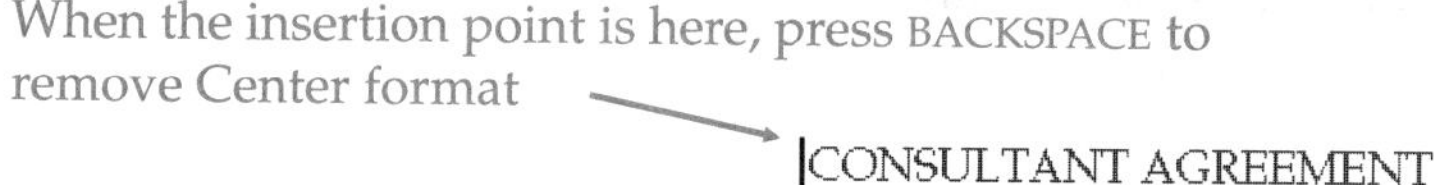

This agreement dated August 6th, 1992, is made by and between Stephen G. Dyson, whose address is 1078 Wilshire Boulevard, Los Angeles, California 90210, referred to hereinafter as "Client", and Severn Consulting, Inc., whose address is 27 East Main, Westlake, California 91361, referred to hereinafter as "Consultant."

Then press BACKSPACE, and WordPerfect removes the centering from the line. When you do this, you delete the formatting code that WordPerfect inserted to create the centered line. Usually, formatting codes are invisible when you create your documents, but you can view and edit them when the Reveal Codes feature is turned on.

As described here, the Center feature works for only a single text line. You can center two or more lines at once by first selecting the lines and then choosing the Line Center feature. This is explained in Chapter 11, "Commands and Features," under the heading Center Text.

Flush-Right Text

In addition to centering, you can also align text at the right margin. This is useful for certain types of documents where dates, labels, or notes should appear at the right edge of the page.

To create a text line at the right margin, begin with the insertion point at the left margin of a new line. From the menu bar, choose Layout/Line, and then choose Flush Right. Keyboard users can simply press ALT+F7 to turn on the Flush Right feature. The insertion point moves to the right margin. Type the text line you want aligned at the right margin and then press ENTER to end the line. If text is already typed below the line, you can simply press DOWN ARROW to move the insertion point to the next line. Flush-right text remains at the right margin. If you change the margin settings, WordPerfect adjusts the placement of flush-right text for the new right margin.

To align a text line that is already in your document, first move the insertion point to the beginning of the line. Choose Layout/Line, and then choose Flush Right. If you prefer to use the keyboard, press ALT+F7. This aligns the existing text at the right margin.

You can cancel or remove the flush-right format with the BACKSPACE key. To do so, first move the insertion point before the first character of the flush-right text; then press BACKSPACE. WordPerfect removes the flush-right format and moves the text to the left to fill the empty space. When you do this, you actually delete the formatting code that WordPerfect inserted to create the flush-right text.

If you want to align two or more lines of text at once, first select the text lines; then choose the Flush Right feature. For the complete procedure, see Flush Right in Chapter 11, "Commands and Features."

Moving the Insertion Point

When you work with documents, you need to move the insertion point to perform most editing tasks. The location of the insertion point determines where you will insert new text and delete existing text, and indicates where font changes and formatting options should be applied. You can use the mouse or the keyboard to move the insertion point to different places in the document text. Although this is often easier with the mouse, several keyboard commands provide quick ways to move the insertion point to individual pages and to the beginning or end of the document.

NOTE: You can move the insertion point only within the boundaries of the document text. In other words, you cannot move the insertion point to a place in the document where you have not typed text or pressed the ENTER key to insert blank lines.

Using the Mouse to Move the Insertion Point

When the mouse pointer is positioned over document text—or any place where you can type text—it appears as an I-beam, like this:

I

The movement of the mouse controls the position of the I-beam on the screen. When you click the mouse button, the insertion point moves to the location of the I-beam. This is the easiest and quickest way to move the insertion point to another place in the on-screen text. For example, suppose you want to move the insertion point to the beginning of the word "Charlie" in your text. First, use the mouse to move the I-beam before the C in "Charlie"; then click the mouse button once. The insertion point is placed before the word.

NOTE: If you do not have a mouse connected to your computer, you cannot move the I-beam cursor; however, you can move the insertion point with keystroke commands.

When you want to move the insertion point to another page, use the scroll bar or the ALT+PGUP and ALT+PGDN combinations. Then, move the I-beam to the desired location and click the mouse once, and the insertion point moves to the new location.

Using the Scroll Bars

WordPerfect's scroll bars allow the mouse user to quickly move through a long document. Figure 2-4 shows the vertical scroll bar. Click the arrow at the bottom of the scroll bar and you'll scroll down one line in your document; click the arrow at the top and you'll scroll up one line in your document.

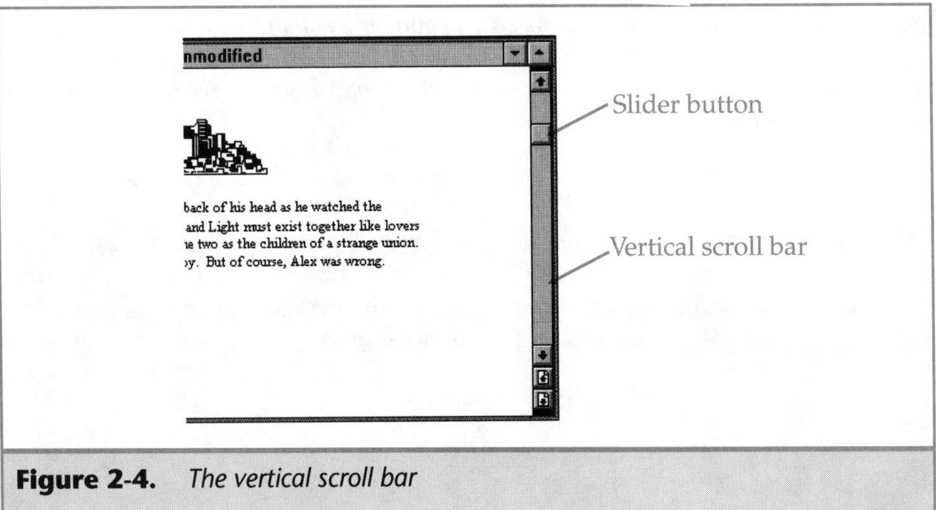

Figure 2-4. *The vertical scroll bar*

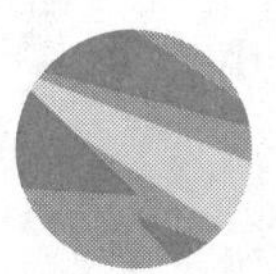

NOTE: *If you do not have a mouse connected to your computer, you cannot use the scroll bars.*

The length of the scroll bar represents the total length of the current document. The button in the middle of the bar, called the *slider button,* indicates your place in the displayed document. If the slider is at the top of the scroll bar, the page shown on the screen is located at the beginning of your document; if the slider is at the bottom of the scroll bar, the displayed page is located at the end of your document. You can position the mouse pointer over the slider button, hold down the mouse button, and then drag the slider up or down. When you release the mouse button, WordPerfect displays the page in your document that is represented by the new location of the slider button.

When you use the scroll bar to scroll through the text of your document, the insertion point does not move with your view of the text. Instead, the insertion point stays at the last place where you typed or inserted new text. After using the scroll bar, simply move the I-beam to a place in the text and click the mouse; this will bring the insertion point to the displayed page.

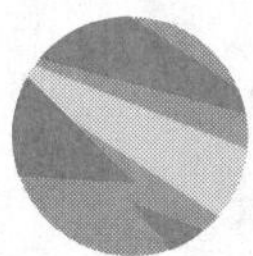

NOTE: *You can also move the insertion point to the displayed page by pressing* UP ARROW *or* DOWN ARROW *on your keyboard.*

WordPerfect shows both the vertical and horizontal scroll bars on the screen only when they are required. If you are displaying a document that is wider or longer (or both) than the WordPerfect screen, the horizontal or vertical (or both) scroll bar(s) will appear.

To change this default method of display, choose File/Preferences/Display from the menu bar. Then, select either Vertical or Horizontal; An X in the box next to either of these options tells you that the scroll bar is turned on. If and when the scroll bars display is determined by whether Show Always or When Required is selected. If you select Show Always, WordPerfect will always display the scroll bars regardless of whether or not text fits on the screen.

Using the Keyboard to Move the Insertion Point

Although the mouse lets you move the insertion point with ease, you can also use the keyboard to move the insertion point through your document—and in some cases, with more precision than the mouse allows. Generally, there are three categories of keyboard commands for moving the insertion point: moving through characters and words, moving through text lines and paragraphs, and moving through document pages. Table 2-1 provides a list of the keystroke commands for moving the insertion point.

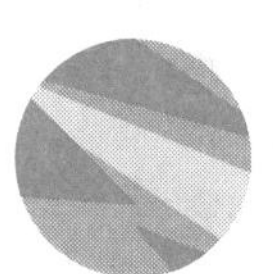

NOTE: *The keystrokes listed in Table 2-1 are from the default WordPerfect for Windows keyboard, which includes keystrokes common to other Windows programs. If you decide to use the WordPerfect 5.1 (WPDOS)-compatible keyboard, your keystroke assignments will be different from those described here. Refer to Appendix B, "WordPerfect Keyboards," for information about the WordPerfect 5.1 (WPDOS)-compatible keyboard.*

Characters and Words

To move the insertion point to the next text character on the line, press the RIGHT ARROW key. Press the LEFT ARROW key to move the insertion point to the previous text character.

When you want to move the insertion point to an adjacent word, hold down the CTRL key while pressing the RIGHT ARROW or LEFT ARROW key. Pressing CTRL+RIGHT ARROW moves the insertion point to the beginning of the next word in your document. CTRL+LEFT ARROW moves the insertion point to the previous word.

Lines and Paragraphs

To move the insertion point to the previous line in your document, press the UP ARROW key. Press DOWN ARROW to move the insertion point down to the next

UP ARROW	Move up to previous line
DOWN ARROW	Move down to next line
RIGHT ARROW	Move to next character
LEFT ARROW	Move to previous character
CTRL+LEFT ARROW	Move to previous word
CTRL+RIGHT ARROW	Move to next word
CTRL+UP ARROW	Move to previous paragraph
CTRL+DOWN ARROW	Move to next paragraph
HOME	Move to beginning of line
HOME, HOME	Move to beginning of line (before codes)
END	Move to end of line
ALT+PGUP	Move to top of previous page
ALT+PGDN	Move to top of next page
PGUP	Move to top of screen
PGDN	Move to bottom of screen
CTRL+HOME	Move to beginning of document
CTRL+HOME, CTRL+HOME	Move to beginning of document (before codes)
CTRL+END	Move to end of document
CTRL+F6	Move to next open document
SHIFT+CTRL+F6	Move to previous open document

Table 2-1. *Keystrokes for Moving the Insertion Point*

line. Press HOME to move the insertion point to the beginning of the current line; press END to move it to the end of the line.

You can also move the insertion point from one paragraph to the next. WordPerfect considers a paragraph as any section of text that begins or ends with a hard return code—that is, a place in the text where you have pressed the ENTER key. (You can use the View/Reveal Codes option to view the hard return codes in the text.) To move the insertion point to the beginning of the previous paragraph, press CTRL+UP ARROW. Press CTRL+DOWN ARROW to move the insertion point to the beginning of the next paragraph. When you press CTRL+UP ARROW or CTRL+DOWN ARROW, WordPerfect simply moves the insertion point to the text following the next hard return code in your document, which may be a complete paragraph or a single line of text. The insertion point skips blank lines when you use these keystrokes.

Pages

When you have a document with several pages, press ALT+PGUP to move the insertion point to the top of the previous page; if the insertion point is on the first or second page of the document, ALT+PGUP moves it to the top of the first page in the document. Press ALT+PGDN to move to the top of the next page in the document; if the insertion point is on the last page, ALT+PGDN moves it to the end of the text.

When you want to move directly to a specific page, choose Edit/Go To. Figure 2-5 shows the dialog box that appears. Type a page number in the text field, and then click the OK button. The insertion point moves to the top of the page number you specified. Keyboard users can press CTRL+G, type a page number, and then press ENTER to move to a specific page.

NOTE: *At the Go To dialog box, if you enter a page number that is greater than the actual pages in your document, WordPerfect moves the insertion point to the top of the last page.*

Sometimes you'll want to move the insertion point only half a page, which is approximately equal to one screen of text. Press PGUP to move the insertion point up one screen of text; press PGDN to move the insertion point down one screen of text.

Beginning and End of Document

Sometimes you will need to move the insertion point to the beginning or end of your document. Mouse users can move to the beginning or end with the vertical scroll bar, but in this case, keystrokes perform these tasks more quickly.

Figure 2-5. *The Go To dialog box*

To move the insertion point to the beginning of your document, press CTRL+HOME. This places the insertion point at the beginning of the document text, but after any formatting codes that are embedded at the top of the document. If you want to move the insertion point before the codes at the beginning of the document, press CTRL+HOME twice. To move the insertion point to the end of the document, press CTRL+END. This places the insertion point to the right of the last word, character, or code in the document.

After moving the insertion point to the beginning or end of the document, you can return the insertion point to its original position. First, press CTRL+G to display the Go To dialog box. Then highlight "Last Position" from the Position box. Click OK and the insertion point is moved to its previous location, before you pressed CTRL+HOME or CTRL+END.

Fonts and Attributes

The appearance of printed text is determined by *fonts* (also called *typefaces*). WordPerfect supports various font and text attributes, according to the capabilities of your printer. While fonts control the general appearance of text, *attributes* help to emphasize specific words and phrases. These include bold, italics, and underline. Some text attributes can be turned on with the press of a shortcut key; all may be selected from the Font dialog box.

You can choose an attribute or font while you are typing text, or you can select a passage of text and apply an attribute or font to it. See the section "Basic Editing Skills" later in this chapter for information about selecting text.

When you choose different fonts and attributes, the left edge of the status bar displays the current font name with the attributes you have selected. As you move the insertion point through your document, the font name on the status bar is updated to reflect the font and attribute changes in your text.

Bold Text

The bold attribute is used to emphasize a title, headline, or passage of text. To turn on the bold attribute, do any of the following:

- Choose Layout/Font and click the Bold checkbox.
- Click on the bold button on the power bar.
- Press the shortcut key for bold, CTRL+B.

Type the text that you want to appear boldface, then again use one of the same three methods to turn off the bold attribute.

Underlined Text

Choose the underline attribute to create text with an underscore. Similar to the bold attribute, underline may be used to emphasize a title or headline, but it can also be used to create an underlined space where signatures or other information should be written on the finished document. WordPerfect for Windows provides two attributes that create single- and double-underlined text.

To turn on underlining, use any of these methods:

- Choose Layout/Font and click the Underline checkbox.
- Click on the underline button on the power bar.
- Press the shortcut key for underline, CTRL+U.

If you want to use the double underline attribute instead, choose Layout/Font and click Double Underline. (This is the only method you can use to apply double-underline formatting.) Type the text that should be underlined, or press the SPACEBAR several times to create a blank line. To turn off the underline attribute, use one of the underline options again.

When an underline attribute is turned on, WordPerfect underlines the text and character spaces. Initially, spaces inserted with the TAB key are not underlined. This is the standard setting of WordPerfect, but you can change the underline method to underline tab spacing, too. First move the insertion point to the place in your document where the new underlining method should begin; this is necessary because WordPerfect inserts a code to indicate the change. Then, choose the Layout/Font option from the menu bar, and select the Spaces check box, Tabs check box, or both to indicate your preferences. When you exit the dialog box, the text that follows the insertion point will be affected by the underlining method you selected.

Italic Text

The italic attribute is commonly used to offset a quote in a document or to emphasize phrases and terms. You can use any of the following methods to turn on the italic attribute:

- Choose Layout/Font and click on the Italic checkbox.
- Click on the italic button on the power bar.
- Press the shortcut key for italic, CTRL+I.

Use any of these methods a second time to turn off the attribute. If your printer cannot apply the italic attribute to the selected font, WordPerfect displays italics as underlined text in your document.

Redline and Strikeout

The redline and strikeout attributes are often used as tools for editing contracts and manuscripts. Generally, redlined text appears red in the document editing window and indicates text that has been added to the document. On the printed page, the Redline attribute usually appears as shaded text. Choose Layout/Font and click on the Redline checkbox to turn on the Redline attribute. Type the desired text and then choose Redline again to turn off the attribute. Strikeout text appears with a line scored through the middle of the text, like this:

2. Terms of Agreement. This agreement will begin on August 6th, 1992, and will end on October 31st, 1992. ~~Either party may cancel this agreement on ten (10) days notice to the other party in writing, by certified mail or personal delivery.~~

The strikeout attribute is usually applied to existing text, to indicate information that will be removed from the document. This is done by first selecting the text and then choosing the strikeout attribute. To turn on the strikeout attribute while you are typing text, choose Layout/Font and click on the Strikeout checkbox. Type the desired text and click Strikeout again to turn off the attribute.

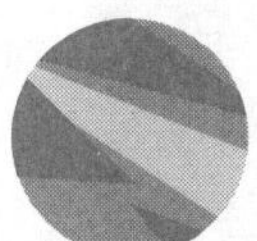

NOTE: *Redline and strikeout do not have shortcut keys, but you can easily create on-screen buttons for these and other attributes with WordPerfect's Button Bar feature. For more information, see the section "Using the Button Bar" in Chapter 3, "Tools and Techniques."*

Superscript and Subscript

The superscript and subscript attributes help you create symbols and notations in your documents. Choose Layout/Font and choose Superscript or Subscript from the Position option button to turn on the desired attribute. Type the text that should appear superscripted or subscripted; then choose the attribute again to turn it off.

The size of superscripted and subscripted text is approximately 60 percent of the current font size. You can control the size of superscripted and subscripted text by entering a percentage preference in the File/Preferences/Print dialog box, under the Size Attribute Ratio options.

Hidden Text

One of the more unusual attributes that can be applied to text is to make it hidden. In WordPerfect for Windows, hidden is an attribute the same as bold or italic—it simply means that the text formatted with this attribute does not display or print unless you specifically direct it to.

You can apply the Hidden attribute only to text you have already typed in your document. Select the text, and then choose Layout/Font and click on the Hidden checkbox. To control the display of text with the Hidden attribute, choose View/Hidden Text. If a checkmark appears next to this menu option, then hidden text is displayed; otherwise it is not. Instead of using this menu option, you can also choose File/Preferences/Display/Hidden Text.

Other Attributes

The Bold, Italic, Underline, Double Underline, Redline, Strikeout, and Hidden options appear in the Font dialog box, but these are not all the text attributes that WordPerfect supports. You can also specify three other attributes—Outline, Shadow, and Small Cap. Simply check the boxes of the attributes you want; when you choose the OK button, WordPerfect applies all the attributes that are checked. This allows you to create combinations such as bold and underlined; italic and bold; or outlined, underlined, and shadowed. The results on the printed page depend on the capabilities of your printer and the fonts you have installed for use with your printer. For example, you can apply the outline and shadow attributes to your text, but they will appear on the printed page only when your printer can produce a font with these attributes.

Changing the Font

WordPerfect lets you choose various fonts for the text of your document. The fonts available to you depend on what is supported by your printer. Although many printers have a variety of fonts built in, most fonts must be purchased as separate cartridge or software packages and then installed for use with your printer. You probably noticed as you installed WordPerfect for Windows that some new fonts were installed along with your software.

To choose a different font for your text, first move the insertion point to the place in the document where the change should begin. Then choose Layout/Font from the menu bar to display the Font dialog box shown in Figure 2-6. Click the desired font name in the list box; if you have a long list of fonts installed, a scroll bar appears to help you move through the entire list. Once you highlight a font name, the box at the bottom left of the dialog box shows how text will appear when printed with the selected font.

If your printer allows different sizes for the font you have selected, you can choose a font size from the Font Size list. If the size you want does not appear in the list, you can click on the box at the top of the Font Size list, and type in a specific size. When you have selected a font and size, choose OK to accept the change, and WordPerfect inserts a font change code, which affects the text that follows the insertion point. The new font will affect the text until the end of the document, unless, of course, you change the font again later in the document.

To change the standard font for the entire document, use the Layout/Document/Initial Font option, instead, to choose a specific font for all document text.

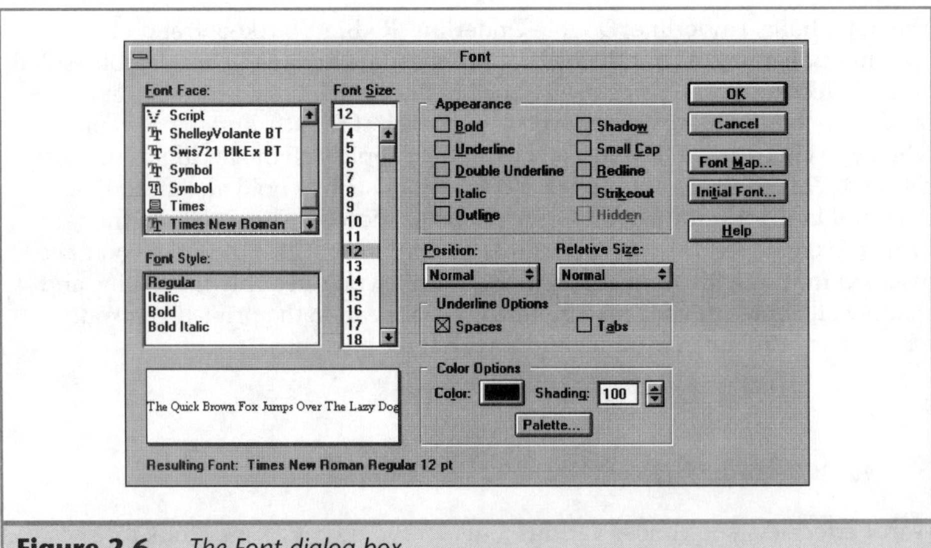

Figure 2-6. *The Font dialog box*

Basic Editing Skills

There are several ways to edit and manipulate the text of your documents, including the basic tasks of inserting new text, deleting unwanted text, copying, and moving things to other places in your document. You often need to select the section of text you want to manipulate before you choose an editing option. Chapter 11, "Commands and Features," includes complete information about the editing features mentioned here.

Selecting Text

Selecting lets you specify a word, paragraph, or passage of text for editing. The Select feature in WordPerfect for Windows is similar to the Block feature in earlier versions of WordPerfect. Once a section of text is selected, you can choose an editing feature or text attribute and apply it to the selected text.

If you have a mouse, it is easy to select a passage of text. First move the I-beam to the beginning of the text you want to select. Then hold down the mouse button and drag the I-beam to the end of the text. As you move the mouse, the text is highlighted and appears in reverse video on the document window—usually as white text on a black background. Release the mouse button when the desired passage is selected, and then choose the editing command that you want to apply to the text (such as Layout/Line/Center or Edit/Copy). Sometimes, text remains selected even after you have chosen an editing command. To turn off the Select feature, click the mouse anywhere in the text; this turns off Select and also moves the insertion point to the place where you click.

The mouse also provides a fast way to select a word, sentence, or paragraph. To select a word, move the I-beam onto it and quickly click the mouse button twice—called a *double-click.* This selects the word and the space that follows the word. Click the mouse button three times—a triple-click—and you select the sentence where the I-beam is located. A quadruple-click selects the current paragraph. If you prefer to use the keyboard, you can choose Edit/Select and then choose Sentence or Paragraph to select a complete sentence or paragraph. A menu option is not available for selecting a single word, but you can press CTRL+SHIFT+RIGHT ARROW to select the word where the insertion point is located.

NOTE: *When you type something while a passage of text is selected, the text you type replaces the selected text. You can also select and replace text items and measurements that appear in dialog boxes.*

For larger sections of text, the SHIFT key can help you select passages that extend beyond the screen. First, move the insertion point to the place in your text where the selection should begin. Without moving the insertion point, use the scroll bar to display the end of the text that you want to select. Move the I-beam to the end of the text you want selected, hold down the SHIFT key, and click the mouse button. This tells WordPerfect to select all text between the insertion point and the I-beam. Then choose the desired editing feature.

If you don't have a mouse, there are a few keystrokes you need to remember. Table 2-2 shows the valid commands for selecting text with the keyboard; many of these keystrokes are practical for mouse users as well. To select a passage of text with the keyboard, first move the insertion point to the beginning of the text you want to select. Then, press F8 to turn on the Select feature; the "Select" indicator appears undimmed near the center of the status bar. Use the arrow keys to extend the selection to the end of the text you want to change, move, or copy. Then choose the desired editing command. Press F8 again to turn off the Select feature.

You can also use the SHIFT key with other keys to select sections of text. Press SHIFT+END to select all text between the insertion point and the end of the text line. Note that a text line is simply the line of text where the insertion point is found, and that the end of the line is not necessarily the end of the current sentence. Press SHIFT+HOME to select all text between the insertion point and the beginning of the line. CTRL+SHIFT+HOME selects the text between the insertion point and the beginning of the document; CTRL+SHIFT+END selects text from the insertion point to the end of the document.

Inserting New Text

You can easily add new text to a document displayed in the document window. First move the insertion point to the place where the new text should be inserted, and then type it. Before you type, make sure the typeover mode is turned off, as described earlier in this chapter. As you type, WordPerfect reformats the document paragraphs to accommodate the new text.

Deleting Text

There are several ways to delete text from your document. You can use keystrokes to delete characters and words, or you can use the Select feature to remove or cut a section of text from your document. To delete single characters, press the BACKSPACE key. This deletes the character that lies to the left of the

Keystroke	Action
F8	Select on/off
SHIFT+LEFT ARROW	Select from insertion point to previous character
SHIFT+RIGHT ARROW	Select from insertion point to next character
SHIFT+UP ARROW	Select from insertion point to previous line
SHIFT+DOWN ARROW	Select from insertion point to next line
SHIFT+CTRL+UP ARROW	Select to the beginning of current paragraph
SHIFT+CTRL+DOWN ARROW	Select to the end of current paragraph
SHIFT+HOME	Select from insertion point to beginning of line (after codes)
SHIFT+HOME, SHIFT+HOME	Select from insertion point to beginning of line (before codes)
SHIFT+END	Select from insertion point to end of line
SHIFT+ALT+HOME	Select from insertion point to top of current column
SHIFT+CTRL+HOME	Select from insertion point to beginning of document (after codes)
SHIFT+CTRL+HOME, HOME	Select from insertion point to beginning of document (before codes)
SHIFT+ALT+END	Select from insertion point to bottom of page or column
SHIFT+PGUP	Select from insertion point to top of screen
SHIFT+PGDN	Select from insertion point to bottom of screen
SHIFT+ALT+PGUP	Select from insertion point to top of page
SHIFT+ALT+PGDN	Select from insertion point to end of page
SHIFT+F8	Select cell in table
SHIFT+CTRL+RIGHT ARROW	Select current word
SHIFT+CTRL+LEFT ARROW	Select previous word

Table 2-2. *Keystroke Commands for Selecting Text*

insertion point. If you hold down the BACKSPACE key, you will continue to delete characters to the left of the insertion point. Press the DELETE key to delete the character where the insertion point is located; hold down the DELETE key, and you will delete characters to the right of the insertion point.

To delete a complete word, move the insertion point to the word and press CTRL+BACKSPACE. This deletes the word and the space that follows it. You can also delete a passage of text by first selecting it and then pressing the BACKSPACE key to remove the selected text. After you delete text from the document, WordPerfect automatically reformats the text to fill any empty space.

NOTE: *You can also use the Edit/Cut feature to remove selected text from your document. For more information, see "Copying and Moving Text" later in this chapter or the section "Cut Text" in Chapter 11, "Commands and Features."*

Restoring Deleted Text

You can restore deleted text by choosing Edit/Undelete from the menu bar. When you do so, a dialog box appears that lets you restore the last text you deleted or view and restore a previous deletion.

Choose Edit/Undelete to display the dialog box shown in Figure 2-7. WordPerfect displays the last thing you deleted, or the last text removed by typeover mode, as selected text at the insertion point. Command buttons on the Undelete dialog box provide options for restoring the text. Choose Restore to restore the highlighted text at the insertion point. Choose Next or Previous to

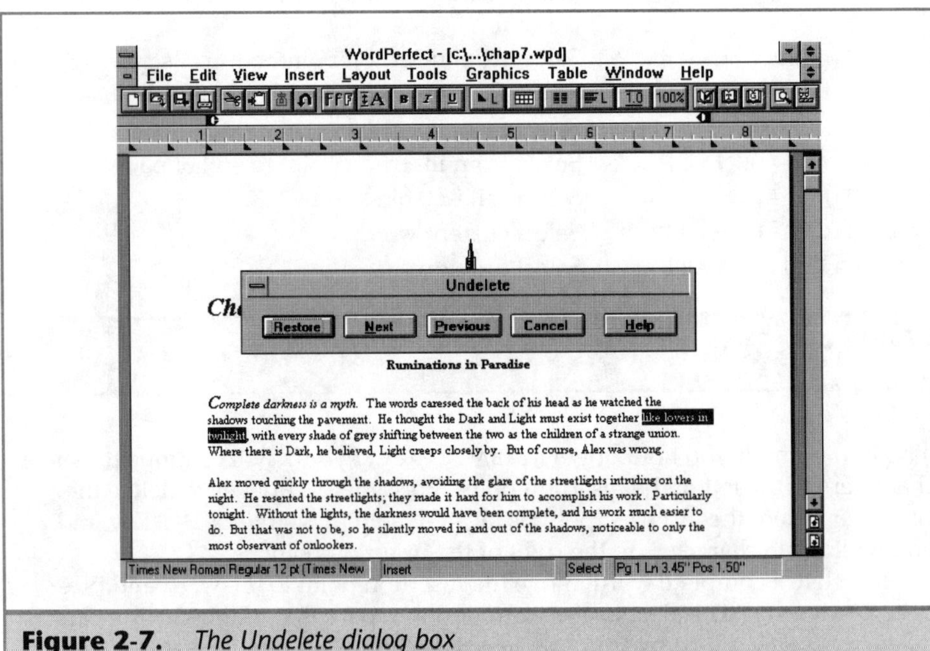

Figure 2-7. *The Undelete dialog box*

display items previously deleted. WordPerfect can remember the last three things you deleted from the document. Once a deleted item is displayed, choose Restore to restore it, or choose Cancel to close the dialog box without restoring any text.

Copying and Moving Text

The Cut, Copy, and Paste options on the Edit menu are standard features for programs running under Windows. These features let you move and copy text to another location in your document. To move a section of text, select it and then choose Edit/Cut. This removes the selected text from your document and places it in the Windows Clipboard. Then, move the insertion point to the place in your document where the text should be moved, and choose Edit/Paste. The text is retrieved from the Clipboard and inserted at the insertion point. The procedure for copying text is similar: simply choose Edit/Copy instead of Cut.

The Cut, Copy, and Paste features all have keystrokes assigned to them, and in many cases, you'll work faster by pressing the keys instead of choosing the features from the menus. Once text is selected, you can press SHIFT+DELETE or CTRL+X to cut the text, or CTRL+INSERT or CTRL+C to copy the text to the Clipboard. Then, press SHIFT+INSERT or CTRL+V to retrieve the text from the Clipboard and into the document at the insertion point.

WordPerfect for Windows includes a feature that allows you to use the mouse to drag a block of text from one place to another in your document. To do so, first select the text. Then, move the mouse pointer over the selected text and hold down the mouse button. The mouse pointer changes to the "move text" icon, which looks like two overlapping boxes. While holding down the mouse button, move the mouse pointer to position the insertion point at the place where the selected text should be moved. When the insertion point is where you want it, release the mouse button and the selected text is inserted at the new location.

Creating a Document Layout

The general appearance of a document is determined by formatting codes, which specify page margins, line spacing, justification, tab settings, and other characteristics of the document layout. WordPerfect has predefined settings for each of these layout options, but you can easily change them for any document.

The tools for formatting your document are found on the Layout menu, and are divided into different categories for Line, Paragraph, Page, and Document commands. Before you choose a command from these menus, you should move the insertion point to the place in your document where the format should occur. If, for example, you want to indent a paragraph, the insertion point should be located at the beginning of the paragraph before you choose the indent feature. If a formatting change should affect the entire document, move the insertion point to the beginning of the document before choosing the desired feature. You can also use WordPerfect's Layout/Document/Initial Codes Style feature to apply layout options to all text in the document.

The following sections explain how to change the standard document layout settings. See Chapter 11 for complete information about these and other options found on the Layout menu.

NOTE: *Initially, all layout options are measured in terms of inches, but you can choose the File/Preference/Display and select the Units of Measure feature to change the measurement type that WordPerfect uses.*

Margins

The standard document margins allow one inch of space at each edge of the paper, but you can change the margins anywhere in your document. First, choose Layout/Margins, or press CTRL+F8, to display this dialog box:

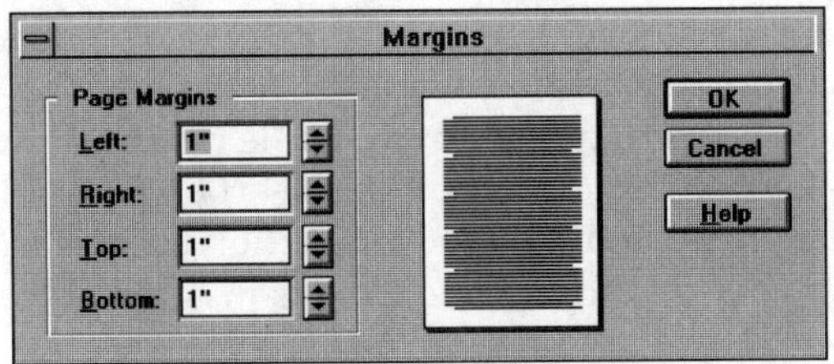

Type the desired measurement for each of the margin settings, choose OK, and codes for the new margins are placed in your text. As you move the insertion point down the left and right edges of the pages, the "Ln" and "Pos" labels on the status bar will indicate the margin settings. If you choose to display the formatting ruler (View/Ruler Bar), the new left and right margins are shown there, as well.

Remember that margins are measured from each edge of the page. For example, suppose you want margins set at 1.25 inches and 7 inches on a sheet of 8.5" x 11" paper. You would enter **1.25"** for the left margin and **1.5"** for the right margin; 1.5" is entered because a right margin set at the 7-inch mark leaves 1.5 inches of space at the right edge of the page.

Line Spacing

Line spacing determines the vertical spacing of text lines in your document. Text lines are usually single-spaced, but you can change this measurement to any number, including fractional numbers such as 1.5, 1 3/4, or 2.2. You can change the spacing for the entire document, or as often as you like within parts of a document.

To change the line spacing, begin by moving the insertion point to the place in your document where the line spacing should change. If you want to change the spacing for the entire document, press CTRL+HOME to move to the top of the document. Then, choose Layout/Line/Spacing to display the Line Spacing dialog box. In the dialog box text field, type a number for the spacing you desire. Choose OK to accept the change, and WordPerfect inserts a line spacing code into the text. The new line spacing affects all text that lies below the insertion point, until, of course, another line spacing change is made.

Justification

Justification determines how text is distributed between the left and right margins of the page. WordPerfect provides five ways to justify the text in your document:

- Left justification, the standard of WordPerfect for Windows, means that all text is aligned at the left margin.
- Right justification aligns text at the right margin.
- Center justification centers all text lines between the left and right margins, even when the text is in paragraph form.
- Full justification stretches each line so that the text extends to each margin; this produces a perfectly straight edge at both the left and right margins.
- All justification is the same as full justification, except that the last line of a paragraph is also stretched between the left and right margins. In some desktop publishing programs, this is referred to as forced justification.

To change the justification setting, choose Layout/Justification from the menu bar. Then select Left, Right, Center, Full, or All to indicate your preference.

WordPerfect provides shortcut keys that let you quickly change the justification setting. For left justification, press CTRL+L. Press CTRL+R for right justification and CTRL+E for center justification. For full justification, press CTRL+J. There is no shortcut key for All justification, however. When you select from the menu or press a shortcut key, WordPerfect inserts a justification code at the insertion point, which affects the text that follows.

Besides using the menus, you can also choose the justification tool from the power bar. When you click on this tool and hold down the mouse button, you will see the five types of justification. Move the mouse to select one of the types, and then release the mouse button.

Tabs

The Tab Set feature lets you define the tab stops for your document. The standard tab stops are set at every half-inch across the page. You can define as many tab settings as you need in your document. In addition to the standard left-aligned tab stop, WordPerfect lets you create special tabs that align text over decimal points, center text, and tab-align at the right edge of the text. You also have the option of setting tabs at absolute positions, measured from the left edge of the page, or at positions that "float" according to the position of the current left margin. Each time you define or change the tab settings, WordPerfect inserts a code into your text to indicate the change.

There are two ways to change or define tab stops for your document: you can choose Layout/Line/Tab Set to define the tabs from a dialog box, or you can quickly move and change tab stops with the formatting ruler. See Chapter 11, "Commands and Features," for detailed information about defining and using the Tab Set and ruler features.

Indenting a Paragraph

For your documents, you may use the TAB key to indent the first line of a paragraph. However, the *Indent* feature lets you indent the entire paragraph from the left margin or both margins. Paragraph indentation can help you offset certain passages of text—like quotations—from the rest of the text in your document. The Indent commands affect only the paragraph or text line where the insertion point is located; you cannot indent two or more paragraphs at once.

Before you indent a paragraph, you must move the insertion point to the beginning of the text that should be indented. To indent the left edge of the paragraph, choose Layout/Paragraph/Indent, or simply press F7. To indent both edges of the paragraph, choose Layout/Paragraph and then choose Double Indent; if you prefer to use the keyboard, you can press CTRL+SHIFT+F7.

WordPerfect indents text according to the next tab stop on the line. Using the standard tab stops, paragraphs are indented at half-inch increments. If you want to indent a paragraph more than half an inch, you can choose the indent feature again to indent to the next tab stop. Or, you can define new tab stops to indicate where the text should be indented.

Some documents require hanging indents (where the first line of text is flush left, but the rest is indented) for paragraphs and other text items. To create a hanging indent, move the insertion point to the beginning of the paragraph. Then, choose Layout/Paragraph and select Hanging Indent; if you prefer to use the keyboard, simply press CTRL+F7. This creates a format where all lines in the paragraph—except the first line—are indented to the first tab stop.

Changing the Predefined Document Layout

When you start WordPerfect, margins, tabs, line spacing, and other layout options are predefined according to standard document settings. This allows you to begin working without defining new layout settings. If, each time you start WordPerfect, you want margins or tab stops that are different from the standard settings, you can change the predefined layout to suit your own needs.

To change the predefined layout, choose Layout/Document/Initial Codes Style. This displays the Styles Editor screen. At this screen you can choose or create any styles which you have defined. These can then be saved so they apply to any new document you create. These styles can contain any of the features that define and control the document layout, including margins, tab settings, line spacing, justification, column definition, and graphics box options.

When you are finished, click on the Close button to return to the document editing screen. The codes you inserted become the standard format for WordPerfect.

NOTE: *The predefined layout does not cancel any layout changes you make within the document text; it simply provides a default layout when you do not make any explicit formatting changes.*

Templates

In WordPerfect for Windows, a *template* is a special document you create to use as a pattern for future documents. This gives you the ability to make a blank layout for the document type you create most often. For instance, if you find yourself constantly typing business letters which must be laid out with the same spacing, fonts, and so forth, you can create a single template document instead of reformatting each letter. Then each time you create a new document, you affix the template and all the formatting and preparation is done for you—you simply type the letter. In this example, templates can also help your letters maintain a uniform appearance since the formatting is the same.

Templates also allow you to alter the way WordPerfect works, as you can designate which button bar, keyboard, and menu bar to use.

Creating a New Template

You can create templates from existing template styles or from scratch. Select File/Template and choose Create Template from the Options button in the Template dialog box. Creating a template actually begins a new, separate document. You are presented with the Create Document Template dialog box where you enter appropriate information about the template. Type a unique name for this template or, to base the name on an existing template, click on the File icon to the right of the text box and browse through the existing template filenames. Press TAB to move to the Description text box and enter a brief description of the template and its purpose. Click on OK to access the Template editor screen.

From the Template editor screen, design your document template just the way you want. You can design the paragraph styles, headings, font sizes, and so on.

Editing a Template

Once you have created a template, you can edit it by selecting File/Template and highlighting the template name in the Document Template to Use list. Select Edit Template from the Options button. The Template editor screen appears from which you can make any adjustments to the template you want.

You can also create variations of a template so that, for example, you can customize several different styles of business letters. To do this, select Create Template from the Options button. Type a name for the template and press TAB to move to the Description text box and enter a description of the template. Click on the down arrow in the Name text box and choose a name from the drop-down list to base this layout on an existing template file. Choose the filename and click on OK. Select OK from the Create Document Template dialog box. All the styles, attributes, and other settings are copied to the new template. Make your changes as necessary.

WordPerfect Codes

WordPerfect for Windows usually hides the codes that create the layout of your document. Codes are inserted into your text, at the insertion point, whenever you choose WordPerfect formatting, font, and graphics options. These codes help WordPerfect display and print your document according to the format you have specified.

The Reveal Codes feature (View/Reveal Codes) lets you see the hidden codes. When the Reveal Codes window is displayed, you can move, copy, and delete any formatting codes and also edit the text and format as needed.

Displaying the Codes

To display the codes in your document, choose View from the menu bar and then select Reveal Codes. Keyboard users can press ALT+F3. Your screen will appear similar to the one shown in Figure 2-8. The document window is divided by a bar into two parts: the top part shows your document as it appears during editing; the bottom part is the Reveal Codes window.

NOTE: *If you have a mouse, you can use the mouse pointer to drag the dividing bar up or down to adjust the size of the Reveal Codes window.*

The text in Reveal Codes is displayed in any font you desire. To change the appearance of the font in Reveal Codes, refer to the section "Reveal Codes" in Chapter 11, "Commands and Features." Codes appear in graphical boxes within the document text; see Appendix C, "WordPerfect Codes," for a list of all codes that WordPerfect displays.

Types of Codes

Codes are organized into different categories, according to the different layout options for your document. Some codes affect the layout of pages in your

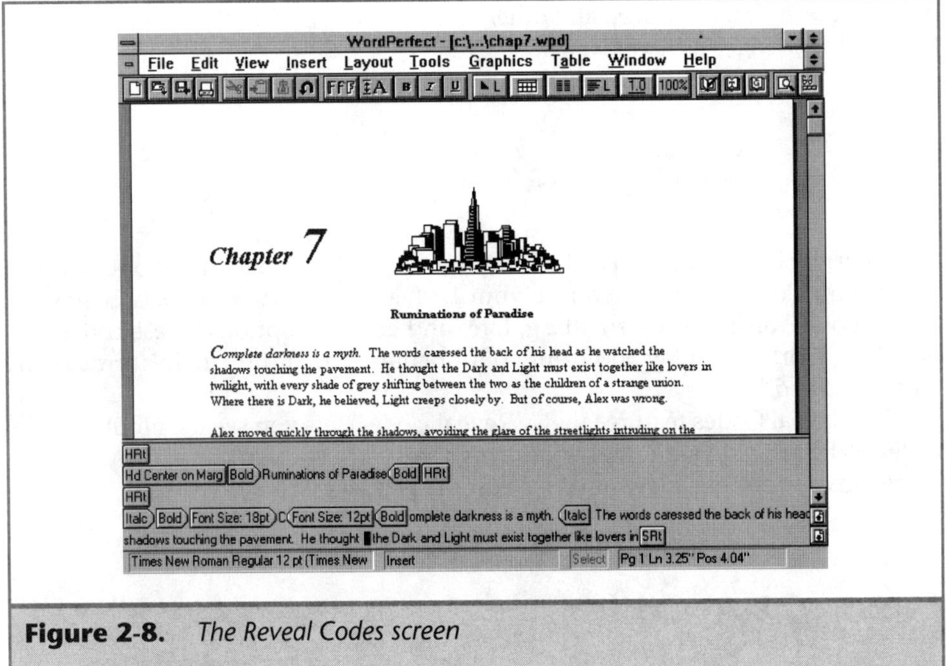

Figure 2-8. *The Reveal Codes screen*

document, while some format single lines or paragraphs of text. Other codes determine the appearance of text, create tables, represent graphic images, and structure tables and columns. Sometimes, codes are inserted in pairs, to turn a feature on and off at specific places in the document. You probably noticed some of these paired codes in Figure 2-8. For instance, a Bold code appears before and after the text that is formatted as bold. The different appearance of the starting and ending codes indicates their purpose—turning the attribute on or off.

Other codes, such as the column definition code, depend on other codes (in this case, the "column on" code) to complete a layout function. Most formatting options, however, insert a single code, such as a margin change, to affect all text that falls after the code.

The codes you insert are often called *hard codes,* but there are also *soft codes* that WordPerfect inserts to help format the document text. The term "soft" refers to codes that WordPerfect automatically inserts when necessary, or codes that will become dormant under certain circumstances. Hard codes are those that continue to affect the text, regardless of the state of the document.

For example, the hard return code (HRt), mentioned earlier in the chapter, ends a paragraph or text line and is inserted when you press ENTER. The hard return code stays where you place it in the text and will not change unless you move or delete it. The soft return code (SRt) is inserted by WordPerfect to wrap lines and create paragraph text and is automatically inserted and removed by WordPerfect as needed to keep text wrapped in the paragraph format.

There are other types of codes that will become familiar to you as you work with WordPerfect. Code names often indicate the purpose of each code, but several are somewhat cryptic. See Appendix C, "WordPerfect Codes," for a complete list of WordPerfect codes, descriptions, and the menu options for inserting each of the codes.

Moving Through Codes

When the Reveal Codes window is displayed, each code is considered one "character" in the text. Notice that a position marker appears in the Reveal Codes window. This indicates the position of your insertion point within the document.

NOTE: *At the standard document screen—when the Reveal Codes window is not displayed—the insertion point skips over the hidden codes in the text. If you use the arrow keys to move the insertion point, you do not need extra keystrokes to move past the hidden codes.*

You can use the scroll bars or the UP ARROW and DOWN ARROW keys to scroll through the document text. As you do so, WordPerfect updates the Reveal Codes window to show the codes surrounding the position of the insertion point. If you move the insertion point with the mouse or the arrow keys, the marker in the Reveal Codes window will also move to reflect the current location of the insertion point. Mouse users can simply click a code in the Reveal Codes window to move the marker and the insertion point to the code.

Deleting Codes

Sometimes, you may need to delete formatting codes after they are placed in your document. To delete a code, first move the reverse-video marker (the marker in the Reveal Codes window that represents the insertion point in your document) so it is adjacent to the code. If the code is to the right of the marker, press the DELETE key to remove the code; if it is to the left, use the BACKSPACE key.

Generally, WordPerfect will allow you to delete codes only when the Reveal Codes window is displayed; however, the following Preferences option, File/Preferences/Environment/Confirm Deletion of Codes, Stop Insertion Point at Hidden Codes, lets you delete hidden codes without the Reveal Codes window being displayed. When this option is turned on, WordPerfect will prompt you about deleting when you press BACKSPACE or DELETE with the insertion point near an embedded code.

NOTE: You can also move and copy codes from one place to another in your document. See Chapter 11, "Comands and Features," for more information.

Correcting Spelling Errors

Spelling and typing errors creep into most documents, and WordPerfect provides an online Speller that lets you correct these misspellings quickly and easily. Unlike earlier versions of WordPerfect, the Speller for WordPerfect for Windows is installed as a separate application that works with WordPerfect—and other Windows programs produced by WordPerfect Corporation.

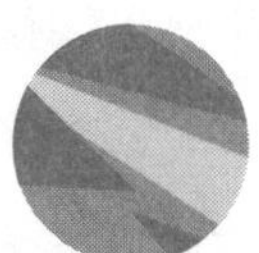

NOTE: You should save your document before you attempt a spell-check in WordPerfect. Once the Speller makes changes to the text in your document, you cannot undo the changes without retyping the corrected text. If you save your document before spell-checking, you can recover the saved file should something go wrong with the spell-check in the displayed document.

When you are ready to check the spelling of your document, choose Tools/Speller from the menu bar. The Speller appears on the screen, as shown in Figure 2-9. Command buttons on the Speller provide different options for

Figure 2-9. *The WordPerfect Speller*

checking your document text. Choose Start and the Speller begins checking the spelling of your document. If a word is not found in the Speller dictionary, the Speller will prompt you to correct the word and displays a list of suggested corrections. Double-click on the correct spelling from the list of suggestions; keyboard users can press UP ARROW or DOWN ARROW until the appropriate spelling is highlighted and then press ENTER.

The Speller replaces the misspelled word with the word you selected from the suggestion list. If the same word is misspelled in the same manner later in the document, these misspellings are automatically corrected for you. The Speller will stop at all words it does not recognize—including words that may be spelled correctly, like names and technical terms. Choose Skip Once or Skip Always when the Speller stops at a word you know is spelled correctly, and the word is ignored.

When the Speller is finished checking your document, you will see the "Spell check completed. Close Speller?" message box. Choose Yes to close the Speller and return to your document. You can also leave the Speller open so that you can check spelling in another document. See Chapter 11, "Commands and Features," for more information about the Speller and Speller options.

Inserting a Picture or Illustration

Some documents require pictures, illustrations, or diagrams to help communicate a message. You can insert any graphics image into your document from a file saved on disk. Graphics files can come from a number of sources, including:

- Images you have created with graphics software
- Illustrations from professional clip-art software packages
- Graphs created in a spreadsheet program
- Scanned photographs

Also, there are a large number of graphics images stored in files with the WordPerfect for Windows software; these images include business illustrations, symbols, and cartoons to suit a variety of business and personal documents. If you do not have other software that can create graphics files, the WordPerfect graphics images will help you get started with the graphics features. See the section titled "Graphics, Inserting" in Chapter 11, "Commands and Features," for some sample graphics.

Graphics images are placed into your document as *graphics boxes.* Once an image is retrieved into a graphics box, you can move and resize the box within your document. Graphics in your document will appear on the editing screen, just as they will appear on the printed page.

The following sections explain how to retrieve a graphics image into your document and how to move and resize a graphics box; the WordPerfect graphics features can do much more than the basic information described in this chapter. The graphics features can also produce horizontal and vertical lines, equations, and graphics boxes that include text. For complete information about the graphics features, see Chapter 11, "Commands and Features."

Retrieving a Graphics File into Your Document

When you have a graphics image file that you want to include as part of your document, you can easily retrieve it with the following procedure. First, display the page in your document where the graphics image should appear. Then, choose Graphics/Figure from the menu bar. WordPerfect displays the Insert Image dialog box. The list on this dialog box shows the files stored in the WordPerfect graphics directory, which is specified by the File/Preferences/Files feature. If your graphics files are stored in a different directory, browse through the Directories list to display the appropriate directory. Once your graphics directory is displayed, select the graphics file from the list that you want to insert in your document. Then, choose the OK button. WordPerfect creates a graphics box on the document page and retrieves the graphics file into it.

NOTE: *When the Insert Image dialog box is displayed, you can select a graphics filename and choose the View button to look at the contents of the selected file, without actually retrieving the graphics image. This will help you find the image you want when you don't remember the exact filename.*

Here is an example of how to retrieve one of the graphics images from the WordPerfect graphics directory. It is assumed that the WordPerfect graphics files are stored in a directory called "\wpwin60\graphics"; this directory is created for you when you install the WordPerfect program. First, choose Graphics/Figure. At the Insert Image dialog box, make sure the "\wpwin60\graphics" directory is displayed above the Directories list; if it is not, navigate through the directories by double-clicking directly on the directory names until you reach the graphics subdirectory, or you can type **\wpwin60\graphics** in the Filename text field and press ENTER. From the file list, select the SAN_FRAN.WPG file name. Then, choose the OK button. WordPerfect retrieves the graphics image from the file and creates a graphics box, similar to the example shown in Figure 2-10.

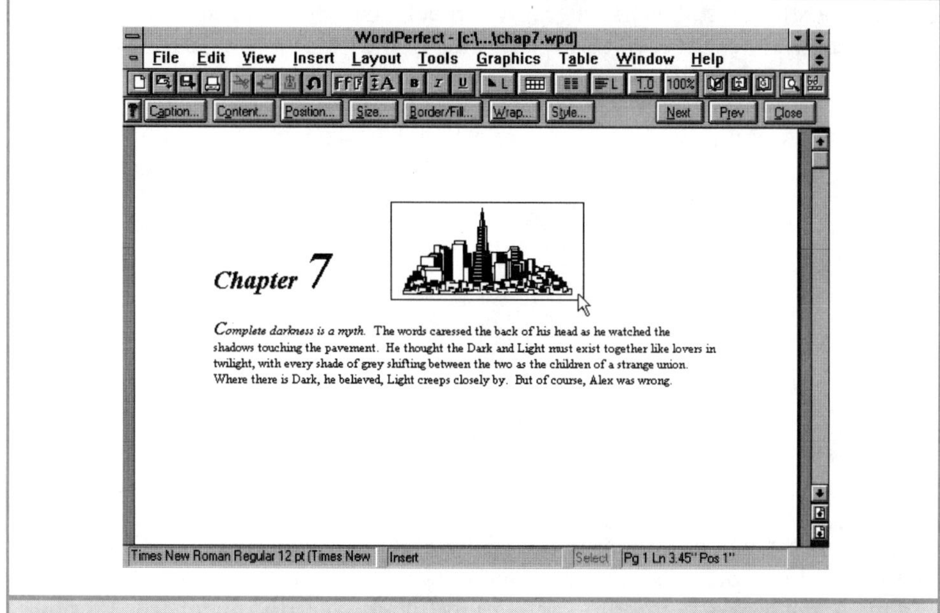

Figure 2-10. *Inserting a graphics image into your document*

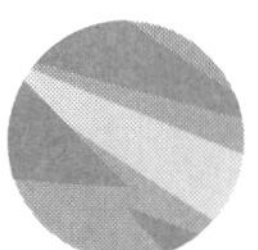

NOTE: *WordPerfect can accept graphics files from a wide variety of software programs. For a complete list of the supported graphics programs and files, see Appendix D, "Graphics Programs and Files," later in this book.*

NOTE: *If you need to remove a graphics image from your document, simply click on the graphics box and press the* DELETE *or* BACKSPACE *key.*

Moving a Graphics Box

WordPerfect makes it easy to position a graphics box in your document. You won't need to enter measurements or select a position from the menu; simply use the mouse to move the graphics box where you want it. First, click on the graphics box to select it. When a graphics box is selected, small square boxes called *handles* appear at each corner and side of the graphics box, as shown here:

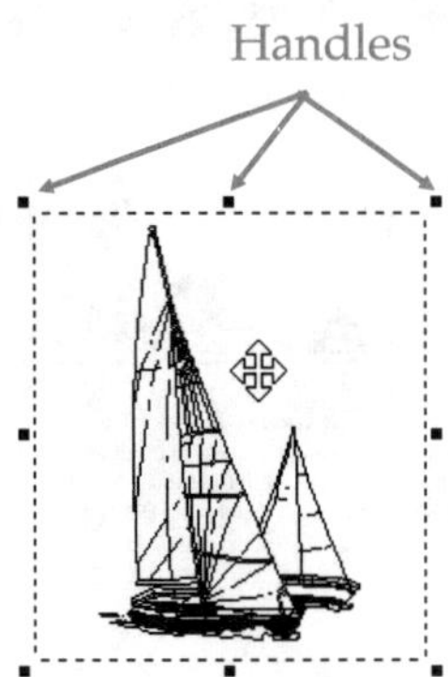

Then, move the mouse pointer to the center of the box; when you do so, the mouse pointer appears as a "four-arrow" cursor. Hold down the mouse button and move the mouse pointer to another location in your document. The graphics box will move with the mouse pointer. When you release the mouse button, the graphics box is placed at the new location. It's that simple. You can move the box as often as you like, and even make fine adjustments for positioning.

NOTE: *If you are not using a mouse, you cannot move or size graphics boxes as described here; refer to Chapter 11 for information about alternatives for keyboard users.*

Sizing a Graphics Box

You can also change the size of any graphics box in your document. First, click on the graphics box to select it. When the graphics box is selected, note the handles that appear at each corner and side of the graphics box border. You use these handles to size the graphics box, just as you would a document or application window. Move the mouse pointer onto one of the handles. Then, hold down the mouse button and move the mouse pointer to change the size of the box.

The following illustration shows how a graphics box appears while you are sizing it; the dotted border shows what the size of the graphics box will be when you release the mouse button. If you move a handle at one of the border sides, you will change the height or width of the box; move a handle at one of the corners, and you will change the height and width at once. When you release the mouse button, the box and the graphics image are resized.

Printing

WordPerfect makes it easy to send your documents to the printer, with options for printing single pages, nonconsecutive pages, or the entire document. Other options let you print multiple copies of the same document, choose draft quality for faster printing, and select adjustments for binding.

WordPerfect works with the Windows Print Manager to send your documents to the printer. Resource files called printer drivers help WordPerfect format your document for your particular printer, and store font information for text. When printing, you can use WordPerfect printer drivers or the printer drivers supplied with Microsoft Windows. You do not need to reinstall WordPerfect or make changes at the Windows Control Panel to change the driver type; you can choose either WordPerfect or Windows printer drivers from within the WordPerfect program at any time.

The following sections explain basic information about sending your documents to the printer. For complete information about the printing features, see the Print reference headings in Chapter 11, "Commands and Features," and in Chapter 5, "Working with Your Printer."

Selecting a Printer

Before you can print a document, you must create and select the correct printer definition for the printer you are using. WordPerfect's Print dialog box lists the printer definitions that you have created; you may have already created one or more of these definitions when you installed the WordPerfect program. Usually, you will have only one definition for the printer attached to your computer, but there are some situations—such as network installations—where you may need two or more printers defined. Once the definitions are created, you can select the printer you want to use.

WordPerfect for Windows supports the use of Microsoft Windows printer drivers, but it also includes its own drivers for printing. From the Select Printer dialog box, you can choose which driver type you want to use. Only the WordPerfect drivers support all of the printing features of WordPerfect. For more information, see the Printing sections in Chapter 11, "Commands and Features."

To select a printer, choose File from the menu bar, and then choose Select Printer. The Select Printer dialog box appears, which is similar to the example shown in Figure 2-11. The list of available printers will vary depending on the printer definitions you have created. Move the mouse pointer onto the name of the printer you want to use and double-click the mouse button. Keyboard users can use the arrow keys to highlight a printer name and then press ENTER or ALT+S to choose the Select button. This selects the highlighted printer name and clears the dialog box from the screen. The selected printer remains in effect until you change it or until you retrieve a document that is formatted for another printer definition that you use.

Information from the selected printer is saved with the documents you create. The selected printer definition determines which fonts are available for the text and also influences certain formatting options—such as the sizes of

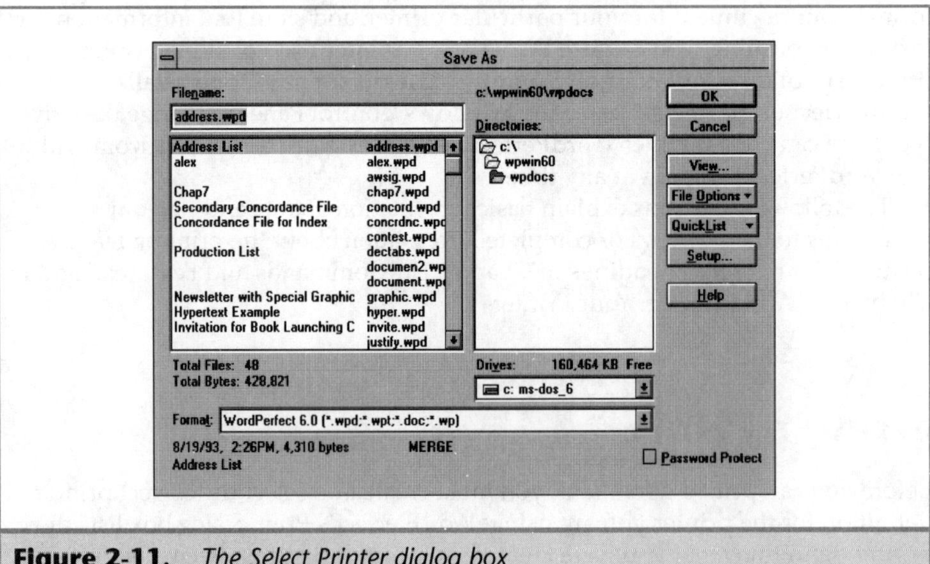

Figure 2-11. *The Select Printer dialog box*

paper that you can use to create your documents. Fonts, text spacing, and paper sizes vary between different printers, and so WordPerfect saves printer information with each document to ensure proper formatting when the document is retrieved again. This helps WordPerfect make adjustments when the document is opened on a different copy of WordPerfect, where printer definitions are different from the one used to create the initial document.

Printing Your Document

When you choose the Print feature, WordPerfect sends a copy of the document from the active document window to your printer. Before you attempt to print a document, make sure the printer is turned on and ready to print. To print the document displayed on your screen, choose File/Print from the menu bar, or simply press F5. WordPerfect displays the Print dialog box shown in Figure 2-12. You will notice that the Full Document option is selected; if you want to print only the page displayed on the document window, select the Current Page option instead. Then, choose the Print command button on the dialog box and WordPerfect sends a copy of your document to the printer.

This is the basic procedure for printing the entire document or a page from the active document window; for detailed information about printing and print options, see the reference headings for Print in Chapter 11, "Commands and Features."

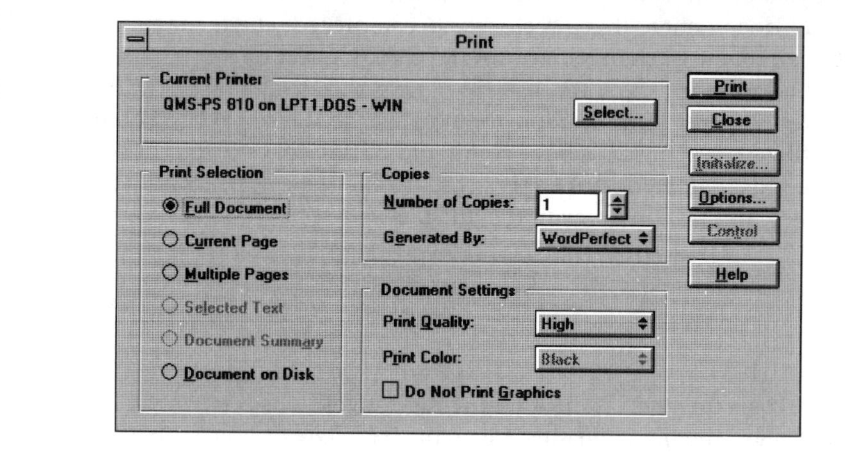

Figure 2-12. *The Print dialog box*

Saving and Retrieving Documents

Programs that run under the Windows environment include different ways to save and retrieve documents, and these are supported by WordPerfect for Windows. The method you choose to save or retrieve a file depends on whether you are working with a new document or editing an existing one. You can quickly save editing changes from the displayed document without entering a filename. Or you can choose a Save option that prompts you for filename information; this option appears automatically when you save a new document. When you open an existing document, you retrieve a file into a new document window. When you want to insert file information into the current document, you retrieve it into the active document window.

NOTE: The Save and Retrieve options use list boxes to display files and directories. For complete information about list boxes and the Save and Retrieve options, see Chapter 11 "Commands and Features."

Saving a New Document

To save a new document to a file on disk, choose File/Save As from the menu bar. Figure 2-13 shows the dialog box that appears. In the Save As text field, type the name of the file to be saved. The current directory label on the dialog box shows the default directory path, where the file will be saved. If you do not want to save your document to this directory, you can precede the filename with a complete path name or change the current path by selecting a drive/directory combination from the Directories list. (See List Boxes in Chapter 11, "Commands and Features," for more information about using these lists.) When you have typed the filename, choose the Save command button to save your document to the specified file. After a document is saved, its filename appears next to the "WordPerfect" application name in the title bar.

Filenames

When you type a filename, it must follow the conventions established by MS-DOS. That is, the filename must be eight characters or less, with a period at the end of the name and an optional three-character extension. For example, these are valid filenames: MEMO_1.DOC, REPORT.93, and FLETCHER.LTR. Some words and characters are reserved by DOS for certain functions and

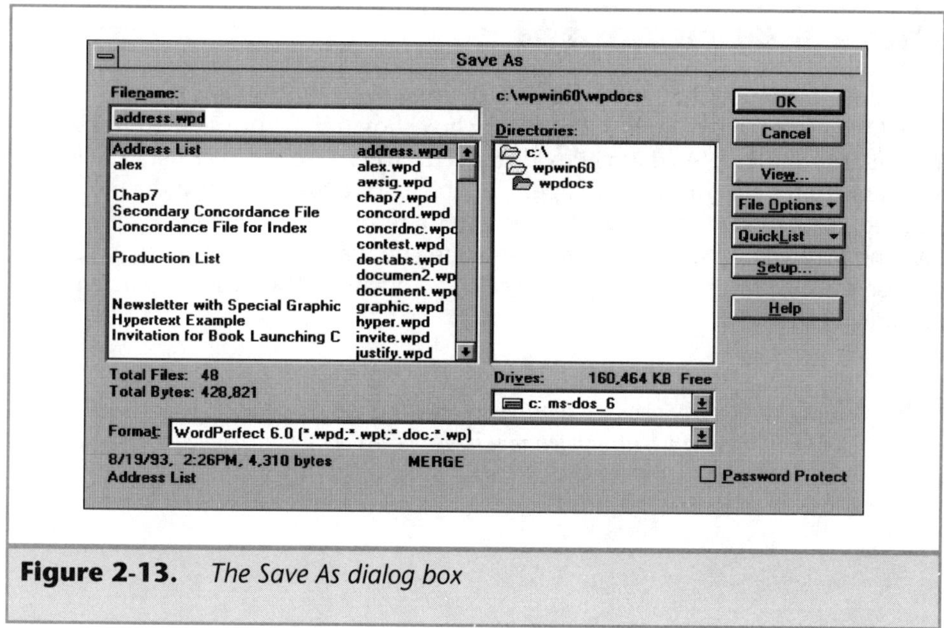

Figure 2-13. *The Save As dialog box*

operations and may not be included in filenames. Generally, you cannot type a filename that includes spaces or slashes, a plus (+) or equal (=) sign, square brackets ([or]), an asterisk (*), a comma (,), a colon (:), a semicolon (;), or quotation marks (" "). Some invalid filenames are JAN/DEC.RPT, MON+TUE.DOC, and DR.MORRIS.LTR. Check your DOS manual for a complete list of reserved characters and words.

Saving an Edited Document

When you are editing a document that has already been saved to a file, you can quickly update your editing changes by choosing File/Save. This instructs WordPerfect to save the current document to the original filename.

NOTE: *When you choose File/Save for a document that exists as a file on disk, WordPerfect will not prompt you about replacing the existing document file. The document on the screen is automatically saved over the original disk file. If you want to open an existing file and use it as a model to create a new document, make sure you choose File/Save As to save the new document under a different document name.*

Opening a Document File

To open a document that you have already saved as a file on disk, choose File/Open from the menu bar. The dialog box shown in Figure 2-14 appears; this is similar to the Save As dialog box discussed earlier. Use the Files list to select the name of the file you want to open. Double-click a filename, and the file is opened in a new document window. If you prefer to use the keyboard, use the TAB and arrow keys to highlight the filename you want, and then press ENTER to choose the OK command button. The selected document is retrieved into a new document window.

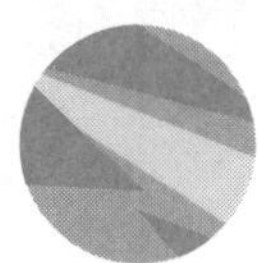

NOTE: You can open up to nine document windows at once, but WordPerfect will run more efficiently when you have fewer documents opened.

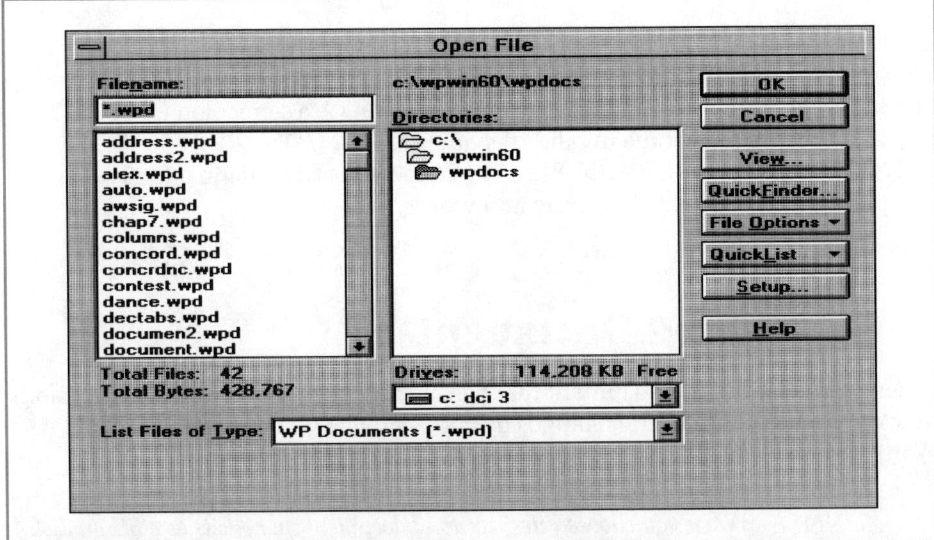

Figure 2-14. *The Open File dialog box*

Closing a Document

When you are finished working with a document, you should close it before you start a new document. To close a document, choose File/Close from the menu bar, or press CTRL+F4. If you have made changes to the document that you have not saved, WordPerfect prompts you to save the changes before you close the document.

Basic File Management

WordPerfect provides an Option button on the Open dialog box, and other similar list boxes, that allows you to perform some basic file management tasks. These include copying, moving, deleting, and renaming files. To perform any of these tasks, display a list box, select a filename, and choose one of the file options from the pop-up list.

For example, assume you want to delete a file from a specific directory. Choose File/Open from the menu bar to display the Open File dialog box. Use the directory list to display the directory where the file is located. Highlight the file, and then choose the File Options button; a pop-up list of file options appears. Choose the Delete option from the list, and WordPerfect displays a message box that prompts you to confirm the file deletion. Choose Delete and the file is removed from your directory. The other file options—Copy, Move, and Rename—display the current filename and location and prompt you to type a new path or filename. When you choose the appropriate command button on the message box, the file is copied or moved to the new directory or renamed with the new name you entered. When you are finished with the file options, choose the Cancel button to close the list box.

For information on how you can perform advanced file manipulation with WordPerfect for Windows, see Chapter 4, "Managing Files with WordPerfect."

Getting Help

The help feature displays on-screen information about the WordPerfect program. You can display information through an index of program features, view a list of assigned keystrokes, use a special pointer to find out the function of displayed buttons and menu items, or look up terms in an online glossary. The help feaure also includes a Search feature, which lets you look for help screens that contain key words and phrases.

Using the Help Feature

There are two ways to access the help feature. You can choose a help option from the Help menu, or you can press the F1 key to display context-sensitive information about the feature you are currently using. For example, suppose you want to know more about WordPerfect's Button Bar feature. You can display information about this feature by choosing Help/Contents from the menu bar. From the displayed help screen, click on the Search menu button. An index of program topics through which you can search is displayed. Type "Button Bar" in the text box and click on Show Topics to narrow the topic. You can also use the scroll bars until the "Button Bar" heading appears in the list. Select a topic in the lower portion of the dialog box and click Go To, or press ENTER, and a help screen about the Button Bar feature is displayed.

When help information is displayed, it appears in its own window, within the WordPerfect program. Buttons at the top of the window let you display the Help Contents, Search for another term, go Back to a previously displayed help screen, see a History of help topics you have recently viewed, Print the displayed help screen, or Close the help feature. Within the help text you will see underlined terms or topics, called *jump topics*. Click a jump topic, and a help screen is displayed for it. When you are finished reading the information, click the Back button to return to the previous help screen. Terms shown with a broken or dotted underline are glossary terms; click a dotted underline term and a definition of the term is displayed. When you are finished with Help, click on Close to close the Help window and return to your document.

When a WordPerfect menu item is highlighted, or when a dialog box is displayed, press F1 to display context-sensitive help about the feature. When you are finished reading the help information, press ALT+F4 to return to the WordPerfect program.

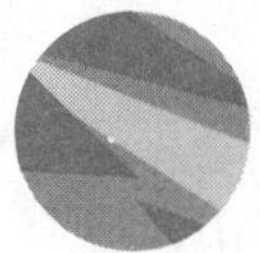

NOTE: *See the section Help in Chapter 11, "Commands and Features," for complete information about the help feature.*

WordPerfect Customer Support

WordPerfect Corporation provides toll-free customer support to all registered users of WordPerfect software. Call the support hotline, listed in your WordPerfect manual, when you have problems with the program that you cannot solve on your own. When you call, the customer support operator may ask you for your registration number; if so, this number is found on a card included with the WordPerfect package. If you entered your registration number during the WordPerfect installation procedure, you can view the number on the screen by choosing Help/About WordPerfect from the WordPerfect menu bar. Before you call, make sure you know the brand and model number of your computer and printer, as well as information about other software programs that you are running with Windows. This information will help the operator find a solution to the problems you are encountering.

CHAPTER 3

Tools and Techniques

WordPerfect for Windows incorporates many tools to help you create and edit your documents efficiently. Special features simplify many editing tasks; an on-screen ruler lets you quickly create the layout you want; the power bar includes many common tasks; and the button bar feature lets you create on-screen buttons for the features you use most often. This chapter covers these and other basic procedures to help you increase your productivity in WordPerfect. The general use of each feature is described here; for complete details on these and other features, see Chapter 11, "Commands and Features."

This chapter also explains how to customize the Windows program by choosing screen colors, desktop options, and mouse settings. Because these options are selected from Microsoft Windows (and not from WordPerfect for Windows), they affect the display and operation of all programs that run within the Windows environment—including WordPerfect. Finally, this chapter assumes you know the basics of typing, selecting, and editing text. See Chapter 2, "WordPerfect for Windows Basics," for a review of these word processing tasks.

Editing Tools

The WordPerfect menus list several options and tools for editing. Most of these are provided to help you with common editing tasks, such as converting text from lowercase to uppercase; canceling, or "undoing," an editing command; and moving to specific places in the document. You can also search for certain text or codes, insert comments as references for editing, and count the total number of words in a document.

Converting Lowercase and Uppercase Text

An option on the Edit menu lets you quickly change selected text to all lowercase or uppercase letters. After using the mouse or the keyboard to select the text you want to convert, choose Edit/Convert Case. A submenu appears with the options for Convert Case. Choose Lowercase, Uppercase, or Initial Capitals to indicate your preference, and the selected text is converted. After converting the text, click the mouse or press F8 to turn off the select mode.

When you choose a Convert Case option, WordPerfect changes the capitalization of all selected text to the case you've specified. There are, however, some exceptions when WordPerfect keeps certain letters capitalized. For example, when you select the pronoun *I* or related contractions like "I'm" and "I've," WordPerfect keeps the *I* capitalized, regardless of whether you choose Uppercase or Lowercase. Also, when you choose the Lowercase option, any capital letters that follow a period are kept as uppercase letters; WordPerfect assumes that these letters begin a new sentence and must remain capitalized. These exceptions help ensure correct capitalization for words in your document.

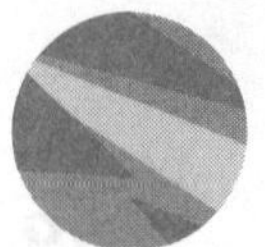

NOTE: When converting an uppercased sentence to lowercase letters, include the ending punctuation from the previous sentence as part of the selected text. This tells WordPerfect to convert all selected text to lowercase letters—except the first letter of the sentence, which remains capitalized.

Moving to a Specific Place in the Document

The Go To dialog box lets you move quickly to a specific page number, to the top or bottom of the current page, or to the previous position of the insertion point. Before you can display the dialog box, you must have a document open in WordPerfect. To display the Go To dialog box, shown in Figure 3-1, choose Edit/Go To, or simply press CTRL+G. If you want to move to a specific page, type the page number in the Page Number text field and choose OK. WordPerfect displays the page and also moves the insertion point to the top of the page.

The Position radio button in the Go To dialog box gives you additional options for moving the insertion point. The current option appears as the name on the command button. From the Position button, you can select one of the options, which vary depending on what you are doing in the document window. You can choose Top of Current Page or Bottom of Current Page to move the insertion point to the top or bottom of the displayed page. Another option, Last Position, moves the insertion point to its previous location, where text or formatting codes were last inserted or edited. The Last Position button is useful when you need to "jump back" to the last place you were editing your document. After you have chosen an option, choose OK, and the insertion point moves to the new location. Or, choose Cancel to close the Go To dialog box without moving the insertion point.

When text is selected, the Position button provides additional options for Beginning of Selection, End of Selection, and Reselect Text. Beginning of Selection and End of Selection moves the insertion point to the beginning or the end of the selected text, respectively; Reselect Text selects the text from the beginning of the current selection to the location of the insertion point before Select was turned on; in most cases, this reselects the previously selected text.

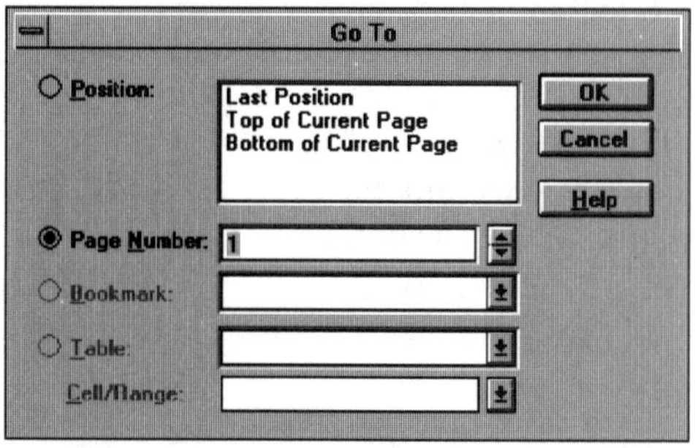

Figure 3-1. *The Go To dialog box*

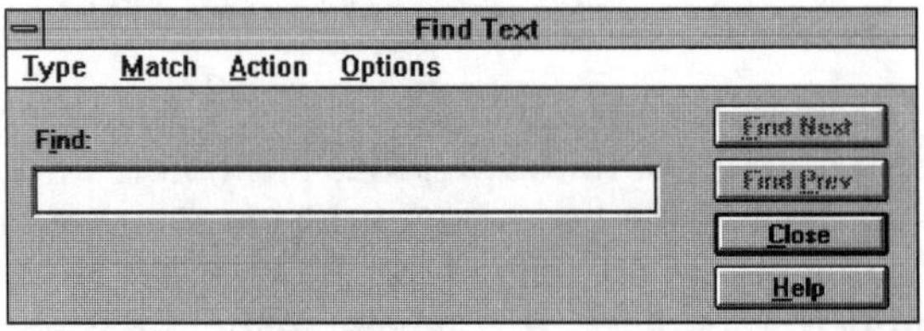

Find Text
Type Match Action Options
Find:
Find Next
Find Prev
Close
Help

Figure 3-2. *The Find Text dialog box*

When the insertion point is located within text columns, the Position button displays options for moving to the top or bottom of columns and for moving between the columns across the page. If the insertion point is located within a table, the Position button displays options for moving between the cells and columns of the table.

Other options within the Go To dialog box allow you to jump to a specific bookmark within your document. A bookmark is a named position within the document. You select the bookmark, by name, and WordPerfect moves the insertion point to that location. See the entry "Bookmarks" in Chapter 11, "Commands and Features."

Searching for Words and Phrases

WordPerfect's search feature lets you move the insertion point directly to a specific word or phrase in your document. You can also search for document codes, such as margin changes or tab settings, and locate the layout commands that are hidden in the text.

To search for a word or phrase, choose Edit/Find from the menu bar. Keyboard users can simply press F2. This displays the Find Text dialog box, shown in Figure 3-2. Type the word or phrase you want to find; this word or phrase is called the *search criterion* or *search string*. WordPerfect saves the search criterion in the dialog box until you change it or until you exit the WordPerfect program.

You can use the Find Text dialog box to indicate other criteria you want to use in your search:

- The choices under the Type menu allow you to specify how WordPerfect should treat what you have typed in the Find field.

- The Match menu allows you to specify whether WordPerfect should match only whole words, and whether uppercase or lowercase (as you entered them) are significant. You can also use this menu to specify text attributes or formatting codes that you want to search for.
- The Action menu is where you specify what WordPerfect should do when it locates a match. You can instruct it to position the insertion point either before or after the match. You can also choose to select everything between the current insertion point position and the match by choosing the Extend selection option.
- Finally, the Options menu includes choices on where WordPerfect should begin searching, how it should act when it reaches the end of the document, and whether nondocument text should be searched. This includes items such as footers, headers, and so on.

Whenever you search for something in your document, WordPerfect begins the search at the insertion point, unless, of course, you have indicated it should begin at the top of the document using the Begin Find at Top of Document choice under the Options menu. When you have specified your search criterion, choose the Find Next command button, and WordPerfect looks for the next occurrence of the text you typed in the Find field. If you want to search toward the beginning of the document, instead choose the Find Prev button.

If a match of the search criterion is found, WordPerfect moves the insertion point to the text that matches, in the manner you specified under the Action menu. If the search criterion is not found, WordPerfect displays a "Not found" message, and the insertion point remains at its original position.

If you want to continue searching, you can continue to click on the Find Next or Find Prev command buttons. If you close the Find Text dialog box, you can later continue a search by using SHIFT+F2 (find next) or ALT+F2 (find previous). If you want to change the search criterion, choose Edit/Find to redisplay the Find Text dialog box, and enter the new settings.

Replacing Words and Phrases

Another WordPerfect feature, called Replace, lets you search for specific text and replace it with new or corrected text. This is useful when you want to quickly change a date, number, or phrase that is repeated often throughout the document. The Replace feature is initiated by choosing Edit/Replace from the menus, and works very similarly to the search function. For information about the Replace feature or more information about the Search features, see Chapter 11, "Commands and Features."

Canceling an Editing Command

Many dialog boxes in WordPerfect include a command button called Cancel. You choose this button when you do not want to accept the action or settings of the displayed dialog box. When you want to cancel an action or setting that you have already accepted, use the Undo command.

Undo is a standard feature for programs running under Windows. This command lets you recall the last program operation you performed; this can be anything from removing the sentence you just typed to canceling the defined document layout. Whatever you last did in WordPerfect, Undo will most likely reverse its effect. Choose Edit/Undo or press CTRL+Z, and WordPerfect cancels the last operation you performed. If, for example, you changed your document margins, Undo can restore the original margins as if no change had been made. If you selected a new text color or attribute, Undo can remove it from your text.

Remember that Undo can undo only the last command you selected. This includes commands performed with keystrokes. Generally, you can undo only those commands that affect the appearance and text of your document. Commands that affect the WordPerfect program, like File/Preferences/Display and View/Ruler Bar, cannot be undone.

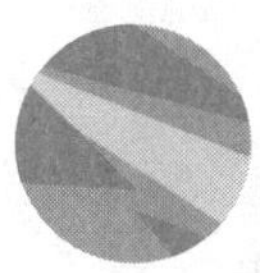

NOTE: See Chapter 11 for complete information about the features and commands that may be canceled with Undo.

Inserting Document Comments

The Comment feature of WordPerfect for Windows lets you insert references and notations that are visible only when your document is displayed on the screen. You can place comments, as notes to yourself, for revisions, inquiries, or even confidential information. When you print your document, the comments do not appear on the printed pages.

Unlike hidden text, you do not have the option to print comments. However, for the sake of flexibility, you can easily convert comments into normal, printable text. For more information on converting comments into text, see the entry "Comments" in Chapter 11, "Commands and Features."

Before you create a comment, move the insertion point to the location within your document where the comment should appear. Then choose the option Insert/Comment/Create. You will then see the Comment window, which you use to insert your comments. When this window is displayed, type the comment or note you want to insert. When you have finished typing the text, choose the

Close button to insert the comment into your document. Comments will display differently depending on the view mode you are using. In draft view, an inserted comment appears as a grey bar across your document with the comment displayed inside. In Page view and Two Page view, a comment symbol appears in the left margin as a caption balloon with quotes inside. To view the comment, click on or near the comment symbol. When you do so, a balloon appears at the insertion point of the comment that displays the comment, as shown in Figure 3-3.

Each comment you create appears on the document screen but is actually inserted as a code in the text. You can edit a comment by moving the insertion point just beyond the displayed comment and choosing Insert/Comment/Edit from the menu bar. If you are using a mouse, simply move the I-beam onto the grey comment bar and double-click the mouse button. This displays the Comment window again, where you can edit the text you typed. When you have finished, choose Close, and your editing changes are updated in the comment. You can remove a comment by deleting the code that creates it. First, choose View/Reveal Codes or press ALT+F3 to display the document codes. Then position the marker before or after the Comment code in the codes window, and press the DELETE or BACKSPACE key. This removes the comment from your document.

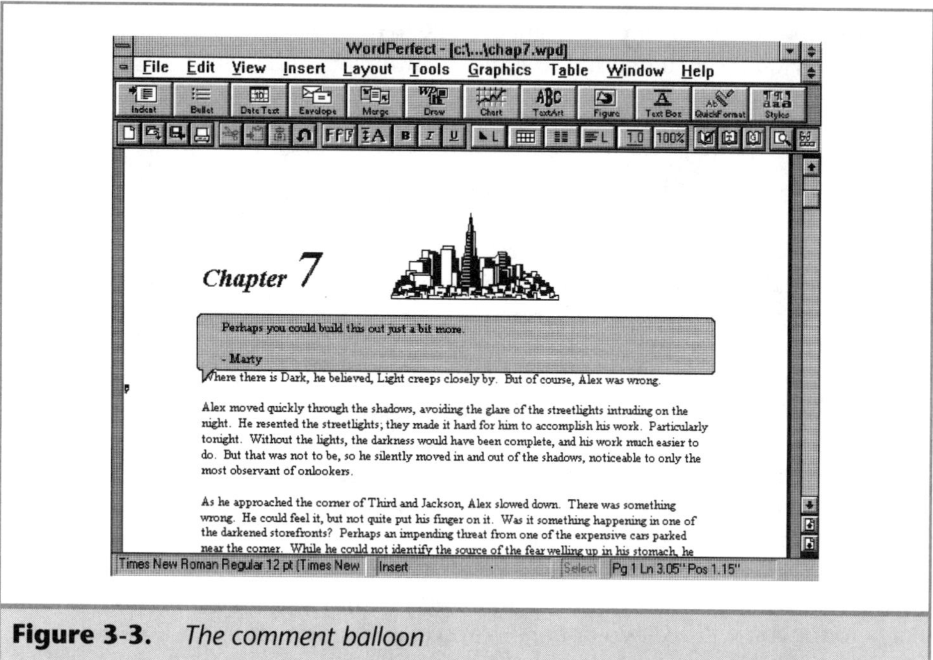

Figure 3-3. *The comment balloon*

Displaying Document Statistics

Sometimes, it is important to know the number of words that your document contains. This is true for term papers, magazine articles, and other documents that require a specific word count. You may also want to know other statistics about your document and how it is written. To display a word count, along with other document statistics, choose File/Document Info. WordPerfect displays the Document Information dialog box:

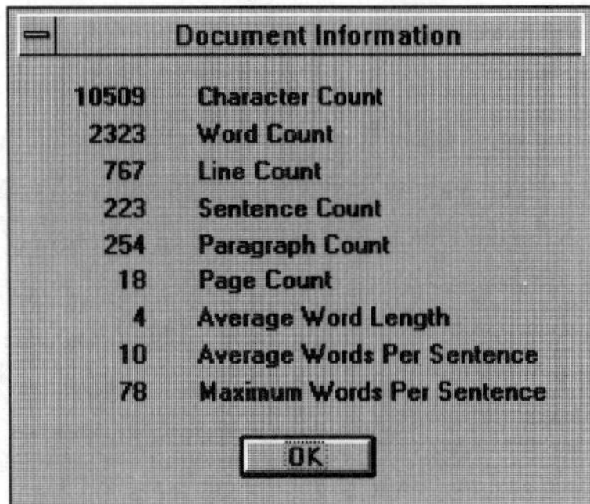

When the count is completed, choose OK to remove the dialog box from the screen. Only text is included in the statistics; numbers and graphics are ignored.

Displaying Vertical and Horizontal Scroll Bars

WordPerfect has two scroll bars—one for vertical scrolling and one for horizontal scrolling—that may be turned on and off as needed. Initially, WordPerfect displays only the vertical scroll bar on the document window because many documents do not require horizontal scrolling. For most documents that are 8 1/2 (or fewer) inches wide, WordPerfect's WYSIWYG (what you see is what you get) display can show the entire document width on the screen at once. When your document extends beyond the width of the screen, the horizontal scroll bar helps you scroll to each side of the document. For example, the horizontal scroll bar is useful when you are printing your document in *landscape mode*—that is, sideways on the paper.

To turn one or both scroll bars on or off, choose File/Preferences/Display. A dialog box then appears with different display setting options. Under the Scroll Bars group, you will see two options, Vertical and Horizontal. An X in the box next to each option indicates that the scroll bar is turned on. Click a scroll bar option and it is turned on or off, depending on whether the box was already checked.

You can also specify how WordPerfect should display the horizontal scroll bar. If you choose the Show Always option, then the scroll bars will always be visible. If, however, you choose When Required, the scroll bar will only be on the screen when it makes sense, based on the width of your document.

Click the OK button to accept the changes, and the WordPerfect screen is redisplayed with the scroll bars you turned on. The scroll bar setting remains active until you turn them off from the Display Preferences dialog box.

The horizontal scroll bar works just like its vertical counterpart: click the arrows at each end of the bar to scroll one direction or the other. Drag the slider button to move quickly to one end of the document. When you use either scroll bar, the insertion point does not move with your view of the document; instead, the insertion point remains at the last place in your document where you typed or inserted text or selected a formatting command. Once you've used the scroll bars to move within a document, click on the screen to regain your insertion point. Otherwise, as you begin typing, you will return to the location of the insertion point.

Formatting with the Ruler Bar

WordPerfect's ruler bar (or ruler, for brevity) makes it easy to create and change a document layout. With the ruler, you can see document measurements, change margins and tab settings, adjust text alignment and line spacing, and apply fonts and predefined layout styles to your text. You can also create and edit tables and columns with convenient on-screen controls. These formatting options may be selected from the Layout menu; also, the advantage with the ruler is that layout adjustments are more visual than they are when you use menus and dialog boxes. Instead of entering numbers and choosing options, you simply move markers on the ruler to create or edit your layout. If, for example, you want a tab stop to be located elsewhere, simply use the mouse to drag it to the new location on the ruler. Any changes you make are shown instantly on the screen, and they can be quickly changed if necessary. This type of control is possible only from the ruler.

NOTE: *You must have a mouse connected to your computer if you want to use the ruler to create or change the layout settings of your document.*

Before you make any changes to the margins, tab stops, or other ruler settings, make sure the insertion point is located at the place in your document where the change should occur. Although the ruler appears at the top of your screen, the changes made on the ruler are inserted as codes at the insertion point in your text. As you move the insertion point through your document, the markers on the ruler change to show the current margin and tab settings.

Displaying the Ruler Bar

You can display the ruler bar by choosing View/Ruler Bar from the menu bar. If you prefer to use the keyboard, press ALT+SHIFT+F3. Figure 3-4 shows how the ruler will appear on your screen. The ruler is divided into two different parts. The top part of the ruler is the margin bar; this is where the left and right margins are displayed. When you define columns and tables for your document, the margin bar also shows margin divisions for each text or table column. With the exception of top and bottom margins for your pages, all margin settings, including those for columns and tables, may be changed from the ruler. When the ruler is displayed, choose View/Ruler Bar again or press ALT+SHIFT+F3 to remove the ruler from the screen.

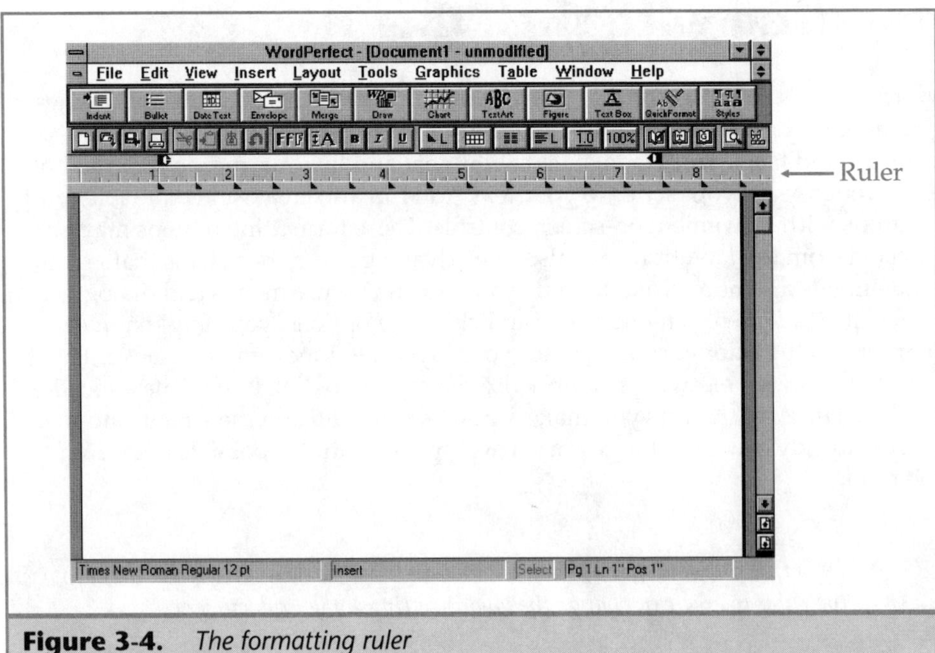

Figure 3-4. *The formatting ruler*

If you want the ruler displayed each time you start WordPerfect, you can choose an option from the Display Preferences dialog box. Choose the option File/Preferences/Display to access the Display Preferences dialog box. Then choose Ruler Bar from the display categories at the top of the screen. The dialog box now appears as shown in Figure 3-5.

Now select the checkbox labeled Show Ruler Bar on New and Current Document. When you choose the OK button to accept the change, the ruler will be displayed at all times. This affects only the initial display of the ruler; you can always turn the ruler on and off from the View menu while you are working with WordPerfect.

Changing the Ruler Measurements

Initially, the measurements on the ruler are displayed in terms of inches. You can easily change the unit of measurement to centimeters, to typesetting points (72 points per inch), or to 1200ths of an inch, which is the internal measurement that WordPerfect uses. WordPerfect gives you two options for changing the unit of measure. The first option controls the measurement type for layout settings, such

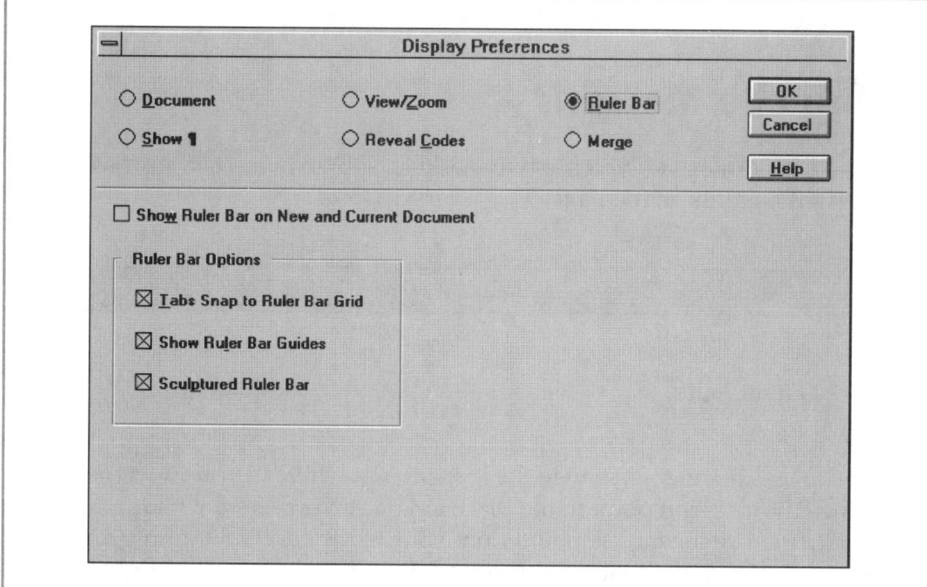

Figure 3-5. *The Display Preferences dialog box*

as margins, tab settings, and columns. Generally, this option affects only the measurements displayed in dialog boxes. The second option determines the unit of measurement for the status bar and the ruler.

Both measurement options are controlled from the Display Preferences dialog box. To change them, choose File/Preferences/Display. In the Measurement section, choose either Units of Measure or Status/Ruler Display. When you click on the button to the right of these options, you can choose one of the available measurement units:

- Inches (displayed with an inch mark)
- Inches (displayed with an *i*)
- Centimeters (*c*)
- Millimeters (*m*)
- Points (*p*)
- 1200ths of an inch (displayed with a *w*)

Then choose the OK button to accept the change. The displayed ruler will now use the measurement type you selected to show the location of document margins and tab stops.

Changing the Margins

At the top of the ruler, you will see two markers, shown here, that represent the left and right margins on the page:

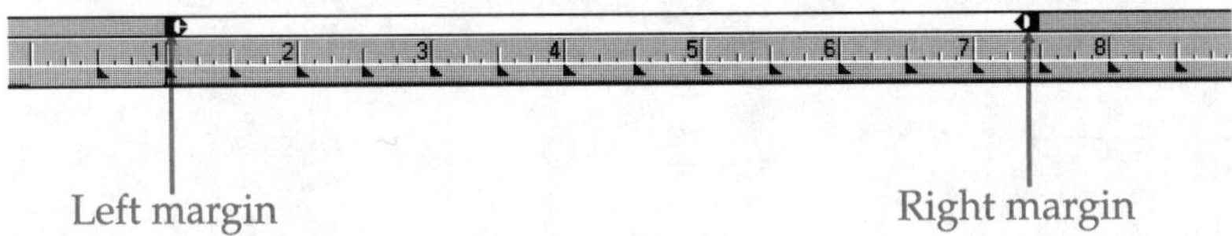

You can use the ruler to change the margins anywhere in your document. First, move the insertion point to the place in your text where the margins should change. Then move the mouse pointer onto one of the curved margin markers on the ruler. Hold down the mouse button, and drag the marker left or right to move it to the new location. As you drag the mouse, a vertical dotted line extends from the marker, along the side of the page, as a guide for the new margin location. When you release the mouse button, a margin code is placed at the location of the insertion point, and the ruler indicates the new margin.

NOTE: *If you change your mind and want to restore the original margins, choose Edit/Undo from the menu bar.*

When the ruler is displayed, you can change the margins at any time, but remember that each time you do so, a margin change code is placed at the location of the insertion point. You can view the margin code by choosing the View/Reveal Codes option. This code affects the text positioned after it until you change the margins again. As you move the insertion point through your document, the markers on the ruler will change to reflect the margin settings you have defined.

Changing Paragraph Indents

Besides the margins, you can also change the indents for a paragraph by using the ruler. Take a look, again, at the top part of the ruler:

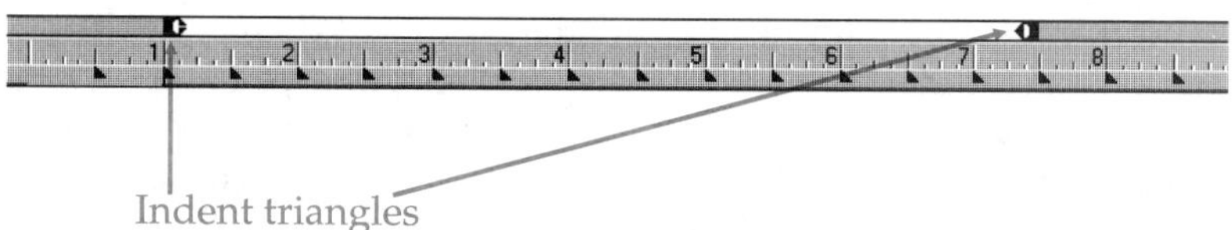

Notice that just inside the curved margin markers are some triangles that point toward the center of the screen. The triangle on the left is actually broken into two pieces. The top part of the left triangle controls the first line indent, and the bottom part controls the regular paragraph indent. The right triangle controls the right indent. By adjusting these three triangles, you can modify how you want paragraphs to appear.

You adjust the indents by moving the mouse pointer over the triangle that controls the indent you want to change. Click and hold the mouse button, and, as you drag the mouse, the indent triangle moves as well. As you move the triangle, a vertical dotted line appears on the page so you can see where your indents will occur. When you release the mouse button, the indent is set at that location, and your text is reformatted.

Moving and Deleting Tab Stops

You can create and adjust tab stops from the Tab Set dialog box, but it is much easier to work with tabs from the ruler. When you move and delete tab stops, any text formatted with the tabs is instantly reformatted to reflect the changes. Tab stop markers appear on the ruler, like this:

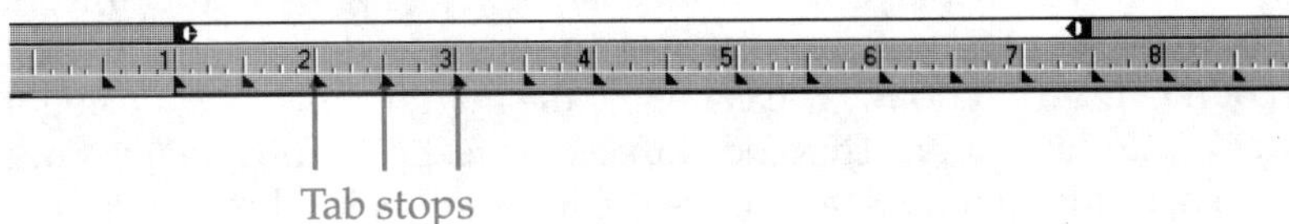

Tab stops

Before you move or delete tab stops, make sure the insertion point is located at the place in your text where the changes should occur. If, for example, the tab stops should affect the entire document, press CTRL+HOME to move the insertion point to the beginning of the document. If the new tab stops should affect only a specific paragraph or table, move the insertion point to that place in the document.

To move a tab stop, first position the mouse pointer over the tab stop marker. Then hold down the mouse button and drag the marker left or right to move it to the new location. As you drag the mouse, a vertical dotted line extends down from the marker as a guide for positioning the tab stop. When you release the mouse button, the tab stop is set at the new location. After you move a tab stop, tabbed text on the screen is adjusted to show the correct layout in your document.

To delete a tab stop, drag the marker down off the ruler, instead of left or right; this removes the marker from the ruler and deletes the tab. After you move and delete tabs, WordPerfect inserts a Tab Set code into your text for the new tab stops. If you change your mind and want to restore the deleted tabs, choose Edit/Undo from the menu bar.

Defining New Tabs

Adding new tab stops is as easy as moving and deleting tabs. But before you do so, make sure the insertion point is located where the new tab stops should begin. Then use the mouse pointer to point to the location on the ruler where you want the tab stop placed. Click on the *right* mouse button, and you will see a tab definition list appear, as shown in the following:

✓Left
Center
Right
Decimal
...Left
...Center
...Right
...Decimal
Clear All Tabs
Tab Set...
Hide Ruler Bar
Preferences...

Move the mouse pointer to select the type of tab you want set at the ruler location. You can select from any of the following types:

- Left-aligned
- Centered
- Right-aligned
- Decimal-aligned

These tab stop types are repeated twice on the menu—once without leading periods, and once with. The selections that have the leading periods result in placing a tab that uses a *dot leader.* The dot leader places a line of dots between text columns formatted with the tab stops. For complete information about the tab stop options, refer to Chapter 11, "Commands and Features."

NOTE: *You can also define and edit tab settings from the Tab Set dialog box. To display this dialog box from the ruler, choose the Tab Set options from the tab setting menu.*

When you have finished setting the tab stops, a Tab Set code, which includes the changes you made on the ruler, is inserted into your document, on the line where the insertion point is located. This code affects the text positioned after it

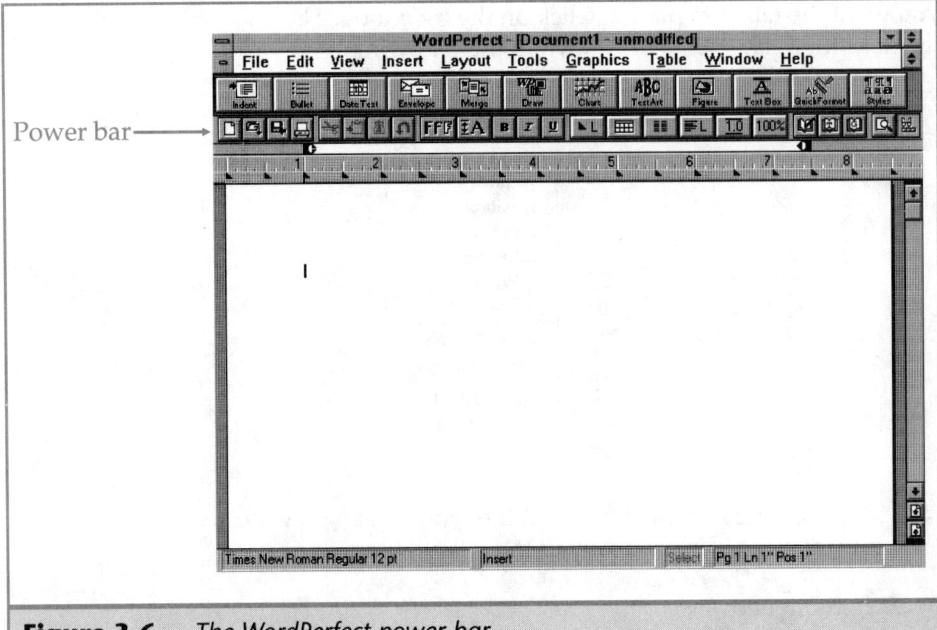

Figure 3-6. *The WordPerfect power bar*

until you change the tab stops again, later in the document. You can view the Tab Set code, and other codes in your document, by choosing View/Reveal Codes or by pressing ALT+F3.

Using the Power Bar

WordPerfect for Windows has a new feature called the *power bar.* The power bar includes many different buttons that allow you to perform common WordPerfect functions without resorting to using the menus. For instance, you can save your document, undo changes, and apply formatting. To display the power bar, choose View/Power Bar. Your screen will appear as shown in Figure 3-6.

You may have noticed that many of the figures and illustrations used in this book have had the power bar displayed. This is because it provides an ease-of-use you won't want to be without as you are using WordPerfect for Windows. Notice that there are 24 buttons on the power bar. These perform the following functions:

Creates a new document

Opens an existing document

Saves the current document

Prints the current document

Cuts the selected text

Copies selected text or graphics to the Clipboard

Pastes the Clipboard at the insertion point

Undoes the last action

Changes fonts

Changes font size

Turns on/off bold text

Turns on/off italic text

Turns on/off underlined text

Accesses the Tab Set dialog box

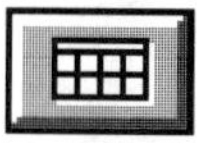

Creates a table

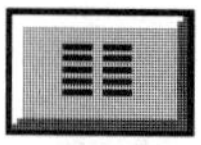

Applies/changes the number of text columns

Changes text justification

1.0	Changes line spacing
100%	Zooms in or out
	Accesses the spelling checker
	Accesses the thesaurus
	Accesses the grammar checker
	Views full page
	Show/hide the current button bar

Many of the functions performed by buttons on the power bar have already been discussed in this book. There are a few, however, that may require additional explanation. The next few sections address several of the buttons.

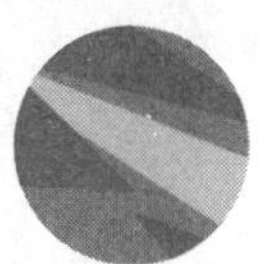

NOTE: *You must have a mouse to use WordPerfect's power bar feature.*

Changing the Font

The Font Face button on the power bar lets you apply different fonts to the text in your document. Before you choose a font, move the insertion point to the place in your text where the font change should occur. Then move the mouse pointer over the Font Face button on the power bar and click the mouse button. This displays a pop-up list of fonts that are assigned to the power bar, as shown in Figure 3-7.

While still holding down the mouse button, move the pointer down the list until the font you want is highlighted. Then release the mouse button to select the font. After you do so, a Font code is inserted into your text to start the font change; this affects all text placed after the code until another Font code is placed later in the document.

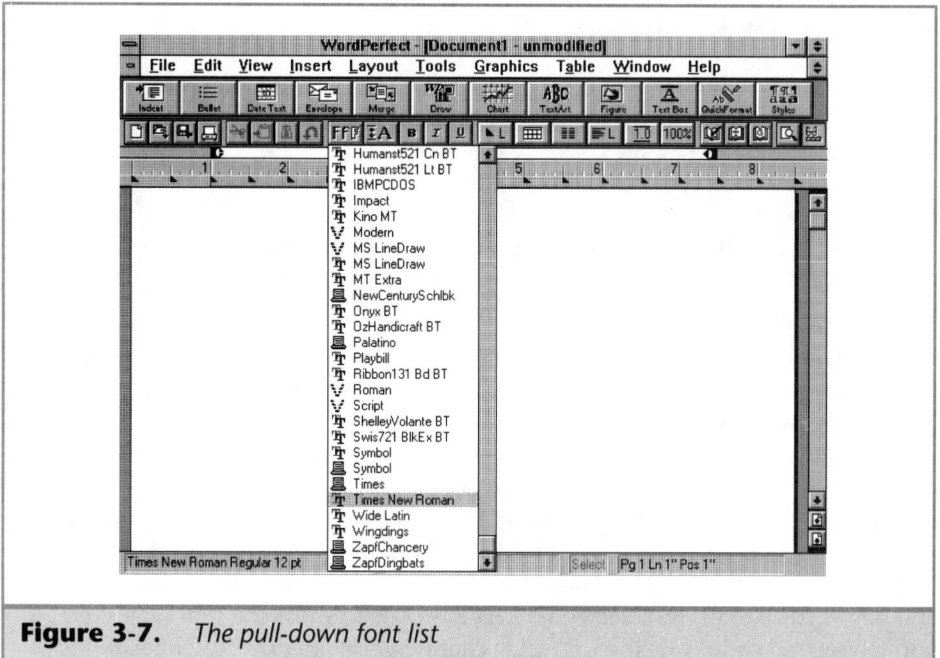

Figure 3-7. *The pull-down font list*

You can apply a font change to selected text also. First, select the text that should be affected by the font change. Then choose the desired font from the pop-up list on the power bar. In this case, WordPerfect inserts two font change codes: one to start the font change at the beginning of the selected text, and one at the end of the selected text to change back to the original font.

You can select any of the available fonts from the power bar. Since the font name and font size options are accessible from the power bar, this means you can also modify any of the fonts displayed by the font button. To designate which fonts you want to display from the font name and/or font size buttons, select File/Preferences/Power Bar and click on the Fonts option button. All of the available fonts are then listed along with their respective sizes. Those items that have check marks next to them are the currently accessible items from the Font Face button (and the sizes from the font size button). Make the desired selections and click OK.

Once this is done, you do not need to do it again until you change your printer or fonts. For complete information about printer setup and fonts, see Chapter 5, "Working with Your Printer."

Changing the Font Size

The Font Size button on the power bar lets you choose different text sizes by inserting a new font code for the current typeface. You can also choose font sizes from the Layout/Font menu.

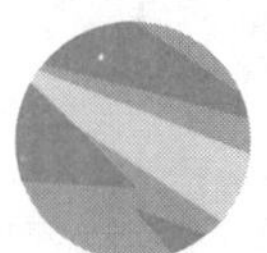

NOTE: You can also display the Font dialog box from the power bar by double-clicking the power bar's Font Face button or the Font Size button.

To select a new size for the current font, move the mouse pointer over the Font Size button. Then hold down the mouse button to display the font size pop-up list. While holding down the mouse button, move the pointer into the list to highlight the size you want. Release the mouse button; the highlighted size is selected, and WordPerfect inserts a new Font code at the insertion point to create the change. You can also apply a font size to selected text by first selecting the text and then choosing the desired font size from the pop-up list on the power bar. In this case, WordPerfect inserts two font change codes: one at the beginning and one at the end of the selected text. The first code starts the font/size change, and the second code ends the font/size change, returning the font back to the original size.

The sizes you can select from the list are shown as point sizes. A point is the standard typographical unit of measurement for fonts, with 72 points equaling one inch. For scalable fonts, WordPerfect chooses standard sizes and displays them on the list. If you need to select a font size that is not displayed on the power bar's Size list, you should choose the font and the point size from the Font dialog box.

Creating a Table

WordPerfect's Table feature lets you create tables for lists, accounting ledgers, and other similar documents. You can create tables with options provided under the Table menu, or you can use the table button on the power bar.

To create a table from the power bar, move the mouse pointer onto the table button. Then hold down the mouse button, and a table grid pops up over the power bar. Each square on the grid represents a possible cell for the table. While holding down the mouse button, move the pointer into the grid to highlight the desired dimensions for the table. Figure 3-8 shows how the grid might appear on your screen. The area at the top of the grid displays the size of the table. When you release the mouse button, WordPerfect creates the table with the selection from the grid. Figure 3-9 shows a table in the document window.

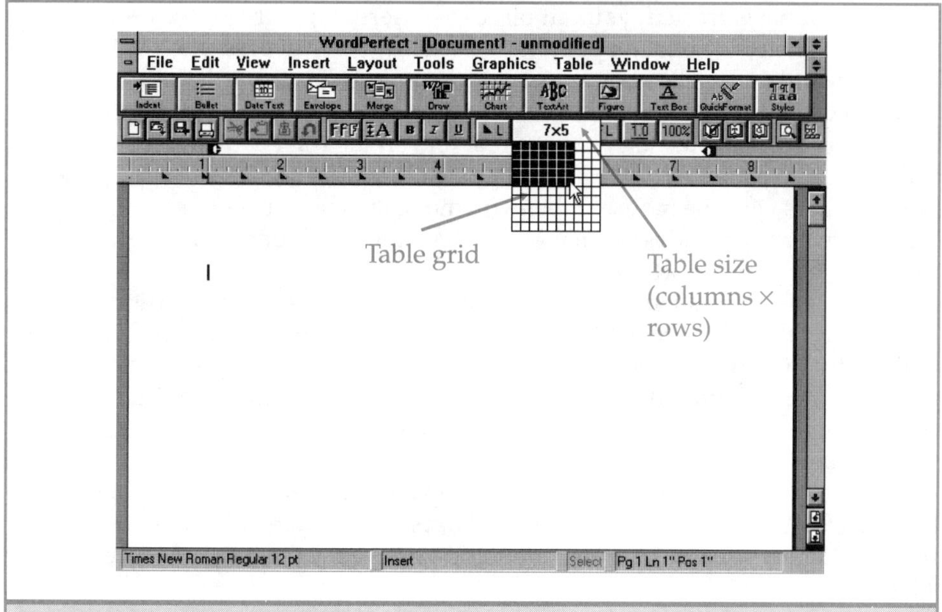

Figure 3-8. *The table grid*

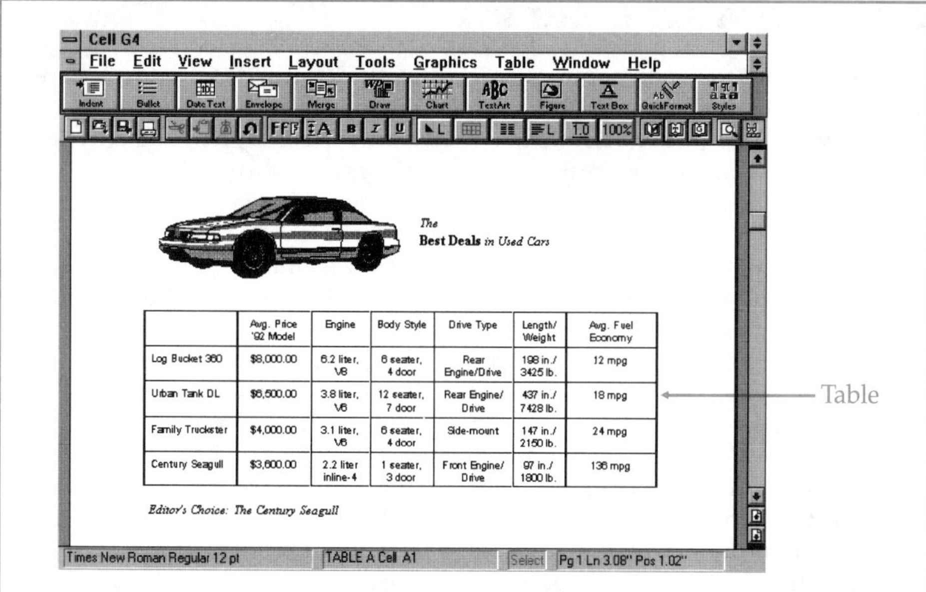

	Avg. Price '92 Model	Engine	Body Style	Drive Type	Length/ Weight	Avg. Fuel Economy
Log Bucket 360	$8,000.00	6.2 liter, V8	6 seater, 4 door	Rear Engine/Drive	198 in./ 3425 lb.	12 mpg
Urban Tank DL	$6,500.00	3.8 liter, V6	12 seater, 7 door	Rear Engine/ Drive	437 in./ 7428 lb.	18 mpg
Family Truckster	$4,000.00	3.1 liter, V6	6 seater, 4 door	Side-mount	147 in./ 2150 lb.	24 mpg
Century Seagull	$3,600.00	2.2 liter inline-4	1 seater, 3 door	Front Engine/ Drive	97 in./ 1800 lb.	136 mpg

Figure 3-9. *A WordPerfect table*

Once a table is created, you can place the insertion point into the cells and type text. When the insertion point is in the table, you can press the TAB key to move forward from cell to cell and SHIFT+TAB to move backward. If the text you type in a cell fills more than one line, WordPerfect expands the current row to allow more room for the text. Margin markers on the ruler show where the table is divided into columns; you can adjust the width of columns by dragging the table markers with the mouse. When you move the markers left or right, WordPerfect adjusts the other markers to keep the width of columns relative to the original table proportions.

When you create a table, a Tbl Def code is placed where the insertion point is located, and this is where the table appears in your document. You can view the table codes by choosing View/Reveal Codes or simply pressing ALT+F3. Row and Cell codes are also placed to divide the rows and columns in the table. If you make changes to the column widths or table format, WordPerfect updates the Tbl Def code with your changes.

Options on the Tables menu let you define the appearance of table lines, choose text alignment and attributes, and apply math calculations to the information in the cells. For complete information about the table features, see Chapter 11.

Formatting with Columns

The Columns button on the power bar lets you quickly divide your text into two or more *newspaper columns*—that is, columns where the text flows from one column to the next, just like newspaper text. WordPerfect supports other types of columns, which can also be created using the Columns button.

To create columns from the power bar, move the insertion point to the place in your document where the columns should begin. Move the mouse pointer onto the Columns button, then hold down the mouse button to display the Columns pop-up list. While still pressing the mouse button, move the pointer to the number of columns you want, and then release the mouse button. WordPerfect creates the number of columns you selected, with a code placed at the insertion point. The Col Def code determines the format of the columns. This affects all text that falls after the insertion point. If you do not want all text formatted into columns, move the insertion point to the end of the text that should be formatted with columns. Then use the Columns button to display the pop-up list and choose "Columns Off" from the list. This inserts a Col Def: Off code at the insertion point.

When the insertion point is located within text columns, markers for the column margins appear on the ruler, as shown here:

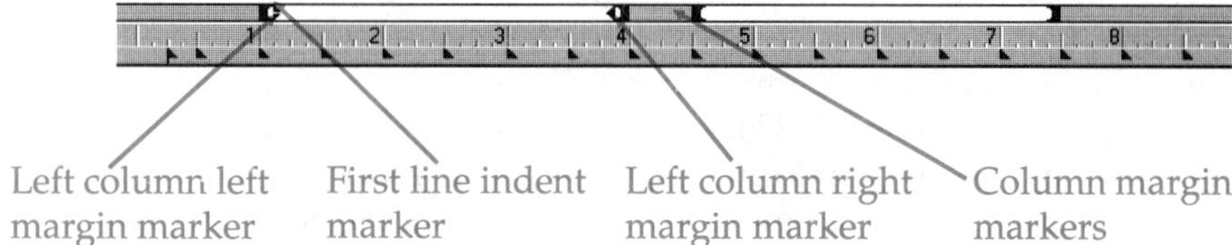

Each marker represents a column margin, and the shaded space between markers represents a column *gutter*—that is, the space between columns.

The default space between columns is one-half inch. To change the width of a column or the amount of space between columns, use the mouse to drag the curved margin markers right or left on the ruler. To adjust the width of columns without changing the space between them, move the mouse pointer over the shaded space between markers; then hold down the mouse button and drag the mouse pointer right or left. This adjusts two column margins at once, while keeping the space between them equidistant.

If you prefer to enter precise measurements for the column layout, you can use the Columns dialog box. Double-click the Columns button, and the Columns dialog box appears on the screen. You can also choose Define from the Columns pop-up list that is visible when you click on the Columns button. Figure 3-10 shows what the Columns dialog box looks like.

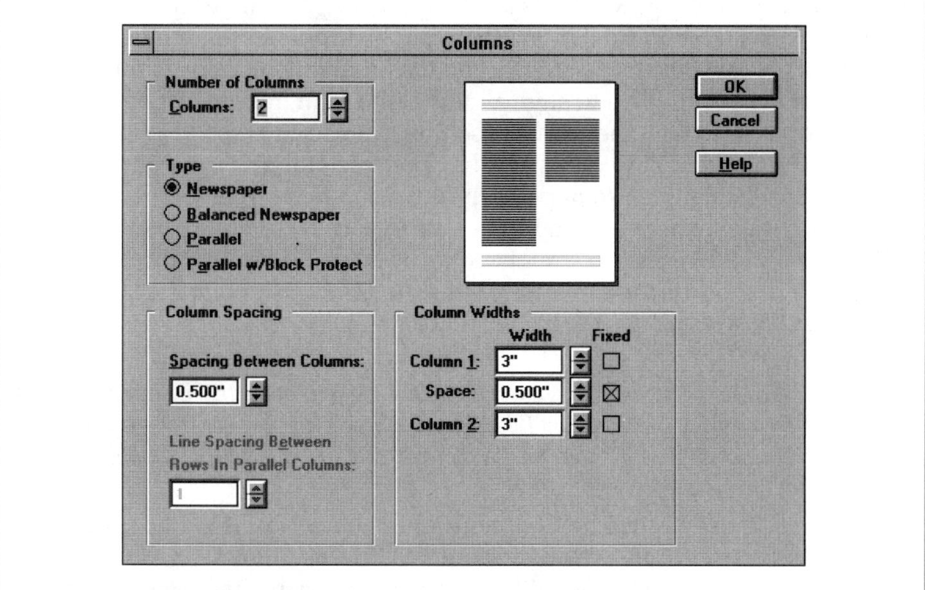

Figure 3-10. *The Columns dialog box*

Using the Columns dialog box, you can enter exact measurements for column margins and widths. You can also create column layouts with one of the other column types, such as parallel columns. For more information on parallel columns, see the entry "Columns, Parallel" in Chapter 11, "Commands and Features."

When you create the column format from the power bar, you are limited to a maximum of five evenly spaced newspaper columns. WordPerfect is actually capable of producing up to 24 columns across the width of the page, but only five can be created from the power bar. If you need more than five columns across, you can choose a greater number of columns from the Columns dialog box. For complete information about the Columns feature, see Chapter 11.

Justification

The Justification feature determines how text is aligned or distributed between the margins of the page. The Center and Flush Right features align single lines of text, but the Justification feature can align paragraphs, pages, or the entire document, if you wish. From the power bar, you can display a pop-up list of the five types of justification: left, right, center, full, and all (discussed momentarily). Before you choose one of these options, move the insertion point to the place in your document where the justification change should occur. Then move the mouse pointer onto the power bar's justification button. Hold down the mouse button to display the pop-up list, and then move the pointer to highlight one of the options. Release the mouse button, and the highlighted option is selected.

For example, if you want to align all text at the right margin, choose Right from the pop-up list. Left, the standard setting, aligns text at the left margin. Choose the Center option to center text lines between the left and right margins; this works even when the text appears in paragraph form. The Full Justification option extends each line of text to fill the entire space between left and right margins; this produces a clean straight edge of text at each side of the page. Finally, the All option is the same as Full Justification, except that the last line of the paragraph is also justified to the left and right margins.

NOTE: *Keyboard shortcut keys are available for four of the five justification types, and they may be faster for you than choosing from the power bar or Layout menu. See Chapter 2, "WordPerfect for Windows Basics," for more information.*

After you choose a justification option, a Just code is inserted into your text at the insertion point location. If you change your mind, you can cancel the justification change by choosing Edit/Undo from the menu bar or by clicking on the Undo button on the power bar.

Line Spacing

The line spacing feature determines the amount of space between text lines when you press the ENTER key or when lines are wrapped. The standard setting is single-spaced text, but other line spacing options are available. From the power bar, you can display a pop-up list with four options for line spacing: 1.0, 1.5, 2.0, and Other. Before you choose one of these options, move the insertion point to the place in your document where the line spacing change should occur. Move the mouse pointer onto the power bar's Line Spacing button and hold down the mouse button; you will see the pop-up list displayed. Move the pointer to highlight one of the options, and then release the mouse button.

WordPerfect supports any spacing measurement you want. Besides the predefined settings of 1.0 (single space), 1.5 (one and one-half space), and 2.0 (double space), you can use the Other selection to specify a different setting. When you choose this option, or when you double-click on the Line Spacing button, you will see the Line Spacing dialog box:

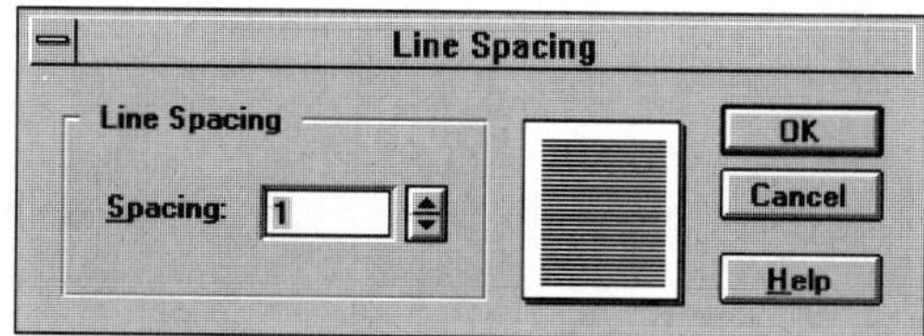

After you choose a line spacing option, a Ln Spacing code is inserted into your text at the insertion point location. This affects the spacing of all text lines that follow the code, and remains in effect until you change the line spacing later in the document. If you change your mind, you can cancel the line spacing change by choosing Edit/Undo from the menu bar or by using the Undo tool from the power bar.

Zoom In/Out

WordPerfect for Windows allows you to zoom in for a closeup view of your document or shrink your document and get an overview of the page. These *zoom* features let you see different views of the document you are editing, but they do not actually change the size of the document or the text on the pages. To change the view of your document, click on the power bar's Zoom button. When you do this, you will see the following pop-up list with different zoom options:

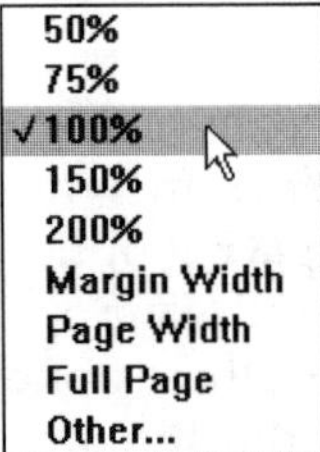

Choose 50%, 75%, 100%, 150%, or 200% to reduce or expand the view of the current document. You can also choose the Margin Width, Page Width, or Full Page options to adjust the zoom level to what is appropriate for your video card and monitor.

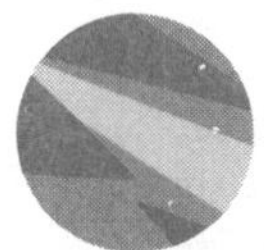

NOTE: *If you choose 150% or 200% for a closeup view, the entire width of the page may not be visible on the screen. In this case, you can press* CTRL+PGUP *or* CTRL+PGDN *to scroll from one end of the page to the next.*

If you prefer to choose your zoom option from a dialog box, you can double-click on the Zoom button on the power bar, or choose View/Zoom. Both methods will display the Zoom dialog box, as shown in Figure 3-11.

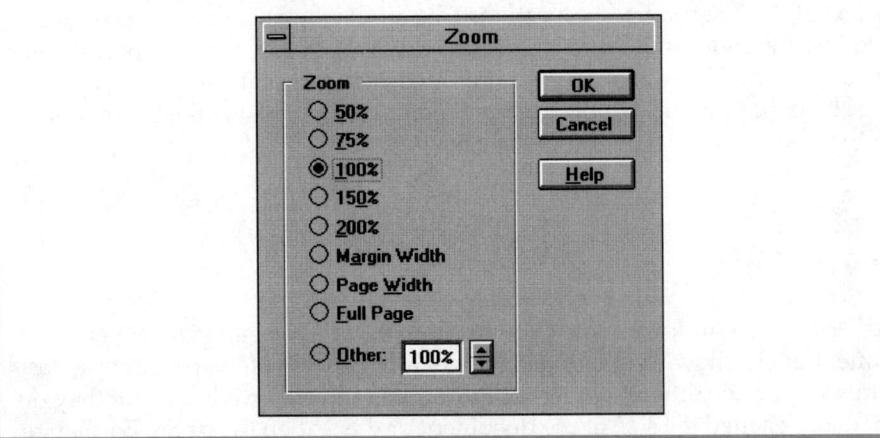

Figure 3-11. *The Zoom dialog box*

From this dialog box you can select one of the predefined zoom levels, or you can specify any zoom factor you desire between 25% and 400%.

After you use a zoom option, you can continue to create or edit your document. You can reset the view of your document by choosing 100% or Page Width from the Zoom pop-up list.

Using the Button Bar

Programs running under Windows have screen buttons that let you quickly access program features. Some of these buttons include the arrows on the scroll bars and the command buttons that appear in dialog boxes. WordPerfect for Windows takes this concept a step further by allowing you to define a set of on-screen buttons for the features you use most often. This is accomplished with the button bar feature. You can define your own button bars or you can choose from the predefined bars that are included with the WordPerfect program files.

You should not confuse the button bar with the power bar. While both can be customized in any way you desire, they both perform different functions. The power bar largely provides predefined features that can normally be accessed through the menus. While you can also do this with the button bar, the button bar is even more flexible, in that you can define specialized macros to run at the click of a button.

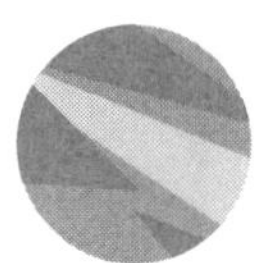

NOTE: *You must have a mouse to use WordPerfect's button bar feature.*

Displaying the Button Bar

Figure 3-12 shows the standard WordPerfect button bar displayed on the screen. Initially, WordPerfect's button bar is displayed, but you can hide it by choosing View/Button Bar. Each of the buttons on the bar represents a WordPerfect feature that can be selected from the menus. Icons and labels on the buttons show the action that each button performs. Instead of browsing through the menus, you can just click the button for the feature you want. The following are the functions of each button on the default (uncustomized) button bar:

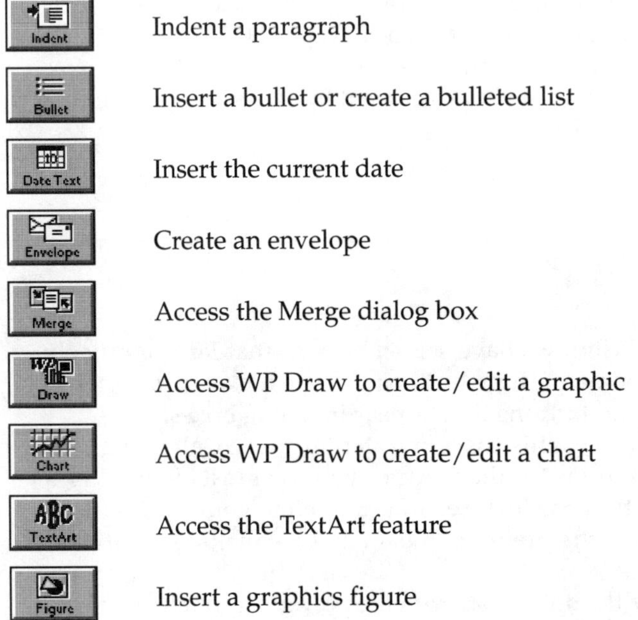

Indent
Indent a paragraph
Bullet
Insert a bullet or create a bulleted list
Date Text
Insert the current date
Envelope
Create an envelope
Merge
Access the Merge dialog box
Draw
Access WP Draw to create/edit a graphic
Chart
Access WP Draw to create/edit a chart
TextArt
Access the TextArt feature
Figure
Insert a graphics figure

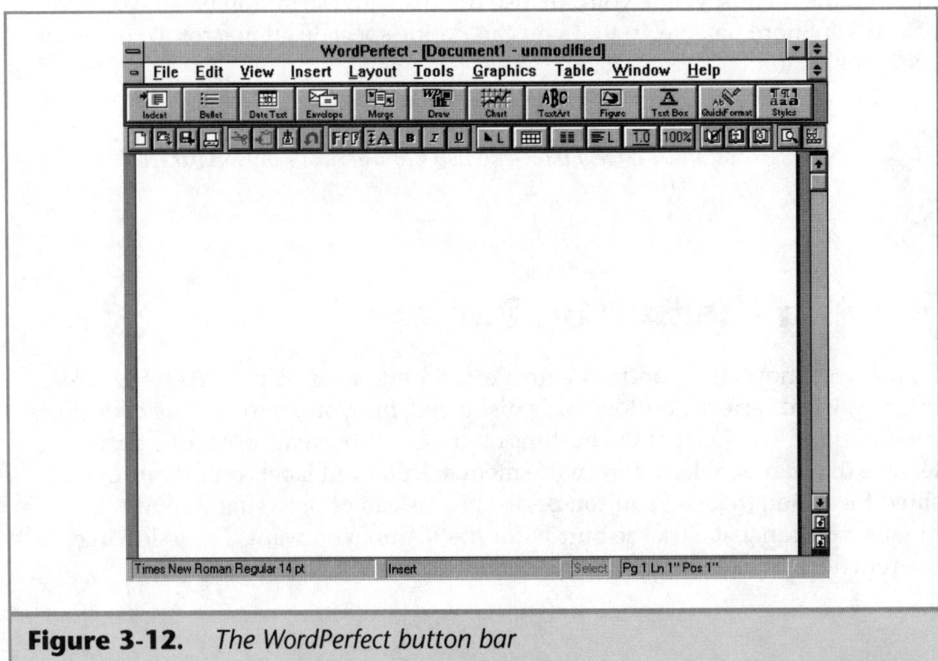

Figure 3-12. *The WordPerfect button bar*

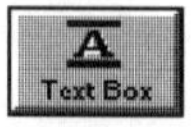
Insert a text box

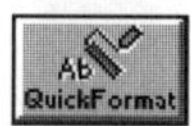
Apply the current format to another area in a document

Access the Styles dialog box

If your button bar does not appear like the one shown here, don't despair. WordPerfect for Windows is flexible enough that you can actually choose any of 12 different predefined button bars, and countless other ones that you can define yourself. The default button bar, previously described, is known as the WordPerfect button bar. It is only one of the available button bars, as detailed in Table 3-1.

To select any of these predefined button bars, use the File/Preferences/Button Bar menu choices. You can switch to any button bar at any time you desire.

Remember that button bars are designed to help you accomplish specialized tasks. That is why they are divided into individual button bars the way they are. The functions available from the various button bars are the same ones you can access through menus in WordPerfect for Windows. Because of this, they are not described

Button Bar Name	Purpose
Equation Editor	Tools used when working with equations
Font	Tools used to manipulate text fonts
Generate	Tools used to create lists, tables, indices, and subdocuments
Graphics	Tools used to work with graphics
Layout	Tools for adjusting the layout of your document
Macros	Tools used for working with macros
Outline	Tools for manipulating outlines
Page	Tools for working with entire pages
Preferences	Tools for customizing WordPerfect
Tables	Tools for working with tables
WordPerfect	The WordPerfect for Windows button bar
WordPerfect 5.2	The WordPerfect 5.2 for Windows button bar

Table 3-1. *Predefined WordPerfect for Windows Button Bars*

in their entirety at this time. If you want to know how a certain button works, you should refer to the description of the corresponding menu choice in Chapter 11.

Creating a New Button Bar

The predefined button bars include buttons for most all of the WordPerfect features, and you can create your own button bars for the features you use most often. This is done from the Button Bar Preferences dialog box. To display this, choose File/Preferences/Button Bar. The dialog box will appear as shown in Figure 3-13.

Choose Create from the dialog box. You are asked to provide a name for the button bar you are creating. Enter a name, and then click on OK. An "empty" button bar appears on your screen, and the Edit Button Bar dialog box appears, as shown in Figure 3-14. While this dialog box is displayed, you can choose the features you want to include as buttons on the bar by selecting options from the menu bar.

There are three major parts to this dialog box. The first part consists of the three selections at the top of the dialog box. Here you can specify what you want the button to do. Your buttons can

- Activate a Feature
- Play a Keyboard Script

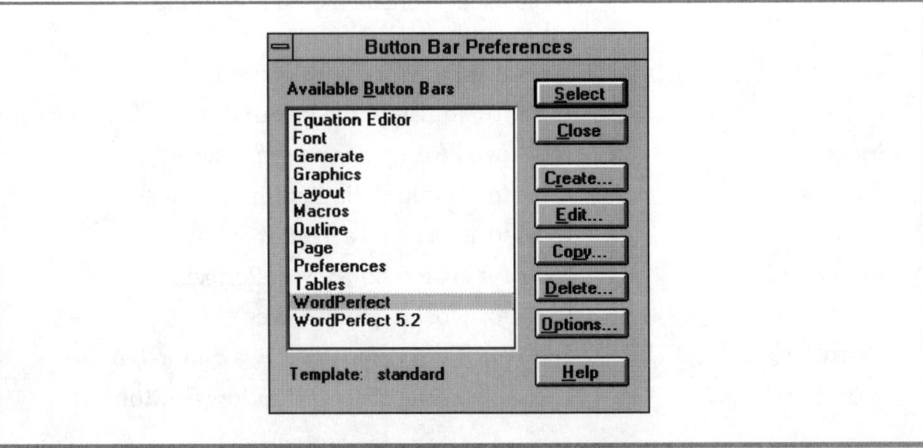

Figure 3-13. *The Button Bar Preferences dialog box*

- Launch a Program
- Play a Macro

The choice you make in this section controls what is displayed in the other two sections of the dialog box. For instance, if you choose Activate a Feature, then you will see lists of feature categories and actual features within those categories. If you specify that you want the button to perform a different action, then you will see different choices.

For example, suppose you want to add the Reveal Codes feature to a new button bar. Make sure you choose Activate a Feature, then choose the View from the Feature Category. Finally, choose Reveal Codes in the Features list, and then click on the Add Button button. You will see the button appear on the empty button bar on your screen.

You can assign as many features as you need for the button bar; there is no limit to the number of buttons you can add. If you add more buttons than WordPerfect can display at once on the bar, a pair of scroll arrows will appear at one end of the bar. Click the arrows, and the line of buttons will scroll up or down to show the buttons that extend beyond the width of the screen. This allows you to display and choose from a large number of buttons.

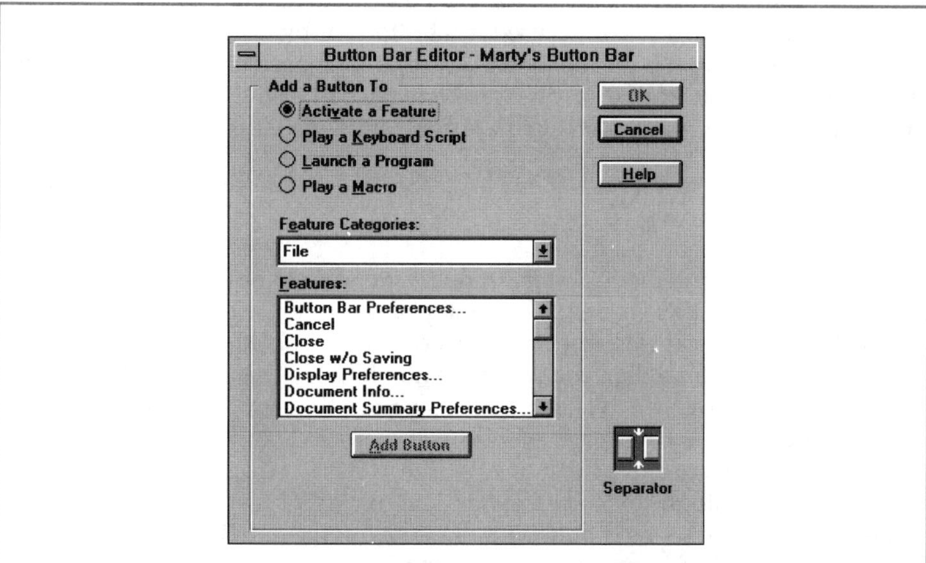

Figure 3-14. *The Button Bar Editor dialog box*

When you have finished assigning features to the button bar, choose OK from the Edit Button Bar dialog box. Choose Select to pick the button bar you just created.

NOTE: You can create different button bars for various word processing applications. For example, you could create one button bar for the features you select for legal contracts, one for employee lists or database operations, and one for desktop publishing. You can also create WordPerfect macros and assign them as buttons on the button bar.

Changing How the Button Bar Is Displayed

Normally the WordPerfect for Windows button bar is displayed just below the menu and above the power bar. You can, however, make it appear anywhere you desire on the screen. This is done by moving the mouse cursor to an empty place on the button bar, one in which there is no button. Notice that the pointer changes to a hand. When this occurs, click the mouse button and drag the button bar elsewhere on the screen. The button bar then appears in its own window, which you can position and size as desired. WordPerfect for Windows remembers the position and shape of your button bar, as well. This way, whenever your turn on the button bar, it will be displayed in the same manner.

You can also change the fonts used in a button bar by using the Options button from the Button Bar Preferences dialog box. Choose the button, and then specify the fonts you want used by WordPerfect when displaying the button bar. When you click on OK, your changes are made immediately.

Editing a Button Bar

WordPerfect lets you remove and rearrange buttons that appear on a button bar. To edit a button bar that is already created, you must first select and display the button bar file, as explained earlier in this chapter. Then you must choose the option File/Preferences/ Button Bar, and select the Edit button. This displays the Button Bar Editor dialog box, which is the same dialog box that appears when you are creating a new button bar.

To delete a button, move the mouse pointer—which will appear as the "button hand"—onto the button you want to remove. Click and hold the mouse button and drag the selected button up or down, off the bar. Release the mouse button, and WordPerfect removes the button from the button bar. If you change your mind and want to put the button back on the bar, you need to choose the feature again from the menus.

To rearrange the order of the buttons, use the mouse pointer to drag a button left or right on the bar. For example, suppose you want to move a button from the beginning to the end of the bar. Move the mouse pointer onto the button you want to move, and hold down the mouse button. Then drag the button to the end of the bar. The location of the screen button determines where the button will be placed. When you release the mouse button, the screen button is moved to the new location.

While the Button Bar Editor dialog box is displayed, you can also add new buttons to the button bar by choosing the appropriate features from the dialog box. When you have finished editing the button bar, choose OK from the dialog box, and WordPerfect updates your changes to the button bar.

Working with Document Windows

The WordPerfect program consists of at least two windows: the application window and one or more document windows. The WordPerfect application window shows the "WordPerfect" title bar, the menus at the top of the screen, and the status bar, where font choices, prompts, and document measurements are displayed. A document window appears inside the WordPerfect application window.

When you first start WordPerfect, one document window is open, and it is maximized to fill the workspace in WordPerfect. Click the Document Restore button, or press ALT+HYPHEN (-) and choose Restore, to see the main document window. Figure 3-15 shows a document window within WordPerfect. You can open up to nine document windows and move or resize them to suit your needs. (The default is for a cascade window arrangement to offer the greatest flexibility for moving around multiple windows.)

NOTE: *If you notice that your document does not display a filename, it is likely you have the Descriptive Names option enabled but have not yet given the document a descriptive name. For more information on this topic, see the entry "Descriptive Names" in Chapter 11, "Commands and Features."*

Minimize and Maximize

The minimize and maximize buttons appear at the upper-right corner of every document window; the minimize button shows a triangle pointing down, and the maximize button shows a triangle pointing up. These buttons let you shrink or expand a document window.

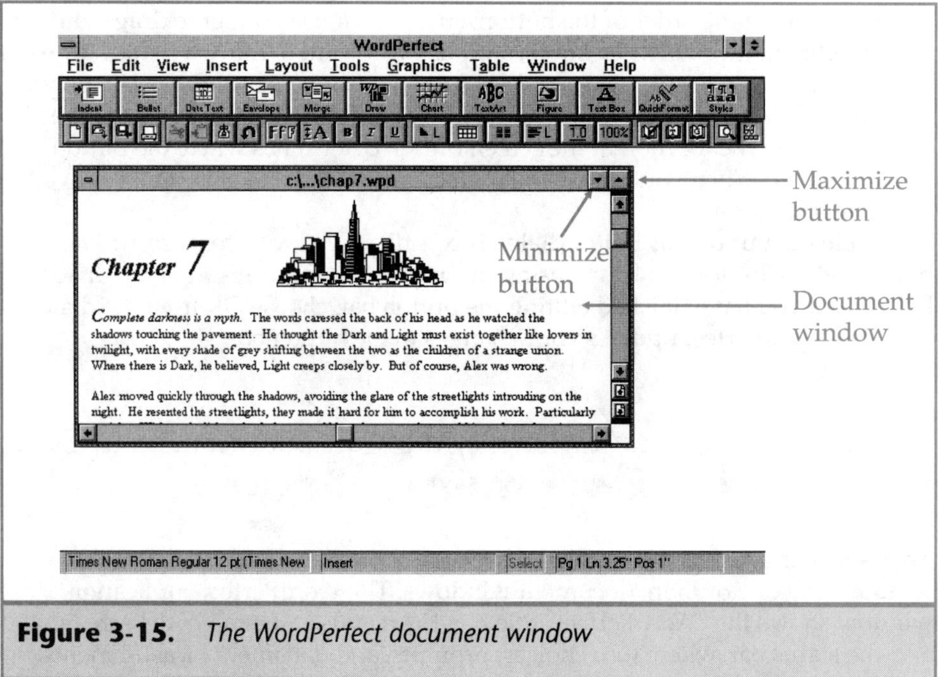

Figure 3-15. *The WordPerfect document window*

Click the maximize button, and the active document window expands to fill the entire WordPerfect application window. When a document window is maximized, the maximize and minimize buttons are replaced with the restore button, which appears as a single button with a pair of triangles. When the restore button appears, this tells you that the window or application is now maximized. This is the state of the first document window when you start the WordPerfect program. Click the restore button, and the window returns to the original size.

NOTE: *When you maximize a window, its border disappears, and the window cannot be sized or moved. Use the restore button to restore the window, and the border reappears.*

Click the minimize button, and the active document window shrinks to an icon at the bottom of the WordPerfect screen. If the document has been saved once, the filename appears beneath the icon. Minimizing one or more documents helps to clear the WordPerfect workspace, but it does not free computer memory for other documents or applications. A minimized document is still open. To actually close the document and free computer memory, choose File/Close.

Double-click the document icon, and its window is opened to display the document again.

Opening Multiple Documents

Each time you open a document with the File/Open option, you retrieve a document into a new document window. You can also open the same document in different windows; this is useful when you are working with long document files because it allows you to simultaneously view two different places in the same document. However, if you do this, be careful not to edit both document windows at once, because the changes made in one window will not be updated to the other open window, and the latest saved version replaces the original file. In WordPerfect, you can open up to nine different document windows on your screen at once; when all nine windows are open, the File/Open and File/New options are greyed, and you cannot open or create another file until you close at least one of the open document windows.

Keep in mind that each document window requires a certain amount of memory, depending on the size of the document. Each document you open takes some of the available memory that WordPerfect and Windows could use. If you find that WordPerfect is running slowly or that the program is displaying "Out of Memory" error messages, consider closing the displayed documents that you are not editing and unused applications that are running outside of WordPerfect.

Switching Between Documents

When two or more documents are open in WordPerfect, you can edit the document in the active document window. The active window has a shaded title bar; the actual appearance of the bar depends on the screen colors you are using. You can switch from one document window to another by pressing CTRL+F6 or CTRL+SHIFT+F6. If document windows overlap or are tiled on the screen (see the next two sections), you can simply move the mouse pointer on the document you want to edit and click the mouse. This activates the selected window. Another way to switch to other open documents is with the Window menu. When you open a new document window, WordPerfect adds it to the document list on the Window menu. If the document has been saved, the document name is shown on the list. You can move to another document by choosing Window from the menu bar and then choosing the name of the document you want to edit next.

NOTE: If document windows are maximized or overlap, the active document always appears on top of the other windows in the "stack" of documents.

When you have multiple documents open, make sure the correct document window is active when you choose file features like Save As, Close, and Print. Otherwise, you may send the wrong document to the printer, or inadvertently change the name of a file.

Tiling Document Windows

Sometimes, you will want to view all open documents on the screen at once. You could resize and move document windows until all documents are visible, but there is an easier way. An option on the Window menu lets you tile all document windows in WordPerfect. Figure 3-16 shows how tiled documents look on the screen; the size and arrangement of the windows depends on the number of

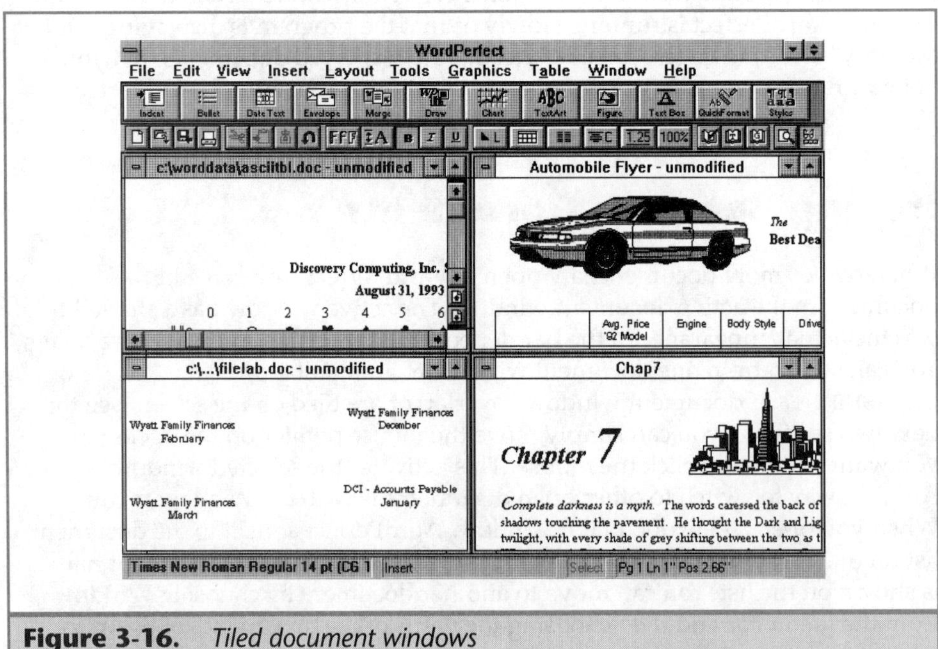

Figure 3-16. *Tiled document windows*

documents you have opened. To tile your documents, choose Window/Tile from the menu bar.

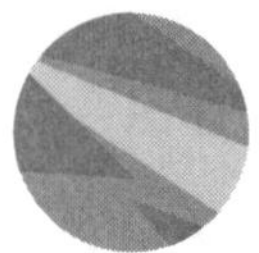

NOTE: If you tile with only one document open, the document window fills the WordPerfect application window, with the maximize and minimize buttons intact.

WordPerfect arranges the windows according to the order in which they were most recently accessed. If you have three or fewer documents opened, each document window is tiled to fill the width of the screen. If you have five or fewer documents open, the latest opened document will be placed on top and will extend the full width of the screen. If you have six or more documents opened, WordPerfect tiles all the windows to fit on the screen, but it will be difficult to work in any window unless you first maximize it.

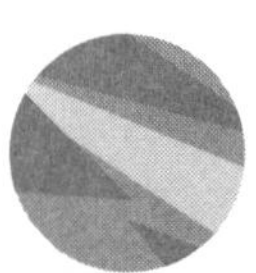

NOTE: You can bring any tiled window to the top of the screen by first selecting the window and then choosing Window/Tile again. This changes the order of the tiled windows so that the active window appears at the top of the screen. If you open other documents after you have tiled the windows of the already opened documents, the newly opened documents appear as windows in the middle of the screen. To tile these with the other document windows, simply choose Window/Tile again.

Cascading Document Windows

The Cascade option arranges documents with overlapping windows. This lets you see which documents are open but allows maximum use of the screen area for editing. To cascade the open document windows, choose Window/Cascade from the menu bar. Figure 3-17 shows an example of cascading document windows on the screen.

When you arrange windows with this option, the document of the first window is shown, while the other document windows are "stacked" behind, with only their title bars displayed. To display one of the other documents in the stack, simply click its title bar. This activates the selected window and brings the document to the front of the stack. You can also press CTRL+F6 or CTRL+SHIFT+F6 to cycle through the document windows.

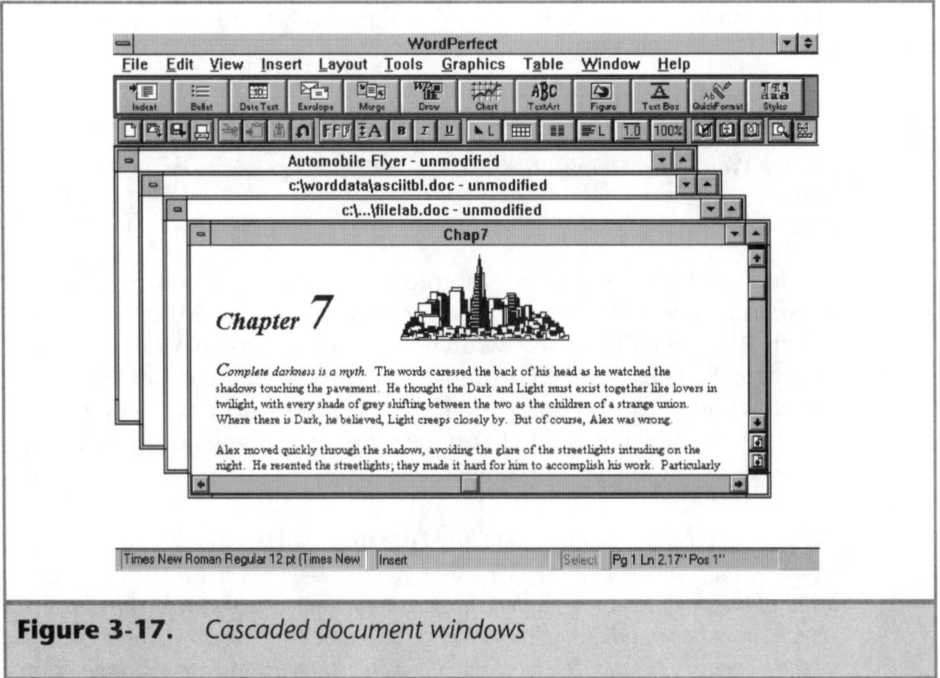

Figure 3-17. *Cascaded document windows*

Choosing WordPerfect Preferences

WordPerfect for Windows allows you to customize many different features. By using the Preferences dialog box, you can specify how you want WordPerfect to behave each time you start the program.

To display the Preferences dialog box, choose File/Preferences from the menu bar. The dialog box shown in Figure 3-18 appears. Each icon in this dialog box represents a different setup area with its own set of options. If you have worked through this book so far, you have already accessed many of these different areas.

There are 12 options available from the Preferences dialog box. In short, these options provide the following capabilities:

Lets you specify your preferences for the document windows, scroll bars, the unit of measurement, the ruler, and merging. Here you can also specify a character or symbol to be shown as the hard return character in your document, and you can specify screen color preferences for the Reveal Codes window.

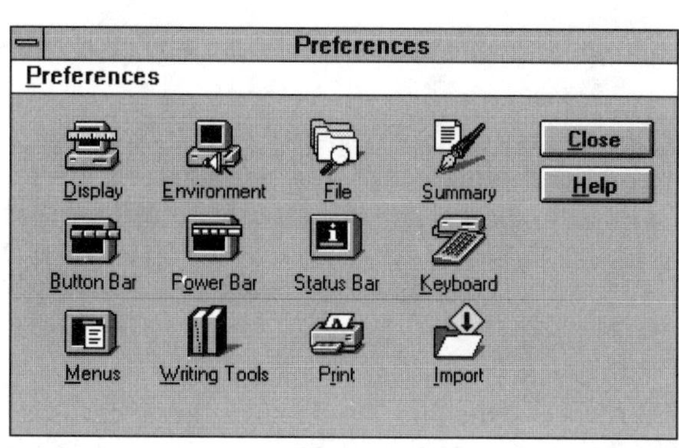

Figure 3-18. *The Preferences dialog box*

This option lists standard program settings for user information, formatting procedures, speaker use, and menu options.

WordPerfect can store documents and other system files in virtually any place you desire. This option allows you to specify where various files used by WordPerfect should be stored.

Allows you to specify how document summary information should be maintained.

Used for setting up the various button bars, as described earlier in this chapter.

Used for setting up how the power bar should appear.

Used for setting up what should appear on the status bar.

Allows you to select or create different keyboard layouts.

Allows you to select or create different menu layouts.

 Used to specify which writing tools are available on the Tools menu.

 You can use this option to specify how the printing functions of WordPerfect should work. This includes settings for number of copies, print quality, and font size relationships.

 This can be used to define how text should be imported from a DOS text file.

The changes you make at the File/Preferences menu become the standard settings for WordPerfect and remain in effect until you change them again. Because these preferences are selected within WordPerfect, they generally do not affect other programs that run under Windows. However, some of the options—such as Location of Files—do affect other WordPerfect Corporation software that is running under Windows. For complete information on these and other preference options, see Chapter 11.

Customizing the Windows Program

WordPerfect for Windows uses information from the Windows Control Panel to determine many desktop settings, including the date and time for your system, screen colors, mouse settings, and other desktop options. The following sections explain how to customize the basic system settings for Microsoft Windows; detailed information about these options may be found in your *Microsoft Windows User's Guide*.

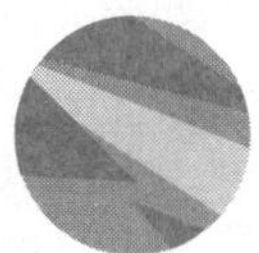

NOTE: *Changing the settings as mentioned here will affect all programs you use in the Windows environment. Make sure you follow the directions closely; otherwise, the settings may not be what you expect.*

Displaying the Windows Control Panel

To display the Windows Control Panel from WordPerfect, choose Switch To from the application control menu, or simply press Switch To (CTRL+ESC). Select "Program Manager" from the list that appears, and then choose the Switch To button. This displays the Program Manager. From the Main group window, double-click the Control Panel icon to display the Control Panel shown in Figure 3-19. The icons displayed in this window let you change the system settings for Microsoft Windows. These affect all programs that run under Windows, including WordPerfect.

Setting the Date and Time

The Control Panel includes an option that lets you set the date and time that are stored in your computer. To do so, choose the Date/Time icon from the Control Panel. The Date & Time dialog box appears. To change the month, day, or year, click the appropriate number in the Date box and type the correct number, or click the incremental buttons (shown as arrows at the side of the date) to change the number. To change the time, click the hour, minute, or second number, and type the correct number. Or click a number and use the incremental buttons to change the

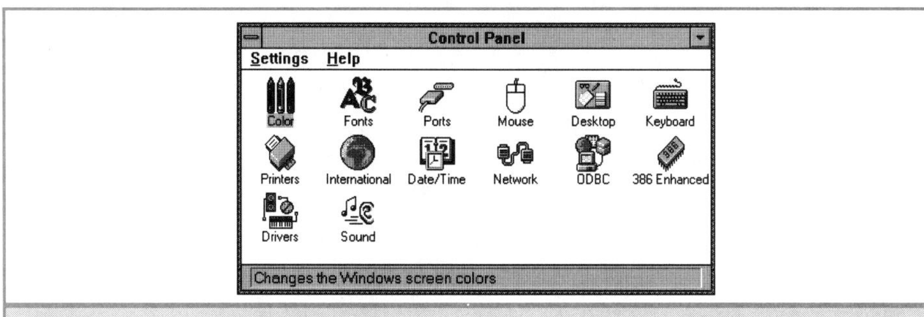

Figure 3-19. *The Windows Control Panel*

hour, minute, or second. When you have finished with the date and time settings, click the OK button to save your changes and return to the Control Panel.

Changing the Screen Colors

Screen colors are defined from the Color dialog box, which determines the system screen colors for all programs running under Microsoft Windows. You can choose one of several predefined color schemes, or you can create your own scheme from a palette of supported colors. The number of colors you can choose depends on the type of display monitor you are using. From the Control Panel,

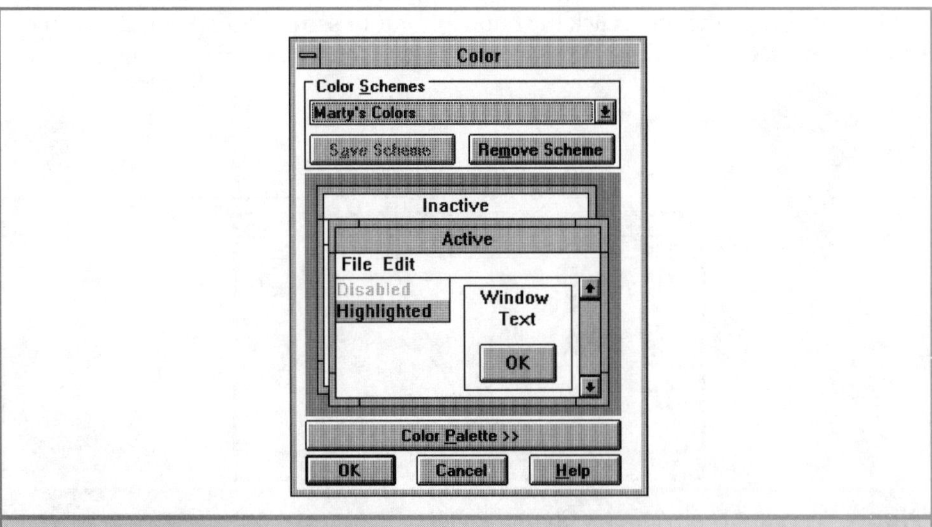

Figure 3-20. *The Color dialog box*

double-click the Color icon to display the Color dialog box, shown in Figure 3-20. Sample windows appear at the middle of the box to show the current color selections for all window elements. Choose the Color Schemes option, and a pop-up list appears with the predefined color schemes that are available to you. When you select one of the schemes from the list, the sample windows show you the colors for that scheme.

If you do not want to use one of the predefined schemes, you can define your own color scheme by choosing the Color Palette >> button. When you choose this button, the dialog box expands to include a color palette and a list of screen elements. First, choose the Screen Element that you want to change (or click on an area of the sample screen whose color you want to change); then choose the desired color for the element from the Basic Colors palette. Repeat this procedure for each of the screen elements you want to change. The sample windows in the dialog box will show how your color choices will look if you accept the new screen colors.

When you have selected the screen colors you want to use, choose Save Scheme to save the changes. Provide a name for the new scheme, or click OK to accept the displayed name. Click OK to accept the changes. The Windows program will update the display to show your new color choices for the screen. These system colors will be used for all programs that run under Windows and will remain in effect until you change them again from the Control Panel.

In addition, WordPerfect for Windows uses the system screen colors to display text in your document windows. If you have a color printer, you can select different print colors for text from WordPerfect's Font dialog box, but these colors are not displayed when the Windows system colors are active. From WordPerfect, you can choose File/Preferences/Display and turn off the Windows System Colors option to show color text on the screen as it will appear on the printed page. This change affects only WordPerfect; other programs running under Windows will continue to use the Windows system colors to display text.

Modifying the Desktop Settings

Choose the Desktop icon from the Control Panel to display the dialog box shown in Figure 3-21. At this dialog box, you can choose different options to customize

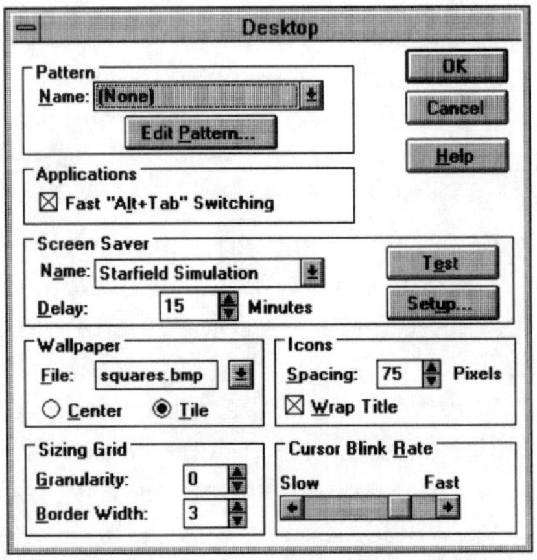

Figure 3-21. *The Desktop settings dialog box*

the desktop display. Choose Name in the Pattern section to select a pattern for the Windows desktop. You can use one of the predefined patterns or edit one of the existing patterns with the Edit Pattern option button. The color of the selected pattern depends on the background color you have chosen for the desktop, which is selected from the Color dialog box, described earlier.

To provide the ability to switch quickly between open windows, enable Fast "Alt+Tab" Switching. A screen saver is built into Windows. You can enable it by clicking on the down arrow to the right of the Name text box. Adjust the delay between minutes of inactivity before the screen saver activates.

Choose Spacing in the Icons section to adjust the space between icons displayed in windows. The number entered here represents a number of screen pixels; the higher the number, the greater the space between icons. The Granularity option in the Sizing Grid section lets you specify an invisible grid that forces windows and icons to be aligned when you are sizing or moving screen elements. Each increment for this option represents eight screen pixels. The higher the number, the larger the grid coordinates. When set to 0, no grid exists, allowing icons to overlap. The Border Width option determines the width of window borders; change the standard setting of 3 to make the borders thicker or thinner.

The Cursor Blink Rate setting lets you increase or decrease the blinking speed of the insertion point (cursor) on your screen. Use the slider button on this option to select a speed; the sample beside the scroll bar will show you how the insertion point will look at the current rate.

When you have finished with the desktop settings, choose OK to accept your changes and return to the Control Panel.

Using a Graphics File as the Desktop Background

Microsoft Windows includes a few graphics images that are saved in files with a .BMP extension, which is the extension for Paintbrush files saved under Windows version 3.0 or greater. You can select one of these files and display it as the desktop background to give your desktop a more colorful look, or you can use the Paintbrush program (included in the Accessories group window) to create your own graphics image for the desktop.

To select a file for the desktop, choose the Desktop icon from the Control Panel. Then click the down arrow to the right of the File option to display a pop-up list of all bitmap (BMP) files in the Windows directory. Select the name of the file you want to use and select Tile to evenly spread the graphic over the screen. Choose the OK button on the dialog box to accept your choice. The selected file becomes the background screen for the Windows program.

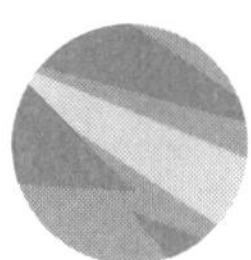

NOTE: *If you use the Wallpaper option, the desktop setting for the Pattern Name option should be set to None.*

Changing the Repeat Speed of the Keyboard

When you hold down a key on the keyboard, the Windows program pauses before the key is repeated. You can change the repeat speed of the keyboard to adjust the length of the pause for your typing speed. If, for example, you are a fast typist, you might want to increase the repeat speed. If you find that keystrokes are repeating when you don't want them to, consider decreasing the repeat speed. To change the keyboard speed, choose the Keyboard icon from the Control Panel. This displays the Keyboard dialog box. Move the slider button for Repeat Rate to indicate the speed you desire; click the Test field and hold down a letter key to test the repeat rate. You can also alter the delay before the key is repeated by moving the slider button in the Delay Before First Repeat option. When you have made the changes that are comfortable for you, click the OK button to accept the change. The new repeat rate affects the keyboard speed for all programs running under Windows.

Adjusting the Mouse for Left-Handed Users

When you first install the Windows program, the mouse is configured for right-handed users. You can easily change the button assignment for left-handed users by choosing the Mouse option from the Windows Control Panel.

To designate a mouse for left-handed users, open the Windows Control Panel, and then double-click the Mouse icon. The Mouse dialog box shown in Figure 3-22 appears. Move the mouse pointer onto the Swap Left/Right Buttons option. Click the left mouse button once to place an *X* in the box. After you check

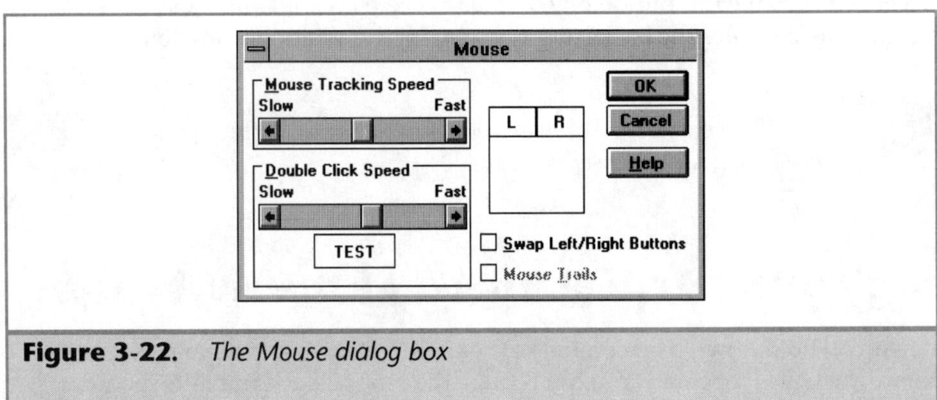

Figure 3-22. *The Mouse dialog box*

the box, the mouse buttons are reassigned immediately. This means you will have to use the right mouse button, instead of the left, if you change your mind and want to uncheck the box. Using the right mouse button, make any additional changes to the mouse settings that you desire. Then click the OK button to accept the changes, and the Control Panel window reappears. Double-click the Control Menu button to close the Control Panel and return to the Program Manager.

If you save the desktop settings when you exit the Windows program, these changes remain in effect until you change them again from the Control Panel.

PART TWO

Exploring More Advanced Features

CHAPTER 4

Managing Files with WordPerfect

Within the WordPerfect program, you can view a list of files and directories from several different dialog boxes including the Open File and Save As dialog boxes. From these and other similar dialog boxes you can perform many basic file manipulation tasks, including copying, deleting, renaming files, and changing file attributes. You can also create and delete directories. Along with displaying files and directories, you can display a QuickList, which is a customized list of your most frequently accessed files and/or directories. Another powerful file management tool included with WordPerfect is the QuickFinder, which provides powerful file searching capabilities. With the QuickFinder you can search for files containing specific words or phrases. You can also create indexes that contain specific files and directories that WordPerfect can search. This chapter covers the use of the many file management tools within WordPerfect.

Using the File Management Dialog Boxes

When you display one of the file management dialog boxes, the current directory is displayed in the top center of the dialog box so you always know what directory you are working with.

A File List for the current directory is displayed in the far left of the dialog box, under the Filename text field, as shown in Figure 4-1. From the File List window, you can copy, delete, move, rename, view, open, print, and retrieve files. By default the filenames are sorted alphabetically and only the filename is shown in the File List. While in the File List window, quickly move to a file, and type the first few letters of the filename. When you highlight or select a file, the date and time the file was last modified and the size of the file are shown in the left corner of the dialog box.

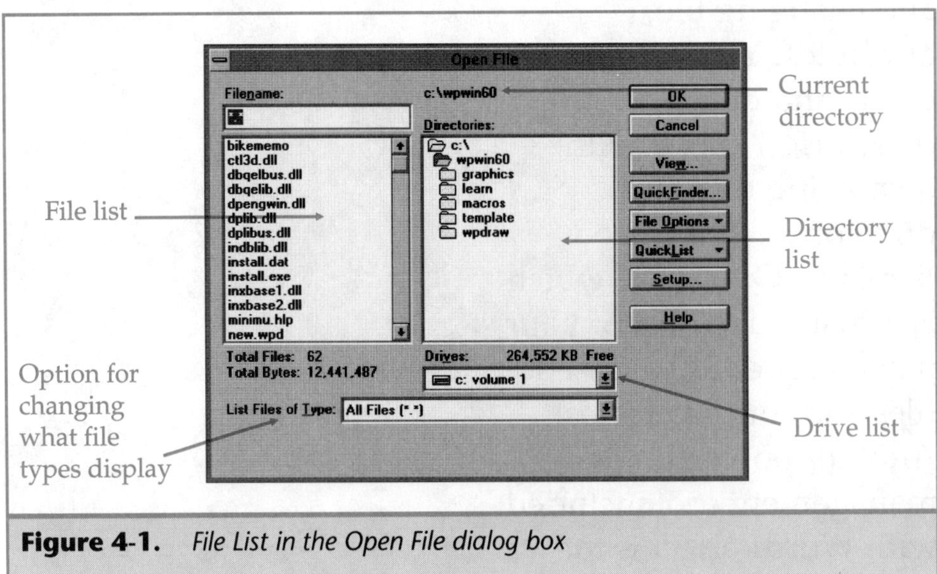

Figure 4-1. *File List in the Open File dialog box*

The Filename text field at the top of the File List window lets you select files or change what files are displayed in the File List. To change the files displayed, move the mouse pointer to the text field directly below the Filename option; when you first open a file management dialog box your cursor is positioned in this field. Type the desired directory path, and press ENTER. When entering a directory name, you can use wildcard characters to display only files that match a certain filename pattern. For example, if you want to display only files that end with an .LET extension, type ***.LET** in the text field. Directly below the File List, WordPerfect displays the number of total files and total bytes used in the directory.

NOTE: *In some file management dialog boxes, such as the Open File dialog box, you can specify which type of file you want to display in the File List. Choose List Files of Type and then select the type of files you want to display. For example, if you are performing a merge and have named your form files with an .FRM extension, you could choose WP Merge Forms to display only the files ending with the .FRM extension.*

HINT: *If you use wildcard characters to limit the files that are displayed, the information given for Total Files and Total Bytes is only for the currently displayed files.*

A list of directories is also displayed in the file management dialog boxes. By default your WordPerfect directory and subdirectories are shown along with the directory one level above your WordPerfect directory, which is usually C:\. If you want to see the files and subdirectories contained within a directory, simply point to the directory in the list and double-click the mouse button. If you are using the keyboard, press ALT+D to move to the Directory list box, use the arrow keys to highlight the desired directory, and then press ENTER. The File List to the left of the dialog box displays the names of the files stored in the selected directory and lists the directory name in the Filename text box. For example, if you want to see all the directories on your C:\ drive, simply double-click on that entry. When you select a directory, the Directories list also updates and displays the directories in the path above the selected directory and its subdirectories.

HINT: *If you change directories from a file management dialog box and then choose OK or close the dialog box using the control menu, that directory becomes your default directory. This means that any files you save without specifying a full path will be saved to the new default directory. In addition, when you retrieve files, WordPerfect will try to retrieve the files from the new*

default directory unless you specify a full path. If you do not want WordPerfect to automatically change your default directory, choose Setup from a file management dialog box, then choose Change Default Directory to turn off the option.

The Drives option allows you to display the contents of another drive in the File List and Directory List. Choose the Drives option and select the drive you want to display. WordPerfect lists all available drives, including disk drives, RAM drives, and network drives. The total number of available bytes on the selected drive is also listed.

Customizing the Display of File Management Dialog Boxes

There are several setup options that allow you to customize the display of the file management dialog boxes. You can change what information is displayed in the File List and how the information is given. In addition, you change which file management list boxes are displayed in the dialog box. For example, you can display your QuickList instead of a Directory listing. Any changes you make to the setup of a file management dialog box affect all file management dialog boxes. For example, if you change the setup to display the QuickList from the Save As dialog box, the QuickList will also be displayed in the Open dialog box.

Displaying a QuickList

By default WordPerfect displays a File List, Directory List, and a Drive List. However, you can also display your QuickList. Remember, the QuickList is a customized listing of files and directories you use most often. For more information on creating a QuickList, see Chapter 11, "Commands and Features." To display the QuickList, choose QuickList from any file management dialog box (such as the Open dialog box), and choose Show QuickList to replace the Directory List with a QuickList or choose Show Both to display both the QuickList and the Directory List, as shown in Figure 4-2. When the QuickList is displayed, you can double-click a descriptive name or directory to display the corresponding File List. With the QuickList displayed in the file management dialog boxes, you can easily access the files and directories you use most often without scanning through an entire directory structure.

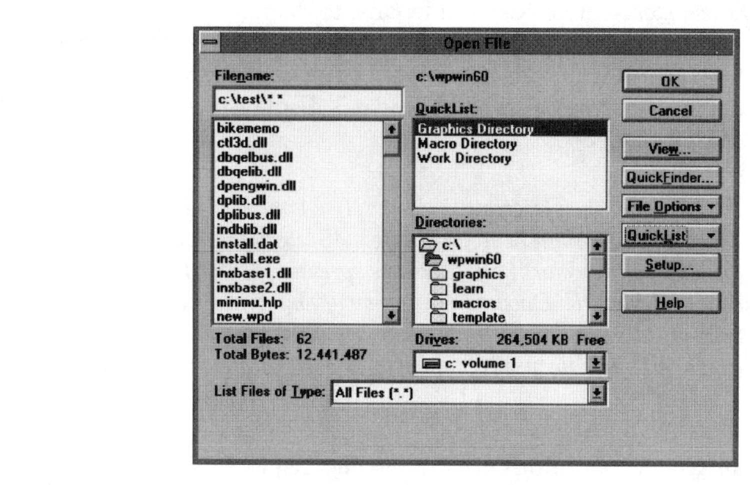

Figure 4-2. *Displaying a QuickList and a Directory List*

Customizing the File List Information

When you display a file management dialog box, only the filename is displayed in the File List; the date and time the file was last modified and the size of the file are shown in the bottom left-hand corner of the dialog box. If you would like to see more information for each file, you can customize the display of the File List. To change the File List display, choose Setup from a file management dialog box and the Open/Save As Setup dialog box will be displayed as shown in Figure 4-3. Choose the Show command button to view the different display options. Choose Filename only to display only the filename (the default setting); choose Filename, Size, Date, and Time to display all the information

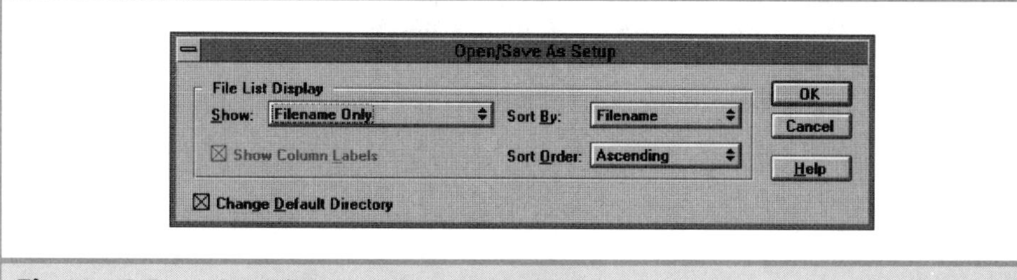

Figure 4-3. *Open/Save As Setup dialog box*

in the File List; choose Descriptive Name, Filename to display and sort the File List using the Document Summary Descriptive Name followed by the actual filename; or choose Custom Columns if you want complete control over what information is displayed in the File List and how it is displayed. After selecting the desired option, choose OK.

NOTE: If you choose the Descriptive Names, Filename option, or Custom Columns, WordPerfect prompts you to create a directory for Speedup Files. If you create this directory, WordPerfect creates speedup files that contain the Descriptive Name from the Document Summary. This greatly increases the amount of time it takes to display a file management dialog box that uses Descriptive Names since the program no longer has to scan each Document Summary.

When using the Custom Columns option, the File List looks something like this:

Filename	Size	Date
attend.wpt	30,339	9/7/93
balance.wpt	26,332	9/7/93
cal_side.wpl	91,717	9/7/93
cal_up.wpt	179,567	9/7/93
certif1.wpt	27,894	9/7/93
certif2.wpt	30,934	9/7/93
classchd.wp	27,128	9/7/93
costanyl.wpl	24,570	9/7/93
creditap.wpl	27,630	9/7/93
envlpe.wpt	29,556	9/7/93
estimate.wpl	24,881	9/7/93
expense.wpl	47,311	9/7/93

You can change the order, size, and type of information displayed in the File List. To move a column of information to a different location in the File List, point to the column heading with the mouse pointer, hold down the mouse button, and drag the column heading to a new location at the top of the list. To change the size of a column, move the mouse pointer to the edge of the column heading you want to size. When the mouse pointer changes to a double arrow, press and hold the mouse button and move the mouse to size the box as desired.

If you want to remove a column from the File List, simply use the mouse pointer to drag the column heading off the heading bar. To add information to the File List, point to a blank space on the heading bar and hold down the right mouse button. The following pop-up list displays the options for possible column headings:

Descriptive Name
Descriptive Type
Filename
Size
Date
Time
Attributes

Choose an item from the pop-up list to add a column of information to the File List window. The Attributes column displays the file attributes; see the section "Changing File Attributes" later in this chapter for more information. The Descriptive Name and Descriptive Type columns display document summary information from the Document Summary. If a column heading is already used in the current File List window, the corresponding item appears grey in the pop-up list and cannot be selected. After you choose an item from the pop-up list, a column for that information is added to the File List.

If you display more file information than can be viewed on the File List box, the direction buttons (< and >), at the left edge of the column headings window, allow you to scroll horizontally through the information. You cannot change the size of the File List box.

NOTE: *If you are not using a mouse, you cannot change the layout of the File List columns.*

HINT: *If you do not want to display the title of each column, such as Filename, Size, etc., deselect the Show Column Labels option on the Open/Save As Setup dialog box.*

You can change the sort order of the files displayed in a File List from the Open/Save As dialog box. To change the sort order, choose Setup from a file management dialog box. Then, choose the Sort By command button to specify the field by which the list is sorted. The standard File List is sorted by Filename. You can also sort according to the Date and time when files were last modified by specifying those choices. If, for example, you want to see all files that were modified within the past two weeks, you can display these files chronologically on the list. You can sort the list by file Extension, Size, Descriptive Name, or Descriptive Type. Each of these options represents a possible column of information in the File List. When using the Sort By option, you can specify only one field as the key for sorting. You can also specify the Sort Order (Ascending or Descending) for the File List window. After you have selected the desired options, choose OK. The File List automatically updates to reflect the changes you made.

Viewing File Contents

One of the powerful features available in the file management dialog boxes is the ability to look at a file without retrieving it. When you select a filename from the File List, you can choose View to display the contents of the file in the Viewer window. The Viewer displays the name of the file in the Viewer title bar.

If the selected file is a WordPerfect file, you will see some of the original document layout, similar to the example shown in Figure 4-4; however, some types of formatting, such as font changes and columns, will not appear in the Viewer window. You can also view the contents of all graphics file formats supported by WordPerfect. If a file contains both text and graphics, only the text is shown in the Viewer window.

Some types of files do not automatically display in the Viewer. If the file is not a WordPerfect file, a Convert command button is displayed on the Viewer that you must select to have the file converted into WordPerfect format before viewing. WordPerfect does not actually convert the file, it simply makes a temporary conversion for viewing purposes. You can view any file as long as WordPerfect can convert files from that format. See "File Conversion" in

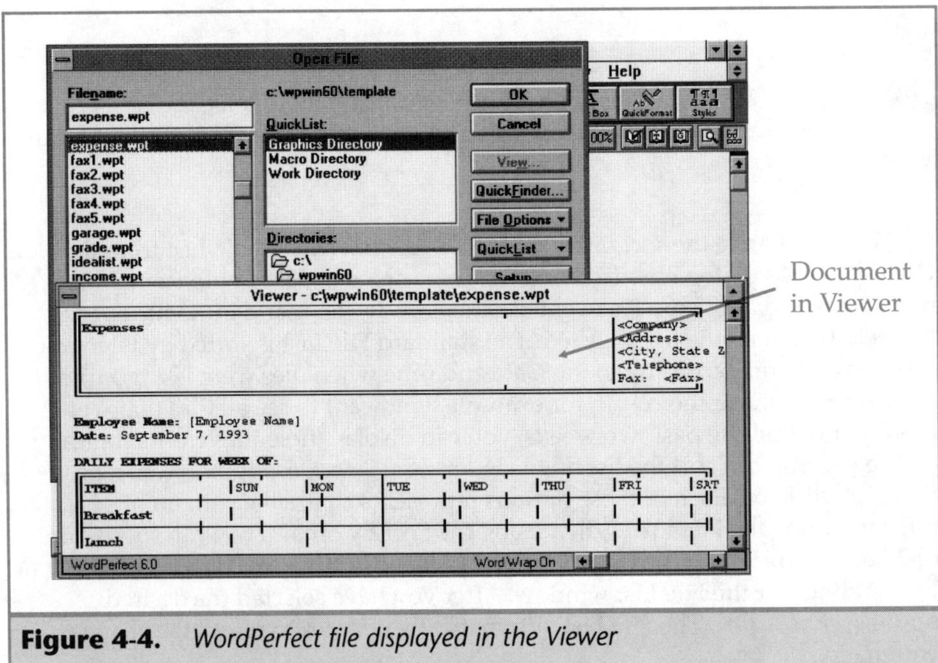

Figure 4-4. *WordPerfect file displayed in the Viewer*

Chapter 11 for a list of supported file formats. If you want WordPerfect to automatically convert files for viewing purposes, you can change the Viewer Setup. While in the Viewer window, press the right mouse button, then choose Viewer Setup to display the Viewer Setup dialog box. Choose Automatically convert document files to have WordPerfect convert text files. You can also choose Automatically convert graphic files to have WordPerfect convert supported graphics files. If you want WordPerfect to display Document Summaries when available instead of the document text, choose Show Document Summary (if available).

Viewing Documents in the Viewer

Once the Viewer is open, any file you select from the File List is displayed in the Viewer window. The Viewer must be open to display file contents, but it does not need to be active. If you want to move or resize the Viewer window, or if you need to scroll through the contents of the displayed file, you do need to activate the Viewer. To activate the Viewer window, simply place the mouse pointer anywhere in the window and click the mouse button once.

Once the Viewer window is active, you can use the vertical and horizontal scroll bars to move through the file. When all information in a file can be displayed within the boundaries of the Viewer window, the scroll bars remain on the window but become inactive. If you want to see more information in the Viewer, you can resize the window or maximize it for a full-screen view of the file contents.

HINT: When viewing files you can press the right mouse button to access the Viewer options. From the pop-up list displayed in Figure 4-5, you can see the file format and choose several other options.

Searching for Text in the Viewer

While the Viewer window is active, you can use the Find feature to move quickly to a specific word or phrase. From the Viewer window, press the right mouse button and choose Find or press F2 to display the Find dialog box. In the Find text field, type the text you want to find. Choose Match Whole Word Only if you only want to find complete words. Choose Case Sensitive if you want to match the case of the text entered in the Find text field. Choose Find Next if you want to perform a search from the cursor forward, or choose Find Prev if you want to perform a search from the cursor backward. If text that matches the search string

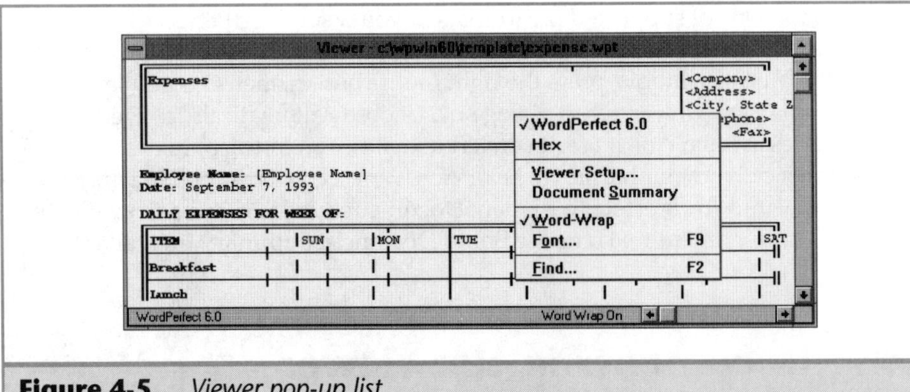

Figure 4-5. *Viewer pop-up list*

is found in the displayed document, it is highlighted and shown in the Viewer window. Sometimes the Find dialog box may display on top of the text you are searching for. In this case, you might want to move or resize the window. Otherwise, a message is displayed notifying you that the search string was not found in the displayed document; if the "not found" message appears, choose OK to return to the Find dialog box. Once a search string is defined, you can choose Find Next to search ahead for the next occurrence of matching text, or Find Prev to search back for the previous occurrence. After completing a search choose Close to close the Find dialog box.

NOTE: *You cannot use the DOS wildcard characters (* and ?) when using the Find option in the Viewer.*

Saving Displayed Text to the Clipboard

When the Viewer is active, you can select text and save it to the Windows Clipboard. Saving text from the Viewer to the Clipboard lets you clip passages of text from a file without actually retrieving the file into WordPerfect. When you save text to the Clipboard, it replaces previously stored information in the Clipboard.

To save text to the Clipboard, first select the text displayed in the Viewer; you can select only complete lines of text. Press the right mouse button and then choose Copy to Clipboard. Once you save text to the Clipboard, you can paste the information in a WordPerfect document or even use it in another Windows application. To insert the information into a WordPerfect document from the document window, move the cursor to the location where you want to insert the text, then choose Edit/Paste. To insert the information in another Windows application, consult the documentation for the specific application.

Changing the Viewer Font

You can change the font for the text in the Viewer window. For example, if you want to see more information in the window, you could change the font to a smaller size. This option affects only the text on the screen; it does not change any printed output. To change the Viewer font, press the right mouse button and then choose Font or press Font (F9) to display the Font dialog box. Select the desired font typeface from the Font list box, then select the font size from the Size list box. Not all font sizes are available for each font, so when you select the font, the Size list box updates accordingly and you can choose the desired size. From the Font dialog box you can also select whether you want the text displayed boldfaced and/or italicized by selecting the Bold or Italics check box, respectively. Once you highlight a font typeface, the box below the list shows how the text will appear on the screen. Once you have made your selections, choose OK to accept the new screen font.

Closing the Viewer Window

When you have finished with the Viewer, you can close it by double-clicking on the control menu in the Viewer window.

Selecting Files

For many file management functions, you can select multiple files before you perform a task. This is true for functions such as delete, copy, rename, and move. To select a single file, click the filename. If you are using the keyboard, simply use the UP ARROW and DOWN ARROW keys to highlight the filename.

To select a group of consecutive files, point to the first file in the list, hold down the mouse button, and drag the pointer until the rest of the files you want to select are highlighted. While selecting multiple files, you can hold down the

CTRL key while highlighting a file and skip over the file, so you do not have to select a continuous range.

You do not always have to select individual files when copying, deleting, or moving files. You can enter a filename pattern in the appropriate text field when copying, moving, or deleting a file. A filename pattern allows you to select files that meet certain criteria by using wildcard characters. WordPerfect recognizes two wildcard characters: the question mark (?) and the asterisk (*). The ? represents one character and the * represents zero or more characters. (A zero character simply means there is no character.) For example, if you wanted to delete all files that have the filename prefix of REPORTS, you would enter REPORTS.* in the "Files to Delete" text field. This would delete all files with a prefix of REPORT and any combination of extensions, including no extension.

Copying Files and Directories

From a file management dialog box you can copy a single file or a series of selected files from the File List. You select the file or files you want to copy, choose the Copy feature, and then specify where the copies of the files should be stored.

To copy a file or files, select the file(s). Then, with the mouse pointer in the File List, click the right mouse button and choose Copy. In the To text field, type the drive or directory where you want the file(s) copied. If you want to make a copy of the file in the same directory, simply type a new filename, then choose Copy. The file(s) are copied to the destination directory, or to the new filename.

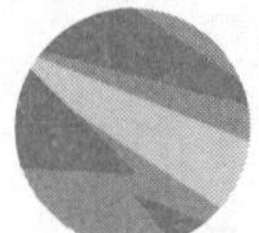

HINT: *If a file with the same name exists, WordPerfect will prompt you before replacing the file. If you know that the exact file or files exist in the destination directory, you can choose the Don't replace files with the same size, date, and time check box. WordPerfect will not replace the files and will not prompt you if these conditions are met.*

Deleting Files and Directories

From a file management dialog box you can delete a single file, multiple files, a directory, or an entire directory structure. As a safeguard, WordPerfect prompts you to confirm all deletion operations. To delete a file or multiple files, select the file(s) from the File List. With the mouse pointer in the File List, press the right mouse button and choose Delete, then choose Delete again.

Along with deleting files, you can also delete directories. When you delete a directory, any subdirectories and files in the directory are also deleted. To delete a directory choose File Options from the file management dialog box, then choose Remove Directory. The following dialog box is displayed.

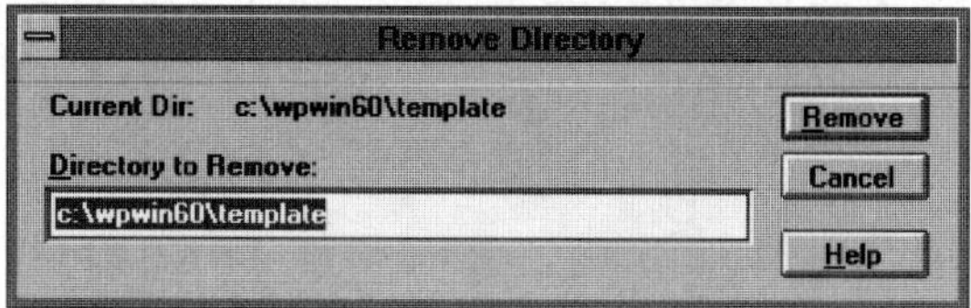

Enter the name of the directory you want to delete in the Directory to Remove text field, then choose Remove. If the directory contains files or subdirectories, WordPerfect displays a warning; choose Yes to confirm that you want to delete the directory.

Moving and Renaming Files

The Move/Rename feature helps you rearrange files and directories. With the Move/Rename feature you can change the name of a file or directory or move a file or directory to a new location.

HINT: If you specify a directory that does not exist when moving files, WordPerfect prompts you to create the directory.

To move or rename a single file, select the file from the File List. With the mouse pointer in the File List, press the right mouse button and choose Move; the Move File dialog box is displayed. In the To text field, enter the directory to which you want to move the file. If you want to rename the file, enter the new filename in the To text field. If you want to move and rename the file, enter the new directory and new filename, then choose Move. The file is moved and/or renamed.

To move or rename multiple files, first select the files with the mouse pointer in the File List, then press the right mouse button and choose Move or Rename. In the To text field, enter the directory to which you want to move the files and choose Move. If you are renaming the files, type a filename pattern in the To text field and then choose Rename. For example, if you type ***.DOC** in the To text field, the selected files are renamed with .DOC file extensions; if you type **LETTER.*** the files are renamed as LETTER but keep their original extensions. Carefully consider the filename pattern you type, and make sure it will not create duplicate filenames when all the selected files are renamed; if the pattern does create duplicate filenames, WordPerfect will ask you whether you want to replace the renamed files. Usually, you will not want to replace the recently renamed files with other files in the selection. If you want to rename the files, but not with a file pattern, you will need to select and rename each file individually.

Creating Directories

There are several ways to create directories in WordPerfect. The standard method for creating a directory is to choose File Options from a file management dialog box and then choose Create Directory. The Create Directory dialog box appears, as shown in Figure 4-6. In the New Directory text field, enter the name of the directory, including the path, you want to create, and choose Create. If you do not include a full path, the directory you specify is created as a subdirectory under the current directory. You can also create directories when copying, moving, or changing directories by specifying a directory that does not exist. WordPerfect will prompt you to create the directory.

Changing File Attributes

There are several DOS file attributes you can assign to a file from a file management dialog box: Read-Only (r), Hidden (h), Archive (a), and System (s).

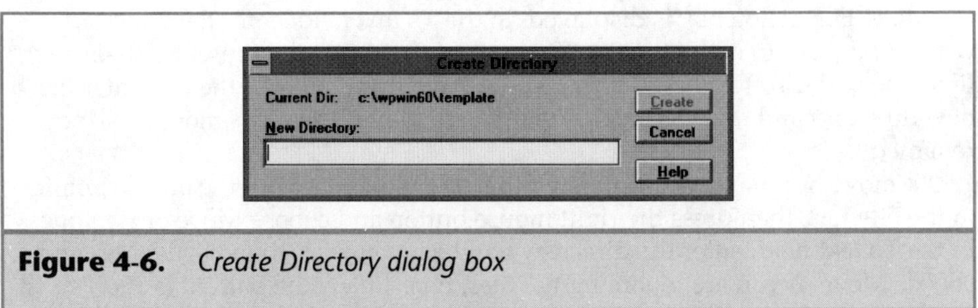

Figure 4-6. *Create Directory dialog box*

When a file is marked Read-Only (r), it cannot be deleted or modified, but it can be copied, moved, and renamed. If you are on a network and save files to a directory where many users have rights, it may be a good idea to change the attribute of files you do not want modified to Read-Only. You need to be sure that you remove the Read-Only attribute before you try to modify the file(s).

When a file is marked Hidden (h), it is not displayed when you use the DIR command from DOS to display a directory list or in the File List in WordPerfect. You can still perform all file operations such as move, copy, delete, and so on, on a hidden file if you know the filename, but a hidden file is not easily accessible to those who do not know the filename. Marking a file as Hidden is a good way to prevent others from tampering with it.

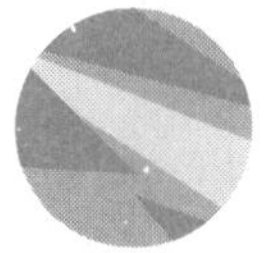

HINT: *Each time you create or modify a file, it is marked with the Archive (a) attribute. This informs backup programs which files have been modified since the last backup. The backup may be performed with the DOS BACKUP command or with a backup utility program. Once a backup copy or archive of the file is created, the Archive attribute is removed. This helps you quickly identify which files have changed since your last backup, thus alleviating the need to back up all files each time you perform a backup.*

A file marked as System (s) signifies that the file is needed to run your computer. System files are not displayed when you use the DIR command from DOS to display a directory list, nor are they displayed in the File List in WordPerfect. You should not modify or delete system files.

To change the attribute of a file or files, first select the file or files from a File List. Then choose File Options/Change Attributes; the Change File Attributes dialog box appears. Select the desired attribute or attributes and then choose OK.

Assigning a Password to a File

Assigning a password to a document locks the document so only those who know the password can retrieve, view, print, copy, move/rename, or delete the file while in WordPerfect. Assigning a password to a file adds security to confidential files. If you are using a network and save files in a shared directory or share a computer, assigning a password ensures that other users will not be able to retrieve and modify your document unless they know the password.

To assign a password to a file in a document window, choose File/Save As. If the document has not been saved, type a filename but do not press ENTER. Choose the Password Protect check box in the lower right-hand corner, then choose OK. Enter a password. Reenter the password. WordPerfect asks you to reenter the password to ensure you entered it correctly the first time.

To remove a password with the file on screen, choose File/Save As. Choose Password Protect to deselect the option, then choose OK. Choose Yes when prompted to Replace the file.

Each time you try to retrieve, print, copy, move, delete, or look at a file with a password, you will be prompted to enter the password. If you do not know the password WordPerfect does not allow you to perform the operation. The password encrypts the file so it cannot be used in other applications. Other users can delete the file.

Printing from a File Management Dialog Box

From a file management dialog box you can print a file or selected files without retrieving the files. You can also print a list of the files in the File List.

To print a file(s) from the File List, select the file(s) and choose File Options/Print. From the Print dialog box, choose Print. The file is automatically printed from WordPerfect. You can select multiple files and then choose Print. WordPerfect will automatically print each file.

To print the contents of the File List, choose File Options/Print List. The Print File List dialog box appears; choose Print List of Selected Items to print only selected items, or choose Print Entire List to print all the information. Then choose Print.

Finding Files with the QuickFinder

The QuickFinder is a powerful tool that helps you find files that match certain search criteria. Using the QuickFinder can be as simple as finding a file in a directory containing the name "Brooke Taylor," or as complicated as searching selected directories and finding all the files that contain the word "Florida," but not the word "California," that were created between 9/1/94 and 10/1/94. With the QuickFinder you can search specific directories, drives, and even customized indexes that you create. Once you narrow down where you are going to search, you specify what you are going to search for.

Follow these steps to use the QuickFinder:

1. Choose File/QuickFinder; the QuickFinder dialog box is displayed, as shown in Figure 4-7.
2. If necessary, choose File Pattern and type a directory and/or file pattern that you want to search. For example, **C:\LETTERS*.LET** would search only the files in the LETTERS directory that ended with a .LET extension. You can combine multiple filename patterns by separating them with a comma. If you do not enter anything in the File Pattern text field, the contents of whatever is specified for Search In will be searched.
3. Choose Search For and enter the text you want to find. For more information on what you can enter in the Search for text field, see "Entering the Search Information" later in this section.
4. Choose Search In and choose Directory, Disk, Subtree, or QuickFinder Index to specify where you want to search. The Subtree option searches all subdirectories below a specified directory.
5. If necessary, enter a Date Range in the From and To text fields. You can click on the calendar icon to display the current month's calendar and select a date from it. Entering a Date Range can speed up a search since WordPerfect only has to search the files last modified during a certain period of time. Entering a Date Range also gives you more control over a search.
6. Choose WordPerfect Document Only if you want to search only documents created in WordPerfect.
7. Choose Find to begin the search. After completing the search, WordPerfect displays the Search Results List containing a list of all files that met the criteria specified.

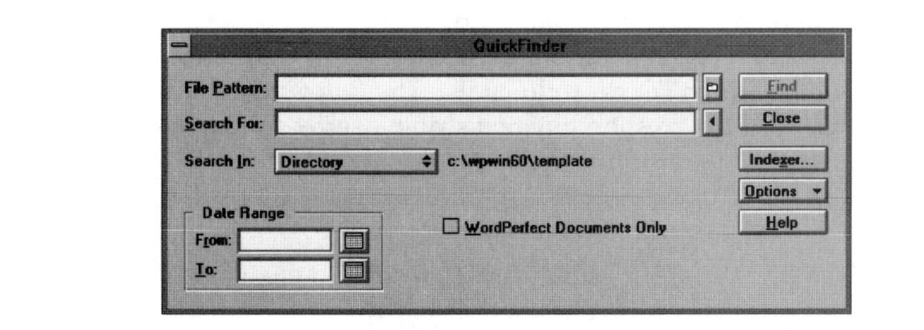

Figure 4-7. *QuickFinder dialog box*

Viewing the Search Results Dialog Box

The Search Results dialog box is very similar to the other file management dialog boxes found in WordPerfect. The File List displays the names of all files that meet the specified search criteria, along with the Full Path of the file and several other columns of file information. You view the contents of a file by selecting the desired file and choosing the View option. Viewing the file can help you further determine if it is the file you are looking for. For more information on viewing files see "Viewing File Contents" earlier in this chapter.

You can save the results of your search by choosing the Save Search Results. This allows you to go back and look at the results at a later time.

Entering the Search Information

WordPerfect gives you numerous options for defining the search criteria in the Search For text field. You can specify logical operators, what components of the document you want to search, case sensitivity, and how thorough you want the search. The following sections describe the different options available for specifying search criteria.

Using Logical Operators

In addition to entering words and phrases in the Search For text field, you can also use the Operators option to limit your search even further. Sometimes the word or word pattern you are looking for is not clear cut. For example, you may want to find files with two words that are not always displayed together, or you may want to find files that do not contain a certain word. These and other situations are handled by *logical operators*. Logical operators are text strings that tell WordPerfect that certain conditions exist. To access the operators, choose Operators from the Search For drop-down list. The following table lists the operators available, the corresponding text string inserted, and a description and example of how each operator functions.

Operator	Text String	Function
AND	&	Finds files that contain the word pattern that is on each side of the &. For example, enter **Defendant & Charles Morgan** to find all files with both defendant and Charles Morgan.

Operator	Text String	Function
OR	|	Finds files that contain the word pattern on each side of the |, or files that contain either word pattern. For example, enter **Profits | Deficits** to find files with both "profits" and "deficits" or files with either word.
NOT	-	Finds files that do not contain the word following the -. For example, enter **- April** to find all files that do not contain the word "April."
Followed By	..	Finds files that have the first word preceding the second word somewhere in the document. For example, enter **rain..February** to find all files that contain the word "rain" somewhere in the document before the word "February."
Group	()	Finds files that contain specific words or phrases in various groupings.
Match Single Character	?	Finds words containing a single character. For example, enter **report?** to find "report1," "report2," "report3," etc.
Match Multiple Characters	*	Finds words containing multiple characters. For example, enter **sail*** to find "sailor," "sailboat," "sails," etc.

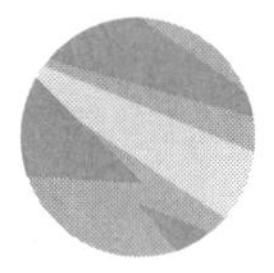

NOTE: *Logical operators can be combined to limit the search even further.*

Specifying the Parts of a Document to Search

You can specify exactly what parts of the document you want searched when using the QuickFinder. Choose Document Components from the Search For drop-down list. The following table describes the available options.

Document Component	Description
Entire	Searches the entire document, including headers, footers, footnotes, and the Document Summary.
Text Only	Searches the text body of the document, but does not search headers, footers, and Document Summaries.

Document Component	Description
First Page	Searches the first page of the document and the Document Summary.
Summary Only	Searches only Document Summary fields.
Summary Fields	Searches selected Document Summary fields.

Specifying Case Sensitivity

When you enter text in the Search For text field, WordPerfect ignores all case sensitivity. If you want the search to be case sensitive choose Case Sensitivity from the Search For drop-down list and then choose Case Sensitive.

Specifying the Search Level

If you are searching for word patterns that are specified with the Operators option, you may want to change the level at which WordPerfect searches. From the Search For drop-down list, choose Closeness of Words and then choose the level you want WordPerfect to search for word patterns. Document is the most global option. The more specific the level of searching, the longer the search will take. For example, if you specify Page, the word pattern must be together on the same page. If you specify Sentence it must be found in the same sentence.

Creating a QuickFinder Index

In addition to searching specific files and directories, you can also create your own indexes to search. Creating your own index allows you to include only those files and directories you need in a search. Once the index is created, you can use the QuickFinder to quickly search the information contained in the index for specific text. Using the QuickFinder allows you to expand your search to include multiple directories. It also allows you to limit your search to contain only specific files from specific directories.

To create a QuickFinder index definition:

1. Choose File/QuickFinder.
2. Choose Indexer.

3. Choose Create. The QuickFinder File Indexer screen is displayed. Choose Create.
4. Enter a name for the index such as Employee Expense Reports and choose OK. The Create Index dialog box is displayed.
5. Choose Add Directory or File and enter the directory or filename you want to index, then choose Add. You can use the Browse option to list files and directories from which you want to choose. You can also choose the Include Subtree option to automatically include all subdirectories under the specified directory.
6. Repeat step 5 until you have added all directories and/or files you want to include in the index.
7. Choose Generate to create the index file. WordPerfect displays the Generating Index dialog box followed by the Index Completed dialog box. Choose OK.
8. If necessary, choose the index you want to use in a search from the Search In text box, displayed here:

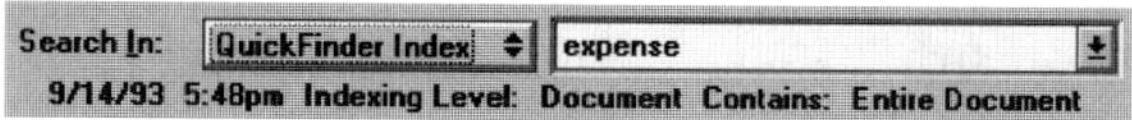

9. Enter any additional information in the QuickFinder dialog box and then choose Find.

When you make changes to files and directories in an index, you must update the index so it includes the changes. The following sections explain how to update indexes when you make changes to the files and directories in the index, and how to change index options.

Updating Indexes

Any time you make changes to the files and/or directories in an index, you need to update the index to reflect the changes. When you update the index, WordPerfect reads the files and directories and updates the index file. To manually update your indexes, choose File/QuickFinder. Then choose Indexer, highlight the index you need to update, and choose Generate. The Index Method dialog box is displayed, as shown in the following illustration.

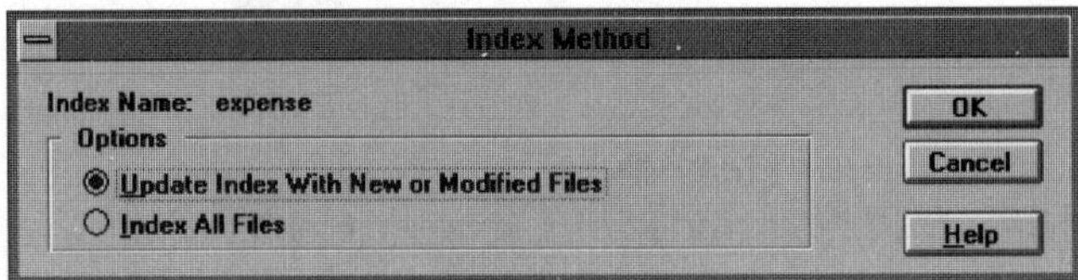

Choose the desired option and then choose OK. If no changes have been made to the files or directories, WordPerfect will not update the index. Choose OK and Close to return to the document window.

WordPerfect has a utility program called Kickoff that automates the process of updating QuickFinder indexes. Once you set up the Kickoff utility program, WordPerfect will automatically update your indexes at specified intervals. To set up the Kickoff program to update your indexes:

1. Exit WordPerfect to the WordPerfect group window.
2. Double-click on the Kickoff icon.
3. Choose Add.
4. In the Command Line text field enter **C:\WPC20\QFWIN20.EXE /ia**. Make sure to add a space before the startup option (/ia). If you have changed your default WordPerfect directories, you may need to alter the information you enter in the Command Line.
5. Enter a Start Date and Time to specify when you want the index update.
6. Enter a Repeat Interval, such as 1 for Days to have Kickoff update the indexes once a day at the specified date and time. The Edit/Add dialog box appears:

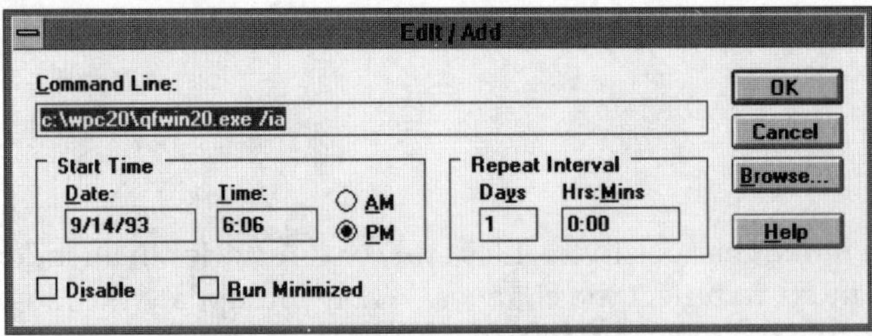

7. Choose OK, then choose Close to return to the WordPerfect group window.

WordPerfect will now update all your indexes whenever changes have been made to the files and directories at the specified intervals. You can still manually generate your indexes within WordPerfect, but this will save you time by automating the process.

If you want to remove the automatic update of indexes from Kickoff, run Kickoff, highlight the appropriate line in the Events list box, then choose Remove. Choose Close to return to the WordPerfect group window.

Changing Index Options

You can define specific options for each index you create. You can define global index options for all newly created indexes, or you can define individual index options when you create an index. You can also edit an existing index. To define global index options:

1. Choose File/QuickFinder.
2. Choose Indexer.
3. Choose Options/Preferences; the Preferences dialog box is displayed, as shown in Figure 4-8.

The following table lists the default Index options available and a brief description of each option.

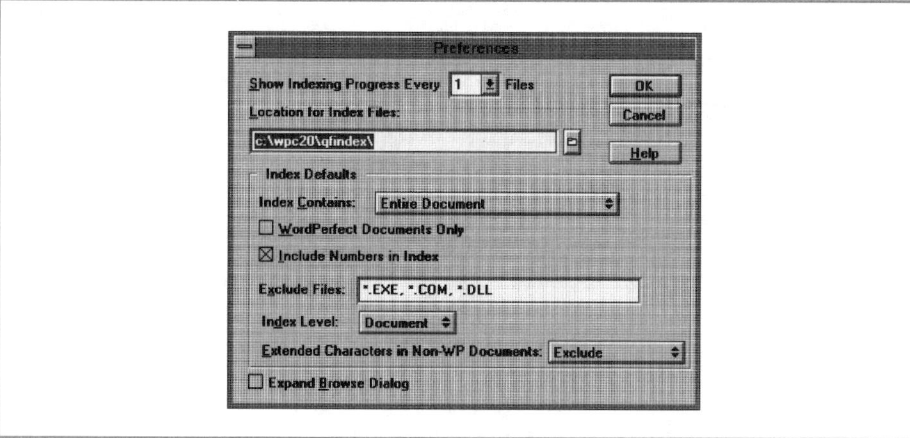

Figure 4-8. *QuickFinder Preferences dialog box*

Option	Description
Index Contains	Lists what information in the files has been indexed. By default the entire document is indexed.
WordPerfect Documents Only	Indexes only WordPerfect documents, when selected. This will speed up indexing.
Include Numbers	Includes numbers in the index when selected.
Exclude Files	Lists files to exclude from indexing. By default all files ending with an **.EXE**, **.COM**, and **.DLL** extension are excluded.
Level	Lists the level of indexing. You can choose from document, hard page, page, paragraph, sentence, and line. The level of indexing is used when searching for word patterns. Document is the most global option and line is the most specific option. The more specific the level of indexing, the larger the index and the longer the search will take.
Extended Characters in Non-WP Documents	Specifies whether to exclude extended characters or interpret them as ASCII or ANSI text in the index.

CHAPTER 5

Working with Your Printer

An important function of word processing is getting your words on the printed page. The WordPerfect printing features are powerful, and they are also flexible so they can suit your needs. You can print an entire document, print a specific page, or print a series of selected pages. You can choose different print qualities and create draft copies for proofreading.

Special software files, called *printer drivers*, enable WordPerfect to communicate with your printer. Since each printer is different, WordPerfect for Windows includes printer drivers for over 900 printer models—about 700 more than the Microsoft Windows 3.0 program supports and about 600 more than Microsoft Windows 3.1. These include standard laser printers, PostScript printers, dot-matrix and daisy-wheel printers, and some plotter output devices. Complete font support is included to make the best use of your printer's capabilities. Color printing is also supported for printers with color capabilites.

This chapter shows you how to set up and use your printer with WordPerfect. You'll learn how to view a document in Full Page mode and at different magnifications, how to print a document, and how to choose special options for printing. The last section in this chapter explains how to solve common printer problems.

General Printing Information

Printing is usually a simple task, provided that you have correctly set up your printer equipment and software. When you send a document to the printer, the printer drivers help WordPerfect communicate with your printer. Most software programs that run under Microsoft Windows use the printer drivers supplied with the Windows program. WordPerfect, however, lets you use the Windows printer drivers or its own WordPerfect printer drivers, which are usually activated when you first install the WordPerfect program; that is, if you choose to set up printer information when you installed the WordPerfect program, the WordPerfect software should be ready to work with your printer. If you prefer to work with the Microsoft Windows printer drivers, you can easily change the driver type from within the WordPerfect program.

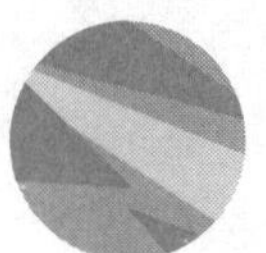

NOTE: *You can use WordPerfect 6.0 for DOS printer files with WordPerfect 6.0 for Windows, but you cannot use WordPerfect for Windows 5.1 or 5.2 printer drivers.*

Printer Drivers and Files

WordPerfect uses two types of printer files to store information about the printers it supports. Files ending with an .ALL extension contain complete information for several printers. Each file ending with a .PRS extension—called printer resource files or printer drivers—contains information about one specific printer. This includes information about text spacing, fonts, and the paper sizes the printer can accept. When you installed the WordPerfect program, at least one

.ALL file and one .PRS file were copied to your WordPerfect directory, according to the printer name that you selected during installation. WordPerfect uses the .PRS file to communicate with the printer that is connected to your computer. If you use two or more printers with your computer, you need a .PRS file for each unique printer. The .ALL file is copied because it contains complete information about the type of printer you have selected; if, for example, you add a new cartridge for your printer, WordPerfect needs the .ALL file to update the font information stored in your .PRS file.

When you create a document, WordPerfect saves printer information with your document file and specifically formats the text for the printer you have selected. This ensures correct fonts and text spacing when your document is sent to the printer. If you select a new printer definition while a document is displayed, WordPerfect automatically adjusts fonts, formatting, and text spacing according to the capabilities of the selected printer. This "auto-adjustment" allows you to exchange files with other WordPerfect users without having to make formatting changes for the current printer.

Fonts and Attributes

Fonts determine the general appearance of text in your documents. Common fonts include Courier, Helvetica, and Times Roman. Most printers have two or more "built-in" fonts—that is, fonts that are always available for printing. You can purchase font software, called *soft fonts,* and *font cartridges* to add more font capabilities to laser printers and other similar printers. WordPerfect also supports *graphical fonts*. Graphical fonts print the text in a graphics mode. In order to use these fonts, your printer must be able to print graphics. WordPerfect ships a set of TrueType graphics fonts with the package; you install these fonts when you install WordPerfect.

When you purchase additional font software, you need to tell WordPerfect which fonts you have added to your printer. When installing graphics fonts in Windows, WordPerfect automatically recognizes those currently installed and adds them to your selection of fonts. If you need to install more graphics fonts, the easiest way is to use the Windows Font Installer program. As soon as they are installed in Windows, WordPerfect will add them to the list of available fonts. If you have soft fonts you need to install the soft font files to your hard disk and install the information to your WordPerfect .ALL file.

From the list of installed fonts, you can select different fonts to change the appearance of the document text. When you do so, WordPerfect inserts a code for each font change and reformats the text according to the size and spacing of the new font. Font codes do not appear on the document window but can be viewed when you choose the Reveal Codes feature (choose View/Reveal Codes or press ALT+F3). The font style changes on screen so you can see what the text will look like when you print the document.

Certain printers limit the number of font changes per document page; refer to your printer documentation for any such limits.

Text attributes, such as bold, underline, and italics, are variations of the font you are currently using. The text attributes you can select from the Font dialog box are shown here:

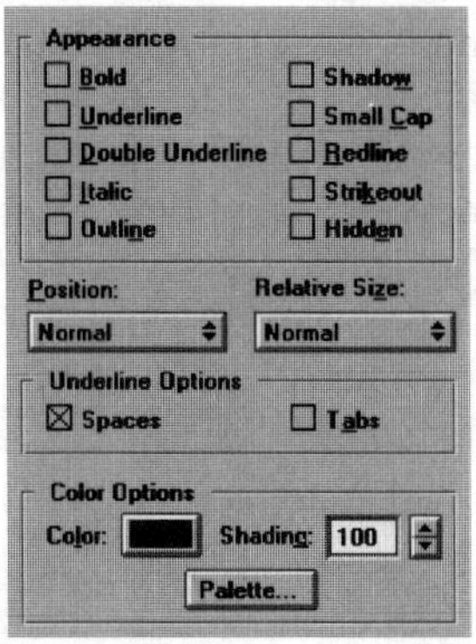

When you select an attribute from one of the Font menus, WordPerfect inserts codes at the insertion point to start the attribute. If, for example, you choose Bold, WordPerfect inserts a code into your document that turns on the bold attribute. Select the attribute again to turn it off. When the text is sent to the printer, the bold code is translated as a font change that instructs the printer to use a bold version of the current font. Because font changes for attributes are handled at print time, you can easily retrieve and print documents created for other printers.

Although WordPerfect lets you select ten different text attributes, six generic text sizes, and three position options, the results you get depend on the font capabilities of your printer. If you do not have an internal font or a printer font, WordPerfect will print the text graphically as long as you have installed graphics fonts.

From the Fonts dialog box you can also select color options for your documents. Selecting a color is very similar to selecting a font. To change the color of the text choose Layout/Font, then choose Color. Highlight the color you want to use and click the mouse button. If you want to change the Shading of the color to make it more or less intense, choose Shading and enter a number between 1 and 100, indicating the percentage of the color.

Printing Through Microsoft Windows

WordPerfect works with the Windows software to send your documents to the printer. A file called WPCPRINT.DRV was copied with the program files when you installed the WordPerfect program. This is a driver file that allows WordPerfect to send print jobs through the Windows software while using its own printer drivers to format documents for printing. WordPerfect for Windows does not have a Printer Control screen where you can view and manage print jobs. Instead, WordPerfect uses the Microsoft Windows Print Manager to handle the printing process. The Print Manager also generates the error messages that appear when a printing problem occurs.

When you print a document, WordPerfect sends information through the WPCPRINT.DRV driver to the Windows Print Manager. The WP Print Process dialog box briefly appears on your screen and displays information about the printing process. As soon as you send a print job, you can continue working in WordPerfect. This is called print spooling; it means the computer can handle the printing process in memory while you are working with other tasks. If the Print Manager is not available, you can still print from WordPerfect and take advantage of print spooling.

WordPerfect allows you to work with its own printer drivers, or you can use the printer drivers included with the Microsoft Windows program. The Microsoft Windows printer drivers let you use the same printer drivers you may be using with other Windows applications. Your printer, however, may not be supported by the Microsoft drivers. In addition, WordPerfect printer drivers provide extensive support for kerning. Because of the advantages of both types of printer drivers, WordPerfect lets you select either driver type at any time while you are working with the program.

WordPerfect automatically displays both Windows drivers and WordPerfect drivers. An icon displays to the left of each printer name in the Select Printer dialog box shown in Figure 5-1 designating if the driver is WordPerfect or Windows. To select and/or edit a Microsoft Windows printer driver, follow these steps:

1. From the WordPerfect menu bar, choose File/Select Printer.
2. Highlight the printer name that displays a Windows icon and choose the Setup button to adjust the printer settings. The Windows Printer Setup dialog box appears, in which you can change many of your printer options. After making the necessary changes choose OK to return back to WordPerfect.

This is the same dialog box that appears when you choose the Printers option from the Windows Control Panel.

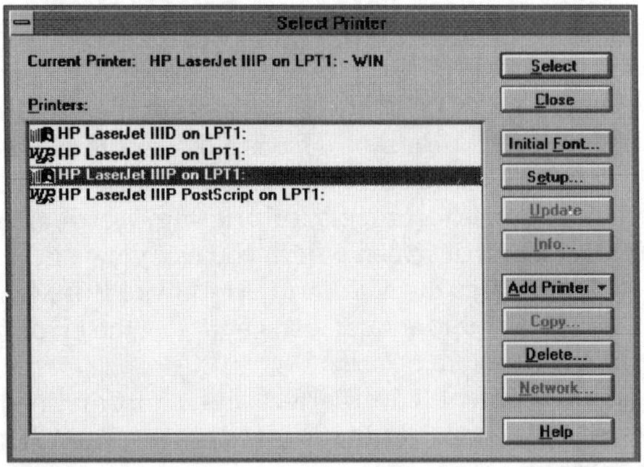

Figure 5-1. *The Select Printer dialog box*

3. Choose Select. The highlighted printer driver becomes active and the Select Printer dialog box is closed. When you change from WordPerfect drivers to Windows drivers (and vice versa), WordPerfect automatically adjusts your documents for the new printer driver type.

If you are using WordPerfect in an office environment where Windows programs are already in use, you may want to select the Windows printer drivers; if you need accurate text spacing and kerning, or if you use a printer that is not supported by Microsoft Windows, choose the WordPerfect printer drivers. You don't need to commit to one driver type; you can switch between the two at any time, from within WordPerfect.

Throughout this book, it is assumed you are using the WordPerfect printer drivers, because these are automatically selected when you install WordPerfect for Windows. If you are using the Windows printer drivers instead, refer to your Microsoft Windows User's Guide for additional information about printer setup and use.

Getting Help

Sometimes it is easy to get lost in WordPerfect's numerous printing features, which are distributed across several menus and dialog boxes. As you are working with these features, you can press Help (F1) to display information about the command or menu that is currently on your screen. This will answer questions you may have about the displayed menu or dialog box. You can also activate the help pointer, which lets you display help information about a specific item within a menu or dialog box. When a dialog box or menu is displayed, press What Is (SHIFT+F1), and the mouse pointer changes to this:

Move the help pointer to an item or command button and click the mouse once. You will see a help screen about the selected item. When you have finished reading the help information, choose Close to exit the Help utility.

If you are using the WordPerfect printer drivers, you can also display help information about the specific printer you are using. This includes the date of the *.ALL printer file you are using and information about printer fonts, memory, color printing settings, and certain problems that can occur with your printer. If you have selected a sheet feeder for your printer, you can also display information about the sheet feeder. To display printer help information, first display the Select Printer dialog box (File/Select Printer) and highlight the name of your printer on the list of available printers. Then choose the Info command button. Figure 5-2 shows an example of the Printer Information dialog box WordPerfect displays. This dialog box displays specific information about the printer you selected; if necessary, use the scroll bars to view all the help text.

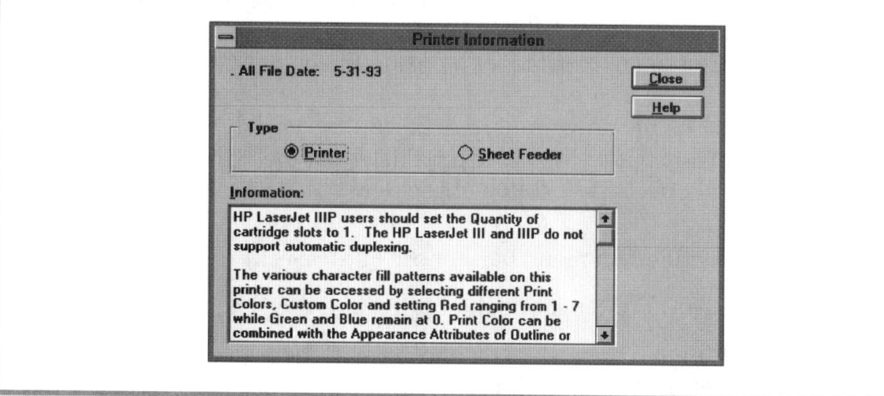

Figure 5-2. *Displaying printer information*

Not all printers have information displayed in the Printer Information dialog box. Sometimes this dialog box is left blank because there is no special information or problem associated with your printer. When you have finished viewing the printer information, choose the Close command button to return to the Select Printer dialog box. Choose Close from this dialog box to return to the WordPerfect document window.

Printer Setup

Installing a printer for WordPerfect involves two basic steps. First, the correct printer driver files must be copied to your WordPerfect directory. Second, you need to select the printer definition before you create and print your documents.

If you specified a printer when you installed WordPerfect, the installation program performed these tasks for you, and WordPerfect should be ready to work with your printer. If you work with two or more printers, you can install as many additional printer drivers as you need. Then select the printer definition you want to use before you create and print your documents. The following sections show you how to install and set up your printer for use with WordPerfect.

Installing Printer Information

When you installed the WordPerfect program, printer information was copied to your \WPC20 directory, and your printer was set up for use with WordPerfect. You can install information for additional printers using the Add Printers dialog box if the .ALL file has been installed, or by using the Install program to install a new .ALL file.

If you have an .ALL file on your hard disk, you can add the new printers to the Select Printer dialog box in WordPerfect. First, start the Windows program, and then start WordPerfect. Then follow these steps:

1. From the WordPerfect menu bar, choose File/Select Printer.
2. Choose the Add Printer command button and then choose WordPerfect.
3. Choose Additional Printers to display a list of the printers contained in the .ALL files, as shown in Figure 5-3.

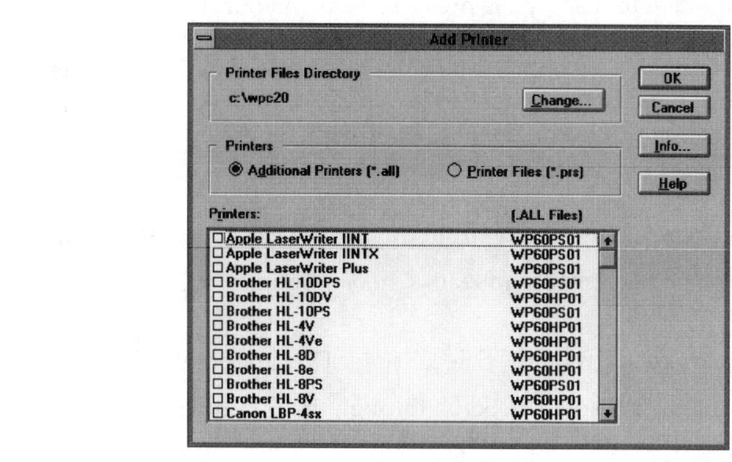

Figure 5-3. *Adding a printer to the Select Printer list*

4. Select the printer you want to use; if necessary, use the scroll bar to move through the list. An X in the check box indicates the printer is selected.
5. Choose the OK button. WordPerfect prompts you for the printer filename; choose OK to accept the default .PRS filename or choose Printer Filename and enter a new filename, then choose OK. WordPerfect adds the printer to the list of available printers on the Select Printer dialog box.
6. In the Select Printer dialog box, choose the Select button to select the highlighted printer. If you do not want to select the printer at this time, choose the Close button instead.

When you add a new printer to the list, WordPerfect copies information from the .ALL file to create a printer driver (.PRS file) for the selected printer. The .PRS file is stored in the directory where the other WordPerfect printer files are located.

If the list of Printers in the Add Printer dialog box displays no printer names, this means an .ALL file is not found in the current directory. Make sure the path name shown at the top of the dialog box is the directory where your WP printer driver files are located. If this is not the correct directory, choose the Change command button, and WordPerfect displays a Select Directory dialog box; if you know the path name where the printer files are stored, type it in the Directory Name text field. Otherwise, you can double-click the items in the Directories list to browse through the directory structure and find the correct path name.

Double-click the [..] item to display the previous level in your directory structure; double-click a directory name to display the next level in the directory structure.

If your printer is not listed in the Add Printers dialog box and WordPerfect is accessing the correct directory, you need to install the printer .ALL file using the WordPerfect installation program. The following steps show you how to add a printer using the WordPerfect installation program.

1. Choose WPWin 6.0 Installation from the WordPerfect program group.
2. The main installation menu appears. Choose Options/Printers to install printer information.
3. Follow the instructions on the Select Printer Directory dialog box.
4. A list of printers is displayed. Scroll through the list until the printer you want is displayed. You can also type the first letter of the printer name to quickly move through the list. Then double-click on the printer name.
5. Select as many printers as you need, and then choose OK.

The installation program copies an .ALL file for the selected printer to the directory where your other WordPerfect printer files are stored (by default this is the \WPC20 directory). Choose Close and then Exit to return to Windows. Now you need to start WordPerfect and select the newly added printer.

Selecting a Printer

When you have two or more printers listed in the Select Printer dialog box, you can select the printer definition you need before creating or printing a document. To select a printer, follow these steps:

1. Choose File/Select Printer from the WordPerfect menu bar. This displays the Select Printer dialog box shown in Figure 5-4.
2. Highlight the name of the printer you want to use. If you are using a mouse, simply point to the printer name and click the mouse button. If you are using the keyboard, press the UP ARROW and DOWN ARROW keys until the printer name is highlighted.
3. Choose the Select command button to select the highlighted printer.

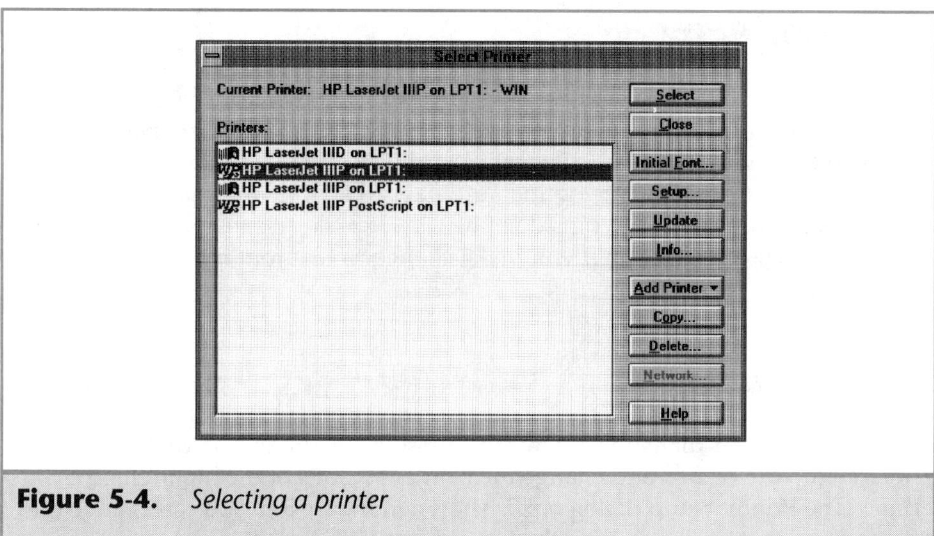

Figure 5-4. *Selecting a printer*

HINT: When selecting a printer you can also choose the Initial Font command button to choose the initial font for the highlighted printer. The initial font is used whenever you create a new document with the specified printer.

You do not need to select your printer each time you print a document; WordPerfect remembers the last printer selection and continues to work with that printer until you select a different printer definition or until you retrieve a document created with a different printer definition.

WordPerfect uses information from the selected printer's .PRS file to calculate text spacing and to determine which fonts are available for printing. When you save your documents, some of the printer information is stored in the document file to help WordPerfect make formatting adjustments when you open (retrieve) the document into a copy of WordPerfect where the original .PRS file is not available.

Once you open a document, you can convert it for printing on a different printer by simply selecting the desired printer definition. When the new printer is selected, WordPerfect converts all font codes and text spacing to match the capabilities of the new printer. If you want to convert the document back to its original form, simply reselect the printer definition you initially used to create the document.

Updating a Printer

The Update option available on the Select Printer dialog box lets you update your .PRS file with changes in an .ALL file. This option is extremely beneficial if you receive a new printer .ALL file from WordPerfect containing fixes and changes. Choosing the Update option automatically copies the changes to the .PRS file. Using this option avoids deleting the .PRS file and reselecting it again. You must also use this option if you make changes to the font map.

Changing Settings of WordPerfect Printers

At the Select Printer dialog box, you can choose the Setup option to display the Printer Setup dialog box and change the printer settings of the highlighted printer. The Printer Setup dialog box is shown in Figure 5-5. You can change the printer name that is displayed in the Select Printer dialog box and enter a directory path name to tell WordPerfect where your printer's soft font files are located. You can specify the computer port to which your printer is connected or a filename if you want the printed output to go to a file (if your computer does not have access to a printer). This file can then be printed with the DOS Print

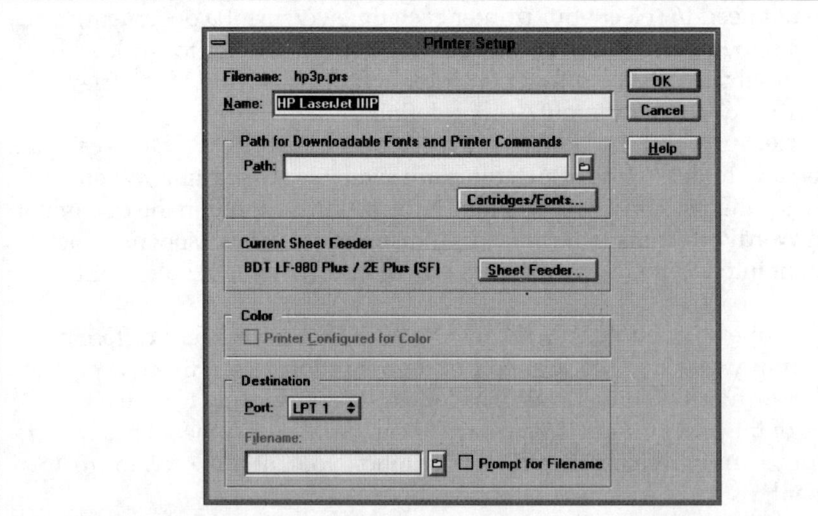

Figure 5-5. *Changing the printer settings*

command or copied to the printer with the DOS Copy command. You can also indicate which sheet feeder you are using (if any), and tell WordPerfect which fonts you have available for printing. If you have added color capabilities to a printer you can specify if your printer is configured for color. To change the printer settings, follow these steps:

1. Choose File/Select Printer from the WordPerfect menu bar and highlight the name of the printer you want to change.
2. Choose the Setup button to display the Printer Setup dialog box.
3. Make the desired changes to the printer settings.
4. Choose OK to close Printer Setup.
5. At the Select Printer dialog box, choose Select to select the printer and return to your document.

The changes you make in the Printer Setup dialog box are saved to the .PRS file for the selected printer and to WordPerfect's program setup file. If you have changed the printer name, displayed in the Select Printer dialog box, WordPerfect tries to find a printer definition with the older name when you open documents created under that name. If the older definition cannot be found, WordPerfect simply reformats your document for the current printer definition.

Defining Printer and Graphics Fonts

When you install WordPerfect printer drivers, WordPerfect recognizes the "built-in" fonts that are stored in your printer. These are the standard fonts that your printer can produce without additional software or hardware. If you purchase font cartridges and software to add more font capabilities to your printer, you need to change the printer setup to indicate the fonts you have added. You can add font cartridges from the Cartridges and Fonts dialog box (from the Setup menu), where a list of possible cartridges is displayed. You mark the cartridges you have added for your printer, and WordPerfect updates the printer's .PRS file to include the fonts.

If you have purchased printer soft fonts, you must install these fonts using the manufacturer's installation program. The actual soft font files must be copied to your hard drive or network drive. In addition, the soft font information must be copied to the WordPerfect .ALL printer file. If your soft font software does not copy the information to the WordPerfect .ALL file, you must use the WordPerfect

Font Installation utility. You must order the WordPerfect Font Installation utility from WordPerfect—it is not included with your WordPerfect for Windows software.

If you have installed graphics fonts for use with Windows, WordPerfect automatically recognizes these fonts and adds them to the list of available fonts.

Installing Cartridge Fonts

Cartridge fonts are the easiest to install. Simply plug the cartridge into your printer and follow these steps to tell WordPerfect which font cartridge you have added:

1. From the WordPerfect menu bar, choose File/Select Printer.
2. Highlight the name of the printer that has the font cartridge, and then choose the Setup command button.
3. In the Printer Setup dialog box, choose the Cartridges/Fonts button. This displays the Select Fonts dialog box shown in Figure 5-6.

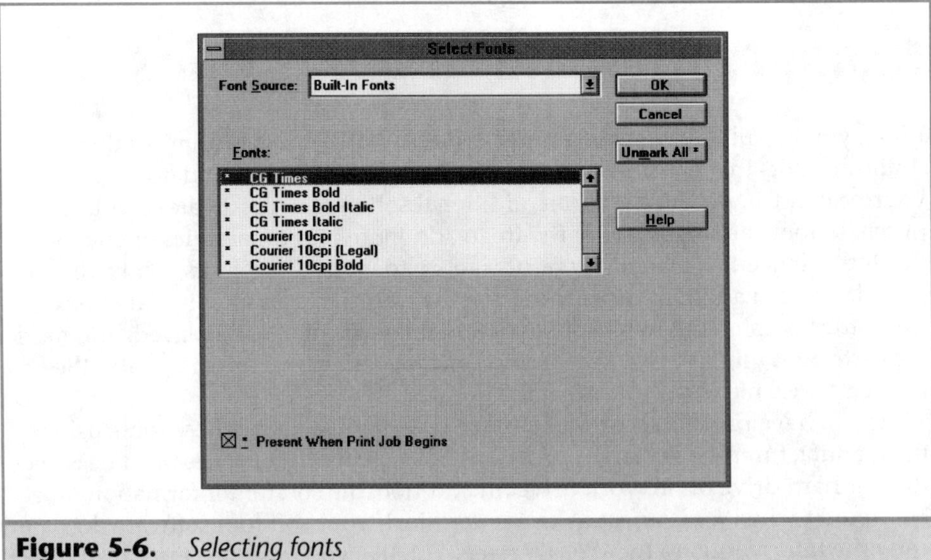

Figure 5-6. *Selecting fonts*

4. Choose Font Source and select Cartridges. A list of available cartridges is displayed. From this list, you need to indicate the cartridges you have installed for use with your printer. The Total option shows the number of cartridge slots in your printer. If this number is incorrect, choose Total and enter the correct number of slots. The Available option lists how many more cartridges you can select.
5. Use the scroll bars to move through the list of cartridge names. Highlight the name of the cartridge installed in your printer, and then check the box for "*Cartridge Installed." This marks the cartridge name for use with WordPerfect. The number of cartridges you can mark depends on the quantity of cartridge slots you have indicated.
6. Choose the OK button to return to the Cartridges and Fonts dialog box. Then, choose the OK button and the Close button until all Print dialog boxes are closed.

WordPerfect adds the fonts from the selected cartridge to the list in the Font dialog box. You can choose these fonts to change the style of text when you are creating and editing your documents.

Defining Soft Fonts

Soft fonts contain font information that is stored in software files instead of in a printer cartridge. When you install font software, note the directory where the soft font files are stored. You will need to enter the directory path name for soft fonts in the Printer Setup dialog box. Once the soft font files are copied to your hard disk and to your printer .ALL file, follow these steps to tell WordPerfect which soft fonts you have installed:

1. From the WordPerfect menu bar, choose File/Select Printer.
2. Highlight the name of the printer that will use the soft fonts, and then choose the Setup command button.
3. At the Printer Setup dialog box, choose the Cartridges/Fonts button.
4. Choose Font Source and select Soft Fonts.
5. Choose Font Groups and select the group that represents the font software you have purchased and installed. The Fonts group box displays the fonts in that font group, as shown in Figure 5-7.

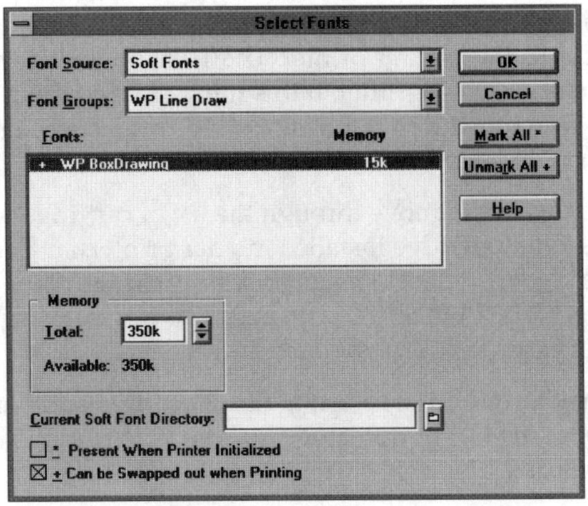

Figure 5-7. *Selecting soft fonts*

6. Choose Fonts and use the scroll bars to move through the list of soft font names. Highlight the name of each soft font file you have copied to your hard disk, and check the box for "* Present When Printer Initialized" or "+ Can be Swapped out when Printing."
7. If necessary choose Total and enter the correct amount of printer memory, listed in kilobytes. For example, enter 700 if your printer has 700K of free memory. Check your printer manual for information about the memory in your printer.
8. The last thing you need to do is add the soft font directory path name to the information stored in the printer setup. To do so, choose Current Soft Font Directory and enter the directory where the soft font files are actually stored.
9. Choose the OK button to return to the Cartridges and Fonts dialog box. Then, choose the OK and Close buttons until all Print dialog boxes are closed. WordPerfect adds the marked soft fonts to the list on the Font dialog box. (Choose Layout/Font from the WordPerfect menu bar to display the list.) When you create documents, you can choose these fonts to change the style of text.

If you mark a font "* Present When Printer Initialized," WordPerfect expects the software for that font to be resident in the printer at all times. When you mark a font "+ Can be Swapped out when Printing," WordPerfect loads and unloads the software for that font as necessary to make room for other fonts used during printing.

It is possible to mark a font with both options, provided there is enough printer memory available to load the marked fonts at once. Each font requires a certain amount of printer memory, as noted in the Memory column. As you mark each font, the amount of memory required is subtracted from the amount of available printer memory. If a font is marked as both "* Present When Printer Initialized" and "+ Can be Swapped out when Printing," WordPerfect expects the font to be resident (downloaded) at the printer before any documents are printed; WordPerfect will also load or unload the font as necessary during the printing process.

Whenever you start a new WordPerfect session, you should initialize the printer so that the fonts marked as "* Present When Printer Initialized" can be downloaded to the printer before you attempt to print any documents. You need to do this only once, when you start a new session. To initialize your printer, choose File/Print and select the Initialize Printer command button. WordPerfect then copies the font information for fonts marked as "* Present When Printer Initialized" to your printer. Fonts that are marked as "+ Can be Swapped out when Printing" are copied to the printer when you print documents that require them.

The fonts you marked in the Cartridges and Fonts dialog box appear on the list of fonts you can choose for your text; to see the list, choose Layout/Font from the WordPerfect menu bar. The list of available fonts is specific to the printer you have selected. When you select a different printer, the list is updated to reflect the fonts available for use with the new printer.

Defining Graphics Fonts

When you installed WordPerfect you had the option to install TrueType fonts, which are graphics fonts. If you installed these fonts they are automatically displayed when you choose Layout/Font and are indicated by the TrueType icon. You can also install additional graphics fonts using the Microsoft Windows Font Installer. Once you add the fonts in Windows, WordPerfect automatically recognizes them.

Sending Documents to the Printer

WordPerfect provides various ways to print your documents, allowing you more control over the printing process. You can print the entire document, but you can also print a single page or a range of selected pages. Before you send your documents to the printer, you can choose View/Zoom/Full Page option to view the layout of your document and correct any problems before you waste paper at the printer. In addition to printing documents from within WordPerfect, you can also print a document directly from a file on disk, without opening the document in WordPerfect. You can also print a document directly from the Open File dialog box.

Viewing Your Document

The WordPerfect document window displays your document in Page mode, which is almost identical to the way it is going to print. From the document window you can view document elements—like headers, footers, and footnotes.

If you want to see the exact layout of the entire page you can choose View/Zoom/Full Page, and then choose OK or press SHIFT+F5. WordPerfect displays a screen similar to the example shown in Figure 5-8. You can edit your document while displaying it in Full Page mode. If you want to display the next or previous page you can click on the Next or Previous Page buttons at the bottom of the vertical scroll bar. When you have finished viewing your document in Full Page mode, choose View/Zoom/100% to restore the document window to the default display. In addition to viewing the document in Full Page mode, you can also view two pages side by side, by choosing View/Two Page.

You can also change the magnification of the document window so you can "zoom in" on an area of a document to see some of the finer details, such as graphics. To change the magnification of the document window choose View/Zoom, then choose any of the percentages listed or choose Other and enter your own percentage, and then choose OK.

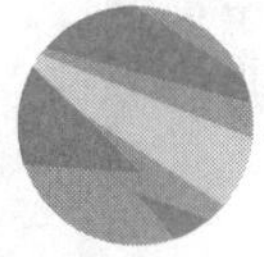

HINT: *You can also choose the magnification button on the power bar to change the display of your document.*

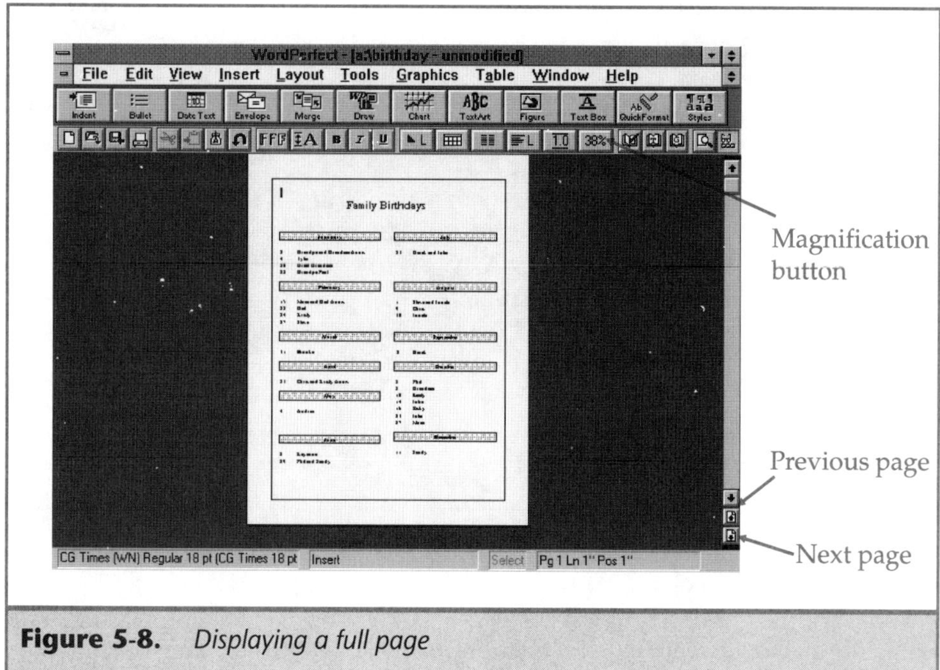

Figure 5-8. *Displaying a full page*

Printing the Entire Document

To send the active document to your printer, choose File/Print from the WordPerfect menu bar, or press Print (F5). The Print dialog box appears, as shown in Figure 5-9. If it is not already selected, choose the Full Document button and then select the Print command button. WordPerfect briefly displays the WP Print Process dialog box. If you need to cancel the print job immediately, choose the displayed Cancel button. You can display the WP Print Process dialog box at any time to see the status of print jobs that have not yet been sent to the Windows Print Manager. To view the WP Print Process dialog box choose File/Print, and then choose Control. This window remains open until you close it. After WordPerfect has prepared the print job it is handled by the Windows Print Manager. If you have sent a number of print jobs to the printer, you can view their progress at the Print Manager screen; refer to your Microsoft Windows User's Guide for more information about the Print Manager.

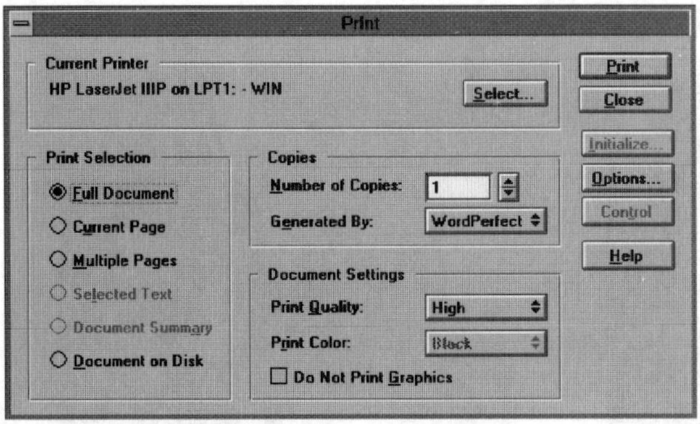

Figure 5-9. *The Print dialog box*

Printing a Single Page

Sometimes you will want to print only one or two pages from a long document file. To print a single page, first display the page on your screen. You can use the Page Down and Page Up button directly below the vertical scroll bar to quickly move up and down one page at a time, or use the Page Down (ALT+PGDN) and Page Up (ALT+PGUP) keystrokes to display the page. It is important that the insertion point appear on the page you want to print. Make sure you click the mouse pointer on the page or press the UP ARROW or DOWN ARROW key to move the insertion point to the current page. Then choose File/Print to display the Print dialog box. Select the Current Page option and choose the Print command button. WordPerfect sends a copy of the displayed page to your printer.

Printing a Range of Pages

The Multiple Pages print option lets you select and print a series of pages from your document. To use this option, choose File/Print and select Multiple Pages. Then choose the Print command button, and the Multiple Pages dialog box is displayed, as shown in Figure 5-10. In the Pages text field, type the numbers of the pages you want to print, separated by commas. If you have used the WordPerfect Page Numbering feature to create secondary pages, chapters, or volumes, you can use these options to have greater control over what you want

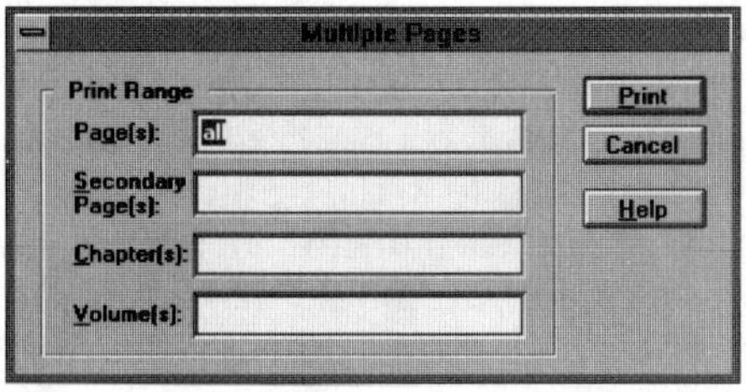

Figure 5-10. *Selecting multiple pages*

to print. Choose the Print command button, and WordPerfect sends the specified pages to your printer.

When you enter the series of page numbers in the Pages text field, you must type them in numerical order. For example, if you want to print pages 2 and 11, you would enter 2,11. If, instead, you enter 11,2, page 11 is printed, but 2 is ignored because it does not follow the logical order of the pages in the document. If you specify chapters and volumes, WordPerfect only prints the pages in the specified chapters and volumes.

You can insert numbers in the Pages field in a variety of ways:

Pages	Printed Output
2-6	Prints pages 2 through 6
2-	Prints from page 2 to the end of the document
-6	Prints from the beginning of the document to page 6
2,6,8-10	Prints pages 2, 6, 8, 9, 10

Printing from a Disk File

You do not need to open a document file to send it to the printer because WordPerfect lets you print documents directly from the files on disk. To do so, choose File/Print from the WordPerfect menu bar, or press Print (F5). Select the Document on Disk option and choose the Print command button, and WordPerfect displays the Document on Disk dialog box.

In the Filename text field, type the name of the document file you want to print. If you do not remember the filename, click the Directory button at the right of the text field to choose a filename from a Directories List box. If you want to print only a certain range of pages, secondary pages, chapters, or volumes from the file, type the appropriate numbers in the Range text fields. When you have selected the print options you want, choose the Print command button, and WordPerfect sends the document file to the printer.

Because WordPerfect formats each document for the printer that was selected when the document was created, you should make sure the correct printer is selected when you print files from the disk. If you open a document that was formatted for a printer other than the one you are now using, WordPerfect automatically reformats the document when you open the file for the current printer.

Printing from the Open File Dialog Box

You can also print documents from a Directories List or File List from the Open File dialog box. To do so, choose File/Open from the WordPerfect menu bar. Use the Directory and Filename options to display the File List where the document you want to print is stored. Select the filename and choose File Options/Print. When WordPerfect displays the Print File dialog box, choose the Print command button to send the document to the printer.

Printing Options

WordPerfect's Print dialog box includes features for printing multiple copies, color printing, and adjusting print quality. The Print Options dialog box, accessed by choosing the Options button from the Print dialog box, includes features for printing a Document Summary, printing a booklet, printing in reverse order, and whether to print odd, even, or both pages. You can also change several Output options for printers with sorting, grouping, and jogging (or stacking) capabilities.

You can permanently change some of the printer settings by choosing File/Preferences/Print to display the Print Preferences dialog box. The changes you make here are saved with the WordPerfect setup file and become the default print settings for the program.

Printing Several Copies

To print multiple copies of a document at the printer, choose File/Print and select the Number of Copies option. In the corresponding text field, type the number of copies you want, or click the incremental buttons to increase or decrease the number of copies. When you send the next document to the printer, it will produce the number of printed copies you specified in the text field. When you close the current document, the number of copies will return to the previous setting—most likely 1, for single copies. If you normally print more than 1 copy of a document, you can change this setting in Printer Preferences.

Duplicate copies can be generated by WordPerfect, or by your printer, if your printer has the capability to do so. In the Print dialog box, choose WordPerfect or Printer from the Generated By pop-up list. When WordPerfect produces the copies, it simply repeats the print job for the specified number of copies. When your printer produces the copies, WordPerfect sends a command to the printer that instructs it to print each page in the document until the desired number of copies is generated. If you are running WordPerfect from a network, you may also see a third option in the pop-up list, Network, which instructs the network software to generate the copies for you.

HINT: *It is usually faster to have the printer or network, instead of WordPerfect, generate multiple copies.*

Changing the Print Quality and Color

The Print dialog box also includes options for controlling the quality and color of your documents. The Print Quality affects both graphics and text in your document. You can choose draft, medium, or high quality. From the Print dialog box, choose the Print Quality option and select High, Medium, Draft. The Draft option lets you speed up the printing process, while the High quality is slower but produces crisper images.

For some printers—such as laser printers and plotters—the Draft, Medium, and High options for text quality have no effect on the printed document. This is because these printers cannot produce different print qualities for fonts.

If you do not want to print graphics choose the Do Not Print Graphics option. When selected, WordPerfect leaves blank spaces on the printed page where the figures or illustrations would normally appear. This option is useful when you want to proofread only the text in a large document that has graphics, when graphics may slow printing to an unacceptable level.

If your printer supports color printing, the Print Color option lets you print in Full Color or in Black. From the Print dialog box choose Print Color and select Full Color to print the document in color, using the color codes you inserted when creating the document or select Black to print the document in black ink. This option is useful when you want to proofread a document and do not need to view the colors of text and/or graphics.

When you save a document with the print quality and color settings, these are recorded with your document file and will automatically take effect whenever the document is retrieved. For this reason, make sure you check the quality settings in the Print dialog box before you choose the Print command button to print your document.

Formatting Options

The Formatting options on the Print Output Options dialog box give you control over specific printer formatting options. You can print a Document Summary for a document, print a booklet, reverse the order of printing, and determine if you want to print odd, even, or all pages. To access the formatting options choose Options from the Print dialog box. Check the Print Document Summary box if you want to print the summary information stored in the document file. Check Booklet Printing if you are using the Subdivide Page feature and want WordPerfect to print the document in booklet form. If your printer does not support duplex printing, WordPerfect prompts you to reinsert the appropriate physical page in order to print on both sides of the page to create the booklet. If you want the last page in a document to print first, check the Print in Reverse Order (Back to Front) option. If you are using a printer that does not support duplex printing and you want to print on both sides of the paper by reinserting the paper into the printer, choose Print Odd/Even Pages, and then select Odd or Even. After printing odd or even pages, turn the pages over and reinsert them in the printer, and then select the opposite option (Odd or Even) and print the document again.

Output Bin Options

The Output Bin Options are only available for printers that have special bin options and only available when printing multiple copies. To select Output Bin Options choose Options from the Print dialog. Select Sort to have WordPerfect sort each copy of the document into a different bin. Select Group, to group the same pages together in a bin. Select Jogger to have the printer automatically jog the paper after each copy. Select Output Bins to specify which bins are available for printing.

Binding Space

Many large documents, like corporate reports and thesis papers, need to be bound before they are presented. For your own documents, you may need to punch holes to fit the pages into a three-ring binder. WordPerfect includes a feature called Binding Offset that instructs WordPerfect to shift the text over on the page to allow extra space for the binding.

To add binding space to a document, choose Layout/Page/Binding. Choose the appropriate radio button to specify where you want to add the binding width, and then choose Amount and enter the amount of space you want the document to shift for the binding area. When you print your document, all printed text is moved over according to the measurement you entered. The extra binding space is added only when you send your document to the printer; it does not actually change your margin settings or change the spacing of text in the document editing window. If you are printing on both sides of the paper, text printed on odd pages is shifted to the right to add binding space; text printed on even pages is shifted left.

Printing on Both Sides of the Page

If your printer supports duplex printing and you want to print a document on both sides of the page you need to turn on Duplexing in WordPerfect. When Duplexing is on WordPerfect automatically prints the document on both sides of the page. To turn on Duplexing choose Layout/Page/Binding, and then choose Duplexing; select From Short Edge if the document is going to be bound on the top of the page or select From Long Edge if it will be bound on the long edge of the page.

Printing Sideways on the Page

Some types of documents do not fit on a sheet of paper that is 8 1/2 inches wide. This is common with charts and tables, which often need to be printed sideways on the page to accommodate several columns of data. The Paper Size feature lets you tell WordPerfect to print your document sideways on the page to allow enough space for wide documents. Paper size definitions determine the dimensions of the paper on which you are printing and also indicate the orientation of the text on the page. The standard is called *portrait orientation*, meaning that the text is printed as it would appear on a normal business letter. The second type is called *landscape orientation*, which means the text is printed sideways on the page, but only if your printer has fonts that can be printed sideways or you are using a graphics font, such as the TrueType fonts shipped with WordPerfect.

For laser printers, WordPerfect uses landscape fonts or graphics fonts to print sideways, and you will need to select a new paper type that specifies this orientation. To do so choose Layout/Page/Paper Size. As shown in Figure 5-11, WordPerfect displays the paper definitions that are defined for use with your printer. Highlight the Letter Landscape Paper Definition, and choose the Select command button. This inserts a [Paper Sz/Typ:11" by 8.5",LetterLandscape] code into your document, indicating that each page that falls after the [Paper Sz/Typ:] code will be printed sideways on the paper.

WordPerfect can print sideways only if your printer has the right fonts, which include landscape fonts and fonts that can be rotated sideways.

If your printer does not support landscape fonts and cannot print graphics fonts, you can print sideways by feeding the long edge of the paper into your printer. For example, most dot-matrix printers do not support landscape fonts, and printing a lot of text with a graphics font is very slow so you can adjust how the paper goes through the printer in order to print sideways on the page. Just

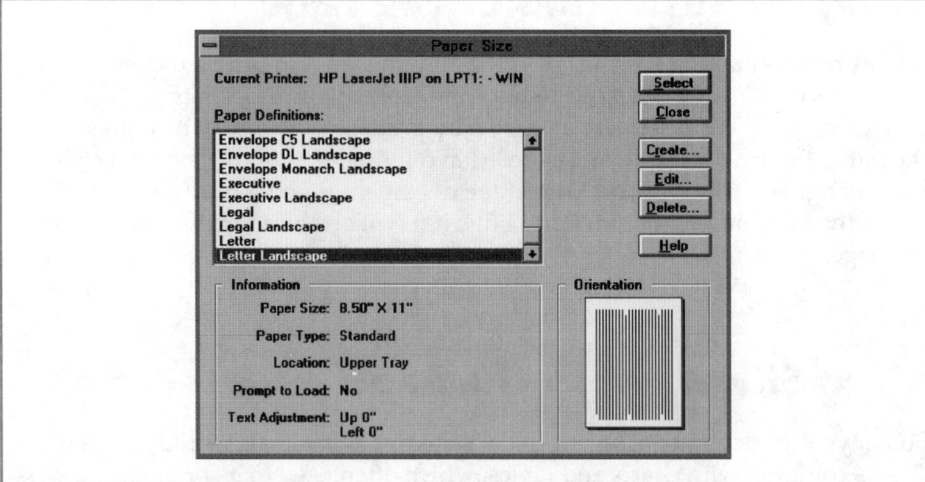

Figure 5-11. *Choosing a paper size for landscape (sideways) printing*

feed the 11-inch (long) edge of the paper into the printer, instead of the 8 1/2-inch (short) edge. If you are using a tractor paper feeder, you may need to remove your regular paper and insert standard sheet paper to print the document. Then, select the Standard 8.5" x 11" paper type from the Paper Size dialog box, choose the Wide Form checkbox, and then print your document.

Printer Troubleshooting

When you have problems with printing, there are several things you can do to correct each situation. Most printing problems are easy to fix, provided you know what to do. The following sections cover common problems that occur when printing from WordPerfect. It is assumed that you are using the WordPerfect printer drivers. If you are using the Microsoft Windows printer drivers instead, the information presented here will help you correct some printer problems; however, you may want to read the "Print Manager" section of your Microsoft Windows User's Guide for additional troubleshooting tips.

Basic Troubleshooting

Most printer problems occur because the printer equipment or printer driver software is incorrectly installed. This section covers the troubleshooting procedure for general printing problems; specific problems and solutions are discussed in the next sections.

When you encounter a problem with printing, first check your computer equipment. Make sure the printer cable connectors are securely attached to your printer and computer. Also, make sure your printer is turned on, with paper correctly loaded into the paper feeder. The printer's Online indicator shows whether the printer is ready to receive information; if the indicator is not lit, press the Online button on your printer. This puts the printer back online and allows WordPerfect to send document information to your printer.

If, after checking your computer equipment, you are still having printing problems, check the printer driver setup in WordPerfect. Start the WordPerfect program from Windows, and choose File/Select Printer from the menu bar. WordPerfect displays the Select Printer dialog box; the printer driver that is currently in use is listed at the top of the dialog box. If this is not the printer that is connected to your computer, select the correct printer driver from the list. If your printer is not on the list, choose the Add Printer command button to copy the correct printer driver from a larger list of printers. When the correct printer driver appears on the Printers list, highlight the printer name and choose Select. Then, send a document to the printer.

If, after selecting the correct printer, your document does not print, check the setup options for the printer. Redisplay the Select Printer dialog box (File/Select Printer), highlight the name of the printer you are using, and choose the Setup command button. This displays the Printer Setup dialog box, described earlier in this chapter. Make sure each of the settings in this dialog box is correct, particularly the port setting; an incorrect setting will cause printing problems. When you are finished with this dialog box, choose the OK command button to return to the Select Printer dialog box. Choose the Select command button to select the highlighted printer and close the dialog box. Then send a document to the printer to see if the printing problem has been corrected.

If the printer is still not printing anything, try printing from the DOS prompt. First, exit WordPerfect and the Windows program. At the DOS prompt, type **copy con lpt*n*** or **copy con com*n***, where *n* represents the port number, and then press ENTER. If you don't know your port, type **copy con prn** and press ENTER. Then, type **This is a printing test** and press ENTER. Press CTRL+Z followed by ENTER. The CTRL+Z keystroke appears as ^Z on the command line and indicates the end of the text you want to send to the printer. If you have a laser printer connected to your computer, press CTRL+L followed by CTRL+Z, and then press ENTER; the CTRL+L keystroke appears as ^L and indicates a formfeed command after the text is printed. If the printer is ready but the text does not print, there is a problem with your printer equipment; your printer may be connected to the wrong computer port, you may have incorrect equipment settings, or your computer or printer may need to be serviced. If the printer test does print from DOS but not from within WordPerfect, you probably need to change one or more options under the printer setup.

To check the printer setup, start the Windows program, and then start WordPerfect. Choose File/Select Printer, and highlight the name of the printer you are using. Then choose the Setup command button to display the setup options, described earlier in this chapter. Verify that the correct settings are indicated in this dialog box. When you have finished, choose OK to return to the Select Printer dialog box. Then choose Select to choose the highlighted printer. If you need further assistance, contact the WordPerfect Customer Support Group. (The phone number is listed in your WordPerfect manual.)

The Print Manager Cannot Write to the Port

The Windows Print Manager displays an error message when it cannot send information through the printer port. This occurs when the printer is offline or when the port specified under Printer Setup is not the port to which your printer is connected.

To correct this problem, check that the printer is online and that the printer cables are securely attached to the correct computer port. If your computer has two or more printer ports, try connecting the cable to each of the ports, and send something to the printer from WordPerfect. Also, make sure the correct port setting is specified under Printer Setup. To do so, choose File/Select Printer and highlight the printer name. Then choose the Setup command button and choose the correct port setting from the Port pop-up list. Choose OK to close the dialog box, and select the printer name.

For some printers, such as dot-matrix printers, you must set internal hardware switches, called DIP switches, to specify port and communication options; if these are not set correctly, your printer may not be able to receive document information. Refer to your printer manual for more information about DIP switch settings.

After receiving the "cannot write to port" message from the Print Manager, you must either cancel or resume the printing process for the document you sent to the printer. To do so, press CTRL+ESC to display the Windows Task List. Select the Print Manager application from the list and choose Switch To. This displays the Print Manager application window. The Print Manager lists the active printer and WP Document as the name of the document. If you have corrected the port problem and the printer is now working, select the printer name and choose the Resume command button to continue printing. Or you can select the document name from the list and choose Delete to remove the print job from the list. When you have finished, press CTRL+ESC, select the WordPerfect application name, and choose Switch To to return to the WordPerfect program.

The "Out of Memory" Error Message

"Out of memory" error messages can appear if you attempt to print documents when there is not enough computer memory or disk space available for the printing operation. When an "out of memory" message appears, you can free up memory by closing unused documents and application windows. Remember that minimized document windows do not fill the entire screen, but they are still open documents and take up some memory to remain active. Screen controls, like the ruler bar, button bar, and power bar, also require additional memory that may prevent the printing of your documents. You can turn off the ruler bar, the Reveal Codes screen, power bar, and the button bar to free some memory for printing.

Only Part of the Document Prints

If you are printing documents with several fonts or a document with graphics, it is possible that your printer does not have enough memory to print all the information on the page. If only part of the document prints, or you receive an error on your printer indicating that it does not have enought memory, there are several things you can do. First, you can try changing the Print Quality on the Print dialog box to Medium or Low. You can also try printing your document without any graphics by choosing Do Not Print Graphics on the Print dialog box. It is possible that your printer may not be able to provide you with the desired results. In this case, you should consider purchasing additional printer memory from your vendor.

When you are printing documents with graphics, you will need about 1 MB of printer memory to print half a page of graphics. This is in addition to the memory in your computer. If you need to print full-page graphics at high quality, you should have at least 2 MB of memory in your printer.

The "Disk Full" Error Message

When you send a document to the printer, WordPerfect uses computer memory to prepare the document for printing. If there is not enough computer memory available, the Windows program may use space on your hard disk to store and transfer information. A "disk full" error message appears when your hard disk does not have enough available space for the printing operation. To correct this problem, use the Open File dialog box to examine the files in your directories. You need to free some of the memory on your hard disk, and you can do this by removing software programs that you do not use, deleting unneeded files, and copying important older files to archive disks for storage. You can delete files within WordPerfect by selecting the file on the Open File dialog box and then choosing File Option/Delete.

If the "disk full" message appears when you believe there is sufficient available disk space, find out which directory the WordPerfect program is currently using. When you open or save files to a floppy disk, WordPerfect changes the default directory to the floppy drive where the file is stored. This happens when the Change Default Directory box is checked in the Open/Save As Setup dialog box. If the default directory is a floppy drive, there may not be enough available disk space to complete the printing operation, and you will see the "disk full" message. You can correct this problem by displaying the Open File dialog box (File/Open) and then, in the Drive list, choosing the drive letter assignment for your hard disk (for example, [-c-]). Then, when you send a document to the printer, the program will look to your hard disk for available disk space.

WordPerfect Cannot Find the Font Information

If you are using downloadable soft fonts with your laser printer, WordPerfect needs to know where the soft font files are stored on your hard disk. The soft font directory is specified under Printer Setup in WordPerfect, but the directory path name is not automatically entered for you. If you do not specify a path name under Printer Setup or if you specify the wrong path name, WordPerfect will not be able to locate the soft font files. When you attempt to print your document, an error message may be displayed.

To correct this, find the correct directory path name where the soft font files are stored. Then start the WordPerfect program and choose File/Select Printer. Highlight the name of the printer you are using and choose the Setup command button. This displays the Printer Setup dialog box; one of the text fields in this dialog box is labeled Path for Downloadable Fonts and Printer Commands. In this text field, type the path name where the soft font files are stored. Then, choose OK to return to the Select Printer dialog box. Select your printer from the Printers list and choose the Select command button to return to your document.

Text Is Printed with the Wrong Fonts

When you apply different fonts to your document text, WordPerfect uses the font information from the printer driver to instruct your printer to change fonts. If the font information under Printer Setup is incorrect, WordPerfect cannot send the correct font change information to the printer. When this happens, either WordPerfect or your printer will substitute other fonts for the font indicated in the document. This happens often with laser printers when you use fonts that have not been downloaded to the printer; you may have the correct soft fonts installed on your hard disk, but WordPerfect and your printer cannot access the font information. When the printer does not have the information to print the requested font, a standard font, such as Courier, is used instead.

To correct this problem, first check that the soft font directory is indicated under Printer Setup. Choose File/Select Printer. Highlight the name of your printer and choose Setup. In the Printer Setup dialog box, type the full path name for the directory where the soft font files are stored. Next, make sure you have marked the correct fonts for your printer.

Sometimes text attributes, like bold, italics, and underline, do not print or are printed with a font that does not match the font you are using in your document. This happens often with non-PostScript laser printers because WordPerfect cannot find a font with the specified attribute that matches the font you are using in your document. For example, suppose you are using the Helvetica font in your document. When you turn on the italics attribute, WordPerfect uses the italics version of the Helvetica font. This is called an automatic font change because your printer needs to use a different font to create the text attribute you want. If your printer does not have the Helvetica italics font, WordPerfect substitutes an available italics font. If your printer has no font with the italics attribute, the attribute change may appear as underlined text or regular text.

When the text attributes are not printing correctly, check your list of fonts (choose Layout/Font) to see if you have fonts with the desired attributes. If you do have the correct fonts available, WordPerfect is probably choosing the wrong font when an attribute code is encountered in your document.

To correct the problem, use the Font Mapping feature to edit your printer driver file and modify the selections for automatic font changes. First select the printer for which you want to change the font mappings.

1. Choose Layout/Font/Font Map and the Edit Printer/Document Font Mapping dialog box is displayed as shown in Figure 5-12.

2. Select Automatic Font Change as the Item to Map.

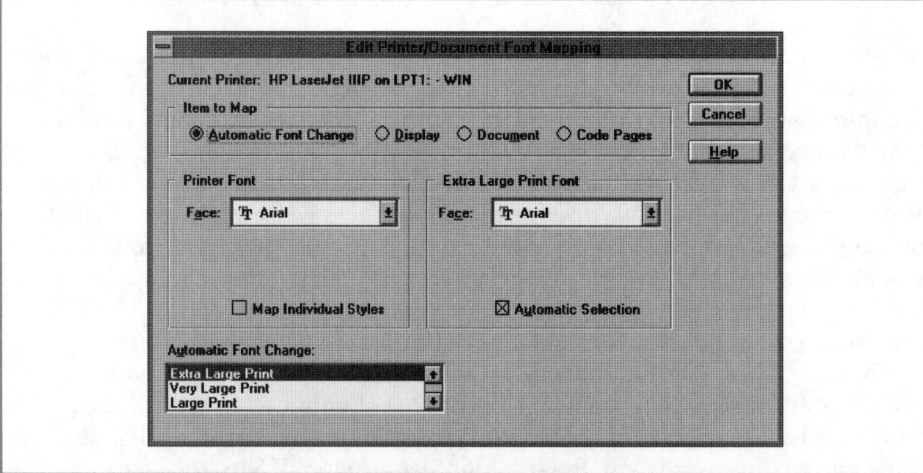

Figure 5-12. *Mapping automatic font changes*

3. Choose the Face you want to change in the Printer Font group box. For example, if you want to change the Automatic Font Changes for Times Roman, select that font here.
4. Choose Automatic Font Change at the bottom of the dialog box and highlight the attribute, character set, or orientation that does not change to the right attributes when you change the text style in your document.
5. Choose the Face and select the font face you want to use as the new Automatic Font Change.
6. Choose OK until you return to the document window.
7. Choose File/Select Printer.
8. Make sure the printer for which you changed the Automatic Font Changes for is highlighted, and then choose Update. This adds the changes to the printer's .PRS file.

Printed Pages Include "Garbage"

When jumbled characters and codes are printed instead of your document, make sure that you have selected the printer driver for the printer you are now using. This is the most common reason for "garbage" coming out of your printer. The garbage characters are actually the code sequences that WordPerfect sends to communicate with another type of printer. To correct the problem, turn off your printer to clear any unprinted portion of your document and then turn it back on. Choose File/Select Printer. Highlight the name of the printer that is currently connected to your computer, and choose the Select command button. Try printing the document again. If there are still problems with unwanted characters, check your printer manual for information on emulation modes and correct DIP switch settings. It is possible that your printer can emulate other types of printers and that the mode that is currently active does not match the printer driver you have selected. For example, many laser printers accept cartridges that allow them to behave as PostScript printers; when one of these cartridges is installed, you must select a printer driver that recognizes the new PostScript capabilities of your printer.

Page Margins Are Incorrect

When page margins are not printing as you would like, make sure the paper is feeding correctly into the printer; this is important for dot-matrix and daisy-wheel printers, where the paper is fed manually or with a tractor-feed device. If the paper is inserted too high or low on the printer platen, the top and bottom margins will be incorrect. If the feed mechanism is moved too far to the left or right, the left and right margins will be incorrect. Although laser printers do not allow you to make such adjustments to the paper-feed mechanism, you may still have some problems with the position of the printed text on the page; WordPerfect does allow some adjustments here, as explained later in this section.

If the paper seems to be feeding correctly into the printer, check the margin settings in your document. The easiest way to do this is by viewing your document in Full Page mode (choose View/Zoom/Full Page or press SHIFT+F5). While in Full Page mode, press Page Down (ALT+PGDN) and Page Up (ALT+PGUP) to view each page of your document. If you find a page where the margins are wrong, choose View/Page to return to the document window. Then, use the Reveal Codes window (choose View/Reveal Codes or press ALT+F3) to find and delete the margin codes that are causing the problems. If necessary, choose Layout/Margins or press CTRL+F8 to insert new margin codes.

If the page margins are wrong for the entire document but you cannot find any margin codes in the text, check the Initial Codes screen (choose Layout/Document/Initial Codes Style). The Styles Editor dialog box is where the standard document layout is defined; if margin codes are inserted here, they affect the entire document.

If the margin settings appear to be correct but are still not printing correctly, you can make slight adjustments to the paper size definitions to fix problems with the margin spacing. This is particularly useful when you are using a laser printer since you cannot adjust the way paper is fed into the printer. To make adjustments, choose Layout/Page from the WordPerfect menu bar. Then, choose Paper Size to display the paper definitions. Choose the paper definition that you want to adjust. If, for example, you want to adjust the standard paper type, highlight Letter, and then choose the Edit command button. The Text Adjustments options on the Edit Paper Size dialog box let you adjust where text is printed on the page; each option has a pop-up list to select the direction of the adjustment (up, down, left, or right) and a text field that lets you enter a measurement for the adjustment. From the Top pop-up list, choose Up or Down and then type a measurement for the adjustment. If, for example, each page of text is printed 0.25 inch lower than it should be on the paper, choose Top/Up and type 0.25" in the text field next to the Top adjustment. From the Side pop-up list, choose Left or Right, and then type a measurement in the text field to indicate horizontal adjustment. When you have finished, choose OK to return to the Paper Size dialog box. Then choose Close to return to your document.

After you edit the paper definitions, you need to delete any paper size codes from your documents that included the previous settings. Select the paper sizes with the text adjustments, and then save and print your document. Experiment with different measurements until your pages print correctly.

The text adjustment settings do not change the margin settings in your document; they simply adjust the position of the printed document—including margins—on the pages.

The Document Is Printing on the Wrong Paper

Printers with sheet feeders or multiple paper trays let you load two or more types of paper into your printer. You can set up WordPerfect to recognize the trays or bins and thus print pages from the same document on different types of paper. For example, suppose you have one paper bin with letterhead and another bin with envelopes. You could create a document for a business letter and include a page to print the recipient's address on an envelope. Layout commands tell the printer when to feed paper from the desired paper bin.

When your document is not printing on the correct paper, there are two things you need to investigate. First, you must check that the correct sheet-feeder definition is selected for your printer and note the numbers assigned to the bins or paper trays. Second, you need to make sure the WordPerfect paper definitions indicate the correct locations (according to bin or tray numbers) for the types of paper you are using.

To check the sheet-feeder definition for your printer, choose File/Select Printer from the WordPerfect menu bar. Highlight the name of the printer you are using and choose the Setup command button; this displays the setup information about your printer. Choose the Sheet Feeder command button, and a list of sheet feeders is displayed. First, make sure the sheet feeder you are using is selected. Highlight the name of the sheet feeder you are using. Then choose the Info command button to display information about the sheet feeder, and note the numbers assigned to each bin or tray. When you have finished reading the information, choose the Close button, and then choose the OK command button to choose your sheet feeder. In the Printer Setup dialog box, choose OK to continue. Finally, choose Close from the Select Printer dialog box.

To check the bin assignments for the paper definitions, choose Layout/Page and choose the Paper Size option. This displays the Paper Size dialog box, where the paper definitions for your printer are shown. The Location shows the bin location for each of the paper definitions displayed in the Information group box.

Compare the bin assignments listed here with the information from the Sheet Feeder Info screen.

If a paper definition lists an incorrect bin number, highlight the name in the Paper Definitions list and choose the Edit command button. This displays the Edit Paper Size dialog box, where you can specify the correct location for the paper type. From the Location pop-up list, select the correct tray or bin option, and then type the correct number in the Bin Number text field. Choose OK to return to the Paper Size dialog box. When you are finished with the paper definitions, choose the Close button to return to the document window. After you edit the paper definitions, you will need to delete any paper size codes from your documents that included the incorrect settings. Then, select the paper sizes with the correct bin location settings.

The .ALL File Cannot Be Found

In the Select Printer dialog box, you can add new printers to the list of available printers. You do this by choosing the Add Printer command button and choosing your printer from a list of supported printers, stored in an .ALL file. After you choose a printer, WordPerfect creates a .PRS file for the selected printer by copying information from the .ALL file. Then the printer is added to the list of printers you can select in WordPerfect. When you make changes to the printer setup—such as adding fonts with the Cartridges/Fonts option—WordPerfect needs the information stored in the .ALL file that was used to create your printer's .PRS file. If WordPerfect cannot find the .ALL file for your printer's .PRS file, an ".ALL file not found" message is displayed. To correct this, exit WordPerfect and the Windows program and insert the original WordPerfect Printer disk into a floppy drive. Run the WordPerfect installation program, and choose Options/Printer to reinstall the .ALL file for your printer.

The Printer File Is the Wrong Version

When you receive updated versions of WordPerfect software, some of the printer files you have used previously may not work with the current software. For example, you can use WordPerfect 6.0 (DOS version) with WordPerfect for Windows, but if you attempt to use printer files from WordPerfect 5.1 or earlier versions, you will receive an error message that the printer file is the wrong version.

When this happens, choose File/Preferences and choose the File option. Choose Printers/Labels to display a list of the directories where WordPerfect expects to find certain files. Verify that the Default directory is the directory where the WordPerfect for Windows printer files are stored. If it is not, enter the correct directory in this field. If the printer directory is listed correctly, you may have invalid versions of the printer files, or the printer files may be damaged. To correct this, run the WordPerfect Install program (INSTALL.EXE) and choose the Printer option to reinstall the .ALL file for your printer. If the "wrong version" error message continues to appear, contact the WordPerfect Orders department (the phone number is in your WordPerfect manual) for information on obtaining the recent WordPerfect for Windows printer files.

CHAPTER 6

Merge Applications

WordPerfect's Merge feature is a powerful tool for automating form letters, contracts, preprinted forms, and other documents that you create and use on a regular basis. Most people use the Merge feature to create form letters for mass mailings, which is why this feature is also called *mail merge.* But the Merge feature can do much more than create form letters. An extensive programming language allows you to create your own applications that prompt for information and generate documents based on variable information.

This chapter shows you how to create common merge documents and applications. You will see how to set up form letters and address lists for mass mailings and how to merge address information onto mailing labels, envelopes, and business memos. You will also see how you can use the Merge feature to merge information onto preprinted forms and how to create documents that prompt the user for information.

Because of the complexity of the merge commands and options, the first part of this chapter explains merge commands within the structure of common applications. This will help you understand the concepts of the merge process. The examples shown here are only one way of completing the desired task; the great advantage of the Merge feature is that you can structure your documents and applications as you wish, and there are many ways to achieve the same end result.

The second part of this chapter explains the programming functions of the Merge feature and discusses the merge commands supported by WordPerfect. These include commands for displaying prompts and messages for the user, for storing and manipulating information with variables, and for managing the merge process with programming structures. Many of these commands let you create a merge application with "decision-making" capabilities, to account for a variety of situations. Although the programming aspect of Merge can be complicated, it allows you to create powerful applications for a more productive office environment.

General Information

You can think of the merge commands as tools that you use to create automated documents; Merge is a powerful feature, but it requires you to design and create files according to the desired result. The success you achieve depends on how well you have designed your application.

The Merge feature does what its name implies; it merges information from two or more sources into a finished document. Generally, there are two types of files involved in this process: the *form file*, which is the model for the finished document; and the *data file*, which contains the information that should be combined with the model document. When the form and data files are created, you use WordPerfect's Merge tool to combine the information from both files to create a new finished document.

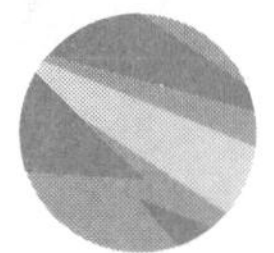

NOTE: WordPerfect 6.0 for Windows uses different terminolgy for merge files than was used in earler versions of WordPerfect. In earlier versions, a form file was known as a primary file, and a data file was known as a secondary file. If you are familiar with earlier versions of WordPerfect, you will want to keep this change in mind.

For complex applications, you can insert merge commands into the form file and create *conditional statements* for the merge process—that is, places where the Merge feature will do different things depending on the information coming from the data file. You can even insert prompt commands that ask the user to supply information to control the content of the completed document.

Although very powerful, the merge features are not forgiving when you enter the wrong commands or structure your files incorrectly. Ultimately, Merge does exactly what you tell it to do; unfortunately, this is not always what you want. Thus, it is important to understand a few basic concepts before you create your first merge application.

The Form File

A form file is simply a WordPerfect document that is the model for a merge application. A common example of this is the form letter shown in Figure 6-1; the format and content for the letter are created as a WordPerfect document with special commands called *merge field codes*—represented as FIELD()—placed where a recipient's name and address should be inserted. Other types of merge codes can perform functions like inserting the current date. When you merge the form file with a data file that contains address information, the Merge feature can create a separate personalized letter for each person in your address list.

Any WordPerfect document can be converted to a form file, including documents with tables, graphics, and columns. Simply determine which information in the document will change and replace it with field codes that indicate the variables. When you create form files, remember that the field codes represent information coming from one or more data files; in many cases, it is better to create your data files first so you know how to structure the field codes in your form file.

When you merge form and data files, the information from both files is combined to create new documents. The Merge feature generally does not alter the original documents unless you create a specific merge application to do so. When a merge is finished, the form and data files remain intact on your disk, and the finished document or documents are displayed in the document editing window. Once a merge operation is complete, you can edit, save, and print the document like any other WordPerfect document file.

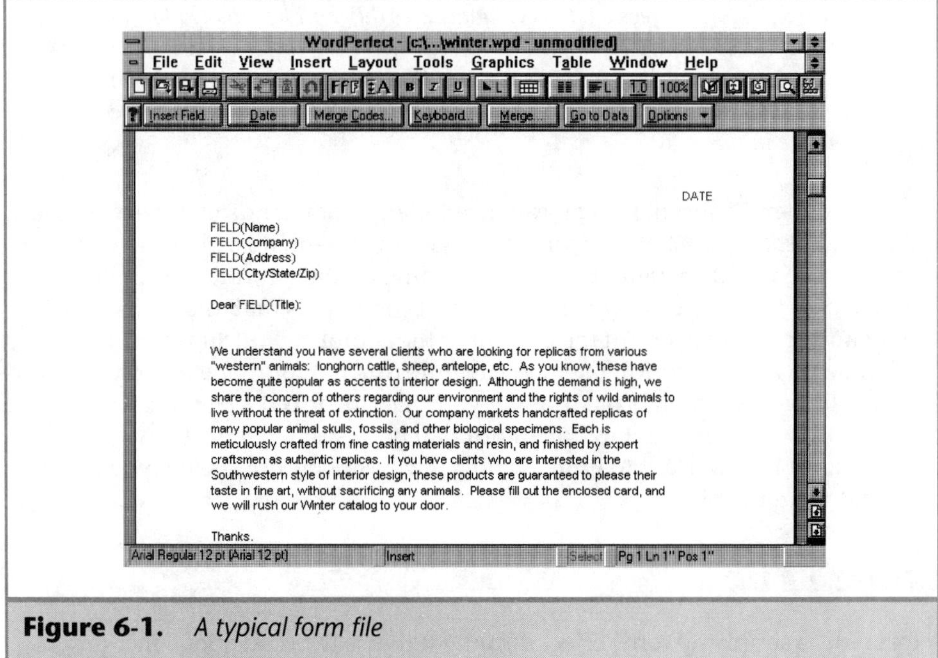

Figure 6-1. *A typical form file*

The Data File

A data file is a special WordPerfect document that contains the variable information for a merge application. The information in a data file is divided into *records* and *fields,* as shown in Figure 6-2. Again, the most common example of this is the form letter application; in this case, the data file contains address information for each person who will receive the form letter. A *record* contains all the information for one person in the address list. A *field* contains one piece of information within the record, such as a city or zip code. When you merge a data file with a form file, the Merge feature creates a finished document for each record in the data file.

Although the address example is the most common data file, you can structure the file any way you want; the data file can contain inventory information, catalog entries, sales figures, stock quotes—any variable information that you want to merge with a standard document format. The only requirement is that each record have the same number of fields as the other records in the file—even if the fields are empty for some records. For example, you may have a field in the data file that contains the company name for each record. Although you don't know the company name for everyone in the list, the

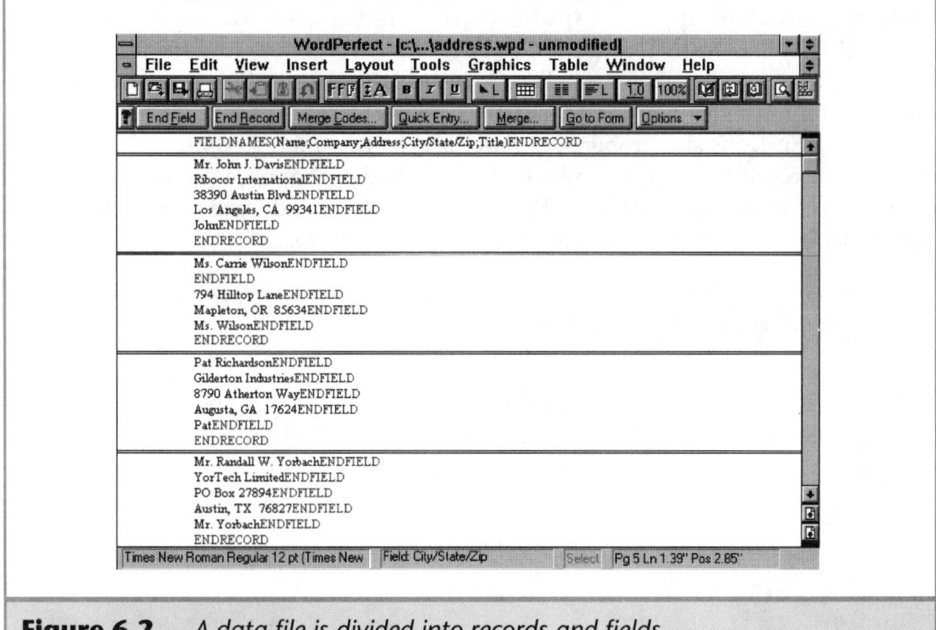

Figure 6-2. *A data file is divided into records and fields*

Company Name field must exist in each record; otherwise, the merge will not work correctly. This is very important.

Once you have created your data file, you can use it with any form files you have created—provided that each form file is created for the record structure of the data file. For example, you can create a data file that contains the names, addresses, phone numbers, and insurance information for all employees in your company. You can use this data file to supply information for employee announcements, invitations, envelopes, mailing labels, insurance statements, and other documents that will be distributed to the company employees. The finished documents do not need to include all information stored in each employee's record; when you create the form file, you choose which information the merge should insert, based on what is required for the finished documents.

Merge Commands

You can insert merge commands into form and data files by using the Tools/Merge menu choice. On the document editing screen, merge codes appear in a different color than the rest of your text, and they are always in capital letters. Merge codes have descriptive names like DATE, PRINT, and QUIT. Although merge codes appear as text in the document window, in the Reveal

Codes window, they appear as special WordPerfect codes with names like MRG:DATE, MRG:PRINT, and MRG:QUIT. When you merge the form and data files, WordPerfect performs the action or inserts the information indicated by the merge codes in the form and data files.

The applications shown here contain the common merge commands and codes that appear in form and data files. Later in this chapter, you'll find complete information about WordPerfect merge commands and syntax, as well as instructions on using merge variables and expressions.

Standard Form Letters

Following is a description of how to set up a mail merge with the Merge feature. The documents in this section are only one example of how a form letter and address list can be created for a mail merge application.

Creating the Address List

The address list is usually the first document you create for a form letter application. This is important because you need to know how your address information is organized before you create the form letter which will use the information.

Follow these steps to create your own data file with address information:

1. Start WordPerfect for Windows.
2. Choose the Tools/Merge menu choice. You will see the Merge dialog box shown in Figure 6-3.
3. Choose the Data button. This informs WordPerfect that you want to create a data file. You will see the Create Data File dialog box, shown in Figure 6-4.
4. Enter the names of each of the fields in your data file. These are the names you will use to tie the information in your data file to your form file. These field names can be anything you desire, so make them descriptive. If you look back at Figure 6-1, the field names were names such as Name, Company, Address, and City/State/Zip. You do not have to use these names, however. You can use any names you desire, but you need to make sure that you provide a name for each field in your data file.

Figure 6-3. *The Merge dialog box*

5. When you are through defining field names, click on the OK button. You will see the Quick Data Entry dialog box, similar to what is shown in Figure 6-5. Notice that this dialog box contains all the fields you have defined for your records.
6. Enter your data, one field at a time. If you don't have the information for a certain field (for instance, you don't have a company name for an individual), then leave that field blank.

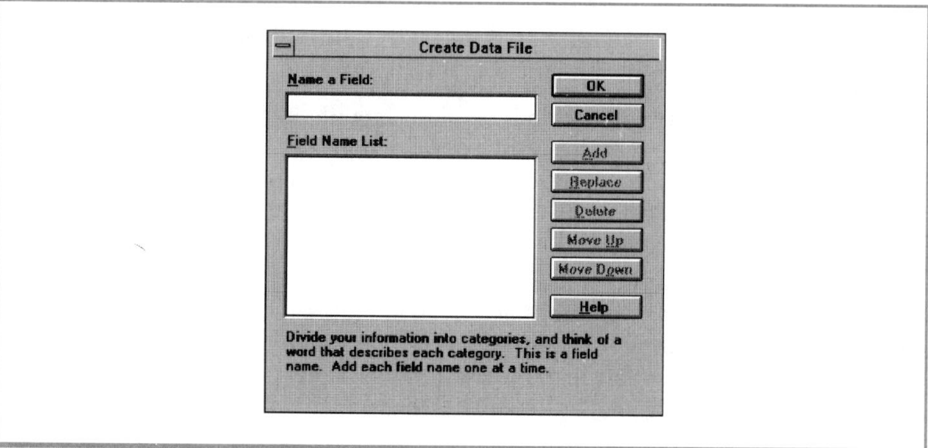

Figure 6-4. *The Create Data File dialog box*

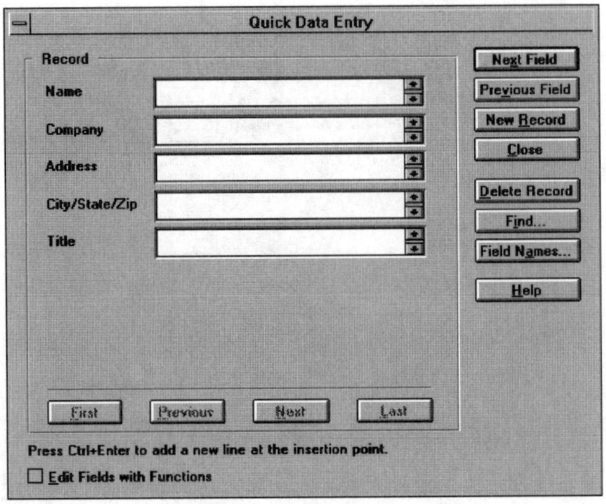

Figure 6-5. *The Quick Data Entry dialog box*

7. When you get to the final field and press ENTER, or you click on the New Record button, the information is formatted properly for a data file by WordPerfect. You may even notice it being added to your document, behind the dialog box.
8. Repeat steps 6 and 7, as necessary, to include additional names and complete your address list.
9. You can use the navigation buttons on the Quick Data Entry screen, as desired, to move through the records in your data file.
10. When you are satisfied with how your data file looks, choose Close. You will be asked if you wish to save your changes to disk. Click on the Yes button. Supply a filename, and the file is saved to disk as is done with any other WordPerfect file.

When you have completed these steps, you have completed your data file. Your screen will appear similar to that shown in Figure 6-6. This looks like any other WordPerfect document, except there is a feature bar at the top of the document window. This feature bar is useful when you later want to edit your data file by adding, changing, or deleting records.

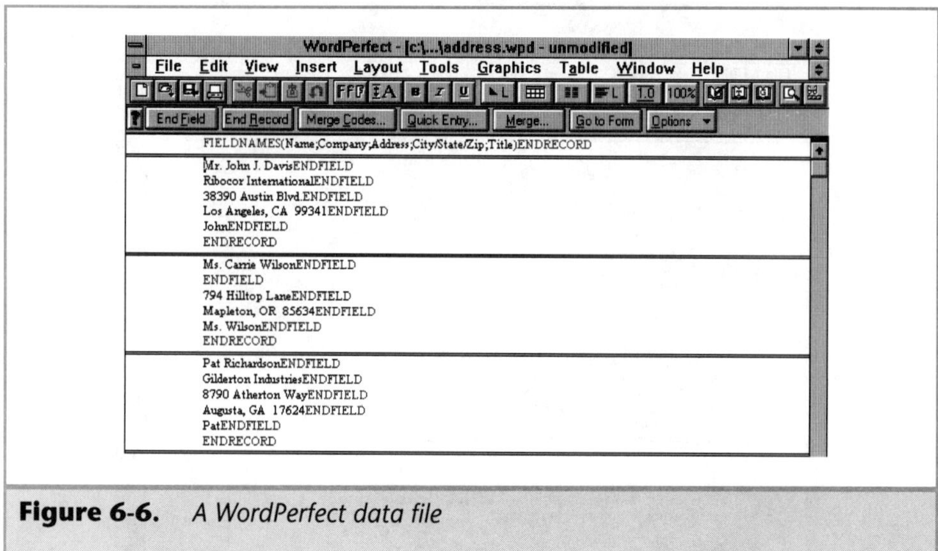

Figure 6-6. *A WordPerfect data file*

This feature bar is displayed every time you load this data file, and removed whenever you close the document. If you later add records to your data file, it is your responsibility to make sure that:

- Every field ends with an ENDFIELD code.
- Every record ends with an ENDRECORD code.
- Every record has the same number of ENDFIELD codes.

If you do not make sure of these things, you will have problems using your data file at a later point.

Creating the Form Letter

The form letter looks the same as a regular letter you would create, with one exception: instead of the name and address information, you insert codes that reference the information in your data file. Figure 6-7 shows an example of what a form letter looks like.

Follow these steps to create the form file shown in Figure 6-7:

1. Start WordPerfect for Windows.

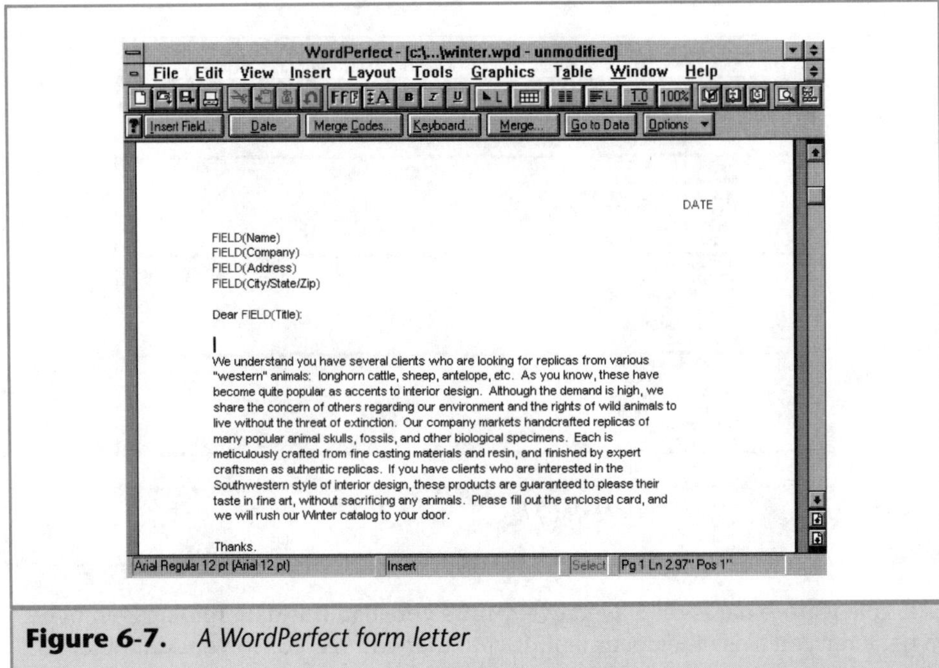

Figure 6-7. *A WordPerfect form letter*

2. Choose the Tools/Merge menu choice. You will see the Merge dialog box shown in Figure 6-8.

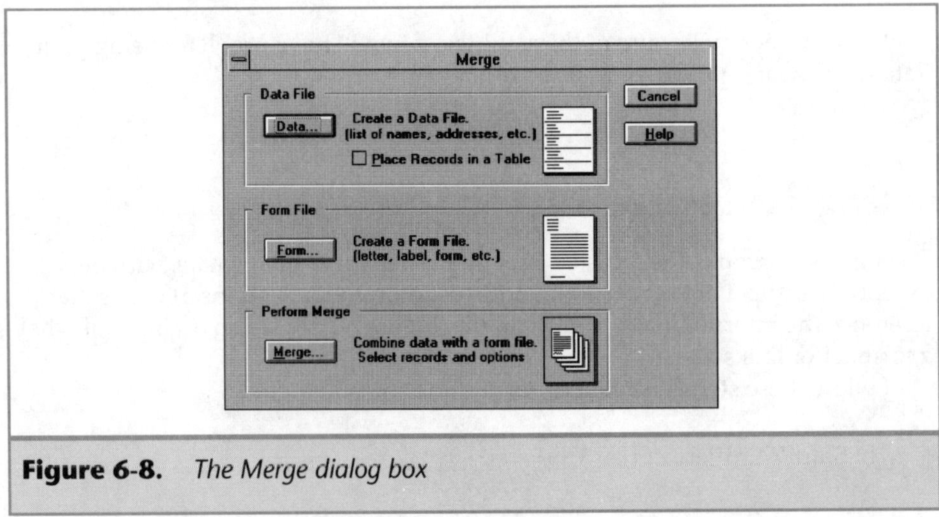

Figure 6-8. *The Merge dialog box*

3. Choose the Form button. This informs WordPerfect that you want to create a form file. You will see the Create Form File dialog box, shown in Figure 6-9.
4. Enter the filename (and extension) of the data file you created in step 10 of the last section, then click the OK button. You will see a regular document screen, with the merge form file feature bar at the top of the document window.
5. Choose the Date button. This inserts the DATE field in your document.
6. Press CTRL+R to right justify the DATE field and press ENTER three times to end the current line and add two blank lines. Be sure to left justify your text afterward by pressing CTRL+L.
7. Choose Insert Field. You will see the Insert Field Name or Number dialog box, as shown in Figure 6-10. From this dialog box, you can choose the names of fields you want inserted in your document where the insertion point is located.
8. Choose the Name field, and press ENTER or choose Insert. Notice that the Select Field Name dialog box stays on the screen, but you are free to still enter the text of your letter. Press ENTER to move to the next line.
9. On the next three lines, repeat step 5, but instead choose the Company, Address, and City/State/Zip fields, in order.
10. Press ENTER another time to move down an extra line.
11. Type **Dear** and then choose the Title field from the Select Field Name dialog box. Click on Insert, and then on Close. This hides the Select Field Name dialog box, which is OK since you don't need it any more.

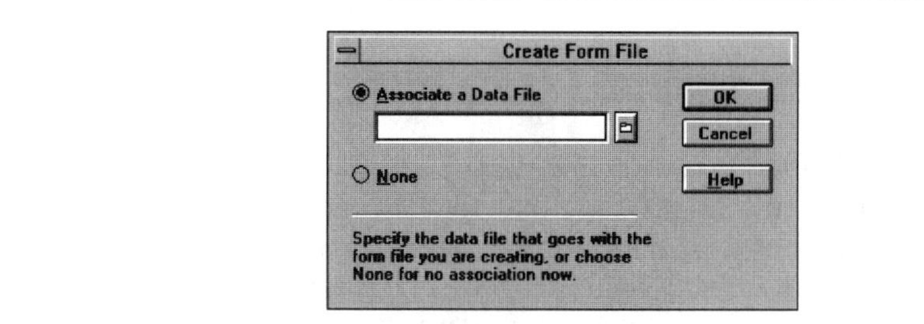

Figure 6-9. *The Create Form File dialog box*

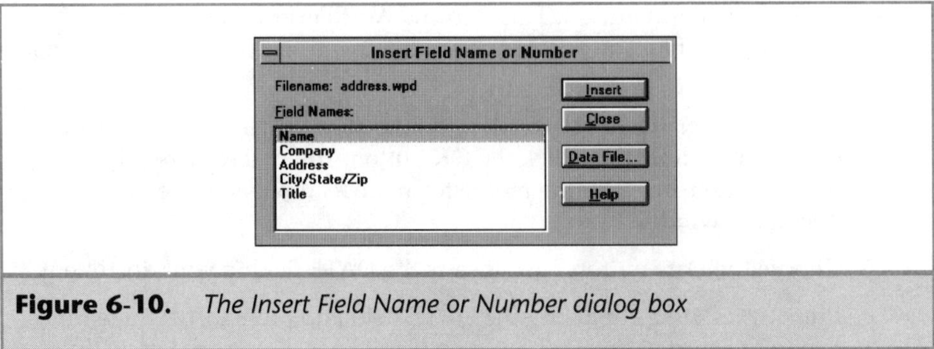

Figure 6-10. *The Insert Field Name or Number dialog box*

12. Press ENTER twice to move down two lines. Type the body of the letter. Make sure you add any desired formatting, such as to make the DATE field right justified.
13. Save your letter, using a filename such as **MERGE.WPD**.

Accounting for Blank Fields

If any fields in your data file do not contain information when you perform the merge, WordPerfect inserts blank lines in their place. Here is an example of a merged record that had no information in the Company field:

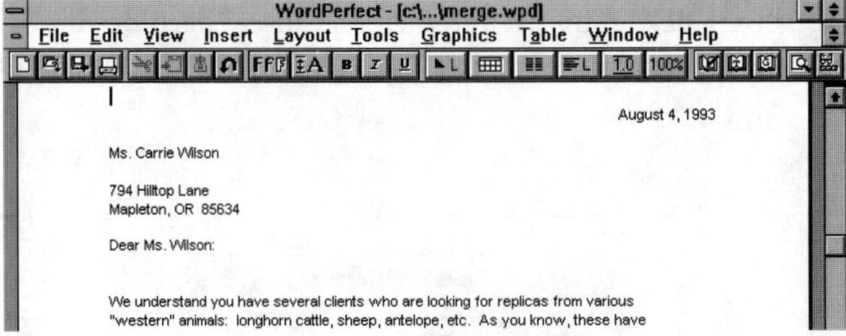

The blank line was inserted because WordPerfect considers a field to be everything—text and formatting codes—that appears between the ENDFIELD merge codes. If you look at your data file with Reveal Codes turned on, you'll see a hard return code after the ENDFIELD code that precedes each field. The hard return code indicates a place where a line or paragraph ends. When a field is left blank, WordPerfect merges the hard return code into the location where the field information would be.

To fix the problem, you could delete the hard return code from all the blank fields, but WordPerfect provides a faster, easier way. While you are working with the form file, simply type a question mark after the field name, but before the closing parentheses, for those fields that *might* be empty in some records. Here is an example of what you would type in the form file if you suspect some of the Company fields might be blank in the data file:

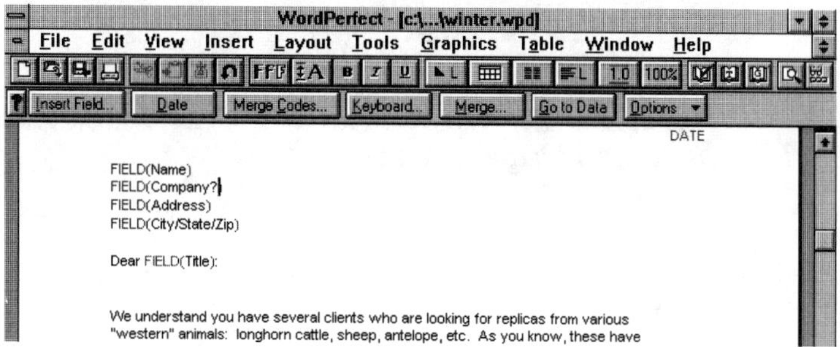

During a merge, the question mark in the field name tells WordPerfect to check the contents of the field before merging the information into the form file. If the field does not contain any characters, WordPerfect skips it and moves to the next field. This ensures that no blank lines will appear in the merged document for fields that are empty.

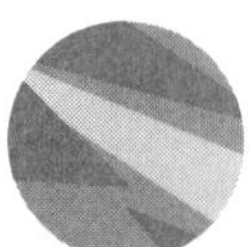

NOTE: Later in this chapter, you will find information about the IFBLANK merge code. Like the question mark, the IFBLANK code also compensates for empty fields, but it allows you to control what the merge will do when field information is left blank.

Merging the Address List and Form Letter

When you merge the form file with a data file, WordPerfect uses the form file as a template and replaces the field codes with the corresponding information from each record in the data file. To merge the two files, follow these steps:

1. Choose the Tools/Merge menu choice. You will see the Merge dialog box that was shown previously in Figure 6-8.
2. Choose the Merge button. This informs WordPerfect that you want to merge a form file with a data file. You will see the Perform Merge dialog box, shown in Figure 6-11.
3. In the Form File field, type the name of a form file, such as **MERGE.WPD**.

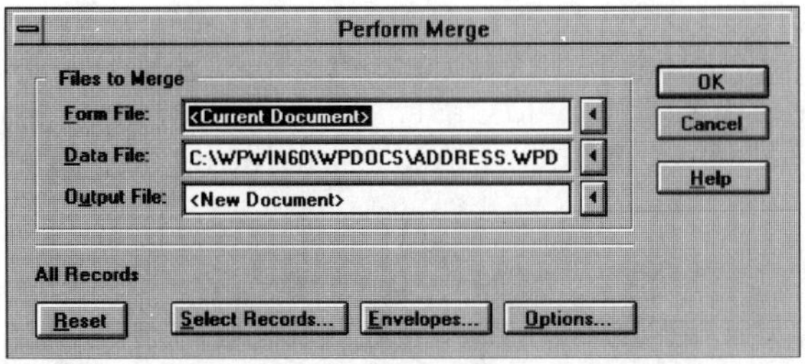

Figure 6-11. *The Perform Merge dialog box*

4. In the Data File field, type the name of a data file, such as **ADDRESS.WPD**.
5. Choose the OK button to start the merge process.

When the merge is finished, the result is a document with personalized letters for the records in the address list. As shown in Two Page view in Figure 6-12, each page in the document is a completed form letter. WordPerfect inserts a hard page break (HPg) code at the end of each letter to help separate the merged documents. At this point, you can send the entire document to the printer, or you can scroll through the document and print specific pages. You do not need to save the merged document because you still have the form and data files intact on disk, and it takes only a few moments (for smaller files) to run the merge again.

Merging to the Printer

When your data file includes a large number of records—for example, 200 or more—the merge process can be slow and difficult to manage. The PRINT merge command lets you send each merged document to the printer as it is created during the merge process. This lets you merge a large number of records when you have limited computer memory. The PRINT code is often used with the PAGEOFF code to turn off the extra hard page codes that WordPerfect inserts after each record is merged. When you merge to the printer, you do not need the page breaks between the record documents.

To use this option, you must place the PRINT merge command into your form file. First, retrieve the form file and move the insertion point to the end of the document, or to the place where WordPerfect should send the merged

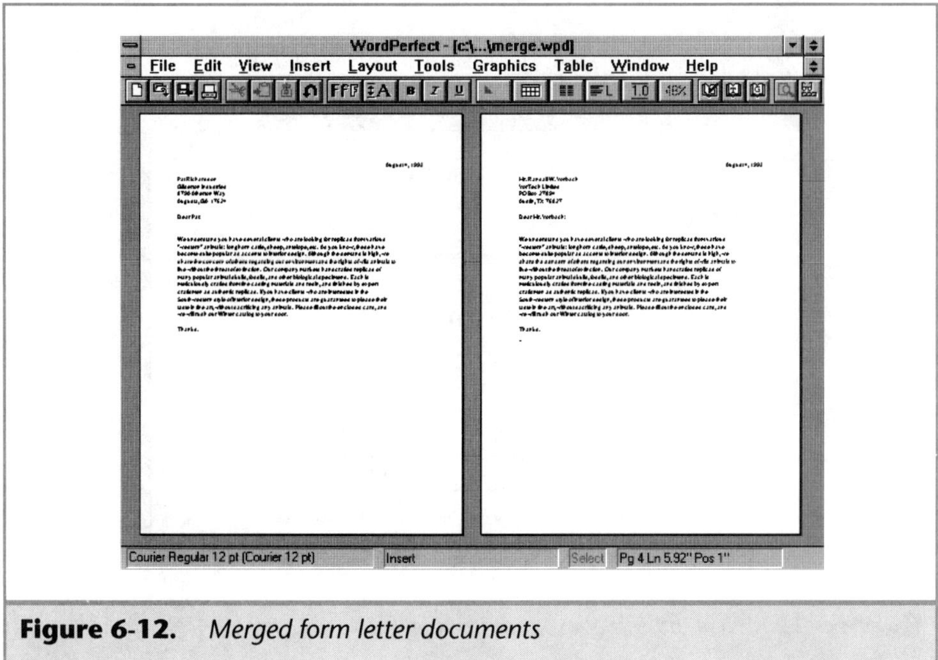

Figure 6-12. *Merged form letter documents*

information to the printer. Then choose the Merge Codes button. Select PRINT from the list of available merge codes, and choose Insert. If you want to cancel the extra page breaks between record documents, move the insertion point before the PRINT command and insert the PAGEOFF merge command. When you are finished, save the form file to replace the existing file on disk. When the merge is performed, WordPerfect sends to the printer everything merged to the place where the PRINT command is located.

Merging from the Keyboard

When you use the Merge feature, you must have a form file to use as a model for the document you want to create. However, you can merge information into a form file document without using a data file. You can insert merge KEYBOARD codes into the form file that prompt the user to type information as required during the merge process.

The document in Figure 6-13 is an example of a form file with KEYBOARD codes. This document follows an accepted format for business memos. The

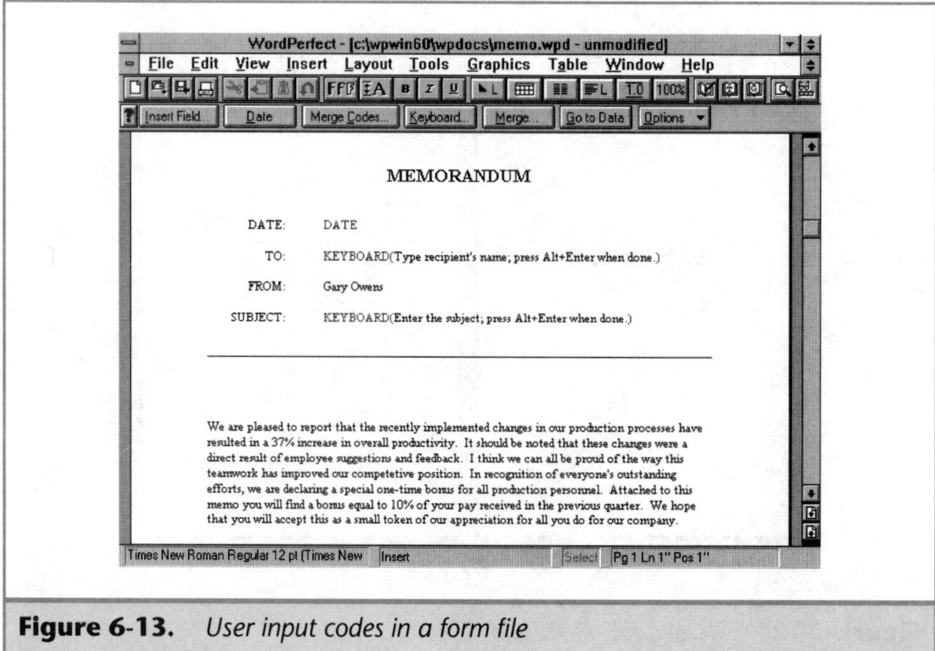

Figure 6-13. *User input codes in a form file*

information that will not change—the title, the memo labels, and the sender's name—are typed as regular text. The variable information—the date, the recipient's name, and the subject—are represented with merge codes.

The DATE code inserts the current date whenever a merge is performed with the form file. (You insert the DATE code using the same procedures described earlier in this chapter, when you created the form letter.)

During the merge process, the KEYBOARD code tells WordPerfect to suspend the merge and prompt the user to type text or perform an action from the keyboard. The message between the parentheses after the KEYBOARD code is the prompt that appears for the user. To insert a KEYBOARD code into your form file, follow these steps:

1. Designate your document as a form file, as described earlier in this chapter.
2. From the Merge feature bar, choose the Merge Codes button. The Insert Merge Codes dialog box appears.
3. In the Merge Codes list, choose the KEYBOARD([prompt]) selection.
4. Click on Insert, and the Insert Merge Code dialog box appears.

5. In the text field, type the message that you want to appear as the prompt for the user. For example, if the user should type the recipient's name at this point in the document, you could type **Type recipient's name; press Alt+Enter when done.**

6. After typing the message in the Insert Merge Code dialog box, choose the OK button to insert the KEYBOARD code.

After you have placed the KEYBOARD codes that you need, save the form file. With the form file still open, click on the Merge button on the Merge feature bar. Click on the Merge button again (to perform merge), and then click on OK to start the merge. WordPerfect will perform the merge up to the point where the first KEYBOARD code is located, where it suspends the merge process. The insertion point moves to the place in the document where the KEYBOARD code was placed, and a message box appears with the prompt you entered for the KEYBOARD command. When you are finished typing the required text, press ALT+ENTER to continue the merge, or click on the Continue button on the feature bar. ALT+ENTER is used because this is the keystroke that ends a field when you are creating a data file.

At each KEYBOARD code in the form file, WordPerfect will stop the merge and prompt you to enter information. When the merge is completed, you will have a finished document. Again, the Merge feature simply uses the form file as a template for the finished document; the original document remains unchanged in the file on disk.

Mailing Labels and Envelopes

You can apply the principles explained in this chapter to create a form file for mailing labels or envelopes. Start from a new document window and choose Layout/Labels. From the Labels dialog box, choose the Labels type. If you do not have a paper size defined for envelopes or labels, see the entries for "Envelopes" and "Labels" in Chapter 11, "Commands and Features."

After you select the paper size, insert merge codes to access the information from your data file. You need to create only the first label or envelope as the form file. When you are finished, save the form file. Then, from a new document window, merge the form file with the data file. When you merge with the data file, WordPerfect automatically creates a label or envelope for each person in your address list. When the merge is completed, you can send the entire document to be printed on the labels or envelopes in your printer.

Merging to Preprinted Forms

You can use WordPerfect's Merge feature to merge information for a preprinted form. Figure 6-14 shows an example of an invoice for a service garage. The invoice forms are preprinted, and a WordPerfect form file is created to print information in the appropriate columns and rows of the table.

You can create a merge application to print text on preprinted forms like the one shown here. First, you need to measure the form, and then you can use WordPerfect's Advance feature to position merge codes in the form file. In this example, KEYBOARD codes are used so the service representative can enter information from the keyboard, and the advance codes in the form file position the responses where they need to be on the page.

Measuring the Form

If you need to print information on a preprinted form, start with a blank copy of the form and a ruler. Measure the form carefully to find out exactly where the text lines should fall on the page. For each text item that you want to print on the form, you need to take two measurements: one measurement from the top of the form to the line where the text should appear (a vertical measurement), and one measurement from the left edge of the form to the place where the text item should begin to print (a horizontal measurement), as shown in Figure 6-15.

Edwardo's Garage
1630 Thousand Oaks Blvd., (805) 555-3728
"In Beautiful Downtown T.O.!"

Date: 01/12/94 Mechanic's I.D.: 078

Customer Name: Brent Averett Phone: (801) 555-7231

Address: 2179 Lindsay Avenue
Encinitas, CA 92024

Service I.D.	Problem/Description	Time	Charges
02311	Computer Tune-Up	1:20	50.00
01779	Front Alignment Adjustment	0:45	75.00

Figure 6-14. *Information merged with a preprinted form*

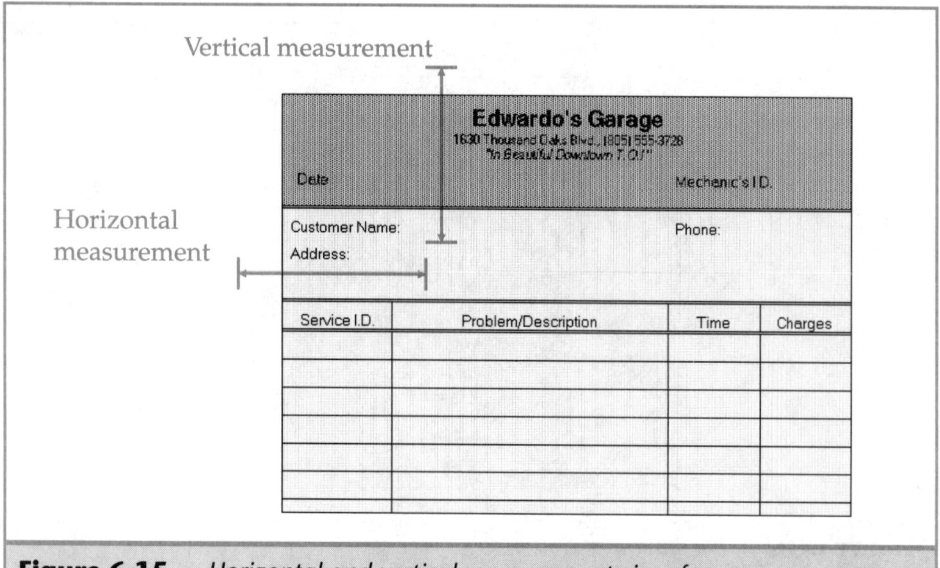

Figure 6-15. *Horizontal and vertical measurements in a form*

When you take the vertical measurements, remember to measure to where the top of the text line should begin—not where the baseline of the text should be. The Advance feature allows you to define both the horizontal and vertical positions and where the text will print in relation to those positions. Generally, placing the text above the baseline is preferred since the font and size of the text may change the display when placed below the baseline.

Creating the Form File

Once you have these measurements for each text item to be printed on the form, you can use WordPerfect's Advance feature to create a document with precise placement of the merge codes. For example, suppose you need to print to the form shown in Figure 6-15. For the Date information, suppose the vertical measurement is 1.25 inches and the horizontal measurement is 0.75 inch. For the Customer Name information, suppose the vertical measurement is 2.2 inches and the horizontal measurement is 1.75 inches. To begin the procedure, follow these steps:

1. Create a new form file document, as described earlier in this chapter.
2. From the menu, choose Layout/Typesetting/Advance. You will see the Advance dialog box, as shown in Figure 6-16. Here you can position text anywhere on a printed page.

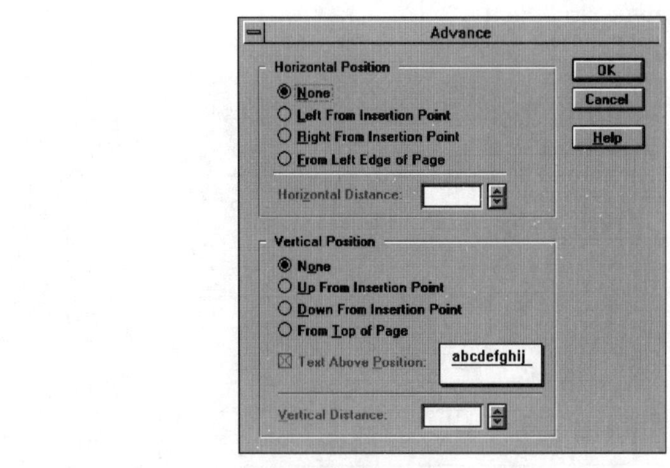

Figure 6-16. *The Advance dialog box*

3. In the Horizontal Position box, choose how you want the text positioned. In this case, choose From Left Edge of Page, and then enter **.75"** in the Horizontal Distance field.
4. In the Vertical Position box, choose how you want the text positioned. In this case, choose From Top of Page, and then enter **1.25"** in the Vertical Distance field.
5. Choose OK, and WordPerfect inserts the necessary codes to move the insertion point to the specified position.
6. Now that the insertion point is positioned where it should be, you can insert the DATE merge code.
7. Choose the Date button. This inserts the DATE field in your document.
8. Position the insertion point and place the merge code for Customer Name. From the menu, choose Layout/Typesetting/Advance. You will see the Advance dialog box, as shown in Figure 6-16.
9. Repeat steps 3 through 5, this time using measurements of 1.75" and 2.2", respectively.
10. From the Insert Merge Code dialog box, insert a KEYBOARD code to prompt for the customer name. In the prompt field, type **Type the Customer Name and press Alt+Enter to continue.** Choose the OK button to insert the merge code.

Continue this procedure to insert advance codes and merge codes for each of the items to be printed on the form. When you are finished, save the form file and close the document.

Correcting the Position of Text Items

Form fill-in is often a matter of trial and error. When you print your document to the form, some of the text items may not be positioned correctly. This is sometimes the case when tractor-fed paper is loaded too low or too high in dot-matrix printers. You can fix this problem by adjusting the position of the paper in your printer.

Most laser printers add a small unprintable region of space around the edges of the printed page; if you do not account for this space when you measure, the text items will not be positioned correctly. The simplest way to find out the unprintable region for your printer is from the Margins dialog box. First, choose Layout/Margins and change all the margin settings to zero (0); when you choose OK from the dialog box, WordPerfect will display a message that tells you what the valid margin settings are for your laser printer; any measurement less than the valid range is in the unprintable region. Once you have determined the unprintable region for your printer, you can use the Reveal Codes screen (ALT+F3) to locate and delete the advance codes with the incorrect measurements. Then insert new codes to adjust the measurements.

Using the Merge Commands

Merge commands let you manipulate text, display prompts and messages, and control the merge operation. Some commands let you repeat or loop a procedure until a specific condition is satisfied. Others let you create a merge structure called a *subroutine* that performs calculations or other singular tasks. Many of the merge commands follow standard programming structures, with IF statements, FOREACH or FORNEXT loops, and subroutine calls.

This section discusses general information about merge commands and procedures. If you have previously worked with computer programming, you'll quickly discover how to incorporate these commands into your merge applications. If you are new to programming, the examples in this chapter will show you how to use the merge commands to perform common tasks. For a complete reference of all commands, see the "Merge Command Reference" section later in this chapter.

Placing Merge Commands in Your Files

As you have learned, merge commands are usually placed in the form file that serves as the model for the merged documents. For some applications, merge commands may also be placed in data files or other files that contain information accessed during the merge. Each merge command tells WordPerfect to perform one task during the merge process. These tasks include inserting information from another file, storing text in memory, sending a document to the printer, or repeating a certain procedure.

Some merge commands are not complete without parameters. A *parameter* is a piece of information, provided by you, that allows the merge command to perform a certain task. When you insert a merge command that requires parameters, a dialog box appears that lets you enter parameter information. For example, the FIELD merge command is not complete without a field name that indicates into which field information should be inserted during the merge. When you select the FIELD command from the Merge Code list, a dialog box appears and prompts you to enter the field name for the command. The complete command might appear like this in the form file:

```
FIELD(Address)
```

In this case, the parameter is "Address"; this tells WordPerfect to insert information from the field named "Address," which is found in the data file records. You can type parameters for merge commands as either upper- or lowercase letters. Many of the merge commands have other merge commands as their parameters. When a merge command that requires a parameter is nested within another command, it looks like this:

```
ONCANCEL(GO(labelname))
```

Some merge commands require two or more parameters. For these commands, a semicolon is used as a *delimiter* to separate multiple parameters. Here is one example of parameters required for the FOREACH command:

```
FOREACH(variable;exp1;exp2;exp3)
```

Notice that each parameter ends with a semicolon, to separate it from the next parameter in the command.

Merge structures can be quite long and complex, depending on the number of parameters required by the commands. It is important that you do not type extra hard returns, spaces, or tabs between the commands in a merge structure. When the merge is performed, all merge commands are either executed or stripped from the finished document; if you insert extra spaces or hard returns between the merge commands, these will appear with the text in your merged document and will change the document format you have created.

NOTE: *For many of the merge examples in this chapter, the commands are placed on separate lines to clearly show each step of the merge; however, when you insert merge commands into your own documents, make sure each command immediately follows the previous command or text, without extra spaces, tabs, or hard returns.*

Using Variables to Store Merge Information

Merge variables let you store information in memory during the merge operation. There are several reasons why you need to do this. Some merge commands let you create menus and prompts that appear on the screen during a merge; for these commands, you need a way to store the responses from the keyboard until they can be evaluated for an appropriate action. In other cases, you will want to take a piece of information and compare it to something else. Sometimes, you may need to perform a calculation based on the number of records in your data file or perform a specific action when one of the merge fields is blank. These and several other operations deal with variable information that you can use to control the actions of the merge application.

WordPerfect includes merge commands that let you store, control, and evaluate variable information. Variables make it possible to create many of the programming structures supported by the WordPerfect merge commands. The name of a variable will not change, but the information stored in the variable can.

There are different types of variables to perform specific functions in the program. *User-defined variables* are variables created by you, the person who creates the merge; these variables can store numeric values or text. The information stored in user-defined variables usually changes during the course of the merge operation. *System variables* are numeric codes that indicate what the WordPerfect program is doing; these are described later in this section.

Creating User-Defined Variables

The ASSIGN and ASSIGNLOCAL merge commands let you create a variable to store text or a number. You do not need to indicate what the variable contents will be; the WordPerfect variables can store numbers or text at any time. Up to

128 standard characters or numeric digits can be stored in a variable. Font attribute codes, like bold and underline, are ignored when assigned to a variable. If you assign text to a variable, each space between words is considered 1 character.

Variables created with the ASSIGN command are considered *global,* which means the variable contents persist, even after the merge is completed. Here is the command you would enter to create a variable with the ASSIGN command:

```
ASSIGN(variable;expression)
```

The *variable* parameter becomes the name of the variable; for this, you can type any number of characters, but only the first 15 characters are recognized as the unique variable name. You can use any combination of characters to create the variable name, and each name must be unique. For the *expression,* you can type any number, text, or variable expression to assign contents to the variable; remember, the total length of the *expression* can be no more than 128 characters. For more information about variable expressions, see the upcoming sections, "Comparing and Manipulating Numeric Values," and "Comparing and Manipulating Text Strings."

Variable information created with the ASSIGN command remains in memory until you change or clear the variable or until you close the WordPerfect application. The information in these variables can be retrieved with the VARIABLE(*variable*) merge command or with other macro commands.

As the name implies, variables created with the ASSIGNLOCAL merge command are local, or confined, to the merge application or file where they are placed. Here is the command you would enter to create a variable with the (ASSIGNLOCAL) command:

```
ASSIGNLOCAL(variable;expression)
```

The *variable* and *expression* parameters must follow the same guidelines explained earlier for the ASSIGN command. When the current merge operation is completed, LOCAL variables are cleared, and their values do not exist outside the merge environment.

Retrieving and Using Variable Contents

After a value is assigned to a variable, you can use the VARIABLE merge command to retrieve variable information into the merged document or as a parameter into another merge command. Simply insert the VARIABLE(*variable*) command at the position where the variable information is needed. For example, the following merge structure prompts the user to enter a name, which it stores in the variable called "First Name." Then the VARIABLE command inserts the information into the merged document:

```
GETSTRING(First Name;Enter your name: ;User Info)
VARIABLE(First Name)
```

Variables can also be retrieved as the parameters for other merge commands. The following sections explain how to compare and evaluate the information stored in merge variables.

Comparing and Manipulating Numeric Values

The ASSIGN, ASSIGNLOCAL, CASEOF, FIRSTCAP, FOREACH, IF, IFEXISTS, STRLEN, STRPOS, SUBSTR, SWITCH, TOLOWER, TOUPPER, and WHILE commands accept a parameter that may be an expression. An *expression* can be a number, a text value, or a VARIABLE command. An expression can also be a calculation or comparison performed with variables and logical operators. Here is an example of a merge command with a numeric expression:

```
IF(10<21)Sale made profitENDIF
```

In this example, the "less-than" logical operator (<) is used to compare the values 10 and 21. Because the statement is true, the text "Sale made profit" is inserted into the merged document. If the statement were false, the merge would continue with the next command that follows the ENDIF command. In this case, there is no point in creating an expression like "10<21" because the answer or result is obvious. That is why you use variables, combined with a logical operator, to create a statement that is conditional according to the information stored in the variables. The previous example could be modified to read like this:

```
IF(VARIABLE(Cost)<VARIABLE(Net))Sale made profitENDIF
```

In this example, the expression compares the values stored in the "Cost" and "Net" variables. If "Cost" is less than "Net," the text "Sale made profit" is inserted into the merged document. If the amount of "Cost" is greater than "Net," then the merge continues with the command that follows the ENDIF command. Expressions are important structures because they allow your merge applications to make decisions based on information merged from the data file or typed from the keyboard. Table 6-1 shows a list of the valid logical operators for numeric expressions. Use these with the VARIABLE command to compare and manipulate variables with numeric values. For information on comparing variables with text values, see the next section, "Comparing and Manipulating Text Strings."

Numeric Expression	Action or Result
x=*y*	Compares two values to see if they are identical. If they are, a true value (–1) is returned; otherwise, a false value (0) is returned.
x!=*y*	Compares two values to see if they are not identical. If not, a true value (–1) is returned; otherwise, a false value (0) is returned.
x<*y*	Checks whether *x* is less than *y*. If so, true (–1) is returned. If not, false (0) is returned.
x>*y*	Checks whether *x* is greater than *y*. If so, true (–1) is returned. If not, false (0) is returned.
x+*y*	Adds the values of *x* and *y*. This operator can be used to combine two values as one, like this: ASSIGN(Total;VARIABLE(Total)+VARIABLE(Subtotal)). In this case, the current value of the "Subtotal" variable is added to the value of the variable called "Total." The result is then reassigned as the new value for the "Total" variable.
x–y	Subtracts the value of *y* from the value of *x*.
x*y*	Multiplies the value of *x* by the value of *y*. When multiplying values, WordPerfect places the restriction that one of the values cannot exceed the amount of + or – 65,535.
x/*y*	Divides the value of *x* by the value of *y*. When dividing values, WordPerfect places the restriction that one of the values cannot exceed the amount of + or – 65,535.
x%*y*	Returns the remainder of the quotient of *x* and *y*. For example, the expression 14%4 returns the value of 2, because 14 divided by 4 equals 3 with a remainder of 2. This is also known as the MOD operator.

Table 6-1. *Numeric Expressions*

Numeric Expression	Action or Result
–x	Returns the negative value of x. For example, if VARIABLE(Sum) contains the value 24, then –VARIABLE(Sum)=–24. If VARIABLE(Sum) contains –18, then –VARIABLE(Sum)=18.
x&*y*	The AND (&) operator. Examines the binary equivalents of *x* and *y* and compares the values. When both values have a 1 bit in the same binary number column, a 1 is placed in that column for the result, which is converted to an integer and returned as the value.
x | *y*	The OR (|) operator. Examines the binary equivalents of *x* and *y*. If a 1 bit exists in a binary number column for either value, a 1 bit is placed in that column for the result. The resulting binary number is returned as an integer value.

Table 6-1. *Numeric Expressions* (continued)

In Table 6-1, *x* and *y* can be numeric values or VARIABLE commands. When an expression is true, –1 is returned. When an expression if false, zero (0) is returned.

NOTE: *In any numeric expression, WordPerfect will not correctly recognize values that exceed the number +2,147,483,647. Values greater than this number are interpreted as negative numbers.*

Comparing and Manipulating Text Strings

Because variables can also store text information, you can create expressions to compare text values. The structure and concepts are similar to those explained earlier for the numeric expressions. One difference for text expressions is that variables or items in the expression must be enclosed in quotes. This is the only case where you need to use quotes around text items; you do not need to use quotes when you use ASSIGN or ASSIGNLOCAL to assign text items to variables.

Suppose you have a merge application where the user is prompted to enter a city name. For this application, the merge will need to perform differently if the city name "Washington DC" is entered than for the other city names that might be entered. A text expression is created to compare the value stored in the city name variable with the text string "Washington DC". Here is the structure of the merge commands for this example:

```
GETSTRING(CityName;Enter the Name of Your City;City Name)
IF("VARIABLE(CityName)"="Washington DC")GO(Capitol)ENDIF
```

Notice that quotes enclose the entire VARIABLE command; this is necessary to compare the contents of VARIABLE(CityName) with the text string "Washington DC". The equal sign (=) operator is used to specify that the contents of "CityName" must exactly match the "Washington DC" text string. If so, the next command, GO(Capitol), is executed; if not, the command that follows the ENDIF command is executed. This is only one example of a valid text expression; Table 6-2 shows a complete list of the valid logical operators for text expressions.

Table 6-2 shows how operators can be used to compare text values. In the table, *text1* and *text2* can be text values or variables that contain text. Remember that these expressions compare the characters represented by *text1* and *text2* and are sensitive to the case of the text values. For example, in the expression "First Security"="First Security", the text values are identical; however, in the expression "First Security"="first security", the text values are not identical.

NOTE: The greater-than (>) and less-than (<) operators make their comparisons based on the WordPerfect character set numbers of the text values. The CTON and NTOC merge commands can help you determine what the character set numbers are.

Text Expression	**Action or Operation**
"text1"="text2"	Checks to see whether *text1* and *text2* are identical. If so, a true value (–1) is returned. If not, false (0) is returned.
"text1"!="text2"	Checks to see whether *text1* and *text2* are not identical. If not, a true value (–1) is returned. If the text values are identical, false (0) is returned.
"text1"<"text2"	Checks whether the combined character set numbers of *text1* are less than the character set numbers of *text2*. If so, true (–1) is returned; if not, false (0) is returned.
"text1">"text2"	Checks whether the combined character set numbers of *text1* are greater than the character set numbers of *text2*. If so, true (–1) is returned; if not, false (0) is returned.

Table 6-2. *Text String Expressions*

Using Subroutines to Perform Repeated Tasks

Within a merge file, you can create a *subroutine* to perform a specific task in your document. Generally, subroutines let you organize your merge application into different sections according to tasks or functions; these are often procedures that need to be repeated several times during the merge process. Subroutines can also be structured to perform different actions, depending on the results of an IF or SWITCH command.

The LABEL(*labelname*) command is used with the RETURN command to create a subroutine in your merge file. The merge commands that are placed between LABEL(*labelname*) and RETURN comprise the task that the subroutine will perform. Elsewhere in the merge file, the CALL command can be used to call or redirect the control of the merge to the subroutine specified by *labelname*. The commands of the subroutine are executed until the merge encounters the RETURN command; then, control of the merge continues with the command that follows the CALL command.

For example, suppose you create a merge application that prompts the user to choose an option from a menu. Depending on the user's choice, the merge will perform a task indicated by the menu item. The following shows how this example could be structured with merge commands:

```
CODES(
CHAR(Choice;Choose an Option: 1 State, 2 County, 3 City:)
SWITCH(VARIABLE(Choice))
   CASEOF(1)
      CALL(StatePop)
   CASEOF(2)
      CALL(CountyPop)
   CASEOF(3)
      CALL(CityPop)
ENDSWITCH
VARIABLE(Pop)STOP()
LABEL(StatePop)
     ASSIGNLOCAL(Pop;3,100,500)
     RETURN
LABEL(CountyPop)
     ASSIGNLOCAL(Pop;70,000)
     RETURN
LABEL(CityPop)
     ASSIGNLOCAL(Pop;20,500)
     RETURN
)
```

In this example, there are three subroutines at the end of the merge file: StatePop, CountyPop, and CityPop. The CHAR command displays the "Choose an Option: 1 State, 2 County, 3 City" message as a menu to prompt the user to type **1**, **2**, or **3**. When the user types an option, the number is stored in the variable called "Choice." Then, the SWITCH structure compares the contents of "Choice" with the three possible case statements. If one matches, control of the merge is transferred to the label named after the case.

The commands in each subroutine assign a population figure to the variable called "Pop." When the merge encounters the RETURN command, control returns to the command that follows the SWITCH structure. There, the VARIABLE(Pop) command inserts into the document whatever figure was assigned in the subroutine. The STOP command simply ends the merge when none of the valid choices is made, and it serves to separate the subroutines from the rest of the merge file. This is only one example of how you can structure and use subroutines in your merge applications. These can become quite complex, but they can also provide powerful capabilities for decision making in your merge applications.

Formatting the Merge Commands

Remember that, unlike WordPerfect's Macro language, the merge commands are actually inserted into a document. As each command is executed, the command is removed from the document, leaving only the text generated by the merge. Although some of the merge structures can be quite long and complex, it is important that you do not type extra hard returns, spaces, or tabs between the commands in a merge structure. If you insert extra hard returns, spaces, or tabs between merge commands, these will appear with the text in your merged document and will change the document format you have created.

Sometimes a merge structure can become too complicated to read. The IF and SWITCH commands provide good examples of structures that are difficult to understand without some kind of formatting, especially when there are several parameters. Consider these two examples:

```
SWITCH(VARIABLE(City))CASEOF(New York)CALL(Zone1)
CASEOF(Chicago)CALL(Zone2)CASEOF(Denver)CALL(Zone3)
CASEOF(Dallas)CALL(Zone4)CASEOF(Los Angeles)CALL(Zone5)
CASEOF(San Francisco)CALL(Zone6)ENDSWITCH

IF("VARIABLE(State)"="New Haven")CALL(Sam's District)
ELSE CALL(Corporate Accounts)VARIABLE(District)ENDIF
```

Without any formatting, it is difficult to see the logic of the commands. You can use the COMMENT merge command to add temporary formatting that can separate the commands but not be printed in the final document. The COMMENT(*message*) command lets you insert any text or codes that should not be inserted into the completed merged document. The *message* parameter of this command represents the text or codes you want in the comment.

Although the COMMENT command is generally used to insert notes about the form file, you can use this command to insert tabs and hard returns to format the command structures. Simply end a merge command line with the COMMENT command, insert the type of formatting you want (tabs or hard returns), and type a right parentheses before the next command, to end the COMMENT command. Using the previous examples of SWITCH and IF, you can use the COMMENT command to apply formatting, like this:

```
SWITCH(VARIABLE(City))COMMENT(
   )CASEOF(New York)CALL(Zone1)COMMENT(
   )CASEOF(Chicago)CALL(Zone2)COMMENT(
   )CASEOF(Denver)CALL(Zone3)COMMENT(
   )CASEOF(Dallas)CALL(Zone4)COMMENT(
   )CASEOF(Los Angeles)CALL(Zone5)COMMENT(
   )CASEOF(San Francisco)CALL(Zone6)COMMENT(
)ENDSWITCH

IF("VARIABLE(State)"="New Haven")COMMENT(
   )CALL(Sam's District)COMMENT(
)ELSE COMMENT(
   )CALL(Corporate Accounts)COMMENT(
   )VARIABLE(District)COMMENT(
)ENDIF
```

In these examples, a hard return is placed after each COMMENT code to end the current command line. Then a tab is inserted to indent and start the next line; before the next command begins, a right parentheses is inserted to end the COMMENT code. Everything between the parentheses, after the COMMENT command, is ignored when the application is merged.

Another option for formatting your merge codes is to use the CODES command. When you use this command, you are permitted to enter your merge codes in free-form fashion, without the need to worry about white space such as spaces, tabs, or hard returns; these are ignored by WordPerfect. For instance, you could rewrite the IF and SWITCH example using CODES in the following way:

```
CODES(
SWITCH(VARIABLE(City))
   CASEOF(New York)
      CALL(Zone1)
   CASEOF(Chicago)
      CALL(Zone2)
   CASEOF(Denver)
      CALL(Zone3)
   CASEOF(Dallas)
      CALL(Zone4)
   CASEOF(Los Angeles)
      CALL(Zone5)
   CASEOF(San Francisco)
      CALL(Zone6)
ENDSWITCH

IF("VARIABLE(State)"="New Haven")
   CALL(Sam's District)
ELSE
   CALL(Corporate Accounts)
   VARIABLE(District)
ENDIF
)
```

Notice that this form is even more readable than the previous example that used the COMMENT command. All the spaces, tabs, and hard returns between the parentheses following CODES are ignored.

Merge Command Reference

This section lists all the merge commands supported by WordPerfect for Windows. Instead of a strict alphabetical reference, the commands are divided into categories according to different merge operations. These categories will help you easily locate the commands you need, based on the type of task you want to perform. Following is a list of the merge commands supported by WordPerfect for Windows and described in this chapter.

ASSIGN
ASSIGNLOCAL
BEEP
BREAK
CALL
CANCELOFF
CANCELON
CAPS
CASEOF
CHAINDATA
CHAINFORM
CHAINMACRO
CHAR
CODES
COMMENT
CONTINUE
CTON
DATE
DEFAULT
DISPLAYSTOP
DOCUMENT
ELSE
EMBEDMACRO
ENDFIELD
ENDFOR
ENDIF
ENDRECORD
ENDSWITCH
ENDWHILE
FIELD
FIELDNAMES
FIRSTCAP
FOREACH
FORNEXT
GETSTRING
GO
IF
IFBLANK
IFEXISTS
IFNOTBLANK
INSERT
KEYBOARD
LABEL
LOOK
MRGCMND
NESTDATA
NESTFORM
NESTMACRO
NEXT
NEXTRECORD
NTOC
ONCANCEL
ONERROR
PAGEOFF
PAGEON
POSTNET
PRINT
PROCESSOFF
PROCESSON
PROMPT
QUIT
RETURN
RETURNCANCEL
RETURNERROR
REWRITE
STATUSPROMPT
STEPOFF
STEPON
STOP
STRLEN
STRPOS
SUBSTDATA
SUBSTFORM
SUBSTR
SWITCH
SYSTEM
TOLOWER
TOUPPER
VARIABLE
WAIT
WHILE

Cancel and Error Handling

During a merge operation, you can use the following commands to manage the use of the Cancel key, which is usually the ESC key. If you use the WordPerfect Keyboard feature to change the keyboard layout, the Cancel key can be any key to which the Escape function is assigned.

Also included in this section are the commands that let you specify what the merge should do when error messages are generated by WordPerfect, by Microsoft Windows, or from DOS. An *error message* is any signal or message that indicates when an action cannot be performed. This can be a "File not found" message generated when a form or data file cannot be found or a "Disk full" message when there isn't enough disk space to save a file or continue with the merge. With the following merge commands, you can include error-checking to control how the merge will continue when a problem occurs during the merge operation.

CANCELOFF

During a merge, you can press ESC, or the key that is assigned the Escape function, to stop or cancel the merge. The CANCELOFF command disables the Cancel feature so that the person performing the merge cannot stop the merge operation. This command is also useful when you want the user to press the Cancel key to reject an option you have programmed into the merge; because of the CANCELOFF command, the user can press the Cancel key to reject a displayed option without stopping the entire merge process. When you use this command, you cannot stop the merge with ESC, or with the key assigned the Escape function, until a CANCELON command is used to restore access to the Cancel feature.

CANCELON

The CANCELON command enables the Cancel feature, allowing the merge operation to be stopped with the Cancel key. You can use this with the CANCELOFF command to protect part of the merge operation from being stopped by the user.

ONCANCEL(*action*)

The ONCANCEL command instructs the merge to perform a specific *action* if the Cancel key is pressed or when the RETURNCANCEL command is executed within a merge. The *action* can be one of the following merge commands: BREAK, CALL(*labelname*), GO(*labelname*), QUIT, RETURN, RETURNERROR, or STOP. Generally, this command should be placed at the beginning of the merge file, before the place in the file where the Cancel key might be pressed, or before the subroutine where a RETURNCANCEL command is used.

The ONCANCEL command is valid only when the merge is operating within the file where the command is placed. For example, suppose your merge application includes multiple form or data files, and you want to define a cancel action that exists for the entire application. In this case, you need to insert the ONCANCEL command into each of the files. If the ONCANCEL command is placed in only one of the files, the cancel action is valid only while the merge is working with that file. If you place two or more ONCANCEL commands in your merge file, only the last occurrence of the command is recognized.

ONERROR(*action*)

The ONERROR command instructs an *action* to be performed if an error is generated during the merge by the WordPerfect program, by the Microsoft Windows program, or from MS-DOS. Possible errors include attempting to access a file that does not exist or cannot be found, memory limitations that do not allow the merge operation to continue, and problems with printing. This command also determines the *action* that will be performed when the RETURNERROR command is executed from within a merge subroutine.

The *action* parameter is the merge command that should be executed when an error has been detected. Possible actions include BREAK, CALL(*labelname*), CHAIN(*filename*), GO(*labelname*), QUIT, RETURN, and STOP. When you use the CHAIN(*filename*) command as the *action*, WordPerfect will not chain to the specified file until the merge is finished with the current form or data file.

You should place the ONERROR command at the beginning of the merge file or before the subroutine where a RETURNERROR command is used. The ONERROR command is valid only for the file where the command is placed; it does not affect other files accessed during the merge.

RETURNCANCEL

When you use the CALL command to move merge control to a subroutine, you can use the RETURNCANCEL command to exit the subroutine and simulate the pressing of the Cancel key. When RETURNCANCEL is executed from a subroutine, merge control returns to the previous level in the merge and the *action* of the ONCANCEL command is performed. If ONCANCEL is not used in the merge file, the function of the Cancel key is performed at the previous level.

RETURNERROR

When you use the CALL command to move merge control to a subroutine, you can use the RETURNERROR command to exit the subroutine and signal an error to the previous level of the merge. This is useful when the ONERROR(*action*) command is defined earlier in the merge file, to specify what action will be performed when an error occurs. For example, suppose you use the GETSTRING command in a subroutine to prompt the user to enter a filename; if the user enters the wrong type of name, the RETURNERROR command can return from the subroutine and signal an error to the previous level of the merge. Then, the *action* defined by the ONERROR command will be executed.

Macro Execution from Merge

The following commands allow you to play a macro from the merge operation. During a merge, macros can help you perform calculations, format text, apply font attributes, and perform any other operation that cannot be accomplished by the merge commands alone. There are two ways to play a macro from within a merge. You can chain a macro and nest a macro. When you *chain* a macro, you start a macro that performs a task when the merge is finished. A *nested macro* performs the macro operation within the merge; when the macro is finished, the merge continues.

NOTE: *Any macros you access must be created or converted for use with WordPerfect for Windows. You cannot use macros from earlier versions of WordPerfect under DOS.*

CHAINMACRO(*macroname*)

The CHAINMACRO command instructs WordPerfect to play the macro specified by *macroname*, when the merge is completed. If necessary, the *macroname* may be preceded by a full drive/directory path. The specified macro is played at the end of the merge, regardless of where the CHAINMACRO command is located in the merge file. The *macroname* can be any valid WordPerfect macro filename (.WCM), including a full path, if necessary. You can use this command only once in a merge file; when two or more CHAINMACRO commands are placed in a merge file, only the last command is executed.

NOTE: *If a merge is terminated by a cancel or error operation before completion, the chained macro is not played.*

EMBEDMACRO(*macro*)

While you can use the NESTMACRO command (described next) to call a macro from your merge file, there may be times when you don't want to use an entire macro file to run a few simple macro commands. In these instances, you can use the EMBEDMACRO command to place a macro in your merge file, in-line. All you need to do is supply the macro codes between the parentheses of the

EMBEDMACRO command. WordPerfect then translates these codes as macros, not as merge commands.

NESTMACRO(*macroname*)

The NESTMACRO command instructs the merge to play the macro specified by *macroname,* which can be any valid WordPerfect macro filename (.WCM). If necessary, the *macroname* may be preceded by a full drive/directory path. When the specified macro has performed its task, the merge resumes with the command that follows the NESTMACRO code. Unlike the CHAINMACRO command, you can insert multiple NESTMACRO commands in a single merge file.

Merge Execution Control

The following sections explain each of the commands that control the direction and flow of the merge operation. These include commands for loop structures, subroutine calls, and decision-making procedures. See the section "Using the Merge Commands" earlier in this chapter for examples of how these commands can be incorporated into your merge applications.

BREAK

The BREAK command lets you break from a subroutine or from a loop structure. This command is often used as the *action* for the ONCANCEL and ONERROR commands, to break from a level of nested loops created with the IF, WHILE, and FOREACH or FORNEXT commands. For complete information about the BREAK command, see the section "Stopping the Subroutine or Merge" later in this chapter.

CALL(*labelname*)

The CALL command moves merge control to the subroutine represented by *labelname.* When this command is executed, merge control moves to the subroutine structure that begins with LABEL(*labelname*). The merge executes the commands placed after the LABEL command until a RETURN command is found. Then the merge returns and continues with the command that immediately follows the CALL command.

CASEOF(*condition;expression*)

The CASEOF command is used in conjunction with the SWITCH and ENDSWITCH commands to determine what should happen when a certain *condition* is met. If the *condition* is met, then the *expression* is executed. For instance, consider the following:

```
CODES(
SWITCH(FIELD(Children))
    CASEOF(1)
        INSERT(one child)
    CASEOF(2)
        INSERT(two children)
    CASEOF(3)
        INSERT(three children)
ENDSWITCH
)
```

In this instance, the content of the Children field is checked. If it is 1, then the text "one child" is used. If it is 2, then the text "two children" is used, and 3 results in "three children" being used.

For a complete understanding of the CASEOF command, you should also refer to the SWITCH, ENDSWITCH, DEFAULT, and CONTINUE commands.

CONTINUE

The CONTINUE command is used in a SWITCH structure to indicate that execution of the code should skip to the next CASEOF command. You will typically use CONTINUE statements within an IF command in the SWITCH structure, as in the following:

```
CODES(
SWITCH(FIELD(Bedrooms))
    CASEOF(1)
        IF(VARIABLE(Children)>2)
```

```
            CONTINUE
        ENDIF
         INSERT(one bedroom)
      CASEOF(2)
         INSERT(two bedrooms)
      CASEOF(3)
         INSERT(three bedrooms)
      DEFAULT
         INSERT(many bedrooms)
ENDSWITCH
)
```

In this case, the text "one bedroom" is inserted in the document only if the Bedrooms field is equal to 1 and the Children variable is less than 3.

DEFAULT

Typically, when you are building a SWITCH structure, you define a condition, and then a group of possible matches for the condition. The SWITCH command allows you to define the condition, and the CASEOF statements are used to define the possible matches and what should occur if there is a match. However, there may be times when you want to define an "all other times" condition, as in the following:

```
Your commission rate is CODES(
SWITCH(FIELD(Sales Rep))
   CASEOF(John Davis)
      INSERT(8%)
   CASEOF(Marilyn Barnes)
      INSERT(7.5%)
   CASEOF(Andrea Smith)
      INSERT(8.25%)
   DEFAULT
      INSERT(6%)
ENDSWITCH)
```

ELSE

You can use the ELSE command to provide an alternative action within IF structures—that is, structures created with the IF, IFBLANK, IFNOTBLANK,

IFEXISTS, and ENDIF commands. Place this command between the IF... and ENDIF commands to start a series of commands that should be executed when the IF expression is false (a value of zero).

ENDFOR

The ENDFOR command marks the end of a FOREACH or FORNEXT loop structure. For more information, see FORNEXT.

ENDIF

The ENDIF command marks the end of an IF, IFBLANK, IFNOTBLANK, or IFEXISTS structure. For more information, see the headings for these commands.

ENDSWITCH

The ENDSWITCH command is used to mark the end of a SWITCH structure. For more information, refer to the SWITCH command.

ENDWHILE

The ENDWHILE command marks the end of a WHILE loop. See WHILE for more information.

FOREACH(*variable;expression1;expression2;...;expressionN*)

The FOREACH command is used, in conjunction with the ENDFOR command, to repeat a process for a certain list of items. The variable defines the *variable* to be replaced, one at a time, with each of the expressions (*expression1* through *expressionN*).

For example, you may have just been assigned a position where you are acquiring several new clients who had previously been handled by different account reps. If you wanted to replace all occurrences of the old account rep names with your name, you could use the following:

```
FOREACH(Old;John Davis;Aaron Kilmer;Maryanne Summers)
   IF("VARIABLE(Name)"="VARIABLE(Old)")ASSIGN(Name;Allen
Wyatt)ENDIF
ENDFOR
```

This removes the necessity of writing, in this instance, three different IF statements to check for the old account rep names. Instead, you have created a flexible structure, which you can use for one or a dozen account rep name replacements.

FORNEXT(*variable;start#;stop#;step#*)

The FORNEXT and ENDFOR commands let you create a loop structure, where a task or operation is repeated a certain number of times. When FORNEXT is executed, the commands in the loop are repeated once for each of the increments between the *start#* value and the *stop#* value, with the increment defined by the *step#* parameter. Initially, the *start#* value is automatically assigned to the *variable* when the FORNEXT command begins execution; you do not need to assign a value to the *variable*, but you do need to specify values for *start#, stop#,* and *step#.* You can type numbers for these parameters or insert variables that store the parameter information.

The *variable* parameter acts as a counter to increment each time the commands in the FORNEXT loop are executed. As each pass of the FORNEXT loop is completed, the increment specified by *step#* is added to the value stored in the *variable.* When the FORNEXT command completes the specified number of repetitions, the value stored in the *variable* indicates the number of successful passes through the loop structure.

The following example shows how the FORNEXT command can be structured to repeat a specific task. In this case, the FORNEXT command creates a numbered list with merge information from a data file.

```
FORNEXT(number;1;5;1)VARIABLE(number): FIELD(VARIABLE(number))
ENDFOR
```

In this example, the FORNEXT command completes a pass through the loop for each increment between 1 (the *start#* value) and 5 (the *stop#* value). The commands between FORNEXT and ENDFOR are executed for each pass through the loop. The "number" variable is incremented by 1 each time the FORNEXT command successfully completes a pass through the loop. When the merge is finished, this FORNEXT structure will produce a list like this:

```
1: Craig Saavedra
2: 1432 Camino Los Flores
3: Mission Viejo
4: California
5: 92691
```

The VARIABLE(number) command inserts the incrementing numbers in the list. The colon and character space are typed immediately after the command VARIABLE(number) in the merge file, followed by the command, FIELD(VARIABLE(number)), which inserts field information to match the numbers at the beginning of each line.

GO(*labelname*)

The GO command transfers control of the merge to a subroutine, specified by *labelname*. This is similar to the CALL command, except there is no RETURN command in the subroutine. Use the GO command when you want to skip to another part of the merge file but do not need to return from the subroutine to continue the merge operation. Use the LABEL(*labelname*) command to mark the place in the merge file where the merge should continue when the GO(*labelname*) command is executed.

IF(*expression*)

The IF command performs a task or series of commands when the *expression* equals a nonzero value (indicating "true"). If the *expression* returns a zero value (indicating "false"), the commands between IF and ENDIF (or the IF and an optional ELSE command) are ignored, and the merge continues with the command that follows the ENDIF (or ELSE) command.

The *expression* is usually a logical expression, but it can also be a single VARIABLE command that stores a value or a FIELD command that retrieves information from the data file. Using the logical operators, you can create an expression like VARIABLE(number)<12 or you can also create an expression like VARIABLE(balance)=FIELD(payment) that compares values of variables and numbers. When the variables contain text strings, you can compare variable or field contents by placing the VARIABLE or FIELD command in quotes, like this: "VARIABLE(name)"="Charlie" or "FIELD(name)"="Charlie".

The following example checks the contents of a variable for the text string "New York"; if the specified variable contains the text, then the GO(East) command, between IF and END IF, is executed.

```
IF("VARIABLE(state)"="New York")GO(East)ENDIF
```

You cannot have an IF command without an ENDIF command to indicate where the IF structure ends. You can place practically any commands in the IF structure. When two or more conditions must be specified, you can include another IF structure within the first IF structure; this is called a nested structure. You can also insert the ELSE command between IF and ENDIF to provide an alternative to the IF statement when the expression returns a zero (false) value. The following shows one example of a nested IF structure, with the ELSE command. In this example, each command is placed on a new line to show the structure of the IF command.

```
CODES(
IF(FIELD(Route#)=25)
   IF("FIELD(City)"="Fredmire")
      GO(Midwest)
   ELSE
      CALL(Find Account)
      CALL(Add Name)
   ENDIF
ENDIF
)
```

Here, the commands within the IF structure are executed when the contents of the field named Route# equals 25 and the field named City contains the text string "Fredmire". If the Route# field does contain 25, but the City field does not contain "Fredmire", the command or commands between the ELSE statement and the following ENDIF statement are executed. When you nest IF statements in this manner, remember to include an ENDIF command for each IF command in the structure.

IFBLANK(*field# or name*)

The IFBLANK command checks to see whether the specified field is blank for the record that is currently being merged with the form file. The parameter for the IFBLANK command can be either a *field#* or an assigned field *name.*

This command has a structure similar to the IF command and must be grouped with an ENDIF command. The following is an example of how the IFBLANK command can adjust the opening greeting for a business letter, when information may be missing in one or more of the fields in a given record. In this example, the MrMs field is checked to see whether a name title (Mr., Mrs., or Ms.) is stored in the field. If the field is blank, a true value is returned, and the commands listed after the IFBLANK command are executed.

```
IFBLANK(FIELD(MrMs))Dear FIELD(First Name):
ELSE Dear FIELD(MrMs) FIELD(Last Name):ENDIF
```

If the MrMs field is blank, the merge inserts the "Dear" text with the contents of the First Name field from the data file, followed by the closing punctuation for the greeting—a colon; the spaces and punctuation will be inserted into the merge file when the commands are executed. If the field is not blank, a false value is returned, and the commands after the ELSE are executed: the "Dear" text is inserted with the title stored in the MrMs field, followed by the surname stored in the Last Name field. The ENDIF command is required to indicate the end of the IFBLANK structure. The ELSE command is optional and should be used only when you want the merge to perform an alternate task when the IFBLANK expression returns a zero (false) value.

IFEXISTS(*variable*)

Use the IFEXISTS command to verify that a value has been assigned to the specified *variable*. If so, the commands between IFEXISTS and ENDIF are executed. The ENDIF command must be used to complete the IFEXISTS structure.

IFNOTBLANK(*field#* or *name*)

The IFNOTBLANK command is similar to the IFBLANK command, except it examines the specified field to see if it is *not* blank—that is, it checks to make sure the field contains something. If the field does contain something, the commands between IFNOTBLANK and ENDIF are executed. The ENDIF command must be used to complete the IFNOTBLANK structure.

LABEL(*labelname*)

You use the LABEL command to mark a place in the merge file or to mark the beginning of a merge substructure, called a subroutine. You enter the *labelname* parameter to create a unique name for the label, which can be up to 15 characters; actually, you can use as many characters as you want, but only the first 15 characters are recognized as the label name. You can use any characters, including spaces, to create the label name. Each label name must be unique; if duplicate label names are used, only the first occurrence of the name is recognized. You cannot enter a label name that is identical to a name used to define a local variable with the ASSIGNLOCAL command. Each name used for the LABEL and ASSIGNLOCAL commands must be different than the other LABEL and ASSIGNLOCAL names in the file. If two or more names are identical, a "Label is already defined" error message is displayed when you run the merge.

Once a LABEL command is inserted, you can use the CALL and GO commands to transfer merge control to the place where the LABEL command is located. If you use CALL to access a subroutine marked with a LABEL command, you must insert a RETURN command after the commands of the subroutine. RETURN transfers control of the merge back to the previous level after the commands of the subroutine are executed.

NEXT

The NEXT command is placed within a FOREACH, a FORNEXT, or a WHILE loop to force the merge to start the next pass in the loop structure. This is useful when you want to immediately skip to the next pass of the loop because a certain condition has been met. Unlike the BREAK command, NEXT does not cancel the loop procedure; it simply stops the current pass through the loop and begins the next.

QUIT

The QUIT command terminates the merge operation. For complete information about the QUIT command, see the section "Stopping the Subroutine or Merge" later in this chapter.

RETURN

You place the RETURN command at the end of a subroutine to return control to the previous level of the merge. When this command is executed, the merge continues with the command that follows the CALL command that was used to transfer control to the subroutine. The RETURN command must be used to return from a CALL command. If the RETURN command is encountered when a CALL command was not executed, an error message is displayed.

RETURNCANCEL

The RETURNCANCEL command is used to exit a subroutine and simulate the pressing of the Cancel key to return to the previous level of the merge. When RETURNCANCEL is executed from a subroutine, control returns to the previous level in the merge and the *action* of the ONCANCEL command (if defined) is performed.

RETURNERROR

You use the RETURNERROR command to exit a subroutine and signal an error to the previous level of the merge. This is useful when the ON ERROR(*action*) command is defined earlier in the merge file, to specify what action will be performed when an error occurs. The RETURNERROR command lets you generate your own error messages from within the merge application. For example, suppose you use the GETSTRING command in a subroutine to prompt the user to enter a filename; if the user enters the wrong type of name, the RETURNERROR command can signal an error to the previous level of the merge. Then the action defined by the ONERROR command will be executed.

SWITCH(*expression*)

The SWITCH command is used in conjunction with the CASEOF, DEFAULT, and ENDSWITCH commands to create a structure that executes different code under different conditions. The *expression* defines the condition or variable you are testing. In the following example, the contents of the Children field is the condition being tested:

```
CODES(
SWITCH(FIELD(Children))
   CASEOF(1)
      INSERT(one child)
   CASEOF(2)
      INSERT(two children)
   CASEOF(3)
      INSERT(three children)
ENDSWITCH
)
```

The CASEOF command determines what should happen when the SWITCH condition is met. For more information on this type of structure, refer to the ENDSWITCH, CASEOF, DEFAULT, and CONTINUE commands.

WAIT(*number*)

The WAIT(*number*) command suspends the merge operation for a certain length of time, with *number* representing tenths of a second. For example, suppose you want to use the PROMPT command to display a message, and you want the message to appear for five seconds before the merge continues. After the PROMPT(*message*) command, enter WAIT(50) to pause the merge for five seconds during execution. You can also use the WAIT command to slow the merge process, when certain text items or merged information should be seen by the user.

WHILE(*expression*)

This command continues to execute the commands that are placed between the WHILE and ENDWHILE commands until the *expression* becomes false. With the commands between WHILE and ENDWHILE, you must include a command that can change the *expression* from true (a nonzero value) to false (a zero value) during the course of the loop execution. This can be a GETSTRING or CHAR command, or an incremental loop with variables that will change the *expression* to false when the variable increments to a certain number. When the *expression* returns a false value, the merge continues with the command that follows the ENDWHILE command.

Merge Programming and Debugging Aids

Some of the merge commands exist to help you fix—or debug—your merge file when the merge doesn't run as expected. You can insert the BEEP, STEPON, and STEPOFF commands anywhere in your merge files to help you track the course of the merge operation. Insert the commands you want to use, and then run the merge to see the desired results; once the merge files are working correctly, you can remove these codes to run the merge as intended. The COMMENT command is used to insert notes into the merge files, for yourself or others; when structured correctly, the COMMENT command does not affect the merge process. The following commands do not fix problems with your merge files; they are simply tools that can help you locate mistakes in the merge file structures.

BEEP

The BEEP command causes the computer to beep once. When you are testing your merge applications, you can use the BEEP command to signal when a specific merge task is finished. You can insert the BEEP command as often as you need, to flag different points along the merge process.

CODES(*merge codes*)

The CODES command allows you to instruct WordPerfect to ignore all spaces, tabs, and hard returns inserted in your merge codes for formatting purposes. For instance, consider the following merge codes, which use the COMMENT command for formatting:

```
SWITCH(VARIABLE(City))COMMENT(
    )CASEOF(New York)CALL(Zone1)COMMENT(
    )CASEOF(Chicago)CALL(Zone2)COMMENT(
    )CASEOF(Denver)CALL(Zone3)COMMENT(
    )CASEOF(Dallas)CALL(Zone4)COMMENT(
    )CASEOF(Los Angeles)CALL(Zone5)COMMENT(
    )CASEOF(San Francisco)CALL(Zone6)COMMENT(
)ENDSWITCH
```

```
IF("VARIABLE(State)"="New Haven")COMMENT(
   )CALL(Sam's District)COMMENT(
)ELSE COMMENT(
   )CALL(Corporate Accounts)COMMENT(
   )VARIABLE(District)COMMENT(
)ENDIF
```

While this is readable, the following example, using the CODES command instead, is much more readable:

```
CODES(
SWITCH(VARIABLE(City))
   CASEOF(New York)
      CALL(Zone1)
   CASEOF(Chicago)
      CALL(Zone2)
   CASEOF(Denver)
      CALL(Zone3)
   CASEOF(Dallas)
      CALL(Zone4)
   CASEOF(Los Angeles)
      CALL(Zone5)
   CASEOF(San Francisco)
      CALL(Zone6)
ENDSWITCH
)
```

You can use the INSERT command (described momentarily) to temporarily reverse the effects of the CODES command.

COMMENT(*message*)

The COMMENT command lets you insert a *message* into your merge file that serves as a note for future reference. With the COMMENT command, you can add notes that explain the purpose of each command in the merge file. This is useful when others will need to edit or examine the merge files that you create. The comment *message* does not appear in the merged document, nor is it printed when you send the merged document to the printer. When you merge the form file, the COMMENT command, and all text between the COMMENT command parentheses, is ignored.

You can also use the COMMENT command to turn a section of the merge file into a comment. When you do so, the commands between the parentheses following the COMMENT command will not be executed when the merge is run. When you are trying to discover the source of a problem or error, this can help you turn off segments of the merge and isolate specific procedures or subroutines. Simply place the COMMENT command before the section you want to disable, and type an end parenthesis at the end of the section. When you perform the merge, any text, codes, or commands between the parentheses after the COMMENT command are ignored. When you want to enable that section of the merge again, simply delete the COMMENT command that you inserted.

INSERT(*text*)

The INSERT command is used to temporarily reverse the effects of the CODES command. Normally, WordPerfect ignores any spaces, tabs, or hard returns within the parentheses of a CODES command. You can, however, use INSERT to cause WordPerfect to pay attention to a specific occurrence of these characters. The following is an example of how this works:

```
CODES(
SWITCH(VARIABLE(Tickets))
   CASEOF(1)
      INSERT(You have one ticket. Be sure you avoid future
trouble.)
   CASEOF(2)
      INSERT(You have two tickets. If you get one more, your
privileges will be suspended.)
   CASEOF(3)
      INSERT(You have three tickets. Please make sure you
stop by the office as soon as possible.)
ENDSWITCH
)
```

In this example, the hard returns and spaces of the text between the INSERT parentheses are inserted in your document. After the closing parenthesis, the CODES command is again in effect, and WordPerfect assumes you are only using spaces, tabs, and hard returns for formatting your merge codes.

STEPON

The STEPON command causes the merge to pause as each command in the file is executed. At each point, messages or text appear to indicate the command that is executing. If the merge is producing text, the characters are displayed one at a time, and the merge pauses after each character. If the merge encounters a merge command, the entire command appears on the status bar. This helps you identify what is happening in the merge when there are no other visible signs on the screen. After each step, press any key from the keyboard to continue to the next step in the merge process. In some cases, you may need to display the Reveal Codes window to see the effect of all merge commands during the merge process.

The STEPON command should be inserted at the point in your merge file where you want to begin tracking the progress of the merge. If, for example, you want to monitor the entire merge process, insert the STEPON command at the beginning of the form file. For a section of the merge, insert the STEPON command at the beginning of the section you want to monitor; at the end of the section, insert the STEPOFF command to turn off the effect of STEPON.

STEPOFF

The STEPOFF command turns off the effect of the STEPON command. See STEPON for more information.

Merge Variables

WordPerfect includes merge commands that store different types of information for use during the merge. Because the information produced by the commands may change, these merge commands are called *variables.* Some variables let you store information in memory to be used at a later point in the merge. This information can be an item of text, a number, or the result of a calculation or operation between two or more items. Earlier in this chapter, a few examples are provided with variable merge commands.

Variables are also required as parameters for several of the merge execution commands. These variables provide information that helps the commands perform a specific task. Some merge commands help you determine how many characters are stored in variables or let you convert text values to numbers and vice versa. Other merge variables provide the system date stored in your computer or help you monitor what is happening inside WordPerfect during the merge process.

ASSIGN(*variable;expression*)

The ASSIGN(*variable;expression*) command assigns the value or text string represented by *expression* to the variable represented by *variable.* If the named variable does not exist, the ASSIGN command creates it and assigns the value of the *expression* to it. The *expression* can be a number, a text string, or an expression with variables and logical operations. You should never enclose the *expression* in quotes, even when the *expression* is a text string.

Suppose you want to create a variable named "account" and assign the number 25 to it; you would enter the following command:

```
ASSIGN(account;25)
```

Within the merge application, you can retrieve the contents of a variable by inserting the VARIABLE(*variable)* command. If, for example, you enter the VARIABLE(account) command in your merge file, the contents of the variable are inserted at the point where the command is located.

The *expression* of the ASSIGN command can also be a numeric or text expression with logical operators. Here are two examples of this:

```
ASSIGN(account;200+1000)
ASSIGN(Monthly Balance;VARIABLE(account)/12)
```

You can clear the contents of a previously assigned variable by using the ASSIGN command without typing an expression, like this:

```
ASSIGN(variable;)
```

You should clear global variables at the beginning of the merge application, when the variables were earlier in use. Global variables continue to store information until you exit the current WordPerfect session.

Remember that variables created with the ASSIGN command are *global variables,* which means the information stored in the variable can be accessed with merge commands and macro commands. Variables created with the other variable command, ASSIGNLOCAL, can be accessed only from a merge application.

Although the *variable* parameter can be any number of characters, only the first 15 characters are recognized as the unique variable name. You can use any combination of characters to create the variable name, and each name must be unique. These conditions apply to all merge commands that create and assign information to variables. If duplicate variable names are used, only the first occurrence of the name is recognized. You cannot enter a variable name that is identical to a name already defined, as with the LABEL command. Each name used for variable and LABEL commands must be different than the other variable and LABEL names in the file. If two or more names are identical, a "Label is already defined" error message is displayed when you run the merge.

ASSIGNLOCAL(*variable;expression*)

The ASSIGNLOCAL command performs the same operation as the ASSIGN command, except that the ASSIGNLOCAL command creates a local variable that can be accessed only through merge commands. Local variables are cleared when the current merge operation is completed. The value or text string represented by *expression* is assigned to the variable represented by *variable.* The *expression* can be a number, a text string, or an expression with variables and logical operators.

CHAR(*variable;message;title*)

The CHAR command lets you prompt the user to select an option from a list of characters. The *message* parameter is a text string that appears in a dialog box when the CHAR command is executed. The ***title*** parameter is used in the title bar of the dialog box. When the dialog appears, the merge is suspended until you type a single character from the keyboard; the character you type is then assigned to the specified *variable.* The CHAR command is usually followed by a command that evaluates the *variable* and performs an action based on the results. Here is an example of the CHAR command:

```
CHAR(YesNo;File was not found. Do you want to continue?
Y/N;File Error)
SWITCH(VARIABLE(YesNo))CASEOF(y)CALL(continue)CASEOF(n)CALL
(quitnow)ENDSWITCH
```

In this example, the message "File was not found. Do you want to continue? Y/N" is displayed in a dialog box on the screen, with a dialog box title of "File Error." In the text field of the dialog box, you can type a single character. Suppose you type **N** for "No"; the *N* character is assigned to the variable named "YesNo." Then, the SWITCH structure evaluates the contents of the variable and the CASEOF commands transfer execution to the place in the merge file where the

LABEL(*quitnow*) command is located. If you type **Y** instead, merge execution goes to the label named "continue." In this example, *Y* and *N* are the only valid characters that the user can type. If another character is typed, the SWITCH structure accomplishes nothing. For this example, you could add the DEFAULT command within the SWITCH structure to specify an action when the contents of the *variable* do not match one of the valid characters. You do not need to use a SWITCH command to evaluate the result of the CHAR statement; you can use other merge commands to evaluate or manipulate the contents of the variable.

CTON(*character*)

The CTON (Character TO Number) command converts a text character, represented by *character*, to a unique key number from the WordPerfect character sets. You can use this command to convert characters for use with the SYSTEM command, which works with numeric values instead of characters. To find the character set number, use the CTON command to convert a character to its key number; then divide the result by 256. The remainder is the WordPerfect character set number for the specified *character*.

DATE

The DATE command inserts the current date as text in the merged document. To insert the date, the command takes the date information stored in your computer system and displays it using the format defined for the WordPerfect Date feature. You can change the date format, before performing the merge, by choosing Insert/Date/Date Format and then selecting the format you want from the dialog box. If included in the defined date format, the current time also can be inserted with the DATE command. Remember that this command displays whatever date and time information is stored in your computer; if that information is incorrect, the wrong date and time will be displayed in your merged document.

You can use WordPerfect's Date Code feature instead of the DATE command. The difference between the two is that the DATE command inserts the current date only when the file is sent through the merge process; the WordPerfect Date Code inserts the current date, regardless of file type or conditions. To insert a WordPerfect date code, choose Insert/Date/Date Code or press CTRL+SHIFT+D.

IFEXISTS(*variable*)

Use the IFEXISTS command to verify that a value has been assigned to the specified *variable*. If it has, the commands between IFEXISTS and ENDIF are executed. You must use the ENDIF command to complete the IFEXISTS structure. Here is an example of how you might use this command:

```
IF EXISTS(Name)GO(Type Name)
   ELSE GETSTRING(Name;Enter Your Name)
ENDIF
LABEL(Type Name)VARIABLE(Name)
```

In this example, the IFEXISTS command checks to see if the "Name" variable contains something. If it does, the merge control moves to the label named Type Name. If the variable is empty or does not exist, the ELSE statement instructs the merge to perform the GETSTRING command, which prompts the user to enter a name. Once a value is found in the "Name" variable, merge control moves to the LABEL(Type Name) command, where the VARIABLE command inserts the variable contents into the merged document.

LOOK(*variable*)

The LOOK command notes the last keystroke pressed and assigns it to the specified *variable*. This command is useful when you need to monitor whether a specific key is pressed during a continuous loop. The following example shows how the LOOK command can be used in a merge:

```
LABEL(Begin Loop)
LOOK(Key)
IF("VARIABLE(Key)"="?")
   GO(GetHelp)
ELSE
   GETSTRING(Item;Type an item for the list. Type ? for Help.)
   VARIABLE(Item)
   GO(Begin Loop)
ENDIF
```

In this example, the LOOK command does not record a keystroke during the first pass through the loop. During the successive passes, the LOOK command notes the last keystroke that was pressed during the previous pass through the loop and assigns the keystroke as the current value for the "Key" variable. The IF command evaluates the contents of the "Key" variable; if the last key pressed was a question mark (?), then merge control moves to the label called "GetHelp". This is only one example of how the LOOK command can be used to monitor keystrokes pressed during the merge.

NTOC(*number*)

The NTOC (Number TO Character) command converts a unique key number, represented by *number,* to its corresponding text character from the WordPerfect character sets. You can use this command to determine the findings of the SYSTEM command, which returns numeric values instead of characters. To find the unique key number for a given character, multiply its character set number by 256, and then add the character set number to the product. The result is the unique key number.

SYSTEM(*number*)

The SYSTEM command lets you check the current state of the WordPerfect program. This command can help you determine what information is displayed in your document or on the screen during the merge operation. The *number* parameter represents a possible value or system variable for a condition in the WordPerfect program.

One application of the SYSTEM command is in checking to see whether text exists in the active document window before you start the merge. This can be useful when you are working with several document windows to prevent a merge from occurring in a window where a document already exists.

```
IF(SYSTEM(Document)!=256)
   NESTMACRO(cleardoc)
ENDIF
```

In this example, 256 is the number that represents the "Document blank" system variable. The IF(SYSTEM(Document)=256) command simply checks to see if the active document is blank. If so, the GO(Begin Merge) command transfers control to the LABEL(Begin Merge) command, where the merge can begin. If the active document is not blank, the ELSE statement executes the NESTMACRO(cleardoc) command; the CLEARDOC macro was created to clear all text from the active document window; this macro could be programmed to prompt the user about saving the existing document. When the document window is clear, the merge begins. This is only one example of the many uses for the SYSTEM command. In the next section, you will find a table of all valid system variable numbers, with descriptions of the WordPerfect conditions each monitors.

VARIABLE(*variable*)

The VARIABLE command retrieves information from variables and inserts it as text into the merged document, with *variable* representing the name of a variable you have created with the ASSIGN or ASSIGNLOCAL merge command. You can also use the VARIABLE command to retrieve variable information as a parameter for other merge commands.

String Manipulation

You have already learned that there are two types of variables—strings and numerics. In this section you will learn about WordPerfect merge commands created specifically for working with string variables. While some of the commands presented earlier in this chapter allow you to assign string values to variables, the commands presented here are intended to be used to work with the variables once the string value has been assigned.

CAPS(*expression*)

There may be times when you want to make sure that the first letter of each word in a variable is in uppercase. This can be done most easily with the CAPS command. This command ensures that the first letter of each word is uppercase, and that the rest of each word is lowercase. Consider, for example, the following:

```
LOCALASSIGN(ICName,CAPS(Name))
```

In this example, the local variable ICName is assigned the same text as contained in Name, except the first letter of each word is uppercase. Thus, if Name contained the characters "JOHN DOE", then ICName would contain "John Doe".

FIRSTCAP(*expression*)

This command is similar to the CAPS command, except that it capitalizes the entire first word of a string; all the rest of the string is lowercase. In the following example:

```
LOCALASSIGN(FCName,FIRSTCAP(Name))
```

if Name contained "Widgets, Red", then FCName would contain "WIDGETS, red".

STRLEN(*variable or expression*)

The STRLEN command returns the character length of the contents in the specified *variable.* STRLEN can also be used to calculate the length of the value returned by an *expression.* You can also use the FIELD command as the STRLEN parameter, to determine the character length of information stored in a field. The following example shows how the STRLEN command might be used to verify that a name has been entered within certain character limits.

```
LABEL(Get Text)
GETSTRING(NameText;Enter Your Name: )
IF(STRLEN(VARIABLE(NameText))>15)
   PROMPT(Name exceeds character limit. Try again.)
   GO(Get Text)
ENDIF
```

This example starts with the LABEL command to mark the place where the merge should return if the name is not entered correctly by the user. At the GETSTRING command, the user is prompted to enter a name. The STRLEN command is included as the expression for the IF command, which states: if the length of the value stored in the "NameText" variable is greater than 15 characters, prompt the user with "Name exceeds character limit. Try again." Then, the GO command moves control of the merge back to the "Get Text" label. If the length of the value in "NameText" is less than or equal to 15, the merge continues with the command that follows the ENDIF command.

STRPOS(*expression; subexpression*)

The STRPOS command is used to determine where the *subexpression* (or variable) exists within the *expression* (or variable). If it exists, then STRPOS returns a number representing the character position where it starts; otherwise, it returns 0. For instance, look at the following code lines:

```
ASSIGN(Var1,"harvesting")
ASSIGN(Begin,STRPOS(Var1,"vest"))
```

After these run, the variable *Begin* will contain 4, which is the character number where the letters "vest" begin in the string "harvesting", which is stored in the variable Var1.

SUBSTR(*expression*;***offset***;***count***)

The SUBSTR command takes a fragment of the text string stored in the *expression* parameter. The *offset* parameter is a number that indicates where to begin the fragment, and the *count* parameter specifies the length of the fragment to take. For example, suppose you have a data file field called Dept that stores department information. Each text string stored in this field will begin with "Dept." and have a two-digit number preceded by a single character and a dash. A few examples of the text that may be found in this field are "Dept. J-12", "Dept. G-27", and "Dept. A-07". Suppose you need to take only the department number from the text string stored in this field. You could enter the SUBSTR command, like this:

```
SUBSTR(FIELD(Dept);8;2)
```

In this example, the *offset* parameter is 8, meaning that you want to take the portion of the text that begins after the eighth character in the text string. The *count* parameter specifies how many of the characters you want to take after the eighth character. In this case, 2 is entered to take the last two characters in the text string.

TOLOWER(*expression*)

Earlier you learned about the CAPS instruction, and how it is used to make the first letter of each word uppercase. There may be times when you want to make sure that a variable is entirely in lowercase, however. This is done with the TOLOWER command. This command returns the lowercase equivalent of a string. Consider, for example, the following:

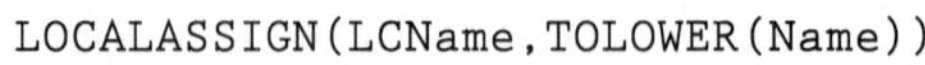

```
LOCALASSIGN(LCName,TOLOWER(Name))
```

In this example, the local variable LCName is assigned the lowercase version of the variable Name.

TOUPPER(*expression*)

The TOUPPER command is the opposite of the TOLOWER command. It results in each letter of a string being coverted to uppercase. For instance, in the following example:

```
LOCALASSIGN(UCName,TOUPPER(Name))
```

if Name contains "Gerald Smith", then after executing this line, UCName will contain "GERALD SMITH".

Form and Data File Control

The commands in the following sections let you switch to other form and data files during the merge operation. Some of these commands will help you merge with multiple files, when the information you need to merge is stored in two or more separate files. One of the commands lets you retrieve document file information during the merge process. Other commands let you control when page breaks are entered as well as process merge commands that are found in data files.

CHAINFORM(*filename*)

The CHAINFORM command indicates that the merge should continue with another form file, specified by *filename*, after the merge with the active form file is finished. This happens at the end of the current merge, regardless of where the CHAINFORM command is placed. Only one of these commands may be used in a given merge file; when you place two or more CHAINFORM commands in a single merge file, only the last command is executed. If you want to immediately stop using the current form file, use the SUBSTFORM command instead (see the section "SUBSTFORM(*filename*)" later in this chapter).

CHAINDATA(*filename*)

The CHAINDATA command indicates that the merge should continue with another data file, specified by *filename*. This happens when all records from the current data file are merged, regardless of where the CHAINDATA command is placed. When a large list of records is divided between two or more data files, use the CHAINDATA command with the PROCESSOFF and PROCESSON commands to "chain" from one data file to the next. Only one of these commands may be used in a given merge file; when you place two or more CHAINDATA commands in a single merge file, only the last command is executed. If you want to cease using the current form file immediately, use the SUBSTDATA command instead (see "SUBSTDATA(*filename*)" later in this chapter).

DOCUMENT(*filename*)

The DOCUMENT command retrieves saved document information at the point in the merge file where the DOCUMENT command is placed. If the retrieved document contains any merge codes, these are ignored. This command is useful for merge applications that are structured to assemble contracts or other documents; you can create separate files for each clause or paragraph that may be assembled with the form file. Then, use conditional merge commands like IF and SWITCH, with the DOCUMENT command, to specify the conditions when each *filename* should be retrieved into the completed document.

ENDFIELD

The ENDFIELD command is used in a data file to indicate the end of a field. You can enter this either by clicking on the End Field button on the feature bar, or by pressing ALT+ENTER.

ENDRECORD

The ENDRECORD command is used to mark the end of a record in a data file. You can enter this either by clicking on the End Record button on the feature bar, or by pressing ALT+SHIFT+ENTER.

FIELD(*fieldname*)

The FIELD command is used to insert information from a specific data file field in your document. If you are using a data file with your form file, the FIELD command is the link between the two. You should make sure that the fieldname parameter is defined and spelled the same in both the data and form files.

You can use FIELD commands in almost any part of a form file document, including headers, footers, and tables.

FIELDNAMES(*fieldname1;fieldname2;...;fieldnameN*)

In a data file, the FIELDNAMES command is used to define the formal names you wish applied to each field in your data records. These fieldnames should appear in the command in the order they will appear in the physical records.

The FIELDNAMES command should be the first record in your data file. The names used here should match those you intend to use in your form file.

MRGCMND(*codes*)

The MRGCMND command lets you insert other merge commands into the merged document, without executing or interpreting the commands. MRGCMND commands are always inserted in pairs, with the *codes* parameter representing the text or merge commands being inserted. This makes it possible for you to structure a merge application that actually creates a new data or form file. For example, the following structure reads information from a data file and creates a new data file with only records that have company information in the field named Company:

```
IFNOTBLANK(Company)
    FIELD(Name)MRGCMND(ENDFIELD)
    FIELD(Company)MRGCMND(ENDFIELD)
    FIELD(Address)MRGCMND(ENDFIELD
    ENDRECORD)
ENDIF
NEXT RECORD
```

In this example, the IFNOTBLANK command checks to see whether the Company field has any text. If not, the current record is skipped and the merge continues with the next record. If, however, the Company field does contain information, the text for each field in the record is inserted into the merged document; the MRGCMND(ENDFIELD) command inserts an ENDFIELD command into the merged document, after each field in the record. The last MRGCMND command also inserts an ENDRECORD command. The result is a new data file that contains only the records with Company fields that are not blank.

NESTDATA(*filename*)

The NESTDATA command causes the merge to take information from the data file indicated by *filename.* While the merge is working with the new data file, no information is taken from the data file that was used to start the merge. When all records from the nested data file have been merged, the merge resumes with the initial data file.

NESTFORM(*filename*)

The NESTFORM command transfers control of the merge to the commands stored in the form file indicated by *filename.* When all commands in the nested form file are executed, control of the merge returns to the command that follows the NESTFORM command in the initial form file.

NEXTRECORD

The NEXTRECORD command instructs the merge to continue the merge operation with the next record in the data file. This is useful when you want to compile field information from each record for a list but do not want a separate document for each record. You simply want to gather information and compile it into one document. When the merge encounters a NEXTRECORD command, it continues to the next record in the data file without inserting a page break for a new merged document. In the following example, the NEXTRECORD command is used to help create a list of names in the data file.

```
ASSIGN(Count;1)
LABEL(list)VARIABLE(Count)) FIELD(name)
ASSIGN(Count;VARIABLE(Count)+1)
NEXTRECORD
GO(list)
```

The ASSIGN command creates a variable called "Count" and assigns the value 1 to the variable. This variable will be incremented during the merge and will provide the entry numbers that begin each entry in the list. The LABEL command marks the place where the merge should return to create each list entry. The VARIABLE(Count) command inserts an item number for the list; the parenthesis character will follow the item number. Then the FIELD(name) command inserts a name from the first record in the data file. The ASSIGN command is then used to add 1 to the value stored in VARIABLE(Count); this increments the value for the next item number in the list. The NEXTRECORD command then instructs the merge to continue with the next record from the data file, without inserting a page break for a new merge document. Finally, the GO command sends the control of the merge back to the LABEL(*list*) to create the next item in the list, with the "name" information from the next record. When this merge is finished, you might see a list on your screen that looks like this:

```
1) Shauna Wilkes
2) Jim Olsen
3) Barbra Carrera
4) Tyler Dyson
5) Alice Lockwood
```

PAGEOFF

The PAGEOFF command prevents a merge from inserting a hard page code after each record from the data file is merged with the form file. This command is useful when you are compiling a list of information from the data file but do not want a separate document for each record. Once the PAGEOFF command has been entered, the merge will not insert hard page codes until a PAGEON command is entered.

PAGEON

The PAGEON command enables the insertion of hard page codes after they have been disabled with the PAGEOFF command. For more information, see the preceding section.

PROCESSOFF

The PROCESSOFF code is used in tandem with the PROCESSON code. For more information, refer to the next section about using PROCESSON.

PROCESSON

The PROCESSON code is inserted into data files when merge commands in the files should be processed and not merged as record text. PROCESSON is always followed by a matching PROCESSOFF, with the commands between the codes representing the merge commands that should be executed from the data file. For example, insert

```
PROCESSON
CHAINDATA(filename)
PROCESSOFF
```

at the end of a data file to chain to another data file when all records of the first file are merged. You can also enclose IF, WHILE, and other merge structures within PROCESSON to control which records will be merged, based on information stored in variables.

When you place a PROCESSON code within the records of the data file—and not at the end of the file—the specified commands are executed whenever they are encountered during the merge process. This can cause problems if the merge performs multiple passes on the records in the data file.

SUBSTDATA(*filename*)

The SUBSTDATA command is similar to the NESTDATA command, except that SUBSTDATA does not return the control of the merge to the original data file. Instead, the merge continues with only the records in the data file indicated by *filename*. When all records in the new data file are merged, the merge ends.

SUBSTFORM(*filename*)

The SUBSTFORM command is similar to the NESTFORM command, except that SUBSTFORM does not return the control of the merge to the original form file. Instead, the merge switches to use only the commands in the form file indicated by *filename*. When all commands in the new form file are executed, the merge operation is finished.

Input and Output Commands

The following commands let you display prompts and messages for the user during the merge. Some of the commands also let you control the screen display and sound a beep as a signal for a task in the merge operation. Finally, a few commands are provided to create printed output.

BEEP

The BEEP command causes the computer to beep once. BEEP is often combined with the user prompt commands to produce an audible signal for the user, when an action should be performed. BEEP is also used to notify you when a specific merge task is finished. For a different application of this command, see BEEP under the heading "Merge Programming and Debugging Aids," earlier in this chapter.

CHAR(*variable;message;title*)

The CHAR command lets you prompt the user to select an option from a list of characters. The *message* parameter is a text string that appears in a dialog box when the CHAR command is executed, and the *title* parameter is what you want to appear in the title bar of the dialog box. When the dialog box appears, the merge is suspended until you type a single character from the keyboard; the character you type is then assigned to the specified *variable*. The CHAR command is usually followed by a command that evaluates the *variable* and performs an action based on the results. For an example of this command, see CHAR under the "Merge Variables" heading earlier in this chapter.

DISPLAYSTOP

When you run a merge, certain merge commands cause text from your document to be displayed on the screen. The DISPLAYSTOP command allows you to turn off the display of this type of text. Including DISPLAYSTOP at the proper places in your merge codes will not only make your file look better on screen, but may also increase the speed at which your merge runs. This is because WordPerfect does not need to take the time to do screen updates. The speed increase will be particularly noticeable if you are working with documents that use graphics extensively.

To update the screen after you have used the DISPLAYSTOP command, use REWRITE.

GETSTRING(*variable;message;title*)

The GETSTRING command lets you prompt the user to type something from the keyboard. The *message* parameter is a text string that appears in a dialog box when the GETSTRING command is executed; the *title* parameter appears in the title bar of the dialog box. When the dialog box appears, the merge is suspended, and the user can type something in a text field that appears in the dialog box. When the user is finished typing, he or she can choose the OK button in the dialog box to continue with the merge. The text entered by the user is then assigned to the specified *variable*. The GETSTRING command is usually followed by a command that evaluates the *variable* and performs an action with the *variable* contents. Here is an example of the GETSTRING command:

```
GETSTRING(name;Enter Your Name;User Info)
Applicant's Name: VARIABLE(name)
```

In this example, the "Enter Your Name" message is displayed in a dialog box on the screen. In the text field in the dialog box, you can type your name. When you are finished, choose OK to continue. The text you type is assigned to the variable named *name*. Then the "Applicant's Name: " text is inserted into the merged document, followed by the information stored in the *name* variable.

KEYBOARD(*message*)

The KEYBOARD command pauses the merge to allow the user to type something from the keyboard, displaying the *message* in a window over the document. To end the input and continue the merge, the user must press ALT+ENTER or choose Continue from the feature bar.

POSTNET(*zipcode string*)

One of the powerful features of WordPerfect for Windows is the ability to print PostNet bar codes. These are used, on envelopes, to lower the cost of mailing and to speed up mail processing. WordPerfect allows you to create PostNet bar codes in a form file simply by supplying a *zipcode string* as a parameter for the POSTNET command.

PRINT

The PRINT command sends all merged information to the printer. When you are merging a large number of records from the data file, you may not have enough memory in your computer to handle the merged document. You can place the PRINT command at the end of the form file to send a document to the printer as each record is merged with the form file. Each time the PRINT command is executed, all previously merged information is cleared from your computer's memory.

When you use this command to merge to the printer, page breaks are indicated after each record is merged. If you do not want the page breaks, use the PAGEOFF command. For more information on the PAGEOFF command, see the section "Form and Data file Control" earlier in this chapter.

PROMPT(*message*)

The PROMPT command displays the specified *message* inside a merge message box on the screen. The message remains on the screen until the screen is rewritten, until a new PROMPT command is issued, or until the merge ends.

REWRITE

The REWRITE command rewrites the screen to display the current state of the merge operation. REWRITE is often placed at the end of the form file to update the screen display with the latest merged document. If you use this command, the merge will run a little more slowly because the Merge feature usually updates the document window only at the end of the merge process.

STATUSPROMPT(*message*)

The STATUSPROMPT command is similar to the PROMPT command, except that the *message* appears on the status bar, at the bottom of the screen, instead of inside a merge message box.

Stopping the Subroutine or Merge

The following commands will terminate a merge subroutine or the entire merge process. The effect for most of these commands will change depending on where the commands are placed in your form or data file.

BREAK

The BREAK command lets you break from a subroutine or from a loop structure. This command is often used as the *action* for the ONCANCEL and ONERROR commands, to break from a level of nested loops created with the IF, WHILE, and FORNEXT commands. The effect of the BREAK command differs depending on where it is placed in the merge file. When BREAK is executed within an IF, WHILE, or FORNEXT structure, merge control moves to the end of the current loop structure, just after the next ENDIF, ENDWHILE, or ENDFOR command.

The BREAK command can also terminate the merge for a single record, or terminate the entire merge operation. When the BREAK command is executed within a form file, the merge for the current record is stopped and the merge continues with the next record in the data file. When BREAK is found in a data file, the entire merge operation is terminated. When BREAK is executed in a nested form or data file, merge control moves back to the parent file.

QUIT

The QUIT command terminates the merge operation and can be placed in either a form or data file. If placed in a form file, the QUIT command should be the last executable command in the file. Also, you should not use the QUIT command as the *action* for commands like ONERROR or ONCANCEL when other commands or text follow QUIT in the form file but should not be recognized after QUIT is executed.

When QUIT is executed in the middle of a form file, the result may be different than you expect. First, the merge is terminated, but any text that follows the QUIT command is still inserted in the merged document without information merged from the data file. Second, any merge commands placed after QUIT are ignored, but their parameters are inserted as text into the merged document. To avoid these problems, make sure the QUIT command is executed after the text from the data file is merged and after other commands that have parameters.

When placed in a data file, the QUIT command terminates the merge at the point where QUIT is found. The merge ignores the portion of the data file that follows the QUIT command but will include the entire form file in the merged document, regardless of whether all text has been merged into it. In a data file, the QUIT command is best used within an IF or WHILE loop or included as the *action* for another command, like ONERROR.

NOTE: *Use the STOP command, instead of QUIT, when you need to terminate a merge from the middle of a form or data file but do not want the remainder of the form file included in the merged document.*

RETURN

Use the RETURN command to indicate the end of a subroutine. When this command is executed, control of the merge continues with the command that follows the CALL command that was used to call the subroutine.

RETURNCANCEL

When the CALL command is used to move merge control to a subroutine, the RETURNCANCEL command can be used to exit a subroutine and simulate the pressing of the Cancel key to return to the previous level of the merge. When RETURNCANCEL is executed from a subroutine, merge control returns to the previous level in the merge, and the action of the ONCANCEL command (if defined) is performed.

RETURNERROR

When the CALL command is used to move merge control to a subroutine, the RETURNERROR command can be used to exit the subroutine and signal an error to the previous level of the merge.

STOP

The STOP command immediately terminates all merge activity, including requests for chained files or macros, that would be otherwise chained at the end of the merge. Unlike the QUIT command, the STOP command prevents the remainder of a form file, if any, from appearing in the merged document.

Checking WordPerfect with the SYSTEM Command

The SYSTEM(*var*) command lets you check the current state of the WordPerfect program. This command can help you determine what information is displayed in your document or on the screen during the merge operation. The *var* parameter represents the name or number assigned for a feature of the WordPerfect program. When you combine a valid *var* parameter with the SYSTEM command, you create a *system variable* that can be used as an expression for other merge commands. The names and numbers assigned to the WordPerfect features are listed in the tables in the next section, "System Variable Numbers."

One application of the SYSTEM command is to check whether text exists in the active document window, before you start a merge; this can prevent a merge from occurring in a window where a document already exists. To check text in the active document, you could place the following set of commands at the beginning of a form file:

```
IF(SYSTEM(Document)!=256)
   NESTMACRO(cleardoc)
ENDIF()
```

In this example, SYSTEM(Document) is the system variable name for the document commands group. The number 256 is the value that represents the "document blank" condition. Using this information, the command IF(SYSTEM(Document)!=256) simply checks to see if the active document is blank. If so, the GO(Begin Merge) command transfers control to the LABEL(Begin Merge) command. If the active document is not blank, the ELSE statement executes the NESTMACRO(cleardoc) command. In this application, the CLEARDOC macro is designed to clear all text from the active document window; when the document window is clear, the merge begins.

Here is another example. Suppose you want to check whether the bold text attribute has been turned on in the document. You could insert this command into the form file to check for the bold attribute:

```
IF(SYSTEM(Attrib)=4096)This is bold textENDIF
```

In this example, "Attrib" is combined with the SYSTEM command to create a system variable that checks for font attributes. The number 4096 is the number assigned to the "bold on" condition. If the expression SYSTEM(Attrib)=4096 is true, then the statement "This is bold text" is inserted into the merged document.

These are only two examples of the many uses for the SYSTEM command. In the next section, you will find tables with all valid system variable names and numbers, including a description of the WordPerfect condition that each monitors.

System Variable Numbers

This section describes the WordPerfect features you can monitor during a merge operation by using the SYSTEM(*var*) command. For the SYSTEM(*var*) command, WordPerfect program features are organized into different categories, with a unique name and number assigned to each group. You can use either the valid name or number as the *var* parameter. When the SYSTEM(*var*) command is executed, the specified condition is checked at the place where the insertion point is located in the merged document.

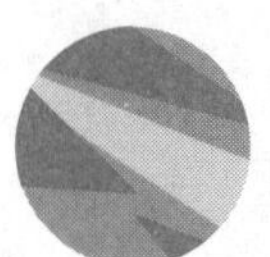

NOTE: *The following tables are not structured alike; each table is organized to show SYSTEM expression information for a particular group of features or conditions. Usually, the SYSTEM expressions must be combined with IF, SWITCH, WHILE, and other command structures to direct an action based on certain conditions in the program.*

Checking for Font Attributes with SYSTEM(Attrib)

When checking for font attributes, the *var* parameter can be either "Attrib" or the number 1, as follows: SYSTEM(Attrib) or SYSTEM(1). Use the information in Table 6-3 to create expressions that check for specific attributes. For example, the expression SYSTEM(Attrib)=256 checks whether the italics attribute is turned on at the current insertion point position. The expression SYSTEM(1)=0 verifies whether all font attributes are turned off or, in other words, whether the text is "normal."

Attribute	Expression Number
Normal (all attributes off)	0
Extra large	1
Very large	2
Large	4
Small	8
Fine	16
Superscript	32
Subscript	64
Outline	128
Italics	256
Shadow	512
Redline	1024
Double underline	2048
Bold	4096
Strikeout	8192
Underline	16384
Small caps	32768

Table 6-3. *Expression Numbers Assigned to Font Attributes*

When you want to check for two or more attributes at once, add their numbers together. For example, the expression SYSTEM(Attrib)=20480 looks to see if the bold *and* underline attributes are turned on; 4096 is the number for bold and 16384 is the number for underline (4096 + 16384 = 20480).

Checking WordPerfect Tables

For WordPerfect tables, the SYSTEM expressions vary depending on whether you are checking for cell locations, attributes, or justification. Following are descriptions of the commands to check for each of these states. If the insertion point is not in a table when these expressions are used, the commands return nothing. For this reason, you may want to precede the following expressions with the SYSTEM(Document)=512 expression, which verifies that the insertion point is located within a table.

The SYSTEM(Cell) and SYSTEM(2) expressions return the cell address where the insertion point is located. For example, when the insertion point is located in cell B5, the SYSTEM(Cell) or SYSTEM(2) expression returns the value B5. The variable is undefined if the insertion point is not in a table.

The SYSTEM(CellAttr) and SYSTEM(23) expressions return the attributes defined for the current cell. Using the attribute number assignments shown in Table 6-3, you can create expressions to check for attributes in a table. For example, to check for bold attributes in a cell, use the SYSTEM(CellAttr)=4096 expression.

The SYSTEM(CellState)/256 and SYSTEM(24)/256 expressions check for the justification and alignment of text within the current cell. As part of the expression, you must include /256 to divide the returned number by 256. The result will be one of the expression numbers indicated in the following table:

Cell Justification	Expression Number
Left-justified	0
Full-justified	1
Center-justified	2
Right-justified	3
Decimal-aligned	4

For example, suppose you want to check the cell at the insertion point for decimal alignment. Since the expression number for decimal alignment is 4, you could use the SYSTEM(CellState)/256=4 expression in the following structure:

```
IF(SYSTEM(CellState)%256=4)
   PROMPT(The current cell is decimal aligned.)
ELSE
   PROMPT(No decimal alignment here.)
ENDIF
```

The SYSTEM(CellState)%256 and SYSTEM(24)%256 expressions check for the justification and alignment of text within the current cell. As part of the expression, you use the MOD operator (the % symbol) to return the remainder of a number after a division by 256. The result will be one of the expression numbers indicated in the following table:

Cell Condition or State	Expression Number
Justification applied to cell	1
Attribute applied to cell	2
Cell text is aligned at bottom	4
Cell text is vertically centered	8
Cell content is a text string	16
Cell content is a formula	32
Cell is locked	64

For example, suppose you want to know whether the cell at the insertion point is locked. Since the expression number for "Cell is locked" is 64, you could use the SYSTEM(CellState)%256=64 expression in the following structure:

```
IF(SYSTEM(CellState)%256=64)
   PROMPT(The current cell is locked.)
ELSE
   PROMPT(The current cell is not locked.)
ENDIF
```

When you need to check for two or more conditions, you can add together the expression numbers. For example, suppose you need to know whether a cell contains a formula and whether that formula is vertically centered in the cell. Add the expression number for "Cell content is a formula" (32) to the expression number for "Cell text is vertically centered" (8), and you get the sum of 40. Thus, the SYSTEM expression for this example would be

```
IF(SYSTEM(CellState)%256=40)
```

Checking the Document with SYSTEM(Document)

You can use the expressions described here to determine the state of the active document window. Use the SYSTEM(Document) or SYSTEM(4) command to create an expression with one of the numbers from the table. For example, the SYSTEM(Document)=1 expression can verify whether the active document window needs to be saved. The following table lists other expression number options for a variety of document conditions:

Document Condition or State	Expression Number
Document was modified but not saved	1
Document was modified since last generated	4
Document window is blank	256

Checking Insertion Point Location

Following are the expressions you can enter to check the insertion point location for tables, columns, and other document structures. Use the SYSTEM(Pos) or SYSTEM(16) command to find the horizontal position (in WP units, 1200ths of an inch) of the insertion point; use SYSTEM(Line) or SYSTEM(10) to return the vertical position. The SYSTEM(Page) and SYSTEM(14) expressions return the number of the page in the document where the insertion point is currently located.

Use the SYSTEM(Left) or SYSTEM(9) command to "look" at the character or code that is found to the left of the insertion point. SYSTEM(Right) or SYSTEM(18) checks the character or code that is to the right of the insertion point.

The SYSTEM(Document)=512 expression verifies whether the insertion point is currently located within a WordPerfect table—that is, somewhere between the (Tbl Def) and (Tbl Off) codes. The SYSTEM(Document)=2048 expression can indicate whether the insertion point is located within (Outline On) and (Outline Off) codes. The SYSTEM(Column) or SYSTEM(3) command returns the number of the current column (within a table or text columns) where the insertion point is located. SYSTEM(Row) or SYSTEM(22) returns the current row number (tables only) where the insertion point is located.

Endnotes, Footnotes, and Graphics

The commands and expressions described here return information to the merge about the numbers of endnotes, footnotes, graphics boxes, and equations. SYSTEM(Endnote) or SYSTEM(5) indicates the number of the current endnote in the document. SYSTEM(Footnote) or SYSTEM(8) returns the number of the current footnote. SYSTEM(Equation) or SYSTEM(6) returns the number of the nearest equation box; SYSTEM(Figure) or SYSTEM(7) returns a figure box number. SYSTEM(TableBox) or SYSTEM(19) indicates the number of the current table box (graphics, not WP tables); SYSTEM(TextBox) or SYSTEM(20)returns the numbers for text and table boxes respectively; and SYSTEM(UserBox) or SYSTEM(21) indicates the box number of the current user box.

NOTE: *For equation boxes and graphics boxes you need to apply a formula to the result of the system command to obtain the correct box number. You need to divide the result of the system command by 32 to get the first number level of the box. For the second number level, use the MOD32 (%32). For example, level 1 = value/32; level 2 = value%32. To determine a figure box number, use an expression like: ASSIGN(Variable)SYSTEM COMMAND(Figure)/32). For more information, see the ASSIGN command discussed earlier in this chapter.*

CHAPTER 7

Desktop Publishing with WordPerfect for Windows

This chapter shows you how to use WordPerfect for tasks typically associated with desktop publishing (DTP). Such tasks include designing newsletters, printing letterhead stationery, and producing announcements and advertisements. In Figure 7-1 you can see an example of a newsletter created with WordPerfect.

Word processing is primarily concerned with putting the right words in the right place, and WordPerfect has many tools for doing just that. The aim of desktop publishing is to improve the appearance of words, augmenting them, where appropriate, with pictures and other visual elements so that information is presented effectively.

Fantastic Sports

The premier sports enthusiasts newsletter

Volume 3, Week 1
September 1, 1994

DARTS OFFICIALLY RECOGNIZED AS OLYMPIC EVENT

September 19, 1994 will officially herald in the long-awaited event of *Darts* in the upcoming summer Olympics. Not since the introduction of the Javelin event has there been such an uproar over the rules and regulations of a sport. Says Jonathan Wilkes of the International Olympic Committee, "Many of the committee members clamored over the news that took many, even me, by surprise." Not all participating countries agree on the style and method of dart-throwing. For instance, since its invention in 1819, darts has evolved to include many strict rules, including the banning of "duplex lobbing" and the ever-popular "ricochet throwing." Many of the sports' enthusiasts in England, where the sport originated, purport that the rules of darts "cannot be loosely interpreted; to do so would result in the degradation of all rules that make the sport such a viable alternative to the more violent sports, such as rugby and some equestrian events." The committee promised, however, that none of the rules will be overlooked or compromised. In any case, darts has long been one of America's favorite pastimes. Now, as an Olympic event, Americans can compete on an even higher level and, perhaps, earn the gold medal.

HUNTER'S PARADISE

Hunters can expect much more excitement as they spend their time in the outdoors this season. No longer are they limited to pursuing the common elk, deer, moose, and antelope. Strangely enough, a new breed of wildlife has been introduced called "bindofers," which offer a faster chase, higher resistance to bullets and razor-tipped arrows, and a keener sense of smell. A spokesman for the Game and Wildlife commission claims that the wild bindofer can achieve speeds in excess of 120 mph! Indeed, this will offer an unsurpassed challenge to even the best hunters. Keep in mind that this new breed may not be for you, particularly if you hunt with guns or long bows. It is anticipated that more than 250 of these beasts will be set loose under authority of the US Game and Wildlife commission in the states of Montana, Wyoming, and northern portions of Colorado. You still need a license to hunt the bindofer, but these are available at

Figure 7-1. *The front page of a newsletter created with WordPerfect*

The Emergence of DTP

Two advances in computer hardware made it possible for programmers to create DTP software: display systems capable of mixing text and graphics on-screen, and printers capable of faithfully reproducing in print what is shown on the screen. With the arrival of EGA and then VGA displays, programs finally have a workable alternative to the old character-mode displays in which text was assembled from a fixed set of letters and symbols arranged in a grid of columns and rows, typically 80 columns by 25 lines. The DOS version of WordPerfect is a classic example of a character-based program, even though WordPerfect 6.0 for DOS has done an admirable job of creating a graphics display that very closely approximates what is printed.

The Appearance of WYSIWYG

By drawing characters in the same way as they draw pictures, graphics mode display systems offer greater flexibility. Text that is to be proportionally spaced on the printed page can be shown proportionally spaced on the screen. Letters can be depicted in the same style that they will print. Printers themselves have advanced. Laser and inkjet technology make it possible and affordable to print in a wide variety of fonts and to reproduce images with impressive clarity.

The emergence of PostScript as a standard for describing the contents of a printed page means that files created on personal computers can be sent directly to typesetting equipment that understands PostScript. Typesetting equipment produces even higher quality output than laser printers. The page shown in Figure 7-1 was printed with a QMS-PS810 Turbo laser printer that is PostScript compatible. The original document is very presentable, but close examination reveals that the letters are less clear cut than the ones you are reading now. This is because the text of this book was typeset at about 1200 dots per inch, whereas the laser printer used only 300 dots per inch.

The close connection between screen and printer gives rise to the term "what you see is what you get," or WYSIWYG (pronounced wiz-ee-wig). Since the programming required to achieve WYSIWYG is complex, Microsoft Windows was developed to provide a complete WYSIWYG environment that can be used by a wide range of programs, including WordPerfect for Windows. Thus, when you load WordPerfect and start typing, you can be fairly sure that the font that appears on the screen will be close to the one that is printed when you select File/Print.

Desktop Publishing Versus Word Processing

Once programmers had the Windows environment to work with, they were able to expand the capabilities of word processing programs. Traditionally, word processors have excelled in text manipulation, editing, proofing, and assembling documents. Users have come to expect features like spell-checking, merging, outlining, and indexing. The first desktop publishing programs concentrated on the one area where character-based word processors were weak: page layout.

Most DTP programs treat the items you need to place on the page—such as sections of text, lines, shading, and pictures—as separate objects that can be moved and sized independently of each other. This is usually achieved with a system of *frames,* which are shapes into which you place text or graphics. The text and graphics are usually created outside the DTP program, with a word processor and a drawing program. The DTP program thus becomes a place in which the various elements of the final page are assembled.

The frames in a DTP program can be sized and moved around the page to achieve a pleasing combination of visual elements. Frames are rather like the boxes you can create in WordPerfect; for example, the boxed quote in Figure 7-1 is a text box. It could be moved lower on the page to achieve a different visual balance. However, the frames in a DTP program are more flexible than those offered in WordPerfect. For example, text can be made to flow from one frame to the next. You can alter the size and shape of the frame and have the text adjust to the new dimensions. Some programs even allow you to create frames that are not rectangular, thus breaking away from the visual limits of column and box layout.

To create a document like the newsletter shown in Figure 7-1 by using WordPerfect, you have to combine several techniques. A format must be created for the bulk of the text in the document, including a two-column section. The graphics are then added, and underlying text is told to flow around them. You can insert lines with WordPerfect, such as the lines between columns shown in Figure 7-2, as well as charts and pictures to enhance your document.

There are some tasks you can perform with a DTP program that you would not expect a word processor to take on. Since the end-target of DTP work is often a typesetting machine rather than a printer, DTP programs offer the ability to create files suitable for use by such machines. You can create this type of file with WordPerfect, as described at the end of this chapter, but it is not particularly convenient to do so. Also, you cannot include specialized information such as *color separations,* a technique used when full-color publications are created.

While WordPerfect for Windows is clearly not a full-fledged DTP program, it can produce impressive results. If you are fairly knowledgeable about WordPerfect and follow the advice given in this chapter, you may well find that WordPerfect can meet most of your DTP needs, particularly in the area of newsletters, letterhead, and presentation materials.

Fantastic Sports
The premier sports enthusiasts newsletter

Volume 3, Week 1
September 1, 1994

DARTS OFFICIALLY RECOGNIZED AS OLYMPIC EVENT

September 19, 1994 will officially herald in the long-awaited event of *Darts* in the upcoming summer Olympics. Not since the introduction of the Javelin event has there been such an uproar over the rules and regulations of a sport. Says Jonathan Wilkes of the International Olympic Committee, "Many of the committee members clamored over the news that took many, even me, by surprise." Not all participating countries agree on the style and method of dart-throwing. For instance, since its invention in 1819, darts has evolved to include many strict rules, including the banning of "duplex lobbing" and the ever-popular "ricochet throwing." Many of the sports' enthusiasts in England, where the sport originated, purport that the rules of darts "cannot be loosely interpreted; to do so would result in the degradation of all rules that make the sport such a viable alternative to the more violent sports, such as rugby and some equestrian events." The committee promised, however, that none of the rules will be overlooked or compromised. In any case, darts has long been one of America's favorite pastimes. Now, as an Olympic event, Americans can compete on an even higher level and, perhaps, earn the gold medal.

HUNTER'S PARADISE

Hunters can expect much more excitement as they spend their time in the outdoors this season. No longer are they limited to pursuing the common elk, deer, moose, and antelope. Strangely enough, a new breed of wildlife has been introduced called "bindofers," which offer a faster chase, higher resistance to bullets and razor-tipped arrows, and a keener sense of smell. A spokesman for the Game and Wildlife commission claims that the wild bindofer can achieve speeds in excess of 120 mph! Indeed, this will offer an unsurpassed challenge to even the best hunters. Keep in mind that this new breed may not be for you, particularly if you hunt with guns or long bows. It is anticipated that more than 250 of these beasts will be set loose under authority of the US Game and Wildlife commission in the states of Montana, Wyoming, and northern portions of Colorado. You still need a license to hunt the bindofer, but these are available at

Figure 7-2. *A variation of the newsletter design seen in Figure 7-1*

Where to Start

The first step in creating documents like those in Figures 7-1 and 7-2 is to assemble the material you need to put into print. Typically, this consists of one or more pieces of text plus some art work. This art work can be divided into pictures that are subject matter and must be included, such as a sales graph or a diagram of the new product you are announcing, and decorative art that is optional, included only to improve the appearance of the document. You can add decorative art work to the layout later on, but essential graphics must be on hand when you begin the design process so you can determine the amount of space you will need.

Working from a Rough Idea

You might find it helpful to make a rough pencil sketch of what you want the finished document to look like. You might also want to collect examples of the type of document you are trying to create; looking at other people's work is a good way to stir your imagination. For example, if you are preparing a newsletter that will be sent to your customers, take a look at similar publications. Do you want a chatty and informal style, or are you trying to project a very polished and sophisticated image? You should decide such issues before you begin work on the newsletter since they affect everything from the font you use to the overall look of the document.

It definitely helps to have pencil and paper beside you as you work at the computer. This does not defeat the purpose of preparing the document on the computer. Bear in mind that you are using a computer to simplify tasks that were traditionally performed by cutting and pasting sections of typeset text and camera-ready art work.

The Select Printer Command

The first WordPerfect command you will want to use is Select Printer from the File menu. This displays the Select Printer dialog box, shown in Figure 7-3. The Printers list contains the names of printers that have already been installed. Check to make sure that the currently selected printer is the one on which you will be producing the final document. This ensures that the fonts you select for the document will be properly supported by the printer you are going to use.

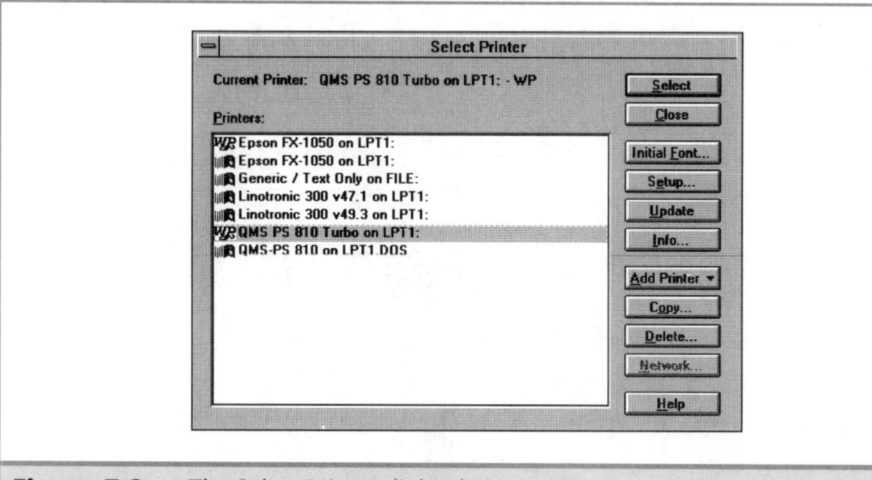

Figure 7-3. *The Select Printer dialog box*

NOTE: *You have a choice between WordPerfect and Windows printer drivers. It is strongly recommended you use a WordPerfect printer driver, as this will give you more accurate control of such adjustments as character spacing (described in the "Spacing" section later in this chapter).*

In the Printers list, highlight the printer you will be using for this document. Now choose Select to make this the default printer. The dialog box will disappear. If you now select Layout from the main menu and pick the Font command, the fonts listed in the Font dialog box will be those available for your printer. For more on the use of fonts, see the "Fonts" section later in this chapter.

A Fresh Start

It is best to begin your project with a fresh document, created by choosing File/New, rather than to try to transform an existing one. To start work on the document, define the page size by choosing Layout/Page. Choose Paper Size, and you will see the dialog box shown in Figure 7-4. This dialog box lists the sizes that are currently available on the default printer. There is a print orientation example displayed in the lower-right corner of the dialog box for any paper definition you select. Portrait orientation is shown in the figure.

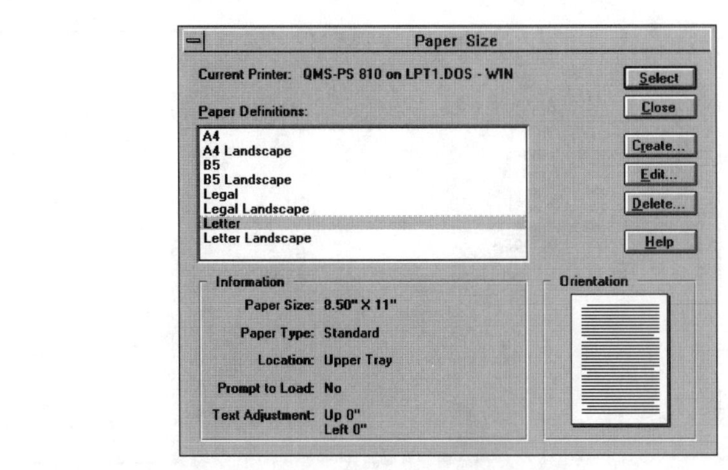

Figure 7-4. *The Paper Size dialog box*

NOTE: *The Paper Definitions list can be scrolled if you have more than nine sizes; if you do not see a suitable paper size for your document when you first select Layout/Page/Paper Size, use the mouse or arrow keys to move down the list.*

If the list does not include a suitable size, you can choose Create to select a new size from those supported by your printer. When you add a new size, it is included in the Paper Definitions list, and you can select it for the current document. When you choose Select in the Paper Size dialog box, you are returned to the document, and a page size code is placed in the document.

Basic Advice

Creating documents like the ones shown in this chapter involves a wide range of WordPerfect commands, as well as a basic understanding of design principles. Such principles are discussed in the section "Design Theory" later in this chapter. This chapter also helps you apply specific commands to typical DTP tasks. All of the commands you need are fully described in Chapter 11, "Commands and Features." For example, many desktop publishing projects involve columnar text, and you can find the information you need under the Columns entries in Chapter 11.

Minor adjustments to a document layout are sometimes required to properly align objects and achieve just the right effect. To do this in WordPerfect, you need to be familiar with the View/Reveal Codes menu choices and be comfortable with moving and deleting codes. You should also be familiar with the Layout/Typesetting/Advance menu choice, which is used extensively to ensure the accurate placement of items on the page.

Bear in mind that success with DTP normally takes time. There is no set formula for turning words into good-looking documents. Be prepared to proceed by trial and error. You can save one version of a document, try some changes, and then abandon them if they don't work. Computers are perfect tools for a "what-if" style of working. Once you have created one layout, don't be afraid to try a radical rearrangement. You can often achieve striking and effective results this way. You should also bear in mind the limits of WordPerfect. You will get further with the program if you look upon it as a word processor that can handle complex layouts rather than as a substitute for a full-featured desktop publishing program.

The Elements of DTP

There is no single WordPerfect command that changes what you do from word processing to desktop publishing. The art of DTP involves combining a variety of features that provide visual enhancement to a document. In the following sections, the main elements of DTP work are described and related to the corresponding features in WordPerfect.

Fonts

One of the basic decisions to be made at the start of a DTP project is which fonts to use. A *font* is a particular style or design applied to letters and numbers across a range of sizes. Fonts can be divided into two categories, *serif* and *sans serif,* meaning those with decorative extensions at the extremities (serifs) and those without.

In Figure 7-5 you can see a variety of serif and sans serif fonts. You will often see sans serif fonts used for headlines and section headings, with serif fonts used for the body of the text. It is generally accepted that large sections of text are easier to read if printed with a serif font. However, you can often achieve pleasing effects by mixing the two types of fonts. Furthermore, you should not be afraid to experiment; you can often achieve effective results by challenging the accepted principles of document design.

This is Helvetica - a sans serif font - 14 point

This is Helvetica - a sans serif font - 12 point

This is Times Roman - a serif font - 14 point

This is Times Roman - a serif font - 12 point

This is Palatino - a serif font - 16 point

This is Gothic - a sans serif font - 18 point

Figure 7-5. *A variety of fonts*

One useful principle that applies to fonts in general is that the longer the line length, the larger the font should be. Short lines, such as those created by placing text into columns, call for a smaller type. Lines of text that extend across the page, as in a typical business letter, require a larger font. Fonts are measured in points, as in Helvetica 12 point. (One point is 1/72 of one inch.)

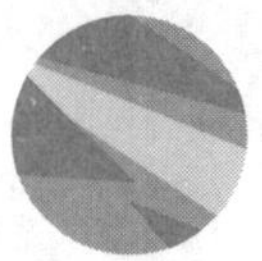

NOTE: An alternative to increasing the font size is to adjust the amount of space in the margins or between columns. You can make a more subtle adjustment by altering the amount of space between letters and words, using the options described in the "Word Spacing and Letterspacing" section later in this chapter.

For each printer you use with WordPerfect, there is an initial font. When you select the default printer for your project and then create a new document, this font becomes the current font, shown at the bottom of the screen. You can choose File/Select Printer/Initial Font to change the initial font.

To change the font or simply to check which font styles are offered by the current printer, select Layout/Font (or press F9). You will see the fonts listed alphabetically by name, as shown in Figure 7-6. The current font is highlighted in the list.

To see what each font looks like, first press HOME to make sure you start at the top of the list. Then simply press the DOWN ARROW key to move the highlighting from one name to the next. WordPerfect shows you a sample of the highlighted font in the lower-left corner of the dialog box. To see what a different size looks

Figure 7-6. *The Font list*

like, select Font Size and adjust the setting. To leave the Font dialog box without actually changing the current font, select Cancel.

You might want to print a document containing a sample of each font in a variety of sizes to help you choose appropriate fonts for the body, headlines, headings, headers, footers, captions, and other sections of your document. You can use a macro to create a font sample document. The macro should select a font, type a piece of text, move down to the next line, and then select another font. In the next chapter you will find a macro of this type described in greater detail.

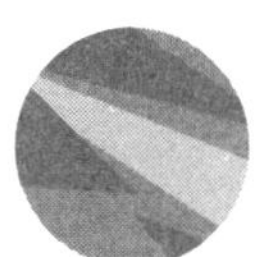

NOTE: *If you find yourself working with fonts quite a bit, consider applying fonts by way of styles. If you format each section of text with a style and decide to change the font later, you can make the font change in the style itself. All text formatted with a particular style will then change automatically. (See the section "Styles for DTP" later in this chapter.)*

Spacing

When you are typing an ordinary business letter, the exact amount of space between characters and lines is not critical; however, spacing can be crucial to the appearance of more complex documents. To achieve DTP-style results with WordPerfect, you will need to be familiar with such terms as kerning and leading.

Kerning

Kerning is the ability to move two characters closer together so they look better; it was devised to overcome the problem illustrated in Figure 7-7. You can see that without kerning, there is too much white space between the first two letters in "WordPerfect." Because this problem is particularly apparent when you are using larger fonts, it often affects headlines in newsletters. Some printers support automatic kerning, which allows WordPerfect to adjust appropriate pairs of characters throughout a document.

If you enter text in a large font and notice an unsightly gap between some pairs of letters, there are two ways you can apply kerning. The first is called *manual kerning.* This allows you to kern one pair of characters at a time. Manual kerning will be described more fully in a moment. The other type of kerning is *automatic kerning.* To activate automatic kerning, select the option, Layout/Typesetting/Word/Letterspacing. The Word Spacing and Letterspacing dialog box, shown in Figure 7-8, allows you to adjust several aspects of word and character spacing.

In the bottom-left corner of the dialog box, you can select Automatic Kerning to turn on kerning for the whole document. The Automatic Kerning option will

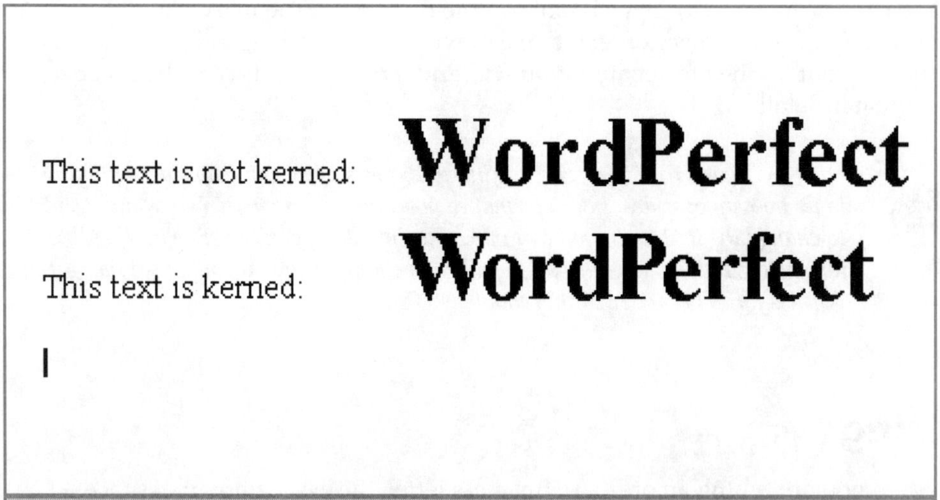

This text is not kerned: WordPerfect

This text is kerned: WordPerfect

Figure 7-7. *An example of kerning*

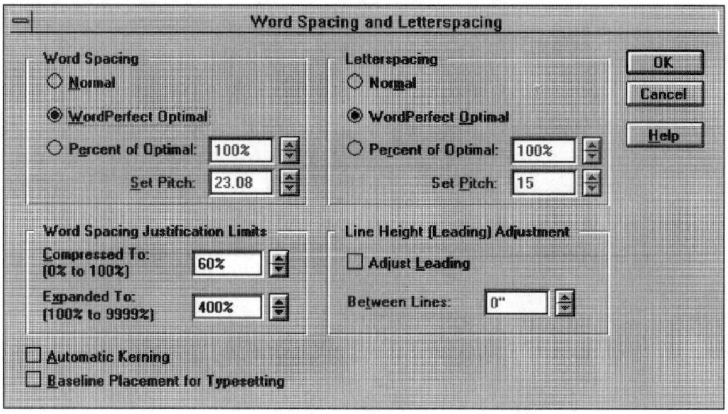

Figure 7-8. *The Word Spacing and Letterspacing dialog box*

not have any effect on your document if your printer font does not support kerning. You can perform automatic kerning only with proportionally spaced fonts and then only if the printer supports this feature.

A quick way to check if automatic kerning is available is to open a new document, choose the printer you want, and then choose the font and size you want. Type some text that would normally require kerning, such as **Word**. Then press ENTER for a new line and select Automatic Kerning from the Word Spacing and Letterspacing dialog box. Select OK, and when you return to the document, select View/Page to make sure you are in high-resolution viewing. Use the Zoom feature to enlarge the text. Check the second line to see if the *W* and *o* are closer together than in the line above. If they are, then the font can be kerned automatically.

Even if the printer and font selections you have made do not support automatic kerning, you can manually adjust spacing between any two characters. To do this, place the insertion point between the two letters that need adjusting. Then select Layout/Typesetting/Manual Kerning; the Manual Kerning dialog box appears, as shown here:

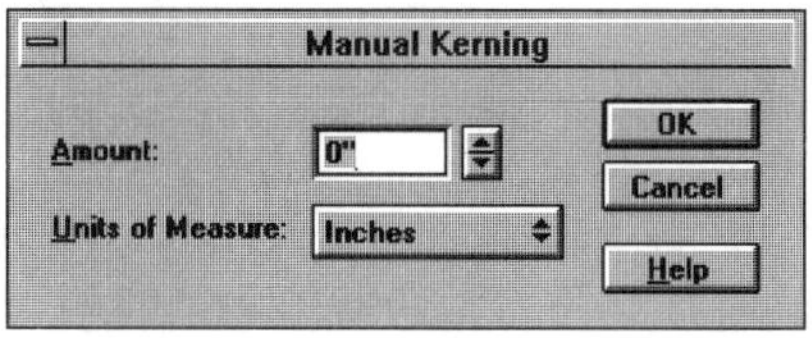

This dialog box will appear in such a way that you can still see your insertion point on the screen. As you adjust the spacing within the dialog box, you will be able to immediately see the effect within your document. The Amount box shows the current spacing between the characters, which is 0 if there is no kerning in effect.

Use the up and down arrows next to the Amount box to increase or decrease the amount of space between letters. (Spacing greater than 0 widens the gaps and is a positive number; spacing less than 0 narrows the gap and is a negative number.) Instead of clicking the arrows, you can type a specific amount, bearing in mind the current Units of Measure setting.

NOTE: *You can enter a value in any unit of measure, regardless of the current setting. For instance, if the document is in inches, you can type* ***-1p*** *to adjust by one point. WordPerfect will convert the point to inches automatically.*

The effect of changing the kerning amount will be shown in your document. When the gap is acceptable, select OK to return to your document. You see the effect of manual kerning right away because WordPerfect has actually inserted an advance code in the text, specifying the exact position of the second character in the pair. If you use Reveal Codes you can see this.

Word Spacing and Letterspacing

The WordPerfect printer definitions include rules for word spacing and letterspacing appropriate to each printer; however, you may want to adjust this spacing. For example, if body text seems too dense, you can increase the letterspacing, word spacing, or both. Similarly, you can tighten up body text that appears to have too much white space in it by decreasing the word spacing and letterspacing.

As you saw in Figure 7-8, the Word Spacing and Letterspacing dialog box contains sections for both word spacing and letterspacing. The choices available for word spacing and letterspacing are Normal, WordPerfect Optimal, Percent of Optimal, and Set Pitch. Normal is the printer manufacturer's suggested spacing. WordPerfect Optimal is the choice made by WordPerfect Corporation when it designed the printer driver. Percent of Optimal is where you tell WordPerfect that you want spacing more or less than optimal. The Set Pitch box allows you to enter a setting in the more familiar measure of pitch, such as 10 pitch. WordPerfect will then convert this to a percent of optimal.

A setting of less than 100 percent in the Percent of Optimal box decreases the space, and a setting greater than 100 percent increases the space. You can use this option to create the effect seen in the letterhead design in Figure 7-9. The first line has normal WordPerfect Optimal spacing. The second line uses a different font, and the letterspacing was increased to 220 percent of optimal to stretch the word.

Since you cannot immediately see the effects of changes you make to word spacing and letterspacing, you will need to use trial and error to create the effects you want. In Figure 7-10 you can see the revealed codes of the document in Figure 7-9.

If you do adjust word spacing or letterspacing, remember to change it back to the previous setting. (If you select the section of text to be adjusted and then issue the command, the code to return to normal spacing is automatically inserted at the end of the selected text.) In Figure 7-10, the typesetting command was used while the word "Corporation" was selected.

Leading and Line Height

The amount of space between lines of text is referred to as *leading* (pronounced *ledding*), a term that comes from the days when type was set by hand. Typesetters adjusted the space between lines by inserting pieces of lead between the rows of type. The amount of leading plus the height of the letters gives the total distance between one line and the next.

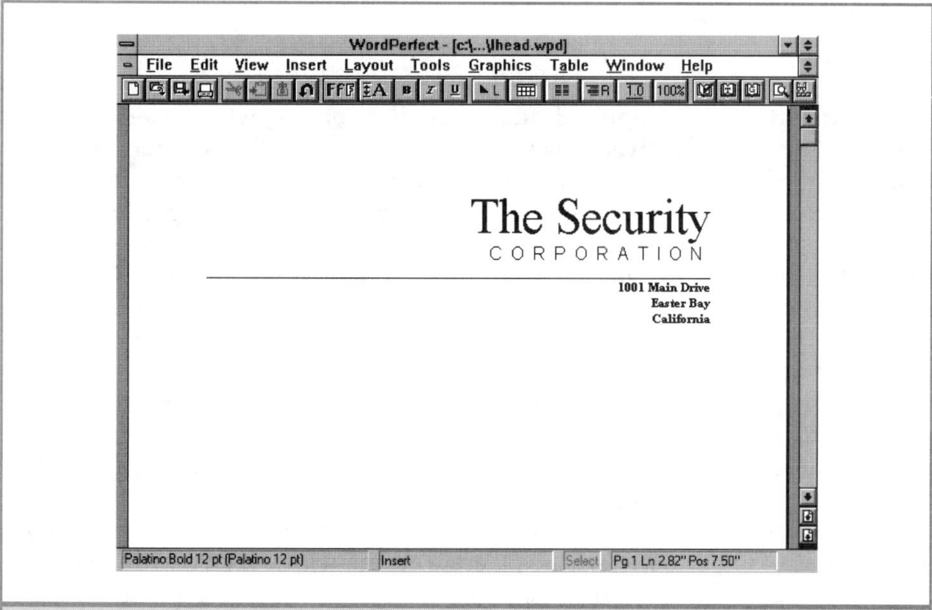

Figure 7-9. *The effect of adjustments to letterspacing*

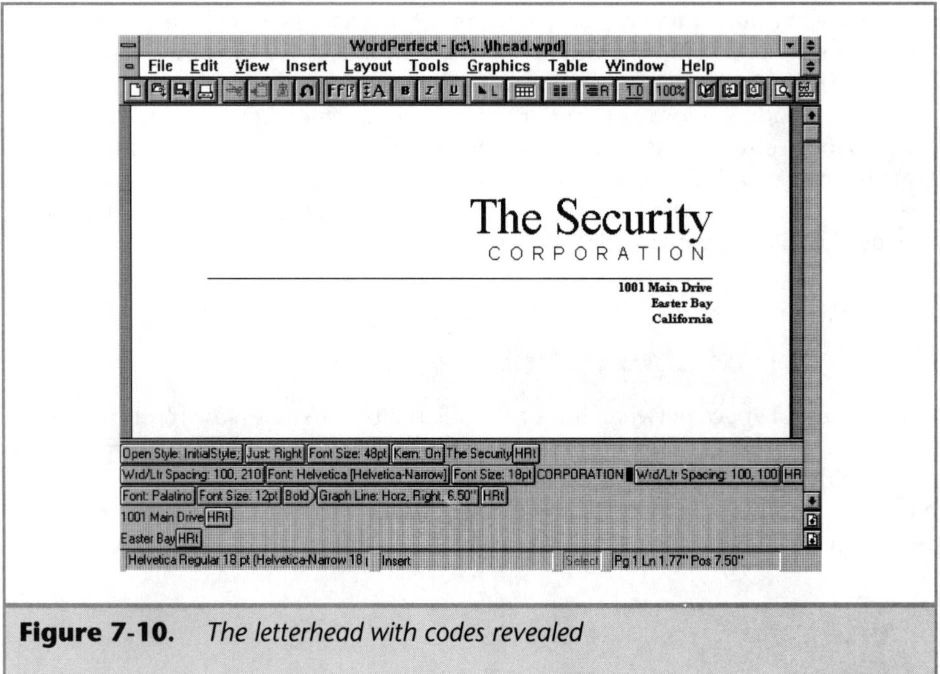

Figure 7-10. *The letterhead with codes revealed*

It is important to distinguish leading from line spacing, which refers to the number of blank lines between lines of text (as in single or double spacing) and which you set by selecting Layout/Line/Spacing. Think of leading as the setting that determines the height of a single spaced line. Typically, leading is from 110 to 120 percent of the font size. In WordPerfect, 2 points are usually added to a font to determine the leading. Thus, a 14-point font with 2 points of leading gives a total line height setting of 16 points.

Most of the time you do not have to worry about leading. WordPerfect adjusts the line height for whatever font you are using. When there is more than one font on a line, the line height increases to make room for the largest font. However, there will be times when you want to use the Line Height (Leading) Adjustment section of the Word Spacing and Letterspacing dialog box to alter the amount of space between lines.

The leading setting is useful when you are trying to fit a section of text into a specific space—for example, when you are working with a text box. (See the section "Text Boxes" later in this chapter.) Here is an example of expanded leading used to fill out a specific space:

> **"Encryption is a special computation that operates on messages, converting them into representation that is meaningless for all parties other than the intended receiver."**

Remember that the amount you specify for the leading setting is applied to all fonts used after the point in the text where the leading adjustment is made.

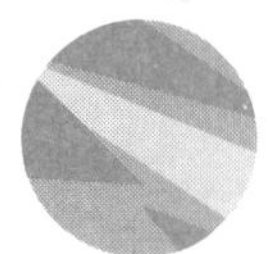

NOTE: *If you select a section of text before applying the leading adjustment, it affects only the selected text.*

WordPerfect also allows you to fix an absolute line height. This is useful in situations where you just have one or two lines to adjust and the same font is used throughout. In Figure 7-11 you can see the earlier letterhead example with increased line height in the address.

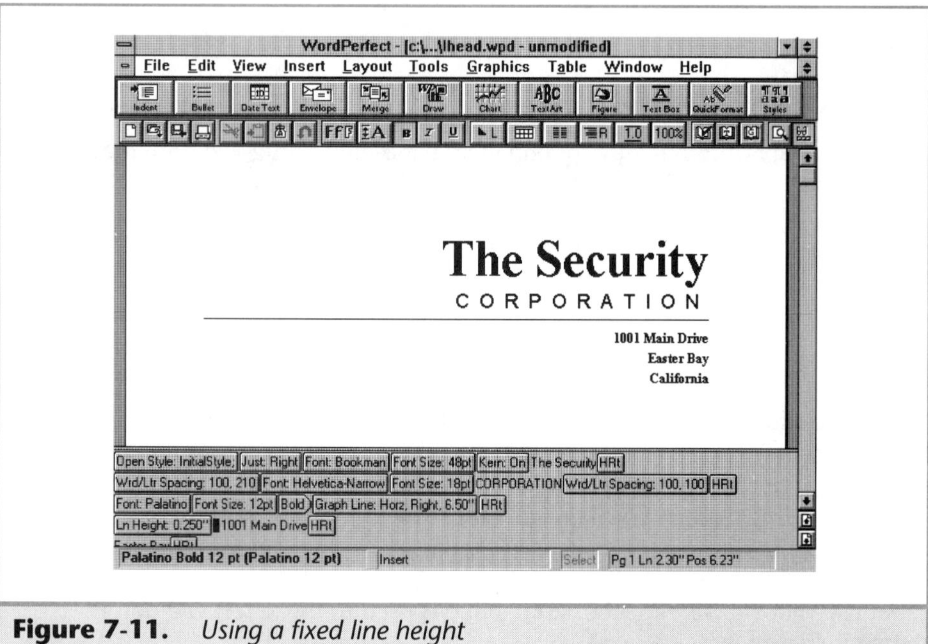

Figure 7-11. *Using a fixed line height*

You set a fixed line height by selecting Layout/Line/Height. This produces the dialog box shown here:

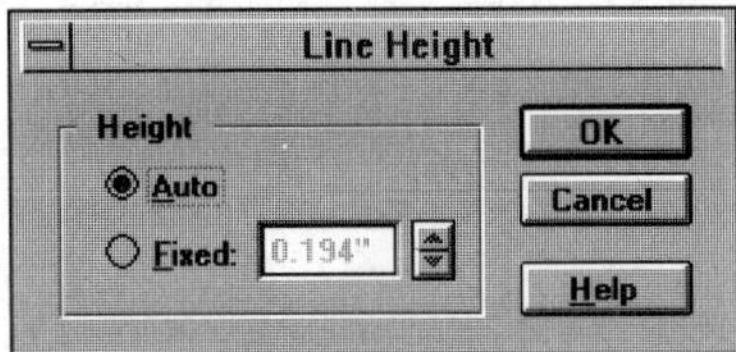

Remember that the line height is measured from the base of one line to the base of the next, regardless of the font you are using. You probably won't want to set a line height for sections of text that include a mixture of fonts. If you select a section of text before selecting Layout/Line/Height, WordPerfect adds the auto code at the end of the selection. However, be sure that the formatting code is placed one line after the last line for which you are fixing the height.

The default measurement for line height displayed when you select the Fixed option is based on the current font and measured in inches. You can enter your setting as inches or follow it with **p** for points. The setting will be converted to the default unit of measurement. Thus, you would enter **36p** for a setting of 36 points, which is half an inch (since there are 72 points to the inch). You could also enter **.5**; WordPerfect will assume you mean inches.

Graphics Elements

There are many different ways of enhancing and enlivening text with graphics elements such as lines, boxes, and pictures. While WordPerfect does not provide drawing tools (outside of a special drawing program), with a little imagination you can use items like lines and boxes to good effect.

Drawing Lines

You can add horizontal and vertical lines of virtually any thickness and shading anywhere in a WordPerfect document. Sometimes referred to as rules, these lines help the eye to distinguish between different sections of a document. Lines can set off a heading or a graphics image. Lines are often used in headers and footers to separate them from body text, as in Figure 7-21 shown later in this chapter. You can place lines at the left and right margins to create a border, or between columns, as in Figure 7-2. A horizontal line is used in the letterhead design shown in Figure 7-11.

You can place lines on your page by using the Graphics menu. Select either Horizontal Line or Vertical Line, and you will see a line appear on your screen. Once the line appears, you have great flexibility in sizing and positioning the line.

In WordPerfect for Windows, you can place lines just about anywhere. Vertical lines can be aligned with the top or bottom margin of the page, centered, or positioned full, meaning from the top to the bottom margin. They can have a horizontal location at the left margin, right margin, or between columns. Location can also be specified with an exact measurement. Horizontal lines can have a specific vertical location or be placed at the baseline, meaning immediately below a line of text. Horizontal lines can be located at the left or right margin, centered, or positioned full, meaning from the left to the right margin.

Once you have placed the line in the document, you can size and move it with your mouse. To move the line, place the mouse pointer over the line. You will see the pointer change from the editing I-beam to an arrow. You can now press the left mouse button to grab the line and move it to a new location. When the line is selected in this way, handles appear around the line, as you can see in Figure 7-12. Handles appear around the line to allow you to stretch or shrink it.

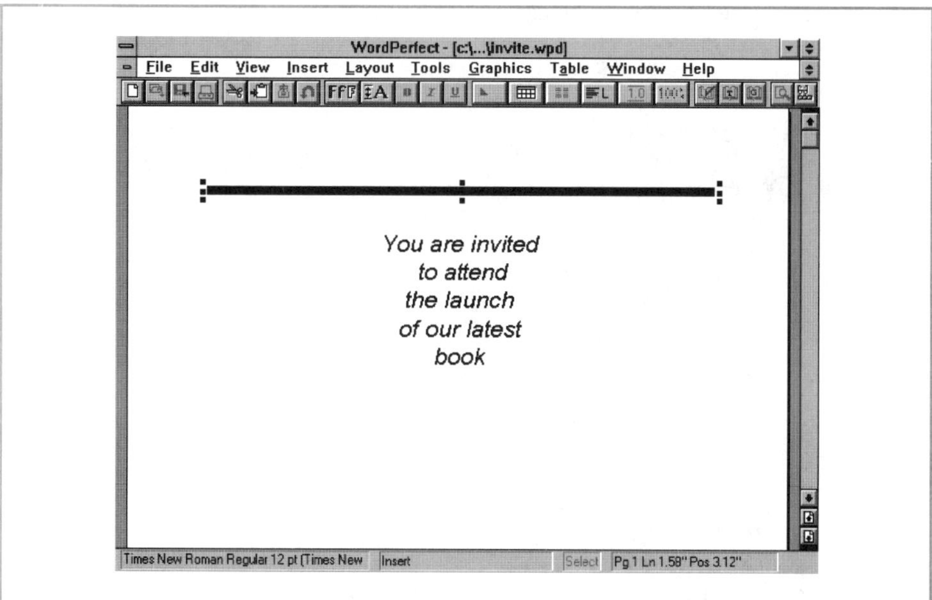

Figure 7-12. *Adjusting a line with the mouse*

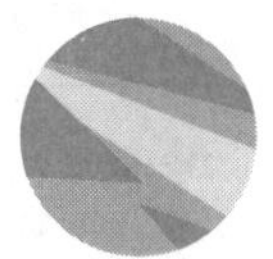

NOTE: Not only can you adjust the length of the line with the mouse, but by moving the handles in the middle of the line, you can also adjust the line's thickness.

When you release the line, WordPerfect records its new size and location. If you double-click the mouse button while pointing to a line, you can pop-up the Edit Graphics Line dialog box. This shows the exact dimensions, location, and attributes of the line, and you can edit these settings. For example, the line in Figure 7-13 has been changed to a light grey color.

Thick lines can be very useful as a drawing tool for making rectangles or solid boxes. Varying the color of lines can add to the visual impact of these objects.

Not only can you maneuver lines with the mouse and alter their size, you can quickly duplicate them. To do so, first select the line and select Edit/Copy. Then select Edit/Paste. A duplicate line will appear next to the original. You can then drag the duplicate to a new location.

Building Boxes

There are four types of boxes you can use to enhance your documents: figure, text, equation, and custom. The commands for creating and editing these boxes

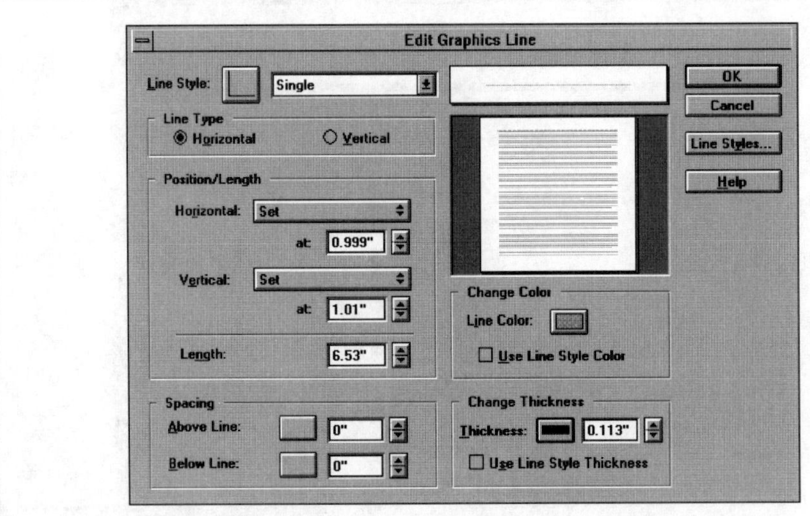

Figure 7-13. *The Edit Graphics Line dialog box*

are covered in Chapter 11, "Commands and Features," in the Graphics entries. Before looking at how these boxes can be used in documents like the newsletter in Figure 7-1, it is useful to point out that the type of box does not necessarily refer to its contents. Images, text, or equations can be placed in any type of box. The main purpose of the box type is to allow consistency when compiling lists of boxes.

When you select Graphics/Custom Box, WordPerfect displays the Custom Box dialog box, shown in Figure 7-14. In the Style Name list, you can select the style of box you want to create.

You can sometimes save time by creating custom boxes instead of text or figure boxes. For example, suppose you want all of your text and figure boxes to have the same border style—a thick border on all four sides. The quickest way to do this is to define the box style for both text and figure boxes, and then use the Custom Box dialog box to insert the boxes as necessary.

If you want to use a variety of border styles for your boxes, you can create a variety of types, each of which has its own border style. In this case, the user box allows you one more style of box.

Box Styles

If you choose Graphics/Graphics Styles from the menu, you will see the Graphics Styles dialog box, shown in Figure 7-15. Here you can select the type of box style you want to modify. The changes you make here will affect how your boxes appear throughout your document. You can even create new box styles that can be used for special purposes.

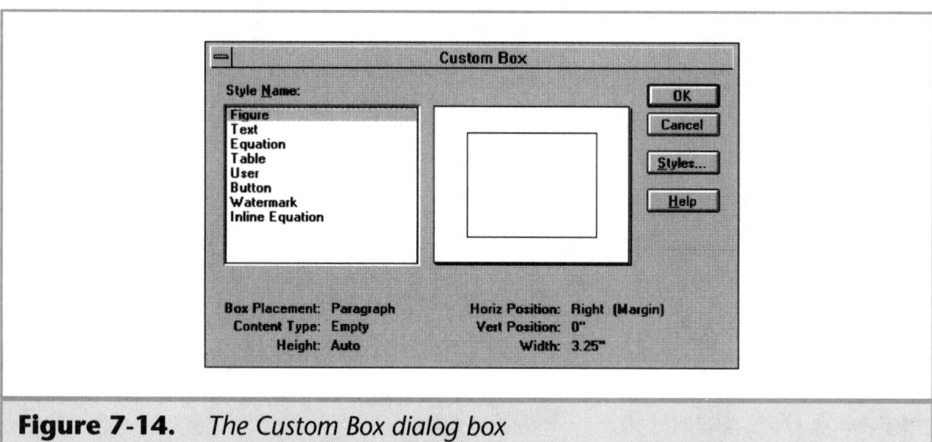

Figure 7-14. *The Custom Box dialog box*

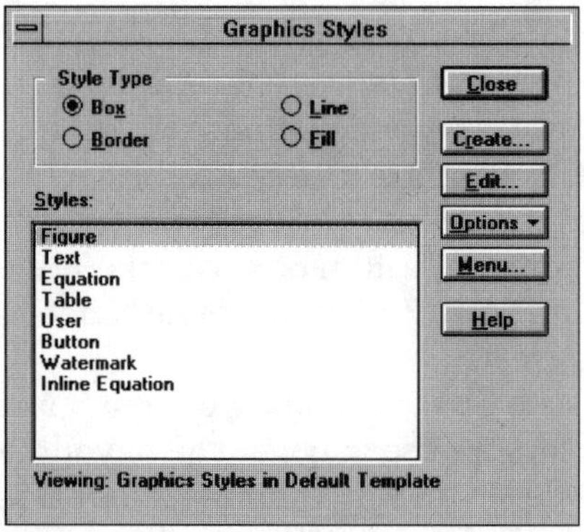

Figure 7-15. *The Graphics Styles dialog box*

To edit a box style, simply choose the style you want to edit from those listed, then click on the Edit button. You will see the Edit Box Style dialog box, as shown in Figure 7-16. Here you can change the attributes used to display and control the box.

You should feel free to experiment with boxes—both creating box styles and using them in your documents. Boxes can be used to effectively present information and to break up the monotony of straight text. If you need information about how to use any of the box style settings, refer to Chapter 11, "Commands and Features."

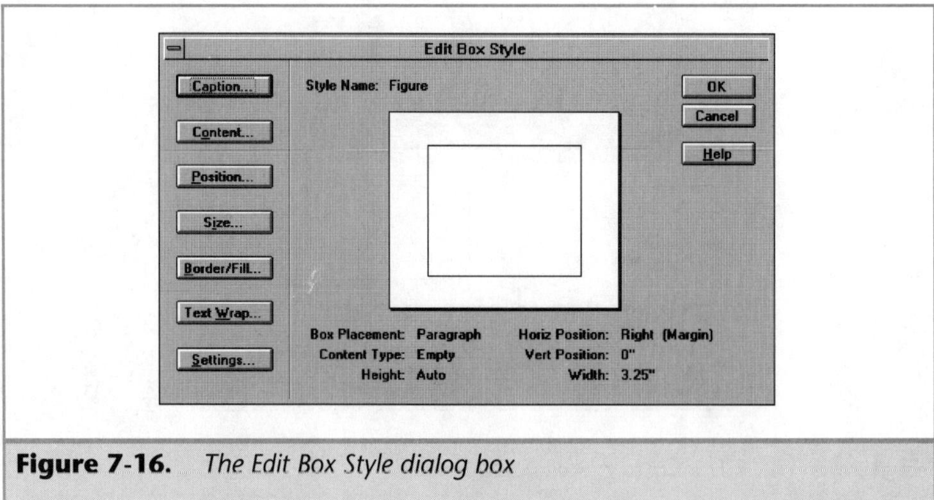

Figure 7-16. *The Edit Box Style dialog box*

Text Boxes

Many magazines make effective use of *boxed text,* sections of text that are set apart from the main body of text. Such boxes, sometimes called *sidebars,* allow authors to address a wider range of readers. A typical example would be an article about espionage, with a sidebar explaining commonly used acronyms. The sidebar avoids the need to define each acronym as it is introduced, which might be boring for the more knowledgeable reader. On the other hand, readers less familiar with the acronyms are not left out.

There are many other uses for boxed text. Important quotes are often boxed out and placed in bold type to draw attention to them. This can be an effective way of arousing the interest of casual readers. Box out a provocative quote, and a reader who might otherwise have ignored the article decides to take a closer look.

Boxes are also useful for sections of text that need quite separate formatting from the surrounding writing. For example, many magazines include a masthead that lists the names of the editors and staff. Centered and formatted in a small font, the masthead may extend the full length of a page, parallel to other text. It is easier to place the text in a box than to use a system of uneven columns.

Since WordPerfect provides all the usual editing tools when you edit a text box, you could place an entire page into a text box to give it a border. However, it is much easier to use the Layout/Page/Border/Fill option than to place that much text into a box. For one thing, boxed text must fit the size of the box. Although you can adjust the size of the box with the mouse, making an exact match between a large amount of text and the size of the box can be tricky. Furthermore, WordPerfect does not allow you to flow text from one box to the next. If you were to box an article starting on the front page of a newsletter and then continue the story on the next page, you would have to manually split the text between the boxes.

Figure Boxes

There is a good chance you are already familiar with figure boxes, and you have seen several examples of such boxes already in this book. The normal use of such boxes is to add illustrations to documents. These can be informative, decorative, or symbolic.

Figure boxes can be used for a wide variety of purposes. For instance, you can place your company logo in a figure box, or you can use them to contain other special flourishes that add to the overall impact of your document.

Bullets

When your documents include a list of items, you can number them by using the new features of WordPerfect for Windows. You can see numerous examples of both bulleted and numbered lists throughout this book. For instance, the following is a three-item bulleted list:

- This is the first item in the list.
- This is the second item in the list, and it is a bit longer than the first (it even runs longer than one line).
- This is the third, and final, item in the list.

The same information can also be formatted as a numbered list:

1. This is the first item in the list.
2. This is the second item in the list, and it is a bit longer than the first (it even runs longer than one line).
3. This is the third, and final, item in the list.

To create a list, first select the text you want included in the list. Then choose Insert/Bullets & Numbers. This displays the Bullets & Numbers dialog box shown in Figure 7-17. There are several different formats listed in the Styles list. These include various types of bullets and numbering.

To apply either a type of bullet or type of numbering to each paragraph in the selected text, simply select the style you want, and then click on the OK button.

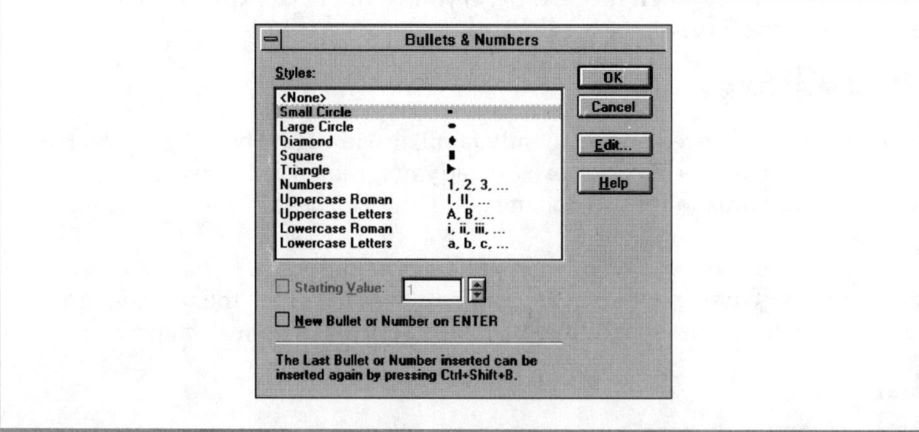

Figure 7-17. *The Bullets & Numbers dialog box*

Adding a Dash

When you want to put a dash between items of text, you probably type a hyphen, like this:

Here is the last-and most important-point.

However, the hyphen does not always look the part. In published documents you will see a slightly different character used for dashes, partly to distinguish them from hyphens, which are used only at the ends of lines and between words that are normally hyphenated. There are two alternatives to the hyphen character: the em dash and the en dash. The em dash is slightly longer than the en dash. Both are printed as thinner lines than hyphens.

Before inserting an em or en dash, place the insertion point in the text at the point where you want the dash to appear. Then select Insert/Character from the menu (or press CTRL+W). You will see the dialog box shown in Figure 7-18. Delete the contents of the Number box and type the letter *m* followed by a hyphen: **m-**. This will change to the Typographic Symbols character set and highlight the em dash in the Characters box. If you want an en dash, type **n-**. Now select Insert and Close, and the character will be placed in your document.

You may want to insert a hyphenation soft return code after the dash. Because em and en dashes are treated like regular characters, not hyphens, words connected with an em dash are normally treated as one for the purposes of word wrapping. Adding the hyphenation soft return code tells WordPerfect that the line can break after the dash. Consider the sentence

This use of dashes makes for attractive text—but beware of line endings.

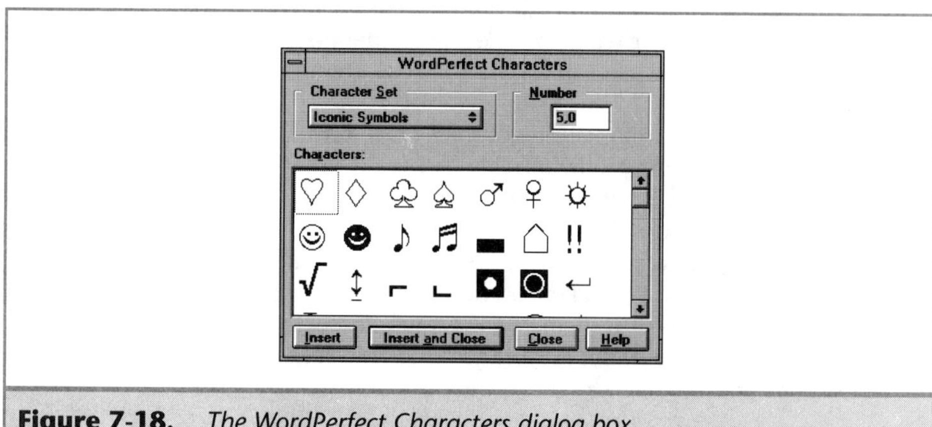

Figure 7-18. *The WordPerfect Characters dialog box*

If you have not inserted a hyphenation soft return code, you may be prompted to hyphenate "text—but" since WordPerfect regards the em dash as a regular character and thus treats both words as one.

You insert the hyphenation soft return code by selecting Layout/Line/Other Codes. Select Soft Hyphen and then Insert. The code will be used to break the line only if the code falls at the end of the line. If the code does not fall at the end of the line, it will not be used. You can use this technique in macros that write em dashes as well as keyboard assignments.

Cross-References

When you are working on newsletter- or magazine-style documents some articles will flow from one page to another. Others will need to be split up, with the article starting in one place and continuing elsewhere. You can use the Cross-Reference feature to insert phrases like "Continued on page 5." On page five the article could begin with the phrase "Continued from page 1." Refer to the section on Cross-References in Chapter 11 for more details on this feature.

Styles for DTP

Choosing Layout/Styles (or pressing the ALT+F8 shortcut key) gives you the ability to store complex collections of formatting codes and apply them in documents without having to repeat all of the formatting steps. A style developed for headings in a newsletter can be applied to each heading very quickly. Simply select the text that forms the heading, select Layout/Styles, choose the style you want, and select Apply.

Although you still have to apply the style for each piece of heading text, the savings from using styles, both in effort and potential errors, are considerable. Even greater savings occur when you decide to change the style. By editing the heading style, perhaps to use a different font, you change all headings formatted with that style.

Remember that you can include graphics lines within styles if you insert the appropriate codes. When you include lines in styles, do not use the Specific option for location; instead, use a relative measurement such as baseline and left, for example, for a horizontal line.

You can make effective use of styles when applying numbering or bulleting to lists. The Edit button in the Bullets & Numbers dialog box, shown in Figure 7-17, takes you to the Styles Editor dialog box. This dialog box, shown in Figure 7-19, allows you to change the bullet or number style you selected before you clicked on the Edit button.

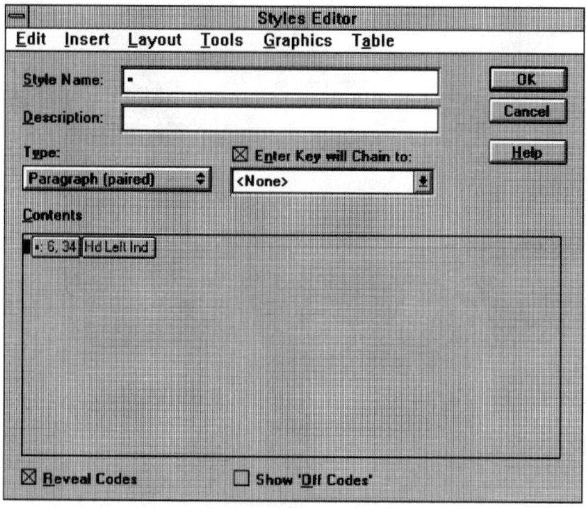

Figure 7-19. *The Styles Editor dialog box*

Notice the setting for the style Type. A paired style is usually best for list items. You can make any changes you desire, with the codes or text for the style appearing in the Contents box. After making any changes you desire, select OK to close the Style Editor.

You can easily use WordPerfect to create custom styles. All you need to do is select Layout/Styles from the menu. You will then see the Style List dialog box, as shown in Figure 7-20.

You can then click on the Quick Create button to create a style based on the paragraph in which the insertion point is located. Or, if you prefer, you can click on Create to access the same Styles Editor dialog box shown in Figure 7-19. You can then define any formatting codes or text that you want assigned to this style. When you click on OK, the style is saved using the name you specify.

To later apply a style, you can use the Layout/Styles menu choice again. When you see the Style List dialog box, select the name of the style you want to use, and then click on Apply.

Building a Newsletter

If you are working on a DTP project like a newsletter, you will want to customize the WordPerfect program settings. Apart from selecting the correct printer and

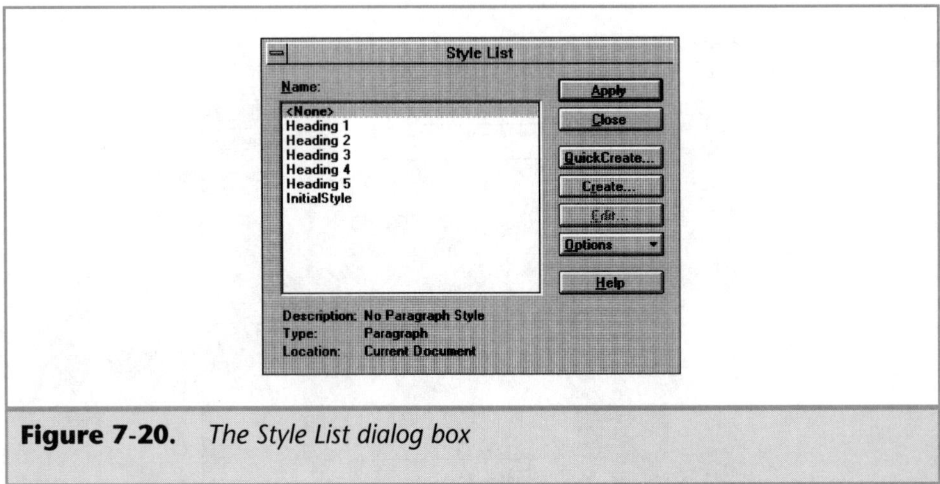

Figure 7-20. *The Style List dialog box*

page size and customizing the button bar, you may want to load a special keyboard. Of course, you will not know exactly which macros you need or which keys and buttons you want to redefine for DTP work until you have had some experience putting together complex documents. The point to bear in mind when you start your first DTP project is that these customization features are there to help as your skills develop.

Headers and Footers

Most newsletters use either a header or a footer to print information such as page numbers, the title, and the issue date on each page. Once you have selected the printer, page size, and basic top, bottom, left, and right margins, defining headers and footers is a good place to begin your newsletter.

An effective way of creating a top and bottom border for your document is to include full-width lines in both a header or footer. You can set the margins of the header and footer wider than those of the body of the document to draw the line wider than the body text. You may want to suppress the header and/or footer on the first page of the newsletter. However, a footer may not be out of place on the first page, as shown in Figure 7-21.

Logos and Headlines

While it is the content of a newsletter that makes it worth reading, the design of the front page, including the title and main headlines, can make a difference in getting people to give the document a second glance. There are likely to be several elements involved in the top half of the front page: the newsletter title, date, issue number, price, and other practical information; the headlines for the main article or articles; and possibly a logo or design.

The details at the bottom of the newsletter in Figure 7-21 were created with a two-column layout, using parallel as opposed to newspaper-style columns. Alternatively, you can arrange text elements like these by using a number of text boxes. Figure boxes without borders can accommodate logos, and these can even be placed behind text if you turn off the feature for wrapping text around the box. You can also use lines of varying width and shading to give a good effect.

Headlines are usually placed in a large font. A sans serif font, as shown in Figure 7-21, can be used for a headline that is above body text in a serif font. Be careful not to make the headline so large that it overpowers the newsletter title or so small that it fails to catch the reader's eye.

Body Text

You can type the content of your newsletter in a simple WordPerfect document that contains no complex formatting codes. This makes it easier to edit and make major corrections to your document than if you typed it directly into a complex layout. Perform a spell-check on the document and store it on disk.

Most newsletters arrange their text in two or more columns, depending on the font style and type size. After setting up any headers or footers and placing the newsletter title and headline, define columns for your text and turn on the columns. Select a small font size appropriate to the width of the columns. Then you can select Insert/File to insert into the columns the document containing the body text.

Once you have inserted the text into the columns, you can still make corrections or alterations to the text, including a final spell-check before publication (something that is not possible with all DTP programs). For example, you will want to alter text if awkward word spacing and placement exist that cannot be fixed by hyphenation (as described in the next section). If you are using full justification in your columns to give them a "newspaper" look, you might want to alter wording to reduce any excess, unsightly white space that can appear. Also check for *stacking*—that is, the same word appearing at the beginning of two or more successive lines—because such occurrences can be confusing to the reader as they are scanning your text.

Fantastic Sports

The premier sports enthusiasts newsletter

Volume 3, Week 1
September 1994

DARTS OFFICIALLY RECOGNIZED AS OLYMPIC EVENT

September 19, 1994 will officially herald in the long-awaited event of *Darts* in the upcoming summer Olympics. Not since the introduction of the Javelin event has there been such an uproar over the rules and regulations of a sport. Says Jonathan Wilkes of the International Olympic Committee, "Many of the committee members clamored over the news that took many, even me, by surprise." Not all participating countries agree on the style and method of dart-throwing. For instance, since its invention in 1819, darts has evolved to include many strict rules, including the banning of "duplex lobbing" and the ever-popular "ricochet throwing." Many of the sports' enthusiasts in England, where the sport originated, purport that the rules of darts "cannot be loosely interpreted; to do so would result in the degradation of all rules that make the sport such a viable alternative to the more violent sports, such as rugby and some equestrian events." The committee promised, however, that none of the rules will be overlooked or compromised. In any case, darts has long been one of America's favorite pastimes. Now, as an Olympic event, Americans can compete on an even higher level and, perhaps, earn the gold medal.

HUNTER'S PARADISE

Hunters can expect much more excitement as they spend their time in the outdoors this season. No longer are they limited to pursuing the common elk, deer, moose, and antelope. Strangely enough, a new breed of wildlife has been introduced called "bindofers," which offer a faster chase, higher resistance to bullets and razor-tipped arrows, and a keener sense of smell. A spokesman for the Game and Wildlife commission claims that the wild bindofer can achieve speeds in excess of 120 mph! Indeed, this will offer an unsurpassed challenge to even the best hunters. Keep in mind that this new breed may not be for you, particularly if you hunt with guns or long bows. It is anticipated that more than 250 of these beasts will be set loose under authority of the US Game and Wildlife commission in the states of Montana, Wyoming, and northern portions of Colorado. You still need a license to hunt the bindofer, but these are available at

Fantastic Sports *September 1994* Page 1 of 5

Figure 7-21. *A newsletter design*

Hyphenation

Your text will fit into columns more neatly if you hyphenate it. However, editing text with hyphenation turned on can be annoying, particularly if you are moving boxes around and the text has to keep rewrapping around them. Try saving the hyphenation process until you are reasonably sure of your layout and the content of the text. After turning on hyphenation and reviewing its effects, you can alter the hyphenation percentages, reducing them if you want more words to be split.

Unfortunately, hyphenation is not a cure-all for word spacing. You may still want to add or reorder words to remove white spaces. You can also adjust the word spacing setting, described earlier in this chapter. It is a good idea to have someone else review a draft of the document for the less fortunate effects of word splitting and stacking; you can then make the necessary changes to the text to remove them.

Creating Letterhead Stationery

Many organizations spend a lot of money on preprinted letterhead stationery. In today's fast-moving business climate, letterhead often needs revising before the current stock is used up. It could be a change to the corporate logo, a change of address, or the need to add a fax number. Using your laser printer to print letterhead onto good-quality stock can save a lot of money. You can even print matching envelopes, which are particularly expensive to order from a print shop. You can see an example of a company letterhead in Figure 7-22.

Because you can print out your design very quickly with a laser or inkjet printer, you can make draft copies of a letterhead design on inexpensive paper for others in your office to comment on or approve. When the design is accepted, you can then print the letterhead on more expensive stock.

There is one practical consideration when creating letterhead with your word processor. Suppose you store the letterhead in a file called LHEAD. When you need to write a letter, you could retrieve LHEAD and add the text of the letter, saving the results in a new file. Unfortunately, this can result in a lot of disk space being taken up by the repetition of the graphics of the letterhead in each letter file. To avoid this problem, slightly alter the process you use when you insert a graphic figure in your document. When you choose Graphic/Figure, you will see the Insert Image dialog box shown in Figure 7-23.

Notice in the bottom-right corner of the Insert Image dialog box there is a checkbox called Image on Disk. If you select this option, WordPerfect will not

Computer Security Network
1001 Solid Place
Safe Haven
California
USA 93575

Figure 7-22. *A letterhead design*

store the actual graphics image with the document. Instead, the graphic will remain separately on disk, and will only be loaded when it is needed for display or printing.

An alternative is to print the LHEAD file without any body text and use the results as a "blank page" when you type a letter. Most laser printers will print twice on the same sheet of paper without any problem. A third possibility is to use a merge operation to combine LHEAD and a file containing the body of your letter.

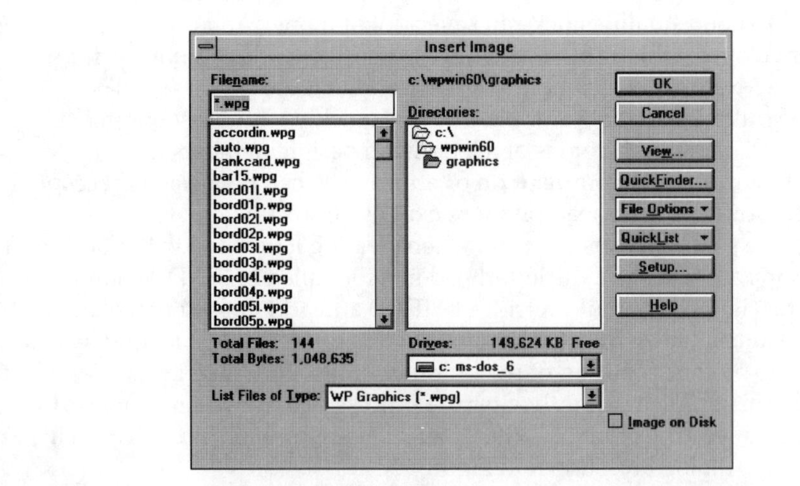

Figure 7-23. *The Insert Image dialog box*

Presentations

These days there is much talk of multimedia and PCs as presentation tools. You can use WordPerfect to make very respectable-looking presentation materials, such as handouts. Because WordPerfect can read a wide variety of graphics formats, you can use figure boxes to read in charts, diagrams, and other visual files used in a presentation such as a computerized slide show. You can then print the slides as part of the handout.

With its ability to display a mixture of graphics and text, there is no reason why WordPerfect itself should not be used to present information. Setting up a series of pages with large figure boxes containing your charts and graphs would allow you to use each page as though it were a slide. Textual information, such as bulleted lists, can be typed in a large font for greater clarity.

DTP Output

While today's laser printers are capable of impressive results, they do not match the clarity of typesetting output devices. Such devices are called *imagesetters,* and are used to prepare the pages sent to a printer for mass production of a publication. You can certainly get away with a laser printer for in-house and informal documents, but crucial documents for public consumption require typesetting. In this case you can use your laser printer for draft output, then send the checked, approved, final version of the files to the typesetter.

The person or agency doing the typesetting can tell you whether they can accept WordPerfect files. However, bear in mind that much of today's typesetting equipment works with PostScript. To ensure that what you preview in WordPerfect comes out exactly the same on a PostScript typesetter, you will want to select a PostScript WordPerfect printer driver for your default printer. Ideally, you will already be printing draft copies on a PostScript laser printer such as the Apple LaserWriter, the Brother HL-8PS, an HP LaserJet with a PostScript option, or one of the QMS PostScript printers.

When the time comes to create a PostScript file from your WordPerfect document, follow these steps:

1. Select File/Print from the main menu.
2. Make sure that the Print Quality button is set to High.

3. Choose Select, and make sure you are using a WordPerfect printer driver for a PostScript printer that is compatibile with the output device the service bureau will be using.
4. Choose Setup, and for the Port setting, choose File.
5. Enter a suitable filename in the Filename box, select OK and then Close to return to the Print dialog box, and choose Print.

The document will be sent to a file on disk, bearing the name you have entered. You can then copy this file to a floppy disk so it can be taken to the typesetter. The next time you print with these settings, the original file you named for the print output will be overwritten.

Design Theory

If you are going to do a lot of DTP work with WordPerfect, you will want to be aware of the five basic principles of graphics design. Awareness of these principles, if not strict adherence to them, should be helpful in the design stage and will probably lead to more professional results.

Seek Propriety

The guiding principle of good document design is the propriety or appropriateness of all items within the design. This means the graphics elements must be appropriate to the purpose of the document and to their surrounding environment. You might like flowery italic fonts, but they might not be appropriate for a technical bulletin. You might want to use a large graphic of a computer in a newsletter about computer security, but it might need to be scaled down to avoid dominating the page and distracting the reader.

Assess the suitability of the different graphics elements you want to incorporate according to both the audience and the content of the document. An advertisement for a new security device might need to look quite different from a proposal to prospective investors. Before adding any graphics element to a document, ask yourself to what extent that element furthers the purpose of the document and how it fits in with the other elements.

Strive for Consistency

One advantage of using styles for formatting is that they encourage consistency, which is critical to a professional design. Unless you are varying them for special effect, keep all margins consistent from one page to the next. Use the same font and alignment for all major headings, the same font and alignment for all subheadings, and so on.

Remember that changes from one font to another or to bold or italic draw the reader's attention. Do not make such changes unless you need to attract the reader's attention; otherwise, the effect is simply confusion.

Evolve Style

One disadvantage of using WordPerfect's Style commands to format a document is that you may be tempted to define all of your styles at once, at the beginning of the project. This is rarely the best way to achieve a pleasing overall style in your design. The general style of a document should evolve as you work toward the elements of the design in light of the principles of propriety and consistency.

The best way to use WordPerfect's Style feature in this context is to define each section of the text and achieve consistency between the sections. Then, when you alter a style, say for the body text, all text formatted with the body style will assume the new look.

Create Tension

Beware of creating documents that look too balanced. The effect can be boring to look at, and it gives the reader no sense of direction, no help in deciding where to look next. Giving more emphasis to one particular area, usually the one that is most important, can help direct the eye and grab the reader's attention. Areas of white can be effective in tilting the balance of a design.

It may help to bear in mind a traditional notion of artist composition within a rectangular frame. The eye naturally looks to a place within the rectangle that can be described as follows: the point on an imaginary line drawn diagonally from one corner to the other, where the line would be intersected by a second line drawn at ninety degrees from the diagonal to one of the other corners. You can see this in Figure 7-24.

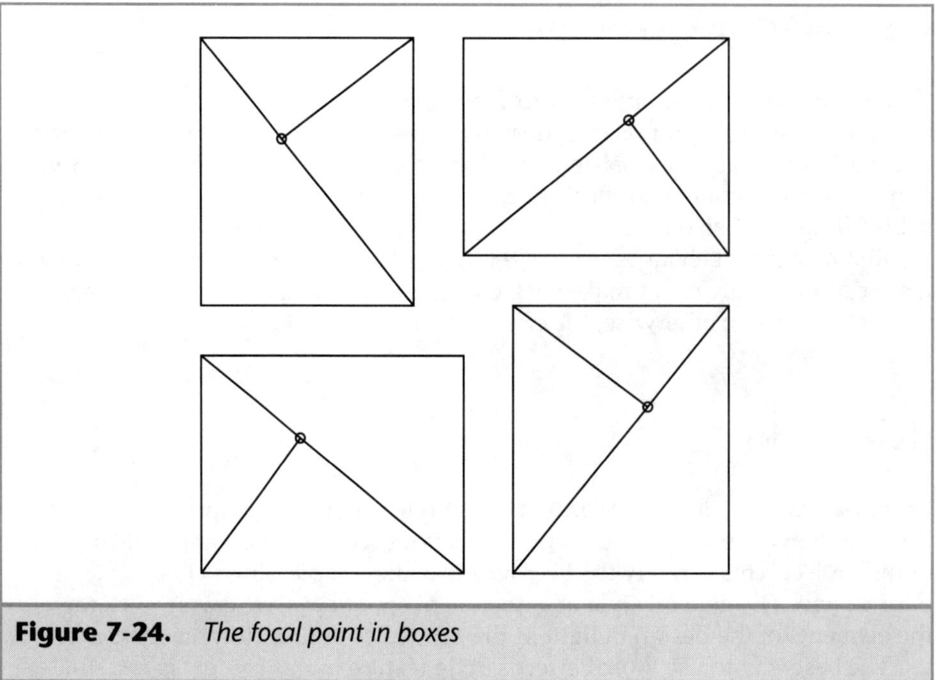

Figure 7-24. *The focal point in boxes*

Provide Unity

The notion of a focal point lies behind the last of the five principles: unity. Selecting one dominant graphics element per page will give each page unity, an appealing visual coherence, plus a starting point for the reader's attention. A sense of unity goes hand-in-hand with propriety, consistency, style, and tension, to create good-looking document layouts.

CHAPTER 8

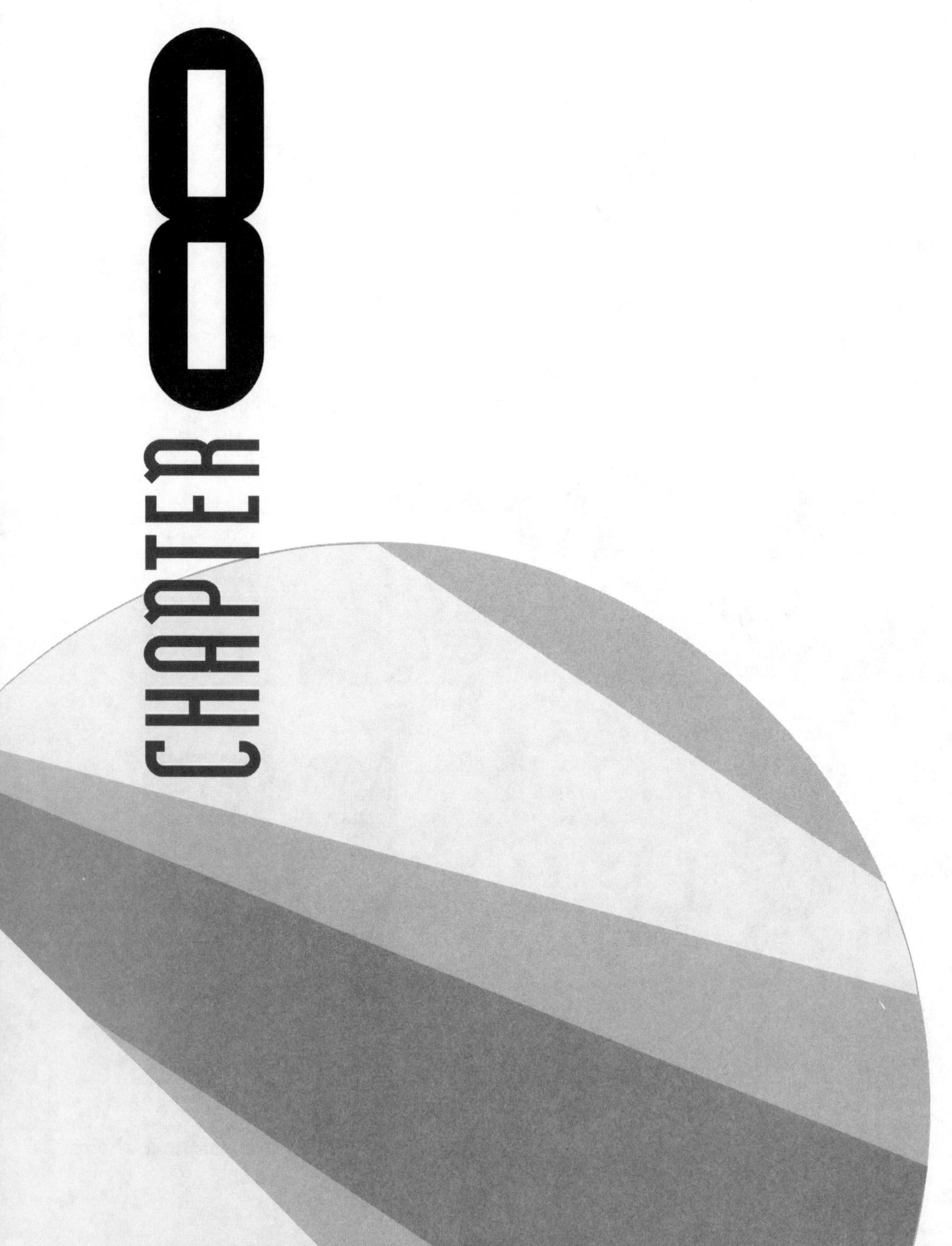

Applications for Macros

This chapter will help you to make the most of the macro facilities in WordPerfect. The purpose of a macro is to automate a repetitive task. This might be typing, such as the closing you use at the end of most of your letters, or a series of commands. A macro can also automate a series of commands, such as selecting a particular view of your document. However, thanks to the WordPerfect macro programming language, macros can be applied to relatively complex tasks, such as copying the address from a letter and printing it on an envelope.

Macros are not just for the people who make them. You can make macros that will be helpful to less experienced users. Through the use of macro programming commands, your macros can ask for input from the person using the macro. Macros request user input through dialog boxes like the one shown here:

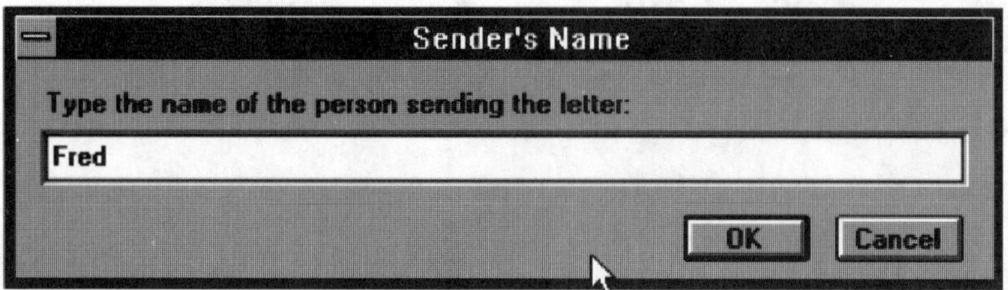

WordPerfect makes it relatively easy to create boxes like this. While Chapter 11, "Commands and Features," describes the basic commands for recording and playing back macros, this chapter looks at how you access macros, edit them, and apply them to typical tasks. The main WordPerfect macro programming commands are then discussed.

Recording Macros

There are two ways of making WordPerfect macros: recording and editing. This section examines the first method and gives you an example of how it works. The next section discusses macro editing and shows you how to edit the macro created in the example in this section.

The Recording Session

To record a macro, you simply carry out the actions you want to automate while WordPerfect is in record mode. For example, suppose you want a macro that types your company name, which always appears in a special font with a registered trademark symbol, like this:

BrightWriter,® Inc.

To see how you would go about recording a macro like this, open a new document and follow these steps:

1. Select Tools/Macro/Record (or press the CTRL+F10 shortcut keys). The Record Macro dialog box appears, as shown in Figure 8-1.

2. Enter the name you want used for this macro (in this case, type **CONAME**). Then, click on the Record button. The dialog box disappears and the "Macro Record" notice appears on the status line.

3. Type **BrightWriter** followed by a comma, and then select Insert/Character (or press CTRL+W) for the WordPerfect Characters dialog box. Don't worry if you make mistakes while carrying out these steps; simply correct each mistake and continue.

4. Select Typographic Symbols from the Character Set pop-up list, and then choose the Registered symbol (®), which is number 4,22. Select Insert and Close to place the symbol in your document.

5. Press SHIFT+LEFT ARROW to highlight the symbol and select Layout/Font. Choose Superscript in the Position field, then click on OK.

6. Press the RIGHT ARROW key once, then type **<space>Inc.** Press CTRL+SHIFT+LEFT ARROW twice to select the complete text of the company name. Select Layout/Font and choose a 14-point font. This example uses Bookman font, but you can use any font different from your usual font for the purposes of illustration.

8. Select OK to confirm the font, and you are returned to the document. At this point, the company name remains highlighted, so press END to move the insertion point past the name and font change.

9. Select Tools/Macro/Record again to turn off macro recording.

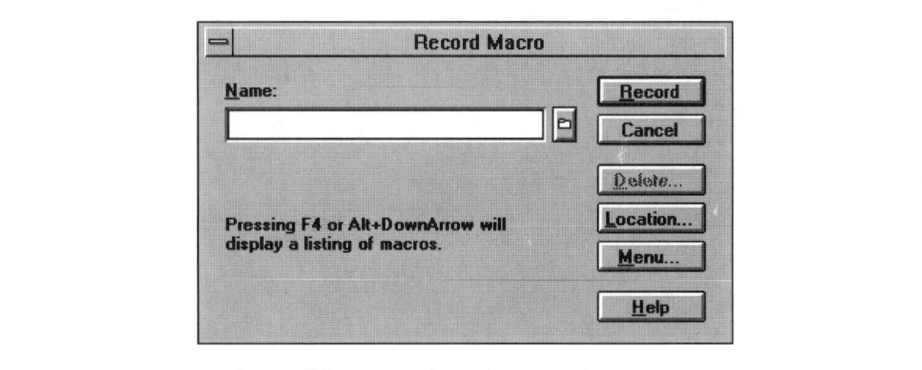

Figure 8-1. *The Record Macro dialog box*

The macro is now recorded. To test the new macro, close the current document without saving it. In a new document, type a few lines of text, and then select Tools/Macro/Play. You will see the Play Macro dialog box, in which you can supply the macro name you want to play. Instead, click on the files button to the right of the name field, and you will see a list of available macros, similar to that shown in Figure 8-2. The name of the example macro (CONAME.WCM) should be included in your list.

Highlight the macro you want to play, and select OK. This inserts the macro name in the Name field of the Play Macro dialog box. Now click on Play. After a moment's wait, the actions you recorded will be carried out. For alternative methods of playing macros, see the section "Running Macros" later in this chapter. Also see the "Editing Macros" section to see how to make changes to macros you have recorded and how to make macros from scratch.

Recording Tips

While recording the macro, you may have noticed that the mouse pointer changed to a "no go" sign (a circle with a line through it), preventing you from using the mouse to move the insertion point during macro recording. (Move the insertion point with the arrow keys or the Find command instead.) However,

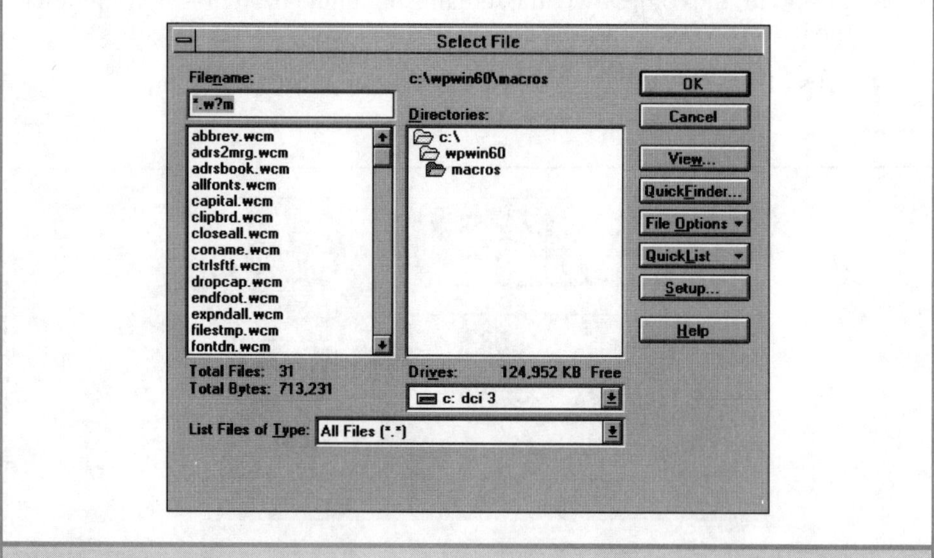

Figure 8-2. *Selecting a macro to be played*

you can still use the mouse to select menu items, and the mouse pointer shape returns to normal if you move it over the menu while recording.

There are some situations in which it is hard to stop a macro recording. For example, there may be times when you cannot access the Tools/Macro menu, or you cannot tell if the macro recorder has stopped because you cannot see the status bar. In these instances, you can make direct use of the WordPerfect Macro Facility. This is a Windows application that is automatically loaded when you start recording a macro. It is the Macro Facility that actually records and executes your macros. To do so, first select the Task List command in Windows (CTRL+ESC) to display a list of currently loaded tasks, as shown here:

Task List
Program Manager
File Manager
WordPerfect Macro Facility
WordPerfect - [Document1]
Switch To | End Task | Cancel
Cascade | Tile | Arrange Icons

To select the WordPerfect Macro Facility, either double-click the task or highlight it and select Switch To.

When you switch to the WordPerfect Macro Facility, you have access to the small dialog box shown in Figure 8-3. Choose Stop record from the Macros menu, and the recording will be ended.

Some WordPerfect actions cannot be recorded in macros. For example, you cannot carry out a spell-check in this way. This is because each time you use select Tools/Speller, a different set of keystrokes is involved. You can have a macro start the Speller, but to do this you need to edit the macro and insert a command, as described in the next section.

You can pause macro recording by selecting Tools/Macro/Pause. The first time you issue this command during a recording, WordPerfect temporarily stops recording. Anything you type or any actions you perform are not recorded until you select Macro/Pause a second time, at which point recording continues. The Pause option can be useful at times, but bear in mind that it does not insert

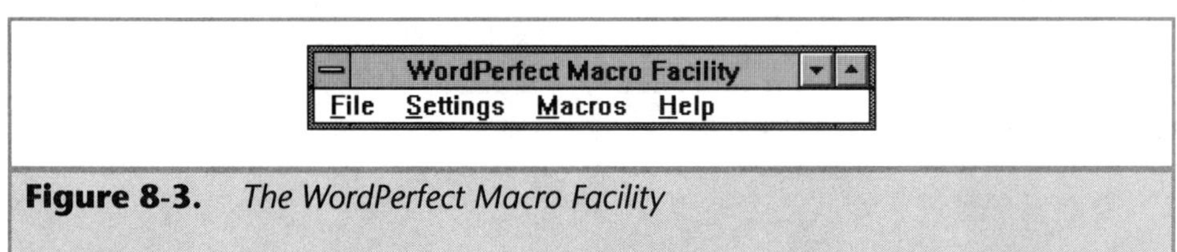

Figure 8-3. *The WordPerfect Macro Facility*

pauses when the macro is played. To do so, you need to edit the macro and insert a special command.

Editing Macros

There are numerous situations in which it is desirable to alter a macro you have recorded: to correct errors in a macro recording, to change the macro action, to add to the macro action, or to insert macro commands that will improve the macro. Macros are easier to alter in WordPerfect for Windows than they are in WordPerfect for DOS. This is because WordPerfect for Windows allows you to edit macros in the same manner as you edit other documents.

Choosing a Macro to Edit

To open a macro so you can edit it, select Tools/Macro/Edit. You will see the Edit Macro dialog box, in which you can specify the name of the macro you want to edit. Click on the files icon to the right of the Name field, and choose the macro you want to edit (CONAME.WCM). Click on OK, then click on Edit. After a moment, you will see a document window that looks like any normal document window, except that it contains some rather strange words. You can see the sample macro in Figure 8-4. (Do not worry if your macro looks slightly different from this.)

Macro File Structure

Once you understand how WordPerfect structures a macro file, you can edit the contents. You can even apply different typestyles if you wish. You might want to change the font to something larger and more legible. As you can see from the complete contents of the sample macro listed here, there are several different types of entries in a macro recording:

```
Application (A1; "WordPerfect"; Default; "US")
Type ({"BrightWriter,"})
WPCharactersDlg ()
Type ({" "})
```

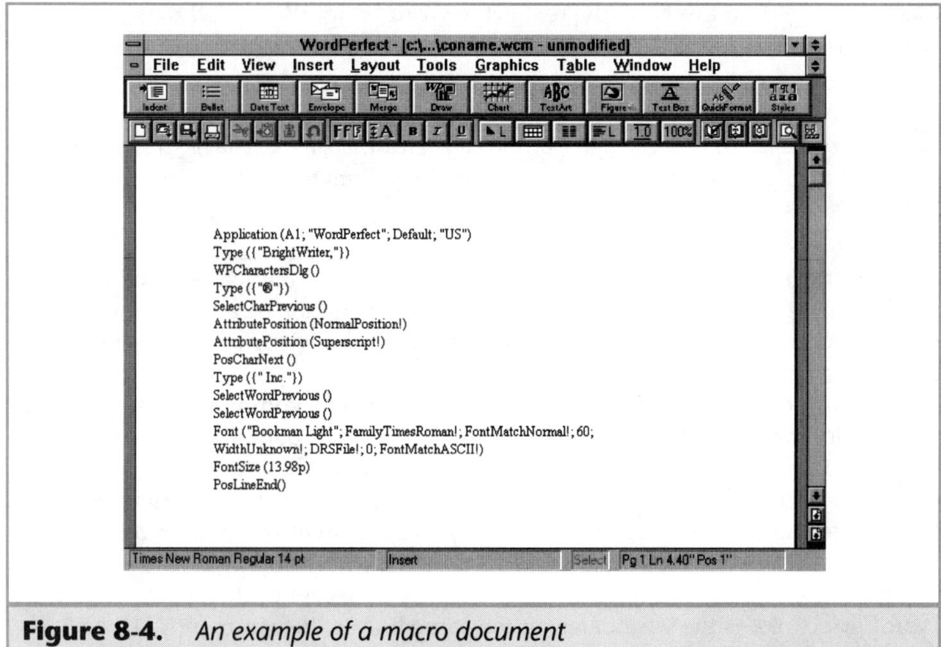

Figure 8-4. *An example of a macro document*

```
SelectCharPrevious ()
AttributePosition (NormalPosition!)
AttributePosition (Superscript!)
PosCharNext ()
Type ({" Inc."})
SelectWordPrevious ()
SelectWordPrevious ()
Font ("Bookman Light"; FamilyTimesRoman!; FontMatchNormal!; 60;
WidthUnknown!; DRSFile!; 0; FontMatchASCII!)
FontSize (13.98p)
PosLineEnd()
```

The first line is a programming statement that tells WordPerfect which applications will be used by the macro. In this case, the application is WordPerfect. The second line of the macro starts the Type command, which tells WordPerfect to type characters into whatever document is current when the macro is played. In this case, the text is the word "BrightWriter"; the text to be typed is placed between double quotes.

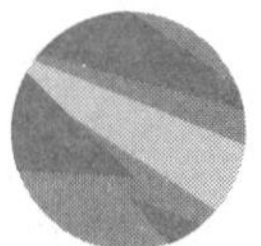

NOTE: *WordPerfect records the result of using the WordPerfect Character command—in the example, for the registered trademark symbol—rather than each of the steps required to choose the symbol and insert it into the text. This makes the macro run more quickly.*

After the type statement is closed, the WordPerfect Characters function is used to insert the registered trademark symbol. Then there is an insertion point location command: SelectCharPrevious(). This tells WordPerfect to select the previous character.

You can see that each item in the macro consists of a command name, such as Application or SelectCharPrevious, followed by a set of parentheses. Within these parentheses is placed any information that affects how the command is executed. Such information is known as an *argument*, or *command parameter.* Some WordPerfect macro commands, such as SelectCharPrevious, do not require arguments, while others, such as Application, definitely do.

When a command requires a parameter, as in the case of the Type command, WordPerfect places the parameter on the same line as the command. This is not necessary, however. You can format your macros so the parameters are on a different line than the command, as in the following:

```
Type({
    "This is the text to be inserted"
    })
```

Capitalization of the command is also optional. Commands can be given all in capitals, or in lowercase letters, like this:

```
type({"This is the text to be inserted"})
```

However, any text you want the macro to type should be capitalized the way you want it to appear in your documents.

More critical and less flexible than the way commands are laid out in the macro document is the way each command is used. The requirements of a command, such as the arguments it takes, are known as the command's *syntax.* If you edit a macro file, you must stick to the syntax. If you open a pair of parentheses, you must close it. If you put text in quotes, you need both opening and closing quotes.

Changing a Macro

Since it is easy to make mistakes during macro recording, you may want to edit the macro to remove the errors. Suppose that in the preceding macro recording example, instead of typing **Bright**, you typed **Brigth**, pressed the BACKSPACE key twice, and then typed **ht** to correct the error. Your macro will contain four extra keystrokes, and the first few lines would look like this:

```
Type({"Brigth"})
DeleteCharPrevious()
DeleteCharPrevious()
Type({"htWriter,"})
```

To correct this problem, you remove the macro code representing the typo and the correction—in other words, everything between the *g* in "Brigth" and the *h* in "htWriter". To do so, simply select this part of the macro document and press DEL. The result is clean code, just like that shown in the original macro example.

When you have made the necessary changes to a macro file, you can save it by selecting Save & Compile, or you can select Save As to save a copy of the macro under a new name. Bear in mind that you must close the macro file before you can run the updated macro.

Besides being useful for correcting mistakes in recorded macros, macro editing allows you to alter the action of a recording. Suppose the boss decides that the company name should be typed without the registered trademark symbol. Instead of rerecording the company name macro, you can simply edit it, deleting the symbol.

Consider the macro in Figure 8-5, used to add the closing to business letters. This is a typical application for a recorded macro. Macro recording was turned on before the user typed **Yours sincerely**, the blank lines for the signature, and her name and title. Macro recording was then turned off. When the user gets a promotion and has to change the title in her closing from "Sales Assistant" to "Sales Manager," she can do so simply by editing the text in the macro. You can see the revised macro in Figure 8-6.

Adding Macro Commands

One of the main reasons for editing macros is to add macro commands. As you have seen from the previous examples of macro editing, a macro file consists of nothing but a series of macro commands. However, there are two types of commands in macros—product commands and programming commands.

```
Application (A1; "WordPerfect"; Default; "US")
Type ({"Yours sincerely,"})
HardReturn ()
HardReturn ()
HardReturn ()
HardReturn ()
Type ({"Jane Dean"})
HardReturn ()
Type ({"Sales Assistant"})
```

Figure 8-5. *A macro to close a letter*

Product Commands

Most of the commands WordPerfect uses to record your actions in a macro are known as *product commands*. They are called this because they are commands that result in a product—a result. Product commands include such actions as typing, selecting text, positioning the insertion point, and selecting menu items. For example, if you record the File/Save command in a macro, it appears as FileSave(). Every action you can perform with WordPerfect has an equivalent product command.

You will often find it useful to edit a recorded macro to add a product command. Suppose you want to expand the letter-closing macro so it issues the Tools/Speller command. (It makes sense to check the spelling of a business letter as soon as you have finished typing it.) In Figure 8-7 you can see the additions necessary to include this step in the closing macro. The WPSpeller() command has been added at the bottom of the macro.

You might wonder how you find out the names of the product commands you want to add to your macros. You will find the commands listed in the WordPerfect for Windows *Macros Manual*, available from WordPerfect

```
Application (A1; "WordPerfect"; Default; "US")
Type ({"Yours sincerely,"})
HardReturn ()
HardReturn ()
HardReturn ()
HardReturn ()
Type ({"Jane Dean"})
HardReturn ()
Type ({"Sales Manager"})
```

Figure 8-6. *The amended macro*

```
Application (A1; "WordPerfect"; Default; "US")
Type ({"Yours sincerely,"})
HardReturn ()
HardReturn ()
HardReturn ()
HardReturn ()
Type ({"Jane Dean"})
HardReturn ()
Type ({"Sales Manager"})
WPSpeller ()
```

Figure 8-7. *Command added to the macro*

Corporation. A third source is covered in "The Macro Command Inserter" section later in this chapter.

Programming Commands

The second type of command is the *programming command*. These commands allow you to introduce decision making and user input into your macros. For example, suppose you want other people to be able to use your letter-closing macro. You want the macro to pause after "Yours sincerely," at the point where the user would normally type his or her name. After the user types a name, you want the macro to issue a hard return and then pause again, ready for the user to type a title. After this you want the macro to carry out the spell-check.

The simplest way of adding a pause is to use the programming command called Pause. Here you can see what the amended macro would look like, with the extra spaces and lines removed:

```
Application (A1; "WordPerfect"; Default; "US")
Type ({"Yours sincerely,"})
HardReturn ()
HardReturn ()
HardReturn ()
HardReturn ()
Pause
HardReturn ()
Pause
WPSpeller ()
```

When this macro plays, it pauses after the fourth hard return. The user can then type a name. Before WordPerfect will resume playing the macro, the user must press ENTER. At this point the macro adds another hard return and pauses again. The user presses ENTER again. The macro then launches the spell-check.

As you can see, the Pause command takes no arguments. When a macro encounters the Pause command during playback, macro activity stops, allowing the user to type text or issue commands. The macro resumes only after the user presses ENTER.

Pauses and Keys

A better alternative to the Pause command is PauseKey. This command allows you to say which key the user must press during the pause in order for the macro to resume playing. If you were to use PauseKey in the letter-closing macro, the last five lines of code would look like the following. Please note that when you type the key to be used by the PauseKey command, it is followed by an exclamation point.

```
HardReturn()
PauseKey(Enter!)
HardReturn()
PauseKey(Enter!)
Speller()
```

When this version of the macro runs, it pauses for the user to type a name. The user types the name and presses ENTER, and the macro carries on to the next line. After the user types a title and presses ENTER, the spell-check is launched. The "continue" key need not be ENTER—it can be Cancel (ESC), Close (CTRL+F4), or just about any other character. To use ESC for the pause key, the code is PauseKey(Cancel!). To use CTRL+F4, the code is PauseKey(Close!).

To use any other character, the code is PauseKey(Character!;"*x*"), where *x* is the character you want to use. For example, if you want the macro to resume after the user has typed an exclamation mark (!) you would use

```
PauseKey(Character!;"!")
```

The exclamation mark does not appear in the text the user is typing, but instead triggers the macro to resume. Note that the quotation marks are required before and after the character you want to use.

Pauses and Prompts

When the Pause and PauseKey commands are used in the manner just described, the user gets little guidance as to what keys should be pressed. One way to solve this problem is to use the Prompt command. This displays a message on the screen, telling the user what to do. You can see an example of this in Figure 8-8.

Here is the macro code that created the prompt in Figure 8-8:

```
Prompt("Name";"Click in the document window, type the name of
the person sending the letter, then choose OK.";4;;)
Pause
EndPrompt
```

This code was placed after the hard returns that follow "Yours sincerely," and before the hard return that creates a new line after the name has been typed. When the message appears, the user clicks in the document window, then places the insertion point where the name should be typed. After typing the name, the user clicks OK, and the macro continues. If the user clicks Cancel, the macro is terminated.

The Prompt command uses several arguments, or parameters. The first is a title for the prompt box. This is text typed within quotes in the command. When the prompt box is drawn by the macro, the text is centered in the title bar.

The second parameter is the text of the prompt, again placed in quotes. The macro displays this text within the body of the box. You type the prompt text as a single line without any hard returns; just allow WordPerfect to wrap the text in the macro document. When the prompt dialog box is drawn, WordPerfect positions the text within the box boundaries, placing about 12 words on each line.

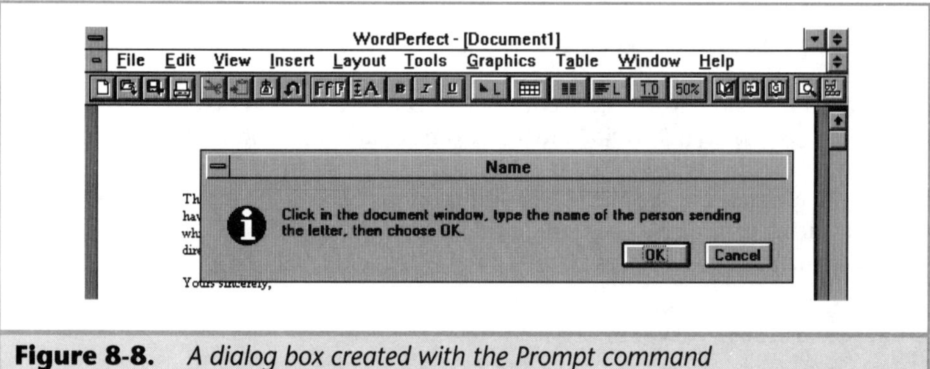

Figure 8-8. *A dialog box created with the Prompt command*

NOTE: The width of the prompt box is fixed, but the depth is adjusted by WordPerfect to accommodate the prompt text. The WordPerfect documentation is decidedly vague as to how long your prompt text can be, but if you use more than a hundred words, the box will start to get quite large and obscure the underlying window. The prompt text will also become difficult to read.

The third prompt parameter is the icon used. In the preceding example, the icon is number 4, the information icon. The other choices are the stop sign (1), the question mark (2), and the exclamation point (3). If you omit the icon parameter or use 0, there will be no icon in the box.

The last two prompt parameters are the horizontal and vertical position of the box. If you omit these parameters, as in the preceding example, WordPerfect displays the prompt in the middle of the screen.

The position parameters are entered as numbers representing pixels (dots on the screen). The horizontal parameter is the number of pixels from the leftmost point of the active application window to the left edge of the prompt box. The vertical parameter is the number of pixels from the topmost point of the active application window to the top edge of the prompt box.

Note that the parameters in a WordPerfect programming command are separated by semicolons. If you leave out a parameter, you mark its place with a semicolon, as in the example, where there are two semicolons at the end of the Prompt command, marking the horizontal and vertical position parameters.

The Pause/Prompt combination is very handy since it is easy to set up and gives welcome assistance to users of the macro. However, it is not without problems. If the user clicks Cancel, the macro ends rather unceremoniously. Also, the prompt message box may appear over the point at which the user must type. While it is possible for the user to drag the prompt box out of the way, this can be disconcerting. See "User Input and Macro Programming" later in this chapter.

Macros from Scratch

So far you have seen how macro commands can be added to macros you have recorded. It is possible to write a macro from scratch, starting with a new document. The first entry in the macro document is often the Application command. You use the Application command to specify which applications will be used during the course of the macro.

All of the macro examples so far have begun with this line:

```
Application(A1;"WordPerfect";Default;"US")
```

This tells WordPerfect important information about the environment in which the macro will be running. The Application command need not be the first command in your macro because it is read when the macro is compiled, not when it is run. The command can be located anywhere in the macro. However, it is probably best placed near the beginning so it is not overlooked. (Without it, the macro will not run properly.)

One command you may want to use ahead of Application is Comment. You represent this command by two forward slashes (//); it allows you to include comments in your macros. When WordPerfect encounters the // command in a macro, it ignores all of the text that follows until the next hard return. For example, the letter-closing macro might begin like this:

```
//This is a macro to close a letter
```

You can add further characters to dress up the macro, as in this example:

```
//************************************************
//Macro Name: CLOSING      Purpose: Close letters
//************************************************
```

The ability to add comment lines such as the row of asterisks just shown is helpful when you have several subroutines in a macro and want to separate them. A *subroutine* is a section of macro code that may or may not be used during the macro's execution, depending upon user input or the existence of certain specified conditions.

After you have issued the Application command and placed any comments you want at the beginning of the macro, you can proceed to add the commands you need. One way of making this process a little easier, whether you are editing recorded macros or writing macros from scratch, is to use the WordPerfect Macro Command Inserter, described in the next section.

The Macro Command Inserter

The WordPerfect Macro Command Inserter is an optional program module designed to help the macro editing process. The program inserts product and programming commands into your macros. You can see the Macro Command Inserter at work here:

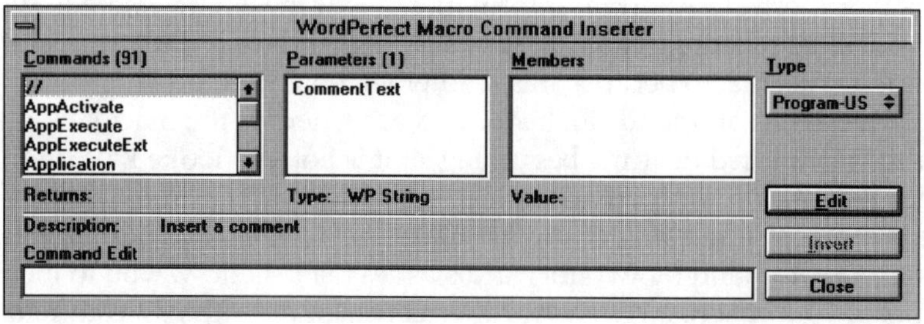

When you insert product commands with the Macro Command Inserter, you can specify parameters and value set members used by parameters. These give WordPerfect information about what options to choose in dialog boxes and whether certain features (such as the button bar) should be displayed or hidden. If you are using programming commands, the Macro Command Inserter displays the proper syntax of the selected programming command.

Using the Macro Command Inserter

If you use the Macro Command Inserter to add commands to your macros, you do not need to worry about spelling or typing errors. Simply choose the commands and parameters you want from the list boxes and insert them into your macro. To choose a command, parameter, or value set member, double-click it, or select the item and then choose Edit (or press ENTER). The Macro Command Inserter places the command in the Command Edit text box and then positions the insertion point at the place in your macro where you may need to enter additional parameters or values.

To insert product or programming commands into your macro, open your macro in the current document window and choose Command Inserter from the Macro feature bar to run the Macro Command Inserter. The WordPerfect Macro Command Inserter dialog box will appear. Choose the type of command you want to insert from the Type pop-up list. Choose the desired command from the Commands list box.

If you choose a product command that has parameters, the parameters will appear in the Parameters list box. If you choose a product command without parameters, the Parameters list box will be blank. In this case, or if you have chosen a programming command, skip to the next paragraph; otherwise, choose the parameter you want to use in the Parameters list box. If the parameter has value set members, the selection cursor moves to the Members list box. Choose the member you want to use in the Members list box.

The insertion point now moves to the place in the macro command where you may need to type additional parameters or values. In the Command Edit text box, type any additional parameters you need. Following is a Prompt command being created in the Token Edit box:

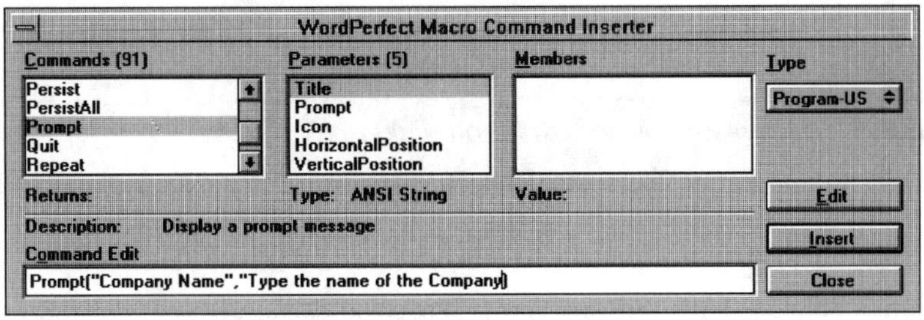

Choose Insert or press ENTER when the product or programming command is completed. This puts the command into your macro. You can use the Macro Command Inserter to include additional commands in your macro and then save and play your macro as usual.

Running Macros

In addition to the basic Tools/Macro/Play command described earlier, there are numerous ways of running the macros you record and edit. When you select Tools/Macro/Play, you are presented with a list of macro files stored in the current macro directory. You highlight the macro you want to run and select Play. There are several shortcuts you can use, including assigning macros to the Macro menu, assigning the Macro/Play command to the button bar, running macros from buttons, and assigning macros to the keyboard.

Macros on the Menu

To gain faster access to a macro, you can add it to the Macro menu. To assign a macro to the Macro menu, follow these steps:

1. Select either Play or Edit from the Macro menu. You will see either the Play Macro or Edit Macro dialog box.

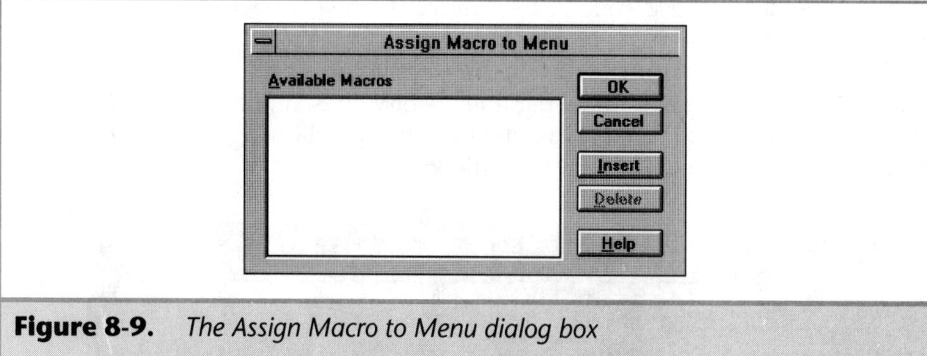

Figure 8-9. *The Assign Macro to Menu dialog box*

2. Click on the Menu button. You will see the Assign Macro to Menu dialog box, as shown in Figure 8-9.
3. Click on the Insert button. You will see the Select Macro dialog box, as shown in Figure 8-10.
4. Enter the name of the macro you want assigned to the menu. In this example, enter the name **CLOSING.WCM**. (This macro was developed earlier in the chapter.)
5. Click on Select, then on OK. You are returned to either the Play Macro or Edit Macro dialog box. From here you can choose Cancel, and you are returned to your document.

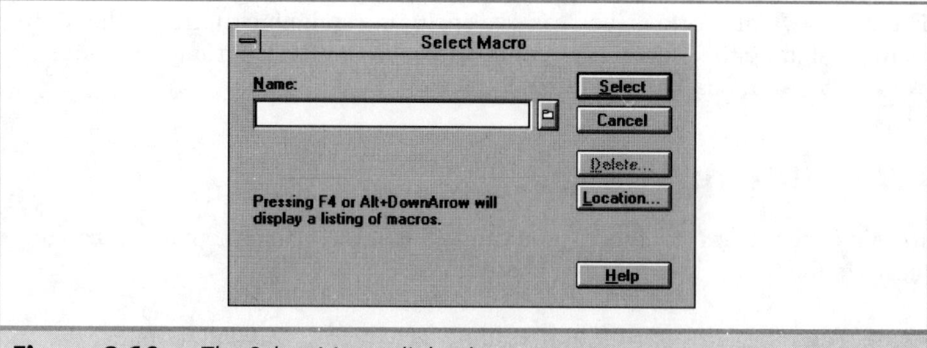

Figure 8-10. *The Select Macro dialog box*

The results of assigning macros to the Macro menu can be seen here:

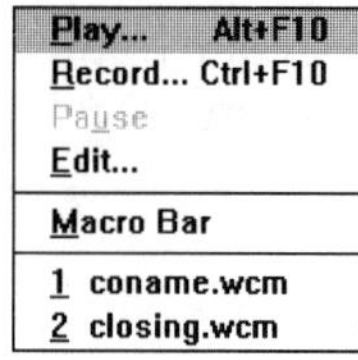

This shows the Macro menu with two macros assigned. To use the first assigned macro, you can select it from the list with your mouse.

Macros and the Button Bar

You can use the button bar to improve access to macros. For example, you can assign the Macro/Play command to a button, or even make buttons out of macros. To customize the button bar, you select File/Preferences/Button Bar. This displays the Button Bar Preferences dialog box, as shown in Figure 8-11. In the Available Button Bars list, you can see the different types of button bars that have been defined.

WordPerfect for Windows allows you to use button bars that are completely customized. The button bar definitions listed in Figure 8-11 represent the button bars that are provided with WordPerfect. Each of these are designed to help you accomplish specific tasks with WordPerfect. You are not limited, however, to only

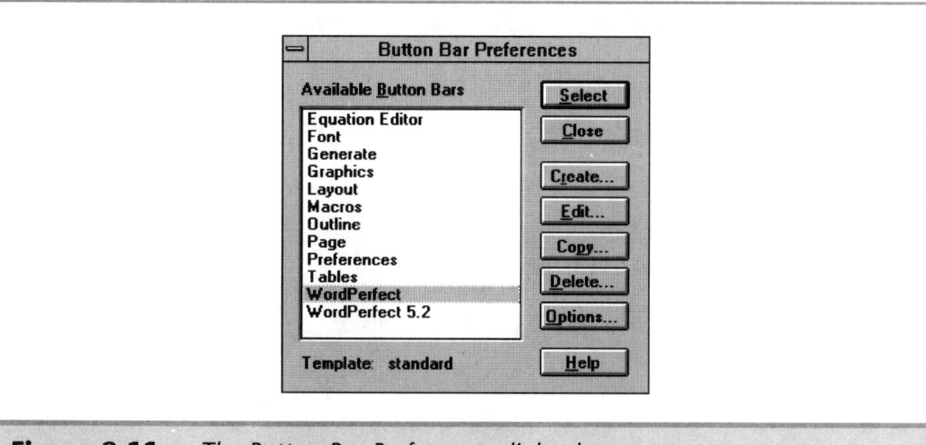

Figure 8-11. *The Button Bar Preferences dialog box*

these button bars. You can also create your own, which is what you will do in this section.

The first step is to click on the Create button. This step is advisable because in this way there is little chance you will mess up any of the previously defined button bars.

TIP: As an alternative to creating a new button bar, you could choose the Copy button to copy an existing button bar definition to a new name. You can then edit the copy of the button bar. This method is advantageous if your new button bar will be very similar to one that already exists.

When you click on the Create button, you will see the Create Button Bar dialog box, as shown in Figure 8-12.

Enter the name you want to use for the button bar. This can be any name you desire, but it should be descriptive of the purpose for which you will use the button bar. When you click on the OK button, you will notice that the button bar at the top of the screen is erased and the Button Bar Editor appears, as shown in Figure 8-13.

To add normal WordPerfect commands to the button bar, you should follow the techniques covered in Chapter 3, "Tools and Techniques." To add a macro, you should first click on the Play a Macro option near the top of the Button Bar Editor. When you do, a single button appears in the editor. Click on this button, Add Macro, to add a macro to the button bar. You can then select the macro as you have done several other times in this chapter. When you add a macro to the button bar, they appear as follows:

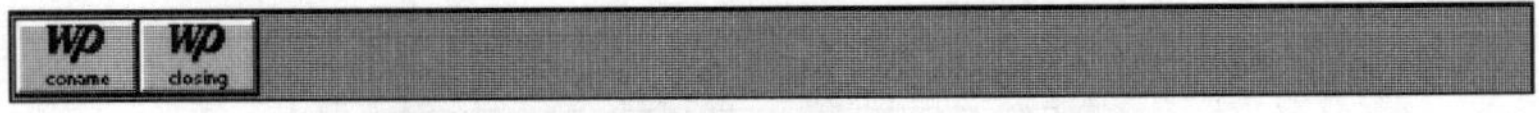

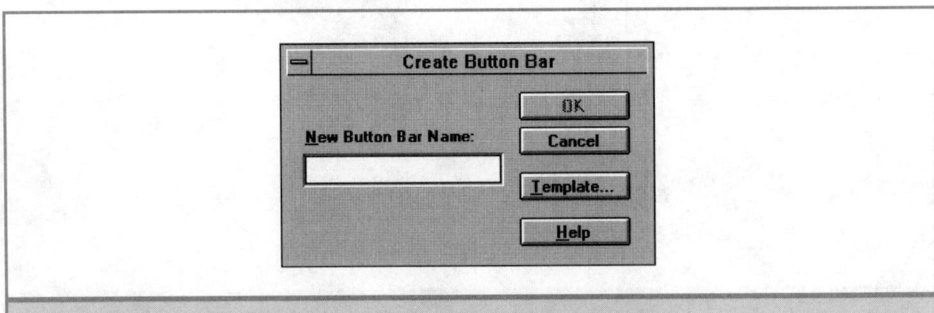

Figure 8-12. *The Create Button Bar dialog box*

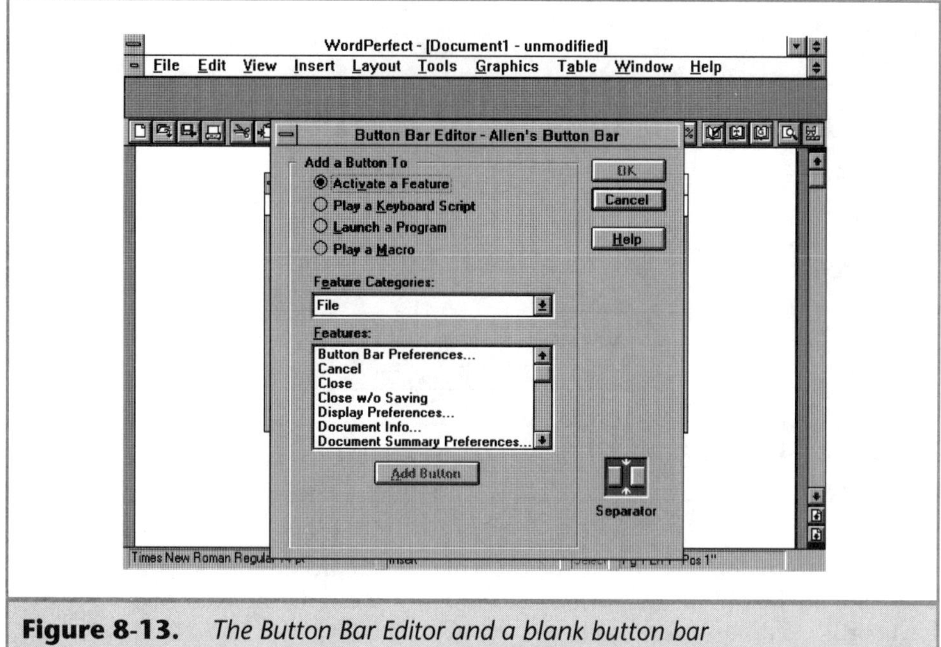

Figure 8-13. *The Button Bar Editor and a blank button bar*

The name of the macro appears under the WP letters on the button. To later use the macro, all you need to do is click on the button.

When you are finished adding, removing, or rearranging buttons, select OK from the Button Bar Editor. You will notice that your new button bar definition appears in the Button Bar Preferences dialog box, and you can select it as you would any other button bar. Unless you select a different button bar before you close WordPerfect, the newly created button bar will be loaded the next time you load WordPerfect.

Macros from the Keyboard

You can also play macros by assigning them to specific keys or key combinations on your keyboard. WordPerfect for Windows allows you complete control over your keyboard, meaning you can specify exactly what happens whenever you press a certain key or key combination.

To find out which keys are already used by a particular keyboard, use the Keyboard Editor. You access this feature by selecting File/Preferences/Keyboard. This presents the Keyboard Preferences dialog box, shown in Figure 8-14.

Figure 8-14. *The Keyboard Preferences dialog box*

From this dialog box you can select which keyboard definition you want to use. As with the button bars discussed earlier, you can define your own keyboards. To do this, simply click on the Create button. You are asked to provide a name for your keyboard, after which you will see the Keyboard Editor appear, as shown in Figure 8-15.

In the upper-left portion of the screen, you can see a list of how the keyboard is *mapped*—meaning what happens when you press a key or a key combination. At the bottom of the screen is the current keyboard layout. Using this layout, you can select different keys with the mouse, and the Keyboard Editor will display in the upper-left corner what the current mapping is for that key.

To change what is assigned to a key—including to assign a macro to a key—you use the upper-right portion of the Keyboard Editor. This portion of the screen may look familar to you. It is very similar to the Button Bar Editor covered earlier in the chapter. Once you select a key for which you want to change the mapping, you can choose what you want assigned to that key.

To assign a macro to a key or key combination, first select the key or combination you want to use, then click on the Play a Macro option. Then click on the Assign Macro button. When you do, you have the opportunity to specify the macro name you want to use. When you click on the Select button, the mapping information in the upper-left corner of the Keyboard Editor is updated.

If you want a keystroke assignment for a menu item to be displayed next to the item in the menu, check the Assignment Appears on Menu option in the Keyboard Editor when making the assignment.

When you exit the Keyboard Editor, you can begin using the keystrokes right away to run your macros.

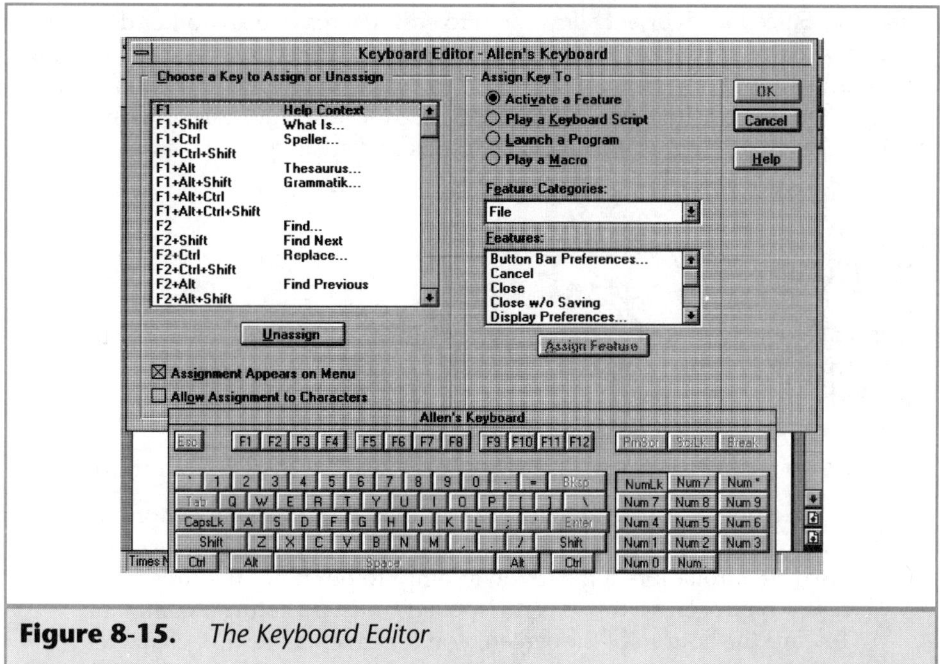

Figure 8-15. *The Keyboard Editor*

Problems with Macros

Using macros in your work can save you lots of time and effort. However, creating macros with some programs can take up a lot of time and effort. Fortunately, as this section describes, WordPerfect can assist the macro-making process in several ways.

Combining Recording and Editing

Recording your actions in a macro is a very efficient way of creating macro code. Recording can save you a lot of typing, and it generates the appropriate product commands for your actions without typos, spelling mistakes, or the need for you to look up commands.

However, as you start to create more sophisticated macros by using macro commands, you might tend to regard macro recording as a beginner's approach to macros. Since WordPerfect allows you to edit macros like any other document, you can combine sections of recorded macro code, cutting and pasting from one document to another. When you need to add program or product commands to a recorded macro, use the Macro Command Inserter described earlier in this chapter. This is another way of avoiding typos and spelling mistakes.

Debugging

The term *debugging* describes the process of testing macros to make sure they work correctly. The following steps represent a typical debugging cycle in WordPerfect:

1. As you are editing a macro, periodically use the Save & Compile option.
2. Make a note of any errors during compilation. These appear on the screen, as shown in Figure 8-16. WordPerfect not only detects errors during compilation, it makes an attempt to point out the cause, in this case a syntax error: the user misspelled the HardReturn() command. Toward the bottom of the screen, you are given a line and character reference for when you edit the file. At this point you can select either Continue Compilation, to check for further errors, or Cancel Compilation, which returns to the macro immediately.
3. Make any necessary changes in your macro, and repeat steps 1 and 2 until there are no more compilation errors.

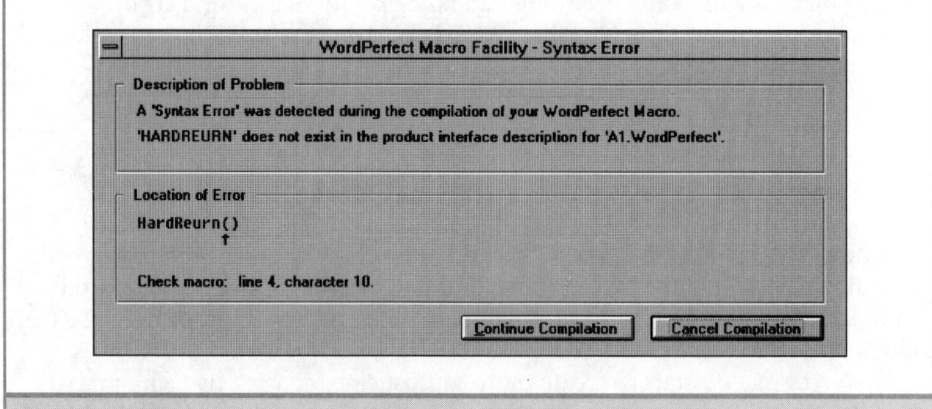

Figure 8-16. *A syntax error while compiling a macro*

4. When you are done editing the macro file, close it.
5. If necessary, open a new document in which to test the macro.
6. Play the macro. Make sure it functions as you expected. If it does not, edit the macro file again, repeating steps 1 through 6.

Macro Tips

A macro that types text may appear to perform incorrectly. Consider the macro described earlier that typed the closing to a letter and then performed a spell-check. You might find that the text typed by the macro does not appear in the document until you reach the end of the macro. This is because the default mode of macro operation in WordPerfect is known as Display(Off!). This means that the screen is not updated until the macro is over. The idea is that your macros will operate more quickly this way. In some circumstances, however, you may want to see the macro actions as they occur. If this is the case, insert the following command on its own line near the beginning of the macro:

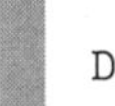

```
Display(On!)
```

Macros can be made to check certain conditions while they play, as described later in this chapter, but many macros are dependent upon the user playing them appropriately. For example, the macro to close a letter should be played when the insertion point is at the end of the letter. You could include a positioning command in the macro to move to the bottom of the text before running the macro, thus assisting the careless user who might try to run the macro while the insertion point is at the top of the letter.

The important point is that macros need to be used carefully, or else made "user-proof" by the addition of safety mechanisms. One of the best macro safety mechanisms is to document your macros, both within the macro document, by using the Comment command, and on paper. Written comments about how and when to run a macro are invaluable, particularly if you are designing macros for others to use.

One type of macro syntax error that can be puzzling is the accidental use of an illegal variable name. To avoid confusion during macro execution, WordPerfect does not allow you to use certain words as variable names. These words include all program and product command names, plus the following words: And, Address, AnsiString, Bool, Byte, Centimeters, Char, Digit, Div, DWord, False, Function, HiWord, Inches, Input, Letter, LoWord, Mod, Not,

OemString, Or, Points, Real, ShortSignature, True, UntilVariable, Version, Word, WPString, WPUnits, Xor.

Finally, remember that many good things come in pairs, and the syntax of most macro commands is no exception. When you edit a macro be sure that you have used pairs of quotes, parentheses, colons, and semicolons. This is probably the most common error to be discovered during macro compilation.

User Input and Macro Programming

The need for user input in macros is only partially met by the Pause, Prompt, and PauseKey commands described earlier in this chapter. This section discusses other ways of soliciting user responses.

Variables, Strings, and the Get Commands

Here is a dialog box requesting the user to enter text:

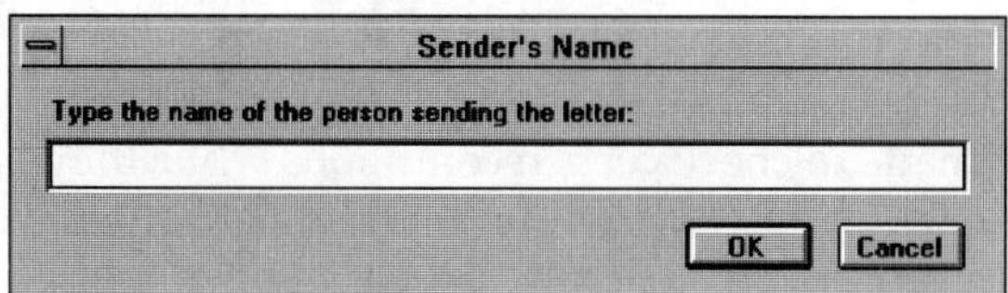

This is part of a variation on the letter-closing macro, and it uses an alternative to the Prompt/Pause approach demonstrated earlier. The dialog box was created by the GetString command. The actual entry in the macro reads

```
GetString(Name;"Type the name of the person sending the
letter:";"Sender's Name")
```

The first parameter is the variable that the GetString command will create. A *variable* is a piece of information stored by a program for use later in the program. In this case, the variable is *Name,* and it stores the text that the user enters in the dialog box. You then type the information in the document by using the Type command with the variable as the argument, as in:

```
Type(Name)
```

NOTE: *The variable is not enclosed in quotes in either the GetString command or the Type command.*

The second parameter in the preceding example of the GetString command is the text of the prompt that is placed in the dialog box. This is enclosed in quotes and separated from the first and third parameters by semicolons. The third parameter is the title of the dialog box, again enclosed in quotes. In Figure 8-17, you can see the full text of the new letter-closing macro. It shows how GetString is used for both the sender's name and the title. Also note the Display(On!) command, which ensures that the text "Yours sincerely" appears in the document before the dialog box is displayed.

There is another parameter that works with the GetString command. This is the optional Length parameter, used to control the length of the user's response. The syntax of this parameter is

Length=*Numeric Expression*

where *Numeric Expression* is the number of bytes that are permissible. Most ordinary characters are one byte in length, so if you wanted to restrict the user to responding Y or N to a prompt, the parameter would be

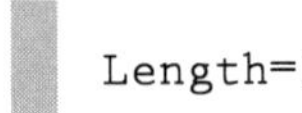

```
Length=1
```

If the user has to type a special character in the dialog box, it may take more than one byte. If the Length parameter is not used, the user can type an entry up to 64K in length, the maximum length allowable for a variable.

```
Application (A1; "WordPerfect"; Default; "US")
Display(On!)
Type ({"Yours sincerely,"})
HardReturn ()
HardReturn ()
HardReturn ()
HardReturn ()
GetString(Name;"Type the name of the person sending the letter:";"Sender's Name")
Type(Name)
HardReturn ()
GetString(Title;"Type the title of the person sending the letter:";"Sender's Title")
Type(Title)
WPSpeller ()
```

Figure 8-17. *A revised letter-closing macro*

The Length parameter is incorporated in the GetString statement as the second parameter, as shown here:

```
GetString(Response;Length=1;"If you are ready to print enter
Y, otherwise enter N:"; "Ready")
```

The command would store the user's reply of Y in a variable called Response.

If you want the user to supply a number in your macro, you can use the GetNumber command. This follows the same syntax as GetString, but it has no Length parameter. When the user selects OK to complete a dialog box created with the GetNumber command, the WordPerfect Macro Facility checks that the user's response is in fact a number, and it requests the user to try again if it is not.

The variable stored by GetNumber is a numeric value. If you want the macro to type the number, you need to convert it to text. Suppose that the user has entered, by means of a GetNumber command, a variable called Copies, used in determining how many copies of a document to print. If you want the macro to type the Copies variable in the document, you can convert it to text with the Numstr command, as shown here:

```
Type({"Number of copies printed: "})
Numstr(CopyText;0;Copies)
Type(CopyText)
```

The first parameter in the Numstr command is the new text variable you are creating. The second parameter is the number of decimal places to be displayed. (The default of six is used if you omit the decimal place parameter.) The third parameter is the existing numeric variable from which you are creating the new text variable. The existing numeric variable is still available in the macro after a Numstr command has been used.

If the user had entered 5 as the number of copies to be printed, the result of the preceding code would be the following text:

```
Number of copies printed: 5
```

Menus, Cases, and Subroutines

Sometimes you want the person using your macro to make a choice among several options. You can do this with the Menu command. For example, suppose you want the user to choose one of four types of text justification: left, right, center, or full. In Figure 8-18, you can see a menu that offers this set of choices. The user can easily select one by typing the appropriate number. At the bottom of the screen, the status bar offers assistance.

The code that creates this menu is

```
Menu(Just;Digit;;;{"Left";"Center";"Right";"Full"})
```

The code that creates the accompanying status bar message is

```
MacroStatusPrompt(State:On!;Prompt:"Select Justification")
```

The first parameter of the Menu command is the name of the variable that will store the user's response. The second parameter is the type of menu you want. Your choices are Digit or Letter. The menu shown in Figure 8-18 is a Digit menu. This means that up to 9 options can be listed, each with its own number. The Letter option allows up to 26 items in a menu, each with its own letter (A, B, C, and so on). The final parameter in the Menu command is the list of menu items, enclosed within curly braces and separated by semicolons. WordPerfect will adjust the width of the menu box to accommodate longer text items.

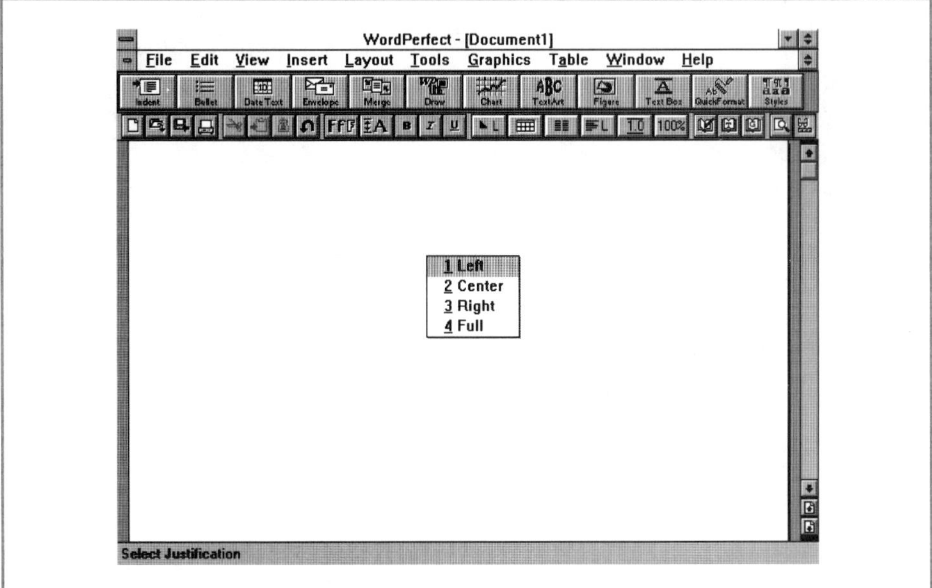

Figure 8-18. *A menu generated by the menu command*

There are two parameters missing from the Menu statement just shown. They are the horizontal and vertical position parameters, represented in their absence by extra semicolons. These parameters work to position the menu box on the screen, just like the same parameters in the Prompt command described earlier in this chapter.

Once you have set up a Menu command, you will need macro code to cope with the user's response. This is a single variable. In the preceding example, it is called *Just* and is one of four numbers.

One way of dealing with user response is to employ the Switch command and a number of labeled subroutines. A *subroutine* is a section of macro code that may or may not be used during the macro's execution, depending upon user input or the existence of certain specified conditions.

The full listing for the sample menu macro is as follows:

```
Application(A1;"WordPerfect";Default;"US")
MacroStatusPrompt(State:On!;Prompt:"Select Justification")
Menu(Just;Digit;;;{"Left";"Center";"Right";"Full"})
Switch(Just)
   CaseOf 1: Call(Left)
   CaseOf 2: Call(Center)
   CaseOf 3: Call(Right)
   CaseOf 4: Call(Full)
Go(End)

//Subroutines
Label(Left)
   JustifyLeft()
   Return
Label(Right)
   JustifyRight()
   Return
Label(Center)
   JustifyCenter()
   Return
Label(Full)
   JustifyFull()
   Return
Label(End)
   MacroStatusPrompt(State:Off!)
```

In this example there are four possible courses of action after the menu: left, center, right, and full justification. These are executed by four subroutines, each with its own label. A *label* is a word of up to 15 characters, such as "Left" in the example. Each of the four possible actions can thus be given a label and entered in the macro in its own section. The Switch and CaseOf commands decide which action is to be used, based on the value of the Just variable returned by the Menu command.

Each CaseOf command within the Switch structure (all the code between the Switch and EndSwitch commands) determines what will happen if the Switch variable (Just, in this case) matches the CaseOf variable. Thus, if Just is 1, then everything after CaseOf 1: will be executed; if it is 3, then everything after CaseOf 3: is run. In this macro, each CaseOf command results in a subroutine being called—a subroutine that performs the actions necessary to complete the menu choice. These subroutines are identified by labels, and end with the Return command, as shown here:

```
Label(Left)
   JustifyLeft()
   Return
```

The Return command tells the macro to go back to the code immediately following where the subroutine was called.

Errors, If, and ForNext

So far you have seen how to create menus and deal with variables derived from user input. You have seen how to structure subroutines that are called into play based on user response. There are several other macro commands that are important when controlling macro execution—for example, if you want to check for a specific condition during a macro and carry out certain actions if that condition exists.

The command you use to check for a condition and then execute other commands based on that check is the If command. This command is handy if you want to do something such as checking if any text was selected when the macro was run. The following code checks the status of select mode and turns off select if it is on:

```
GetWPData(MacroVariable:Select;
      SystemVariable:SelectModeActive!)
If(Select=True)
      SelectMode(State:Off!)
EndIf
```

The GetWPData command can check on many different aspects of WordPerfect, defined as *system variables*. In this case, it evaluates the system variable known as SelectModeActive!. The result of the GetWPData command is a macro variable called Select, which is assigned either the value true or false, depending on the setting of SelectModeActive!. The macro can then take actions based on the value of the Select variable.

The If command is useful in many situations where you need a macro to evaluate a condition or variable and act accordingly, but there are several conditions that can be checked by specialized commands. For example, suppose a user selects Cancel instead of OK in a macro dialog box. The normal response at that point is to end the macro. However, if you use the OnCancel command, you can tell the macro which subroutine to run when the user selects Cancel.

The OnCancel command might look like this:

```
OnCancel(Restart)
```

This command tells the macro to branch to the subroutine labeled Restart. A similar command, OnError, is available to direct macro flow after there is a macro error. If your macro involves the Search command, you can use the OnNotFound command to direct the macro to a suitable subroutine should the search fail to find the target string.

If you want a macro to repeat an action a number of times, you can use the ForNext command. You combine this command with the EndFor command to create a loop. The macro repeats the loop a set number of times. For example, suppose you want a macro to set up a bulleted list, creating as many bullet points as you ask for. The number of points can be obtained with the following code:

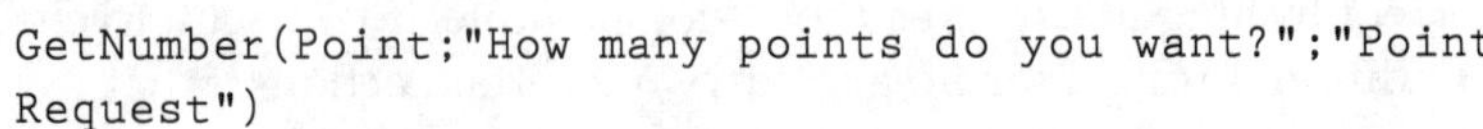

```
GetNumber(Point;"How many points do you want?";"Point
Request")
```

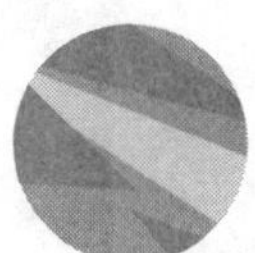

NOTE: *The variable cannot be called Points because that is an illegal variable name, as listed earlier in this chapter.*

Once you have the number of repetitions required, you can issue the ForNext command. This command uses four parameters, the first of which is a variable used as a counter within the ForNext command to keep track of the number of repetitions. In the following ForNext command, the first parameter is called Begin:

```
ForNext(Begin;0;Begin<Point;)
```

The second parameter is the starting value that is assigned to the first parameter when the loop first begins. Thus, Begin is assigned the value of zero. There may be situations where you want the starting value to be other than zero, in which case you can use a variable to supply the value. The third parameter is the limit on the number of times the loop should be executed. In this case, the macro checks to see if the value of Begin is less than that of the variable *Point,* which stores the number entered by the user. If this is true, the code within the loop—that is, between the ForNext and EndFor commands—is executed.

Here is the rest of the code for this macro:

```
    Type(Text:"o")
    ParagraphIndent()
    HardReturn()
    HardReturn()
EndFor
```

The macro simply types the *o* character, a paragraph indent, and two hard returns. The EndFor command marks the point at which the macro loops back to the ForNext command. Each time the code within the loop is executed, the value of Begin is increased by 1. This is determined by the last of the ForNext parameters, which is the amount by which the counter, Begin, is incremented. (If this parameter is left blank, as it is here, then WordPerfect assumes you want to increment the counter by 1.) Obviously, this leads to a point where Begin is equal to Point, at which stage the macro stops looping and carries on after the EndFor command. In this example, you might complete the macro with this code:

```
ForNext(First;0;First<Point;)
    PosLineUp()
    PosLineUp()
EndFor
PosLineEnd()
```

Here you can see another ForNext/EndFor loop. This one moves the insertion point back up the document so it is ready for the user to start typing the text of the bullet points. Note that the ForNext command uses a different name for the counter parameter. This is not necessary; it is done to make the macro code less confusing. The EndFor command is followed by a positioning command that moves the insertion point to the end of the first line of the set of bullet points.

CHAPTER 9

Spreadsheet and Database Files

Personal computers can do a lot more than word processing. This chapter looks at how WordPerfect works with spreadsheet and database programs. You will learn how to convert database files to secondary merge files as well as how to cut and paste text, numbers, and graphics by using the Windows Clipboard. The chapter also looks at how you can use the Windows feature known as dynamic data exchange (DDE) to create links between WordPerfect documents and other programs.

About Spreadsheets and Databases

Spreadsheets are designed to calculate numbers and analyze data. Although WordPerfect can perform arithmetic and sort lists, spreadsheet programs like Microsoft Excel and Lotus 1-2-3 specialize in this type of work. In Figure 9-1, you can see a set of sales figures entered in Excel.

If you are working with a lot of numerical data, it makes sense to use a spreadsheet. However, spreadsheet programs have limited text editing and formatting tools, so you may want to use WordPerfect to write reports that are based on facts and figures stored in a spreadsheet file. In Figure 9-2, you can see a WordPerfect document that uses the data stored in the Excel spreadsheet shown in Figure 9-1. The techniques used to accomplish this are discussed shortly.

A *database* can be defined as a collection of information organized in a meaningful way. A *database manager* is a piece of software designed to help you deal with large collections of information, applying the power of your computer to the tasks of entering, sorting, searching, and reporting data. You may want to use WordPerfect to create letters and other documents that incorporate name and address information stored in files created by database management programs

	A	B	C	D
1		MacLeod Distillers		
2		Summary of Sales for the Year		
3				
4		Casks	Revenue	Per Cask
5	The MacLeod	34	11,560	340.00
6	Old Reaper	23	6,601	287.00
7	Bunachan	19	4,864	256.00
8	Capercaillie	16	2,992	187.00
9	Peat Mist	12	2,376	198.00
10	Ram's Breath	8	3,328	416.00
11	All Brands	112	31,721	283.22

Figure 9-1. *Sales figures in an Excel spreadsheet*

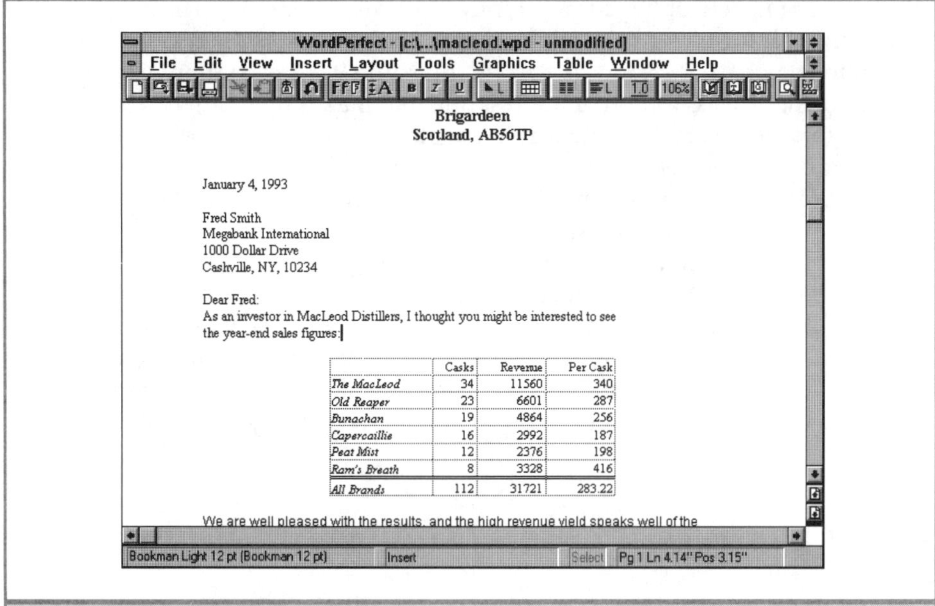

Figure 9-2. *Spreadsheet figures in a WordPerfect document*

such as Paradox and dBASE. In Figure 9-3, you can see a list of customers entered in a Paradox database.

To better understand what a database is, consider your local phone book. It presents three categories of information: name, address, and phone number. The

Viewing Maclient table: Record 1 of 18 Main

MACLIENT	Company	Address	City	State
1	Ashby-Smith	12 The Gables	Oakdale	MA
2	Cal-Deli Corp.	310 North Mary Ave	Sunnyvale	CA
3	FoodWorld Co.	540 Alder Drive	Milpitas	CA
4	GrandTime Inc.	730 Distel Drive	Los Altos	CA
5	Larsons Group	1007 Ridder Parkway	San Jose	CA
6	Liquor Marketing	90 South E Street	Santa Rosa	CA
7	MegaShops	901 Thompson Place	Sunnyvale	CA
8	Parker Inc.	510 Oakmead Drive	Sunnyvale	CA
9	Private Reserve	101 Claridge Dr.	Petrova	MA
10	Redfern Group	2312 Boumont	Sanderville	MA
11	Roundry Corp.	3050 Bowers Avenue	Santa Clara	CA
12	Samsons Inc.	3165 Kifer Road	Santa Clara	CA
13	Spirit Mart	75 Willow Road	Menlo Park	CA
14	SuperFare Corp.	2001 Stierlin Road	Mountain View	CA
15	SuperMart, Inc.	1720 North First St.	San Jose	CA
16	Timeland, Inc.	4401 Great Parkway	Santa Clara	CA
17	Whiskey World	700 Middlefield Road	Mountain View	CA
18	WineTime Corp.	300 Ferguson Drive	Mountain View	CA

Figure 9-3. *A Paradox database*

entries are organized alphabetically, typically one line per entry. The categories or columns of information in a database are referred to as *fields.* Each complete entry in the database is known as a *record.* In Figure 9-3, the columns City and State are fields. The collection of information that makes up CLIENT 1 is a record.

You can arrange database records in a table, as in Figure 9-3, or create a separate form for each one. In Figure 9-4, you can see one of the records shown in Figure 9-3 displayed as a form. Forms are like cards in an index file. Working with data in this form view makes it easier to enter new records. You can easily move from field to field and from record to record.

If you have used the merge feature in WordPerfect, you are already familiar with the terms "field" and "record." In Figure 9-4, you can see the information from Figure 9-3 presented as a WordPerfect merge data document. In the "Data File Conversion" section later in this chapter, you will see how to convert information from a database or spreadsheet into a secondary merge file.

Spreadsheet Data

If you think of a WordPerfect document as a sheet of electronic typing paper, then a spreadsheet is a page out of an electronic columnar pad. A spreadsheet arranges words and numbers in columns and rows. The boxes formed by the intersection of these columns and rows are known as *cells.* A spreadsheet is designed to perform calculations on the numbers it contains. These calculations

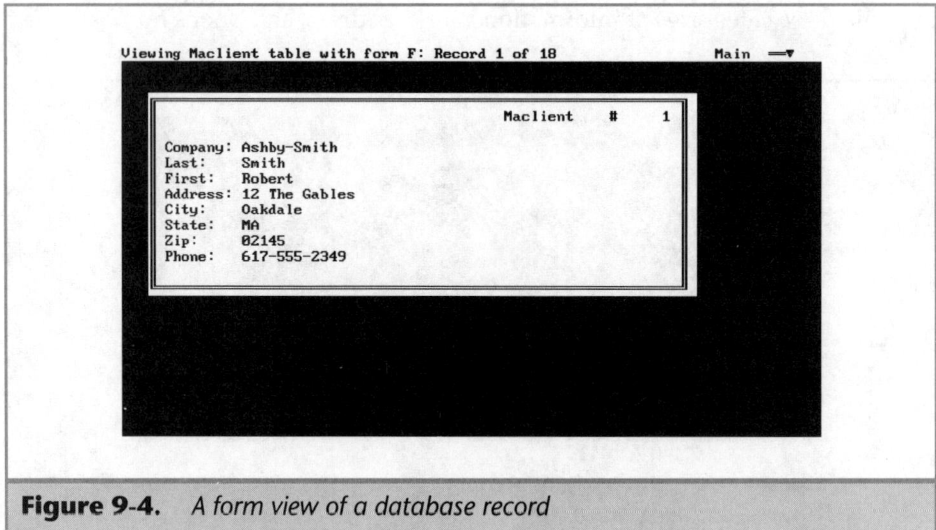

Figure 9-4. *A form view of a database record*

go far beyond the mathematical capabilities in WordPerfect, and a single spreadsheet can be hundreds of columns wide and thousands of rows long.

While the first spreadsheet programs were designed to perform calculations, it soon became clear that users wanted to do more with their facts and figures than arithmetic. Since spreadsheet programs are particularly good at creating tables, they are sometimes used as database managers. In Figure 9-5, you can see a 1-2-3 database of customer information. There are 1-2-3 commands for sorting such information and for searching for selected records.

The most widely used spreadsheet programs today are Lotus 1-2-3, Microsoft Excel, and Borland's Quattro Pro. Data files created by popular database programs such as Paradox and dBASE can be read by these spreadsheet programs. In addition, they can store data in a variety of spreadsheet formats, including WK1, the widely recognized 1-2-3 file format, and delimited text format, a generic format useful for database records. In the "Data File Conversion" section later in this chapter, you can see how WordPerfect handles these file formats.

Spreadsheet Graphics

Besides calculating and storing data, spreadsheets can also graph data, as shown in Figure 9-6. There you can see an Excel graph of the sales revenue listed in the spreadsheet in Figure 9-1. Most spreadsheet graphs are "live." This means that

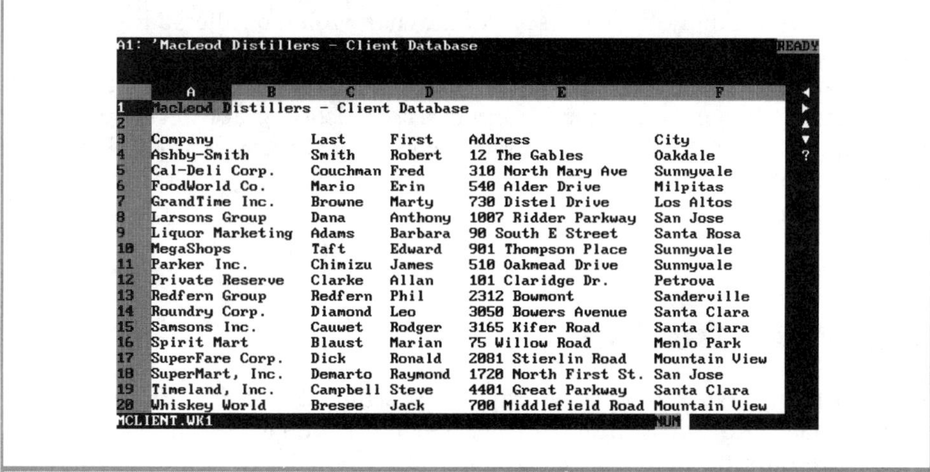
A1: 'MacLeod Distillers - Client Database READY

	A	B	C	D	E	F
1	MacLeod Distillers - Client Database					
2						
3	Company		Last	First	Address	City
4	Ashby-Smith		Smith	Robert	12 The Gables	Oakdale
5	Cal-Deli Corp.		Couchman	Fred	310 North Mary Ave	Sunnyvale
6	FoodWorld Co.		Mario	Erin	540 Alder Drive	Milpitas
7	GrandTime Inc.		Browne	Marty	730 Distel Drive	Los Altos
8	Larsons Group		Dana	Anthony	1007 Ridder Parkway	San Jose
9	Liquor Marketing		Adams	Barbara	90 South E Street	Santa Rosa
10	MegaShops		Taft	Edward	901 Thompson Place	Sunnyvale
11	Parker Inc.		Chimizu	James	510 Oakmead Drive	Sunnyvale
12	Private Reserve		Clarke	Allan	101 Claridge Dr.	Petrova
13	Redfern Group		Redfern	Phil	2312 Bowmont	Sanderville
14	Roundry Corp.		Diamond	Leo	3050 Bowers Avenue	Santa Clara
15	Samsons Inc.		Cauwet	Rodger	3165 Kifer Road	Santa Clara
16	Spirit Mart		Blaust	Marian	75 Willow Road	Menlo Park
17	SuperFare Corp.		Dick	Ronald	2001 Stierlin Road	Mountain View
18	SuperMart, Inc.		Demarto	Raymond	1720 North First St.	San Jose
19	Timeland, Inc.		Campbell	Steve	4401 Great Parkway	Santa Clara
20	Whiskey World		Bresee	Jack	700 Middlefield Road	Mountain View

MCLIENT.WK1 NUM

Figure 9-5. *A database in a 1-2-3 spreadsheet*

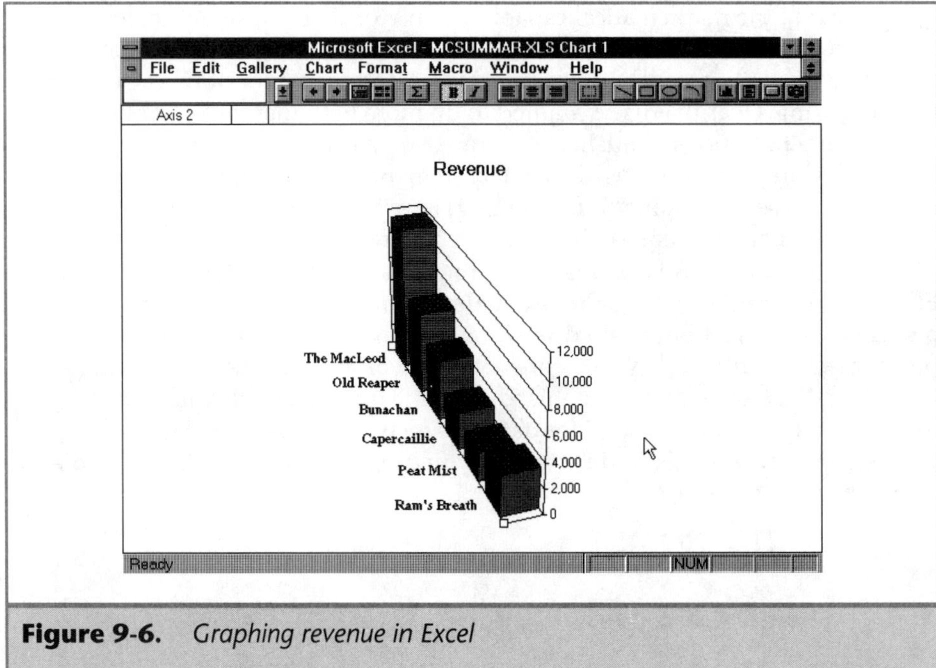

Figure 9-6. *Graphing revenue in Excel*

changes in the data that generate the graph are immediately reflected in the graph. Thus, if revenue from The MacLeod were changed in the worksheet in Figure 9-1 from 11,560 to 14,560, then the chart in Figure 9-6 would automatically be adjusted accordingly. Even the scale of the chart would be altered to accommodate the increased value.

Spreadsheet graphs can make attractive and informative contributions to WordPerfect documents. You can incorporate spreadsheet graphs in documents as figures. If you are working with a Windows spreadsheet such as Excel, you can incorporate charts as "linked" figures that are updated to reflect subsequent changes in the chart.

Spreadsheet Options

There are several ways in which WordPerfect documents can make use of information from a spreadsheet, whether the information is facts and figures, database records, or charts. The technique you use will depend on what you need the data for and the capabilities of the spreadsheet program you are working with. If you are working with a spreadsheet that runs under Windows, you can simply copy spreadsheet cells to the Windows Clipboard and paste them into a WordPerfect document. You can also use this technique to directly link cells in a Windows spreadsheet with a WordPerfect table.

If you are not working with a Windows spreadsheet, then you can select Insert/Spreadsheet/Database/Import from the menus to bring data from a spreadsheet into a WordPerfect document. You can also select Insert/Spreadsheet/Database/Create Link to connect a WordPerfect table with a set of spreadsheet cells.

Pasting, Importing, and the Windows Clipboard

The easiest way to bring spreadsheet data into a WordPerfect document is to use the Windows Clipboard. You can copy both graphics and text to the Clipboard by selecting Copy and Paste from the Edit menu. The Clipboard option is available when you want to use data from applications that are running under Windows.

Basic Copy and Paste

Suppose you are creating the letter shown in Figure 9-2. You have loaded Excel and the sales worksheet. You have also loaded WordPerfect and begun the letter. After typing the colon after "figures," press ENTER to create a new line. Then press CTRL+ESC to call up the Windows Task List. This allows you to switch from WordPerfect to Excel.

After selecting Excel in the list of tasks, select Switch To, and Excel appears in place of WordPerfect. If you are running Excel in full-screen mode, it will completely obscure WordPerfect. If you are running Excel within a smaller window, you will be able to view both WordPerfect and Excel at the same time. In the Excel spreadsheet, select the cells that contain the data you want to use in your WordPerfect document, as shown in Figure 9-7. After you select the cells, select Edit/Copy. Excel places a flashing line around the selected cells to show that they have been copied.

Now that the cells have been copied to the Clipboard, you can switch tasks to the Program Manager and double-click the Clipboard icon. You will see the data recorded there, as shown in Figure 9-8.

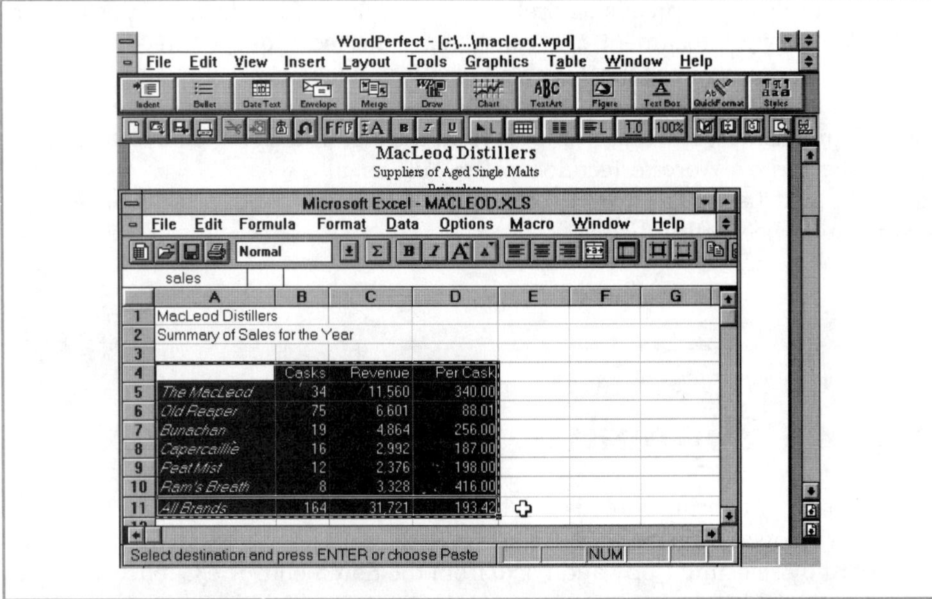

Figure 9-7. *The selected cells about to be copied in Excel*

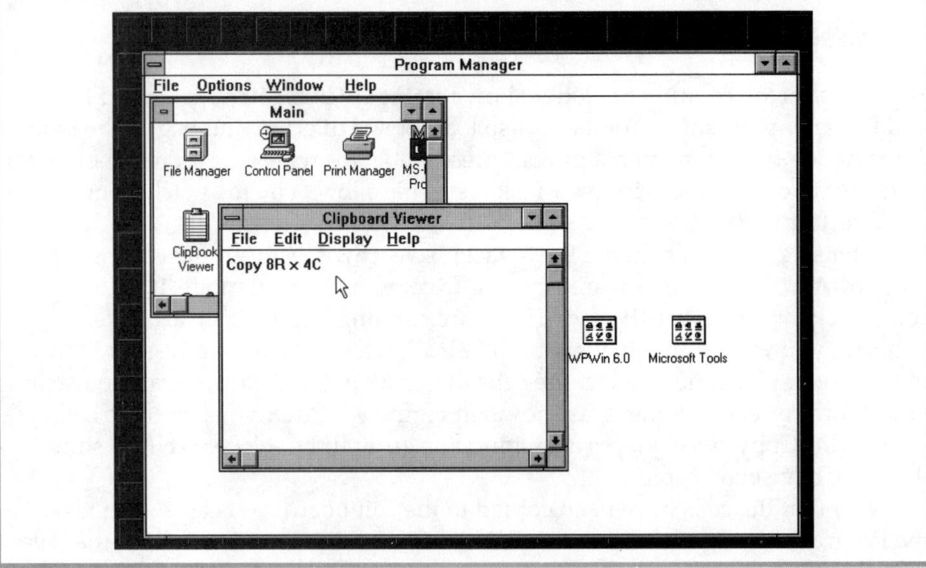

Figure 9-8. *How the Clipboard stores the copied cells*

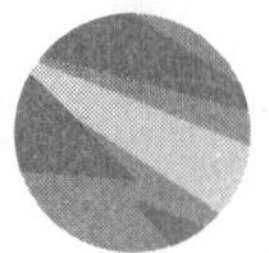

NOTE: Instead of the actual data, the Clipboard shows the notation "8R x 4C." This stands for eight rows by four columns, the size of the section of spreadsheet that has been copied.

You do not need to view the Clipboard to make use of its contents. All you need to do at this point is switch back to WordPerfect and select Edit/Paste. (You can move back to WordPerfect by pressing CTRL+ESC and using the Task List, or, if WordPerfect is visible on your screen, by clicking the title bar of the WordPerfect window to make it the active window.)

When you select Edit/Paste in WordPerfect, the contents of the Clipboard are placed in the current document at the current location of the insertion point. When spreadsheet data is pasted, WordPerfect creates a table to accommodate the data and duplicates as closely as possible the format of the information being copied, including fonts, type styles, colors or shading, and lines.

In Figure 9-9, you can see the initial result of the paste operation using the sample spreadsheet. Notice that the mouse pointer changes to a vertical or horizontal arrow when it is placed over a table cell. If you reveal codes in the document, you will see that WordPerfect has placed table codes around the pasted data. A [Tbl Def] code precedes the data, defining the dimensions of the table, and a [Tbl Off] code marks the end of the table.

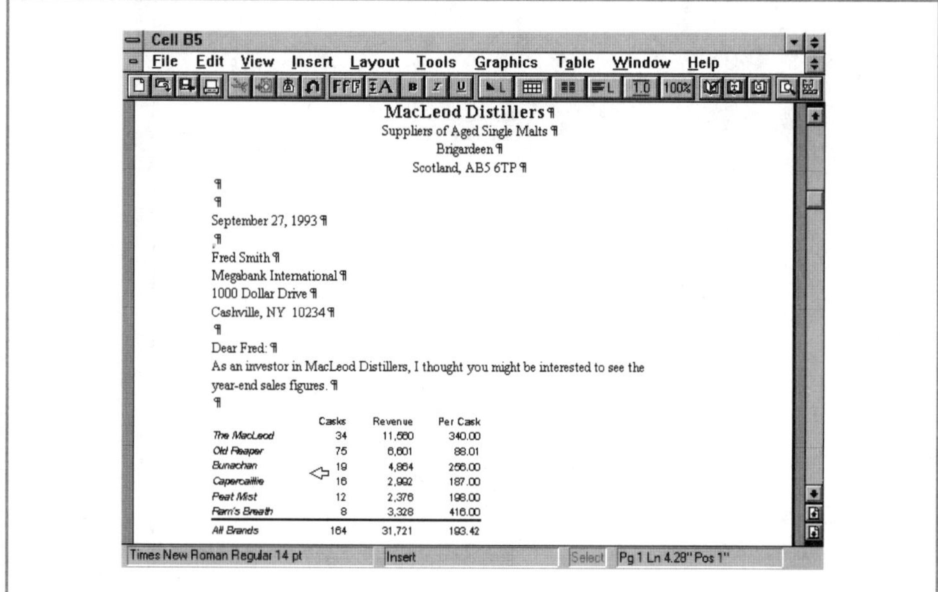

Figure 9-9. *The initial result of pasting the Excel data*

As you can see from Figure 9-9, it may be necessary to tidy up the table. The table looks choppy and unclear compared to the rest of your document. This is because WordPerfect is not always successful at translating the fonts used in the source application (in this case, Excel). The MS Sans Serif font of the original spreadsheet has been turned into a smaller Arial, which looks different in WordPerfect than it did in Excel.

To resolve the problem, you can make adjustments in the table. In this case, the font was changed to be consistent with what was used in the rest of the document, and the table was centered on the page. The result is shown in Figure 9-10, where the table is also centered.

To change table formatting, you select Table/Format from the menu. You will see the Format dialog box shown in Figure 9-11. Don't be surprised if your dialog box looks a bit different; the actual options displayed will depend on what formatting options are selected at the top of the dialog box. You can select Cell, Column, Row, or Table. To change how the table appears, select the appropriate part of the table you want to affect, and then make the change. For instance, to center the table, you would select Table and then choose Center in the Table Position box (bottom-left corner of the Format dialog box).

For more information on table commands, see Chapter 11, "Commands and Features."

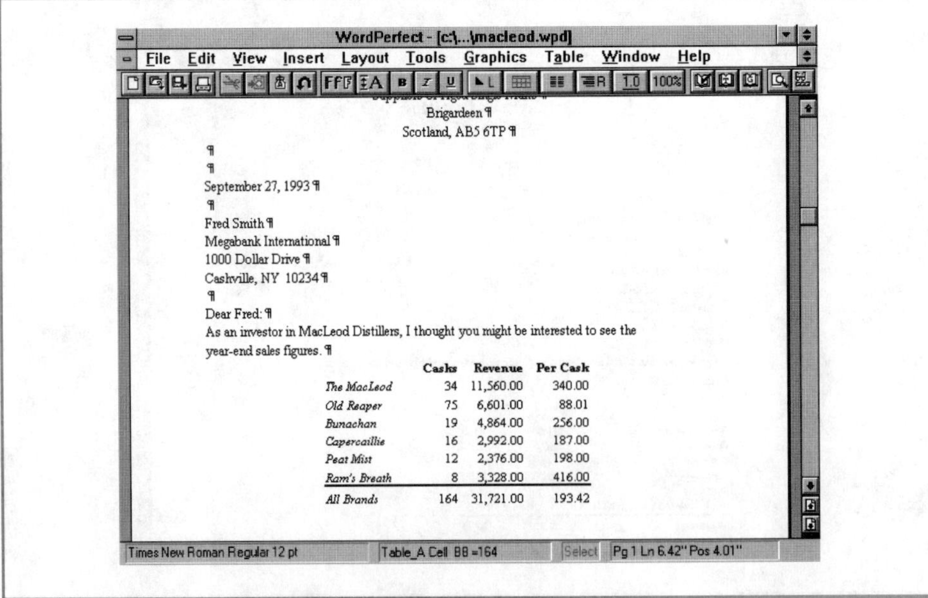

	Casks	Revenue	Per Cask
The MacLeod	34	11,560.00	340.00
Old Reaper	75	6,601.00	88.01
Bunachan	19	4,864.00	256.00
Capercaillie	16	2,992.00	187.00
Peat Mist	12	2,376.00	198.00
Ram's Breath	8	3,328.00	416.00
All Brands	164	31,721.00	193.42

Figure 9-10. *The table with improved formatting*

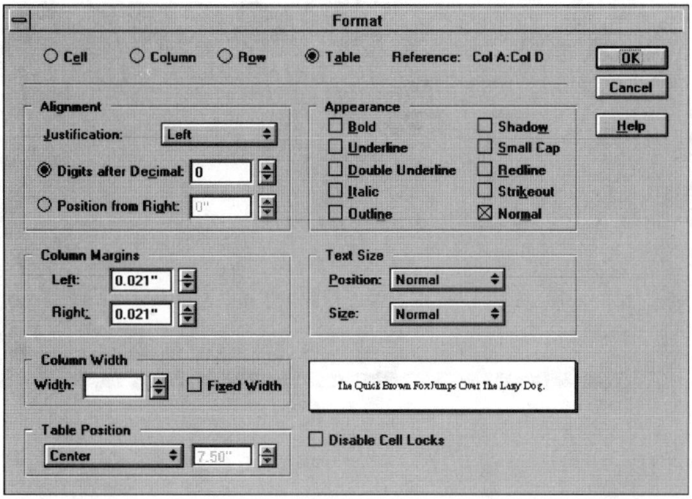

Figure 9-11. *The Format dialog box*

Spreadsheet Imports

The copy-and-paste technique allows a WordPerfect document to use data from a spreadsheet that is loaded into memory in an application running under Windows. However, you may want to use data that is stored in a spreadsheet file on disk rather than loaded into memory. This is possible with the Insert/Spreadsheet/Database/Import menu choices.

Suppose you are writing the letter shown in Figure 9-11 but the spreadsheet data you want to use is stored in a 1-2-3 file like the one shown in Figure 9-12. By selecting Insert/Spreadsheet/Database/Import, you can read the data in cells A4 through D11 directly from disk into a WordPerfect document without having to load the 1-2-3 program. In fact, WordPerfect gives you a choice between reading a select group of cells and reading the entire contents of the spreadsheet file.

If you have worked with a spreadsheet program such as Excel or 1-2-3, you know you can attach a name to a group of cells, known as a *range* or *block.* For example, in the worksheet shown in Figure 9-12, cells A4 through D11 might be named SALES. When you select Insert/Spreadsheet/Database/Import and tell WordPerfect the name of the spreadsheet file you want to import from, WordPerfect checks for named ranges in the file and lists them so you can select a range instead of the entire spreadsheet contents.

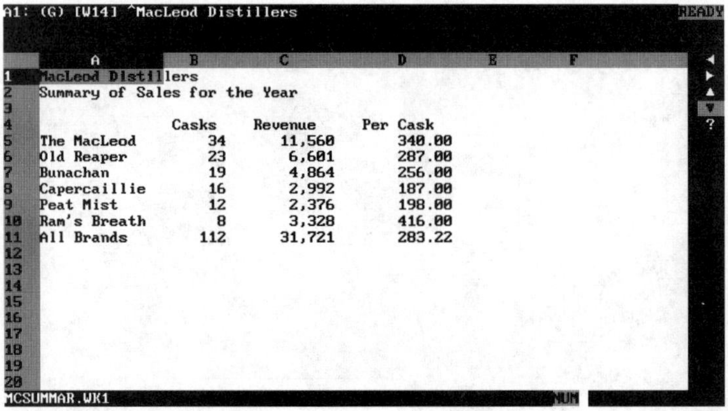

A1: (G) [W14] ^MacLeod Distillers READY

	A	B	C	D
1	MacLeod Distillers			
2	Summary of Sales for the Year			
3				
4		Casks	Revenue	Per Cask
5	The MacLeod	34	11,560	340.00
6	Old Reaper	23	6,601	287.00
7	Bunachan	19	4,864	256.00
8	Capercaillie	16	2,992	187.00
9	Peat Mist	12	2,376	198.00
10	Ram's Breath	8	3,328	416.00
11	All Brands	112	31,721	283.22

MCSUMMAR.WK1 NUM

Figure 9-12. *Data stored in a 1-2-3 spreadsheet*

If there are no named ranges in the spreadsheet file, you can still specify a range by entering its coordinates. You use the top-left cell address and the bottom-left cell address, separated by a colon or a pair of dots. For example, the range of cells from A4 through D11 in a 1-2-3 worksheet would be represented like this: A4..D11. If you are importing an Excel worksheet, you use a colon to separate the cell coordinates. WordPerfect can import spreadsheets from the following programs:

- Lotus 1-2-3
- Microsoft Excel
- PlanPerfect (versions 3.0 and higher)
- Quattro Pro
- Quattro Pro for Windows

In addition, WordPerfect will import files saved in data interchange format (DIF), which is supported by many types of spreadsheets.

To incorporate data from the 1-2-3 file in Figure 9-12 into your letter, you first need to know the name of the file and the directory in which it is stored. Then type the first sentence of the letter and press ENTER to create a new line. Select Insert/Spreadsheet/Database/Import, and WordPerfect displays the Import Data dialog box, shown in Figure 9-13.

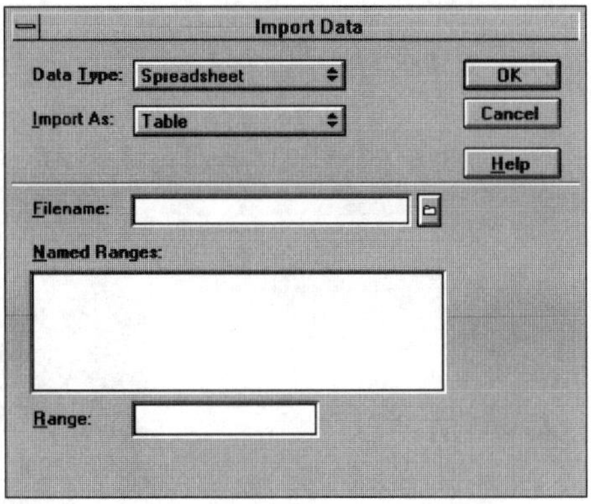

Figure 9-13. *The Import Data dialog box*

This dialog box contains three field choices: Filename, Named Ranges, and Range. All of these fields will be blank unless you have already used the command Insert/Spreadsheet/Database/Import in the document, in which case your earlier file and range choices will appear.

To select the spreadsheet file you want to use, enter the name and path in the Filename field. Alternatively, you can use the File Folder icon to display the Select File dialog box, which has been used in other places earlier in this book.

Once you have specified a spreadsheet filename, WordPerfect displays any named ranges in the spreadsheet in the Named Ranges box, as shown in Figure 9-14. The default range is <Spreadsheet>. The range A1..D11 is not actually all of the cells in the spreadsheet file, which extends from A1 to IV16384. What WordPerfect means by <Spreadsheet> is all of the cells from A1 to the furthest column and row that are occupied—in this case, column D and row 11.

You can see that the named range SALES is also shown in the Range Name list, together with its coordinates. If you want a range other than those listed, you can enter the coordinates in the Range field. In this case, select SALES from the Named Ranges list. The next step is to decide the type of import operation you want. Using the Import As field, you can choose to have the spreadsheet data imported as a table, as text, or as a merge data file.

When you have selected the spreadsheet range and type of import operation, choose OK to complete the command. As the table is imported, WordPerfect may display a message letting you know the table is wider than the current margins. WordPerfect permits tables wider than the current margins and paper selection to be imported (up to 64 columns wide), but you will then want to make adjustments to the document, such as reducing the font size, selecting landscape layout, or narrowing the columns.

Import Data

Data Type: Spreadsheet

Import As: Table

OK

Cancel

Help

Filename: c:\windows\excel\macleod.xls

Named Ranges:

<Spreadsheet>	A1:D11
sales	A4:D11
totals	A11:D11

Range: A1:D11

Figure 9-14. *The Import Data dialog box, showing range information*

As you can see from Figure 9-15, which shows the sample data imported into the letter, WordPerfect uses the current document font for all of the table entries. This is a major difference from the copy-and-paste approach, which attempts to use the format of the data as it appears in the source application.

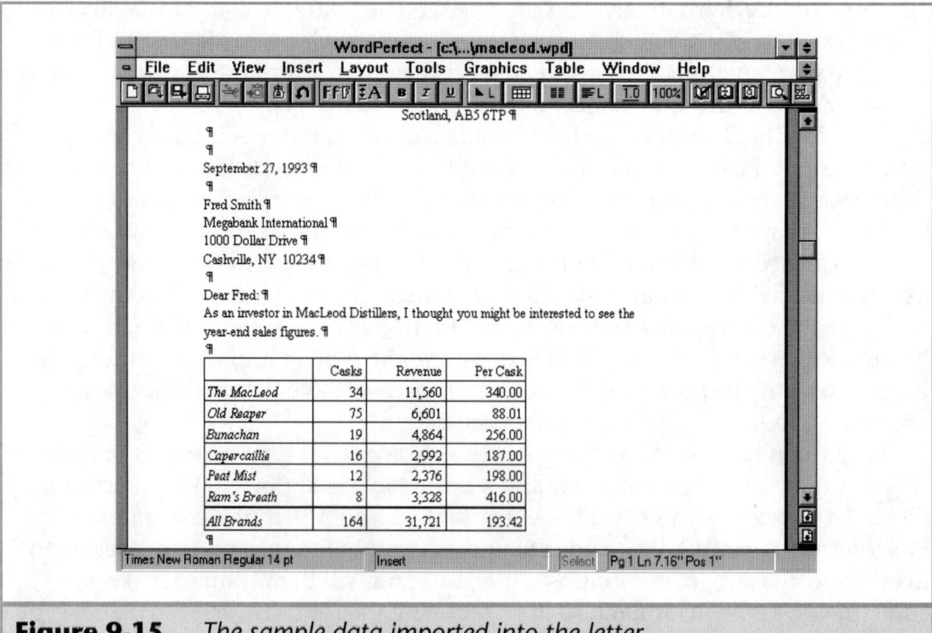

Scotland, AB5 6TP

September 27, 1993

Fred Smith
Megabank International
1000 Dollar Drive
Cashville, NY 10234

Dear Fred:
As an investor in MacLeod Distillers, I thought you might be interested to see the year-end sales figures.

	Casks	Revenue	Per Cask
The MacLeod	34	11,560	340.00
Old Reaper	75	6,601	88.01
Bunachan	19	4,864	256.00
Capercaillie	16	2,992	187.00
Peat Mist	12	2,376	198.00
Ram's Breath	8	3,328	416.00
All Brands	164	31,721	193.42

Figure 9-15. *The sample data imported into the letter*

NOTE: In Figure 9-15, an extra carriage return has been added above the table to distance it from the preceding text. However, no other changes have been made to the document. The line formatting in the table is created automatically by WordPerfect.

In Figure 9-16, you can see the results achieved by importing the sample data after selecting Text rather than Table as the Type setting in the Import Data dialog box. Notice that there are no special lines or borders on the text. Instead, WordPerfect inserts the spreadsheet data as plain text with tab stops defined for the positioning of information on each line. WordPerfect attempted to create a tab ruler that would match the format of the incoming data but was not completely successful. With some adjustment, the tabs can be aligned correctly, but importing spreadsheet data as text is usually less satisfactory than using the Table option.

Possible Links

When you copy and paste spreadsheet data into a WordPerfect document or select Insert/Spreadsheet/Database/Import, the information is copied into the document as words and numbers that become part of the document and have no

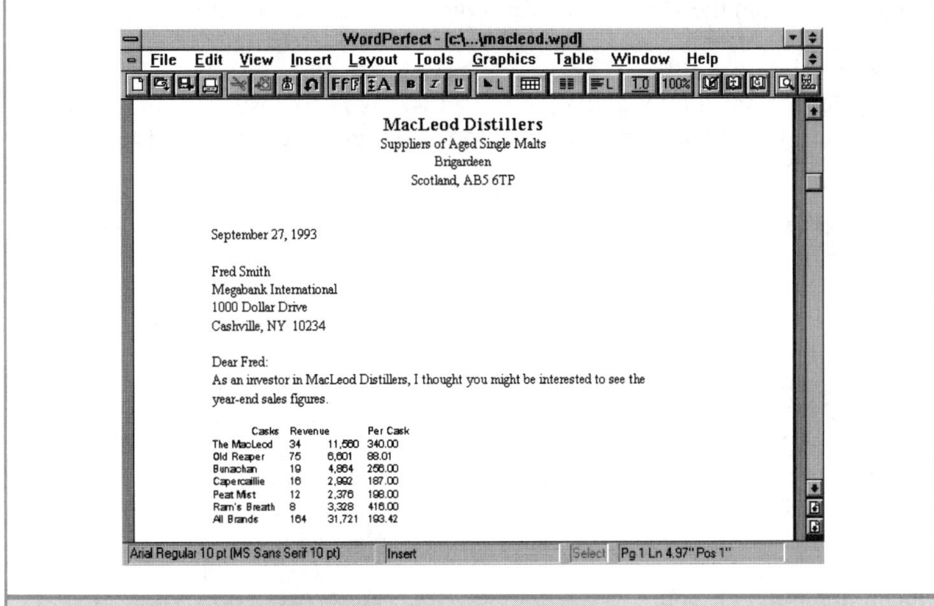

Figure 9-16. *Importing spreadsheet data as text*

further ties to the original spreadsheet. In some situations, this can be a problem. If the sales numbers in the spreadsheets in previous examples were to be altered, then the WordPerfect letter would be out of date, and you would need to manually update the letter.

Link Types

Instead of simply pasting or importing data from a spreadsheet into your WordPerfect document, you can create a link to the spreadsheet, thus ensuring that the document contains the latest numbers. There are two types of links available in WordPerfect, both of which take advantage of Windows technology. The first is a *DDE,* or *dynamic data exchange,* link. You can create a DDE link by selecting Import/Spreadsheet/Database/Create Link. A DDE link can be created only between WordPerfect and another application that supports DDE. However, DDE links can supply graphics as well as text and numbers, and they work with other programs besides spreadsheets.

The second type of link uses a technology called *OLE,* or *object linking and embedding.* Under this technology, an active two-way link can be created. This assumes that you are establishing a link with another application that also supports OLE. Whenever an OLE link is established, one of the applications acts as a client, and the other as a server. The client requests information about the linked object from the server, which supplies the information. Typically, the server is the application used to create the data being exchanged. WordPerfect for Windows can act either as a client or server in an OLE link.

To establish an OLE link, you can use either the Edit/Paste Special function or the Insert/Object function. Either method will produce the desired results.

Link Strategy

The idea behind both types of links is to make a connection between the spreadsheet and the WordPerfect document so that any changes in the spreadsheet are reflected in the WordPerfect document. The main difference between the two types of links is the way you can update information.

In a DDE link, information is updated whenever it is changed in the original spreadsheet. This means that you must manually open the original application that was used to create the spreadsheet, and make your changes there.

When an OLE link is established, you can update the original information by simply double-clicking on the object (the spreadsheet data) you want to update. When you do this, Windows opens the application that created the spreadsheet, allowing you to make your changes. When you close or save the information in that application, it is updated in your WordPerfect document.

Establishing Links

As with many WordPerfect functions, there are a multitude of ways you can establish a link. These methods include the following:

- Copying and pasting
- Inserting an object
- Creating a special link

The examples in this section assume that you want to create links between your WordPerfect document and a spreadsheet.

Copying and Pasting

This method involves the use of the Windows Clipboard, and then pasting the spreadsheet information in your document. This type of action can be used to establish either a DDE or OLE link. To use this method, follow these steps:

1. Load the spreadsheet program and file (the one that will be supplying the linked data to your WordPerfect document).
2. Select the portion of the spreadsheet that you want to appear in the WordPerfect document.
3. Select Edit/Copy in the spreadsheet program. This places a copy of the selected data in the Clipboard.
4. Load the WordPerfect document in which you want the spreadsheet information linked. Position the insertion point where you want the information to appear.
5. Select Edit/Paste Special. You will see the Paste Special dialog box, which indicates the source of the information in the Clipboard.
6. In the Data Type list, select how you want the information pasted. If you select ExcelWorksheet Object, then an OLE link is established. Any other selection results in a DDE link.
7. Click on Paste Link. After a few moments, the data from the Clipboard will appear in the WordPerfect document at the insertion point.

Inserting an Object

This method of establishing a link is used to create only OLE links. It is especially useful if you are creating brand new spreadsheet data—information that has not already been saved in a spreadsheet file.

To use this method, first position your insertion point at the place in your WordPerfect document where you want the object to appear. Then select Insert/Object and you will see the Insert Object dialog box:

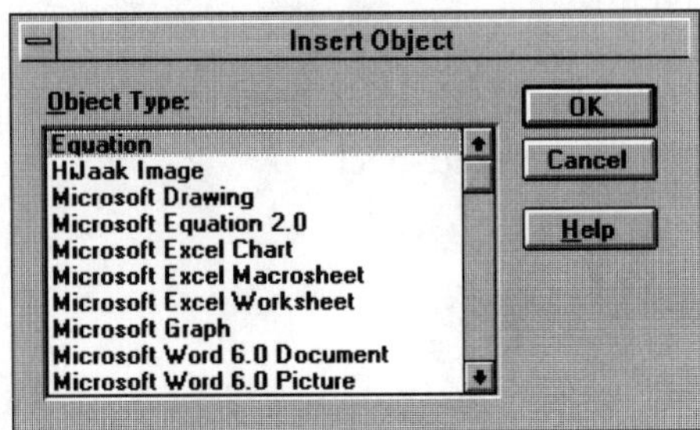

From the Object Type list, select the type of object you wish to insert. For instance, if you want to insert an Excel worksheet, choose Microsoft Excel Worksheet, then click on OK. Windows then loads Excel, with a brand new (blank) worksheet. You can enter spreadsheet data in any way desired. When you are satisfied with your results, close Excel or save the worksheet. The object (the spreadsheet data) is inserted in your WordPerfect document.

If you later want to update the information in the object, simply double-click on it. The original server application is loaded (in this case, Excel), and you can change your data.

Creating a Special Link

The third method of establishing a link between your document and a spreadsheet is done by choosing Insert/Spreadsheet/Database/Create Link. When you do this, you will see the Create Data Link dialog box, shown in Figure 9-17. This dialog box appears similar to the Import Data dialog box, previously shown in Figure 9-13.

This dialog box contains three field choices: Filename, Named Ranges, and Range. All of these will be blank unless you have already linked a spreadsheet before in the document, in which case your earlier file and range choices will appear.

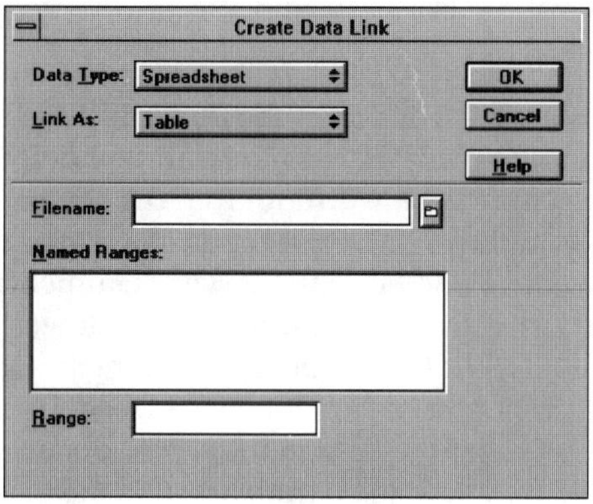

Figure 9-17. *The Create Link dialog box*

To select the spreadsheet file you want to use, enter the name and path in the Filename field. Alternatively, you can use the File Folder icon to display the Select File dialog box, which has been used in other places earlier in this book.

Once you have specified a spreadsheet filename, WordPerfect displays any named ranges in the spreadsheet in the Named Ranges box, as described earlier in the chapter. The default range is <Spreadsheet>, but you can also choose from any other named ranges in the spreadsheet. If you want to link a range other than those listed, you can enter the coordinates in the Range field.

The next step is to decide the type of import operation you want. Using the Link As field, you can choose to have the spreadsheet data linked as a table, as text, or as a merge data file.

When you have selected the spreadsheet range and type of link operation, choose OK to complete the command. After a few moments, the spreadsheet information is inserted in your document, and a link icon appears in your document, to the left side of the linked data. If you use the mouse to click on this icon, you can see the link information appear:

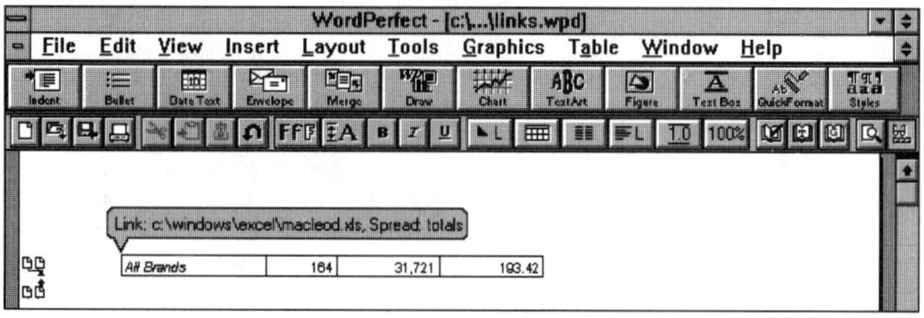

Tips for DDE Linking

Once you have created a link, you can save and close the WordPerfect document. The document stores the latest version of the data supplied by the server document. If you attempt to close the server document before the client document is closed, you may get a warning from the server application. For example, Excel warns you that a link exists and asks you to confirm closing the document. You can go ahead and close the server document; the data in the client document will stay as it was the last time the link was updated.

Whenever you open a WordPerfect document containing a DDE link, WordPerfect looks for the server document. If it is open, the link is updated. This happens regardless of whether the data in the server document has been altered. Since it can take a while for a link to be updated, this means you will have to pause between opening the document and editing it. It also means that simply opening a client document and then closing it will result in the "Save change" message. For these reasons, you may find it easier to use Manual than Automatic for the link update setting.

To change the link settings, select Edit/Links, which works on DDE links or links created with Insert/Spreadsheet/Database/Create Link. You will see the Links dialog box, shown in Figure 9-18.

This dialog box lists all the links within the current WordPerfect document. Select the link for which you want to change the updating method. When you change the Link Options setting to Manual, you must select Edit/Links and then click on Update Now whenever you want to make sure the linked data is current.

Another Technique

You can use one other technique to copy data from an application into a WordPerfect document. This works with applications that run under DOS

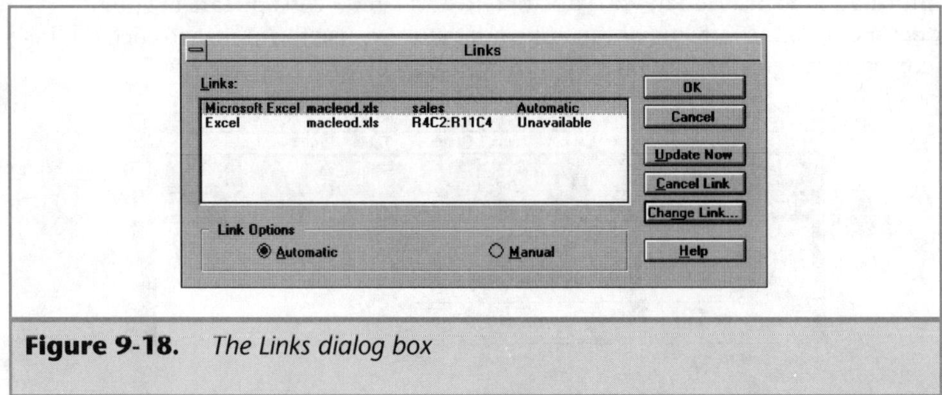

Figure 9-18. *The Links dialog box*

rather than Windows. If you are using Windows in 386 mode, you can launch a non-Windows program such as 1-2-3 Release 2.3 and run it in a separate window from which data can be copied. If you run 1-2-3 from an icon in the Program Manager and it takes up the whole screen, then press ALT+SPACEBAR. This will shrink the program into a window and present the window control menu. Press ESC to clear the menu, and you will be able to carry on with regular 1-2-3 commands.

If you then load a file that contains data you would like to use in WordPerfect, you can select it with the mouse pointer. This changes the 123 window title to Select 123. After highlighting the data you want, press ENTER. This copies the data from the window to the Clipboard.

Once the data are copied to the Clipboard, switch to WordPerfect and select Edit/Paste to copy it into your WordPerfect document. You are limited to one screen's worth of data per copy operation, and the pasted data are not formatted. It arrives in your WordPerfect document as pure text, with spaces instead of tabs.

Data File Conversion

There may be times when you want to merge a WordPerfect document with data from a spreadsheet or database file, such as the Paradox database seen earlier in Figure 9-3. Typically, this is name and address information, but it may also be other data, such as invoicing and accounting details.

About Merge Files

Chapter 6, "Merge Applications," and Chapter 11, "Commands and Features," contain details of the Tools/Merge command. A typical merge operation involves two files. The *form file* is the form letter that is being addressed to a group of people. The *data file* is the names and addresses of those people. In Figure 9-19, you can see a typical merge form file. The address at the top of the letter is made up of fields. It is into these fields that WordPerfect places data from the merge data file during the merge operation, creating a new letter for each record in the file.

In Figure 9-20, you can see a typical merge data file. This consists of a series of records, divided into fields. Each record is placed on a separate page of the document. The first page of the document defines the names of the fields. This is necessary only if the form file uses names for fields. If field names are not used, then each field is known by a number, based on the order in which it appears in the data file. Thus, field 1 corresponds to Company, field 2 to Last, and so on.

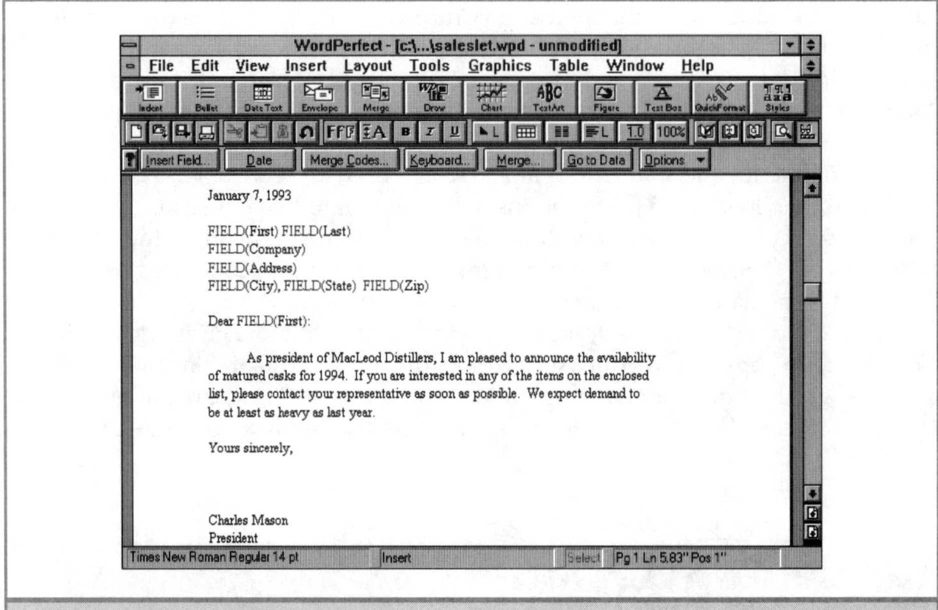

Figure 9-19. *A typical form file*

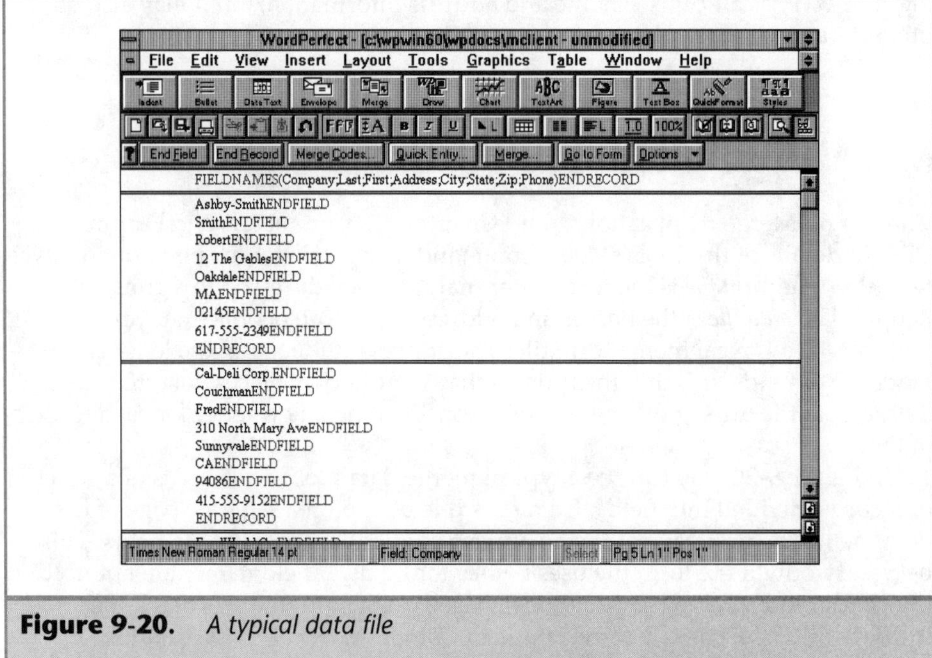

Figure 9-20. *A typical data file*

It is quite possible that the names and addresses you want to use for a merge operation have been stored by a program other than WordPerfect. The following sections discuss how to use such data with WordPerfect.

Delimited Text Files

The most common file format used by database and spreadsheet programs when exporting records is known as *delimited text.* Files in this format consist purely of fields and records and are quite similar to a data file in WordPerfect. Most programs that create delimited text files use a comma to separate, or "delimit," each field. This format is sometimes referred to as *comma separated values.* A carriage return is often used to delimit each record.

When you ask WordPerfect to open a delimited text file, the Convert File Format dialog box appears:

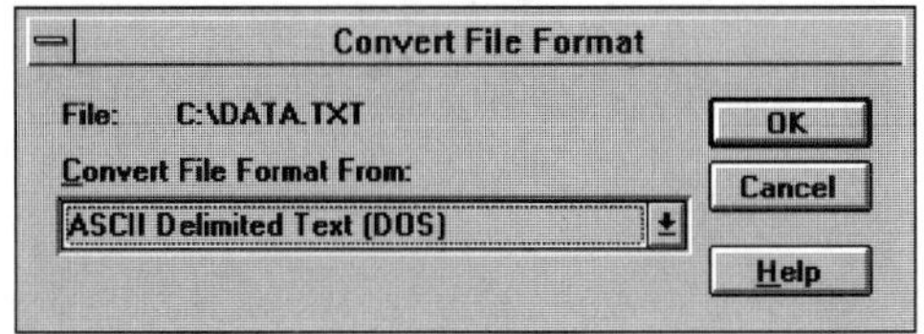

There are two delimited text formats to choose from in the Convert File Format From field: ASCII Delimited Text (DOS), which is for use with files created by non-Windows applications, and ANSI Delimited Text (Windows), used for delimited files generated by Windows applications. Select the appropriate type of delimited text, and then choose OK.

You will then see the Import Data dialog box. Make sure that you indicate the the file should be imported as a Merge Data File. When you click on OK, WordPerfect reads the delimited text file. Each comma is converted to an end-of-field merge code, appearing in the document as ENDFIELD, and each carriage return is converted to an end-of-record merge code, which appears as ENDRECORD, plus a hard page break. WordPerfect will not select the delimited text format when opening files. This is because it cannot tell if a comma is being used to separate fields or simply as part of normal text. This means that if you want this type of conversion, you must select it when you open a file.

There is a possibility of confusion when field information includes commas, such as Oakland, CA. For this reason, quotation marks are often used by programs that create delimited text files in order to enclose the data in each field. This gives rise to a slightly different file format known as *comma and quote delimited text.* WordPerfect understands this type of file and reads it when you select the delimited text format. Quotes around the field data are automatically removed.

You can export name and address data from WordPerfect to a database program by saving a merge data file in the delimited text format. In fact, this creates a comma and quote delimited file. When a WordPerfect document is saved as a delimited text file, all ENDFIELD merge codes are converted to commas. The ENDRECORD merge codes and accompanying hard page breaks are converted to carriage returns. Quotation marks are always placed around the field data during this type of conversion. You should select this format only if the WordPerfect document you are saving is already in the merge data format.

CHAPTER 10

Using WordPerfect for Windows on a Network

If you plan to use WordPerfect for Windows in a network environment, there are special considerations when you are installing and setting up the WordPerfect program files. This chapter explains the preparations you should make before installing WordPerfect. You will also learn how to install WordPerfect on your network and how to organize and manage the WordPerfect directories and files. Also explained here are the global network files that are important for

WordPerfect installation and the specific startup options for running WordPerfect on a network.

This chapter is intended for the system administrator who will be maintaining WordPerfect on the network. Generic network terminology is used so you can apply the information to your specific network.

Installation Preparation

Before you install WordPerfect, you need to designate an area on your network that all users can access. They should be able to access this area through a logical drive assignment or a search drive. You also need to verify that the computer from which you are installing WordPerfect has a logical drive assignment to the network directory where the WordPerfect files should be installed.

If you are using DEC PCSA/Pathworks, you must create a disk service area and mount it as read/write before you install WordPerfect.

Installing WordPerfect

There are four main steps to installing the WordPerfect files on a network; you must install the files on the network server, assign appropriate rights to the directories, create a global setup file that includes any companywide settings you want users to use, and then install the workstation portion of WordPerfect on each user's workstation.

Installing WordPerfect on the Network Server

To install WordPerfect on the network server, start the installation program. From the Installation Type dialog box, choose Network, then choose Server from the Network Installation menu. From the Network Installation Options dialog box, choose Source and Destination to specify where you are installing the files from and where you are installing the files to. Choose Files and specify which WordPerfect files you want to install.

Choose Net Options to display the WPWin 6.0 Supervisor Options dialog box. From this dialog box specify the location of the user's initialization files. The initialization files contain information about the Preferences that are set in the program. If you choose Shared directory on network, users must be able to read, write, execute, create, and open files in this directory. Choosing Shared directory gives you as the administrator more control over user setup files. However, installing setup files in the user's Windows directory may speed up performance.

You then need to specify users' rights. When you choose Yes for a Professional Install, WordPerfect leaves the path blank for template, printer, macros in the Files Preferences dialog box, and inserts the network location that you the supervisor specify as the Supplemental Files location. If you choose No for a Corporate Install, WordPerfect inserts the network directory as the default location for template, printer, macros in the Files Preferences dialog box, and leaves Supplemental Files location blank so users can insert their own directories. Choose Install Bitstream True Type fonts during workstation installation if you want users to have access to the Bitstream True Type fonts shipped with WordPerfect. This option does not copy the fonts to the users' workstations; it just gives them access to the fonts on the network.

The final supervisor option you must specify is a password for network printer initialization. Anyone who tries to initialize a printer, which is necessary when you need to download soft fonts to a printer, must enter this password. The password can contain up to 82 characters. After selecting the Supervisor Options, choose OK.

You then need to select the printers your users will need to access by choosing the Printers option. Make sure you select all printers the users will need to access, including personal printers. If you are unsure of the printers your users will need, or if you do not want to use network space for printer drivers that only a few people will use, you need to make sure that these users have access to copies of the original WordPerfect program disks. From these disks, they can run the WordPerfect Installation program, as described in Appendix A, "Installing Windows and WordPerfect," to install printer drivers to their local drives. Choose Start Installation to begin the installation.

Assigning Rights to WordPerfect Directories

Once the installation is complete, you should assign the appropriate rights or privileges to the newly created directories. The following table lists the default directories, their contents, and the rights users need for each directory. Remember, the terminology for these rights may vary, depending on your network.

Directory	Directory Contents	Rights
\WPWIN60	WordPerfect program files; LEARN, GRAPHICS, TEMPLATE, WPDRAW, and MACROS subdirectories	Read files, open or execute files, and search files
\WPC20	Shared program files and shared DLL files; QFINDEX and TRUETYPE subdirectories for QuickFinder index files and True Type fonts	Read files, open or execute files, and search files
\WPCNET	Setup files (*.BIF) and initialization file (*.INI)	Read files, write files, execute files, create files, and open files

Customizing the Setup of WordPerfect for Network Use

Once the installation is complete, you should open the WPWin 6.0 Setup program group and change any Preferences or other settings that you want all users using the WPCNET Settings option to have. For more information on WPCNET settings see "Global Network Files" later in this chapter.

Installing Individual Users

After installing the files and customizing the necessary setup options, you can complete the installation process by installing the necessary information on the individual user workstations. You can have individual users run the install program on their own machines or you can run it on each machine.

Start the installation program; from the Installation Type dialog box, choose Network, then choose Workstation from the Network Installation menu. Enter the network directory where WordPerfect for Windows is located, such as x:\WPWIN60, and choose OK. Next enter the name of the Program Group where you want the WordPerfect program icons to display. The workstation installation is now complete and the user can select the WordPerfect icon from the Program Group.

Global Network Files

During the installation process and the initial setup process, several global network files are created. These files include the environment files (*.ENV), setup files (*.BIF) and the initializing files (*.INI). Each of these files is read by WordPerfect on startup and passes important network and setup information to the program. This means that each time a user executes WordPerfect from the network, the information from these files is accessed by the user.

Environment Files

The first group of files created during the installation process is the *.ENV files. These files contain pertinent startup options for running WordPerfect on the network. The following environment files are created during the installation process for the WordPerfect program, the File Manager program, the Speller, and the Thesaurus, as shown here:

WP{WP}.ENV
QF{QF}.ENV
SP{SP}.ENV
TH{TH}.ENV

The WP{WP}.ENV file is stored in the WordPerfect program directory; usually, this is x:\WPWIN60, where *x* represents the drive letter you assign. The other three files are stored in x:\WPC20, which is the shared program directory. By default, the WP{WP}.ENV file contains the following startup options:

Option	Description
/ni-x0:\WPCNET	Specifies the path for the WPCNET.BIF and WTAPI.INI file
/wpc-x0:\WPC20	Specifies the path for the shared product files

If you need to edit the environment file, you can retrieve it into a DOS text editor and make the necessary changes. Along with the preceding options, you may want to include the /d and /pi options in the WP{WP}.ENV file. For more information on these startup options and those used in the WP{WP}.ENV file, see "Network-Specific Startup Options" later in this chapter.

BIF Setup Files

As a system administrator, you can create a global setup file that all users will access when they run WordPerfect on the network. This setup file is named WPCNET.BIF. To change the default settings contained in this file, choose the WPCNET Settings icon from the WPWin 6.0 Setup program group. This option starts WordPerfect. While in WordPerfect, make the changes you want to include in each user's setup file. For example, you may want to set up a global printer for all users by choosing File/Select Printer. To specify standard document settings for all users on the network, choose Layout/Document/Initial Code Styles. Then use the WordPerfect layout options to set standard margins, tabs, and other document settings.

Once you make the desired changes, exit WordPerfect. The setup file is stored in the \WPCNET directory. If you need to change or update the information in the global setup file, start WordPerfect again from the WPCNET Settings icon from the WPWin 6.0 Setup program group and make the desired changes. If, for example, you install a new printer on your network, you might need to update the global setup file to change the network printer for all users.

Each time a user starts WordPerfect, the WordPerfect program uses the global setup options you have defined. Although the global setup file is used, any changes a user makes to settings are stored in a personal setup file. The personal setup file is created when you install WordPerfect on the workstation, and its settings override those in the global setup file. The personal setup files are usually stored in the user's Windows directory, unless you specified a shared network drive during the installation process. Storing the setup files in one location on the network allows you to easily manage the BIF files for the system. Make sure the users have the necessary rights to create and modify files in the directory where the personal setup files are stored.

You can use the WPCNET Settings option anytime to make changes to the global setup file. Each time a user enters WordPerfect, the program reads the global setup file.

Initializing Files

The WTAPI.INI file is an initializing file and is similar to WordPerfect BIF setup files. The information contained in the WTAPI.INI file is specific to the Writing Tools options available in WordPerfect. Information about the location of the different programs such as Speller, Grammatik, and Thesaurus are included in this file. When you installed the server portion of WordPerfect, you specified where to store initializing and setup files. The file can be stored in the user's

Windows directory or in a network directory that you specified. Individual users' WTAPI.INI files are stored in the specified location; the global WTAPI.INI file is stored in the x:\WPNET directory.

Once a user modifies any setting stored in an *.INI file, the filename changes to WPXXX20.INI, where *XXX* represents the user's network initials. Once a user modifies settings contained in the WTAPI.INI file, he or she no longer uses the global file.

Network-Specific Startup Options

Startup options let you configure, at the time WordPerfect is started, one or more options for running WordPerfect. Generally, startup options are added as parameters after the WordPerfect program name on the command line. For example, the /d startup option lets you specify a directory for temporary program files; to use this option, you start WordPerfect by typing **wpwin.exe /d-directory** at the command line.

Under Windows, you can edit the command-line properties for the WordPerfect application, or you can use the File/Run feature from the Program Manager to begin WordPerfect with startup options. You can also combine two or more startup options, as shown here:

```
wpwin.exe /d=c:mytemp /nt=2 /ps-setfiles
```

If you prefer, you can add a DOS SET command to your AUTOEXEC.BAT file to assign startup options for the WordPerfect program. For example, if you want to use the /d startup option for WordPerfect, each time you start the computer, you could add set wpwin=/d-c:\mytemp to your AUTOEXEC.BAT file.

The following sections explain the startup options that are especially useful when running WordPerfect on a network. For complete information about all WordPerfect startup options, see Startup Options in Chapter 11, "Commands and Features."

/d- Directory

The /d startup option (directory for temporary files) lets you specify where WordPerfect should create your temporary files. This can be a personal network drive or a directory on the hard drive. Users must be able to create and modify files in this directory. You can place the /d option in the WP{WP}.ENV file, but it is only advisable to do so if you are using a common directory for all users' temporary files. This option is better suited for a DOS set command or in the Windows file properties defined for the WordPerfect application. If you do not use this option, temporary files are created in the \TEMP or \TMP directory for Windows temporary files.

If these directories are not available, the program looks for and stores temporary files in the directory where WordPerfect for Windows is stored, which is usually \WPWIN60.

Setting this option to a local drive or RAM drive may increase the speed at which WordPerfect operates.

/nt-n

The /nt startup option (network type) lets you specify which network software you are using. The *n* represents a number corresponding to the network type; these numbers are listed in the following table.

Number	Network Type
0	Other
1	NOVELL NetWare
2	Banyan Vines
3	TOPS Network
4	IBM LAN Network
5	Nokia PC-Net
6	3COM 3+
7	10NET
8	LANtastic
9	AT&T StarGROUP
A	DEC PCSA (Pathworks)
B	3COM 3+ OPEN
C	Banyan StreetTalk

Table 10-1. *Networks Supported by WordPerfect for Windows*

/pi- Directory

The /pi startup option (path to WTAPI.INI file) lets you specify where your WTAPI.INI file is located. Use this option only when the WTAPI.INI file is not located in the user's Windows directory.

REFERENCE

PART THREE

Command Reference

CHAPTER 11

Commands and Features

This chapter contains all the features found in WordPerfect for Windows, listed in alphabetical order. Each entry describes a feature and, as appropriate, lists shortcut keys and suggestions on how the feature can be used. Many of the entries also refer to sections of this book where the feature is covered in greater detail.

Abbreviations

If you have text that must be typed repeatedly in a document, you can save time by using *abbreviations*. Abbreviations are particularly useful for lengthy phrases, sentences, or even paragraphs.

You first define the unabbreviated phrase and assign it a keyword, or abbreviation. Then, throughout your document, just type the abbreviation. Since an abbreviation is a condensed form of the text you defined, you can expand it later.

Menu Selections

To create an abbreviation, highlight the text you want included in the abbreviation, select Insert/Abbreviations, and click Create. The Create Abbreviation dialog box appears where you type an Abbreviation Name in the text box. Click OK.

NOTE: Generally, shorter abbreviation names are more convenient to type into your document. However, if you use many abbreviations, you may want to provide longer and more descriptive names than, say, "X" or "RE," so that you can more easily distinguish them.

To place an abbreviation in your document, simply type it at the insertion point. Alternatively, you can select from a list of available abbreviations by choosing Insert/Abbreviation and highlighting one of the abbreviations listed. Below the list the full text of the highlighted abbreviation is shown. By double-clicking an abbreviation from the list, you can expand it at the current cursor location.

If you inadvertently placed and expanded the wrong abbreviation, you can replace it by clicking Replace in the Abbreviation dialog box.

To expand an abbreviation in your document, place the insertion point on the abbreviation and select Insert/Abbreviation and click Expand, or press the shortcut key ALT+A. The abbreviation is immediately expanded to its full text.

Advance

The *Advance* command moves the insertion point and any selected text to a specific position relative to the current location of the insertion point. You can also specify the distance from the left or the top edge of the page.

The Horizontal Distance and Vertical Distance features place the insertion point at an exact horizontal or vertical position on the page. You can advance to within .001 inch of a desired position, which permits precise placement of text, graphics, and tables within a document or form.

Although you can set the units of measurement to any of the common units (inches, centimeters, millimeters, points, and so on), the default units of measurement in WordPerfect are inches. To change the default units of measurements, see Display Preferences later in this chapter.

Menu Selections

When you choose Layout/Typesetting/Advance, the Advance dialog box appears, as shown here:

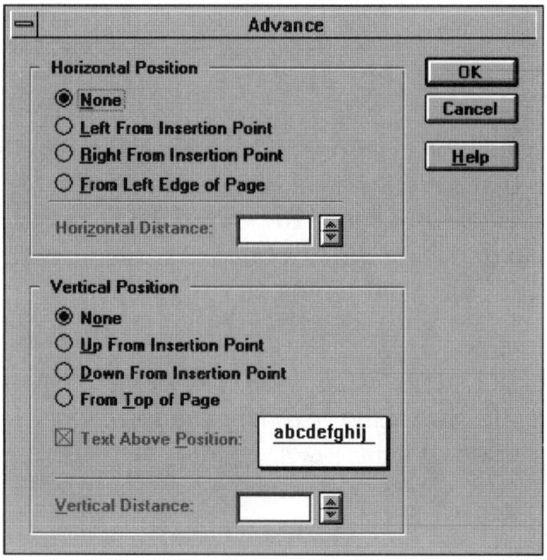

Select the appropriate options to specify the direction that you want the insertion point to move, relative to its current position or from the edge of the page. Specify the distance in inches (horizontal, vertical, or both) that you would like the insertion point to move. The insertion point will move accordingly.

Once you have placed the advance code (HAdv) or (VAdv), you can check the status bar for the exact position of the insertion point. You can also locate the advance code (HAdv) or (VAdv) in your document by choosing View/Reveal Codes.

By using the Advance command, you can also force text to remain above the position you specify. This is done by clicking the Text Above Position command. This is convenient, for instance, if you want to fill in preprinted forms, particularly those with lined boundaries. If you measure to the bottom of a field on the form (identified by a line), you can activate the Text Above Position command and make WordPerfect advance to that location and begin printing text above the line.

Related Entries

See Chapter 3, "Tools and Techniques."

Align Text

See Justification.

Append to Clipboard

The *Append* command can be used only when the Windows Clipboard contains text and/or graphics that have been cut or copied to it. The Append command attaches the selected text or graphic to the end of the current contents of the Clipboard, rather than replacing the Clipboard's contents with new material, as the Edit/Cut and Edit/Copy commands do.

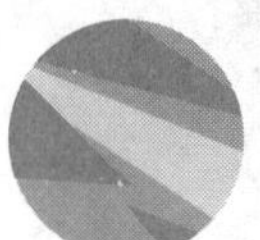

NOTE: *Append will not function when either the Clipboard contents or the selected text in the document is a rectangular block, a bitmapped graphic (.BMP), or a tabular column.*

Menu Selections

Edit/Append

Related Entries

Clipboard
Paste Special

Arrow Keys

The arrow keys on the keyboard are used to move the cursor through the text of the document and also to select commands from menus and dialog boxes. On more recent AT-style keyboards there are two sections containing arrow keys, as shown here:

Numeric keypad/Cursor movement section

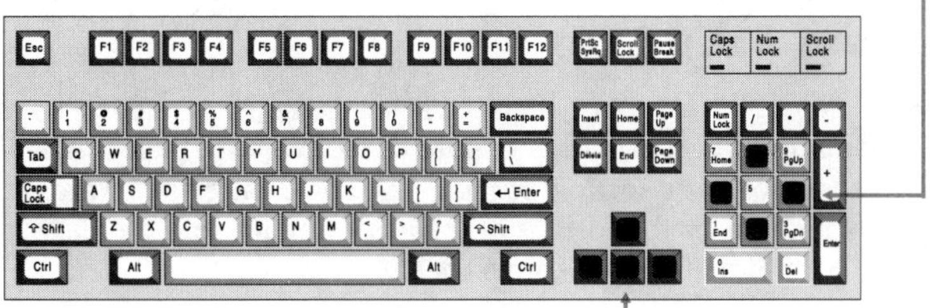

Cursor movement section

The two sections of the keyboard can be used interchangeably, provided the NUM LOCK key is switched off. There is usually a small light on the keyboard indicating when the NUM LOCK key is activated. When NUM LOCK is on, that area of the keyboard serves as a ten-key numeric input pad.

On older XT-style keyboards there are no separate arrow keys. The arrow keys are located on the 2, 4, 6, and 8 keys on the numeric keypad.

ASCII Text Files

You can use WordPerfect to create and edit ASCII files, which are used, for example, to create your AUTOEXEC.BAT and CONFIG.SYS files. There are three file import and export filters that allow you to bring ASCII files into WordPerfect and to save them again as ASCII:

ASCII Delimited (DOS) Text is the type of file that can be brought in from most spreadsheet or database programs and used by WordPerfect as a secondary merge file.

The ASCII Generic Word Processor (DOS) file format replaces each soft return (SRt) with a space and continues the information following the soft return with what was previously on the next line. It continues with this one long line of text until it encounters a hard return (HRt) code, which it honors and puts into the output file.

The ASCII Text (DOS) format places a hard return at the end of every line of text and converts tabs to spaces.

Menu Selections

There are slightly different processes to be followed depending upon whether you are importing or exporting ASCII files.

Importing ASCII Files

To import an ASCII file into WordPerfect, select File/Open and designate the ASCII file to be opened. If you are not sure of the filename, select All Files (*.*) from the List Files of Type section of the Open File dialog box. WordPerfect automatically recognizes the format of the incoming file and displays the Convert File Format dialog box, shown here:

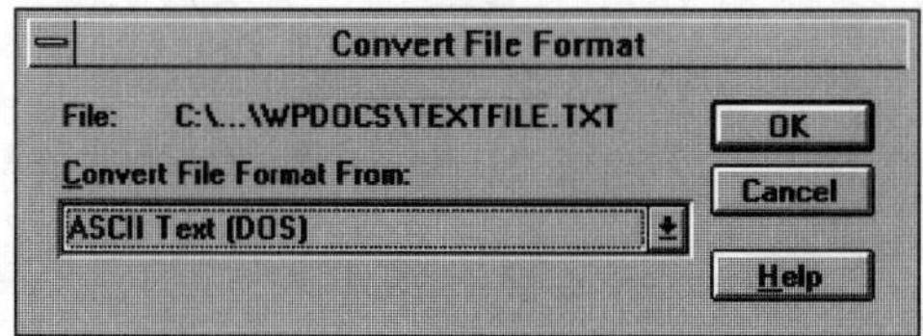

Either click OK, or select another option from the pull-down list and then click OK.

Exporting ASCII Files

To export a file into ASCII format, select File/Save As and indicate the type of ASCII format you want to use in the Format section of the Save As dialog box, as shown in Figure 11-1. In this example, the file is saved as ASCII Text (DOS). Once you have selected the format type, click OK, and WordPerfect converts your text to the designated file type and saves it to disk.

Attributes

Attributes is a term that refers to the way your text appears on your monitor and the way your text appears when printed on paper.

The term attributes also refers to a collection of characteristics applied to text in a document. Text attributes include the font and the actual typeface you select, as well as enhancements you make to the chosen typeface, such as bold, underline, and color.

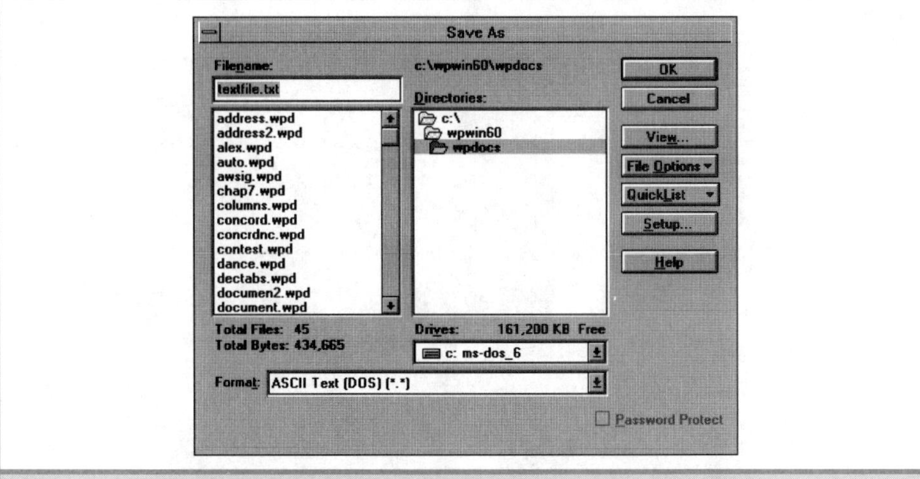

Figure 11-1. *Exporting an ASCII file using the File/Save As command*

Menu Selections

The way text appears on your monitor is controlled by settings you make in the Display Preferences dialog box. You access this by selecting File/Preferences/Display.

Text enhancements are accessed by pressing the F9 shortcut key or through the Layout/Font menu. When you select Font from the Layout menu, you see the dialog box shown in Figure 11-2. From this dialog box you can modify all attributes of your text. You can see a sample of your attribute choices in the Resulting Font section of the dialog box.

Applying Attributes

The general approach to using any of the text attributes is the same. However, you can apply attributes in a number of different ways.

First, you can go into the Layout/Font menu, click the attribute you want to use, and then return to the typing screen and type your text. To apply the common attributes bold, italic, and underline, you can simply click the corresponding icon on the power bar. From that point on, text will reflect the attribute you selected until you change attributes again. If you want to use multiple attributes, return to the Font menu and click any additional ones you need. Turn off the attributes by returning to the Font menu and clicking them again.

Figure 11-2. *The Font dialog box*

A second way to apply text attributes involves typing the text first, highlighting it, and then applying the attribute to it. Once the text is selected, choose Layout/Font, or press F9, and select the attributes you want. Some attributes can be applied by pressing the shortcut keys assigned to them. For example, if you want to underline some text you have already typed, select the text and use the shortcut key CTRL+U to underline it.

Yet another technique for applying a text attribute involves use of the Font button bar and the power bar, as shown here:

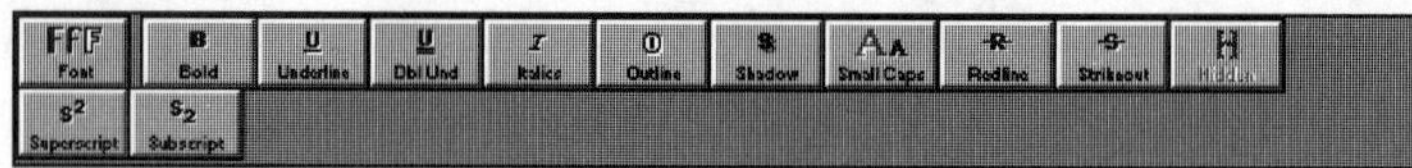

In Chapter 3, "Tools and Techniques," you learned how to create a customized button bar that contains only those buttons you need for your tasks. If you place text attribute buttons on your power bar, you can then turn an attribute on or off by clicking the appropriate button.

Related Entries

Colors, Text
Fonts, Displaying
See also Chapter 3, "Tools and Techniques"

A

AUTOEXEC.BAT File

AUTOEXEC.BAT is a file in the boot drive (usually C:) root directory. It contains DOS commands that are run automatically every time you turn on or restart your computer.

You can use WordPerfect to modify your AUTOEXEC.BAT file. Before you modify your AUTOEXEC.BAT file, you should always make a backup copy of it so that if the new version doesn't work correctly, you can re-create the original version with a minimum of difficulty.

Once you have copied your AUTOEXEC.BAT file to another disk or saved it under a different name, you can modify it. To do so, first create a new document and make the margins on it as narrow as possible, to increase the writing area of the document to its maximum. This prevents word wrap as much as possible. Word wrap causes certain commands in an AUTOEXEC.BAT file not to work correctly. To minimize word wrap even more, you can edit your document using a smaller font. If you do have lines that wrap, you can save the file using the ASCII Generic Text file format, so that soft returns will be disregarded.

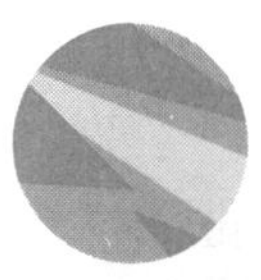

WARNING: AUTOEXEC.BAT must be an ASCII text file. If it is not—if you save it in WordPerfect format—your system will not boot.

Menu Selections

Select File/Open, select the proper drive and directory, and enter AUTOEXEC.BAT in the Filename section of the dialog box. WordPerfect displays a Convert File Format dialog box indicating that the text is in ASCII Text (DOS) format. Click OK. At this point, you can edit the document as necessary. Be sure to press ENTER at the end of each line.

When you have finished your modifications, select File/Save As. Be sure that ASCII Text (DOS) is still indicated as the file format. Then click Save. Your modified AUTOEXEC.BAT will be saved to disk. To test it, exit from WordPerfect and from Windows and type **AUTOEXEC.BAT** at the DOS prompt. If the file executes without errors, then restart your computer. If it does not perform properly, you have the opportunity to correct the problem before rebooting (restarting the computer). Once you restart the computer, the changes you made to the file will take effect.

Related Entries

ASCII Text Files

Back Tab

The *back tab* is similar to a hanging indent, except that a hanging indent tabs right from the left margin. Use back tab whenever you are creating hanging indents to the *left* of the margin.

Menu Selections

To place a back tab, place the cursor at the beginning of the line and select Layout/Paragraph/Back Tab, or press SHIFT+TAB. If you reveal codes at the location of the back tab, you will see a (Hd Back Tab) code.

Related Entries

Hanging Indent
Indent

Backspace Key

The BACKSPACE key deletes the character to the left of the cursor. It is very different from the LEFT ARROW key. The BACKSPACE key deletes text, while the LEFT ARROW key simply moves the cursor to the left by one character. Don't confuse the BACKSPACE key with the DELETE key. Although the two keys function similarly—they delete text—the DELETE key deletes characters to the *right* of the cursor.

NOTE: You can delete an entire word by positioning the cursor anywhere on the word and pressing CTRL+BACKSPACE. *Likewise, you can restore any deleted words by pressing* ALT+BACKSPACE.

Related Entries

Delete Key

Backup, Original Files

A common word processing task is to open an existing file, modify it, and finally save it to disk. Typically, if you save the modified version under the same filename, the modified text overwrites the previous version. The original version will be gone. WordPerfect provides a tool that minimizes the risk of losing the prior version of a file. By using this option, you can always go back to the last version of the file, before modifications were made.

Menu Selections

Select File/Preferences/File and click Original Document Backup to enable this option. Provide a document backup directory, if desired, and exit the dialog box by clicking OK.

When you enable this option, any time you retrieve a file from disk, modify it, and then save it under the same filename, WordPerfect makes a backup of the original file, using the same filename and the extension .BK!. In this way, if you have a file named WORK.DOC on disk and you retrieve, modify, and save it under the same filename, another file will be created on your disk named WORK.BK!. This second file will contain the text of your original, unmodified file named WORK.DOC.

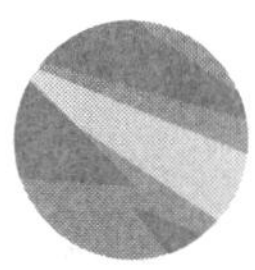

NOTE: *If you have files on disk named WORK.JAN, WORK.FEB, and WORK.MAR, each will create a backup file named WORK.BK!. As you can see, this counteracts the benefit of the Document Backup feature. To prevent this from happening, you must use a different naming convention such as WORKJAN.DOC, WORKFEB.DOC, and so on.*

You can control where WordPerfect stores your backup files on disk by specifying a drive and subdirectory for them in the Backup Directory box.

Related Entries

Descriptive Name
Preferences

Backup, Timed

When you type any document, your text not only appears on your monitor, but it is also held in the random access memory of your computer. Random access memory is usually referred to by its acronym, RAM, and is different from your hard disk. RAM requires an uninterrupted supply of power to remember what you have typed. If the power goes off, even for a second, the contents of RAM are wiped out. Therefore, it is essential that you regularly save your work on disk.

Menu Selections

If you want, WordPerfect will save your work for you at timed intervals that you specify. To have it do so, select File/Preferences/File. In the File Preferences dialog box, click Timed Document Backup every *xx* minutes and enter the number of minutes to wait between backups. You can specify any number of minutes from 1 to 65535.

The backup file is named WP{WP}.BK1 and is placed in the backup file subdirectory you designated as the Default Directory in the File Preferences dialog box. If you have more than one document open at the same time, WordPerfect saves each one and assigns each backup file a name such as WP{WP}.BK2, WP{WP}.BK3, and so on. When you exit WordPerfect properly, the program deletes any timed backup files it has created. However, in case of a power failure or improper exit, the backup files are not deleted, thereby allowing you to resurrect the most recently saved (backed-up) version of your document.

To restore a timed backup file, start WordPerfect. On startup, WordPerfect recognizes that there is a timed backup that has been saved and warns you in a Timed Backup dialog box of the existence of a backup file, as shown here:

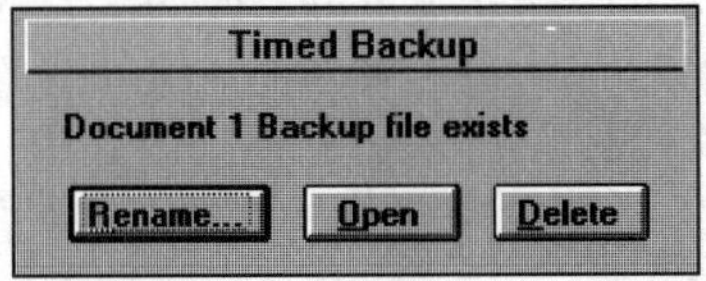

You have the option of assigning a name to the backup file and leaving it on disk, opening it, or deleting it.

Related Entries

Preferences
Save and Save As

Barcode

As technology expands, so do the requirements of the U.S. postal service. WordPerfect provides a POSTNET (Postal Numeric Encoding Technique) barcode system that inserts the appropriate barcode into a document or on an envelope.

A barcode is simply a ZIP code, in either a five- or nine-digit sequence, represented in short and tall lines as shown here:

This is a POSTNET barcode: ||.||.|.||.|.|.||.|....|||.....||.|.|.||..|

Proper use of barcodes on your mail and other correspondence increases the efficiency of the post office and speeds the delivery of your mail. You can also insert an 11-digit delivery point barcode (DPBC).

Menu Selections

To insert a barcode into your document (usually just below or above the addressee line on your document or envelope), position your cursor and select Insert/Other/Barcode. In the POSTNET Bar Code dialog box enter the desired ZIP code and click OK.

Related Entries

Envelopes

Binding Options

If you type text that is to be printed on both the back and front of pages and then bound in some manner, you will want to leave a *gutter margin,* which allows extra space on the left, right, top, or bottom for binding. For instance, if you were to tear a printed page from virtually any published book, you would notice that one side of the page has a wider margin than the other. This is because a gutter margin has been included to allow for the binding which hides a portion of the page from view. In WordPerfect, you too can specify the binding options for the pages of your document. Binding options affect the current and all remaining pages (unless you disable the binding option by setting the amount to 0").

WordPerfect accommodates your binding needs by allowing you to specify from which side of a page the binding will begin. Most often, printed documents begin printing on the odd page (page 1), resulting in a gutter margin on the left side or top edge of the page. However, WordPerfect permits you to specify a binding on the right side or bottom edge of the page, which starts printing the document on an even page number (page 0). A right or bottom binding width might be useful, for example, for the inside cover page of a pamphlet. On the other hand, a gutter margin along the top of the page allows for binding on publications such as flip charts.

Menu Selections

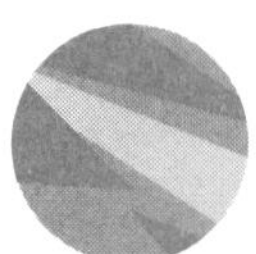

NOTE: *To better view your gutter margins, switch WordPerfect to Two Page View.*

First, position your cursor on the page where the binding options will take effect. Then select Layout/Page/Binding. You must indicate where the gutter margin is to appear on the current page by selecting Left, Right, Top, or Bottom. Specify the binding width in inches in the Amount box. Your subsequent pages will each be offset by the amount you specified, alternating the gutter margin on odd and even pages.

If your printer permits duplex printing (printing on both sides of a sheet of paper in one pass), you can activate it by clicking the Duplexing option button and choosing From Short Edge or From Long Edge. For example, if you are printing on 8.5 x 11-inch paper and your binding is on the long edge, it will place a gutter on the 11-inch edge of the page.

Block

Block is a WordPerfect term for any collection of text you have defined. A block can be as small as a single character or as large as your entire document. It can contain tables, columns, and graphics, as well as regular text. Generally, however, it refers to a highlighted selection of text. As you define a block of text, you activate WordPerfect's *select mode*, indicated on the status bar by the word "Status."

Techniques for Blocking Text

There are various methods you can use for defining a block once you have text on your screen.

Click and Drag

Clicking and dragging is a standard Windows technique. To block text using this method, move the insertion point (cursor) to the beginning of the desired block, press and hold down the left mouse button, and drag the mouse to highlight the text. When you are finished blocking the desired text, release the mouse button. To deselect the block, simply press the left mouse button again. The text will no longer be highlighted.

A related method of highlighting text allows you to position the cursor where you want the text to begin and then to move the I-beam to where you want the block to end. Press and hold down the SHIFT key as you press the left button on your mouse. The text from the insertion point to the I-beam will be highlighted. Often, this method is more precise, because it does not require you to move the mouse with the button depressed.

B

Multiple Clicks

If you double-click a word, the word is selected. Triple-clicking selects the entire sentence your cursor is in. Clicking four times with your mouse button blocks the entire paragraph in which your cursor is located.

Keyboard Blocking

You can also use your keyboard to block and highlight text. To do so, first move the insertion point to the location where you want the block to begin. Hold down the SHIFT key as you press an arrow key. Pressing the LEFT ARROW or RIGHT ARROW key while holding down SHIFT highlights one character at a time to the left or right. Pressing the UP ARROW or DOWN ARROW key highlights to the corresponding point on the preceding or following line. To select one word at a time, use CTRL+LEFT ARROW and CTRL+RIGHT ARROW. To select one paragraph at a time, use CTRL+UP ARROW and CTRL+DOWN ARROW. When you select a block of text, you see the word Select undimmed on the status bar.

Command Line

When your cursor is in a standard text document and you choose Edit/Select, you have the option of selecting a sentence, a paragraph, a page, or all (entire document). If you select a tabular column, like this:

Allen	Sundance	Wyoming
James	Cincinnati	Ohio
David	Ann Arbor	Michigan

and then choose Edit/Select, you are given the additional option of selecting Tabular Column from the menu. When you do, the highlighted block will look like this:

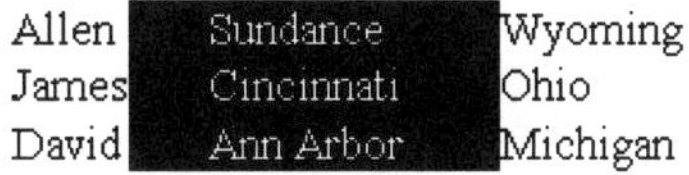

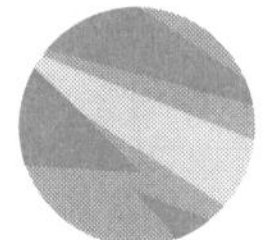

NOTE: Only the middle column is selected. You can then cut, copy, paste, or enhance just that one column of information, separate from all of the others.

You can also highlight a block of text in a document, as shown here:

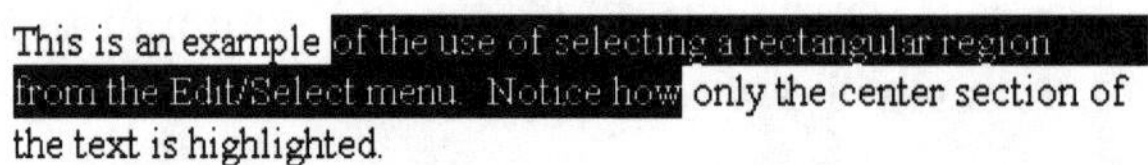

This is an example of the use of selecting a rectangular region from the Edit/Select menu. Notice how only the center section of the text is highlighted.

Choose Edit/Select and then select Rectangle. WordPerfect highlights only the rectangle of text, as shown here:

This is an example of the use of selecting a rectangular region
from the Edit/Select menu. Notice how only the center section of
the text is highlighted.

Menu Selections

Once you have blocked the text you want to alter, there are a number of things you can do to it.

Cut

If you choose Edit/Cut from the menu, click the Cut button on the button bar, or press the CTRL+X shortcut key, you will cut the blocked or selected text out of the current document and place it in the Windows Clipboard.

Delete

If you press the DELETE key after highlighting text, it is deleted from the document. Note that pressing the DELETE key is not the same as Edit/Cut or CTRL+X, which places a copy of the text into the Clipboard.

Copy

If you choose Edit/Copy from the menu or press the CTRL+C shortcut key, you will copy the blocked or selected text from the current document and place it in the Windows Clipboard.

Append

If you choose Edit/Append from the menu, WordPerfect copies and appends the selected text to whatever is already contained in the Clipboard.

B

Convert Case

If you highlight text and select Edit/Convert Case, you are given the option of converting to lowercase, uppercase, or initial capitals. WordPerfect performs a "smart conversion," leaving the pronoun "I" in uppercase, even if it is part of a contraction like "I'm." WordPerfect also leaves the first word of a sentence capitalized when you convert to lowercase.

NOTE: *WordPerfect identifies a sentence as a string of text preceded by a period. Therefore, if you use this case conversion capability, be sure you select the block of text to be converted in such a way that all sentences, including the first one, are preceded by a period.*

Save

If you highlight a block of text and then select File/Save or File/Save As, you are prompted to save the selected text in the Save dialog box. Click OK to save the selected text and a Save As dialog box appears. After you enter an appropriate filename and select OK, WordPerfect will save to the file only the block of text you selected.

Protect

If you want to keep a group of lines together on one page, highlight the lines and select Layout/Page/Keep Text Together. Choose Keep selected text together on same page and WordPerfect will not allow a page break anywhere within the protected block.

Text Enhancements

You can apply font enhancements such as bold, underline, superscript, justification, strikeout, and so on to selected text just by highlighting the text and then selecting the enhancement.

Related Entries

Append to Clipboard
Keyboard Layout
Undelete

Bold Text

Bold text appears darker and heavier than regular text, both on your screen and when printed. You can boldface text in either of two ways. One is to type the text first, select it, and then invoke the Bold option. The second is to activate the Bold feature, type your text, and then deactivate Bold.

Menu Selections

There are three ways to activate boldfacing: select Layout/Font/Bold, click the Bold button if it appears on your button bar or power bar, or press the CTRL+B shortcut key.

Removing Boldfacing

If you decide you do not want bold text, you can remove boldfacing from text in a variety of ways.

One way is to highlight the bold text and select Font from the Layout menu. You will see a check mark next to the Bold entry, indicating that the Bold attribute has been applied. Click Bold to remove the feature. Your text will no longer be boldface. A related method is to highlight the boldface text and press CTRL+B to turn off the Bold attribute.

Another way to remove boldfacing from text is to open the Reveal Codes window and delete one of the (Bold) codes that is placed on both sides of the bold text. When you delete either one, the other member of the paired code disappears as well.

Bookmark

Just as you can place a bookmark between the pages of a book you are reading, you can set a bookmark in a document in WordPerfect. This allows you later to open the file and locate the points you have marked using the bookmark feature.

Menu Selections

To place a bookmark in a document, position the cursor where you want the bookmark and select Insert/Bookmark. Click Create to assign a name to the bookmark. For example, if you set a bookmark in a section of your document that deals with the economy in the midwestern United States, you could type Midwestern Economy in the Create Bookmark dialog box. You can create as many bookmarks in a document as you like.

After you have set bookmarks in a document, you can go to them by highlighting the bookmark you want and selecting Go To from the Bookmark dialog box. You can also use Edit/Go To, or press the CTRL+G shortcut key, and click Bookmark. From the pull-down list, highlight the bookmark you want and click OK.

To move a bookmark to another location in the document, position your cursor at the new location, highlight the bookmark in the Bookmark List, and select Move.

Related Entries

See the section "Set QuickMark on Save" under the entry Environment.

Borders

You can place borders around graphics boxes and columns in your documents. WordPerfect gives many options as to the style, color, and position in conjunction with the graphic or column it surrounds.

You can also create a border for the entire page. A page border surrounds all text and is placed on the left, right, top, and bottom margins.

Menu Selections

Position your cursor on the page where you want to place a page border and select Layout/Page/Border/Fill. The Page Border dialog box appears from which you can select the desired Border Style and Fill Options. When you place a page border in your document, that border will appear on every page from the insertion point on until you either change or turn off the page border. To turn off the page border, move your cursor to the page where you want the page border to end and click Off from the Page Border dialog box.

Related Entries

Graphics, Editing
See also Graphics Styles, Editing for more detail on applying borders.

Box, Custom

See Graphics Styles, Creating.

Box, Editing

See Graphics, Creating and Graphics, Editing.

Box, Graphics

See Graphics, Creating.

Box, Text

See Graphics, Creating.

Bulleted List

See Bullets and Numbers, Inserting.

Bullets and Numbers, Inserting

Bullets and numbers are useful in separating lists from normal text in your documents. *Bullets* are small marks that you can place in front of text to help distinguish a word, sentence, or paragraph from the main text in a document. Numbers help to display consecutive steps, sentences, or paragraphs in an orderly fashion. WordPerfect has defined several special bullets that you can choose from a list. In WordPerfect, a number can be presented in many forms such as standard numbers, Roman numerals, or alphabetic letters.

Menu Selections

To insert a bullet or number in your document, position your cursor where you want the item inserted and select Insert/Bullets & Numbers. From the Bullets & Numbers dialog box, highlight the desired bullet or number from the Styles list. Click OK.

If you already have created a list, you can apply bullets or numbers to a block of text to create a bulleted or numbered list. Make sure you press the ENTER key after each sentence, step, or paragraph, so that it ends with a (HRt) code; otherwise the bullets or numbers will not be applied as you expect.

B

Button Bar

The button bar feature allows WordPerfect users to place a horizontal row of icons (pictures) across the top or bottom of the screen, or vertically on either side of the screen. Macros or menu selections can then be assigned to these icons, providing on-screen access to all of your most frequently used macros or menu selections. Whenever you want to run the macro or choose the menu item, you simply click its icon with your mouse.

Menu Selections

The default button bar, named WordPerfect, can be activated by choosing View/Button Bar. A check mark will appear next to the View/Button Bar selection and the current button bar will be displayed horizontally under the menu bar. This button bar will be displayed until you choose another button bar.

To choose another button bar, select File/Preferences/Button Bar and then double-click the name of the button bar you wish to activate. For example, to display the Tables button bar, choose File/Preferences/Button Bar, and double-click Tables. To deactivate the button bar, simply select View/Button Bar again.

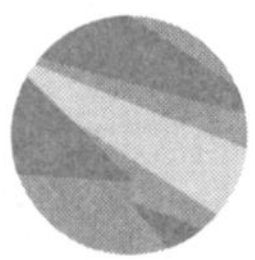

NOTE: *You can change the location of the button bar on the screen by choosing File/Preferences/Button Bar/Options. The button bar can be positioned along the left, right, top, or bottom of your document. You can choose to display the text, the picture, or both on a button by using the controls in the Appearance section of the same dialog box.*

WordPerfect currently comes with 12 standard button bars, each of which is described in Table 11-1.

Button Bar	Comments
Equation Editor	Displays several tools for inserting symbols and editing equations. To display this button bar, double-click Equation Editor. Also, whenever you use the Equation Editor, the same button bar appears. To access the Equation Editor, select Equation from the Graphics pull-down menu.

Table 11-1. *Available button bars*

Button Bar	Comments
Font	Includes buttons for many of the applicable font attributes in WordPerfect. To display the Font button bar, double-click Font.
Generate	Contains buttons for creating and updating a list, a table of contents, and so forth. To display the Generate button bar, double-click Generate.
Graphics	Includes the common graphics tools for drawing and creating text/figure boxes. To display the Graphics button bar, double-click Graphics.
Layout	Displays a variety of buttons that affect your page layout. To display the Graphics button bar, double-click Layout.
Macros	Includes the familiar tape-deck style buttons for recording, playing, and editing macros. To display the Macros button bar, double-click Macros.
Outline	Assists in creating outlines in your document. To display the Outline button bar, double-click Outline.
Page	Includes buttons that let you modify page attributes such as centering, borders, numbering, and so forth. To display the Page button bar, double-click Page.
Preferences	Provides buttons that give you access to the WordPerfect preferences. To display this button bar, double-click Preferences.
Tables	Contains commonly used Table menu selections. To place the Tables button bar on your screen, double-click Tables.
WordPerfect	Contains a number of commonly used menu selections from the File, Edit, Tools, and Layout menus. This is the default button bar that is installed when you load WordPerfect. If you have selected a new button bar and wish to display the default button bar instead, choose File/Preferences/Button Bar and double-click WordPerfect.
WordPerfect 5.2	Displays the buttons used in WordPerfect 5.2 for Windows. Since some users have grown accustomed to the 5.2 button bar layout, this helps ease the transition to the new version. To display the WordPerfect 5.2 button bar, double-click WordPerfect 5.2.

Table 11-1. *Available button bars* (continued)

Related Entries

Button Bar Macros
Button Bar, Creating
Button Bar, Editing
See Chapter 3, "Tools and Techniques," for a more detailed discussion of the button bar.

Button Bar Macros

WordPerfect lets you easily assign macros to your button bar. You may place the macro either on any of the existing button bars or on a new one.

Menu Selections

You must first create a macro before it can be placed on the button bar. To place a macro on an existing button bar, select File/Preferences/Button Bar and highlight the button bar you wish to use. Click Play a Macro, and the Select Macro dialog box appears. Scroll to the macro you wish to use in the Macros in Template list box and double-click that file. The new macro button will automatically appear on the button bar.

To place a macro on a new button bar, choose File/Preferences/Button Bar. Click Create, then type the name of the new button bar. Click OK and the Button Bar Editor dialog box appears. Click Play a Macro. The Add Macro button appears in the lower portion of the dialog box. Click Add Macro to access the Select Macro dialog box. Scroll to the macro you wish to use in the Macros in Template list (not available when playing macro files from the disk) and double-click that file. The new macro button will automatically appear on the button bar.

Related Entries

Button Bar
Button Bar, Creating
Button Bar, Editing
Macros
See Chapter 3, "Tools and Techniques," and Chapter 9, "Spreadsheet and Database Files," for more detailed information.

Button Bar, Creating

WordPerfect provides a simple tool for creating your own button bars from menu selections. This feature enables you to condense a number of keystrokes or menu selections into easy-to-use buttons that you activate with a click of your mouse. For example, rather than selecting Layout/Paragraph/Indent from your menu, you can create a button that will perform all three menu selections at the click of a mouse button.

Menu Selections

To create a custom button bar, choose File/Preferences/Button Bar from your menu. From the Button Bar Preferences dialog box, click Create to access the Create Button Bar dialog box. Specify a new button bar name up to 31 characters in length.

The Button Bar Editor dialog box appears in the center of your screen:

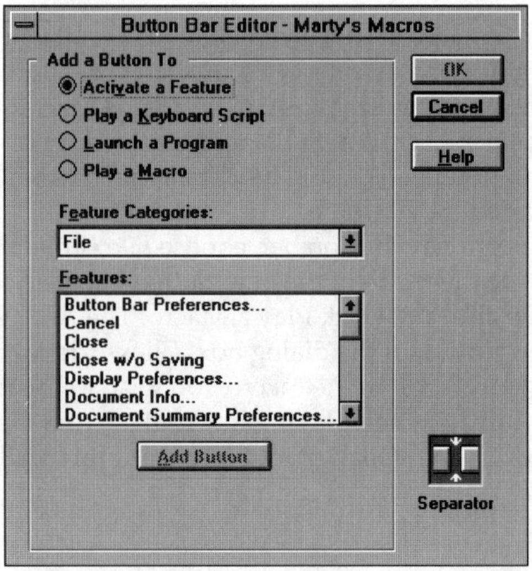

To automatically create a button, point to a sequence of menu selections from the menu bar, such as Layout/Paragraph/Indent, and WordPerfect creates the button relating to those menu selections and places it on the button bar. If the dialog box happens to cover your menu bar, just click the title bar of the dialog box and move it down out of the way.

If you prefer, you can select buttons from a Feature Categories list and a corresponding Features list. This method allows you to view a graphic of the button before you place it on the button bar.

You can separate buttons into logical groups by placing spacers between them. To place spacers, click the spacer and drag it up to the button bar. You can also customize the appearance of a button by modifying its name, modifying the description displayed as you pass the mouse cursor over the button, and by editing and designing the button.

You can remove any button or spacer by clicking it and dragging it anywhere off of the button bar. Once you are satisfied with the buttons on your button bar, click OK in the Button Bar Editor dialog box. To display a button bar, just double-click it.

Related Entries

Button Bar
Button Bar Macros
Button Bar, Editing
See also Chapter 3, "Tools and Techniques," for a more detailed discussion on creating a button bar.

Button Bar, Editing

It is just as easy to edit button bars as it is to create them.

Menu Selections

To edit a button bar, choose File/Preferences/Button Bar, highlight the name of the button bar you wish to change, and click Edit. The Button Bar Editor dialog box appears on your screen.

NOTE: *You can edit any of the 12 standard buttons bars included with WordPerfect or create your own and edit them.*

Once you have the Edit Button Bar dialog box on your screen, you can change the location of a button or spacer on the button bar by clicking the object and dragging it to its new location. The other buttons and spacers will adjust automatically. As soon as the button bar is full, scrolling arrows appear so that you can access buttons that are off the screen to the left, right, top, or bottom.

To remove a button, simply click it and drag it anywhere off of the button bar. The button will disappear and the other buttons will adjust their positions accordingly. Clicking OK in the Button Bar Editor dialog box saves the changes you have made in the button bar file.

NOTE: Should you inadvertently delete the wrong button, just choose Cancel from the Edit Button Bar dialog box, and your button bar will be restored to its original configuration.

Related Entries

Button Bar
Button Bar, Creating
Equation Editor
See also Chapter 3, "Tools and Techniques," for a more detailed discussion on editing a button bar.

Button Bar, Keyboard Scripts

WordPerfect lets you easily assign a keyboard script to your button bar. You can place the keyboard script on any of the existing button bars or on a new one.

When you activate a keyboard script from a button bar, it actually inserts any text you specify with a single click of the mouse.

Menu Selections

To place a keyboard script on an existing button bar, select the command File/Preferences/Button Bar and highlight the button bar you wish to use. Click Edit, choose Play a Keyboard Script from the Button Bar Editor dialog box, and type the text that the button will play in the Type box. Click Add Script to place the keyboard script button on the button bar.

To place a keyboard script on a new button bar, choose the options File/Preferences/Button Bar. Click Create, and type the name of the new button bar. Click OK and the Button Bar Editor dialog box appears. Click Play a Keyboard Script, and enter the text that this script button will play in the Type box. Click Add Script to place the keyboard script button on the button bar.

Click OK to save your changes. Make sure you then double-click that button bar to select it.

Related Entries

Button Bar
Button Bar, Creating
Button Bar, Editing
See Chapter 9, "Spreadsheet and Database Files," for more detailed information.

Cancel

Many dialog boxes include a Cancel button that lets you exit a dialog box without applying settings you may have changed.

Also, in previous versions of WordPerfect the Cancel command allowed you to undo a previous action.

See Undelete and Undo.

Capitalization

Capitalization works virtually the same way it does on a typewriter. To capitalize a single character, hold down one of the SHIFT keys as you type the letter. To capitalize a string of letters, it is generally easier to press the CAPS LOCK key once and then type the text. When the CAPS LOCK key is engaged, a small indicator light is illuminated on many keyboards.

CAPS LOCK works only with letters, not with numbers. To type one of the symbols on top of the number keys, you must hold down one of the SHIFT keys.

Menu Selections

If you type text in uppercase and/or lowercase letters and subsequently decide you prefer to have the text either all capitalized or all in lowercase, you can highlight the text, select Edit/Convert Case, and select Uppercase, Lowercase, or Initial Capitals, as appropriate.

Small Caps

If you have a printer that will support them, WordPerfect offers you an option of printing text in *small caps*. Using small caps creates all capital letters, but the sizes of the letters can differ: for instance, the capital letter at the beginning of a word can be larger than the rest of the characters in the word.

The following line, for example, is typed in regular text:

WordPerfect Corporation is located in Orem, Utah

The same line, in small caps, would look like this:

WORDPERFECT CORPORATION IS LOCATED IN OREM, UTAH

To place text in small caps, select Layout/Font or press the F9 shortcut key. Enable Small Cap in the Appearance section of that dialog box by clicking it. You can either turn on that feature and then type your text or just highlight existing text and then select the option.

Cascading Windows

See the section "Displaying Multiple Windows" in the entry Windows, Working with Multiple.

Cell Formula Entry

Normally, as you enter numbers into the cells of a table, WordPerfect does not perform an automatic global calculation. Instead, it waits for you to manually recalculate with the Calculate command, offering you greater control over your math in certain situations. If you prefer global recalculation, enable this option.

Menu Selections

Select Table/Cell Formula Entry. This is a toggle, meaning that when there is a check mark to the left of the command, the feature is active. The absence of a check mark indicates that the feature is not active.

Related Entries

Math

Center Page(s)

Placing a center page code on a page of text causes WordPerfect to center the contents of that page vertically both on the screen and on the paper when it is printed. You can center just the current page, center the current and subsequent pages, or turn centering off.

NOTE: WordPerfect centers the text between the designated top and bottom margins on the page, not necessarily between the top and bottom of the printed page. The text will be centered on the printed page only if the top and bottom margins are the same size.

Menu Selections

Select Layout/Page/Center. To center the current page only, click Current Page. No other pages will be centered. To center this and all remaining pages, click Current and Subsequent Pages. In addition to the current page, all subsequent pages will be centered until you click No Centering.

To remove automatic centering you can select Layout/Page/Center and click No Centering. Alternatively, you can select Reveal Codes and delete the center page code (Cntr Cur Pg: On) from the top of the centered page.

Center Page affects only the text in the body of your document; footnotes are not centered. The text in the body of the document is centered between the top and bottom margins if there are no footnotes. If there are footnotes, the text is centered between the top margin and the beginning of the footnotes.

Center Text

The Center Text command normally causes your text to be centered between the left and right margins on your page. You can use this feature either before or after you type your text. If you invoke it before you type a line, whatever you type will center itself on the line as you type it. If you invoke this command after typing text, you must place your cursor at the beginning of the line you want centered before you perform the command. Otherwise, only the portion of the line following the center code will be centered.

Menu Selections

Select Layout/Line/Center, or press the shortcut key SHIFT+F7.

Centering at the Middle of the Line

A center text code affects only the line on which it is entered. If you want to center a number of lines of text, you can type them all, select them, and then invoke the Center command. All of the lines will be center justified. Note that this is slightly different from text centered on a line. Text centered on a line is preceded, when Reveal Codes is activated, by a (Hd Center on Marg) code. Highlighting a number of lines and then centering them places a (Just:Center) code at the beginning of the selected text.

To change centered text back to the document's default justification, select Reveal Codes and delete the center code at the beginning of the block.

Centering Other Than at the Middle of a Line

You can also center text relative to a position other than the middle of a line. To do so, position the cursor at the location relative to which you want the text centered. Do this either by tabbing or spacing to the desired location. Invoke the center command and then type your text. The text will be centered relative to the location you indicated.

Related Entries

Justification

Change Dictionary

See Speller.

Character Sets

WordPerfect supplies a number of extra character sets that you can use to insert mathematical, scientific, foreign language characters, and other symbols into your documents. The character sets are divided into 15 categories, including ASCII, Multinational, Phonetic, Box Drawing, Typographic Symbols, Iconic Symbols, Math/Scientific and Extended Math/Scientific Symbols, Greek, Hebrew, Cyrillic, Japanese, Arabic, and Arabic Script. There is also a User Defined category that you can employ to create new characters.

Menu Selections

Position your cursor where you want the desired character to be inserted and choose Insert/Character or press the CTRL+W shortcut key. The WordPerfect Characters dialog box, shown in Figure 11-3, will appear on your screen. Click

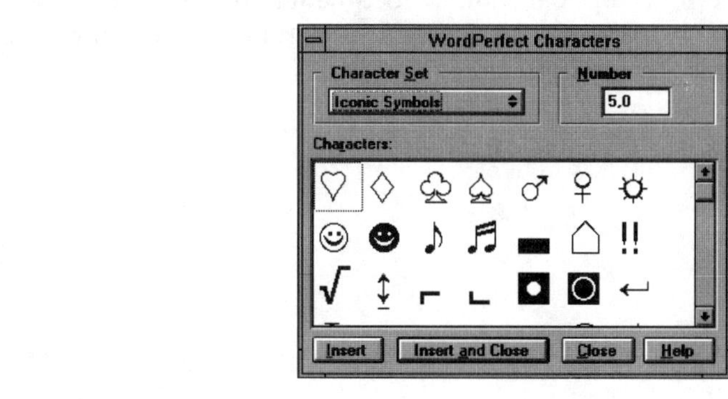

Figure 11-3. *The WordPerfect Characters dialog box*

and hold down the mouse button on the up/down arrow just below the Character Set box to display the list of available character sets. Highlight the character set you wish to use and release the mouse button.

Click the desired symbol and then click Insert. This inserts the character into your document and keeps the dialog box on the screen so that you can choose more characters. If you want to insert only one character, click Insert and Close to exit the dialog box.

Clipboard

The Clipboard is an electronic "holding area" in your computer's RAM (random access memory) for text or graphics that you have either cut or copied from a document. You can paste the contents of the Clipboard into the same document, another document, or into another Windows application.

Menu Selections

To cut text or graphics to the Clipboard, removing it from the document, highlight the text or graphic and select Edit/Cut or press the shortcut key CTRL+X. To copy text or graphics to the Clipboard, select Edit/Copy or press the shortcut key CTRL+C. You can also use the button bar or power bar, if it has a Cut or Copy button.

You can view the current contents of the Clipboard by switching to the Windows Program Manager and opening the Clipboard, usually located in the Main program group.

To paste the contents of the Clipboard into a document at the current insertion point, select Edit/Paste, press the shortcut key CTRL+V, or click the Paste button (if your button bar has one).

Related Entries

Append to Clipboard
Block

Close

The Close command closes the current document and allows you to either save or discard any changes you have made to it since the last time you saved it to disk.

When you select this command and you have changed your document, a dialog box appears in which you can choose one of three options. You can save the changes you made before exiting the document by clicking the Yes button. You can discard your changes, leave the former version intact, and exit the document by clicking the No button. Finally, you can cancel this command and return to editing the document by selecting Cancel.

Menu Selections

Select File/Close or press the shortcut key CTRL+F4.

In the top-left corner of the WordPerfect window are two small icons that look like this:

If you click the Document Control Menu icon, a pull-down menu appears containing a Close option. If you select Close from this list, WordPerfect closes the document in the current window. If you have made changes to the document, WordPerfect prompts you to save the document.

If you select Close from the WordPerfect Control Menu icon, you are again prompted to save any changes that have been made to your document, and then you exit from WordPerfect completely.

Codes, Displaying

See Reveal Codes.

Codes, Finding and Replacing

WordPerfect allows you to search for and replace codes just as if they were text in a document.

Menu Selections

To find and replace codes in your documents, choose Edit/Replace to open the Replace dialog box. Choose Codes from the Match pull-down menu. The Codes dialog box, shown in Figure 11-4, will appear on the screen. Scroll to the code you wish to find, highlight it, and click the Insert button to place the code in the Find area of the Replace dialog box. The Codes dialog box remains open to allow you to search for multiple codes.

Click in the Replace With box in the Find and Replace dialog box. The Codes dialog box stays visible but inactive, so you must click it to make it active again. Select the replacement code and click the Insert button. Click Find to locate the first occurrence of the code and then click Replace to replace the code with the new code. For an automated Find and Replace, click Replace All: WordPerfect replaces all occurrences of the specified code. Keep in mind that by using this option you run the risk of replacing text that you didn't want to replace.

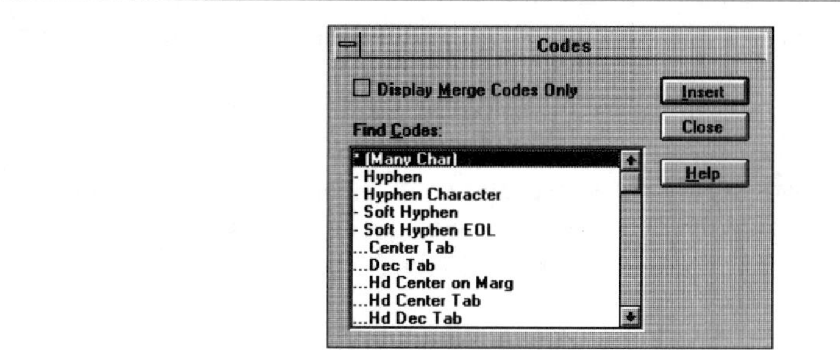

Figure 11-4. *The Codes dialog box from within the Find and Replace feature*

NOTE: To delete a code, you can search for it but leave the Replace With option in the dialog box empty. When WordPerfect finds the code and sees that it is supposed to replace the code with nothing, it deletes the original code. There are some codes that WordPerfect will not let you replace with new ones; if a replacement is not possible, an error message appears.

Related Entries

Finding Text
Replace

Color Printing

If you have a color printer, you can print graphics images in color by using a color printer driver. Keep in mind that it may take a long time to print color graphics.

Menu Selections

To choose a color printer, you must have installed the printer driver using the WordPerfect Installation program. Choose File/Select Printer and double-click the desired color printer in the Select Printer dialog box. Print your document by selecting File/Print.

Colors, Screen

Most programs that operate under the Windows environment display in the colors you have set in Windows. WordPerfect offers you the option to ignore the Windows colors and display your document with the font colors you specify on a white page.

If you enable the Windows System Colors feature, any colors that you apply to your text will display in the default colors dictated by Windows. For example, any text that would normally be displayed in red will show as black text on a white page. Of course, the display will change according to the Windows color settings. However, you can still see the applied font color in the font area of the status bar.

Menu Selections

Select File/Preferences/Display and click Windows System Colors to place an X in the check box. You can change the colors in WordPerfect back to their default by clicking again on Windows Systems Colors.

C

Colors, Text

Text can be formatted on your screen with both predefined and custom colors. Unless you have a color printer and the printer is set to color, however, text will be printed on paper in standard black.

Menu Selections

You can change the screen display of the text color in one of two ways. The first is to select the text to be formatted and choose Layout/Font, then click Color in the Color Options section of the Font dialog box. Select a color from the pop-up list of colors and click OK. Your blocked text will change to that color.

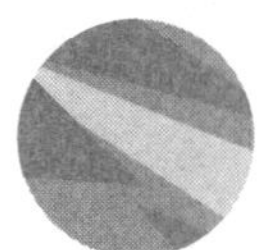

NOTE: The number of available colors depends on the maximum resolution of the video card in your computer. For example, many standard VGA (video graphics adapter) video cards display 256 colors. Other video cards display more or fewer colors.

You can create custom colors by mixing available colors in WordPerfect's palette. Click Palette to display the Define Color Printing Palette, shown in Figure 11-5. Click the white, square marker that is in the middle of the color

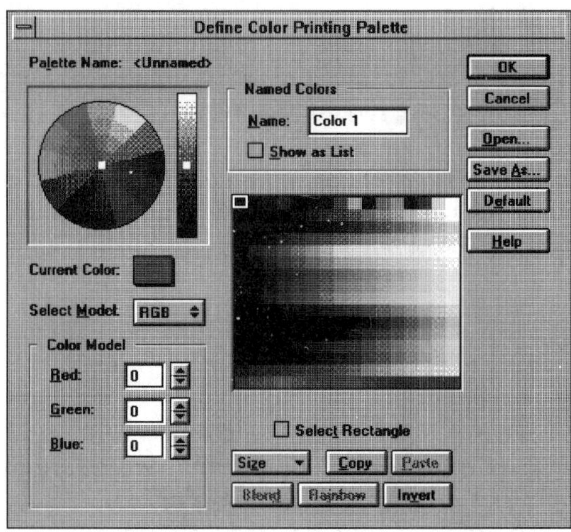

Figure 11-5. *The Define Color Printing Palette dialog box*

wheel and drag it to any location on the wheel. This action automatically adjusts the color shown in the Current Color area of the dialog box. Note also that the Red, Green, and Blue figures change as you move the marker around. You can have colors display in one of three models: RGB (Red, Green, Blue), HLS (Hue, Lightness, Saturation), and CMYK (Cyan, Magenta, Yellow, Black). The vertical column to the right of the color wheel is used to adjust the brightness of the color: drag the marker up, and the Print and Screen colors get brighter; drag it down, and the colors get darker.

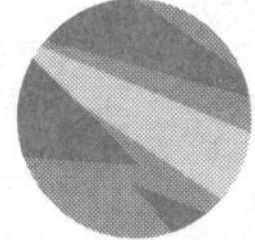

NOTE: To maintain consistency in custom text colors from one document to the next, make sure you write down the figures shown in the text boxes labelled Red, Green, Blue, Hue, Saturation, and Lightness.

If colors are not displayed on your screen, make sure the Windows System Colors box in the Display Preferences dialog box, accessed through File/Preferences/Display, is *not* checked.

Related Entries

Color Printing

Column Breaks

When you have defined a column and turned on column mode, you can force the end of a column by selecting Layout/Columns/Column Break or by pressing the shortcut key CTRL+ENTER. This places a hard column break code (HCol) into your text. When you are in column mode, this has the effect of ending one column and beginning the next if it is on the same page. If no more columns will fit on that page, the (HPg) code ends the current page.

Columns, Balanced Newspaper

One common arrangement of text on a page involves columns. For example, newspapers and newsletters often contain columns which are parallel and balanced. This means that as you type, the text is distributed evenly among the specified number of columns, as shown in Figure 11-6.

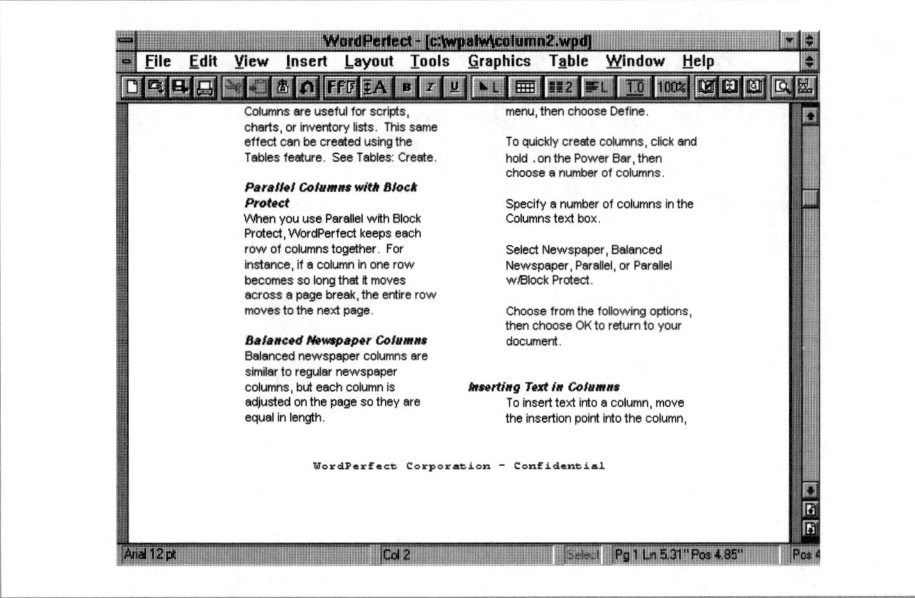

Figure 11-6. *An example of Balanced Newspaper Columns (notice how the text at the end of each column is "parallel" with the other)*

Menu Selections

To create this type of layout, select Balanced Newspaper in the Columns dialog box, shown in Figure 11-7.

Columns, Creating

A common word processing task is to arrange text on a page in columns. One type of arrangement, called newspaper columns, has text flow down one column and then the next (from left to right). A second type of arrangement, called *parallel columns*, is used, for example, in acting scripts and address lists.

Menu Selections

Defining Columns

To set up columns in WordPerfect, position the cursor where you want the columns to begin and select Layout/Columns/Define. The dialog box shown in Figure 11-7 appears.

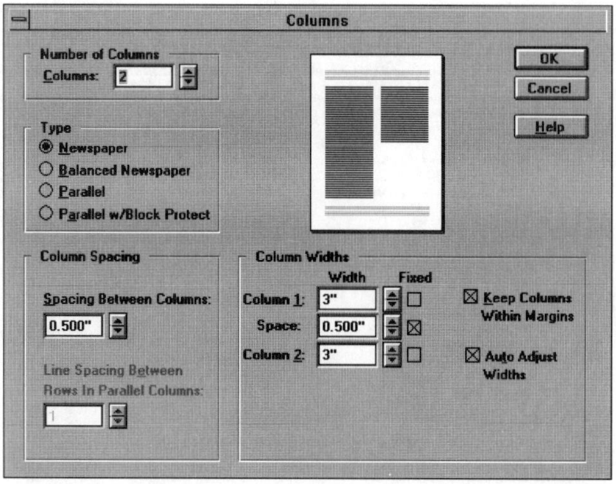

Figure 11-7. *The Columns dialog box*

The first thing you need to do is define the type of columns you want to create—newspaper, balanced newspaper, parallel, or parallel with block protect.

Next, you must define how many columns you want to create on the page. You can specify up to 24 columns. When you type the number of columns, WordPerfect automatically enters appropriate widths for each column in the Column Widths section of the dialog box. It assumes that you intend to have the specified number of columns evenly spaced across the page. This is indicated by the check mark in the Fixed check boxes in the Column Widths section. You can override the column width settings by changing one or more of them manually. If you do so, WordPerfect automatically removes the X from the corresponding Fixed check box. You can specify the default distance you want between columns by entering the appropriate number in the Spacing Between Columns box.

To create simple columns, select Newspaper from the Type section of the dialog box, then click OK. WordPerfect places a column definition code (Col Def:...) and a column on code (Col On) at the location of the cursor. You can see these codes if you open the Reveal Codes window. Your text will change to multiple columns as specified in the dialog box.

Defining Columns from the Power Bar

The Column button is located on the power bar. It looks like this:

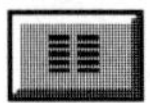

When you click the Column button, you are given the options of turning on two to five columns of equal size.

Turning Columns Off

Once columns have been activated, the remainder of the document will have the same arrangement of columns unless you turn the feature off at some point. To turn columns off, move the cursor to the position where you want the column layout discontinued and select Layout/Columns/Off. You can also turn columns off by choosing the Column button from the power bar and selecting Columns Off.

Removing Column Layout

To remove a multiple-column layout from an entire document, open the Reveal Codes window, locate the column definition code (Col Def:...), and delete it.

Changing the Width of Columns

Once you have columns defined and turned on, you can change the width of one or more of them either by using the Columns dialog box or by changing margins on the ruler bar.

CHANGING COLUMN WIDTHS USING THE COLUMNS DIALOG BOX You can change the column layout by placing your cursor anywhere within the columns and selecting Layout/Columns/Define. In the Columns dialog box, shown in Figure 11-7, change the margin settings as necessary. When you click OK, the columns acquire the new widths.

CHANGING COLUMN WIDTHS USING THE RULER BAR You can also change the widths of columns together or individually from the Ruler, provided that it is displayed. You can display the Ruler by selecting View/Ruler Bar. To change the column widths together, click and drag the column margin markers for the first column, displayed as triangles just above the Ruler, as shown here:

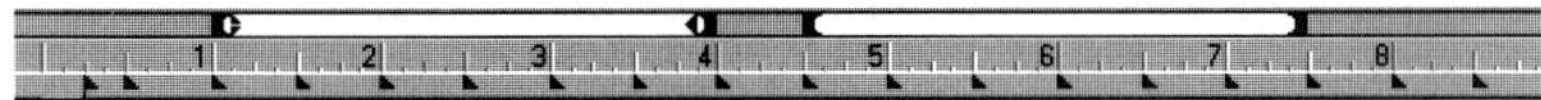

To adjust the widths of individual columns, click and drag the column margin markers for any column, displayed as brackets just above the ruler, as shown in the preceding illustration.

Related Entries

Columns, Balanced Newspaper
Columns, Newspaper
Columns, Parallel
Columns, Parallel with Block Protect

Columns, Line Between

To visually separate and enhance the appearance of your columns, you can place a vertical line between columns. For more information, see the "Vertical Lines" section in the Graphics Lines entry.

Related Entries

Graphics Lines
See also Chapter 7, "Desktop Publishing with WordPerfect for Windows"

Columns, Newspaper

One common arrangement of text on a page involves columns. In newsletters, for example, text typically flows down the first column on the page, then flows into the next column, and perhaps into a third column, as shown in Figure 11-8.

Menu Selections

To create this type of layout, select Newspaper in the Columns dialog box, shown in Figure 11-7.

Columns, Parallel

One common arrangement of text on a page involves columns that are laid out as shown in Figure 11-9.

Menu Selections

To create this type of layout, select Parallel in the Columns dialog box, shown in Figure 11-7.

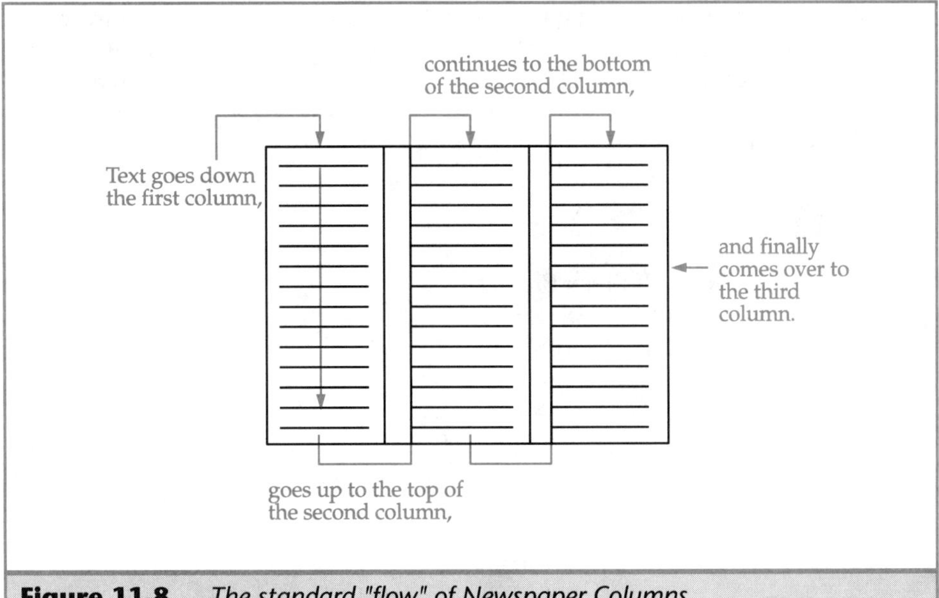

Figure 11-8. *The standard "flow" of Newspaper Columns*

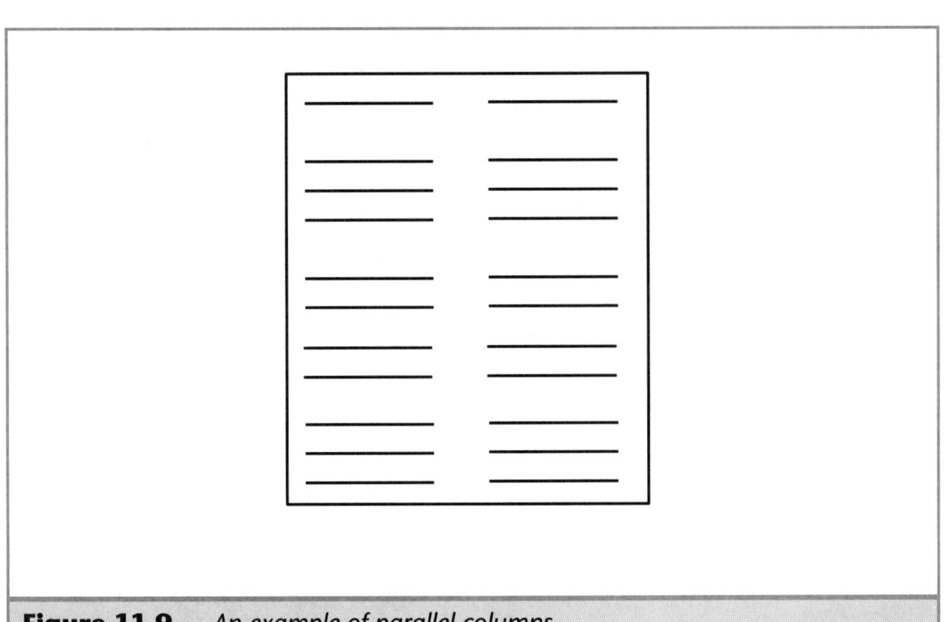

Figure 11-9. *An example of parallel columns*

Note that when you are using parallel columns, one or more lines at the end of an entry in a column can wrap onto another page. This may be fine when you are writing a script, as shown in Figure 11-10. However, this type of a break would not be acceptable in an address list, as shown in Figure 11-11. To avoid this problem, use parallel columns with Block Protect.

Related Entries

Columns, Parallel with Block Protect

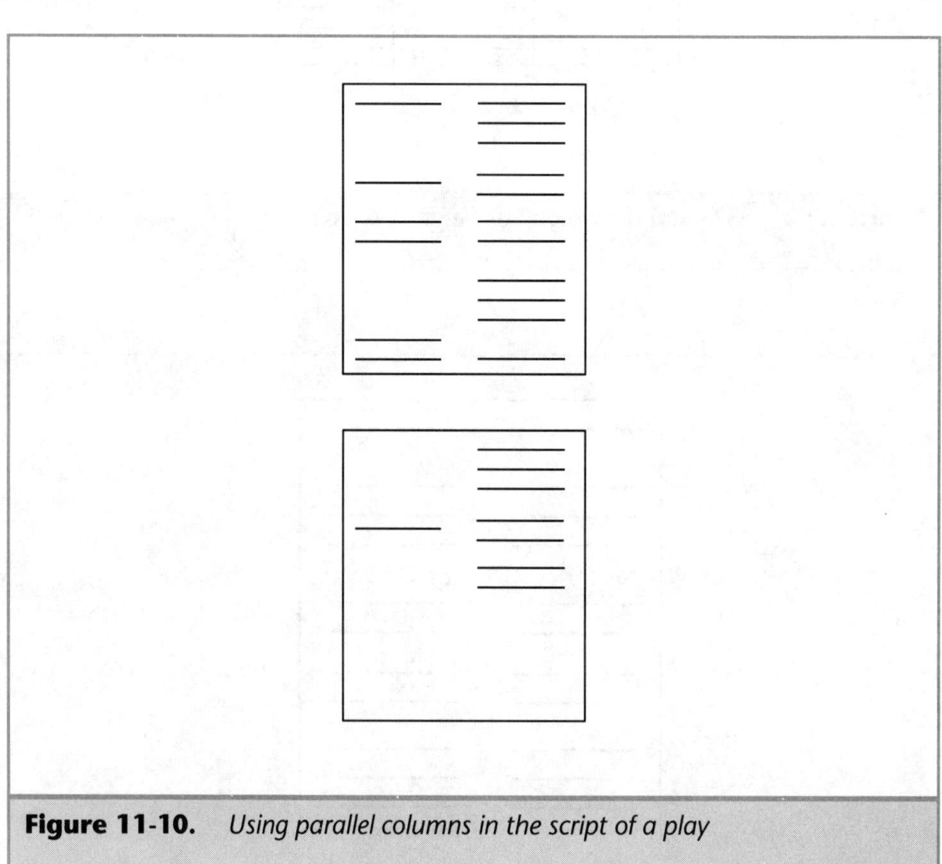

Figure 11-10. *Using parallel columns in the script of a play*

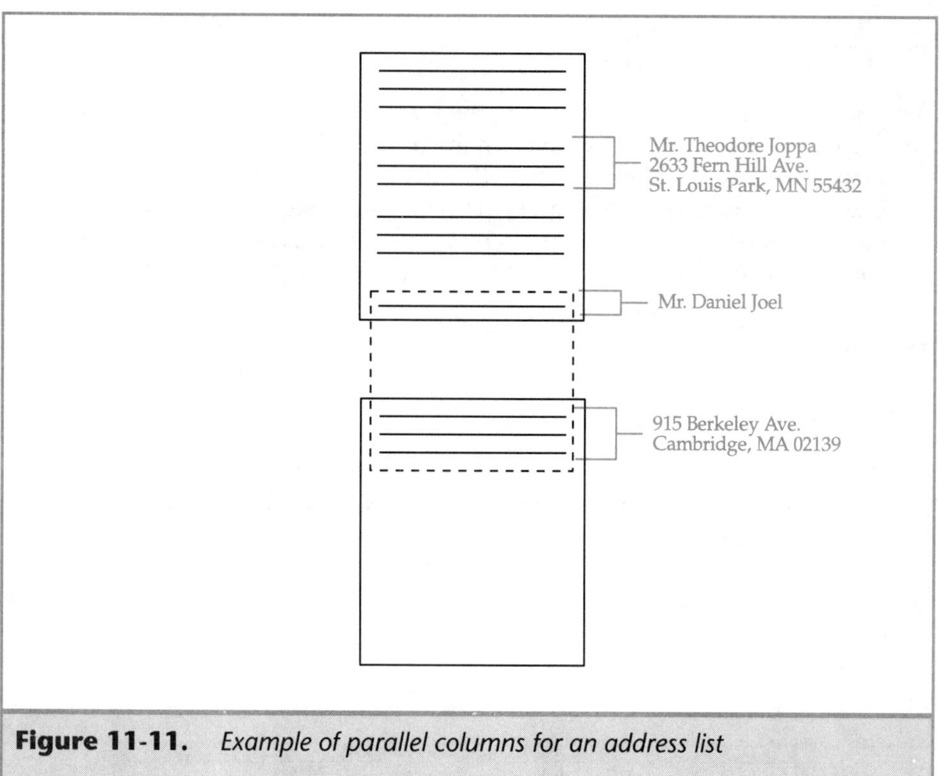

Figure 11-11. *Example of parallel columns for an address list*

Columns, Parallel with Block Protect

Parallel columns with Block Protect are very similar to standard parallel columns. The only difference between the two is that in parallel columns with Block Protect, if a portion of one of the parallel columns needs to wrap to the next page, the entire block will do so, staying together as a unit.

Menu Selections

To activate this option, select Parallel with Block Protect in the Columns dialog box, shown in Figure 11-7.

Comment

A *comment* is text which will appear on the screen in a document, but which will not print. Since they can be displayed in the user's I.D. color marked with a comment balloon on the left margin of the screen, comments are ideal for sending internal messages to people who will read or edit the document on-screen. Any text in a document can be converted to a comment. Conversely, any comment can be converted into printable text.

Menu Selections

Creating a Comment

To create a comment, place the cursor at the location in your text where you want the comment to appear. Select Insert/Comment/Create. You will see the Comment editor screen, shown in Figure 11-12.

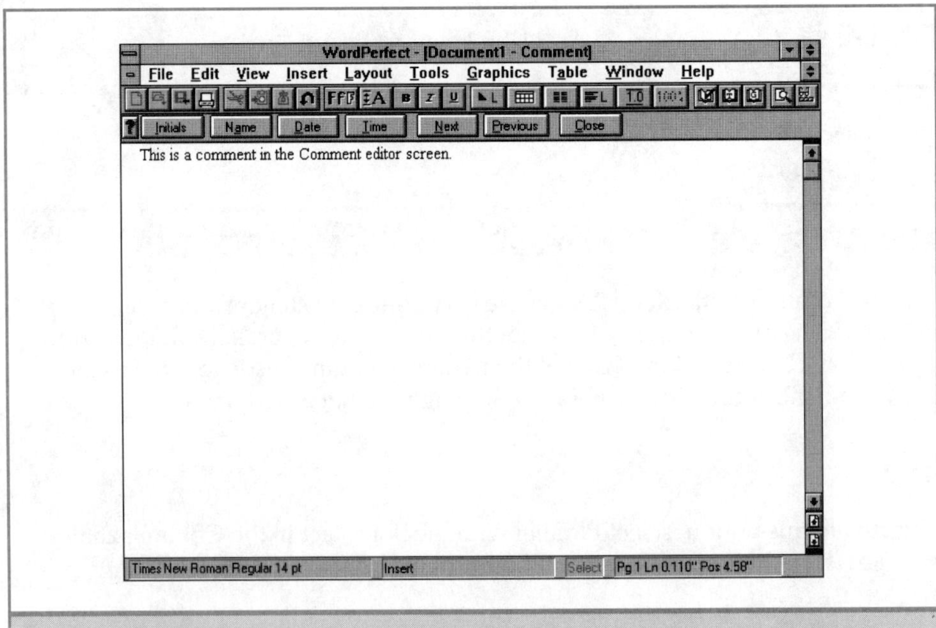

Figure 11-12. *The Comment editor screen*

Comments are typed directly into the text area of the comment editor screen. Comments can contain as much text as you desire and can be formatted. Click Close when you have finished writing the comment.

The way comments are displayed depends on the view mode. If your document is in Page view, you will see a comment balloon icon on the left margin. If you have set the user's Initials and I.D. Color in File/Preferences/Environment, a tag with the user's initials and I.D. color will appear in the left margin. You can view the comment by moving the mouse pointer over the tag and clicking. A caption box appears containing the comment or icon.

If your document is in Draft view, you will not see a tag or icon, but a shaded box across the page containing the comment.

Remember that comments will not appear when you print your document. If you want to print the text of a comment, you must first convert a comment to text.

C

Converting Text to a Comment

You can convert text already in a document to a nonprinting comment by selecting the text and then selecting Insert/Comment/Create. Your highlighted text will disappear from the body of the document and appear inside a shaded comment box.

You can also convert text to a comment while leaving it in the body of the document as well. To do so, highlight the text and select Edit/Copy before you convert it to a comment. Once you have done so, select Edit/Paste to place it back into your document where it was originally located.

Converting a Comment to Text

If you have text in a comment frame, you can insert the text from the comment into the body of your document by selecting Insert/Comment/Convert to Text. If you have more than one comment in your document, WordPerfect will convert to text the comment that immediately precedes the insertion point.

Editing a Comment

You can edit an existing comment in either of two ways.

You can place your cursor just before the comment in your document and then select Insert/Comment/Edit. This brings up the Comment editor screen that contains the text you have already typed. You can edit the text as necessary and then choose Close. Your edited comment will replace the previous one.

Another way to edit a comment is to position the I-beam on the comment balloon (page view) or shaded comment text (draft view), right-click, and then select Edit from the shortcut menu.

Deleting a Comment

To delete a comment, right-click the comment and select Delete from the shortcut menu. You can turn on Reveal Codes and delete the formatting code (Comment).

Viewing/Suppressing the View of Comments

You can choose whether you want your comments to be displayed on the screen by selecting File/Preferences/Display and clicking Comments in the Show section of the Display Preferences dialog box.

Viewing Comments in a Column Layout

Comments are not displayed in a section of a document laid out in columns.

Compare Documents

The Compare Documents feature in WordPerfect is used to compare a document that you have on the screen with one that is on a disk. WordPerfect places redline codes around text that has been added to the current document and strikeout codes around text that has been deleted. Text that has been moved from its original position will be preceded by the phrase "THE FOLLOWING TEXT WAS MOVED" and followed by the phrase "THE PRECEDING TEXT WAS MOVED."

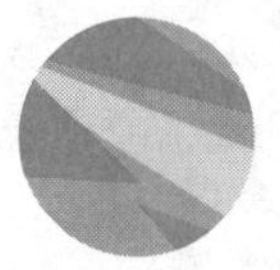

NOTE: *To view the actual redline or strikeout codes, use Reveal Codes.*

Menu Selections

To compare a document on your screen with one on disk, choose File/Compare Document and click Add Markings. Type the drive, path, and name of the file with which you want to compare the current document in the Compare Current Document to box. If you are unsure of the filename, click the File icon to the right of the Compare Current Document to box and browse through the files on disk. Click OK once you have typed or highlighted the correct file. See Figure 11-13 for an example of a document that has been compared to its original.

Once the current file is marked for any deviations from the file to which you are comparing it, you can remove some or all the revision markings by choosing

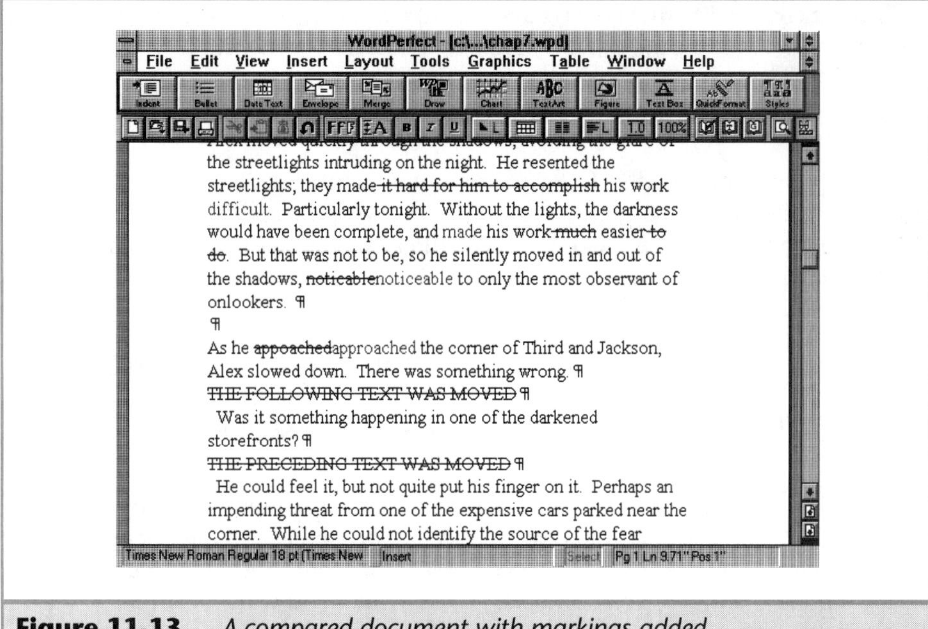

Figure 11-13. *A compared document with markings added*

File/Compare Document and clicking Remove Markings. Click either Remove Redline markings and Strikeout Text or Remove Strikeout Text Only to remove the desired markings. Click OK, and WordPerfect automatically cleans up the revision markings as specified.

Related Entries

Reveal Codes

Concordance Files

A *concordance* file allows you to generate an index for a document without your having to mark each occurrence of a word that you would like to have listed in your index. WordPerfect uses the concordance file to scan a document for the selected words; it then generates an index and sorts the words into alphabetical order.

Later, if you modify the indexed document, you can regenerate a new index, and the page numbers in the index will change to reflect the new locations of the words.

Menu Selections

Start by opening the WordPerfect document you want to index. Next, open a new, empty file by choosing File/New. Type the words you wish to list in the index, pressing ENTER after each entry. WordPerfect will use the entries from this file as a search base.

NOTE: Make sure you enter words the way you want them to appear in the index. Although the index appears with upper- and lowercase entries, WordPerfect will not distinguish case as it scans a document.

Save the concordance file as a normal WordPerfect document. If you do not save the file, the index may function erratically. Switch back to the document you want to index by selecting the open document from the Window menu. To define the location of the index, position your cursor where you want the index to start, usually after the last page of the document, and choose Tools/Index; the Index feature bar appears as shown in Figure 11-14.

Click Define. Select an indexing format from the Define Index dialog box. As you do, WordPerfect shows an example of how the index will appear in the Numbering Format section. In the Filename box of the Concordance File section, type the name of the file you just saved with the index entries. If you are unsure of the filename, click the File icon to the right of the Filename box to browse through the files on disk. Click OK.

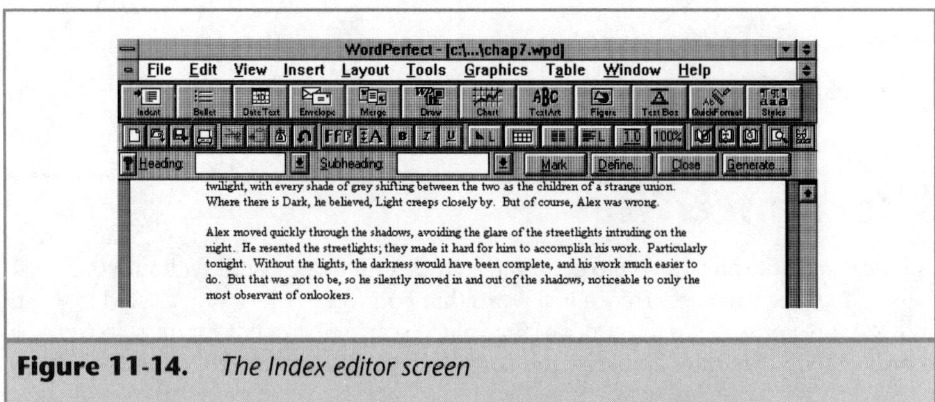

Figure 11-14. *The Index editor screen*

The text marker "<< Index will generate here >>" appears at the insertion point with a (Def Mark: Index, -) code in the Reveal Codes window. These will disappear after you generate the index.

To generate the index, click Generate and select OK. WordPerfect will search the document on the screen for each word listed in the concordance file. When the search is finished, WordPerfect inserts the index into your document at the point you specified. Again, if you later modify the document, you can regenerate a new index easily by choosing Tools/Generate.

To delete an index, turn on Reveal Codes and delete the Index marker (Def Mark: Index, -).

Related Entries

Cross-Reference
Index
Lists

Conditional End of Page

Conditional End of Page can be used to keep a group of lines together on a page. For example, you might use this feature to be sure a section heading in a document does not appear by itself at the bottom of a page, with all of its associated text on the next page.

Menu Selections

To use this feature, you must first determine the number of lines you want to keep together on one page. Then move the cursor just before the first of the lines you want to keep together and select Layout/Page/Keep Text Together. Click Number of lines to keep together to enable the feature. Specify how many lines you want to keep together and click OK. WordPerfect inserts a (Condl EOP:*n*) code, where *n* is the number of lines you specified.

Convert Case

You can convert selected text to either lowercase or uppercase, or you can capitalize just the first letter of each word. To do so, highlight the text to be changed and select Edit/Convert Case. Indicate Uppercase, Lowercase, or Initial Capitals, and the text will be modified accordingly.

Related Entries

Capitalization
Lowercase Text
Uppercase Text

Convert File Type

See File Conversion.

Copy

See Block.

Count Words

See Document Summary.

Cross-Reference

WordPerfect's Cross-Reference feature is a tool that allows you to tie together cross references in your document, such as "See page 4 for further information on this topic." WordPerfect treats the *4* as a reference to a specific target, and WordPerfect will automatically insert the number of the page where the target is located. This way, if the target is ever moved to a new page, the reference will automatically be updated to reflect the new page number when you regenerate the cross-references. You can use this feature to reference a large number of WordPerfect entities, including page numbers, chapters, volumes, paragraph/outlines, footnote and endnote numbers, figure boxes, table boxes, text boxes, user boxes, and equation boxes.

Menu Selections

To cross-reference an item, first choose Tools/Cross-Reference. The Cross-Reference feature bar appears as shown here:

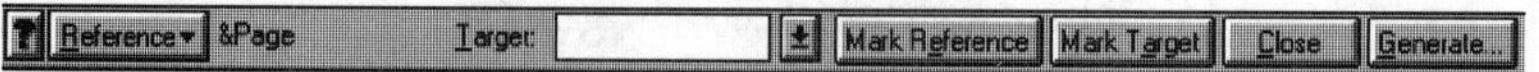

Click the Reference button and choose the item to which you want to make reference, such as a page or chapter number. Move to the Target box and give the target a unique name—something to help you identify it—up to 32 characters in length. Position your cursor in the text where the reference number is to appear. Click Mark Reference. WordPerfect inserts a page reference code (Ref Pg), which appears as a question mark (?).

Now move your cursor to the cross-reference target; that is, go to the page number that contains the text or object to which you are referring, and highlight the text or object. Click Mark Target. WordPerfect has now tied the two parts of the document together as a cross-reference. If you have highlighted any text, click elsewhere to remove any highlighting from the document. Click Generate and then OK to have WordPerfect replace the ? with the actual reference(s). If the target is ever moved to a new page, you will need to regenerate the reference by selecting Tools/Generate or pressing the F9 shortcut key.

NOTE: *Often, it is more convenient to insert the cross-reference in the reference text as you type. For example, when you see a need for a cross-reference such as "See Chapter 8 for more information on this topic," you would first type "See Chapter," enter a unique Target name, press* ENTER, *click Mark Reference, and continue typing the reference text "for more information."*

You can use Reveal Codes to view the target and reference codes in the document.

Related Entries

Codes, Displaying
Generate
Reveal Codes

Cursor

In WordPerfect, your *cursor* is the flashing bar in your document that indicates the location of the insertion point. The I-beam, which appears whenever the mouse is moved over text in a document, is also sometimes called a cursor. You can use the cursor to block or edit text. The different cursors look like this:

| I

Related Entries

I-Beam

Custom Lines

WordPerfect provides 32 different line styles that you can place in your document as lines and borders. You can also create a custom line using the Create Graphic Line dialog box, or edit any of the built-in line styles.

Menu Selections

To create a custom line, select Graphics/Custom Line and choose Line Styles from the dialog box. Click Create and type a name for the custom line in the Style Name text box. Change any of the line options to modify the line shown in the sample. The arrow in the sample points to the line that you are currently changing. If you click Add, another line appears at the position indicated by the arrow. Click OK when you are finished.

The line style you just created is now listed among the built-in line styles and is available from anywhere WordPerfect allows you to place a line or border, such as around graphics boxes. Highlight the line style and click Select to use the custom line in your document.

You can edit any line style in WordPerfect by highlighting the name of the line in the Line Styles dialog box and clicking Edit. From the Edit Line Style dialog box, make the desired changes to the line, then click OK.

Related Entries

Graphics Lines

Cut Graphics

WordPerfect provides two methods for eliminating a graphic that has already been inserted into a document.

Menu Selections

One method for eliminating a graphic is to click the graphic itself so that handles appear around its frame and press the DELETE key. Alternatively, you can use Reveal Codes and delete the code associated with the graphic.

If you select Edit/Cut to remove the graphic to the Windows Clipboard, that object can be pasted to another document or application within Windows.

Related Entries

Append to Clipboard
Clipboard
Reveal Codes

Cut Text

See Block.

Database, Exporting

You can easily export a WordPerfect merge data file to a database by converting it to an ASCII Delimited Text (DOS) file. When the receiving database reads the ASCII Delimited file, it assigns each field a name in the order in which the WordPerfect end field codes appear in the document. (The first end field code will be converted into the database's first field name, say Field 1, the next into Field 2, and so on.)

Menu Selections

Create or retrieve your merge data file to the screen and then choose File/Save As. Type a name between one and eight characters long in the Filename text box.

At the bottom of the Save As dialog box you will see a text box named Format. Click the down arrow to the right of the current format (which is most likely WordPerfect 6.0) to pull down the list of file formats to which WordPerfect will save, as shown in Figure 11-15. Select ASCII Delimited Text (DOS). Click OK, and WordPerfect will save the document in the selected file format. In fact, the extension .TXT will be added to the filename to indicate ASCII Delimited Text format. If you want a different file extension, enter it after the name in the Filename text box.

Related Entries

ASCII Text Files
Database, Importing
Merge

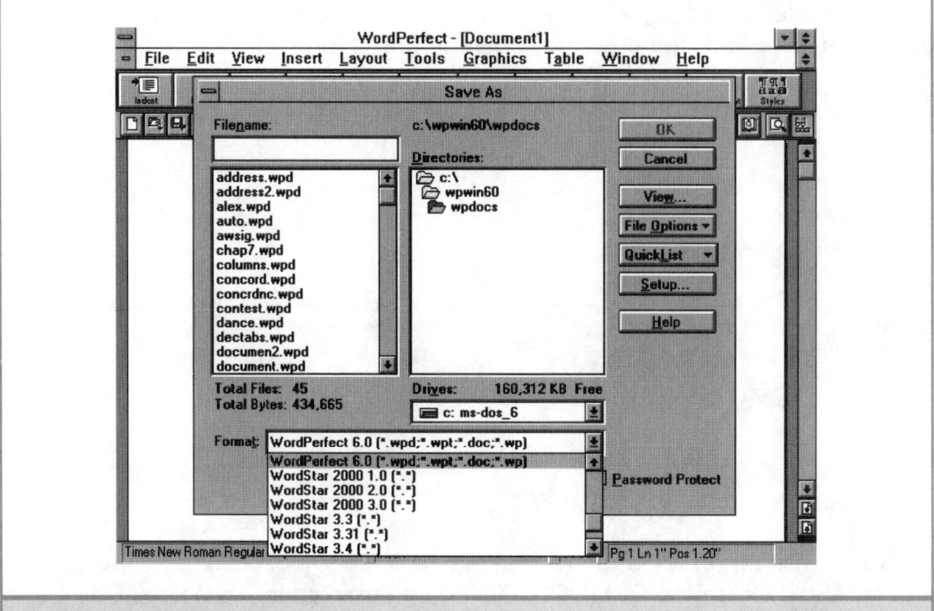

Figure 11-15. *Format list for saving a file*

Database, Importing

Importing database files is an easy task in WordPerfect. As long as the incoming file is saved to an ASCII Delimited format, WordPerfect automatically converts the file when it is opened into a standard merge data file format, with each field ending in an end field code and each record ending in an end record code.

Menu Selections

Choose File/Open and find the ASCII file you wish to open. You may have to specify the ASCII Delimited Text (DOS) file type in the List Files of Type text box to filter out other file types. Also, you can switch directories by selecting the directory and/or drive you need in the Directories or Drives section of the Open File dialog box. Once the file is listed in the Files option, double-click it to open it. WordPerfect will automatically open the Convert File Format dialog box shown here:

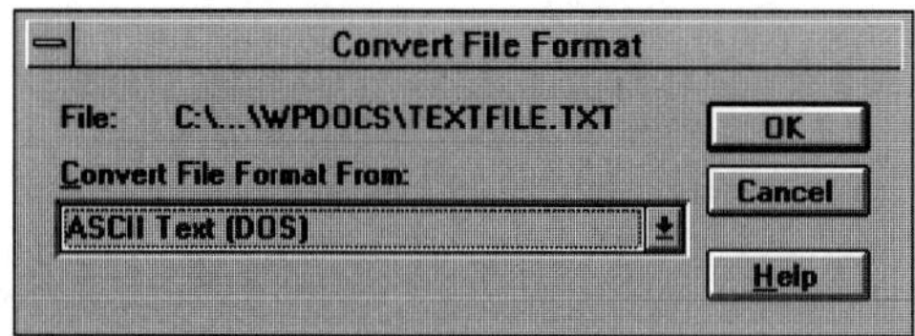

Make sure the program has chosen ASCII Delimited Text (DOS) in the Convert File Format From option box. If it is not, select this format by clicking the down arrow next to the option box and picking the format from the available formats list. Click OK, and WordPerfect converts the database into a standard WordPerfect merge data file.

D

Related Entries

Database, Exporting

Date and Time, Setting

To set your computer to the correct date and time, you need to go into the Windows Program Manager and set the time in the Windows Control Panel. (For more information on your Windows 3.1 Control Panel, refer to your Windows 3.1 documentation.)

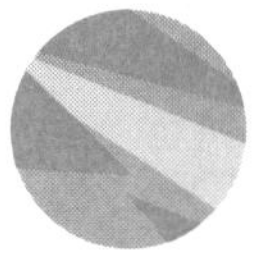

NOTE: *If your date and time continue to be wrong, you may need to replace your computer's internal battery.*

Menu Selections

To set your computer's date and time, you need to switch to the Windows Program Manager. It is not necessary to exit from WordPerfect to set the date or time. To switch to the Windows Program Manager, press CTRL+ESC to view the Task List. Double-click Program Manager. Once the Program Manager appears, activate the Main program group by double-clicking it with your mouse, and double-click the Control Panel to open it. Next, double-click the Date/Time icon, and the dialog box shown below appears:

Click the desired area of the Date or Time, such as the month or the minutes, and increase or decrease their value by clicking the up and down arrows to the right of the item. For example, if you wanted to change the day of the month from the 17th to the 18th, you would select it with your mouse and then click the up arrow once to advance the date by one day. Repeat this process to set the time, if necessary. When you are done, click OK and then switch back to WordPerfect by pressing CTRL+ESC and double-clicking WordPerfect.

If you have already placed a date or time code into your document, they will automatically change to reflect the date or time change as long as you save the document, close it, and open it again.

Date Code

WordPerfect allows you to place a date code in your documents that will display the current date every time you open or print the document. This type of date code is particularly useful when you are working with template documents and forms in which the date at the top of the page should always be current. Note that if you insert a date code into a document on April 5th and then retrieve the document again on August 10th, the date appearing in the letter will be updated to August 10th. If you want the date in the retrieved document always to be the date put in originally (April 5th, in this case), use Date Text instead of Date Code when you create the document.

NOTE: *The way the date code is displayed on your screen is determined by the current date format. If the date is wrong, you will need to update the system date by going into the Date/Time program in the Windows Control Panel.*

Menu Selections

Position your cursor where you want the date inserted into the document and choose Insert/Date/Date Code or press the shortcut key CTRL+SHIFT+D. The current date will be placed into your document. You can see that the date is actually an underlying code, rather than just text, when you reveal codes by pressing ALT+F3.

NOTE: *To delete a date code, position your cursor to the right of the date and press the* BACKSPACE *key. This deletes both the date on your screen and the code from the Reveal Codes screen.*

D

Related Entries

Date and Time, Setting
Date Format
Date Text

Date Format

You can change the way a date code or date text prints by adjusting the date format. When you load WordPerfect, the default date format is set to display [Month] [Day#], [Year####], as in January 1, 1994. You can change this to any date format you want. Once you change a date format, WordPerfect continues to use the new format in date codes and date text until you change it again.

Menu Selections

To change your current date format, choose Insert/Date/Date Format. The Document Date/Time Format dialog box shown here will appear:

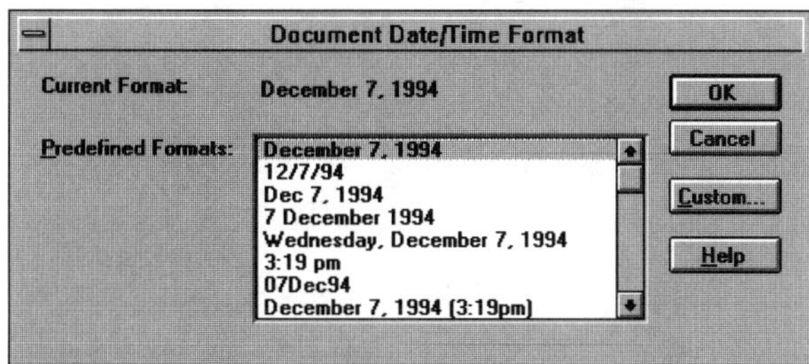

You can then highlight one of the date formats in the Predefined Dates list.

An example of date format appears above the Predefined Dates list so that you can see how the date will appear in the selected date format.

You can also customize date and time formats by clicking Custom. The Custom Document Date/Time Format dialog box appears (as shown in Figure 11-16), in which you can select the date and time format sequence you want. To create a custom date, choose the appropriate codes from the Date Codes button and from the Time Codes button.

For example, suppose you want to create a custom date to appear as Wed 12-7-1994. First, click Custom from the dialog box and delete the date codes displayed in the Edit Date Format box. To do this, simply click in the box and press either the DELETE or BACKSPACE key. Next, from the Date Codes box, double-click Day Abrv. This inserts the abbreviated day code [Day Abrv.] in the Edit Date Format box. Then Double-click Month#, Leading Space to insert the month number with a leading space [Month_#]. Press the - (minus) key to insert a hyhen. Double click Day# to insert the day of the month [Day#]. Press the - (minus) key again and double click Year(4)# to insert the four-digit year [Year(4)#]. Click OK.

Throughout the document, WordPerfect will use the format you just designed as the default. Unfortunately, WordPerfect does not allow you to save the custom date format. In order to use this date format in other documents, you should design a macro to create it for you. Otherwise you must go through the customization steps for each future document.

Date Text

The Date Text feature is very similar to Date Code, except that a date entered using Date Text is not updated every time you retrieve or print the document.

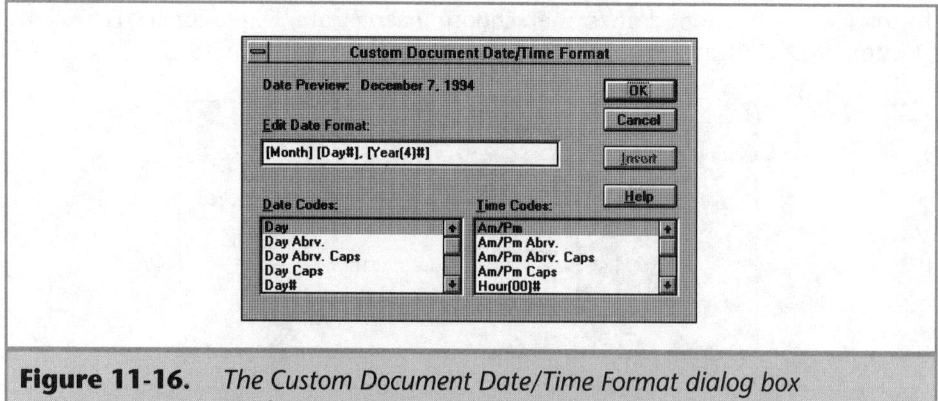

Figure 11-16. *The Custom Document Date/Time Format dialog box*

Placing a date using Date Text into your document is just like typing it manually. Because of this, you can edit date text as though it were regularly typed text.

NOTE: *The way date text is displayed on your screen is determined by the current date format. If your date text is showing the wrong date, you will need to update the system date by going into the Date/Time program in the Windows Control Panel.*

Menu Selections

To place a date text date into your document, position your cursor where you want the date to be inserted and choose Insert/Date/Date Text. The current date will then be placed in your document.

D

Related Entries

Date and Time, Setting
Date Code
Date Format

DDE Link

See Linking.

Decimal Tabs

Decimal tabs are used to line up a column of numbers containing decimal points. When you use decimal tabs, numbers align above and below one another with their decimal points all in line. Decimal tabs allow you to have the numbers in your invoices, expense reports, and order forms all line up automatically.

Menu Selections

The easiest way to set decimal tabs is by using the Ruler. To display the ruler, choose View/Ruler Bar or press the shortcut key CTRL+SHIFT+F3. The ruler will appear just below the power bar. Note that the current tabs look like sideways triangles on your screen; these are left-aligned tabs.

Point to one of the tabs just below the ruler and right-click to view the shortcut menu. Click Tab Set to activate the Tab Set dialog box.

To place a decimal tab on the ruler, click the Type button in the Settings section of the dialog box and choose Decimal. To set the tabs at fixed positions, click Repeat Every. Click the up or down arrow to adjust tab spacing, or set each tab by typing a number in the Position box and clicking Set.

You can move the tabs to any position after they are set. Simply click and drag the tab symbol to the desired location on the ruler. You can remove a tab by clicking and dragging it down away from the ruler bar. Here is an example of how decimal tabs look, both on the ruler bar and in a document:

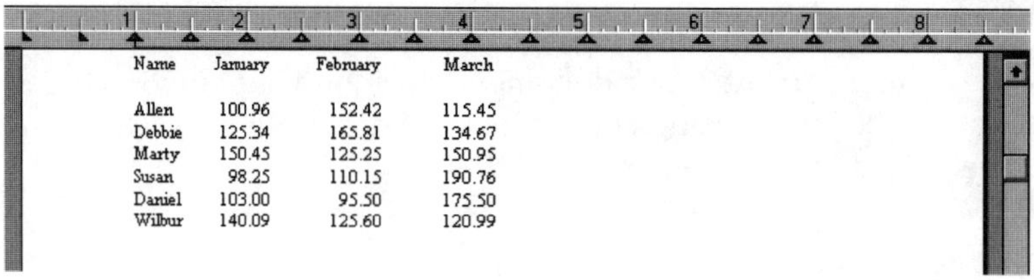

Name	January	February	March
Allen	100.96	152.42	115.45
Debbie	125.34	165.81	134.67
Marty	150.45	125.25	150.95
Susan	98.25	110.15	190.76
Daniel	103.00	95.50	175.50
Wilbur	140.09	125.60	120.99

Notice how the decimal points in all of the numbers align with each other.

Related Entries

Ruler
Tabs, Setting

Delete Formatting Codes

Most of the functions in WordPerfect cause formatting codes to be inserted in the text.

You can delete inserted formatting codes by selecting the code to be eliminated in the Reveal Codes screen and pressing DELETE. You can eliminate certain codes, such as format enhancement codes like bold and underline, by highlighting the enhanced text and selecting the enhancement again. This technique serves as a toggle switch, inserting the codes and then deleting them.

Related Entries

Reveal Codes

Delete Key

The DELETE key on the keyboard deletes the character to the right of the insertion point. If text or formatting codes are highlighted, the DELETE key deletes the selected items.

NOTE: In Reveal Codes, the DELETE key deletes the character or code highlighted by the black (reverse video) cursor.

Related Entries

Backspace Key

Delete Text

See Block.

Descriptive Name

One of the limitations of the DOS operating system is the length of a filename; you can only designate up to eight characters with a three-character extension. Although it is unlikely that you will ever run out of possible document names, it does become tedious to find the document you want in a long list of files.

WordPerfect provides a way to give your documents names of up to 255 characters long called *descriptive names.* This naming method helps you name files accurately and locate files quickly.

Menu Selections

You must first enable the descriptive names option by selecting the options File/Preferences/Summary and placing a check mark in the Use Descriptive Names box. From this point on (unless you remove the check mark), you can save documents with a descriptive name.

In order to view the descriptive names in the Open File dialog box and other locations in WordPerfect, you must select File/Open or File/Save As and click Setup. This accesses the Open/Save As Setup dialog box shown here:

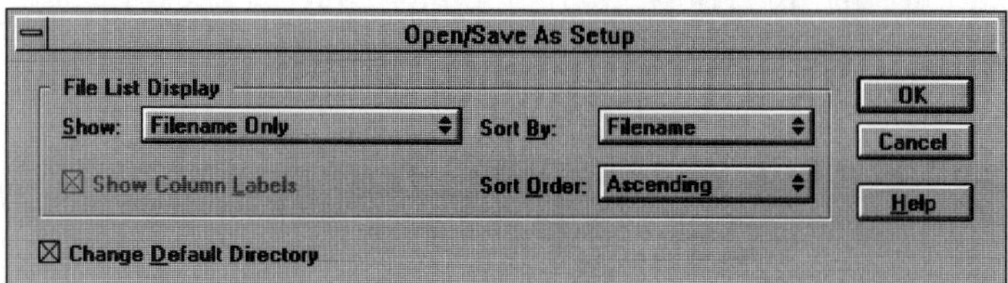

Click the Show option button and select Descriptive Name, Filename. This dictates how the files will be listed in the Open File dialog box. Also, a new area is added to the dialog box allowing you to create Speedup files, which is discussed later. Choose OK and WordPerfect will scan for document summary information in the current directory. If you have any descriptive names, they will be displayed in the file list to the left of the DOS filename.

NOTE: If all you see is blank white space in the file list box, that's because no descriptive names have been assigned to the files yet. To display the descriptive names in the Open File dialog box, first open and save each file with a descriptive name.

Adding Descriptive Names

When you first save a file, the Document Summary dialog box will appear and prompt you for a descriptive name. Type any combination of letters—you can even insert WordPerfect characters by pressing the CTRL+W shortcut key. Click OK, and the Save As dialog box appears. Save the file with an appropriate DOS filename.

Once you have an accumulation of documents with descriptive names, your file list will resemble Figure 11-17.

Modifying a Descriptive Name

Once you've saved a document with a descriptive name, the document summary will not appear the next time you save the document. If you ever need to modify the descriptive name or any of the summary information, select File/Document Summary and make any necessary changes within the Document Summary dialog box.

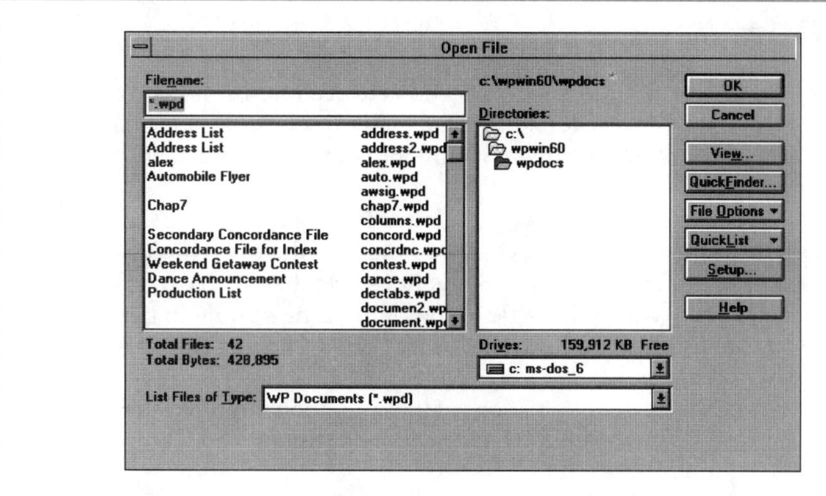

Figure 11-17. *An Open File dialog box with descriptive names enabled*

Creating Speedup Files

Every time you use the File/Open or the File/Save As command, WordPerfect scans through the directory to "compile" and display the document summary information. If you have many files in your document directory, this may take a few moments. To avoid this delay, you can create what are termed *speedup files,* which act as pointers to the document summary information, thereby speeding up the time it takes WordPerfect to scan the directory.

To allow WordPerfect to create speedup files, select File/Open or File/Save As and click Setup. Make sure the Show option button displays Descriptive Name, Filename as described earlier. At the bottom of the Open/Save As Setup dialog box click Create Speedup Files. If you do not want to use C:\WPSPEED as the speedup files directory, type an alternate directory name. Otherwise, just click OK. If the directory does not exist, WordPerfect asks if you want to create it. Click Yes to create the directory.

Related Entries

Character Sets
Document Summary

Dialog Boxes

When you use the WordPerfect menu selections to accomplish tasks, you will often encounter dialog boxes. You know that a menu selection calls up a dialog box if an ellipsis (...) follows the menu command. For example, see the menu command File/Print.

Most dialog boxes contain buttons you can click, such as Open, Cancel, or OK. Some dialog boxes have choices that you mark with an X (check mark) by clicking the box to the left of the item. Some have lists that you pop down or up by clicking the down arrow or triangle to the right of the option. In other dialog boxes you may see lists that you can scroll through by clicking the up and down scroll arrows with your mouse.

Many dialog boxes have combinations of these components. For example, see the Font dialog box shown in Figure 11-18. It contains buttons, check boxes, and lists.

Dictionary, Changing

See the "Selecting a Dictionary" section of the Speller entry.

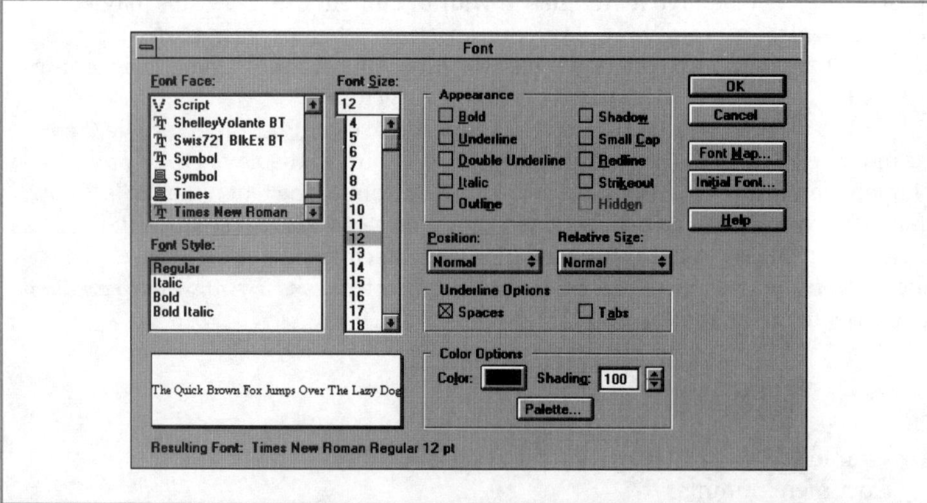

Figure 11-18. *The Font dialog box shows many components that you find in dialog boxes*

Dictionary, Speller

See Speller.

Dictionary, Supplemental

See the "Selecting a Dictionary" section of the Speller entry.

Directories

When you install WordPerfect, certain types of files are automatically copied into predefined, default directories. For example, unless you specify otherwise, the document files are placed in the C:\WPWIN60\WPDOCS directory. The program then looks in this directory for all the document and text files.

You will have to navigate through the directory system in order to find files that are in another directory. Some dialog boxes have a Directories option that lists every location in which files are contained in your computer system. This option lists both drives and directories under the generic heading "Directories."

NOTE: *To change the location of files, you may either use WordPerfect's built-in file management system or exit WordPerfect and copy the files using the Windows File Manager DOS.*

Menu Selections

To find out the default location of WordPerfect files within your computer system, you can choose File/Preferences/File to display the dialog box shown in Figure 11-19.

This dialog box lists the drive and directory where all of your WordPerfect files are located. You may assign a new location for specific files by clicking the File icon to the right of the option. A list of directories will pop up, allowing you to choose an existing drive or directory in which to place the specified files.

If you type in a directory that does not exist, a WordPerfect dialog box shows that the directory does not exist. You can allow WordPerfect to create the new directory by clicking Yes.

It is equally easy to change directories when a Directories list pops up on your screen. For example, when you access the File/Open menu selection, a Directories list is included in the Open File dialog box, as shown in Figure 11-20.

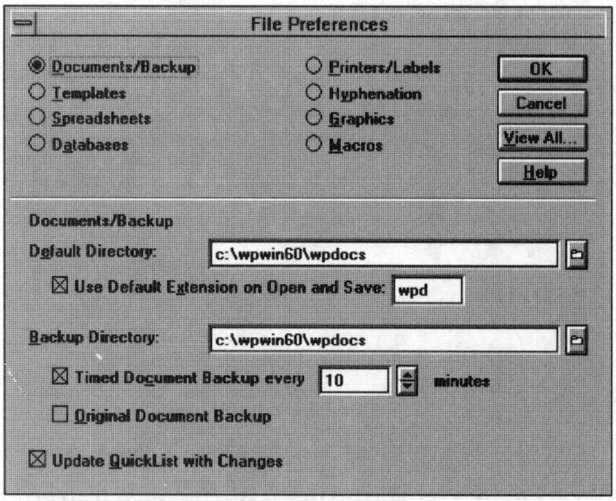

Figure 11-19. *The File Preferences dialog box*

To look for files in another location, double-click the icon or directory that represents that location. For example, to find files on a floppy disk that is in the A: drive, double-click the a: drive icon in the Drives section.

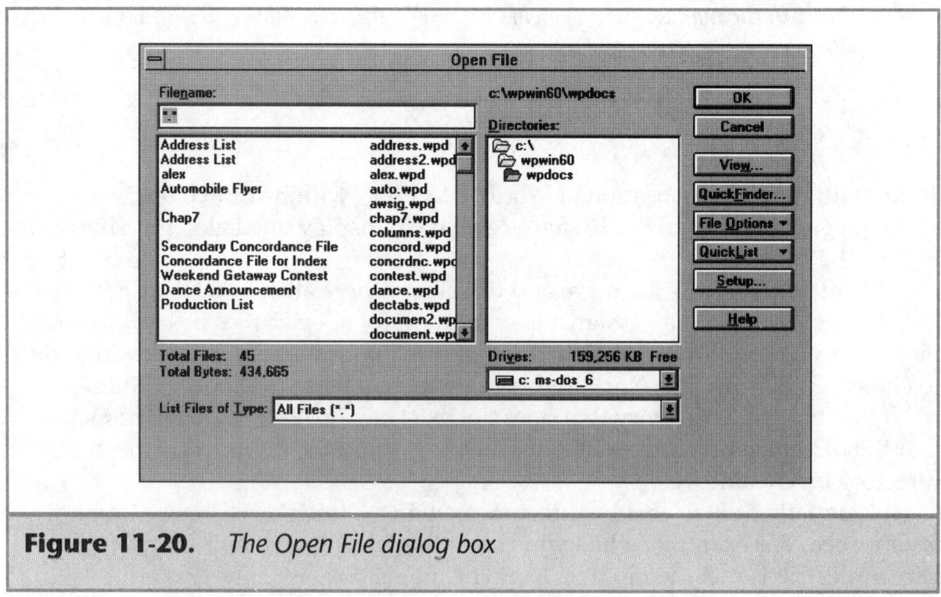

Figure 11-20. *The Open File dialog box*

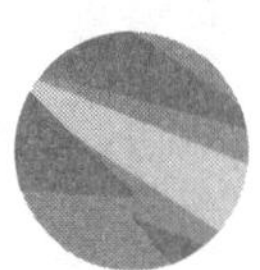

NOTE: The current directory (shown just above the Directories list of the Open File dialog box) in Figure 11-20 is C:\WPWIN60\WPDOCS. To move up one level to the WPWIN60 directory, double-click the WPWIN60 file folder icon in the Directories list. This will display a list of the appropriate file types directly beneath the Filename text box. Also, any subdirectories within WPWIN60 will be displayed under its file folder icon in the Directories list.

Related Entries

File Manager
QuickList

D

Display Fonts

See Fonts, Displaying.

Display Preferences

You can change any of the screen display settings and attributes through the Display Preferences dialog box, shown in Figure 11-21.

Menu Selections

File/Preferences/Display

Related Entries

Colors, Screen
Document Windows
Hard Return Character
Margins
Reveal Codes
Ruler
Scroll Bars
Units of Measure
Zooming

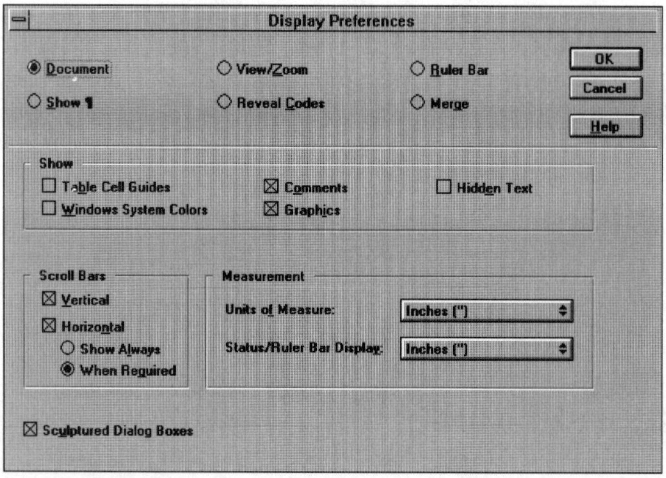

Figure 11-21. *The Display Preferences dialog box*

Document Measurements

See Paper Size.

Document Summary

A *document summary* is used to store useful information about a document, such as the author's name, the typist, the topic, and any comments you would like to attach to the text. You can set up WordPerfect through the menu selection File/Preferences/Summary so that every time you save a document, you are prompted to fill in a document summary. Document summaries are not automatically printed with the document, but you can print one by selecting Print Document Summary from the Options button in the Print dialog box, or by using appropriate commands in the Print dialog box. WordPerfect also allows you to save and delete the document summary.

Menu Selections

To attach a document summary to each of your documents, choose File/Preferences/Summary, and the Document Summary Preferences dialog box appears. Click the Create Summary on Save/Exit check box to toggle it on. Click OK to save the changes. Now every time you save a document you will be given an opportunity to fill in a document summary.

Once you have turned on the Document Summary feature, the Document Summary dialog box, shown here, will appear on your screen each time you save a document for the first time:

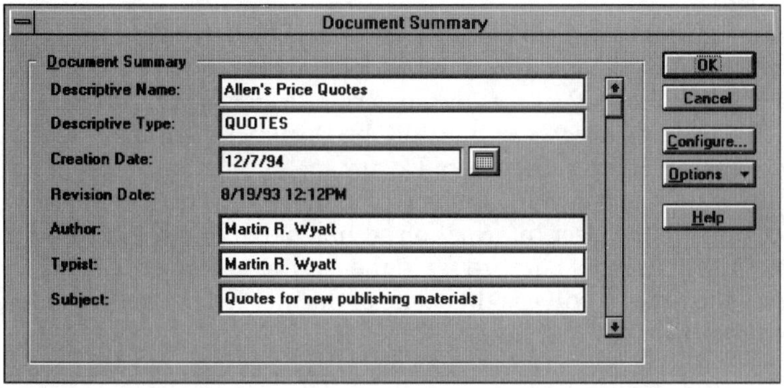

In the Descriptive Name text box you can type a descriptive name up to 255 characters long (descriptive names are not constrained by the 11-character DOS naming convention). The Document Summary dialog box is also accessible by selecting File/Document Summary.

The Descriptive Type text box refers to the general category of the document: you can type an entry in this text box, or, if you always create the same type of documents, you can preset the contents of the text box in the Document Summary Preferences dialog box. The Creation Date text box is filled in with the current date.

The Author, Typist, Account, and Keywords text boxes provide additional information about the file in the document summary. WordPerfect automatically retrieves the author's name from the User Information section of the Environment Preferences dialog box. You can fill in the Subject and Abstract options, or, if you choose Extract Information from Document from the Options button in the dialog box, the Subject and Abstract options will be filled in automatically.

The Options button allows you to print the document summary, delete the summary from a document, extract text from a document for a summary, save the summary as a new document, and obtain document information.

Related Entries

Date and Time, Setting
Document Summary, Extracting
Document Summary, Preferences
Document Summary, Printing
Preferences

Document Summary, Extracting

The Extract Information From Document feature allows you to instantly fill in the Subject and Abstract text boxes of the document summary, as long as you either have chosen to use "RE:" as the subject indicator in your document or have changed the default subject search text in the Document Summary Preferences dialog box. Extract Information From Document automatically fills in the Typist text box using the last entry you made while filling out a document summary. If a name is found in the User Information section of the Environment Preferences dialog box, it will use that name to fill in the Author text box of the document summary. Otherwise, it will use the name of the most recent author entered in a document summary.

Menu Selections

Once the document summary is on the screen, click the Options button in the Document Summary dialog box. Choose Extract Information From Document, and WordPerfect automatically fills in the Author, Typist, Subject, and Abstract text boxes. (The first 400 characters of the document will appear in the Abstract text box.)

Related Entries

Document Summary, Preferences
Preferences

Document Summary, Preferences

The Document Summary Preferences dialog box, shown here, allows the user to set up default search patterns for specific descriptive and subject types:

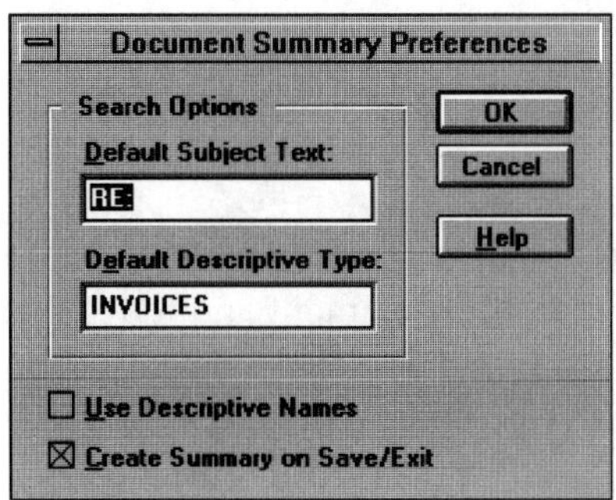

Using the QuickFinder, you can then search for files using any of the document summary text boxes, including type, author, typist, and subject.

Menu Selections

To access the Document Summary Preferences dialog box, choose File/Preferences/Summary. In the Default Subject Text box, you will see the abbreviation "RE:". If you use the word "Subject:," for example, instead of "RE:," to indicate the subject in your document, you should type **Subject:** on this line. WordPerfect will then search within your document for "Subject:" to retrieve text indicating the subject of the document when you use the Extract Information From Document feature in the document summary.

In the Default Descriptive Type text box, you can type a generic topic, like "Invoices," that will always appear on the Descriptive Type line in your document summaries. You can then search for specific descriptive types using the File Manager.

Related Entries

Document Summary, Extracting
File Manager
See Chapter 4, "Managing Files with WordPerfect"

Document Summary, Printing

You can either print your document summary when you print out your document, or you can print it when it is created (when you initially save the document).

Menu Selections

To print the document summary with your document, choose File/Print and select the Options button from the Print dialog box. The Print Output Options dialog box appears, as shown in Figure 11-22. Click the Print Document Summary check box to toggle it on, then click OK to return to the Print dialog box. Click Print to print both the document and the document summary.

To print your document summary when saving a document for the first time, click Print Summary from the Options button in the Document Summary dialog box.

Document Windows

The *document window* is the area on your screen where you type text and place graphics. WordPerfect automatically maximizes the document window when you open a file, so that you have the greatest amount of screen space possible in which to work on your document.

WordPerfect allows you to have a maximum of nine files open simultaneously. The number you can have open at any one time on your system depends, of course, on the memory in your computer and the size of the files. Keeping files open simultaneously makes it easy for you to switch between documents and to copy and move text from one document to another.

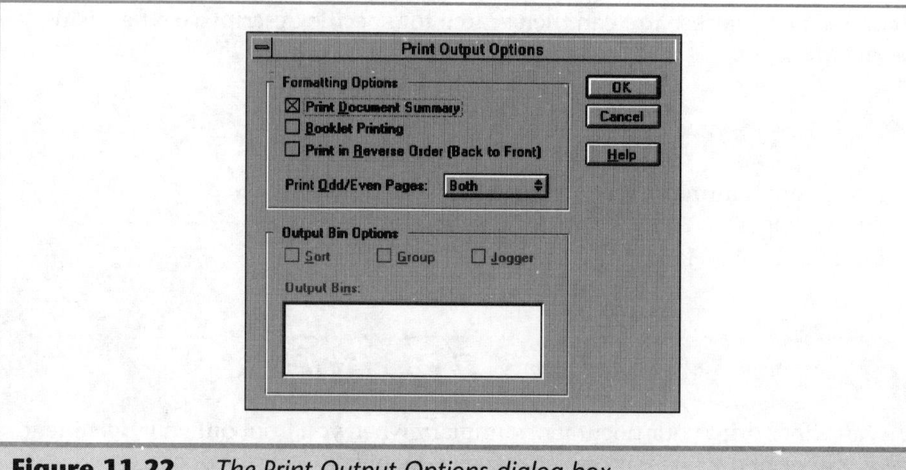

Figure 11-22. *The Print Output Options dialog box*

D

Menu Selections

One way to switch between document windows is to use the Window option on the menu bar. If you have opened a number of files and want to switch from one to another, choose Window from the menu bar and click the name of the file you wish to go to. That file will come forward on the screen and a check mark will appear next to the filename on the Window menu, indicating that it is the currently active file.

One way to display multiple files onscreen is to select Cascade or Tile from the Window menu. If you choose Window/Cascade, the document windows will be shown in overlapping layers on the screen, as shown in Figure 11-23. Notice how the filename of each document is displayed on the title bar of the document window.

When you choose Window/Cascade, the currently active file will be on top of the stack. You may then click the filename of another document to pull it forward. By clicking the maximize button to the right of the filename, you can have the selected file fill the entire screen.

When you select Window/Tile, the document windows are stacked on top of one another, as shown in Figure 11-24.

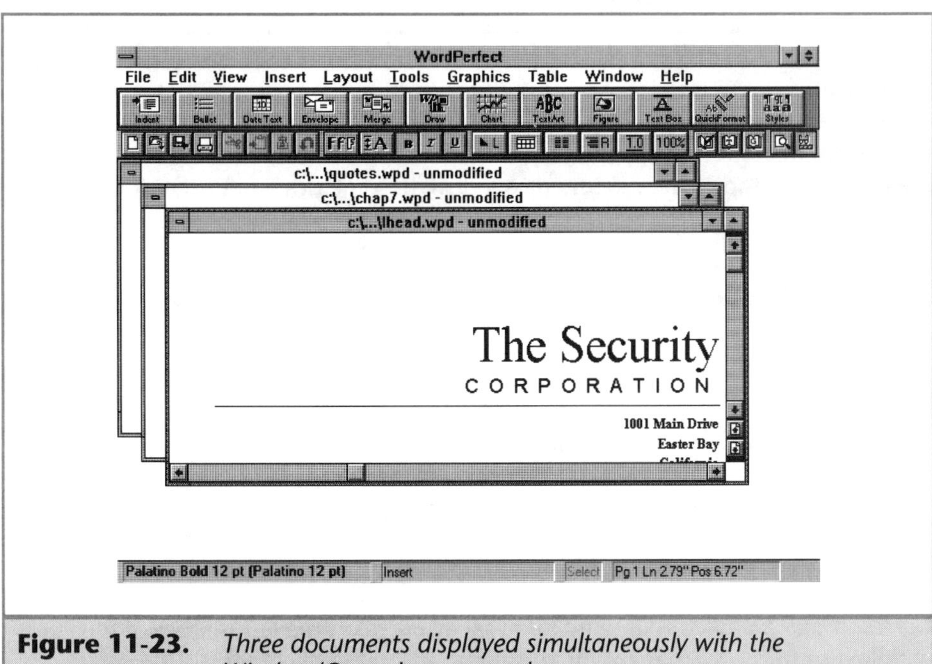

Figure 11-23. *Three documents displayed simultaneously with the Window/Cascade command*

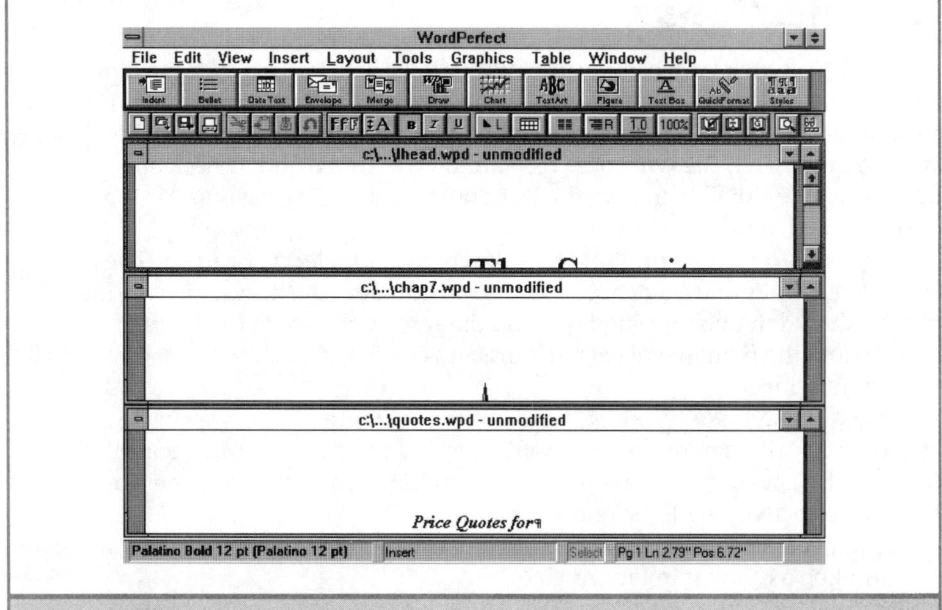

Figure 11-24. *Three documents displayed simultaneously with the Window/Tile command*

To activate a document window in tile mode, click its window. Its title bar will darken and you can then work within the document window. To maximize the current document window, click the maximize button to the right of the filename at the top of the document window, and the document window will fill the screen.

Related Entries

Block
Move
Windows
Windows, Working with Multiple

Dot Leader Tabs

Dot leader tabs are used to line up text that appears on the left margin of the page with text or numbers that are flush right, as in a table of contents. Dot leader tabs automatically put in the dots that connect the text on the left with the text on the right, as shown in Figure 11-25.

You can have left-, center-, right-, or decimal-aligned dot leader tabs in your document.

Menu Selections

The easiest way to set dot leader tabs is by using the Ruler bar. To activate the ruler bar, choose View/Ruler Bar or press CTRL+SHIFT+F3 and the Ruler bar will appear just below the power bar. Note that the current tabs look like tilted triangles on your screen; these are left-aligned tabs.

Point to one of the tabs that is just below the Ruler bar and double-click. This activates the Tab Set dialog box. Click the Clear All button to remove all the default left-aligned tabs.

To place a dot leader tab on the ruler, click the Type list option button and select the Dot Left, Dot Center, Dot Right, or Dot Decimal type. Click Repeat Every to have WordPerfect place tabs every 1/2 inch. Click Set to physically place the tabs on the Ruler bar. Click OK. You can later reposition a tab by clicking and dragging it along the Ruler bar, or you can delete a tab by dragging

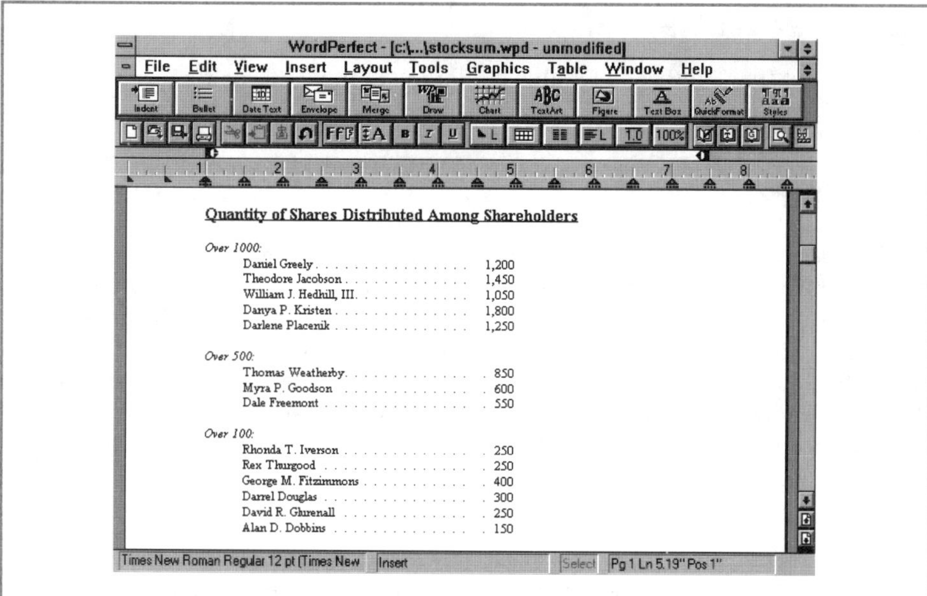

Figure 11-25. *Dot leader tabs applied to text in a document*

it down away from the Ruler bar. Figure 11-25 shows how dot leader tabs look both on the Ruler and in a document.

Related Entries

Ruler
Tabs, Setting

Double Indent

See the "Double Indent" section of the Indent entry.

Double Underlined Text

Text that is double underlined looks like this. To double underline text in WordPerfect, turn on the Double Underline feature and then type the text, or highlight the text and then select Double Underline.

Menu Selections

Select Layout/Font and click Double Underline in the Font dialog box. Click OK.

Draft View

Draft view gives you a different perspective than does Page view in your documents. In Draft view, the pages in your document are not represented graphically. This meaning that page breaks appear as a line across the page, headers and footers are not displayed, endnotes and footnotes are not displayed, and so forth. It may be easier and faster to type text using Draft view, especially if a document contains a lot of graphics or a variety of layout variations. This is because the graphics and other enhancements require less complex screen redrawing in Draft view.

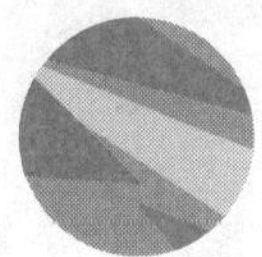

NOTE: *You cannot select Draft view when text is highlighted in a document.*

You can set Draft view as the default mode by selecting File/Preferences/Display and clicking View/Zoom. Change the Default View to draft by clicking the Draft button. Click OK. In order for the default to take effect, you must exit WordPerfect and start it again.

Menu Selection

View/Draft

Related Entries

Page View
Two-Page View

Edit Line

See Graphics Lines.

Endnotes

You can use *endnotes,* like footnotes, to refer to more information on a particular topic. When you use the endnote feature, WordPerfect automatically places a superscript endnote number at the location of your insertion point. WordPerfect numbers your endnotes consecutively, and if you insert text with another endnote inside a document, WordPerfect renumbers all subsequent endnotes. You also have the option of restarting endnote numbering, which is useful for beginning a new sequence after each chapter.

Unlike footnotes, endnotes are placed at the end of a document on a separate endnote page. The endnote number that appears in the document is then tied directly to the one on the endnote page at the end of the document.

NOTE: *It is best to first identify the placement of the endnote by using the Insert/Endnote/Placement option.*

Menu Selections

To place an endnote reference in your document, position the insertion point where you want the superscript endnote number to appear. Then choose

Insert/Endnote/Create to insert the endnote number. You are taken to the end of the document, where the corresponding endnote is placed. Type and format the text of the endnote, and Click the Close button when you are finished. You can view the endnote code in Reveal Codes.

Related Items

Endnotes, Editing
Endnotes, Options
Endnotes, Placement

Endnotes, Editing

To edit existing endnotes you must go to the Edit Endnote dialog box. In Page view, the endnotes appear on a separate endnote page at the end of a file, but you can edit them from any location in the document as long as you know the endnote number. WordPerfect will not let you edit them directly in the document window: you must use the Edit Endnote feature.

Menu Selections

To edit an existing endnote, choose Insert/Endnote/Edit. If you first position your cursor just after the endnote number, WordPerfect will assume that is the endnote you wish to edit and will place that number in the Edit Endnote dialog box. Otherwise, type the number of the endnote you wish to edit, and that endnote appears on your screen. When you are finished editing the endnote, click the Close button to return to the document window.

Related Entries

Endnotes
Footnotes Editing

Endnotes, Options

You can easily change the endnote format by using the Endnote Options dialog box shown here:

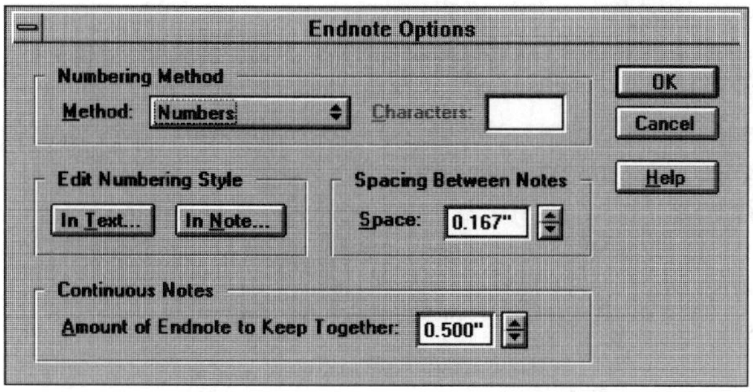

Menu Selections

Insert/Endnote/Options

Numbering Options

In the Endnote Options dialog box, you can change the way the endnotes in your document are numbered by clicking the Method option button. When you do, you are given the option of using numbers, characters, or letters for identifying your endnotes. If you choose Characters, you must specify, in the Characters definition box next to the Method option button, the character you want to use. If, for example, you select the asterisk (*) for numbering your endnotes, your first endnote will be numbered with *, the second with **, and so on.

You can define up to five characters to be used in numbering endnotes. For example, if you enter ***!#** (notice that there are no spaces between characters) in the Character edit box, WordPerfect numbers your first endnote with *, your second with !, and the third with #. The next endnote will be labeled **, the next !!, and so on, until up to 15 symbols of each type are used. Then the cycle begins over again with one of each symbol.

You can use any WordPerfect symbol for endnotes. To select one of the extended WordPerfect characters, click the Method option button, select Characters as the numbering method, and place the cursor in the Characters definition box to the right. Press CTRL+W to activate the WordPerfect Characters dialog box. Select one or more characters to use and insert each into the Characters definition box.

Edit Numbering Style

You can redefine the endnote numbering style by deleting any portion of the default code you don't want to use and clicking either the In Text button or In

Note button in the Endnote Options dialog box. When you do, the Styles Editor dialog box appears, as shown in Figure 11-26. The default format for the endnote designator in the text of the document is a superscript note number. The default format for the endnote designator placed in the endnote at the end of the document is the same as the opening style.

To change any of the style attributes, right-click your mouse in the Contents section of the Styles Editor dialog box to call up the shortcut menu. By selecting among the options given there, you can customize your endnote design. Be sure not to delete the endnote number (EndNote Num Disp) in the list of codes.

Spacing

You can define line spacing within an endnote in units of inches. Spacing between endnotes is .167" by default. This is the single-space height of a standard 12-point line. Double-spacing would be .294, and so on. You can adjust this to leave more or less space between consecutive endnotes.

Continuous Notes

If an endnote is too long to fit completely on a page, WordPerfect continues the note on the next page automatically. Ordinarily, WordPerfect keeps at least 1/2 inch of the endnote together on the page on which it begins. You can adjust this amount as necessary.

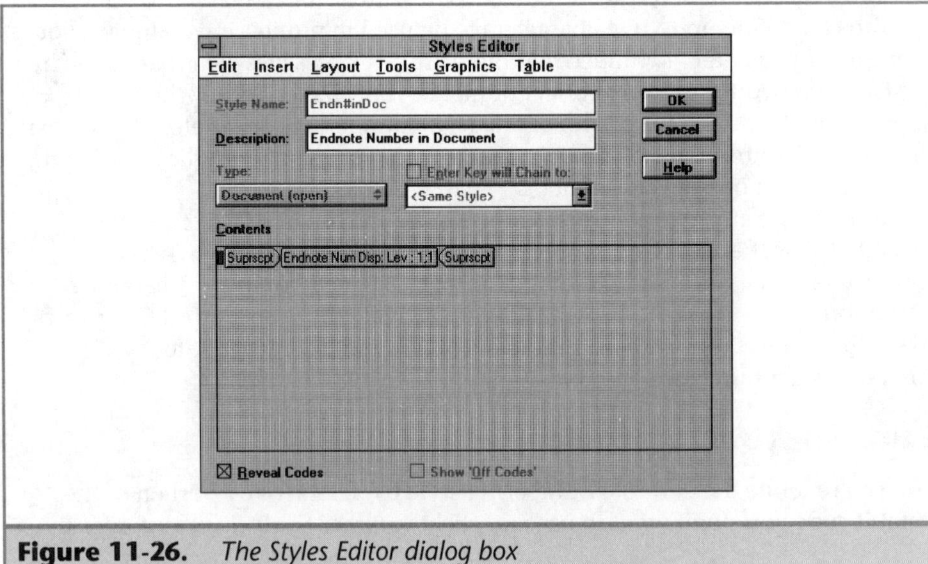

Figure 11-26. *The Styles Editor dialog box*

Related Entries

Endnotes

Endnotes, Placement

Whenever you are using endnotes in your documents, you need to let WordPerfect know where to place them. Endnotes are generally placed on a separate page at the end of the document.

Menu Selections

To place the endnotes at the end of the document, press CTRL+END to go to the bottom of the file. Press CTRL+ENTER to add a required page break (if one doesn't exist), and type any text you wish to use to introduce the endnotes. For example, the word "Endnotes" is usually centered at the top of the page. Position the insertion point where you want the endnotes to begin, and choose Insert/Endnote/Placement. To place endnotes at the location of the insertion point, click Insert Endnotes at Insertion Point. Or, click Insert Endnotes at Insertion Point and Restart Numbering to place endnotes at the cursor's position and restart endnote numbering. When you select either option, WordPerfect adds a page break after the endnote page.

You will need to generate the endnotes when the document is finished by choosing Tools/Generate and clicking OK. This ensures that no endnotes are out of place due to movement or deletion of text, and that the endnotes correspond correctly to the endnote number in the document text. To actually view the endnotes on the page, make sure WordPerfect is in Page view.

Related Entries

Endnotes
Endnotes, Editing

Envelopes

As long as your printer can handle envelope printing, you can use the Envelope feature. Two predefined envelope sizes are available for WordPerfect printers. However, odds are that you have already set up one or more printers in Windows. WordPerfect recognizes and uses these Windows printer definitions, but requires you to define one or more envelope styles before you can print on envelopes. The Envelope feature lets you determine where on the envelope you want the recipient's address and the return address to be positioned. WordPerfect also lets you create envelope types for each individual printer attached to your computer.

Menu Selections

To access the predefined envelope paper size, choose Layout/Envelope, and the Envelope dialog box will appear (see Figure 11-27). The envelope is graphically depicted in the dialog box, allowing you to see exactly how the envelope will appear when printed.

Create a New Envelope Definition

You can design your own envelope layout in WordPerfect by selecting Create New Definition from the Envelope dialog box. You must provide a name for the envelope in the Paper Name text box and then specify any of the parameters you want. You can select from 12 different envelope sizes, whether you want WordPerfect to prompt you to place an envelope in the printer before printing, and the print location of the text on the envelope.

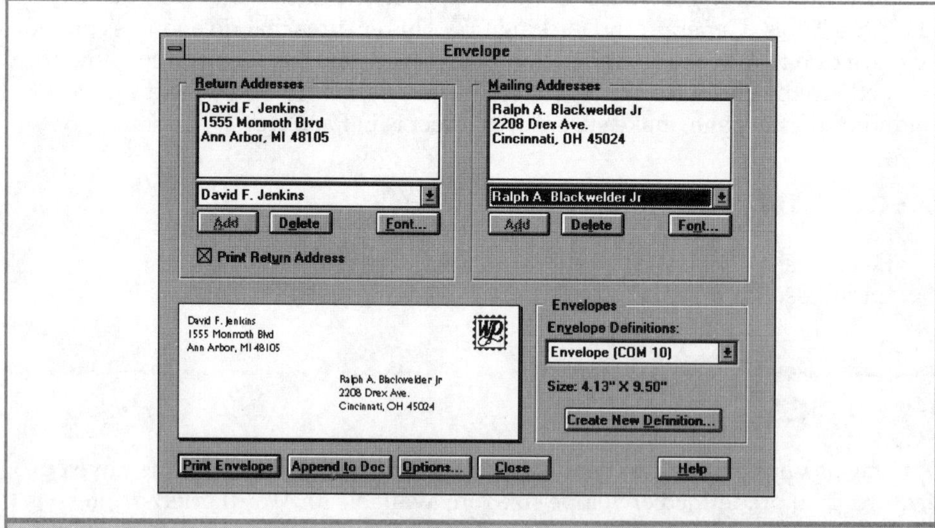

Figure 11-27. *The Envelope dialog box*

Using an Existing Envelope Definition

Type the return address and regular address where you want them to appear and press ENTER after each line of text. You can add these names and addresses to WordPerfect's mailing address list. To select another name from the list, click the down arrow within either address section and highlight the desired name. Any font attribute can be applied to an envelope, just as with regular documents.

Selecting Options from the Envelope dialog box lets you adjust the address positions and whether or not to include the USPS POSTNET Bar Code below the ZIP code of the addressee.

Envelopes can be "attached" to a WordPerfect document by clicking Append to Doc. Each time you print the document, WordPerfect will also print an accompanying envelope, complete with address.

Environment

The Environment dialog box allows you to customize the way WordPerfect operates.

Menu Selections

To display the Environment Preferences dialog box, choose the command File/ Preferences/ Environment. You will see the dialog box shown in Figure 11-28.

User Information

User information is supplied for identification purposes in WordPerfect documents. If your name is in the Name text box, it will automatically be placed in the document summary as the author of the document, provided that document summary is enabled.

Formatting

The Formatting options allow you to change the default settings of several WordPerfect formatting functions.

HYPHENATION PROMPT The Hyphenation Prompt options allow you to specify if and when you want WordPerfect to prompt you for hyphenation assistance. If you select Never, WordPerfect automatically hyphenates words based upon its own hyphenation dictionary. The When Required option causes WordPerfect to prompt you when it needs to hyphenate a word that is not in its hyphenation dictionary. The Always option causes WordPerfect to stop and prompt you whenever it attempts to hyphenate any word—even those in the hyphenation dictionary.

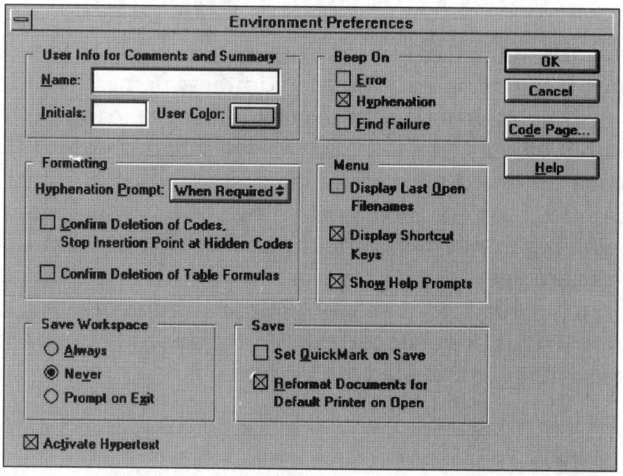

Figure 11-28. *The Environment Preferences dialog box*

The Hyphenation options allow you to select one of two dictionaries to use for hyphenating words in your document. The Document dictionary is built into WordPerfect. The Supplemental dictionary is larger and contains more possible positions for hyphenation than does the internal dictionary. The External dictionary is contained in WPSPELUS.SUP and requires more disk space than does the Document dictionary.

CONFIRM DELETION OF CODES When the Confirm Deletion of Codes option is selected and the Reveal Codes screen is not displayed, the cursor is stopped at hidden codes and you are prompted to confirm any deletion you try to make that would cause removal of an underlying formatting code (for instance, the bold attribute).

CONFIRM DELETION OF TABLE FORMULA When this option is selected, you are prompted to confirm deletion of any formula in a table.

Save Workspace

As you work with one or multiple documents, you might like to have WordPerfect remember them the next time you start WordPerfect. By enabling this option, WordPerfect will save the workspace, that is remember which document(s) you had open last, and reopen it (them) for your next WordPerfect session.

Beep On

If you want your computer to beep to bring your attention to certain actions or results, you can do so by enabling the appropriate option.

ERROR When the Error option is activated, WordPerfect will beep whenever an error warning box appears on the screen.

HYPHENATION When the Hyphenation option is checked, WordPerfect will beep when it attempts to hyphenate a word and present you with the Position Hyphen dialog box.

FIND FAILURE When the Find Failure option is checked, WordPerfect will beep whenever it displays the "String not found" message in the status bar at the bottom-left corner of the screen at the conclusion of a search.

Menu

The Menu options allow you to customize the way certain options appear on your menus.

DISPLAY LAST OPEN FILENAMES When the Display Last Open Filenames option is activated, the names of the last four files you opened appear at the bottom of the File menu. You can open any one of these files by clicking its filename.

DISPLAY SHORTCUT KEYS Certain WordPerfect commands can be accessed by pressing a shortcut key. For example, you can apply boldfacing to text by pressing CTRL+B or underlining by pressing CTRL+U. Similarly, you can select File/Open by pressing CTRL+O and View/Reveal Codes by pressing ALT+F3.

When the Display Shortcut Keys option is checked, the shortcut keys are displayed in the menu to the right of the menu option. This is a good way to remind yourself, as you are learning the program, which shortcut keys go with which feature.

SHOW HELP PROMPTS As you pass your mouse pointer over menu items, icons, and other areas of the screen, WordPerfect displays a brief explanation of the item in the menu bar at the top of the window. When you disable Show Help Prompts, these explanations do not appear.

ACTIVATE HYPERTEXT Hypertext is text within your document that lets you "jump" to related sections in the current or another document, invoke a macro, or link to other documents. You can deactivate hypertext by removing the X next to this option, thereby preventing any inadvertent "jumps" to another document. The hypertext still remains visible in all documents.

Save

These options affect how WordPerfect saves your documents.

SET QUICKMARK ON SAVE As the default, every time you start WordPerfect, a blank document opens for you to begin typing. When you enable this option, WordPerfect will place a QuickMark (like a bookmark) as you exit a file at the last position of the insertion point. The next time you load that document, it automatically opens at the QuickMark.

REFORMAT DOCUMENTS FOR DEFAULT PRINTER ON OPEN When the Reformat Documents for Default Printer on Open option is activated and a document is opened, WordPerfect formats the document for the currently defined default printer. This may modify the appearance of some or all of the text if the document was originally created and formatted for another printer. This is due to the fact that some printers and other Windows programs may use different fonts.

Related Entries

Error Messages
Hyphenation
Ruler
Shortcut Keys

Equation Editor

The Equation Editor in WordPerfect allows you to type mathematical and scientific equations much as you would read them aloud and have WordPerfect create them in a graphics frame. Like all graphics frames in WordPerfect, you can size and position an Equation frame.

The general approach to creating equations is to select commands and symbols from the equation palette, then add arguments to them in the edit pane, and finally redraw the display pane to see the effect of your editing.

Menu Selections

Access the Equation Editor by selecting Graphics/Equation. The Equation Editor screen appears, as shown in Figure 11-29. The Equation Editor screen consists of a number of distinct areas: the command menu and equation bar, the display and edit panes, and the equation palette.

Command Menu

At the very top of the screen is a standard Windows menu.

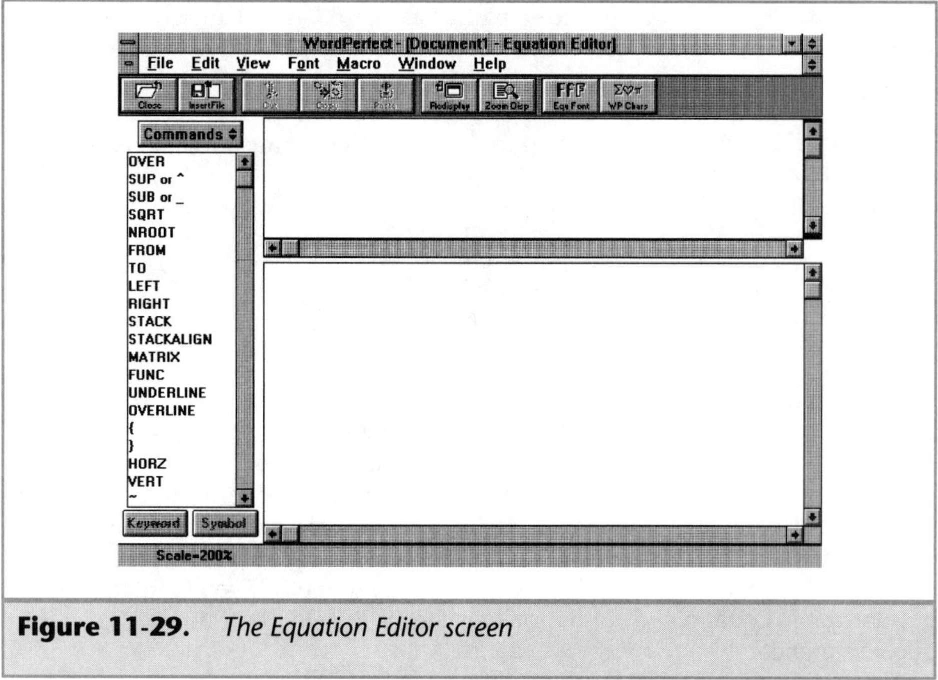

Figure 11-29. *The Equation Editor screen*

FILE COMMANDS The File options are shown here:

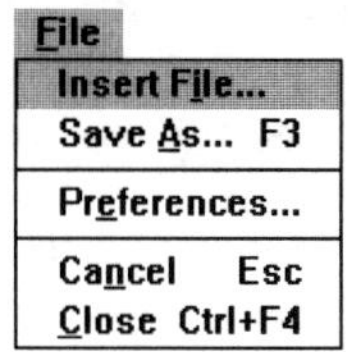

File/Insert File and File/Save As allow you to open and save standard equations on disk. This way you can save an equation to a file that you can open and use whenever you need it, rather than having to re-create it in each document or cut and paste between documents.

File/Preferences brings up the File Preferences dialog box and lets you modify the default WordPerfect settings for the button bar, keyboard, and menu bar.

File/Cancel and File/Close allow you to exit from the Equation Editor and return to your document.

E

EDIT COMMANDS Besides accessing the standard Undo, Cut, Copy, and Paste commands, you can also use the Edit menu to Find and Replace elements matching criteria that you specify.

VIEW COMMANDS The View option displays the menu shown here:

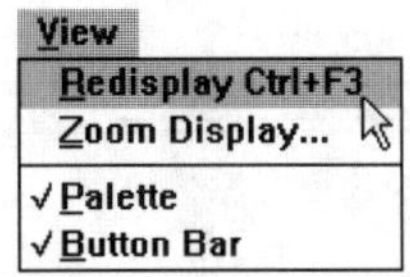

Redisplay causes the equation, shown in the display pane, to be redrawn, based on changes you have made in the editing pane.

Zoom Display accesses a dialog box with options that allow you to increase or decrease the size of the equation on the screen to make it easier to work with it.

Palette is a toggle option that turns on or off the palette of commands and symbols displayed on the left side of the Equation Editor screen.

The Button Bar option toggles the button bar on or off. If you want to customize the Equation Editor button bar, choose Button Bar from File/Preferences.

FONT Equation Font allows you to change the font attributes as they are displayed in the Equation Editor. You can also access any of the WordPerfect extended characters by selecting Character.

MACRO The commands in the Macro menu allow you to play and record macros. These features work much the same as the macro functions when you are not in the Equation Editor. (*See* Macros later in this chapter for more information.)

Equation Palette

WordPerfect's Equation Editor comes complete with virtually every mathematical or scientific symbol needed to create formulas. The equation palette appears on the left side of the Equation Editor window. Commands in the palette are subdivided into eight sets, including Commands, Large, Symbols, Greek, Arrows, Sets, Other, and Function.

To insert a symbol from one of the menus into your editing pane, double-click the symbol, or click the symbol and then whichever button (Keyword or Symbol) is highlighted at the bottom of the palette. Keywords are commands that represent a mathematical symbol; for example, SQRT represents √ and OVERLINE causes a line to be drawn above a symbol or symbols.

Some options cause both the Keyword and Symbol buttons to be highlighted. For example, on the Symbols set, the partial differential symbol, ∂, can be entered into the editing pane either as the symbol or as the keyword PARTIAL. If you prefer, you can type **PARTIAL** into the editing pane, rather than use the palette to enter the word or symbol for you.

Once you have entered the necessary information into the editing pane, either click the Redisplay button or select View/Redisplay to have WordPerfect redraw your equation in the display pane.

Examples of Equations

The following are a examples of types of equations created with the WordPerfect Equation Editor.

E

EQUATION EXAMPLE 1 To create this equation:

$$\int_{x=0}^{\infty} \frac{1}{\sqrt{2+\sin(x)}}dx$$

enter the following in the editing pane:

```
int from {x=0} to inf {1 over sqrt{2+sin(x)}}dx
```

Note how the denominator of the fraction inside the integral is enclosed in braces: { and }. Also, notice that you can nest braces within braces.

EQUATION EXAMPLE 2 To create this equation:

$$\lim_{n \to \infty} \frac{\frac{x^{n+1}}{(n+1)!}}{\frac{x^n}{n!}}$$

enter the following in the edit pane:

```
lim from {n-->INF} {{x SUP {n+1}} over {(n+1)!}}over
{{x SUP n} over {n!}}
```

EQUATION EXAMPLE 3 To create this equation:

crc pickup from pg 453 bottom

enter the following in the edit pane:

```
X={-beta +-SQRT{beta SUP 2-4 alpha gamma}}over{2 alpha}
```

Related Entries

Button Bar
Character Sets
Graphics, Editing
Macros
See also Chapter 8, "Applications for Macros"

Error Messages

Whenever you attempt to do something that WordPerfect can't do, the program places an Error Message dialog box on your screen. With some errors you can either retry or cancel the command (for example, when trying to open a file from the A: drive when there is no disk in the drive), with other errors, you can click OK to find out what went wrong (as in the case of the "Too much text" error). While error messages can be frustrating, in most cases they are straightforward and should be easily understood.

Menu Selections

In order to search for specific error messages using the Help menu, choose Help/Contents and click the Search button. In the Search For text box, type **error**.

This action displays a list of error message topics. Select a topic and click Show Topics; look under the Go To area for available topics; select one and click the Go To button. You may choose File/Exit to exit the help menu or File/Print Topic to print the selected information.

Exit WordPerfect

To quit WordPerfect, select File/Exit or the shortcut key ALT+F4, or double-click the WordPerfect Window Control Option button in the top-left corner of the WordPerfect window.

When you choose to leave WordPerfect, if there are any documents open that have been modified since they were saved to disk, WordPerfect displays a dialog box asking if you want to save the file before exiting.

F

Extended Characters

See Character Sets.

Feature Bar

A *feature bar* provides easy access to all the options related to a specific feature. It contains buttons and text boxes that assist you in performing a set of tasks. For example, here is the feature bar from the Index editor screen.

There are numerous other feature bars available in WordPerfect that are accessible by clicking the red ? (question mark). You can change feature bars by selecting More Feature Bars from the question mark's pull-down menu.

Figures

See Graphics entries.

File

A *file* is information stored in any number of different ways. A WordPerfect document file is your document on the disk.

Related Entries

Close
File Manager
Lock Documents
New Document
Open
Print Document
Save and Save As

File Conversion

WordPerfect automatically converts files from a number of file formats whenever you open them in WordPerfect. The conversion program converts the following file formats into WordPerfect:

Ami Pro 1.2, 1.2a, 1.2b, 2.0, or 3.0
ANSI Delimited Text (Windows)
ANSI Text CR/LF to SRt (Windows)
ANSI Text (Windows)
ASCII Delimited Text (DOS)
ASCII Text CR/LF to SRt (DOS)
ASCII Text (DOS)
DisplayWrite 4.0, 4.2, or 5.0
IBM DCA FFT
IBM DCA RFT
Kermit (7-Bit Transfer)
Microsoft Word 4.0, 5.0, or 5.5
Microsoft Word for Windows 1.0, 1.1, or 1.1a
Microsoft Word for Windows 2.0, 2.0a, or 2.0b
MultiMate 3.3 or 3.6, or 4.0
MultiMate Advantage II 1.0
Navy DIF Standard
OfficeWriter 6.0, 6.1, 6.11, or 6.2
Rich Text Format (RTF)
Windows Write

WordPerfect 2.0 for Macintosh
WordPerfect 2.1 for Macintosh
WordPerfect 3.0 for Macintosh
WordPerfect 4.2 or greater (DOS)
WordStar 2000 1.0, 2.0, or 3.0
WordStar 3.3, 3.31, 3.4, or 4.0
WordStar 5.0, 5.5, or 6.0

Menu Selections

To convert a file into WordPerfect, choose File/Open and find the file you wish to import into WordPerfect. Since other word processors use filename extensions other than .WPD, you may need to select a different file type. Double-click the filename, and the Convert File Format dialog box appears, as shown here:

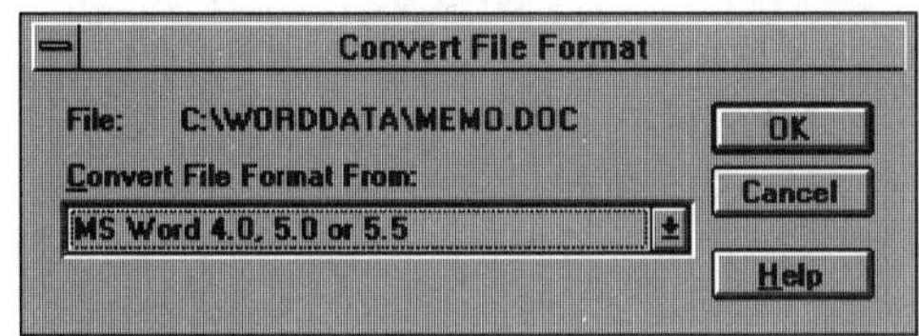

WordPerfect puts into the option box its best guess as to the original file format of the document you are converting. If it is correct, click OK, and the file is converted into WordPerfect format. If the file format is not correct, click the down-arrow to the right of the option box and select the correct option.

Related Entries

Open

File Manager

The File Manager is no longer part of WordPerfect. It has been replaced by the QuickFinder utility. For more information on the QuickFinder, see Chapter 4, "Managing Files with WordPerfect."

Filename Extensions

When you save a file in WordPerfect, you are not required to add a three-character extension to it. WordPerfect automatically adds the default extension .WPD to your file when it is saved. If you name a file LESSON1, then the complete name for the file is LESSON1.WPD. However, you can override the default extension provided by WordPerfect by specifying a different extension. For example, your letter files might have the extension .LET, your invoices .INV, your memos .MEM, and so forth.

You can be quite creative when adding extensions to your WordPerfect documents, but there are several special extensions that indicate specific file types that are used by the program. For example:

File Extension	File Type
.WPG	Graphics images
.WCM	Macro files
.STY	Style sheet files
.BK1, BK2, BK3	Backup files
.HLP	Help files

You must avoid using these extensions for your documents or problems may arise.

Fill

See the "Data Fill" section of the Math entry later in this chapter.

Find Files

WordPerfect allows you to locate files on any drive by filename, or by filename including wildcards. You can also have WordPerfect search for files containing specified text.

Related Entries

See Chapter 4, "Managing Files with WordPerfect."

Finding Text

There are several ways to locate a particular word or text in your document. You can use Edit/Go To or the CTRL+G shortcut keys to move to a page (if you know on what page the text is located), or you can scroll through the document until you find the correct text. A more efficient way is to use the Edit/Find command to look for the text. For example, if you want to know if one of your clients is mentioned in a particular document, you can search that document for the client's name.

Menu Selections

To search for text, place the insertion point where you want to begin searching. Choose Edit/Find or press F2 to display the Find Text dialog box, shown here:

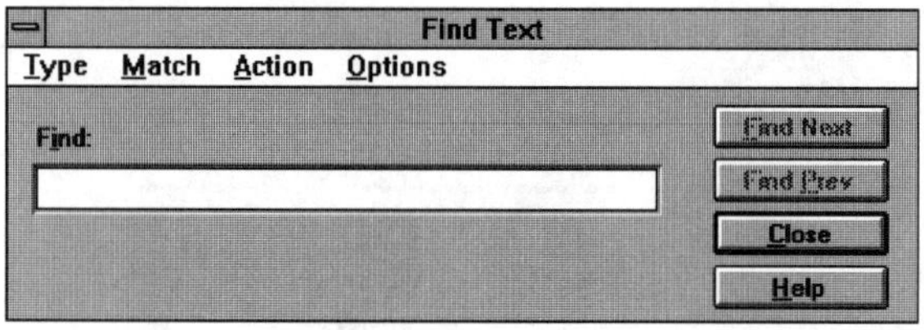

You can move the Find Text dialog box, if necessary, to view more of your document.

If you selected a block of text before choosing the Edit/Find command, the find command will be set initially to search for text that matches the selected block. Otherwise, you can enter a text string of up to 80 characters in the Find text box. You can then determine how WordPerfect performs the search by using the Find Text dialog box menus.

When you are ready to begin your search, click either the Find Next or Find Prev button. The first button searches forward through your document, while the second searches backward.

Searching for Codes

WordPerfect allows you to search either for text or codes. For example, you may need to edit a header code that you placed somewhere in the middle of your document, or you may want to search only for a particular word or phrase that appears in boldface. To include a code in your search, select the Match/Codes menu option. The Codes dialog box appears, displaying an alphabetical list of WordPerfect codes:

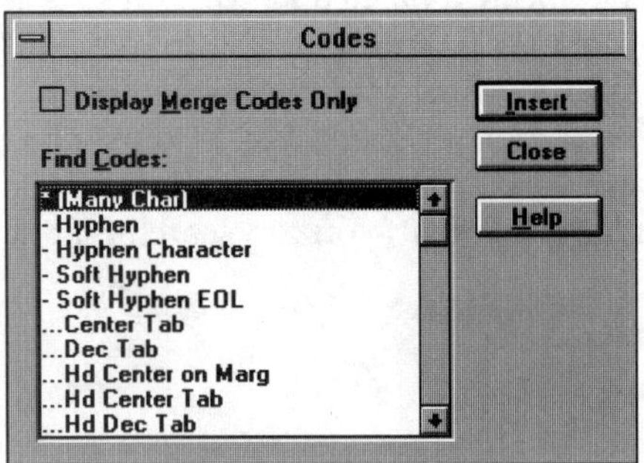

Select the code from the list and select Insert to place it in the Find text box.

If you want to search for specific codes (codes that have values associated with them), you can choose the Type/Specific Codes menu option. This displays the Specific Codes dialog box:

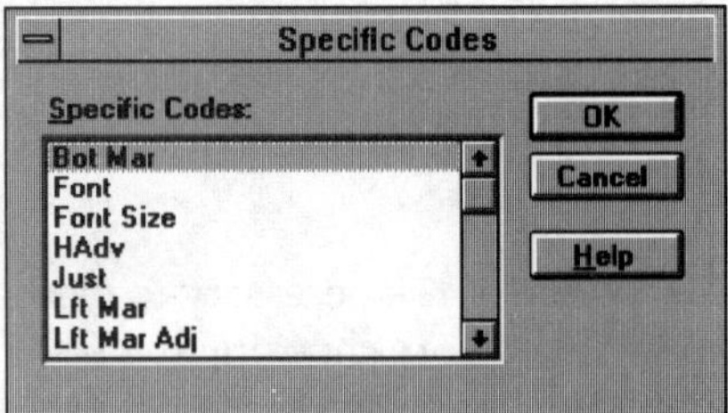

From here, select the code you want to search for, then select OK. You can then enter any additional parts of the code that you want WordPerfect to find.

Specifying Where to Search

Typically, WordPerfect begins searching wherever the insertion point is located. If you want to begin searching at a different place in your document, you can either move the insertion point before issuing the Edit/Find command, or you can use one of the options under the Options menu of the Find Text dialog box.

If you want to begin searching at the beginning of the document, use the Options/Begin Find at Top of Document menu choice. If you want to search only your document, excluding ancillary elements such as the header, footer, and bookmarks, then you can turn off the Options/Include Headers, Footers, etc. in Find option. To limit the search even more, you can make a text selection before using Edit/Find, and then choose the Options/Limit Find Within Selection menu choice. This causes WordPerfect to search only within the highlighted selection.

Usually WordPerfect will stop searching through a document when it reaches the end of the document (if you are searching forward) or the beginning (if you are searching backward). It is possible, however, to cause WordPerfect to behave as if you were at the beginning of the document, regardless of where you begin the search. Thus, if you begin searching forward in the middle of the document, when the end of the document is reached, WordPerfect will begin searching again from the beginning of the document and end the search when it reaches the point where it began. To enable this type of search, select the Options/Wrap at Beg./End of Document menu choice.

If the Include Headers, Footers, etc. in Find option is checked, WordPerfect will also search headers, footers, footnotes, and endnotes rather than just the body text.

Upper- and Lowercase

Normally, WordPerfect does not pay attention to case in a search. For instance, if you enter text in lowercase, then it will match text that is uppercase or a mixture of cases. If you want WordPerfect to find text that matches the case of the text you enter, then select the Match/Case option.

Controlling What WordPerfect Does When a Match Is Found

WordPerfect includes several options that allow you to specify what it should do when it locates a match. These are all accessible from the Action menu. For instance, if you choose Action/Select Match, WordPerfect will highlight (select) the text when it is found. If you choose Action/Position Before, then the insertion point will be placed just before the matched text. Conversely, Action/Position After will place the insertion point just after the text. Finally, you can use the Action/Extend Selection option to select all text between the current position of the insertion point and wherever the matched text is located.

Wildcard Searches

WordPerfect allows you to use wildcards in your search. These are extremely helpful when you are not exactly sure how to spell what you are looking for, or when you want to find words that match a certain pattern.

If you are familiar with wildcards in DOS, you should have no problem with wildcards in WordPerfect. The question mark (?) is used to specify exactly one character. For instance, "d?n" would locate "Dan," "din," and "den," but it would not locate "dawn." The asterisk (*) is used to locate any number of characters. Thus, "d*n" would locate not only "Dan," "din," or "den," but also "dawn," "darn," and "dissertation."

If used effectively, wildcards can greatly expand the power of your searches. To insert a wildcard in your search string, you must use Match/Codes and select * (Many Char) for the * (asterisk) and ? (One Char) for the ? (question mark). You cannot, however, begin a search string with the asterisk wildcard.

Related Entries

Block
Character Sets

Fixed Line Height

You can use the Line Height option to specify the amount of space from baseline to baseline of characters when changing font and point size. Unless you specify otherwise, WordPerfect automatically calculates the best spacing between baselines. Because WordPerfect adjusts your baseline spacing for you, you will not usually want to specify a fixed line height.

Menu Selections

Layout/Line/Height

Related Entries

Line Height

Flush Right

Flush right yields the same result as right justifying text, except that it only is applied to the selected line, lines, or point in a line of text.

Menu Selections

Select Layout/Line/Flush Right, or use the shortcut key ALT+F7.

Related Entries

Justification

Fonts

A *font*, or *typeface*, affects the way text looks when it is printed. Using WordPerfect's Font menu, you can choose a font (the style of letter), its point size (how tall it is), its attributes (such as bold, underline, or italics), and its appearance (small, large, or extra large).

What fonts you can print is in large part a function of your printer. It also depends upon whether you set up WordPerfect to print using its own or Windows printer drivers.

Menu Selections

To access the Font dialog box, shown in Figure 11-30, choose Layout/Font. You will probably see a different list of fonts to choose from, because different printers supply different fonts. If the symbol TT appears to the left of a font name, then it will be displayed on-screen exactly as it will be printed. If a printer symbol appears to the left of the font name, then it is a printer font and will not be displayed on your screen exactly as it is printed on paper. In the Font dialog box, choose the font and size you want. The font will change from the insertion point onward, unless you have selected a particular portion of text, in which case

F

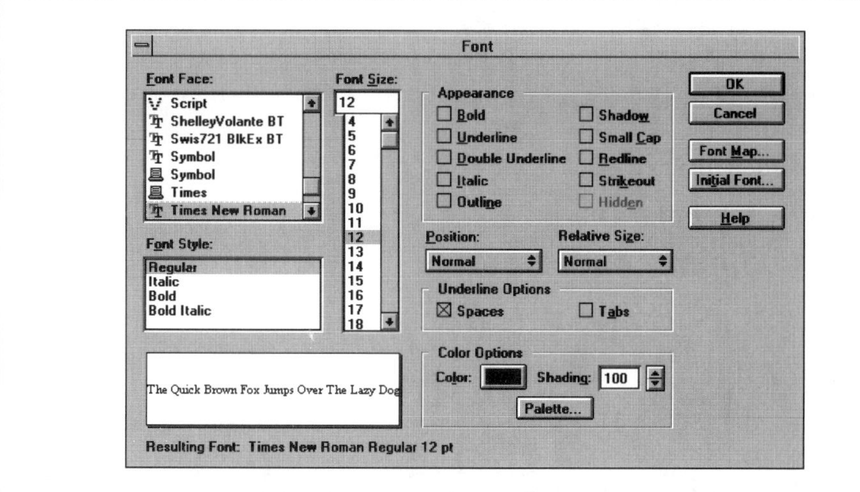

Figure 11-30. *The Font dialog box*

the font will change only within the selection. To find out how to set WordPerfect to use a particular font for every new document, see the Initial Font entry later in this chapter.

Keep in mind, when determining the size of a font, that there are 72 points per inch. The default font size is 12 points. Choose a font first and then choose a point size. After you make your choices, a preview of your selected type in the sentence "The Quick Brown Fox Jumps Over..." is displayed in the Resulting Font box.

Following are some examples of various fonts:

This text is set in the Courier font.
This text is set in the Times Roman font.
This text is set in the Helvetica font.
This text is set in the Century Gothic font.

Figure 11-31 shows some examples of various point sizes, all in the Times Roman font. To add one or more appearance attributes to a font and point size, click the box to the left of the desired options in the Appearance box to enable that attribute. Figure 11-32 shows some examples of different appearance attributes applied to Times Roman, 12-point text.

The Relative Size option in the Font dialog box controls the size of the font relative to the height chosen in the Font Size option. For example, rather than changing the point size (which affects type from that moment on), you can simply change the relative size of that type, which is based on percentages that

This text is 06 point size.
This text is 08 point size.
This text is 10 point size.
This text is 12 point size.
This text is 14 point size.
This text is 18 point size.
This text is 24 point size.
This text is 36 point size.

Figure 11-31. *Examples of various point sizes*

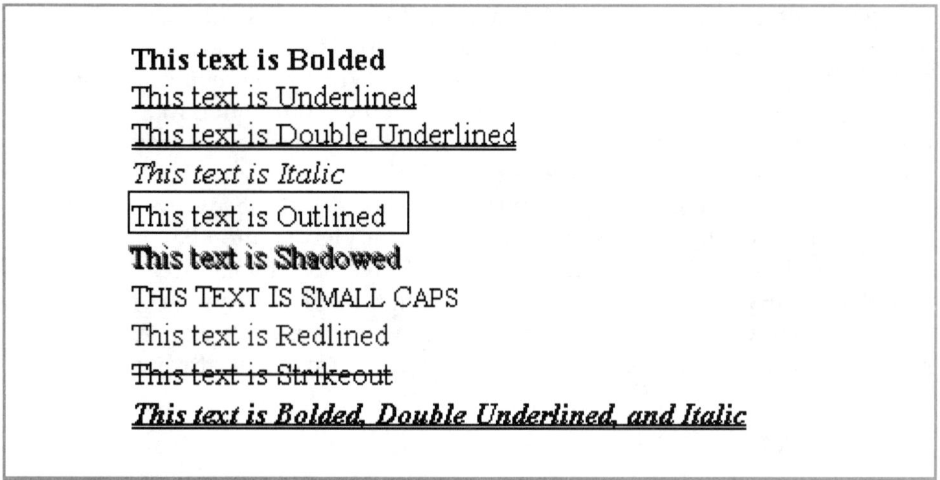

This text is Bolded
This text is Underlined
This text is Double Underlined
This text is Italic
This text is Outlined
This text is Shadowed
THIS TEXT IS SMALL CAPS
This text is Redlined
~~This text is Strikeout~~
This text is Bolded, Double Underlined, and Italic

Figure 11-32. *Examples of appearance attributes*

you define. To define these percentages, select File/Preferences/Print and change the default setting for relative sizes in the Size Attribute Ratio section.

Related Entries

Printer, Selecting
Preferences

Fonts, Assigning to Button Bar

WordPerfect allows you to place your most commonly used fonts on a button bar, giving you quick and easy access to the fonts you use the most. WordPerfect provides a Font button bar with some common attributes. However, you can modify this button bar or create a new one to suit your needs.

Menu Selections

To assign a font to the button bar, choose File/Preferences/Button Bar and highlight Font. Click Edit to access the Button Bar Editor dialog box. Click the arrow to the right of the Feature Categories text box and select Layout. From the Features list box, choose the additional buttons you want to add to the button bar by selecting one and clicking Add Button. Continue until you have added the buttons you want. To remove any unwanted buttons from the button bar, simply drag the button down away from the button bar. When you are finished, click OK. Notice the new buttons that have been added to your Font button bar. To display the Font button bar on your screen, highlight Font in the Button Bar Preferences dialog box and click Select.

To make font changes using the button bar, first select the text you wish to change. With the button bar on the screen (choose View/Button Bar, if necessary), click the desired button and the selected text changes to the desired font. You can also apply a font before you begin typing a letter, word, or sentence by clicking a button from the button bar. Once you complete typing the letter, word, or sentence, simply click the same button to turn off the attribute.

Related Entries

Button Bar

Fonts, Displaying

WordPerfect provides several views for working on documents: Draft, Page, and Two-Page views. While each displays in a WYSIWYG (what you see is what you get) manner, the fonts and the text attributes of some fonts in Draft view may not be displayed the same way that they will when printed. This is because Draft view does not display headers and footers, watermarks, and some other formatting features, such as the graphical page break. As a result, you can move through your document more quickly since WordPerfect does not have to refresh the screen quite as often.

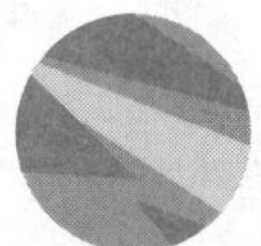

NOTE: *Generally, it is more convenient to work in Page view since you can see all of the printable material in your document.*

Menu Selections

To see if you are working in Draft view, choose View from the menu bar. There will be a check mark next to one of the view modes. Click the desired view and WordPerfect will change to that view immediately.

Related Entries

Draft View
Page View
Two-Page View

Footers, Creating

A *footer* is text, graphics, or a combination of both that appears at the bottom of every page of the document. Often, footers contain the page numbering code for the document, but they also can hold the date, the filename, or any number of other items you may want situated at the bottom of the page.

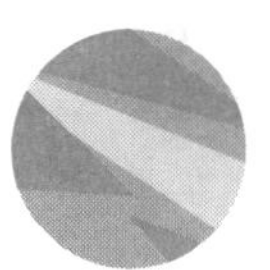

NOTE: *Footers sit on top of the bottom margin of the document in WordPerfect. Therefore, if your bottom margin is set to 1", the bottom line of the footer will be placed one inch from the bottom edge of the document and not between the bottom margin and the bottom edge of the page. Many users change the bottom margin setting to .5" to accommodate footers.*

F

Menu Selections

Choose Layout/Header/Footer.

NOTE: *You can also access the Header/Footer when in Page view by moving the pointer to the bottom of the page and right-clicking to invoke the shortcut menu, and then selecting Header/Footer.*

From the Headers/Footers dialog box, you can select either Footer A or Footer B, as shown here:

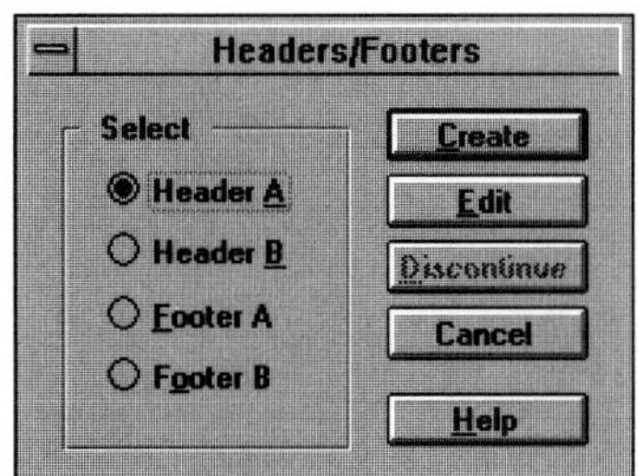

If your footers will be different on odd and even pages, you can use footer A for the odd and footer B for the even. Otherwise, either footer will apply to every page of the entire document.

Once you have selected a footer (Footer A is usually adequate), click Create and the Footer editing screen appears, as shown in Figure 11-33.

The Footer editing screen gives you access to all of WordPerfect's usual text formatting menu options and, in addition, Number, Line, Placement, and Distance buttons located on the feature bar. If, for example, you wanted to center the page number within the footer, you would choose Layout/Line/Center, type the word **Page**, press SPACEBAR, and click the Number button from the feature bar. In Reveal Codes, a (Pg Num Disp) code will appear where the page number will be printed.

NOTE: If you place a page number in the footer, be sure to disable page numbering (Layout/Page/Numbering) or your page numbers will be redundant.

You would choose the Placement button only if you wanted the footer to be different on odd and even pages. The default is for the footer to be the same on

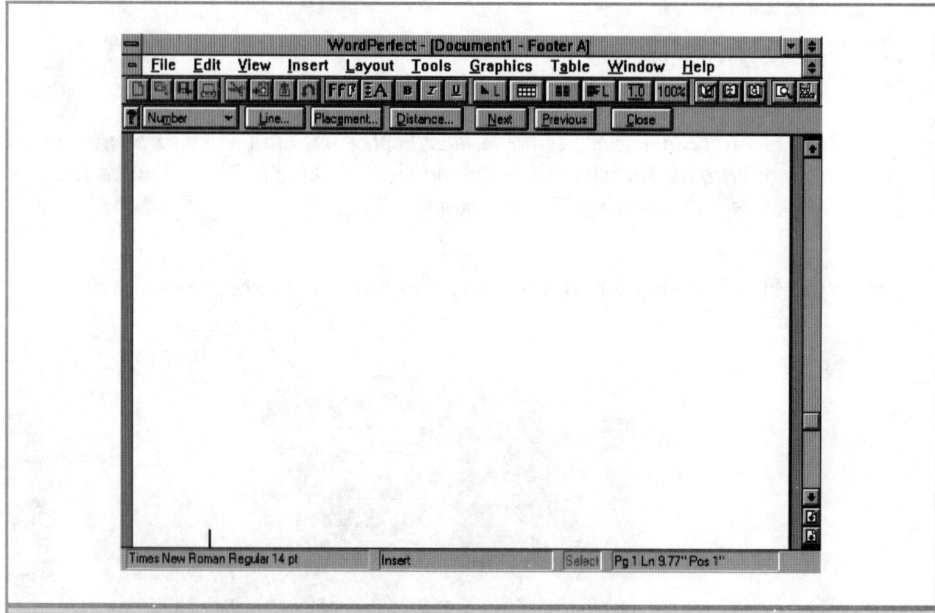

Figure 11-33. *The Footer editing screen*

every page. When you have finished creating the footer, click Close on the feature bar to return to the document.

NOTE: If you want the current footer (either A or B) to end so that you can continue with a different footer, choose Discontinue from the Header/Footer dialog box.

Related Entries

Footers, Editing
Page Numbering

Footers, Editing

If you are in Page view and have created a footer, you can see the footer at the bottom of the page. You can access the Footer editing screen at any time.

F

Menu Selections

Select Layout/Header/Footer, click the appropriate footer (usually Footer A), and select Edit. You are placed in the Footer editing screen with the feature bar across the top of the screen. You can also edit a footer directly from within your document by clicking directly on a footer in your document. This also accesses the Footer editing screen, except that the feature bar is hidden. To access it, right-click in the footer area and click Feature Bar.

When you are editing your document, the footer remains inaccessible, preventing you from accidentally modifying or deleting it. As you edit a footer, you can apply any attributes as you would in the document.

To delete a footer, use Reveal Codes to locate the footer code, such as, (Footer A: Every Page), ([Open Style])footer text.

Related Entries

Footers, Creating

Footnotes, Creating

Footnotes are used to indicate the source of a direct quote or paraphrased material, or to provide additional information on a topic without including that information in the body of the document. As such, footnotes are very similar to endnotes, except that footnotes are usually placed at the bottom of the page and endnotes are located at the end of the document on a separate page.

Because footnotes, like footers, have their last line printed on the top of the bottom margin of the document, you will probably want to adjust your bottom margin to 0.5" to place the footnotes further down on the page. The default is to have a two-inch space above the first footnote on the page to separate the footnotes from the text of the document.

Menu Selections

To create a footnote, position the insertion point where you would like the footnote's reference number to be (usually just after the text you are citing), and choose Insert/Footnote/Create; this brings up the Footnote editing screen, shown in Figure 11-34.

You can then type your footnote and edit it as you would any other text in WordPerfect.

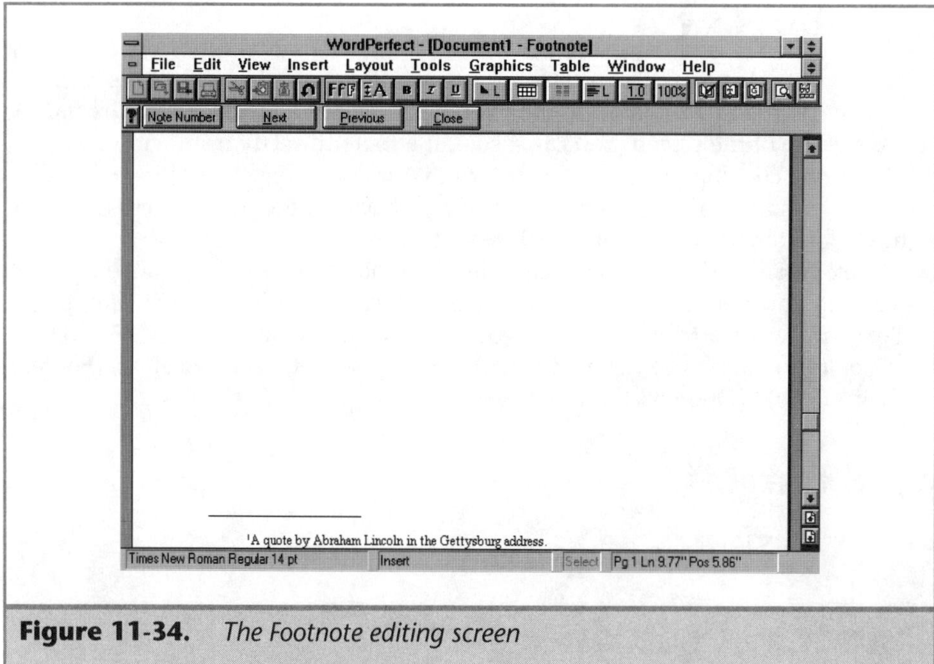

Figure 11-34. *The Footnote editing screen*

Click the Previous or Next button if you want to review footnotes placed before or after the one you are working on. WordPerfect automatically increments the footnote numbers each time you add another footnote. When you are finished creating your footnote, click the Close button to return to your document. You should see the footnote reference number next to the text you are citing. Footnotes are visible near the bottom of the page when you are in Page view.

You can change the way footnotes are numbered by choosing Insert/Footnote/New Number. Type the number you would like the first footnote to be associated with, and all footnotes will be numbered consecutively from that number.

NOTE: *Should you insert or delete a footnote code (in Reveal Codes), the footnote numbers all automatically adjust accordingly. For example, if you insert a new footnote in front of footnote 5, then footnote 5 will become 6, and so on.*

Related Entries

Endnotes
Margins

Footnotes, Editing

In Page view, footnotes appear at the bottom of the document page.

Menu Selections

You can perform some limited editing of footnotes by simply clicking the footnote line and editing text, or by highlighting the text and applying an attribute. However, to delete or change the numbering of footnotes, you must go to the Footnote editing screen through Insert/Footnote/Edit. You will need to input the reference number of the footnote you wish to edit. Make any changes you want to the footnote, and click the Close button to return to the document.

Footnotes, Options

You can change the way your footnotes are formatted by opening the Footnote Options dialog box.

Menu Selections

To access the Footnote Options dialog box shown in Figure 11-35, choose Insert/Footnote/Options. There are a number of footnote features that can be customized.

Numbering Method

CHANGING THE NUMBERING METHOD The default numbering method for footnotes is Arabic numerals (1, 2, 3...). You may change the numbering system to letters, Roman numerals, or characters. If you choose Characters, then you will need to type the characters you wish to use in the Characters text box. Alternatively, you can press CTRL+W to bring up the WordPerfect Characters dialog box, which gives you access to all available WordPerfect characters.

RESTARTING NUMBERING If you select Restart Numbering on Each Page, WordPerfect restarts the numbering sequence on each page, rather than numbering all the footnotes consecutively throughout the document.

EDITING THE NUMBERING STYLE You can also change the numbering style in text and in the footnotes. To adjust the defaults, click either In Text to edit the footnote number in the text, or In Note to edit the number at the bottom of the page. Choose the styles you want from the menu. As you do, notice the codes that are "revealed" in the Contents box.

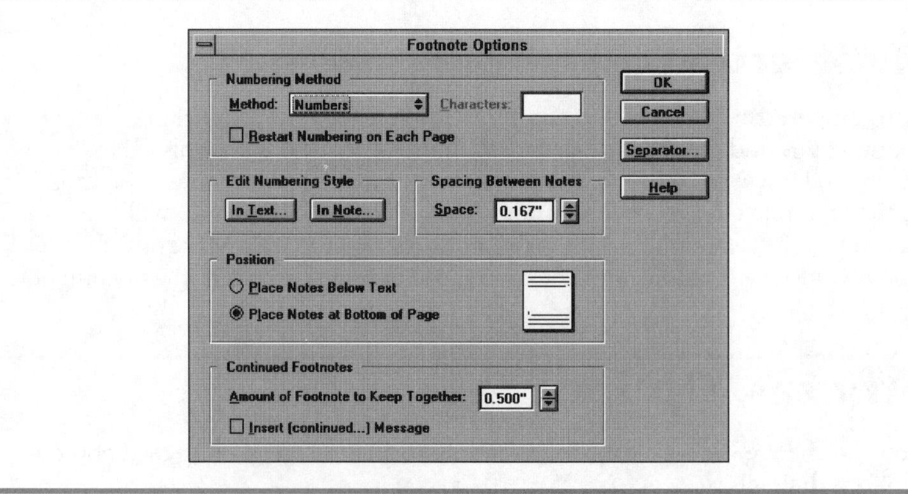

Figure 11-35. *The Footnote Options dialog box*

SETTING SPACING BETWEEN FOOTNOTES In the Spacing Between Notes section, you can adjust the line spacing between the lines of the footnotes and the spacing between notes. The default amount of space between notes is .167"; you can change this to suit your preferences.

CHOOSING A LOCATION FOR THE FOOTNOTES The position of your footnotes within the document can be modified in the Position section. You can place your footnotes either immediately after the footnote (below text) or at the bottom of the page (the default).

INSERTING A "CONTINUED..." MESSAGE In the Continued Footnotes section, you can alter the way WordPerfect deals with footnotes that are too long to fit on one page. If you enable the Insert (continued...) Message check box, WordPerfect places "(continued...)" next to footnotes that are split between two pages of the document. You can adjust how much footnote text should be kept together by changing the default amount of .5" in the Amount of Footnote to Keep Together option.

ADJUSTING THE LINE SEPARATOR If you click Separator, WordPerfect gives you various choices for separating the body of the document from the footnotes. The default separator is a 2-inch horizontal line extending from the left margin. You can adjust the position, length, and line style to suit your preferences.

Related Entries

Character Sets
Fonts

Form Letters

WordPerfect gives you access to a full-featured database. This database gives you the ability to merge names and addresses onto documents, giving them a personalized effect.

Related Entries

See Chapter 6, "Merge Applications."

Forms, Fill-in

You can set up WordPerfect to precisely place your insertion point so that preprinted forms can be filled in quickly.

Related Entries

Advance
See also the "Merging to Preprinted Forms" section in Chapter 6, "Merge Applications."

Function Keys

WordPerfect gives you the ability to run the program without a mouse. Depending on how your program was loaded or the modifications you have made, you should be using the WPWin 6.0 Keyboard. If you don't have a mouse, you can pull down a menu by pressing ALT plus the underlined character of the menu selection. For example, ALT+L pulls down the Layout menu, as shown in Figure 11-36. Note that the function keys are listed to the right of the menu items (assuming the Display Shortcut Keys option is enabled). For example, to get to the Margins option, you would only need to press CTRL+F8.

Another way to list the function key equivalents is to list them by using the Help menu selection. You can then print out the page that lists the function keys and their menu selection counterparts.

Generate

You use the Generate command to create tables of contents, tables of authorities, indexes, cross-references, lists, and endnotes. Use the Generate command once your document has been prepared and modified to your satisfaction.

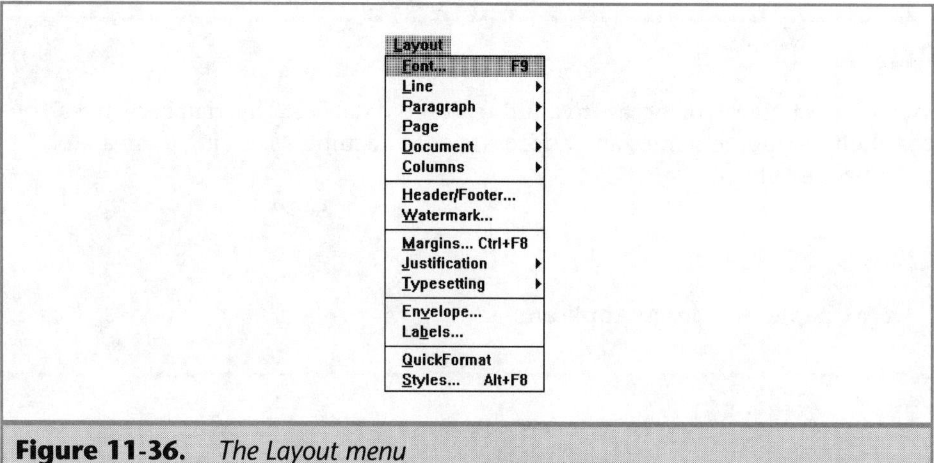

Figure 11-36. *The Layout menu*

Menu Selections

Choose Tools/Generate or the shortcut key CTRL+F9. When you select this option, you see the Generate dialog box, shown here:

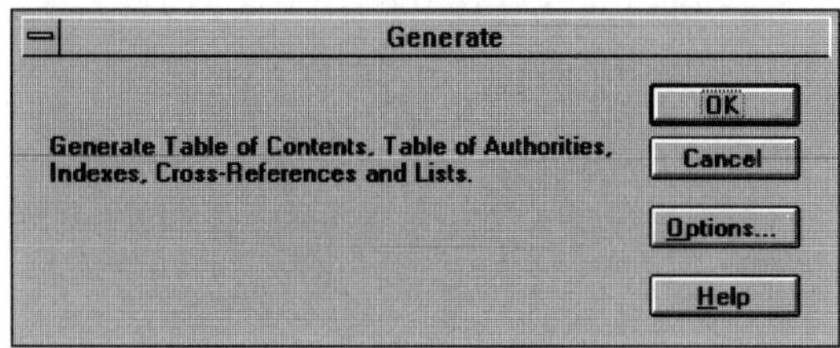

When you click the OK button, WordPerfect generates all of the necessary tables, lists, and so on.

Options

The Options button lets you control how WordPerfect generates indexes, cross-references, and so on. For example, you may create documents which are cross-referenced to other documents, termed master documents and subdocuments. Normally, WordPerfect expands these subdocuments, generates any applicable references, and then saves and condenses the subdocument again. As you can imagine, this operation tends to take more time, particularly on more complex documents. If you do not want the subdocuments expanded, generated, and saved, deactivate the Save Subdocuments option.

If you have any hypertext links in your document that you do not want WordPerfect to generate and save, deactivate the Build Hypertext Links option. Hypertext is text within your document that lets you "jump" to related sections in the current or another document, invoke a macro, or link to other documents.

Related Entries

Cross-Reference
Endnotes
Hypertext
Index
Lists
Master Documents
Subdocument
Table of Authorities
Table of Contents

Go To

The Go To command allows you to move your insertion point easily to any of a variety of locations in your document. This is much easier, for instance, than scrolling through a long document with the PGUP or PGDN key.

Menu Selections

Choose Edit/Go To or press the shortcut key CTRL+G. The Go To dialog box appears, as shown here:

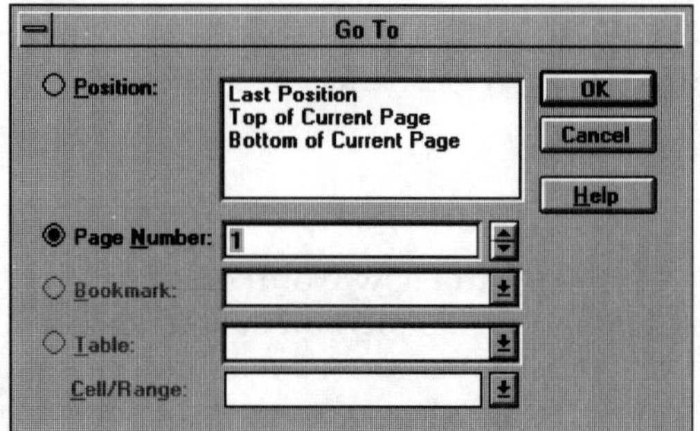

Type the page number to which you want to move the insertion point in the Page Number section and then click OK. Or, you can click the Last Position button to return the cursor to its location prior to your having executed a Go To, Find, or Replace operation.

Using Go To in Standard Text

When you select Go To and your cursor is in standard text (that is, not in a section of the document containing a table or columns), you can click the Position button, which highlights the Last Position option, and automatically go to your previous position in the document.

In standard text you can use the Position option to move the cursor to the top or bottom of the current page. Or, you can simply click Page Number and enter the desired page number.

Using Go To in Columns

When you select Go To with the insertion point positioned in columned text, the Position options change, as shown here:

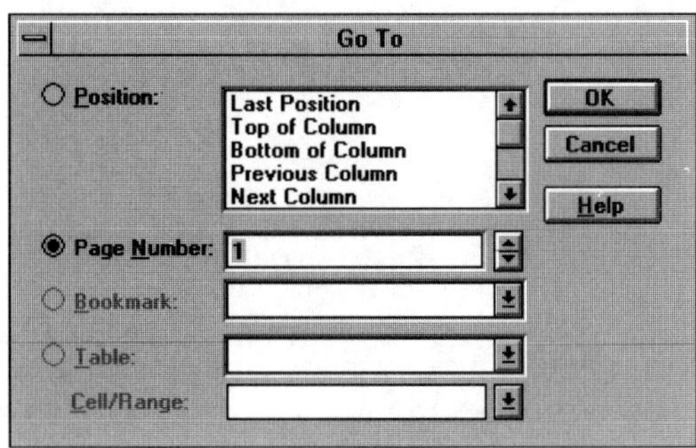

When your cursor is in a section of your document laid out in columns, you can use the Position option to move to the last position, to the top or bottom of the current column, to the previous or next column, or to the first or last column.

Using Go To in Tables

When you have a table defined within your document, you can use the Position option to move to a particular cell or cell range, specified by column letter and row number. You can move to the top or bottom of the current cell, the first or last cell in the table, or the top or bottom cell in the current column.

You can also move to the previous position, to the top or bottom of the current column, to the previous or next column, or to the first or last column in the table.

Using Go To When Text Is Selected

When you have selected text in any mode and use the Go To option, three additional options appear in the Position box: Beginning of Selection, End of Selection, and Reselect Text. Beginning of Selection moves your cursor to the beginning of the selected text and removes the highlighting from the text. End of Selection moves your cursor to the end of the selected text and removes the highlighting. If you then choose to re-highlight the previously selected text, you can use the Reselect Text option to do so for you.

Related Entries

Keyboard Layout
See also Appendix B, "WordPerfect Keyboards."

Grammar-checking

See Grammatik.

Grammatik

After you create a document, you can use the Grammatik utility to check the spelling and verify that the text is grammatically correct. One of the best ways to project a poor image of yourself is to send grammatically incorrect correspondence to businesses or colleagues. Using the Grammatik grammar-checking utility can help you make certain that your documents are properly worded and spelled.

Menu Selections

To grammar-check your document, select Tools/Grammatik or click the Grammatik icon on the power bar. The Grammatik dialog box appears, as shown in Figure 11-37.

Writing Styles

Since there are many possible writing styles, you should specify what writing style you are using in the document that is being checked. This keeps Grammatik from stopping when it encounters an item that it finds questionable, but which you intended to use. To specify the style, select Options/Writing Style from the Grammatik dialog box. In the Writing Style list, you are prompted to choose one of 13 styles. Grammatik uses distinct grammar, style, and mechanical rules to

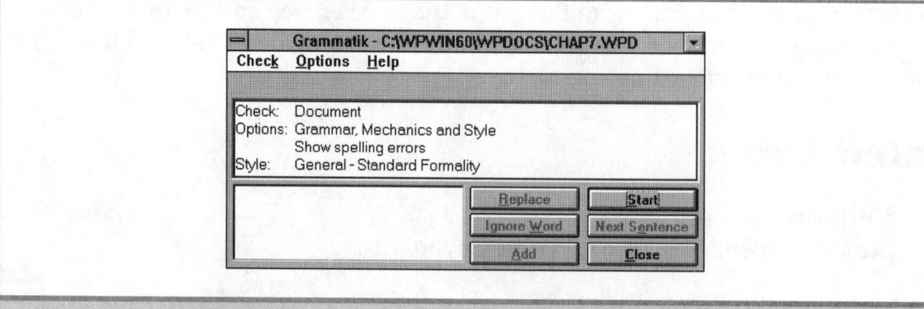

Figure 11-37. *The Grammatik grammar-checking dialog box*

check each style. Highlight the style that most closely matches your document, and pick the formality level at which the document should be checked. For example, because business letters are directed at professionals, you can instruct Grammatik to check the document according to more formal rules. In this case, you would select Formal. Choosing Informal allows for more slang and common usage and is more appropriate for fiction and advertising. Standard applies to the more general types of correspondence such as newsletters and articles, interoffice memos, letters to friends and family, and so on.

CUSTOMIZING A WRITING STYLE In addition to modifying the predefined writing styles, WordPerfect allows you to customize up to three different writing styles of your own. To customize a writing style, highlight one of the custom styles as shown here:

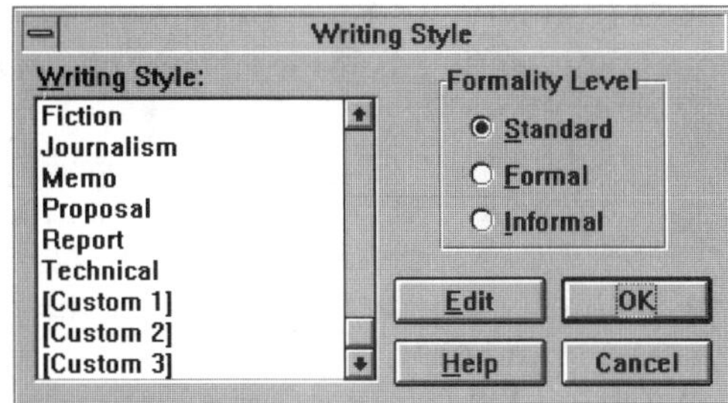

then select Edit from the Writing Style dialog box. You are presented with the Writing Style Settings dialog box, which lets you specify which of the many rules will apply to this writing style. You can create any writing style you want by making the appropriate rule selections.

The Style Rule controls how Grammatik checks for items such as proper abbreviation, sentences ending in a preposition, redundancies, and wordiness. The Grammar Rule examines items such as double negatives, incomplete sentences, subject-verb agreement, and so on. The Mechanical Rule looks for errors in capitalization, punctuation, spelling, and unbalanced parentheses, braces, brackets, and quotes. At the bottom of the dialog box are various options—such as the limiting number of consecutive nouns, prepositional phrases, and passive sentences—for determining how many of each can appear in a document before Grammatik brings the mistake to your attention.

Once you have set the style in all three rule classes, click Save to save the settings in the selected writing style. If you want to restore the predefined styles to their original settings, select Options/Restore Rule Classes from the Grammatik dialog box.

G

Checking Options

To control the way Grammatik uses the style rules, you can set various parameters by selecting Option/Checking Options from the Grammatik dialog box. Indicate by placing a check mark in each box whether you want to Check for paragraph errors, Ignore periods within words, Suggest spelling replacements, or Start checking immediately (upon accessing Grammatik from the power bar).

Grammar-checking a Document

Once you have chosen a writing style, click Start in the Grammatik dialog box. When Grammatik finds a problem in your document, it displays a message in the dialog box. You can choose to Skip the problem, Ignore Word this time and for the remainder of the document, or move on to the Next Sentence. If you Skip the problem, Grammatik will overlook it this time, but will catch the problem if it occurs again. Choosing to Ignore Word will ignore the problem for the remainder of the proofreading session. Selecting Next Sentence performs the same action as does choosing Skip.

If Grammatik finds a misspelled word, you can choose Replace to correctly spell the word. If the word is spelled properly but Grammatik still reports it as misspelled, you can choose Add to append it to the dictionary. You can also temporarily disable the spell-checking feature of Grammatik by selecting Options/Show spelling errors and deactivating it.

In addition to grammar-checking a document, you can also view the Statistics of a document, including the number of words, paragraphs, average words per sentence, and so on. To perform a statistic check, choose Options/Statistics.

As the check progresses and grammatical errors are found, you can get further help or a definition for the rule class that flagged the error by passing the mouse pointer over the Rule Class heading. The pointer appears with a question mark trailing it, meaning you can view help on this item by clicking.

GRAMMAR-CHECKING A PORTION OF A DOCUMENT You can instruct Grammatik to grammar-check just portions of a document, including a sentence or a paragraph, from the insertion point to the end of the document or in selected text.

To specify what portion of the document will be checked, select Check from the Grammatik dialog box and click a menu choice. Or you can highlight the desired sentence, paragraph, or selected text before you enter Grammatik or after it has started. Grammatik will check the entire document if you do not specify any options.

Showing Parts of Speech

If you want to see how Grammatik diagrams sentences, select Help/Show Parts of Speech. You can enable or disable this option once you begin grammar-checking the document. A sentence is presented with each individual word type shown above the word. For example, the word "but" is shown as a conjunction, "quickly" is an adverb, and so on.

Understanding the Rule Class

As Grammatik checks your document, it may display a problem usage or term that you do not understand. To obtain a definition of the rule class, either click the rule class heading that appears below the menu bar or select Help/Rule Class.

Related Entries

Speller

Graphics Files, Supported

WordPerfect supports graphics files created in a wide variety of graphics programs. Appendix D, "Graphics Programs and Files," lists the types of files that can be imported directly into a WordPerfect graphics frame.

Many programs offer a variety of formats in which they can store their graphics files. Experiment with saving graphics to various formats and then bringing them into a WordPerfect document to see which format provides the best combination of image quality and file size. For example, saving a file as TIF generally provides better resolution and shades for color images; but PCX often provides results comparable to TIF with black and white images. WordPerfect Corporation can also advise you as to the most efficient way of importing a particular program's graphics into WordPerfect.

Graphics Lines

WordPerfect allows you to place horizontal and vertical graphics lines in your text. You can define the line style, its position and length, the line spacing, color, and width. For example, you may want a horizontal separator line between a heading and its associated text or a vertical line to separate columns of text.

Menu Selections

To create a line in your document, select either Graphics/Horizontal Line or Graphics/Vertical Line. At any time, you can change the line from one type to the other by making the appropriate selection in the Edit Graphics Line dialog box.

When you select Graphics/Horizontal Line or press the shortcut key CTRL+F11, a horizontal line is placed in your document. When you select Graphics/Vertical Line or press the shortcut key CTRL+SHIFT+F11, a vertical line is placed into your document.

Editing Lines

You can edit already existing vertical and horizontal lines either by using the dialog box invoked by the Graphics/Edit Line command or by using the mouse to select the line and then moving or resizing it by dragging.

EDITING LINES USING THE DIALOG BOX Once you have placed one or more graphics lines in your document, you can easily edit them. To do so, position the insertion point before the line you want to edit and select Graphics/Edit Line. WordPerfect searches for the next line definition code and then displays the Edit Graphics Line dialog box, shown in Figure 11-38, in which you can change the line's settings as necessary.

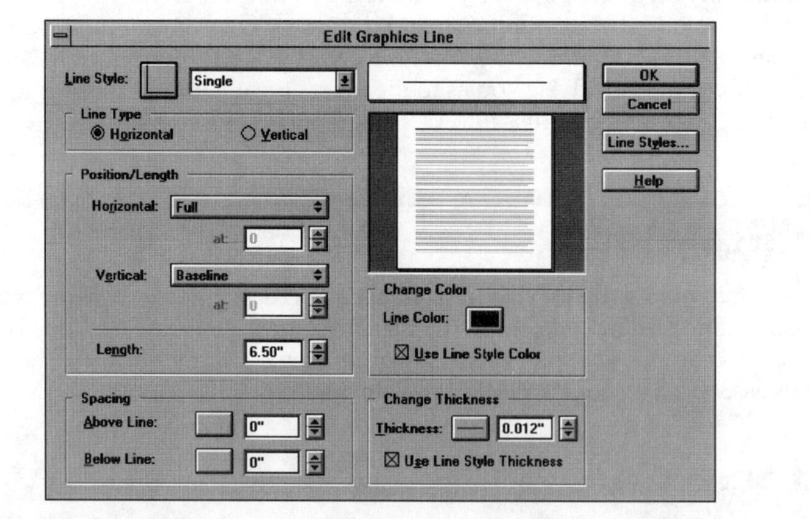

Figure 11-38. *The Edit Graphics Line dialog box*

EDITING LINES USING THE MOUSE You can also access the Edit Graphics Line dialog box by pointing at the line with the cursor. When the cursor is on a line, it changes shape from an I-beam to an arrow. When the cursor is shaped like an arrow, double-clicking brings up the dialog box, in which you can make changes to the line.

Another way of gaining access to a line's settings dialog box is to point at the line so the cursor turns into an arrow and then click the *right* mouse button. A shortcut menu will appear next to the cursor. Depending on the orientation of the line, select either Edit Horizontal Line or Edit Vertical Line and the Edit Graphics Line dialog box appears.

A third way of editing a line is to point at it with the mouse and click the left mouse button. A group of six selection handles will appear around the line:

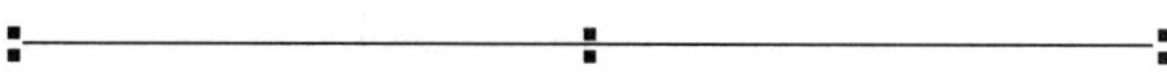

Once a line is selected in this way, if you point at it with the cursor, the shape of the cursor again changes, this time to a four-headed arrow:

G

When the cursor is that shape, you can click and drag the line to any new location you wish. The settings in the dialog box for the line will change to reflect the new position.

You can also change the length or thickness of the line by dragging one of the six selection handles in any direction. For example, you can change the length of a horizontal line by dragging one of the rightmost handles to the left or right.

Likewise, you can change the thickness of the line by dragging one of the middle handles upward or downward.

POSITION/LENGTH If you are editing a horizontal line, you can modify the line's position and length. If you click on the Horizontal option button, you are given the choice of a line that begins on the Left or Right margin of the page, is Centered on the page, extends across the Full width of the page, or is Set to begin at any location you specify.

When you click the Vertical option button, you are given the option of your line beginning at the Baseline of the line of text on which the insertion point is currently located or at any other position you specify with the Set option. If you choose Set from either the Horizontal or Vertical option buttons, you can indicate the exact horizontal or vertical positions by typing the measurement in inches in the "at:" text box.

NOTE: *If you select Baseline as the vertical position of a graphics line and then increase the thickness of the line, the bottom edge of the graphics line will remain on the baseline of the current text line. As the width of the line increases, it can overlap text.*

If you are editing a vertical line, you can modify the line's position and length. If you click the Horizontal Position option, you are given the choice of a line that runs along the Left or Right margin of the page, is Centered on the page, is Column Aligned, or appears in any position you specify. If you choose Set from either the Horizontal or Vertical option buttons, you can indicate the exact horizontal or vertical positions by typing the measurement in inches in the "at:" text box. If you select Column Aligned, you are asked to indicate the number of the column after which you want the line placed. You can choose any one of the options by clicking it.

When you click the Vertical option button, you are given the choice of a vertical line that extends the Full length of the page from the top to the bottom margin, a line Centered vertically on the page between the top and bottom margins, or a line that begins at a location that you specify. You can choose any one of the options by clicking it. If you choose Set from either the Horizontal or Vertical option buttons, you can indicate the exact horizontal or vertical positions by typing the measurement in inches in the "at:" text box.

To adjust the length of the line, click on Length and type the desired length in inches (or other default unit of measurement).

SPACING To set the amount of space above and below the graphic line, click on the appropriate button in the Spacing section, then select a spacing amount or type a precise measurement in the designated text box.

CHANGE COLOR The default color (initially set to black) can be changed to any color available on your palette. Click on the Line Color button to access the color palette and select a color. Selecting a new line color in this way will override any color set in Line Styles unless you click on Use Line Style Color.

CHANGE THICKNESS You can customize the thickness of the line you create by clicking on the Thickness button. This reveals a line palette from which you can choose the desired thickness. If you prefer, you can type the precise thickness in the text box.

LINE STYLE You can define the type of line you want by clicking on the Line Style button and choosing from the style palette. You can also create a custom line style by clicking on Line Styles and choosing Create. You will then see the Create Line Style dialog box, shown in Figure 11-39.

Graphics Styles, Creating

You can create your own style of graphic boxes in WordPerfect to meet your particular needs. You can create custom styles for figure boxes, text boxes, equation boxes, tables, user-defined boxes, buttons, watermarks, and inline equations. For any of these styles, you can also define the default caption, the content of the box (graphic, text, or otherwise), the position and size, the border and fill attributes, the manner that text wraps around the box and/or graphic, and the initial style settings. For example, you may choose not to have the

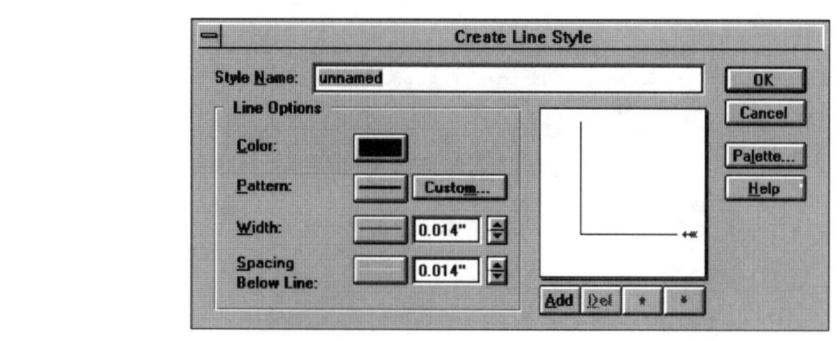

Figure 11-39. *The Create Line Style dialog box*

single-line border style that surrounds a default figure box, or you may choose a different fill pattern for a watermark.

You can also modify any of the predefined graphics box styles. You can even create or change border styles, line styles, or fill attributes that appear in these graphics boxes.

NOTE: *If you are going to create your own style of graphic boxes, it is best to first create the desired style and then use the style in your document rather than the opposite.*

Menu Selections

Select Graphics/Graphics Styles and choose the type of style you want to create from the Graphics Styles dialog box. Each kind of style listed in the Style Type section displays its associated choices in the Styles list, as shown in Figure 11-40. You can modify any of the available graphic box styles. You can also create or change border styles, line styles, or fill attributes that appear in graphic boxes.

Or, if you choose to create a border style, you can click Create to design your own border style or you can click Edit to edit one of the listed border styles.

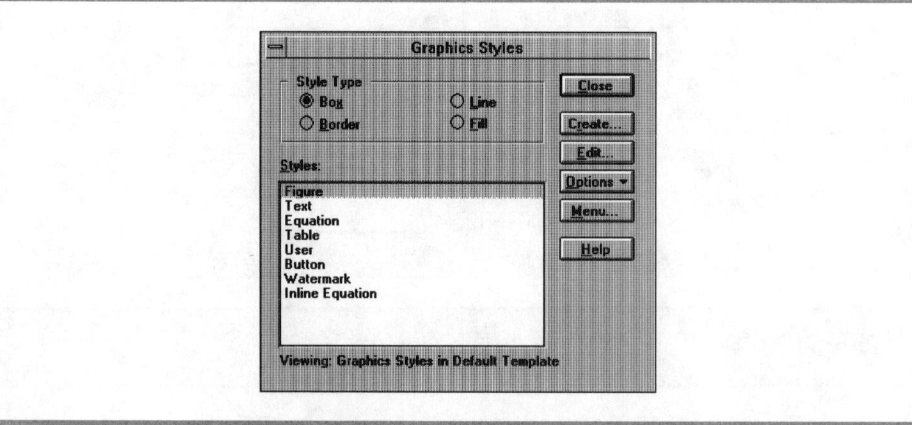

Figure 11-40. *The Graphics Styles dialog box*

Related Entries

Graphics Styles, Editing

Graphics Styles, Editing

You can edit any of the predefined graphics styles or the graphics styles you create.

Menu Selections

Select Graphics/Graphics Styles and click one of the four available style types and then highlight the style you want to edit from the Styles list. Click Edit. Depending on the style type you selected from the Graphics Styles dialog box, you will see an appropriate editing dialog box for the chosen element.

For example, if you want to edit the default border style, which is hairline, you would click Border in the Style Type section of the Graphics Styles dialog box, highlight Hairline from the Styles list, and click Edit. In this instance, you are presented with the Edit Border Style dialog box as shown here:

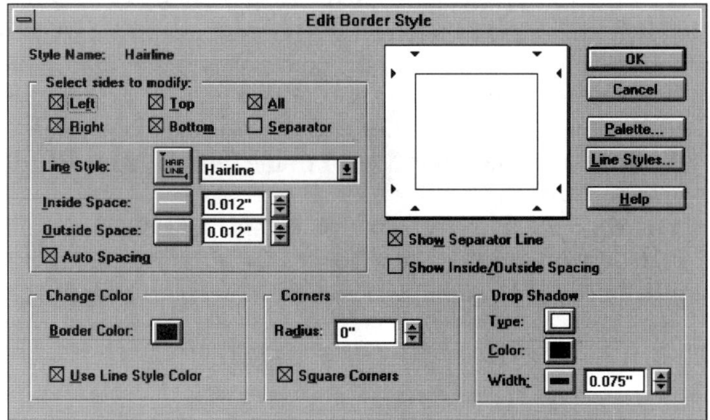

As you edit the style, the results are displayed immediately on the sample screen in the dialog box, thus giving you total control over the appearance of the edited style. After making the desired changes, click OK to save your changes.

Related Entries

Graphics Styles, Creating

Graphics, Creating

Graphics appear in WordPerfect inside a graphic box. There are a number of types of graphic boxes that you can create. To access the Graphics options, select Graphics. You see the menu shown here:

Graphics
- Figure
- Text
- Equation
- Custom Box...
- Edit Box   Shift+F11
- Draw...
- Chart...
- TextArt...
- Horizontal Line   Ctrl+F11
- Vertical Line Ctrl+Shift+F11
- Custom Line...
- Edit Line...
- Graphics Styles...

In practice, the descriptions of the various boxes listed are only that, descriptions. WordPerfect gives each type of box its own set of defaults for attributes such as borders, space between the border and surrounding text, space between the border and the contents of the box, and whether or not the box has a caption. You can, however, override the border and margin settings for any box. Also, WordPerfect allows you to number your figure boxes separately from your other boxes. Figure 11-41 shows the types of frames and defaults WordPerfect sets for each graphics type.

To create a new graphic box, select Graphics, and select the type of box you want to use. The following sections refer to figures, although the techniques described apply directly to the other types of graphic boxes as well.

Graphics, Editing

Using the WordPerfect graphics editing option, you can add a caption, alter the contents of an image, exchange one image for another, size the graphic box, modify the graphic border and fill styles, change the text wrapping method, or change the box style.

Menu Selections

To edit a figure box, select Graphics/Edit Box or press the shortcut key SHIFT+F11, type the number of the figure in the Box Find dialog box, and click OK. If your

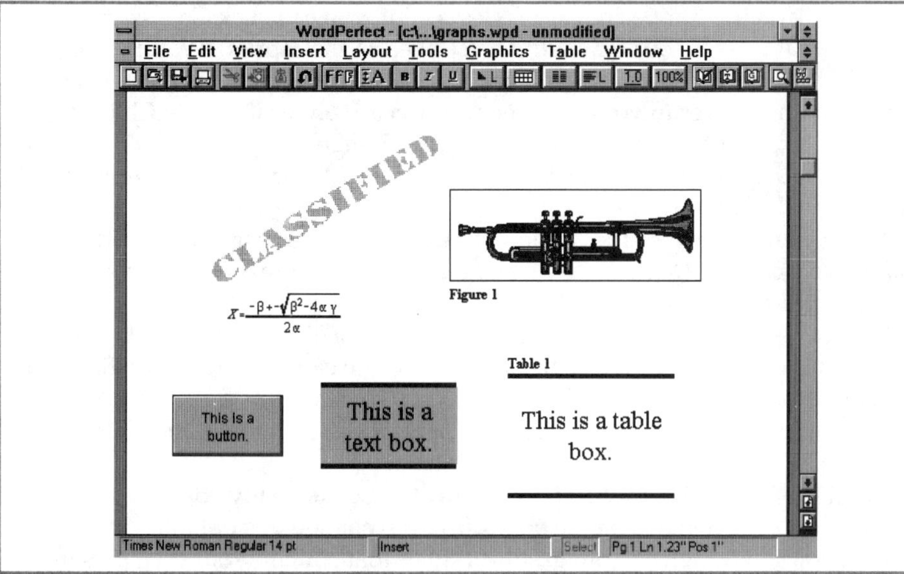

Figure 11-41. *Examples of default settings for WordPerfect graphic boxes*

G

document contains only one figure, the Box Find dialog box will not appear. Instead, handles appear around the figure box and the Figure editor screen appears. You can access a variety of options from the feature bar that extends across the top of the screen.

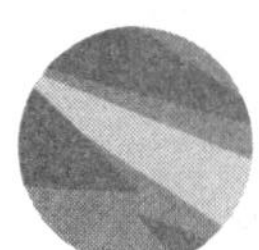

NOTE: You can select and edit a graphic in WordPerfect by right-clicking directly on the graphic and selecting Feature Bar. You can also left-click the graphic and choose Graphics/Edit Box from the menu. WordPerfect also allows you to edit the graphic in the figure by double-clicking the graphic, which loads the graphic into WP Draw.

Adding a Caption

To add a caption to a graphic box, click the Caption button on the feature bar to invoke the Box Caption dialog box. From this dialog box you can select the caption position and its offset from the caption line. Captions can be located on any of the four sides of the box; they can be inside, outside, or on the border; and they can be left-aligned, right-aligned, or centered under the box.

WordPerfect sets the caption width automatically. However, you can adjust the caption width manually by clicking either Fixed and typing a fixed measurement, or Percent, and entering its width as a percentage of the width of the graphic box.

In the Caption Numbering and Styles section you can click Change to indicate what type of counter should be applied to the caption. WordPerfect maintains a separate numbering sequence for each box type. WordPerfect will number all the figures in your document consecutively, as long as each uses the figure box style for the caption number. If you change the style to a different type of box, then the caption (and the box to which it is attached) will be numbered in sequence with that box type.

If you want the text of the caption, for example, to read up the left side of the graphic box, click 90 Degrees to rotate the caption 90 degrees. Make sure that you have selected Left from Side of Box.

To type the text of the caption, click Edit from the Box Caption dialog box. The box number is entered for you; simply type the caption and, when finished, choose another option or click Close.

To restore the default setting for the Box Caption dialog box, click Reset.

CHANGING A DEFAULT CAPTION WordPerfect normally adds the text "Figure 1" as a caption to graphic boxes. You can change this default text or, instead, you can design custom graphics styles that contain your own preset caption text. Both options are discussed in the following paragraphs.

To change the default figure caption, do the following:

1. Choose Graphics/Graphics Styles.
2. Click Box in the Style Type section.
3. Highlight Figure in the Styles list.
4. Click Edit.
5. Click Caption.
6. In the Caption Numbering and Styles section, modify the Number Style by clicking Change.
7. From the Name list in the Style List dialog box, highlight a style and click Apply. If you want no figure caption to appear, select "<None>."

On the other hand, if you want to create a new caption text, such as "Illustration 1," you must follow these steps.

First, create a new counter:

1. Select Insert/Other/Counter.
2. Click Create.
3. Type a name in the Counter Name text box. In this instance, type **IllustrNum**.

4. Click OK.
5. Click Close to exit the Counter Numbering dialog box.

Next, apply the style within a Graphics Box style:

1. Follow the seven steps listed above for changing the default figure caption. In step seven, choose the style you just created, "IllustrNum."
2. Select Graphics/Figure.
3. Highlight a graphic file and click OK.
4. From the Graphics Box feature bar, click Caption.
5. Click Edit. You are placed in the caption area of the figure. The caption "Illustration 1" appears and WordPerfect waits for you to type in the caption text.
6. Type the desired caption.
7. Click Close from the feature bar.

Changing the Contents of a Graphic Box

To replace the graphic in a box with another image, click the Content feature bar button. From the Box Content dialog box, select a different graphic file by clicking the file folder icon to the right of the Filename text box.

To replace the contents of the box with contents of another type, you must first change the box type. For instance, to change an existing text box to a box containing an image, first select the text box, then select the Content option button from the Box Content dialog box and highlight Image. Select an image file by clicking the file folder icon to the right of the Filename text box. Double-click the desired file and click OK to replace the image.

WordPerfect centers the image in the graphic box, but you can adjust the alignment. Click either Horizontal Position or Vertical Position and select the desired position.

If the graphic box contains text, you can rotate it by clicking the desired rotation aspect in the Rotate Text section of the Box Content dialog box.

To restore the default settings in the Box Content dialog box, click Reset.

Changing the Position of a Graphic Box

You can place a graphic box virtually anywhere in a WordPerfect document by clicking Position and specifying the box placement. Graphic boxes can be *anchored* (forced to stay in the same place) to the current page, paragraph, or character in the document. This means that if you anchor a graphic to a character, paragraph, or page, it will move accordingly as you add or delete text around it.

To anchor a graphic box to the current page, click Put Box on Current Page. If one or more page breaks occur before the graphic box, it will remain fixed at the same location on the page.

NOTE: *You can position the graphic box precisely by specifying horizontal and vertical measurements and a point of origin. At the bottom of the dialog box, click Allow Box to Overlap Other Boxes if you want this graphic box to overlap (and possibly hide) other graphic boxes.*

To anchor a graphic box to a paragraph in your document, click Put Box in Current Paragraph. The box will remain anchored to that paragraph as you add or remove text before it in your document.

To anchor a graphic box to a character in your document, click Treat Box as Character. This actually anchors the graphic to the character, thereby reacting as a character as text moves. Making this selection changes the options in the Box Position dialog box.

You can further specify where the box will align by clicking the desired position in the Position Box section. Top aligns the top of the graphic box with the top of the character next to which it is placed, Centered aligns the center of the graphic box with the baseline (not the descenders) of the character, Bottom aligns the bottom of the graphic box with the baseline of the character (not the descenders), and Content Baseline aligns the bottom of the image in the graphic box with the baseline of the character (not the descenders). If you want the graphic box to affect the line height of the text in your document, enable Box Changes Text Line Height. For example, if this option is enabled and the graphic you place is one inch high, that line of text will acquire the height of the graphic box.

Adjusting the Size of a Graphic Box

A graphic box can be resized to meet the spacing needs of your documents. Normally, you would resize a graphic box by clicking and dragging the handles on the edge of the graphic box. However, for a more precise measurement, or to force the graphic box to fit the full width and/or height of the page, you can click Size.

In the Width section of the Box Size dialog box, the Set option allows you to specify the measurement in inches (or whatever you have defined as the default unit of measurement) of the border width of the graphic box. The Full option permits the graphic box to fit the full width of the page. The Size to Content expands the graphic box to fit within the space remaining between text on the page.

In the Height section, the Set option allows you to specify the measurement in inches of the border height of the graphic box. The Full option permits the graphic box to fit the full height of the page. The Size to Content expands the graphic box to fit within the space remaining between text on the page.

Modifying the Border/Fill Styles of a Graphic Box

The default border of a graphic box is a single line around the box's perimeter. You can easily change or remove the border by clicking the Border/Fill feature bar button and making the desired modifications.

Click Border Style and choose an appropriate border style for the graphic box from the visual palette. A list box appears to the right of the Border Style option button with all the palette options listed by descriptive name.

To create a custom border, select a border that is similar to the style you want. Then click Customize Style and choose the options to customize the border style.

You can change the background color and pattern in the Fill Options section of the Box Border/Fill Styles dialog box. Click Fill Style and choose a shading or pattern. To apply color to the shading or fill pattern, select a color from Foreground and Background palettes.

Once you have made the desired modifications, click OK. To turn off previous and current modifications to the border and fill styles, click Off.

Wrapping Text Around a Graphic Box

Normally, when you place a graphic box in text, the text wraps around the border of the graphic box regardless of the shape of the image in the box. WordPerfect lets you alter the way text wraps around a graphic box in a variety of ways.

To change the text wrap feature in WordPerfect, click Wrap to access the Wrap Text dialog box. Square is the default wrapping type and wraps text around the box as a square. Contour wraps the text around the image within the graphic box (you must first indicate NO BORDER in the Box Border/Fill Styles dialog box). Neither Side causes the text to avoid the left and right sides of the graphic box. No Wrap (through) makes the text show through the graphic box, resembling a watermark.

In addition, you can directly control where text should or should not wrap. The default is for WordPerfect to wrap the text around the Largest Side of the graphic box. Left Side keeps the text just on the left of the graphic box and Right Side keeps the text strictly on the right. To make text wrap and flow around both sides of the graphic box, click Both Sides.

Changing the Style of the Graphic Box

The style of a graphic box can be changed. For example, if you want to change an existing graphic box into a text box, click Style and select Text from the Box Style dialog box, as shown here:

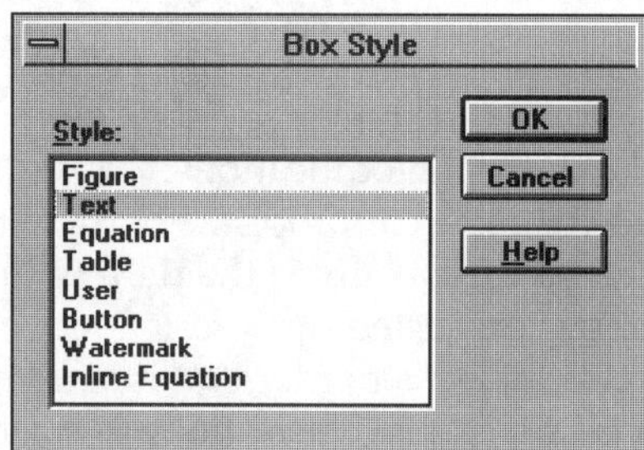

Using the Tools Palette

WordPerfect lets you modify the contents of a graphic box even more with the Tools Palette. These tools enable you to rotate an image around a selected point, move an image around within the confines of the graphic box, scale an image, change the colors on the image to their complementary colors, display a color image in black and white, adjust contrast and brightness levels, reset image attributes, change image attributes, mirror an image around its vertical and horizontal axes, edit the image with WP Draw, and change image settings.

The Tools feature bar button is available for all box types except for text boxes. Select a graphic box and click Tools to access the tools palette shown here:

ROTATE AN IMAGE AROUND A SELECTED POINT To rotate an image around a selected point, click the Rotate icon (the left icon in the first row of the Tools Palette). Handles will appear inside the graphic box (handles are black squares with arrow heads on opposite corners). Click and hold the mouse button as you drag one of the handles with the mouse. The image rotates within the boundaries of the graphic box. Release the mouse button when finished.

MOVE AN IMAGE When an image is selected you can slide it horizontally and vertically by clicking the Move icon (the right icon in the first row). As you position the cursor over the graphic box, the pointer resembles an open hand poised to move the image. Click and hold the mouse button as you drag the image to the desired location. Release the mouse button when finished.

POINTER To reenable the mouse pointer after using another tool, click on the Point icon (the left icon in the second row).

SCALING AN IMAGE Scaling lets you resize certain types of image formats without sacrificing image clarity or resolution. To scale an image, click the Scale icon (the right icon in the second row). Doing so reveals three buttons: a magnifying glass, sizing arrows, and a ratio factor. The magnifying glass lets you scale a specified portion of the image. The sizing arrows permit instant scaling of the image as you scroll up or down. The ratio button restores the image to its original 1:1 scale.

CHANGING THE COLOR OF AN IMAGE To change the colors in an image to their complementary colors (a complementary color is the color that lies directly opposite on a color wheel), click the Complementary Colors icon (the left icon in the third row). Doing so changes red to green, yellow to purple, blue to orange, and so on.

DISPLAYING AN IMAGE IN BLACK AND WHITE To display an image in black and white, click the Black & White icon (the right icon in the third row). Select the desired shading intensity by clicking a shading square.

SETTING THE CONTRAST OF AN IMAGE To set the contrast level for an image, click the Contrast icon (the left icon in the fourth row) and choose a contrast level.

SETTING THE LIGHTNESS OF AN IMAGE You can adjust the brightness of an image by clicking the Lightness icon (the right icon in the fourth row) and choosing a lightness setting.

RESETTING ALL ATTRIBUTES If you need to reset all the image attributes back to their original values, click the Reset Attributes icon (the left icon in the fifth row), and the image will be restored. If you want to reset only specific attributes, use the Image Settings icon, as described later.

CHANGING THE FILL ATTRIBUTES To alter the fill attributes of the image, click the Fill Attributes icon (the right icon in the fifth row). Doing so reveals three buttons: normal color fill, no fill (transparent), and opaque fill.

MIRRORING AN IMAGE, VERTICAL AXIS To mirror an image around its vertical axis, click the Mirror Vertical icon (the left icon in the sixth row).

MIRRORING AN IMAGE, HORIZONTAL AXIS To mirror an image around its horizontal axis, click the Mirror Horizontal icon (the right icon in the sixth row).

EDITING AN IMAGE WITH WP DRAW You can directly edit the image by clicking the Edit Image icon (the left icon in the bottom row). This invokes WP Draw, a utility in which you can modify the image, insert new images, and so on.

CHANGING THE IMAGE SETTINGS INDIVIDUALLY To modify the image settings, including any of the previously discussed attributes, click the Image Settings icon (the right icon in the bottom row). You can reset or adjust any of the image attributes by clicking the appropriate button in the Modify Image Appearance section of the Image Settings dialog box. If you click Reset All, the attributes of the current image will be restored to their original values. This is the same as using the Reset Attributes icon discussed earlier.

Selecting the Next or Previous Graphic Box

To quickly move forward to the next or back to the previous graphic box, click the Next or Prev buttons.

Related Entries

Graphics Styles, Creating
Graphics Styles, Editing
See also Chapter 7, "Desktop Publishing with WordPerfect for Windows."

Graphics, Inserting

You can insert a graphic image directly into a standard figure box and have it placed in the default position on the page. You can later adjust the position and other attributes associated with that graphic box.

Menu Selections

To insert a WordPerfect graphic image into a figure box, choose Graphics/Figure. Double-click the name of the graphics file you wish to insert into the figure box.

You may need to change the file type in the List Files of Type section if the graphic uses an extension other than WPD.

Related Entries

Graphics, Creating
Graphics, Editing

Graphics, New Number

See Graphics, Editing.

Graphics, Printing

When you select File/Print or press the F5 shortcut key, you can specify how you want the graphics in your document to be printed from the Print dialog box. Printing graphics in high resolution can be relatively slow, depending on your computer and your printer. To speed up printing of a document containing many graphics when resolution is not important, indicate in the Document Settings section whether you want the print quality to be High, Medium, or Draft. You can also choose Do Not Print Graphics, which causes WordPerfect to leave blank frames where your graphics will print. This option is helpful when you are printing early drafts of a document, and you don't want to take the time to print the graphics.

Graphics, Viewing

Graphics are always visible in your document, whether you are in Draft, Page, or Two-Page view.

Related Entries

Draft View
Graphics, Creating
Page View
Two-Page View

Hanging Indent

Use a *hanging indent* whenever you want the first line of text to be flush with the left margin and all of the rest of the associated text to be indented to the first tab position. Hanging indents are frequently used to align text that looks like this:

1. This is an example of a hanging indent in a document. Note how the text wraps to the tab position rather than to the left margin.
   a. You can indent your lines to any tab position. In this case, the default tabs are set every .5" across the page.

Once the hanging indent is set up, your text automatically wraps to the tab position. When you have finished typing the text, press ENTER to turn off the hanging indent and return your cursor to the left margin.

Menu Selections

To create a hanging indent, position the insertion point where you would like the indent to start and choose Layout/Paragraph/Hanging Indent or press the shortcut key CTRL+F7. The insertion point will not move, but two codes will be placed at that position: (Hd Left Ind)(Hd Back Tab). You can view these codes by activating Reveal Codes.

Type **1.** and press TAB to send the cursor to the tab position. Type the paragraph of text as usual and press ENTER to turn off the hanging indent; the insertion point will return to the left margin.

To place subpoint "a.", press TAB to send the insertion point to the first tab position. Press CTRL+F7 and type **a.**; then press TAB to send the insertion point to the next tab position and type the paragraph text. Press ENTER to return the insertion point to the left margin.

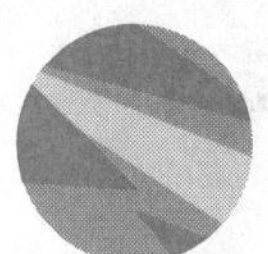

NOTE: *To create multiple subpoints that automatically renumber, expand, and shrink as you add or delete them, such as those found in an outline, see the Outline entry later in this chapter.*

You can also create a double indent, which is similar to a hanging indent, except that it tabs in from the right margin as well.

Related Entries

Indent
Outline

Hard Page Break

WordPerfect automatically calculates how many lines will fit on a page based on your top and bottom margins and the point size of the fonts you are using. However, there are times when you will want to end a page before WordPerfect puts in an automatic page break so you can start typing on the next page. To do this, insert a hard page (HPg) code into the document where you want WordPerfect to move to the next page.

Menu Selections

To place a hard page break into a document, position the insertion point where you want the page break to be and press CTRL+ENTER. A (HPg) code is placed in your text at that location. You will see a new page (in page view) or a double line across your screen (in draft view).

To delete a (HPg) code, position the cursor just below the double line at the left margin and press the BACKSPACE key; the double line on the screen should disappear. In the Reveal Codes screen, you can position the cursor just before the (HPg) code and press DEL.

Hard Return

Whenever you press ENTER, WordPerfect places a *hard return* (HRt) code into your document. To delete a hard return, position the cursor at the end of the line and press DEL.

Hard Return Character

When you install WordPerfect, the default is to have no hard return characters displayed on the screen when you press the ENTER key. You can, however, set the program to display hard returns. While these characters will not print out on the finished document, they are very useful as visual guides.

Menu Selections

To display hard return characters on screen, choose File/Preferences/Display, and the Display Preferences dialog box appears. Click Show ¶. In the Symbols to Display section shown in Figure 11-42, make sure Hard Return is enabled. Click Show Symbols on New and Current Document to activate the display of hard return characters in your current and future documents.

NOTE: From this dialog box you may want to disable symbols such as Space or Advance, which tend to be displayed irregularly in some fonts.

Click OK. Now every time you press ENTER, the paragraph symbol (¶) will appear on your screen.

Related Entries

Character Sets

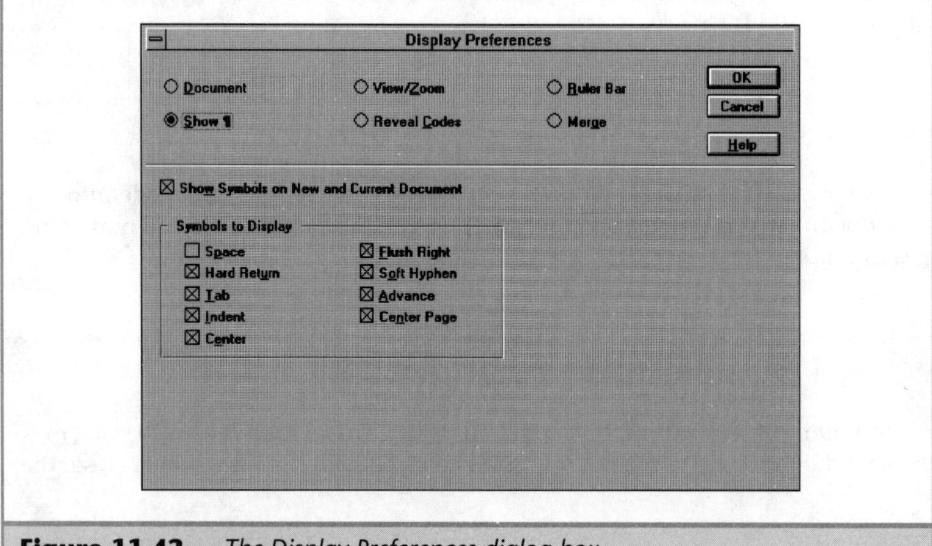

Figure 11-42. *The Display Preferences dialog box*

Hard Space

Use the *hard space* code to keep two or more words together on the same line. For example, if you want the company name "ABC, Inc." to stay together on one line (that is, there will be no case where one line ends with "ABC," and the next line begins with "Inc."), place a hard space code between "ABC," and "Inc."

Menu Selections

To place a hard space code between two words, choose Layout/Line/Other Codes and click Hard Space (HSpace) in the Other Codes section of the Other Codes dialog box. Click Insert, and WordPerfect places a (HSpace) code at the position of the insertion point.

A simpler, more convenient method for inserting a hard space is to press CTRL+SPACEBAR. To view the (HSpace) code, use Reveal Codes.

Hard Tabs

Hard tabs are used in WordPerfect to temporarily change the attributes of either a default or a set tab. You can change a tab from its current alignment to left, center, right, decimal, or dot leader alignment by using the hard tab codes. These attributes last for only one line; after one line, the tabs revert to their original alignment properties.

Menu Selections

To insert a hard tab, position the cursor at the desired tab location and choose Layout/Line/Other Codes. The Other Codes dialog box shown in Figure 11-43 will appear on your screen.

Click the circle to the left of the tab type you wish to use and click Insert to place the code in your document. Use Reveal Codes to view the hard tab code in your document.

Headers, Creating

A header is text, graphics, or a combination of both that appears at the top of every page in the document. Usually headers contain the title of the document, but they also can hold the date, filename, or any number of other items you may want situated at the top of every page.

Other Codes

Hard Tab Codes:
- Left [Hd Left Tab]
- Center [Hd Center Tab]
- Right [Hd Right Tab]
- Decimal [Hd Dec Tab]

Hard Tab Codes with Dot Leaders:
- Left [...Hd Left Tab]
- Center [...Hd Center Tab]
- Right [...Hd Right Tab]
- Decimal [...Hd Dec Tab]

Insert | Cancel | Help

Hyphenation Codes:
- Hyphen [- Hyphen]
- Hyphen Character -
- Soft Hyphen [- Soft Hyphen]
- Hyphenation Soft Return [HyphSRt]
- Cancel Hyphenation of Word [Cancel Hyph]

Other Codes:
- Hard Space [HSpace]
- End Centering/Alignment [END Cntr/Align]
- Thousand Separator: ,

Figure 11-43. *The Other Codes dialog box*

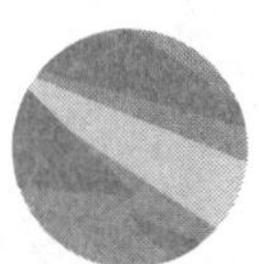

NOTE: Headers are positioned just below the top margin of the document in WordPerfect. Therefore, if your top margin is set at 1", the top line of the header will be placed one inch from the top edge of the document, not between the top margin and the top edge of the page. Most users change the top margin setting to .5" to adjust for this factor.

Menu Selections

Often, you may need to have your header start on the second page of the document to prevent printing a header on letterhead. To do this, place the cursor in the upper left-hand corner of page 2 and choose Layout/Header/Footer. From the Headers/Footers dialog box shown here, select either Header A or Header B:

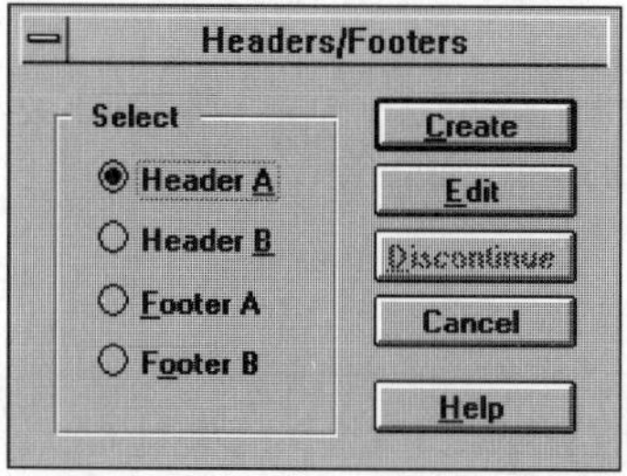

If your headers will be different on odd and even pages, you can use header A for the odd and header B for the even. Otherwise, either header will apply to every page of the entire document.

Once you have selected a header (Header A is usually adequate), click Create, and the Header editing screen appears, as shown in Figure 11-44.

The Header editing screen gives you access to all of WordPerfect's text formatting menu selections, as well as Number, Line, Placement, and Distance buttons accessible from the feature bar. If, for example, you wanted to center the page number in the header, you would choose Layout/Line/Center, type the word **Page**, press the SPACEBAR, and click the Number button from the feature bar. In Reveal Codes, a (Pg Num Disp) code will appear where the page number will be printed.

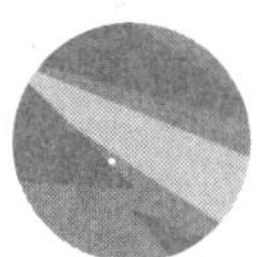

NOTE: If you place a page number in the header, be sure to disable page numbering or your page numbers will be redundant.

You would choose the Placement button only if you wanted the header to be different on odd and even pages. The default is for the header to be the same on every page. When you have finished creating the header, click Close on the feature bar to return to the document.

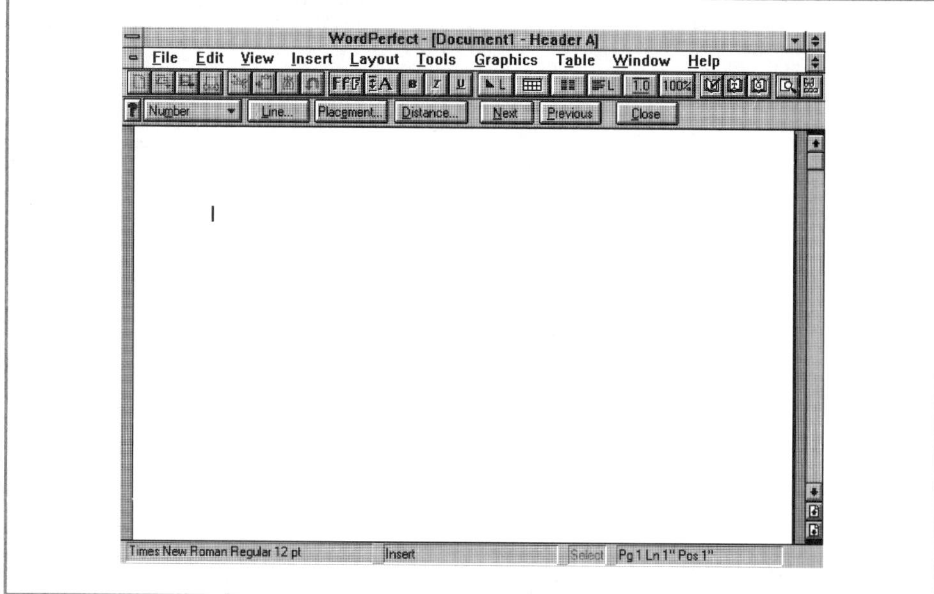

Figure 11-44. *The Header editing screen*

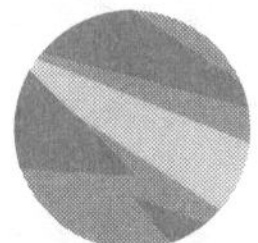

NOTE: *If you want the current header (either A or B) to end so that you can continue with a different header, choose Discontinue from the Layout/Header/Footer menu selection.*

Headers, Editing

If you are in Page View and have created a header, you can see the header at the bottom of the page. You can access the Header editing screen at any time.

Menu Selections

Select Layout/Header/Footer, click the appropriate header (usually Header A), and select Edit. You are placed in the Header editing screen with a feature bar across the top of the screen. You can also edit a header directly from within your document by clicking directly on a header in your document. This also accesses the Header editing screen, except that the feature bar is hidden. To access it, right-click in the header area and click Feature Bar.

The header remains inaccessible as you work in your document, preventing you from accidentally modifying or deleting it. However, as you edit a header, you can apply any attributes as you would in the document.

To delete a header, use Reveal Codes to locate the header code, for example, *Header A: Every Page, [Open Style] header text.*

Related Entries

Headers, Creating

Help

WordPerfect has a powerful and easily accessible help facility. You can use the help menus to look up further information on virtually every function WordPerfect has to offer.

Menu Selections

To access WordPerfect's help system, choose Help from the main menu. The menu selections shown in the following illustration appear.

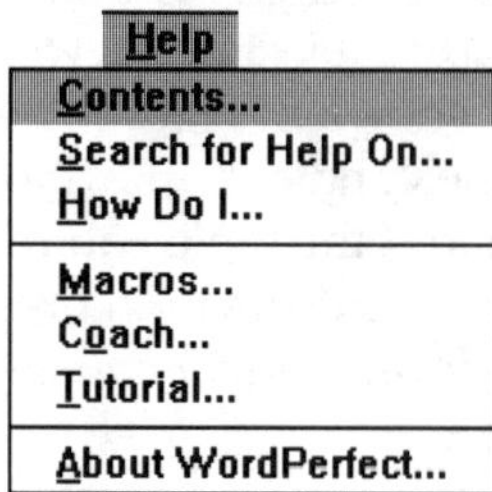

Each menu item is explained separately in the material that follows.

Help Contents

When you choose Help/Contents or press F1, the WordPerfect Help screen shown in Figure 11-45 appears on your screen. If the Help screen appears small, you can enlarge the Help window to full screen by clicking the maximize button. The screen initially shows a table of contents from which you can choose a specific topic.

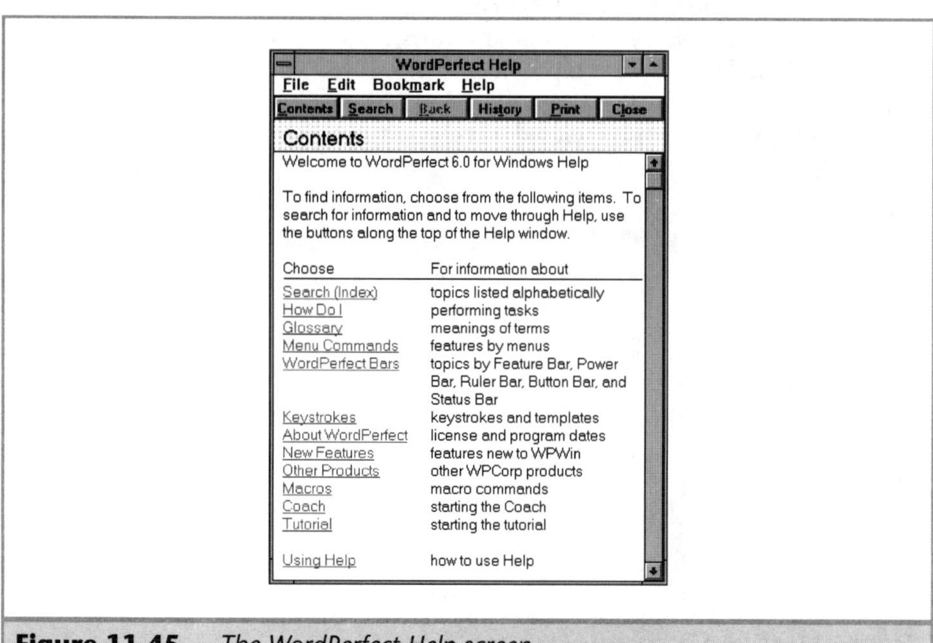

Figure 11-45. *The WordPerfect Help screen*

To return to the Contents screen, click the Contents button just beneath the menu bar. To search for a topic by subject or keyword, click the Search button to bring up the Search dialog box shown in Figure 11-46. You can then type a subject or keyword in the text box and click the Show Topics button. WordPerfect lists all of the available items about the topic you request. Select a topic and click the Go To button. You can read the information presented, choose File/Print Topic to get a printout of the information, or choose File/Exit to return to the document you were working on.

NOTE: If you access Help frequently, click the minimize icon rather than exiting Help completely to save the time it takes to reload the Help program.

To go back to the most recent help topic or level, click the Back button.

To view a list of all the help topics you have accessed, click History. You can also access a topic by double-clicking any of those listed.

To quickly print the onscreen information, click the Print button.

Search for Help On...

Instead of choosing Search from the Help button bar, you can access the Search utility directly by choosing Help/Search for Help On.

To search for a topic by subject or keyword, click the Search button to bring up the Search dialog box shown previously in Figure 11-46. You can then type a subject or keyword in the text box and click the Show Topics button. WordPerfect lists all of the available topics related to your request. Select a topic and click the Go To button.

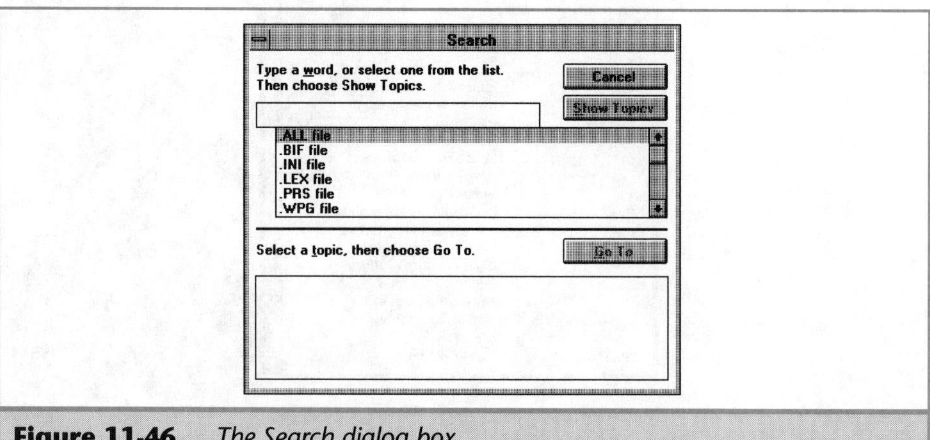

Figure 11-46. *The Search dialog box*

How Do I...

Primarily for new users of the program, WordPerfect has included the How Do I feature shown in Figure 11-47. You can access this option by choosing Help/How Do I. This area of the help system answers common questions like "How do I save a document?" To look at the answers to the questions posed on this screen, click the green, underlined area of the question.

Macros...

An online Macros manual is accessible by clicking Macros. From this Help feature, you can obtain help that is macro-specific instead of the more general help that is available from Help's search feature. The main Help screen for the online Macros manual is shown here:

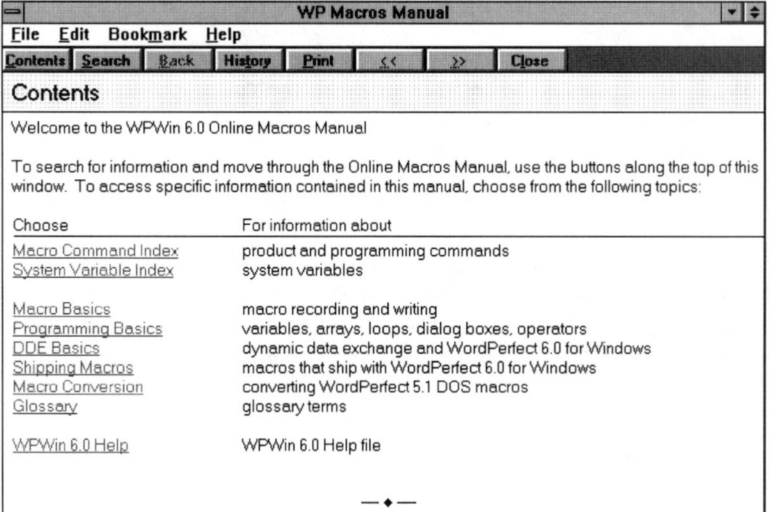

Coach...

WordPerfect includes a handy help feature called *Coach*. The WordPerfect Coach will take you on a step-by-step procedure of how to perform a certain task.

Menu Selections To start a Coach, select Help/Coach, highlight one of the lessons in the Type of Lessons Available, and click OK. WordPerfect will assist you at your own pace through the lesson that you chose.

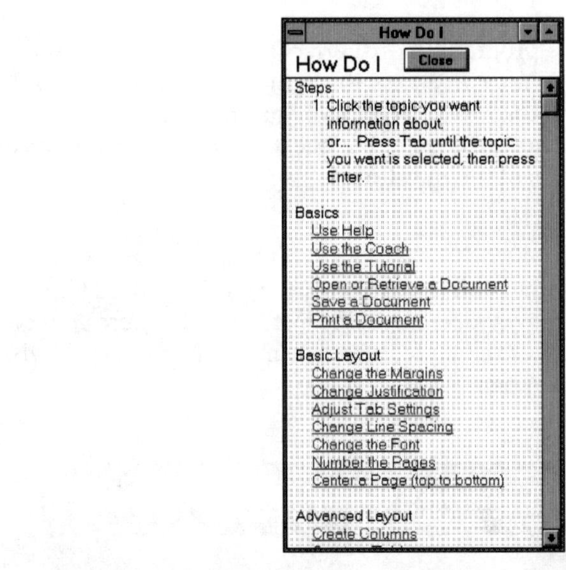

Figure 11-47. *The How Do I feature*

Tutorial...

For those who are new to WordPerfect, a tutorial is available to help you with the basics of the program. There are four lessons that take between five and ten minutes each, instructing you in creating a document, editing text, formatting text, and finishing up.

MENU SELECTIONS To access the WordPerfect tutorial, select Help/Tutorial. Click on one of the four lessons and proceed at your own pace.

About WordPerfect

When you select Help/About WordPerfect, a screen with the license number of WordPerfect, the software's and the shared DLL release dates, network (if any), free memory, and resources available appears. This information is very useful, especially when you call WordPerfect Corporation to get help.

Keyboard Access to Help

You can also get help information from WordPerfect without accessing the Help menu directly. If you press SHIFT+F1, your pointer displays with a question mark in a bubble icon. Point the arrow at any button or portion of the screen about which you have a question, and click. You will be taken to a Help screen relating to that topic.

Help, Bookmark

An interesting feature of WordPerfect's help system is the use of bookmarks to return quickly to help topics you have used in the past. Say, for example, you frequently have questions about tabs. Once you have found the topic, you can define it as a bookmark so that you can return to the same screen without having to navigate through a number of menus.

Menu Selections

To define a help bookmark, access the Help menu, go to a help topic of interest, and choose Bookmark/Define. Click OK to accept the default bookmark name and that bookmark topic will be added to the list in the Bookmark menu. In the future, when you want to return to the same screen, choose Help/Bookmark and select that topic from the Bookmark menu. WordPerfect will take you right to the information screen on that particular subject. To delete a help bookmark, access Help and select Help/Bookmark/Define. Highlight the bookmark as if you were going to rename it and click the Delete button.

Related Entries

Help

Hidden Text

You can place hidden text in your document as notes or messages to yourself or others. The reason it is named hidden text is because, unlike normal text, you can hide it from view on-screen or not have it print.

Menu Selections

To create hidden text, you must first enable Show Hidden Text in the Document option of File/Preferences/Display. Once this option is enabled, you can apply the hidden text attribute just as you apply bold, underline or any other attribute. You can do this in either of two ways. The first way is to enable the attribute, type the text, and then turn off the attribute. The other way is to type the text, highlight or block the text, and then apply the attribute to the selection.

To apply the hidden text attribute, select Layout/Font and place a check mark in the box next to Hidden by clicking it. Click OK.

Once hidden text is placed in your document, you can choose to hide it. This is convenient, for instance, when you have many comments and notes about various subjects in a long report. Simply select View/Hidden Text (this removes the check mark beside it) and any hidden text in the document becomes invisible. It's still there, you just can't see or print it. If you want to print hidden text, you must make it visible by clicking again on Hidden Text (a check mark will appear beside the option).

To turn hidden text into normal text, you must either delete the associated code in Reveal Codes or highlight the text and select Layout/Font and deselect the Hidden option. Remember, it's just another attribute like bold or underline.

Horizontal Lines

WordPerfect makes it very easy for you to place horizontal lines across your screen. You can use these lines to separate headers and footers from the document's main text, to distinguish major headings from the text that appears below them, and to divide pages into sections. A horizontal line has a major advantage over the underscore character in that its width can be adjusted to any thickness.

Related Entries

Graphics Lines

Hypertext

Hypertext is a type of text you can create that lets you invoke a macro, move to another location in the document, or link to other documents. The Help feature in WordPerfect and Windows utilizes hypertext to take you to different help topics or show definitions. You can accomplish a similar task by applying the Hypertext feature in your WordPerfect documents. When you apply hypertext to text, you establish a link with the word, document, location, or macro.

Menu Selections

To create hypertext in your document, you must select the word, group of words, or symbols in your document that you want to behave as hypertext. Depending on what you want the hypertext to do—whether it should invoke a macro, access another document, or move to a bookmark—you should prepare those items first. Choose Tools/Hypertext and the Hypertext editor screen and feature bar appears, as shown in Figure 11-48.

Click Create to access the Create Hypertext Link dialog box. Click Go To Bookmark and choose the bookmark from the Go To Bookmark text box or, if you are linking to another document, provide the document name and choose the bookmark in the Bookmark text box. To link the hypertext to a macro, click Run Macro and provide the macro filename in the text box. Choose the display method of the hypertext in the Appearance section of the dialog box by clicking Text or Button. Click OK when you have finished. To make the hypertext functional after you leave the Hypertext editor screen, click the hypertext and then click the Activate button. When you do, the button changes to a Deactivate button. You can later disable hypertext by clicking Deactivate.

If you are creating more hypertext links, select the new text and repeat the previous steps. The resulting hypertext will appear similar to that shown in Figure 11-48.

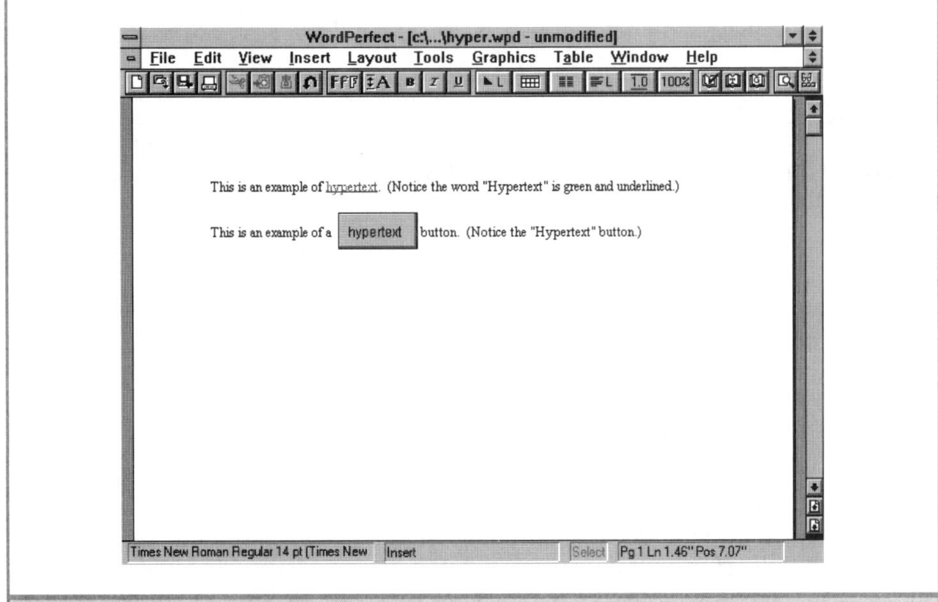

Figure 11-48. *The Hypertext editor screen with two hypertext examples*

H

Editing Hypertext

You can edit and manipulate hypertext just like standard text. If you want to edit the action of the hypertext, place your insertion point in the hypertext and click the Edit button on the featue bar. This accesses the Edit Hypertext Link dialog box, where you can change the action of the hypertext. After you make your changes, click OK.

Changing the Style of Hypertext

You can alter the appearance of the default hypertext in your documents by clicking Style. From the Styles Editor dialog box, change the hypertext as you see fit, perhaps making text red with italics or bold with blue letters.

Related Entries

Bookmark

Hyphenation

WordPerfect allows you to hyphenate your documents automatically. The default setting is to have hyphenation turned off; you need to turn this feature on for WordPerfect to hyphenate your text.

Menu Selections

To turn on the Hyphenation feature, choose Layout/Line/Hyphenation, and the Line Hyphenation dialog box appears:

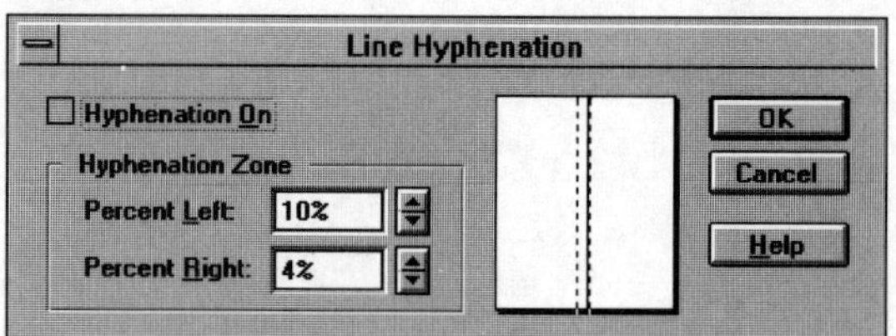

Enable the Hyphenation On check box. Click OK, and WordPerfect automatically begins to hyphenate your document from the location of the insertion point onward.

When WordPerfect encounters a word that fits into the hyphenation zone but doesn't know how to hyphenate it, the program prompts you to indicate where the hyphen should be placed. You can adjust the position of the hyphen in the word or text string by moving the cursor arrows or clicking the mouse inside the text box.

You can also choose to place a nonprinting, nondisplaying hyphen by clicking Hyphenation SRt (hyphenated soft return). A hyphenated soft return divides a word without using a hyphen. This is useful for words separated by a slash (such as "and/or") and *em* dashes (as in "tall—and wide"). The code remains dormant unless it falls within the hyphenation zone where it separates the word as you defined.

To skip a word and continue, click the Ignore Word button. If you want to place a space rather than a hyphen at the location, click the Insert Space button. To stop the Hyphenation process altogether, click the Suspend Hyphenation button (in which case you must re-enable hyphenation later). Naturally, if you accept the placement of the hyphen, choose Insert Hyphen, and WordPerfect inserts the hyphen.

Related Entries

Hyphenation Zone

Hyphenation Zone

When WordPerfect is hyphenating words in a document, it checks to see where the word falls relative to the right margin; if the word falls within the preset hyphenation zone, WordPerfect inserts a hyphen.

The hyphenation zone is an area that you can define by setting a percentage for the hyphenation "cut-off" point in a word. This percentage defines how much of the word must be moved between lines before hyphenation is allowed. For instance, if the hyphenation zone is set to 25%, then at least 25 percent of the word must be movable before hyphenation can occur.

Menu Selections

To adjust the hyphenation zone, choose Layout/Line/Hyphenation and adjust your Percent Left and Percent Right settings in the Hyphenation Zone area. As you increase the percentages, the number of words that are hyphenated in your documents will decrease.

I-Beam

When the mouse pointer is on document text—or any place where you can type text—it appears as an I-beam cursor, as shwon in the following illustration.

I

The movement of the mouse controls the position of the I-beam on the screen. When you click the mouse button, the insertion point moves to the location of the I-beam cursor. This is the easiest and quickest way to move the insertion point to another place in the onscreen text.

Related Entries

See Chapter 2, "WordPerfect for Windows Basics."

Indent

An *indent* is simply one line starting farther in from the margin than another (usually the subsequent) line or paragraph. There are several ways you can indent text in a document. Just remember that all of the indent options depend upon accurate tab settings.

Menu Selections

You access all indents, other than the standard indentation at the beginning of a paragraph, through the Layout/Paragraph menu.

Standard Paragraph Indent

To indent the first line of a paragraph, position the insertion point and press the TAB key. This places a (Left Tab) code, visible in Reveal Codes, at the location of the insertion point.

Indent

Choosing Layout/Paragraph/Indent or pressing the F7 shortcut key causes WordPerfect to indent an entire paragraph one tab stop from the left, as shown in Figure 11-49.

Alex moved quickly through the shadows, avoiding the glare of the streetlights intruding on the night. He resented the streetlights; they made it hard for him to accomplish his work. Particularly tonight. Without the lights, the darkness would have been complete, and his work much easier to do. But that was not to be, so he silently moved in and out of the shadows, noticeable to only the most observant of onlookers. ¶

¶

⁎ As he approached the corner of Third and Jackson, Alex slowed down. There was something wrong. He could feel it, but not quite put his finger on it. Was it something happening in one of the darkened storefronts? Perhaps an impending threat from one of the expensive cars parked near the corner. While he could not identify the source of the fear welling up in his stomach, he could not shake the feeling that something was increasingly wrong. What was it Jim had said just before he had died? *Watch out for the black Mercedes.* Rather cryptic, yet effective, as Alex now watched a passenger-side window roll down on a brand-new black Mercedes 750i. He quickly ducked into the entryway of a drycleaning store, and positioned himself so he had a clear view of the scene. ¶

¶

As he peered into the night, the fear which he felt took form and began to solidify. He caught his breath as he saw the person behind the window of the Mercedes. It was Brenda, the same Brenda that expressed so much grief at Jim's passing. There was no grief evident now as she surveyed the street, looking for something she could not easily find. Alex crouched, silent and motionless, as he continued to watch the odd scene unfold. ¶

Figure 11-49. *A paragraph indented from the left*

Hanging Indent

Choosing Layout/Paragraph/Hanging Indent or pressing the SHIFT+F7 option causes WordPerfect to indent all of a paragraph *except the first line* by one tab stop on the left. The first paragraph in Figure 11-50 has a hanging indent.

You can create a numbered list, as shown in Figure 11-51, by selecting Layout/Paragraph/Hanging Indent or pressing CTRL+F7, typing the number, and then pressing TAB (or choosing Layout/Paragraph/Indent, or pressing F7) and typing the rest of the paragraph.

NOTE: If you are creating lengthy numbered lists, consider using WordPerfect's Outline feature, which automatically renumbers a list as you add or remove list items.

Double Indent

Choosing Layout/Paragraph/Double Indent or pressing the CTRL+SHIFT+F7 shortcut key causes WordPerfect to indent a paragraph by one tab stop on both

Alex moved quickly through the shadows, avoiding the glare of the streetlights intruding on the night. He resented the streetlights, they made it hard for him to accomplish his work. Particularly tonight. Without the lights, the darkness would have been complete, and his work much easier to do. But that was not to be, so he silently moved in and out of the shadows, noticeable to only the most observant of onlookers.

As he approached the corner of Third and Jackson, Alex slowed down. There was something wrong. He could feel it, but not quite put his finger on it. Was it something happening in one of the darkened storefronts? Perhaps an impending threat from one of the expensive cars parked near the corner. While he could not identify the source of the fear welling up in his stomach, he could not shake the feeling that something was increasingly wrong. What was it Jim had said just before he had died? *Watch out for the black Mercedes.* Rather cryptic, yet effective, as Alex watched a passenger-side window roll down on a brand-new Mercedes 750i. He quickly ducked into the entryway of a drycleaning store, and positioned himself so he had a clear view of the scene.

Figure 11-50. *A paragraph with a hanging indent*

the left and the right. To determine the indentation on both sides, the program uses the distance from the left margin to the first tab stop after the left margin. It indents from the right margin by the same amount, regardless of whether or not there is a tab set at that distance from the right margin.

You can indent both sides of a paragraph by two or more tab increments by selecting Layout/Paragraph/Double Indent more than once.

If you want to participate in the weekend getaway drawing, you must remember to follow these steps before the end of this week:

1 Stop by the payroll department and pick up an official entry blank
2 Fill out the entry blank using a number 2 pencil (this is necessary so the data processing department can sort and count the entry blanks automatically)
3 Deposit the filled-out entry blank in the contest hopper in the lunch room

The winner will be announced next Monday morning in a company wide drawing. Remember--you can only enter once, so you should enter early.

Figure 11-51. *A numbered list*

Back Tab

The Layout/Paragraph/Back Tab option or the shortcut key SHIFT+TAB gives you a layout similar to a hanging indent, in that it causes the first line of a paragraph to extend to the left of the rest of the paragraph. In this case, however, the first line extends to the left of the left margin, for a distance of one tab stop.

Related Entries

Back Tab
Hanging Indent
Tabs, Setting

Index

The *index* option allows you to create an index of keywords, subjects, or terms contained in your document. The index can contain only the words, or it can contain the words and the page numbers on which the words appear.

A simple index consists of headings only; a straight list of words or terms with their respective page numbers. A more complex index may have headings listed with subheadings beneath them. You can create both types of indexes.

Creating an index requires three steps:

1. Specify the words and terms you want contained in the index. You can accomplish this in either of two ways: by marking the text in the document one word at a time, or by creating a separate concordance file to specify the words and terms as a group that you want included in the index.
2. Define the index location, numbering style, and heading layout you want to use for the index.
3. Generate the index.

Menu Selections

Marking Text in the Document

One method of defining terms to be included in the index is to go through the document and mark each occurrence of the term manually. To do so, access the Index editor screen, shown in Figure 11-52, by selecting Tools/Index. Use the feature bar in this screen to mark the text for your index.

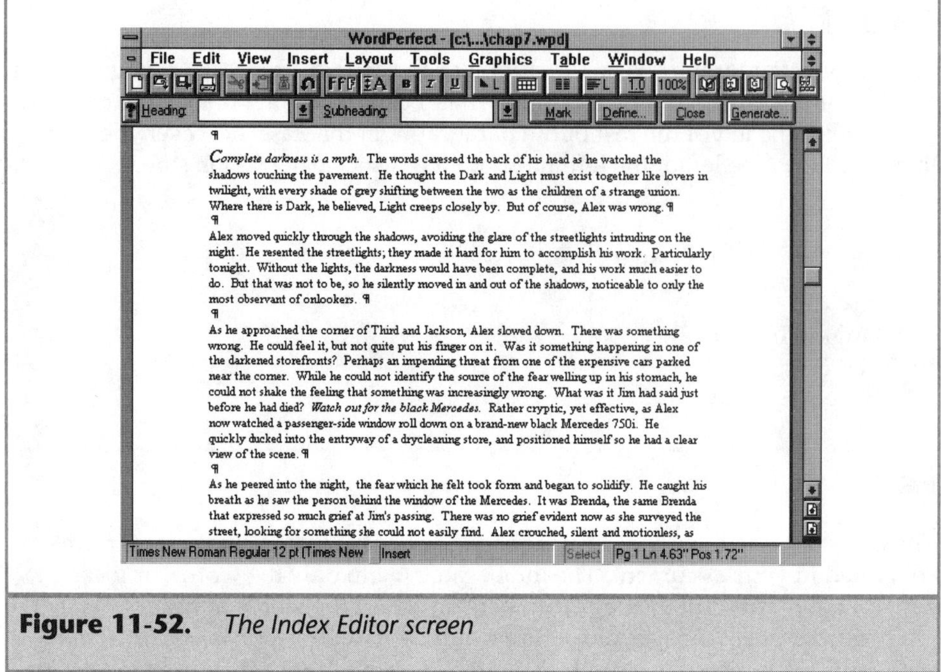

Figure 11-52. *The Index Editor screen*

To make an entry appear as a heading in the final index, as shown here:

Headers 18, 22

you must highlight the word (double-click the word) and then click in the Heading text box in the feature bar. This designates that word as the heading. You must create a heading in order to mark a word.

To make entries appear as subheadings under a heading in the final index, as shown here:

Headers
  creating 18
  editing 22

you must first enter a heading in the Heading text box, as described earlier. Then highlight a word for the subheading and click in the Subheading text box in the feature bar. Click Mark to mark the word for the index. In Reveal Codes, you can see the (Index) code placed immediately before the marked word.

Creating a Concordance File

The other method for creating a list of terms to be included in the index is to create a separate concordance file. A *concordance* is a regular WordPerfect text file that lists all of the entries you want included in the index. While most entries in your index will be only a few words long, an entry in the concordance file can be any length.

NOTE: *Remember that entries that contain more than one word may decrease the number of entries in your final index. This is because you are providing a "search list" that WordPerfect uses to scan the document; the more words there are in an entry, the harder it is to find a match.*

To create a concordance file, open a new, empty file by choosing File/New. Type the words you wish to list in the index, pressing ENTER after each entry. WordPerfect will use the entries from this file as a search base to create the index in an associated document. Save the concordance file as a normal WordPerfect document.

For the index to be generated properly, each entry in the concordance file, whether one word or many, must be followed with a hard return (HRt), created when you press ENTER.

Each entry in the concordance file will be listed as a heading in the final index, assuming, of course, that the term appears somewhere in the document being indexed. If you want a concordance file to include subheadings too, you must mark the words manually in the Index editor screen, as described above. The only difference is that the words are already listed in the concordance file. Simply highlight the desired word for a heading and click in the Heading text box. Then highlight the desired word for a subheading and click in the Subheading text box. Click Mark to mark the word as a subheading.

If the entry is not found in the document text, no entry will be created in the final index.

NOTE: *It is not necessary to sort the concordance entries; WordPerfect automatically puts the final index into alphabetical order when it is created. However, you can sort concordance file entries into alphabetical order by using the WordPerfect Tools/Sort option or pressing the ALT+F9 shortcut key.*

Defining the Index Location, Numbering System, and Layout

The second step in creating an index is to specify where you want the index located, the numbering system (if any), and the heading layout you want to use in the index. First, position the cursor where you want the index to be located, which is usually after the last page of the document. If you want the index to begin on a new, separate page, press CTRL+ENTER to put in a page break.

Then select Tools/Index. From the Index feature bar click Define to access the Define Index dialog box, as shown in Figure 11-53. Use the Position option button to specify the numbering position. When you choose an option, you can see an example of the numbering format in the sample index.

NO NUMBERING The No Numbering option simply lists all entries in the document that are either marked in the text or appear in the concordance file. They are listed in alphabetical order with no page numbers.

TEXT # The Text # option (the default) lists entries with page numbers following each entry.

TEXT (#) The Text (#) option lists entries with page numbers in parentheses following each entry.

**TEXT # ** The Text # option puts index entries on the left edge of the page and puts page numbers right justified on the right margin.

TEXT .... # The Text .... # option puts index entries on the left edge of the page and puts page numbers right justified on the right margin with dot leaders before the numbers.

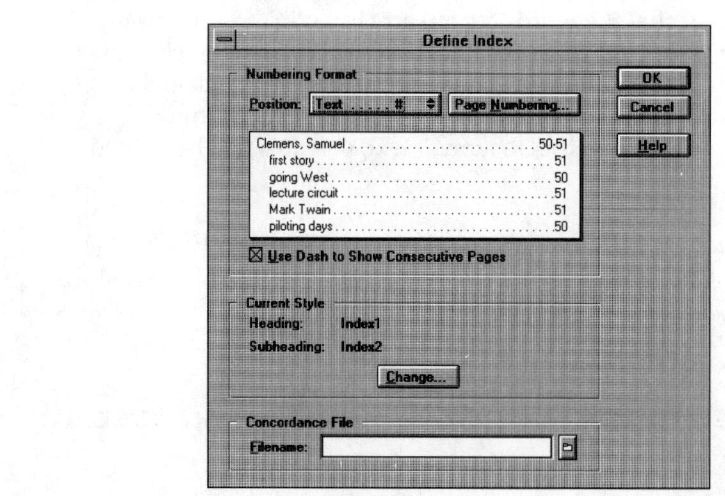

Figure 11-53. *The Define Index dialog box*

PAGE NUMBERING If you want to use a different numbering format, such as "Page 51" or "see chapter 6," click Page Numbering and select User-defined Page Number Format. The default format is [Pg #], which displays as a single number, but you can change it by editing the format text box directly or by clicking Insert to place another numbering code. The text box can contain codes, text, and numbers.

CHANGING THE CURRENT STYLE You can change the heading and/or subheading style to another index style so that you can use the words marked as headings and subheadings to generate a list, table of authorities, or table of contents. To do so, click Change and make the desired changes.

Selecting a Concordance File

If you want to create an index using a concordance file, enter its filename here. If you are unsure of the filename, click the File icon to the right of the Filename text box to browse through the files on disk. Click OK.

Click OK when you have finished using the Define Index dialog box. The text marker << Index will generate here >> appears at the insertion point, and the code (Def Mark: Index, -) is placed in the document (*see* Reveal Codes).

Modifying an Indexed Document

Whenever you make changes to an indexed document, you can select Tools/Generate at any time to update the index, regardless of its location. However, if there are new words that you want to add to the index, you must mark the new words in the document or update the concordance file, and then select Tools/Generate. The existing index will be updated with the new entries.

I

Generating the Index

To generate the index, click the Generate button from the Index editor feature bar. You can also generate an index by selecting Tools/Generate or by pressing the CTRL+F9 shortcut key. You will see the dialog box shown here:

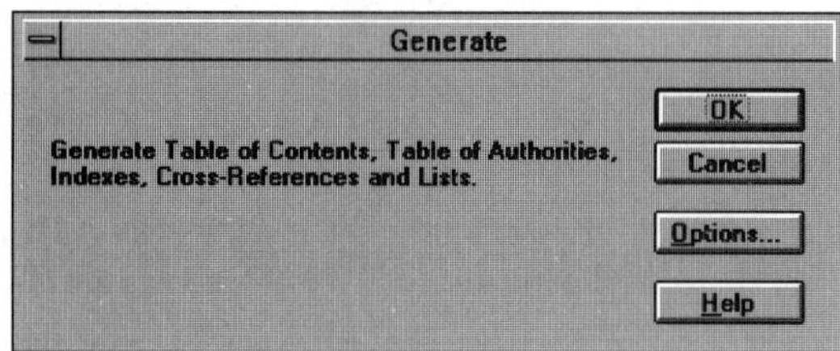

Click OK, and WordPerfect generates your index, based on marked text and/or entries in your concordance file. Click Close on the feature bar to return to the document.

Related Entries

Concordance Files
Generate
Master Documents
Sort

Initial Codes Style, Document

This option allows you to define formatting codes that affect only the current document or that can be used as the default document style. Although the codes you specify here are not directly visible in Reveal Codes, they are contained in the (Open Style: Initial Style) code. Since you cannot delete the Open Style code, this stops you from inadvertently deleting codes.

Menu Selections

Select Layout/Document/Initial Codes Style, to bring up the screen shown in Figure 11-54. On this screen you can insert any page, line, and other formatting

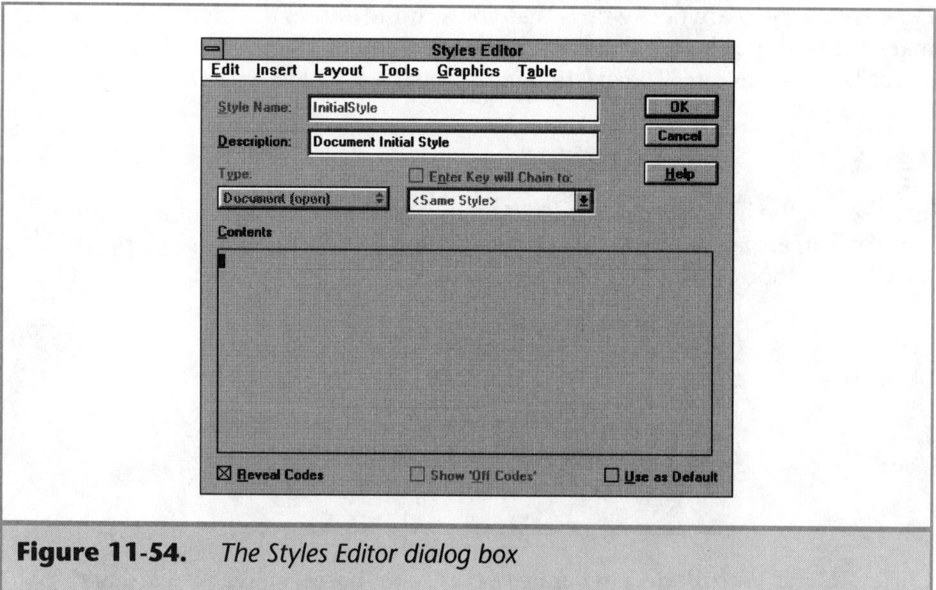

Figure 11-54. *The Styles Editor dialog box*

Column Definition	Letter Spacing
Column On	Line Height
Decimal/Align Character	Line Spacing
Endnote Number	Line Numbering
Endnote Options	Margins
Font	New Page Number
Footnote Number	Page Numbering Style
Footnote Options	Paper Size
Graphic Box Number	Suppress Page Format
Graphic Box Options	Tab Set
Hyphenation On/Off	Text Color
Hyphenation Zone	Underline Spaces and Tabs
Justification	Widow/Orphan On/Off
Kerning	Word Spacing
Language	

Table 11-2. *Optional codes*

codes you wish to have in effect for the document. When you have finished, click OK. The codes are placed at the beginning of the document and take effect immediately.

Codes that you can include in Layout/Document/Initial Codes Style are shown in Table 11-2.

Related Entries

Initial Font

See also the section "Changing the Initial Font" under Printer, Selecting.

Initial Font

You can set the initial font for your document to override the printer initial font. The printer initial font sets the global font for all documents that are set to use that printer.

Menu Selections

Select Layout/Document/Initial Font and choose the appropriate font and size. If you want this font setting to replace the printer initial font (global), click Set as Printer Initial Font.

Related Entries

Initial Codes Style, Document

Initialize Printer

See Print Document.

Insert File

Inserting a file is nearly the same as opening the file. The only major difference is that you can insert a file into another file that is already open. When you open a file, WordPerfect puts it into its own document window; but when you insert a file, WordPerfect places the file at any location in a document that has already been opened.

Menu Selections

To insert a file into a document that has already been opened, move the insertion point to the location where you want the file inserted. Choose Insert/File and locate the document you wish to insert. Double-click the filename, confirm that you want to insert the file, and the document will be placed at the location of the insertion point.

Related Entries

File Conversion
Open

Insert Key

The INSERT key, labeled either "Insert" or "Ins" on your keyboard, is a toggle switch that turns Typeover mode on and off. When you press INSERT, you see "Insert" change to "Typeover" on the status bar at the bottom of the screen.

When "Typeover" appears (in Typeover mode), whatever text you type overwrites any text to the right of the cursor.

When "Insert" appears (in Insert mode) on the status bar, whatever text you type will be inserted at the insertion point, and text to its right will move to the right to make room for it.

Related Entries

See Chapter 2, "WordPerfect for Windows Basics."

Insertion Point

The *insertion point,* commonly known as the cursor, appears as a flashing vertical bar in the typing area of your screen. It indicates where what you type will appear. You can change the location of the insertion point by using the arrow keys, a variety of other keystroke techniques, or the mouse.

Related Entries

See Chapter 2, "WordPerfect for Windows Basics."

International Languages

See Language.

Italic Text

Text printed in italics looks like this sentence. One way to italicize WordPerfect text is to choose Layout/Font and clicking Italic or use the CTRL+I shortcut key, and then type your text. Turn off italics by either selecting Layout/Font and clicking Italic or pressing CTRL+I again.

Related Entries

Fonts

Justification

Justification determines how text is aligned between the left and right margins of the page. WordPerfect provides five ways to justify text in your document, as shown in Figure 11-55. Left justification means that all text is aligned at the left margin with a "ragged" right margin. Right justification aligns text at the right margin with a "ragged" left margin. Center justification centers all text lines between the left and right margins, even when the text is in paragraph form. Full justification, the WordPerfect standard, stretches each line so that the text extends to each margin; this produces a perfectly straight edge at both the left and right

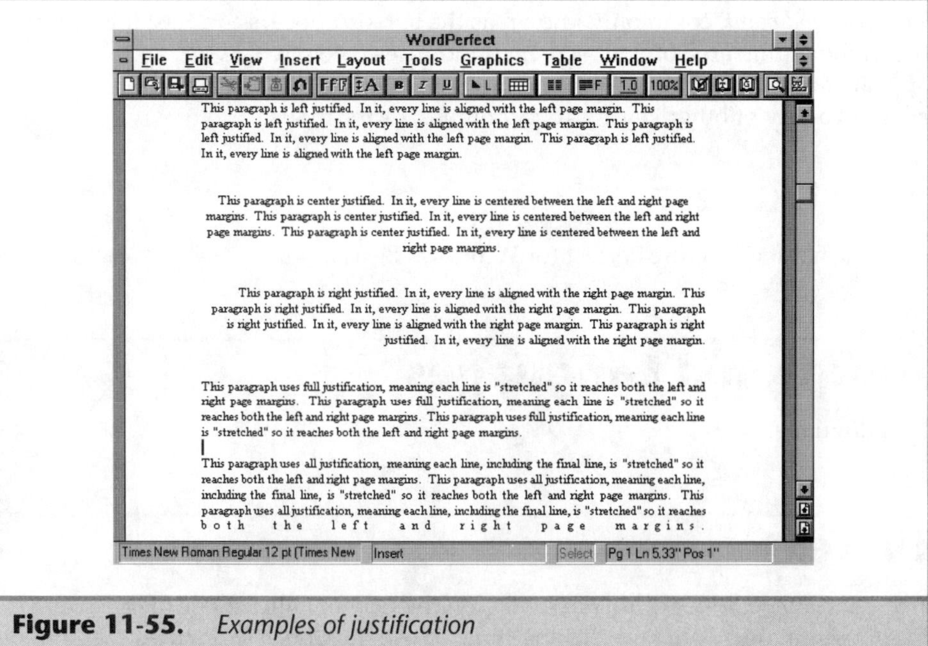

Figure 11-55. *Examples of justification*

margins. All is the same as Full, except that it also justifies the very last line of a paragraph, which sometimes causes it to be spaced widely between margins to compensate for a lack of words.

Menu Selections

To change the justification setting, choose Layout/Justification from the menu bar. Then select Left, Right, Center, Full, or All to indicate your preference. WordPerfect also provides shortcut keys that let you quickly change the justification setting. For left justification, press CTRL+L. Press CTRL+R for right justification and CTRL+E for center justification. For full justification, press CTRL+J. When you select from the menu or press a shortcut key, WordPerfect inserts a justification code at the insertion point, which affects the text that follows.

Kerning, Automatic

Kerning is a typographic feature that deals with the space between adjacent letters. If you choose to have kerning set automatically, WordPerfect scans the document for preset pairs of characters that typically have a lot of space between them, such as *W* and *i*, and then narrows the gap.

Menu Selections

To turn on the Automatic Kerning feature, position the insertion point where you would like the kerning to begin and choose Layout/Typesetting/Word/Letter-spacing to display the Word Spacing and Letterspacing dialog box. Click Automatic Kerning near the bottom of the dialog box and click OK.

J

Related Entries

Kerning, Manual

Kerning, Manual

Manual kerning allows you to adjust the spacing between adjacent letter pairs. A capital *W*, for example, takes up more horizontal space on the screen than a lowercase *i*. You may want to kern the *W* and the *i* so that the unusually large gap between them is narrowed. Depending on the font, its point size, and the printer you are using, manual kerning may or may not be particularly useful.

Menu Selections

To kern a letter pair manually, position the insertion point between the two letters you wish to kern and choose Layout/Typesetting/Manual Kerning, and the Manual Kerning dialog box, shown in Figure 11-56, appears on your screen.

The Units option allows you to change the unit of measure to Inches (the default), Centimeters, Millimeters, Points, or 1200ths of an inch. Once your unit of measurement has been set, you can adjust the amount of space between the two characters by clicking the up/down arrows beside or next to the Amount option as shown in Figure 11-56. Note how the spacing adjusts between the characters in the document.

Related Entries

Kerning, Automatic

Keyboard Layout

See Keyboard, Creating and Editing.

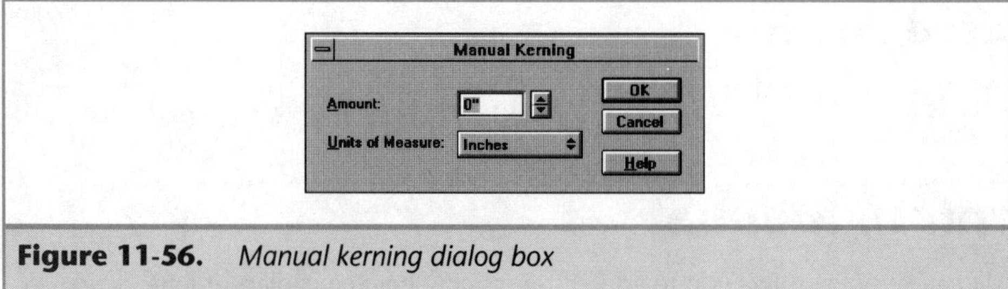

Figure 11-56. *Manual kerning dialog box*

Keyboard, Creating and Editing

WordPerfect allows you to customize your keyboard completely, so that you can define the way you use keys and key combinations to access commands, menus, text, macros, and user-designated items in WordPerfect. This technique is sometimes referred to as *keyboard mapping*, because it lets you "remap" the keyboard to meet your personalized needs. Among the keys you can use are the following:

- Any function key, F1 through F12
- CTRL + any function key or CTRL + any letter or number
- ALT + any function key or ALT + any letter or number
- SHIFT + any function key or SHIFT + any letter or number
- ALT+SHIFT + any function key or ALT+SHIFT + any letter or number
- CTRL+SHIFT + any function key or CTRL+SHIFT + any letter or number

Menu Selections

To personalize your keyboard, choose File/Preferences/Keyboard. The Keyboard Preferences dialog box, shown here, appears on your screen:

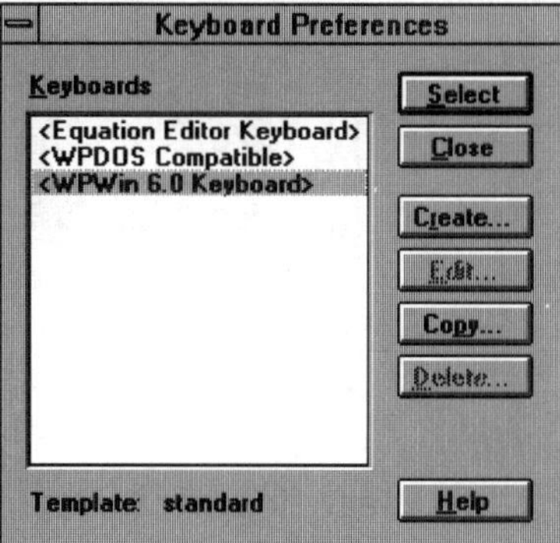

If you would like to select another predefined keyboard, choose Select. To create a new keyboard layout or to edit one that already exists, select the Create or Edit button, and you will see the Keyboard Editor dialog box, as shown in Figure 11-57. If you are creating a new keyboard, WordPerfect will request that you provide a keyboard name.

In the Choose a Key to Assign or Unassign section, you can see all the possible key combinations and the key assignment of each. Those keystrokes that do not yet have a command or other item assigned remain blank. You can add or remove assigned keys from this list by pressing the desired key combination or clicking the keys on-screen with the mouse. For your convenience, you can tell WordPerfect to display the shortcut key you have assigned on the menu by enabling the Assignment Appears on Menu option.

You can assign different key combinations (shortcut keys) to actual program features and commands, keyboard scripts, or macros. This is similar to assigning functions to buttons using the Button Bar editor.

Related Entries

Keyboard Layout
See also Appendix B, "WordPerfect Keyboards."

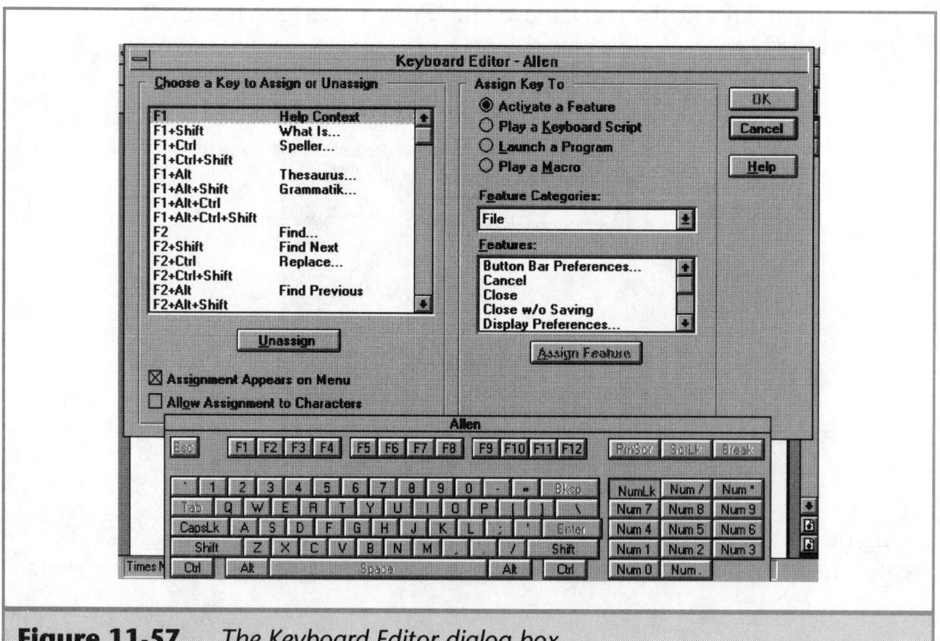

Figure 11-57. *The Keyboard Editor dialog box*

Labels

WordPerfect makes it easy to print addresses or label text on labels sheets, envelopes, or any other type of paper used with your printer. You can create the label text by typing it directly on the screen or by using the Mail Merge feature. If you type the text manually, you must end each label with a hard page break by pressing CTRL+ENTER. The Mail Merge feature inserts hard page breaks for you automatically.

WordPerfect provides a comprehensive list of predefined label styles for both 3M and Avery labels. You can also design your own style and provide the label specifications yourself in the Create Labels dialog box.

Labels are text in a special format placed in a regular WordPerfect document file. You can insert an existing WordPerfect document file containing names and addresses into a label file as long as the fields are consistent throughout the list.

Menu Selections

Creating Text for Labels

When you select Layout/Labels, you are presented with the Labels dialog box, as shown in Figure 11-58. The labels list displays the predefined labels for both laser labels and tractor-feed labels. If you only have one type of printer installed, you may want to click the applicable type to reduce the number of labels displayed in the list.

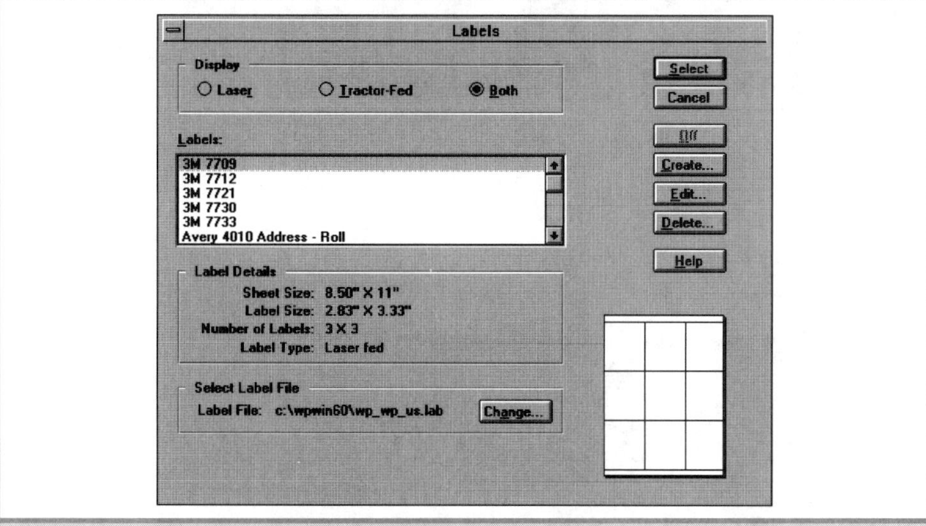

Figure 11-58. *The Labels dialog box*

L

Choose a stock label from the list and confirm that the measurements in the Label Details section are correct according to the specifications that came with your labels. If you have a label file other than WordPerfect's default file WP_WP_US.LAB, click Change and choose that file.

Once you have selected a label style, click Select and you are returned to your document. If you are in Page view, you will notice that the screen is laid out in the label style you chose with one label visible at a time. Adjust the font and type size and begin typing your label information. As you reach the bottom of one label, a new one will appear, allowing you to continue. To move from label to label, use your arrow keys or click the mouse at the desired insertion point. Figure 11-59 shows a group of labels using the Avery 5160 Laser style.

Labels can be part of a regular document as long as they start on their own page. To accomplish this, add a page break by pressing CTRL+ENTER, position the insertion point at the desired location on the new page, and select the label type you want. This will insert a label code and paper size/type code, such as (Labels Form:Avery 5160 Address)(Paper Sz/Typ:8.50" by 11", Portrait). To continue working with normal text in the document, add a page break and select Off from the Labels dialog box. Applying a label style changes your document's page settings to those of the label, so you may want to adjust the margins and other page settings.

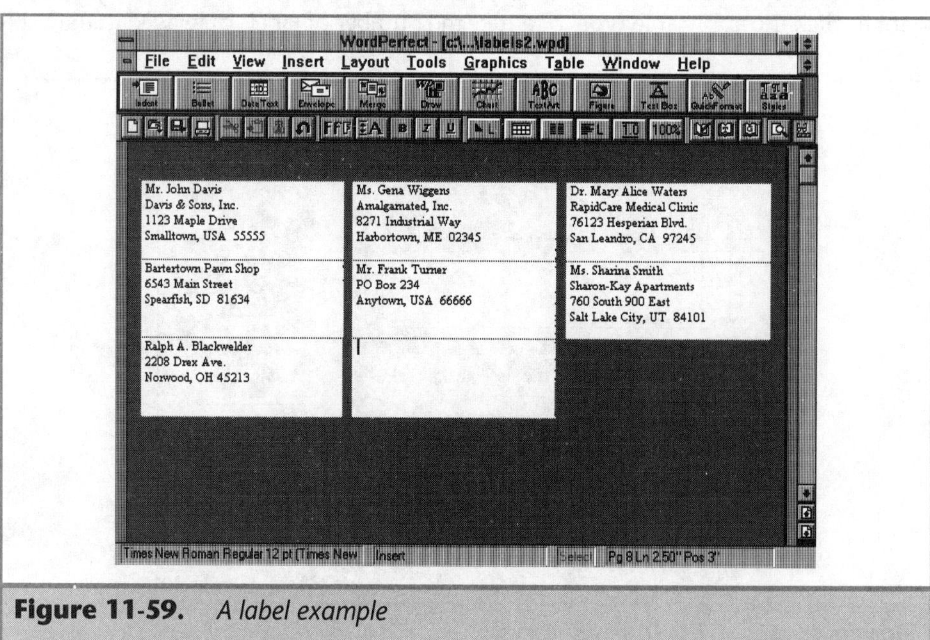

Figure 11-59. *A label example*

Creating New Label Styles

If after looking through WordPerfect's predefined labels you cannot find the exact label style you want, you can create your own label style. To create a new label style, click Create from the Labels dialog box. This accesses the Create Labels dialog box.

In the Label Description text box, type a name that helps you identify the label, usually the brand and stock number. The Label Sheet Size indicates the paper width and length. Leave this set to 8.5 by 11, because most labels, whether laser or tractor feed, break at 11 inches. However, if you do want to change the paper size, click Change and choose the desired sheet size.

Specify the parameters of the label in the corresponding sections of the dialog box. Often this information is printed on the label container. If it isn't, measure the label with a ruler to obtain the measurements. For guidelines on what the settings should be, view some different label definitions by choosing Edit from the Labels dialog box.

Categorize the new label style as Laser, Tractor-fed, or Both by selecting the appropriate type in the Label Type section.

As you specify the various label parameters, observe the changes to the sample label sheet in the example window. Once you are satisfied with the new label style, click OK. The new style is now listed as a predefined label in the Labels dialog box. You can now choose this label style by clicking it and choosing Select.

Printing Labels

When you create text for labels, you first select the label style for the document. This determines where the text is to be positioned on the page and how the labels will be printed.

Print labels as you would an ordinary document: load the document that contains the labels, select File/Print, and click Print.

Landscape Printing

Typically, a document is printed across the width of the paper. This is called *portrait printing. Landscape printing* is often referred to as "sideways printing," because documents are printed horizontally across the length of the paper. Portrait and landscape orientation are illustrated in Figure 11-60.

Menu Selections

To specify landscape printing, select Layout/Page/Paper Size. The Paper Size dialog box displays a list of currently defined paper sizes for the selected printer.

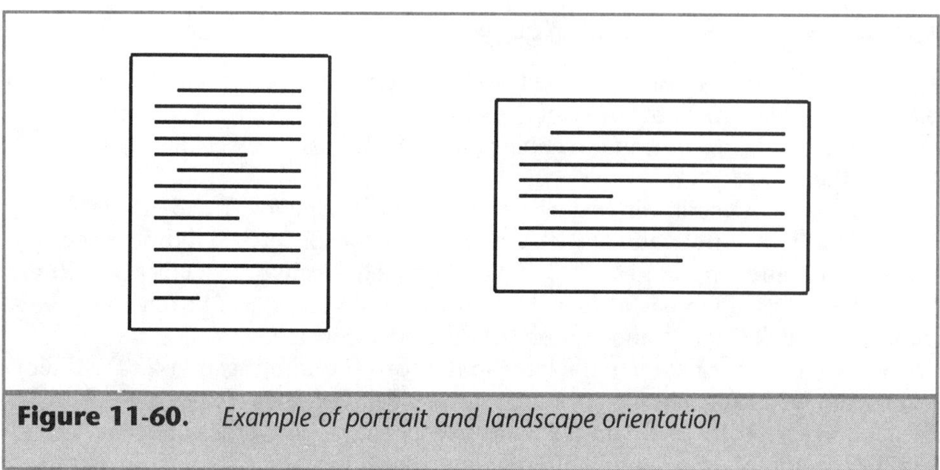

Figure 11-60. *Example of portrait and landscape orientation*

Information on each paper definition is shown in the Information section. You can see an example of the page layout and font direction in the Orientation section.

To choose a paper definition, click one from the list and choose the Select button to make it the active paper type. If you do not find the selection you want, you can design your own paper definition. Select the Create button to display the Create Paper Size dialog box, shown in Figure 11-61.

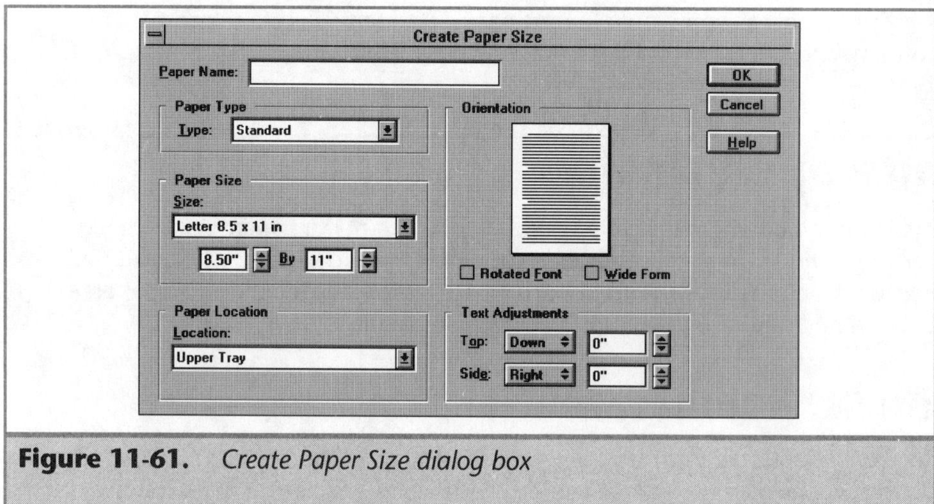

Figure 11-61. *Create Paper Size dialog box*

From this dialog box, define the paper size to suit your needs. In the Paper Name text box, type an appropriate name for the paper. If your paper type is not Standard, choose another kind by clicking the down arrow in the Type text box. If the paper size is not standard 8.5" by 11", click the down arrow to the right of the Size text box and choose the size you want.

You can tell WordPerfect to load paper from different locations, depending on the printer you have selected. For example, to manually feed this paper, select Manual Feed from the Location pull-down list.

You can print the text left to right (the default), rotate the text 90 degrees on the page, or print on wide form paper (commonly termed "wide bar" paper, measuring 8.5" by 14 7/8").

To fine-tune the location where your printing will begin on the paper, make the necessary modifications in the Text Adjustments area. Click OK when finished.

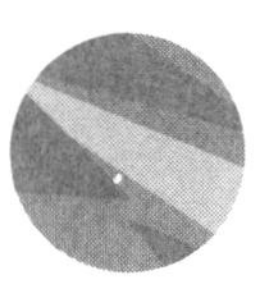

NOTE: If your currently selected printer does not support rotated fonts, the Rotate fonts box as well as the Landscape printer icon will be dimmed (not available). To enable these options, you must select the appropriate printer driver. In addition, if you need to include multiple paper types and sizes in the same document, you must select a WordPerfect printer driver, because Windows printer drivers support only one size or type per document.

Related Entries

Labels
Printer, Selecting

Language

WordPerfect can customize such features as the Speller, the Thesaurus, sorting, and displaying dates to the language of your text. For example, if you include a Spanish word or phrase in your text, WordPerfect can check it against a Spanish dictionary. The Language command allows you to mark foreign words to indicate their language.

L

Menu Selections

To mark foreign-language text you have already typed, first select the text. Then choose Tools/Language to display the Language dialog box. From the Current Language list box, select the appropriate language. Select OK to return to your document.

If you change languages as you type, follow the preceding instructions to select the language and then type the text. After you type the marked text, you must repeat the Language command to insert a code to return to the default language. To cancel the language mark, delete the code. For example, suppose you type the following text into a document:

"Buenos dias" is a greeting often heard in Mexico City.

Mark the text as Spanish, following the steps listed above. In the Reveal Codes screen, your text will look like this:

"(Lang:ES)Buenos dias(Lang:US)" is a greeting often heard in Mexico City.

Listed in Table 11-3 are those languages supported as of this writing, along with the two-character code for each. Also listed are the WordPerfect features that are available for each language. Check the Tools/Language list box to see any additional languages that may have been added.

Other Languages

The -Other- option in the Current Language list box is for languages not yet supported by WordPerfect dictionaries. If the language is not listed, you can select -Other- and enter a two-character code in the -Other- Language text box. This is a way to mark and reserve words for dictionaries installed later, and you can also use it for technical terms that you do not want spell-checked. When WordPerfect encounters an unrecognized language code, it stops and displays an error message dialog box indicating that there is no dictionary. You can then select the Skip Language button and continue spell-checking.

Layout, Document

These options give you numerous ways to change the format of several document features.

Menu Selections

Use the Layout/Document options to change preliminary document settings. The options are as follows:

Initial Font
Initial Codes Style
Redline Method
Character Mapping

Language	Code	Available Features
Afrikaans	AF	Speller, Keyboard
Catalan	CA	Speller, Hyphenation, Keyboard
Croatian	HR	Speller, Hyphenation, Keyboard
Czech	CZ	Speller, Hyphenation, Keyboard
Danish	DK	All Features
Dutch	NL	All Features
English-Australia	OZ	All Features
English-Canada	CE	All Features
English-U.K.	UK	All Features
English-U.S.	US	Speller, Thesaurus, Hyphenation
Finnish	SU	Speller, Hyphenation, Keyboard
French-Canada	CF	All Features
French-National	FR	All Features
Galician	GA	Speller, Hyphenation, Keyboard
German-National	DE	All Features
German-Switzerland	SD	All Features
Greek	GR	Speller, Hyphenation, Keyboard
Hungarian	MA	Speller, Keyboard
Icelandic	IS	Speller, Keyboard
Italian	IT	All Features
Norwegian	NO	All Features
Polish	PL	Speller, Hyphenation, Keyboard
Portuguese-Brazil	BR	Speller, Hyphenation, Keyboard
Portuguese-Portugal	PO	Speller, Hyphenation, Keyboard
Russian	RU	Speller, Hyphenation, Keyboard
Slovak	SL	Speller, Hyphenation, Keyboard
Slovenian	SO	Speller, Hyphenation, Keyboard
Spanish	ES	All Features
Swedish	SV	All Features
Turkish	TR	Speller, Hyphenation
Ukranian	YK	Speller, Hyphenation, Keyboard

Table 11-3. *Languages supported by WordPerfect*

Related Entries

Initial Codes Style, Document
Initial Font
Printer, Selecting
Redline

Layout, Line

These options allow you to change various format features of lines of text.

Menu Selections

The Layout/Line menu selection contains formatting commands that affect the way lines of text appear on the page. These commands control settings for tabs, line spacing, and centering, as well as special features such as hyphenation and line numbering. The options are as follows:

Tab Set
Height
Spacing
Numbering
Hyphenation
Center
Flush Right
Other Codes

Related Entries

Center Text
Hyphenation
Line Height
Line Numbering
Line Spacing
Special Codes
Tabs, Setting

Layout, Page

The Layout/Page options affect the appearance of each printed page, allowing you to create page breaks, headers, footers, page numbering, and set the paper size. You can, when necessary, suppress current headers, footers, or page numbers for individual pages. In addition, special features such as Widow/Orphan Protection, Block Protect, and Conditional End of Page guard your text against unwanted automatic page breaks. The options are listed here:

Center
Suppress

Delay Codes
Force Page
Keep Text Together
Border/Fill
Numbering
Subdivide Page
Binding
Paper Size

Related Entries

See the "Protect" section in the Block entry
Center Pages
Conditional End of Page
Footers, Creating
Headers, Creating
Page Breaks
Page Numbering
Paper Size
Suppress
Widow/Orphan Protection

Leading

See Line Height.

Letter Spacing

Letter spacing refers to the amount of space WordPerfect inserts between letters. This is a common consideration if you are fully justifying your text. If your printer supports incremental spacing, you can adjust letter spacing to suit your preferences.

For best results, the amount of space between letters is generally based on the size, type, and pitch of the font. WordPerfect offers you three different ways to determine spacing between words. You can choose the spacing considered optimal by your printer manufacturer; you can increase or decrease spacing on your own by entering the desired percentage in the Percent of Optimal box; or you can let WordPerfect determine the increase or decrease based on the *pitch* (characters per inch) of the text.

Menu Selections

First, position the insertion point where you want the letter spacing to begin, or select the text in which you want to adjust letter spacing. Then choose Layout/Typesetting/Word/Letterspacing to display the Word Spacing and Letterspacing dialog box, shown in Figure 11-62.

Normal letter spacing is the spacing considered optimal by your printer manufacturer. The default letter spacing is WordPerfect Optimal, which is determined by WordPerfect, depending on the value you enter in the Set Pitch text box. The pitch currently displayed is always that of the current font. You can increase the spacing between letters by entering a smaller number in the box, or decrease the spacing by entering a larger number (more characters per inch). These two settings result in the same letter spacing. (The settings do differ, however, for word spacing.) These settings save you time and trouble by calculating the appropriate spacing based on current font settings.

Alternatively, you can select Percent of Optimal and either enter a pitch relative to which spacing will be adjusted, or enter a percent of optimal spacing based on the current pitch. For example, if you enter 120%, the amount of space between letters will increase by 20%.

When you have made your selection, select OK to close the window and return to your document. WordPerfect inserts a (Wrd/Ltr Spacing:...) code at that point. To return to the default letter spacing, repeat the preceding steps and select the WordPerfect Optimal option. To cancel the letter spacing, delete the code.

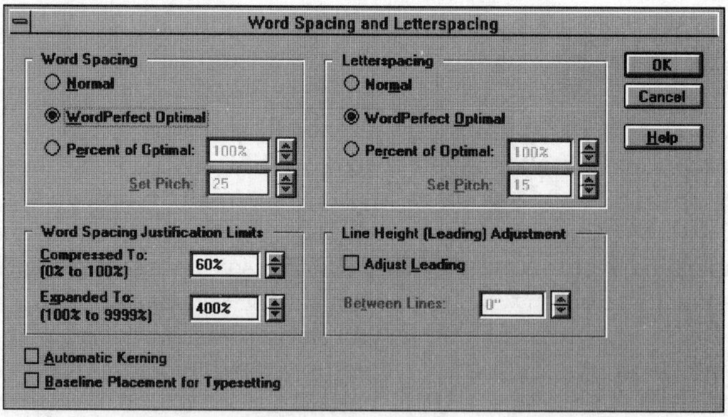

Figure 11-62. *The Word Spacing and Letterspacing dialog box*

Related Entries

Justification
Kerning, Automatic
Kerning, Manual
Word Spacing

Line Height

Line height is the distance between lines of text from baseline to baseline. The *baseline* is an imaginary line on which the bottom of each character rests. *Descenders*, such as those found in *p* and *g*, extend below the baseline. *Leading* (pronounced "ledding") refers to extra spacing between lines.

Line height varies with font types and sizes. Increasing the line height for a font can improve readability. As a general rule, smaller text requires proportionally greater leading than large typefaces, such as those used in headings.

Changing the Line Height

WordPerfect automatically adjusts the line height as you change fonts. However, you can change the line height to suit your own discerning eye. This change affects any subsequent text until the end of the document or until line height is changed again.

To change line height in only a portion of your document, you can first select the text. In this case, WordPerfect enters a code at the end of the selected text that returns the line height to its previous setting.

Menu Selections

Position the insertion point where you want the line height change to begin, or select the text in which you want the change in line height to apply. Select Layout/Line/Height and then select Fixed. Enter a number in the adjacent box. This establishes a fixed line height that will not change even if you select a different font. When you have finished, select OK to return to your document. To discontinue the line height change, repeat the preceding steps and select Auto, or enter another number in the Fixed text box. To cancel the line height adjustment, delete the code in Reveal Codes.

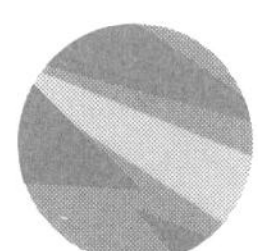

NOTE: *The default unit of measure for distances is inches. However, WordPerfect can be set up to use another unit of measure.*

L

Related Entries

Line Height (Leading) Adjustment
Preferences
Reveal Codes
Units of Measure

Line Height (Leading) Adjustment

One aspect of line height is the amount of extra white space assigned to the soft and hard returns. This extra space, called leading, is in addition to the automatic or fixed line height. Normally, the setting for leading is 0; however, you can change it to suit your needs.

WordPerfect inserts the (Leading Adj: *x*") code at the beginning of the current paragraph, and text is affected until the end of the document or until the line height is changed.

To adjust leading in only a portion of your document, first select the text to which you want the adjustment to apply. In this case, WordPerfect enters a code at the end of the selected text that returns the adjustment to its previous setting.

Menu Selections

First, position the insertion point in your text where you want the adjustment to begin, or select the text you want to adjust. Then choose the commands Layout/Typesetting/Word/Letterspacing. Click Adjust Leading and enter the appropriate number in the Between Lines text box. When you are finished, select OK to return to your document. To discontinue the line height adjustment, repeat the preceding steps and enter 0 or a new number in the Between Lines box. To cancel the line height change, delete the code in Reveal Codes.

NOTE: The default unit of measurement for distances is inches. However, WordPerfect can be set up to use another unit of measure.

Related Entries

Preferences
Reveal Codes
Units of Measure

Line Numbering

Use the Line Numbering feature when you want to print line numbers in the left margin of your document. This feature is most frequently used in legal documents. However, line numbering is also helpful when you are editing lengthy documents, because it allows you to refer to a line by its number rather than search for a text reference or paragraph position. You can number an entire document or just selected text.

You can specify the numbering method, the starting line number, the first printing line number, the numbering interval, the numbering position, and other related options. WordPerfect inserts a (Ln Num: On) code at the point where line numbering begins. Line numbering continues to the end of the document or until WordPerfect encounters a (Ln Num: Off) code. If you line-number selected text, WordPerfect automatically inserts a (Ln Num: Off) code at the end of the text. Once you apply line numbering, it remains visible in your document in any viewing mode.

Menu Selections

To print line numbers, position the insertion point where you want line numbering to begin, or select the text that you want numbered. Choose Layout/Line/Numbering. The dialog box shown in Figure 11-63 will appear.

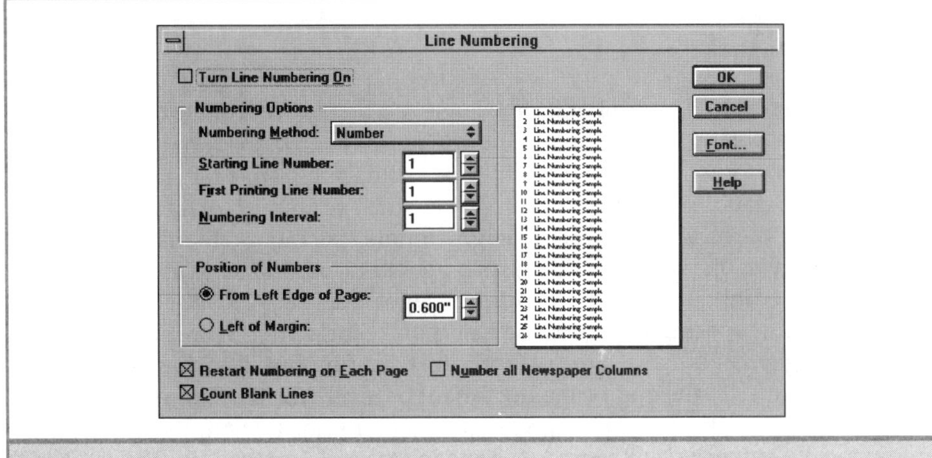

Figure 11-63. *The Line Numbering dialog box*

L

From the Line Numbering dialog box, click the Numbering Method option button and select a numbering method: Number, Lowercase Letter, Uppercase Letter, Lowercase Roman, or Uppercase Roman numerals.

You can choose a different Starting Line Number, First Printing Line Number, and Numbering Interval by clicking their respective up and down arrows. For example, if you want to number lines in increments of five, set both First Printing Line Number and Numbering Interval to 5. Notice how the example displays lines numbered by fives.

Generally, line numbers appear in the left margin of each page. You can position the line number either From Left Edge of Page or Left of Margin by clicking the appropriate button and entering a number in the Position of Numbers text box.

You can select the Restart Numbering on Each Page so that each page starts at the beginning of the numbering sequence. You can instruct WordPerfect not to number blank lines if you remove the check mark in the Count Blank Lines box.

If you enable Number all Newspaper Columns, WordPerfect will place numbers in each column, rather than just on the left margin.

WordPerfect maintains line numbering attributes independent of text attributes, thus allowing you to set a different font for line numbers. To do so, click Font to invoke the Line Numbering Font dialog box and make the desired font changes.

In order for the line numbering options to take effect, you must click Turn Line Numbering On. Select OK to return to your document.

To discontinue line numbering at any point, choose Layout/Line/Numbering and remove the X from Turn Line Numbering On. To remove the line numbering altogether, delete the line numbering code.

Line Spacing

Line spacing refers to the number of lines inserted after a soft or hard return. It is used to control the number of blank lines between lines of text. Line spacing often determines the number of text lines per inch: single spacing is usually six lines per inch; double spacing is usually three lines per inch. However, this varies depending on the font type and line height. Single spacing (no blank lines) is the default; however, one-and-a-half line spacing and double spacing are commonly used to make editing of hard copy (printed pages) easier.

The new line spacing begins at the insertion point, where WordPerfect inserts a (Ln Spacing: *x.xx*) code, where *x.xx* is the spacing amount in inches. This spacing continues to the end of the document or until WordPerfect encounters another spacing code. If you change the spacing for selected text, WordPerfect automatically enters a (Ln Spacing: *x.xx*) code at the end of the text that returns the line spacing to its previous setting.

Menu Selections

To change line spacing, position the insertion point where you want the change to begin, or select the text you want to change. Choose Layout/Line/Spacing. Enter a number that represents the number of lines inserted. The default is 1 line; 1.5 means an additional half line between lines, and so on. When you have entered a number, select OK to return to your document. To discontinue the line spacing, repeat the preceding steps and select the new number of lines or enter 1 to return to the default spacing. To cancel the line spacing selection, delete the code in Reveal Codes.

You need not increase or decrease line spacing in half-line increments. Suppose, for example, you type a letter that is just long enough to move your signature lines to page 2. You can move the insertion point to the very beginning of the document and set the line spacing to 0.9. This reduces the space between lines by ten percent, not a visually noticeable amount, but it is often enough so that your document will fit on one page.

Related Entries

Fonts
Line Height

Lines

See Horizontal Lines *or* the "Vertical Lines" section in the Graphics Lines entry.

Linking

A *link* is a connection between your WordPerfect document and a file from another program. When you create a link, you actually copy the source file into your target document as you create the connection. Then, because your document is permanently linked to this external file, any changes you make to that file will also be updated in your WordPerfect document.

In Windows applications, this type of link between documents is called Object Linking and Embedding (OLE). Although there is no OLE command as such in WordPerfect, it does link files in some programs automatically. For instance, if you create a drawing in WP Draw, that file is linked between two separate programs: WordPerfect and WP Draw.

Related Entries

See Chapter 9, "Spreadsheet and Database Files."

List Boxes

A *list box* is a type of control found in a dialog box. A list box displays a list of choices, such as filenames in the Open File dialog box, as shown in Figure 11-64. You can make only one selection from a list box. A list box is often accompanied by a text box into which you can type your selection instead of selecting from the list.

Some list boxes are the pull-down type; they normally display only the option that is currently selected. They are very much like the menus at the top of the screen, except that they display their set of options only as long as you are holding down a mouse button.

For example, when you first go to the Layout/Line/Numbering dialog box, the Numbering Method is listed as Number, the current selection. If you choose Numbering Method by pointing at it with the mouse and clicking and holding down the left mouse button, you will see a list of additional options, shown in Figure 11-65. To make another selection with the mouse, you must continue holding down the left button and drag the highlight to your choice, for example, to Uppercase Letter. As soon as you release the button, the pull-down list closes, and your new selection becomes active and appears on the list box.

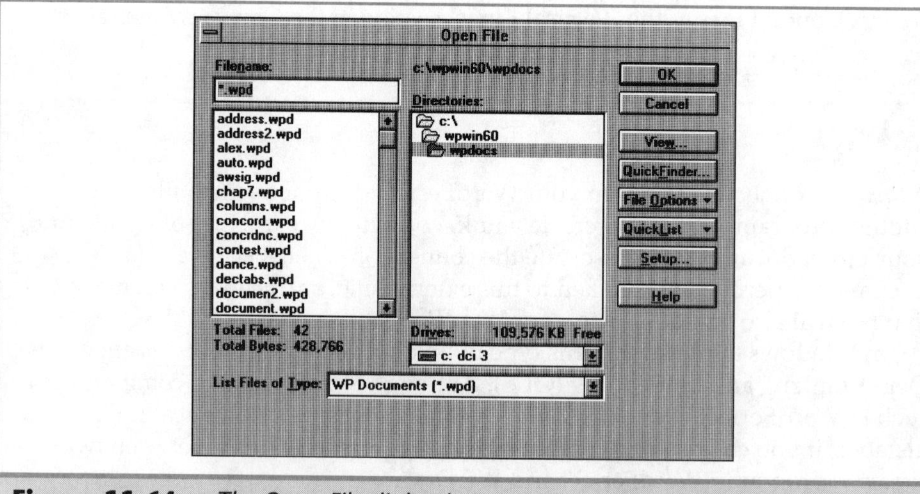

Figure 11-64. *The Open File dialog box*

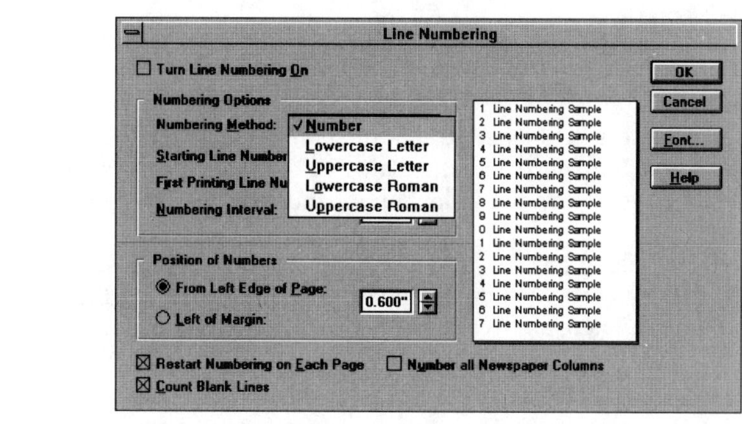

Figure 11-65. *The Line Numbering dialog box showing additional numbering methods*

Related Entries

Dialog Boxes
Text Boxes

Lists

In WordPerfect, a *list* is a reference, similar to a table of contents, that you can use to keep track of topics, tables, charts, figures, and so on. A list can include page number references, but unlike a table of contents, a list can have only one level (no subheadings). You can maintain as many separate text lists as you want for text, figure, table, equation, and user boxes.

Creating a list requires three distinct steps:

1. Specify the list type, its numbering format and style, and its location.
2. Specify the words and phrases that you want to include in the list by marking the text in the document.
3. Generate the list.

Menu Selections

Defining a List Type

Select Tools/List to access the List editor feature bar. Click Define to access the Define List dialog box. If no entries in the dialog box exist or meet your needs, click Create to design your own list style. You must do this if you have not created a list before.

In the Create List dialog box, as shown in Figure 11-66, type a descriptive name in the List box. Select a position for the numbering format by clicking the Position option button. There are five possible numbering options for lists.

Numbering Format

NO NUMBERING This option simply lists all marked entries in the document with no page numbers.

TEXT # This option lists entries with page numbers following each entry.

TEXT (#) This option lists entries with page numbers in parentheses following each entry.

TEXT # This option puts index entries on the left edge of the page and page numbers right justified on the right margin.

TEXT .....# This option puts index entries on the left edge of the page and page numbers right justified on the right margin. The pages are preceded by dot leaders.

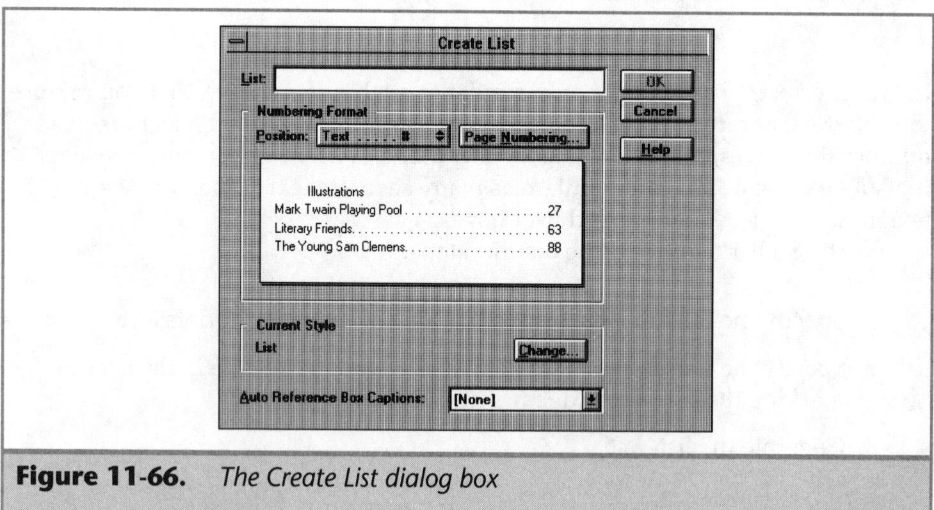

Figure 11-66. *The Create List dialog box*

You can change the list style by clicking Change and choosing from the styles list. If you want the list to automatically generate a caption list, select the box style from Auto Reference Box Caption. Repeat the preceding steps for each additional list you want. Click OK when you are finished. Click Close to return to the List editor feature bar.

Defining the List Location

After you have marked the text for your lists, you must tell WordPerfect where you want each list located. First, position the insertion point wherever you want your list to be located, usually at the end of the document. If you want the list to begin on a separate page, press CTRL+ENTER to create a page break.

Click Define. Your list or lists are displayed in the Define List dialog box, from which you can highlight the desired list, as shown in Figure 11-67.

Click Insert to place the list in your document at the current cursor location. You are returned to the List editor feature bar where you can, if you have more lists to place, move your cursor, create a page break, and repeat the preceding steps.

Marking Text in the Document

Each text item or graphic box you want to include in the list must be marked. You can mark them in any order you want, because they will be sorted and listed in the order in which they appear in the document when you generate the list. After you mark the text or graphic box, WordPerfect inserts the code

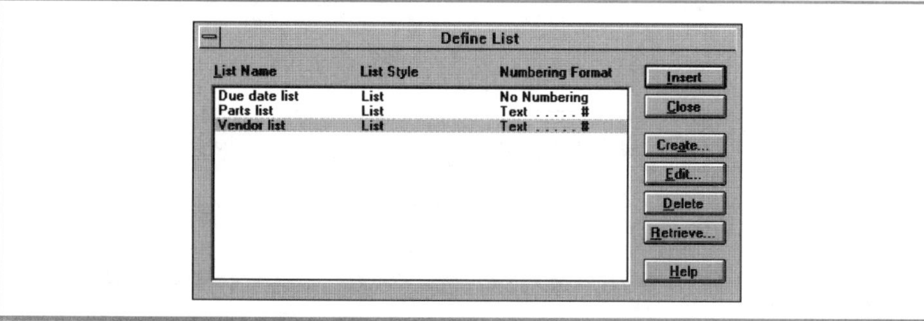

Figure 11-67. *The Define List dialog box*

L

(Mrk Txt List: *name*) on either side of the marked item, where *name* is the name of the list to which the object belongs.

To mark an item for a list, select the text or graphic box, select the list name from the pull-down list, and click Mark from the feature bar in the List editor feature bar as shown in Figure 11-68.

If you are creating only one list of text entries, you do not need to select the list name, because only one exists. However, if you are creating several different lists—for example, one list for figures and another for tables—you must select the list for which you want to mark the entry. To do so, pull down the list options by clicking to the right of the text box. You then see the list options you created previously in the Create List dialog box.

For the example just given, you might assign "Figs" to your figures and "Tables" to your tables. Select the appropriate list name from the options displayed. WordPerfect inserts a [Mark:List,#] code at the beginning and an [End Mark:List,#] code at the end of the selected text. To cancel a list selection, delete the code.

Generating the Lists

After you have marked your text and boxes and defined each list, you are ready to generate the lists. Whenever you mark new text or boxes or make revisions that may cause the page references to change, you need to generate a new list.

To generate the list, click Generate from the feature bar or select Tools/Generate.

Related Entries

Concordance Files
Generate
Index
Sort

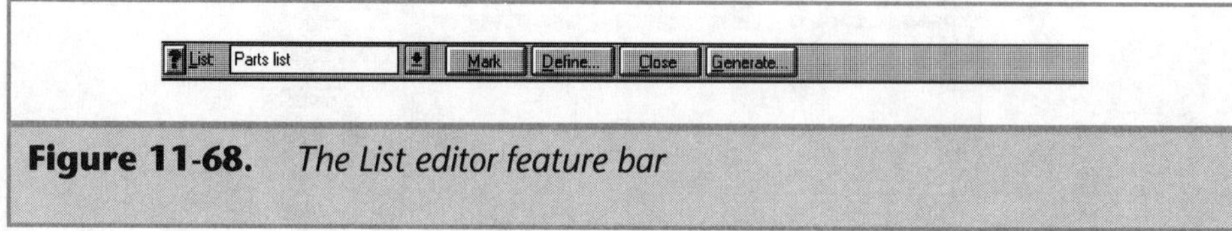

Figure 11-68. *The List editor feature bar*

Location of Files

WordPerfect maintains and creates many types of files, including backup, document, template, database, graphic, printer, label, macro, spreadsheet, and hyphenation files. When you install WordPerfect, it establishes default directories for each of these file types. You can change these default directories at any time.

Menu Selections

To change the location of WordPerfect files, choose File/Preferences/File. The File Preferences dialog box, shown in Figure 11-69, displays the different types of files WordPerfect maintains, each selection having its own directory location.

To change a directory location, select the file type and enter the new directory path in the lower section. If you enter a path that does not exist, WordPerfect displays a dialog box asking if you want to create the directory. Select Yes to create the directory; select No or press ESC to cancel and enter another directory path. If you want your QuickLists updated for speedy reference, check the Update QuickList with Changes box. Select OK when you are finished.

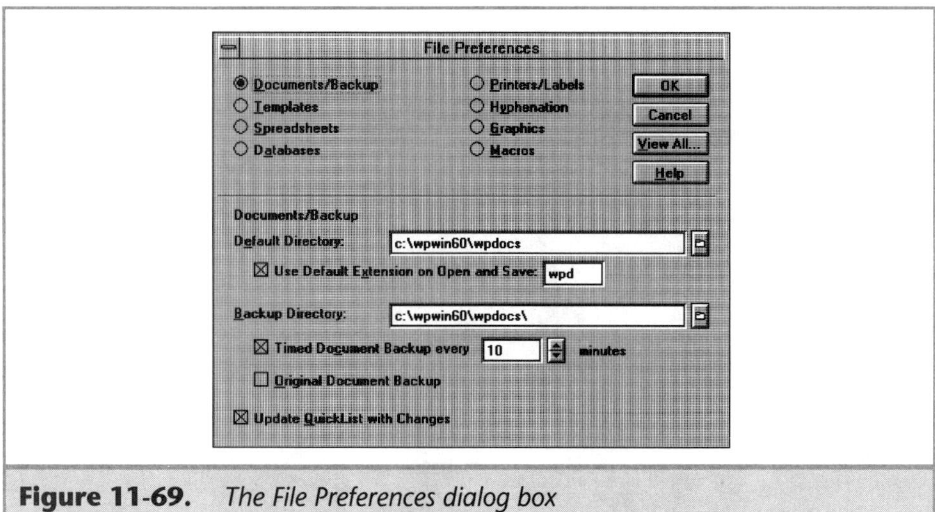

Figure 11-69. *The File Preferences dialog box*

L

Related Entries

QuickList

Lock Documents

WordPerfect allows you to lock your documents (password protect them) so that only you can access the document contents. Only those with knowledge of your password will be able to open, print, or view a protected file.

Menu Selections

Enter or load the document you want to protect. Then choose File/Save As from the menus. You will see the Save As dialog box, shown in Figure 11-70.

Select the Password Protect checkbox in the lower-right corner of the dialog box. When you save the file, you are asked for the password to be used with this document. Because a password is private, only asterisks appear where you type characters. After you press ENTER or select OK, you are asked to type the password again to verify the first entry. To finish saving the protected file, press ENTER or select OK again.

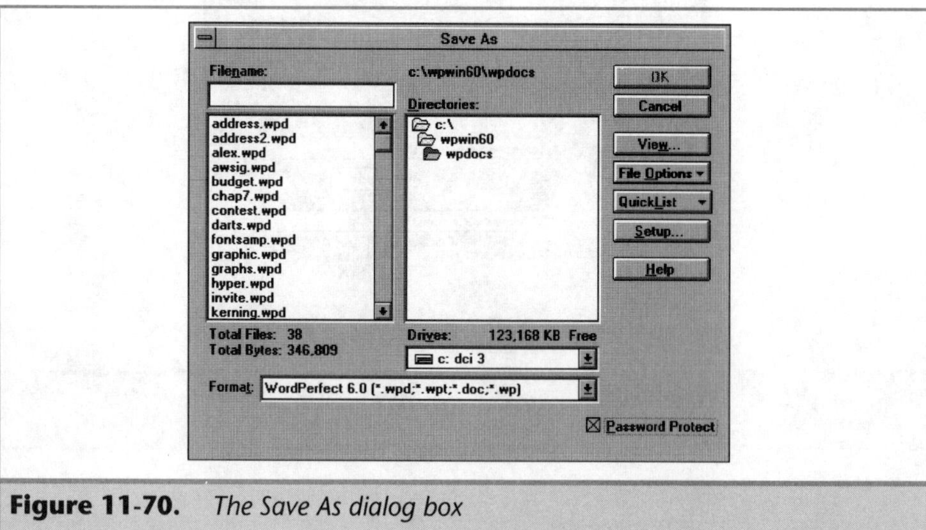

Figure 11-70. *The Save As dialog box*

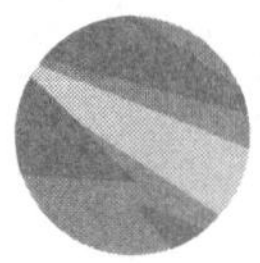

NOTE: Do not forget your password. WordPerfect will not allow access to a password protected file without the password.

Lotus 1-2-3

See Chapter 9, "Spreadsheet and Database Files."

Lowercase Text

Generally, text appears in lowercase as you type unless you press the CAPS LOCK or SHIFT key. However, you can convert case typed in uppercase to lowercase without retyping.

Menu Selections

To convert text to lowercase, first select the text. Then choose Edit/Convert Case/Lowercase. WordPerfect converts all characters to lowercase, except for the pronoun "I" and any word beginning with a capital *I* and followed by an apostrophe, like "I'm" or "I'd." WordPerfect also leaves the first letter of a sentence capitalized, provided the punctuation from the end of the preceding sentence is included in the block selected to be converted.

Related Entries

Convert Case
Uppercase Text

Macros

Macros are files that contain keystrokes or commands, or a combination of both, that can be played back on your screen. Macros are especially useful whenever you find yourself performing the same tasks over and over. In this type of situation, you can record your keystrokes into a macro and then have the macro replay the keystrokes, saving you both time and effort.

At a relatively simple level, you can create a macro that types the text you regularly use when you close business letters. At a more complex level, you can create macros that automatically generate invoices from order forms.

Menu Selections

To create a document closing (signature block) macro, you must type your standard letter closing into a document, while having WordPerfect record your keystrokes. The document into which you type the text could be a real letter—one which you would save on disk. Or instead, you could open a new, blank document, type and record the keystrokes there, then close the document without saving it. Either yields the same results.

Recording a Macro

Choose Tools/Macro/Record, or press the shortcut key CTRL+F10. The Record Macro dialog box, shown in Figure 11-71, appears on your screen. Type a descriptive name up to 31 characters long in the Name text box, such as *Darrel's Signature Block.* Now click the Record button. Note that the status bar displays the message "Macro Record" and the cursor turns into a "no go" sign (a circle with a line through it), which means you should not move the insertion point to another location in the document. It is important that you keep your movements sequential within the macro. If you move the cursor back to information you already typed, the macro will still perform the exact same keystrokes. This could be disastrous if you inadvertently create a macro that overwrites a portion of your document. All of your keystrokes and menu selections (even with the mouse) will now be recorded into the macro.

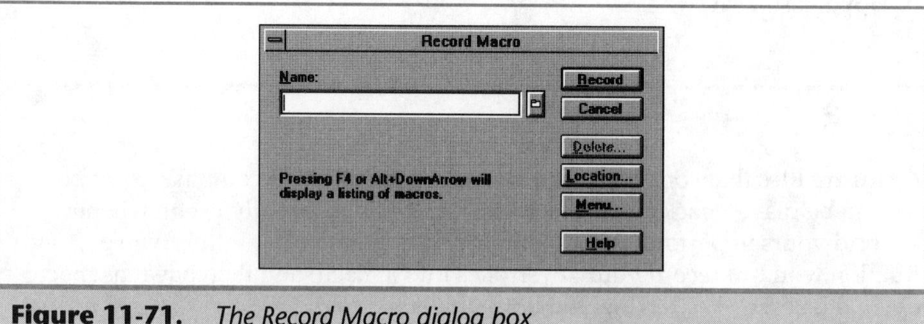

Figure 11-71. *The Record Macro dialog box*

In a signature block you might type something like this:

Sincerely,

Darrel Douglass, Treasurer
Widgets Conglomerated

When you are finished typing the text, choose Tools/ Macro/Record and WordPerfect stops recording keystrokes into the macro.

NOTE: *When creating and editing macros, it may be quicker to utilize the Macros button bar. The buttons are similar to the buttons found on a tape recorder in that you can click a single button to start and stop play, record, and so forth.*

Playing a Macro

To play back a macro, place the insertion point where you want the keystrokes to appear. Choose Tools/Macro/Play or press the shortcut key ALT+F10 and find the macro name under the Files option. Highlight the macro name and click Play to replay the macro keystrokes on your screen.

Related Entries

See Chapter 8, "Applications for Macros."

Macros, Assigning to Menu

An easy way to access macros that you use frequently is to assign them to the Macro menu. Then, whenever you want to use the macro, just choose Tools/Macro menu and choose the macro you want from the list at the bottom of the menu.

Menu Selections

To assign a macro to the macro menu, choose Tools/Macro/Edit and click Menu from the Edit Macro dialog box. The Assign Macro to Menu dialog box appears:

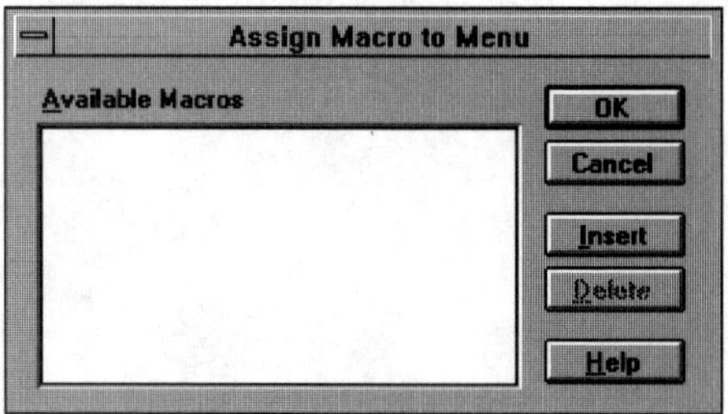

Click Insert and highlight a macro to place on the menu. Choose Select and the macro name is placed in the Available Macros list, which indicates that it will now appear on the macro menu. Click OK.

Related Entries

Macros

Magnification

See Zooming.

Mailing Labels

See Labels.

Margin Release

See Back Tab.

Margins

Your document margins control how much white space is left around the borders of the page—the larger the margins, the more white space. WordPerfect sets one inch margin on the left, right, top, and bottom of the page as the default.

Margins can be changed at any time, and you can even have multiple margin settings on one page. As you set a margin, it will remain in effect until the end of the document or until you change them again.

To permanently set the margins, you must define them by using the option Layout/Document/Initial Codes Style.

Menu Selections

To change the default settings of your margins, choose Layout/Margins. The Margins dialog box appears, as shown in Figure 11-72.

Adjust your margins to the desired settings. You can see an example of the margins in the page sample in the dialog box. Click OK to accept the new margins and return to the document.

Related Entries

Initial Codes Style, Document

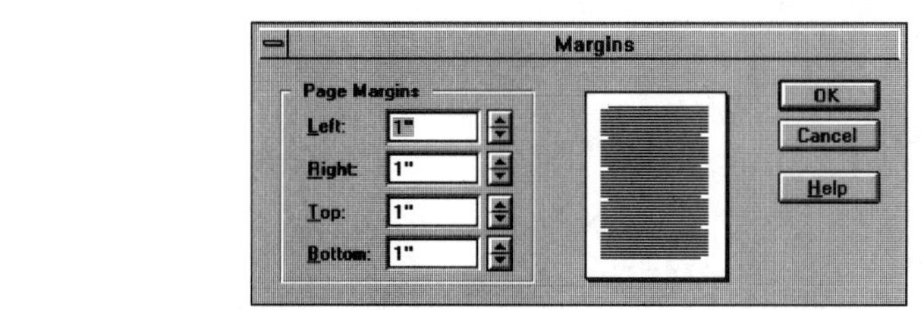

Figure 11-72. *The Margins dialog box*

Mark Text

In order to place text items into WordPerfect-generated lists, the text must first be marked. Text is marked in the same way for a list, index, and table of authorities. However, certain steps precede marking text depending on the type of list, index, or whatever, that you want to generate.

For example, headings must be created for an index and list names must be defined for a list before text can be marked.

Related Entries

Concordance Files
Cross-Reference
Index
Lists
Table of Authorities
Table of Contents

Master Documents

Master documents allow you to create links from a master document file to any number of subdocument files. An example of this would be a computer manual. The master document file would include the title page, table of contents, and any introductory materials, but each lesson in the book would be contained in its own subdocument file. You could now work on each lesson separately (because each lesson occupies its own file) and then pull the whole manual together when you are finished with all the lessons by expanding the master document. Once you have done so, you can generate an index, table of contents, and so on, for the one master document.

Menu Selections

To create a master document, create the document as you normally would, up to the point where you want to tie in a subdocument. Position the insertion point where the subdocument should be and choose File/Master Document/Subdocument. The Include subdocument dialog box will display a list of documents that you can include as a subdocument. Select a filename from the list and click Include. This inserts a small icon in the margin of the master document representing a subdocument of the master. To view the subdocument's name, click the icon in the margin: this displays the full path and filename of the subdocument, as shown in Figure 11-73.

Expanding a Subdocument

When all the files are linked to the master document, you can expand the master to see or print the document in its entirety. To do this, double-click a subdocument icon or choose File/Master Document/Expand Master, then choose OK from the Expand Master Document dialog box. If you have many subdocuments, you can select only those you wish to expand at this time by clicking the individual document names or by using the Mark button to mark the subdocuments.

When a subdocument is expanded within a master document, icons remain in the margin to indicate where the subdocument begins and ends.

Condensing a Subdocument

Expanding a subdocument actually inserts it into the master document in its entirety, but you can condense or return the expanded subdocument to an icon after you are finished viewing, printing, or saving the master document.

To condense some or all of the subdocuments in a master document, double-click a subdocument icon in the margin or choose File/Master Document/Condense Master. The Condense/Save Subdocuments dialog box appears, as shown in Figure 11-74. Notice that the subdocuments listed in the dialog box are shown twice. One is labelled "condense" and the other is labelled

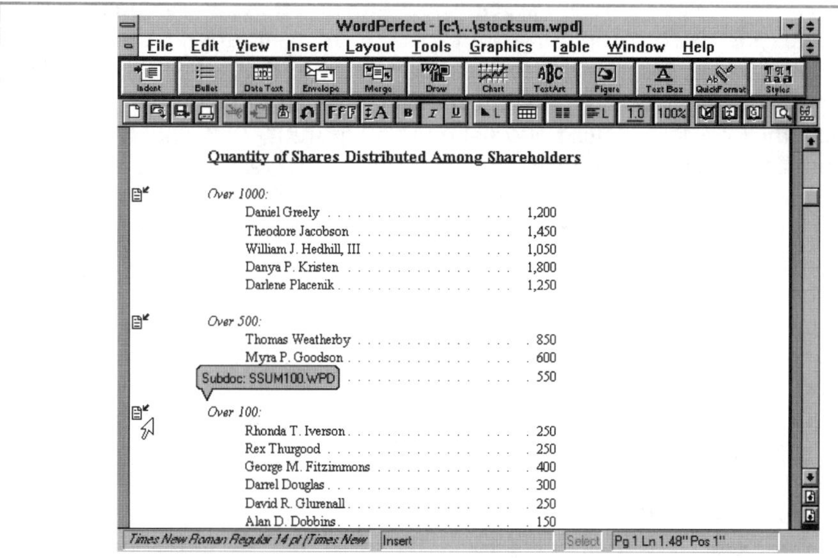

Figure 11-73. *An example of a subdocument in a master document*

M

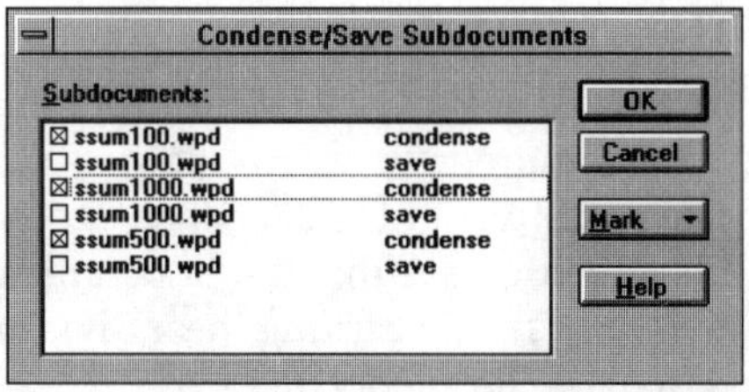

Figure 11-74. *The Condense/Save Subdocuments dialog box*

"save." The purpose for this is to allow you to condense and/or save any of the subdocuments listed. The Save feature is convenient for saving any changes you made in the subdocuments while they were expanded. Select the subdocuments you want to condense and/or save and click OK.

Math

WordPerfect contains its own mini-spreadsheet function that allows you to create basic formulas, just as you would in a standard spreadsheet program. Because all math is done in tables, creating the spreadsheet is easy and fast. For an example of a standard spreadsheet created in WordPerfect, see Figure 11-75.

To create the Quarterly Sales Report shown in Figure 11-75, you first need to center your headings for the report on the page and then create a table below them that is four columns by five rows. To do this, select Table/Create and specify the number of columns and rows in the Create Table dialog box.

Tables are divided into cells that have both a letter column reference and a numerical row reference. The first column is column A, the next column B, the next column C, and so on. The top row is row 1, the next row 2, the next row 3, and so on. Therefore, the cell that is created at the intersection of a column and a row has both a letter and a numerical reference. For example, the upper-left cell of a table (the intersection of column A and row 1) is designated as cell A1. Figure 11-76 shows the column/row designations for the cells in Figure 11-75.

Numbers are usually right aligned in cells. Since the default setting for WordPerfect's tables is left alignment, you need to right justify the cells containing numbers. Occasionally the text at the top of the columns containing numbers is also right aligned, as in the headings January, February, and March in Figure 11-76.

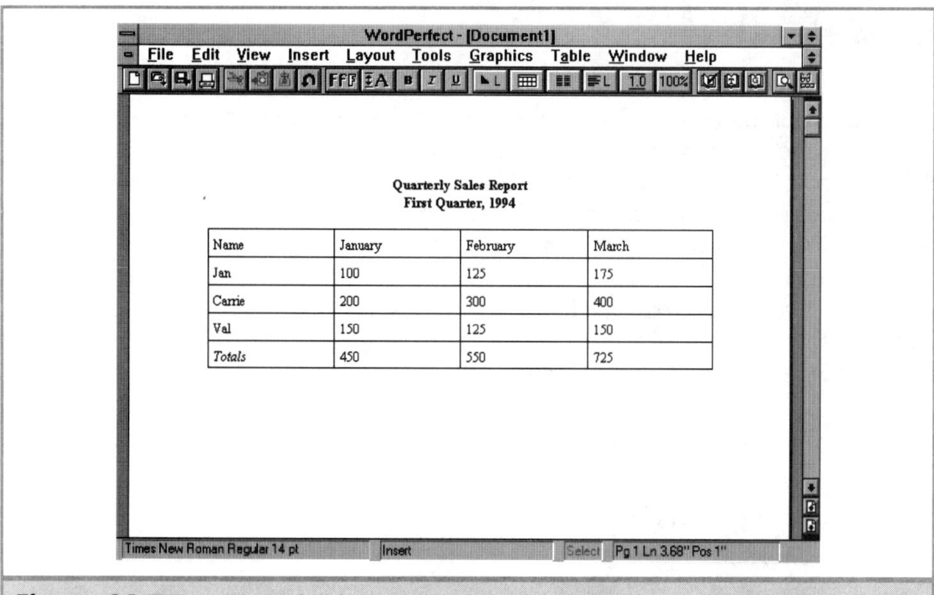

Figure 11-75. *Example of a WordPerfect spreadsheet*

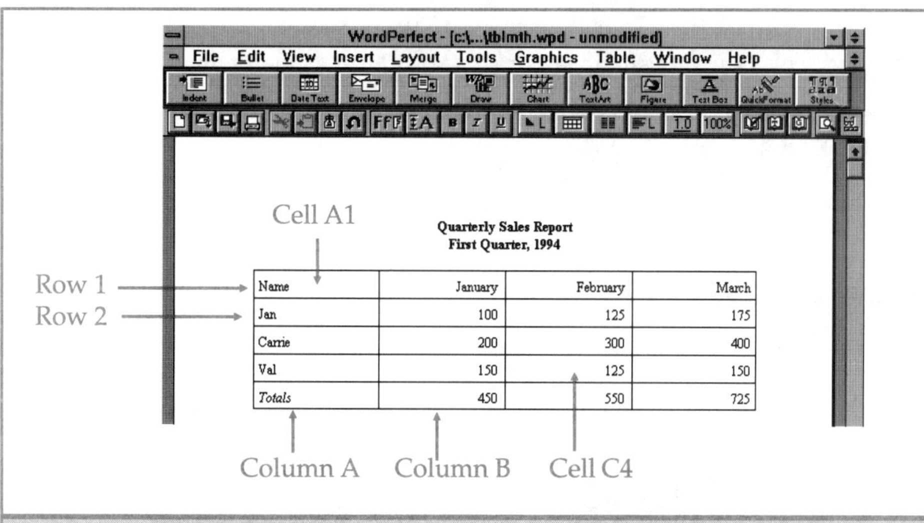

Figure 11-76. *Column and row designations in a table*

Menu Selections

To right justify your numbers and their column headings, select the cells with your mouse (in this case, cells B1 through D5). Choose Table/Format and click the Justification option button in the Alignment section of the Format dialog box. Select Decimal Align and click OK. This aligns the decimals in your numbers, but the decimals are not a fixed length. To remedy this, select Table/Number Type and click Commas from the Number Type dialog box.

You are now ready to type the information for each cell. In the example, you would fill in all the cells except B6 through D6, where the formulas for the totals will be placed.

Keep in mind that the basic mathematical operators are:

+	Addition
–	Subtraction
*	Multiplication
/	Division

Some simple formulas using cell references might look like this:

A2+A3
B5–B6
(C7*C8)/(D7*D8)
D3/D2

Many spreadsheets, including this one in WordPerfect, have a SUM command. This is an automatic feature of WordPerfect when you type a formula in the cell (or use the Sum button from the formula bar) like this:

SUM(B2:B5)

The colon between the cell references means "through" as in "Sum of cell B2 through B5."

Using the Formula Bar

The formula bar lets you enter formulas and perform calculations on cells in the spreadsheet. Choose Table/Formula Bar or right-click with the mouse and select Formula from the shortcut menu to display the formula bar, shown here:

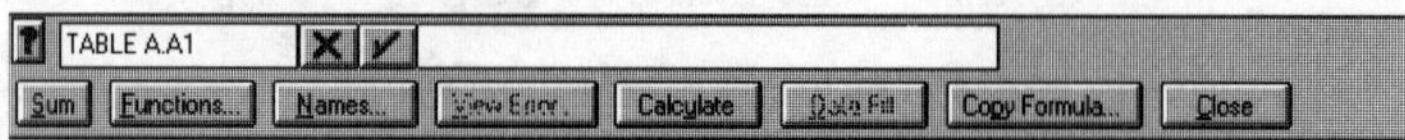

To add the cells in a column, position the cursor where you want the formula to be placed. In the current example, place your cursor in cell B6. Click the formula box (to the right of the green check mark) and type in a formula such as B2+B3+B4+B5. Click OK, and the correct answer to the formula appears in the cell. You can enter any formula in this manner. However, WordPerfect provides several tools that help you enter formulas and data more quickly.

SUM If you need to sum a column or row of numbers, you can position your cursor in the cell where you want to put the formula and choose Table/Sum, press CTRL+=, or click Sum in the formula bar to let WordPerfect generate the formula and add the numbers for you. In this example, place your cursor in cell B6 and click Sum. The formula SUM(B2:B5) is placed in the formula box. Click Calculate to place the result in cell B6.

NOTE: By default, WordPerfect automatically updates the contents of a cell that contains a formula. To disable this feature and permit manual recalculation, select Table/Calculate and click the radio button to the left of Calculate Table. Choose OK to save the setting.

FUNCTIONS A *function* is a predefined formula that performs calculations on values that you specify. WordPerfect lets you insert any function into your spreadsheet from the Table Functions dialog box, shown in Figure 11-77. To insert a function, first position your cursor in the desired cell and click Functions in the formula bar. In the dialog box, choose a function and click Insert to utilize that function. Type or select the parameters of the function and press ENTER.

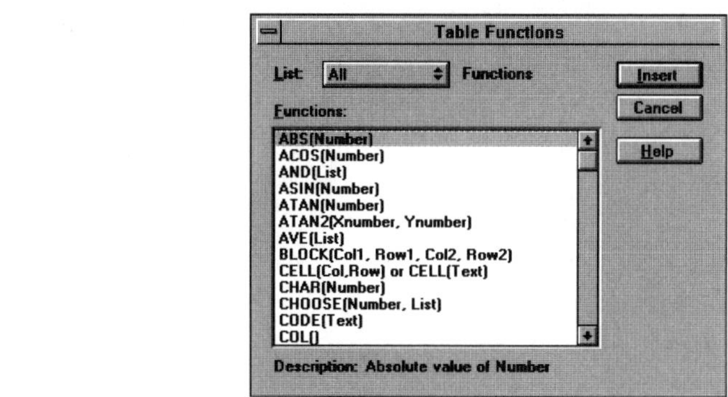

Figure 11-77. *The Table Functions dialog box*

For example, suppose you want to find the average of several numbers. Place your cursor in the cell that will contain the function and click Functions in the formula bar. Highlight the *average* function AVE(List) and click Insert. This places the function in the formula box, where you can specify the cell range you want to average. To specify the cells, you can select the cells with your mouse or type the cell range in the formula bar. After specifying the cell range, the function in the formula bar should display AVE(B2:D2). Press ENTER or click the green check mark to accept the formula and enter it in the current cell.

VIEW ERROR This button is only available when you apply a function improperly. Clicking View Error displays the error message that explains why the function will not work. After you correct the incorrect function, the button dims and is unavailable.

CALCULATE If automatic calculation mode is turned off, you must manually calculate any formulas you have entered in your spreadsheet. To do this, click Calculate after changing numbers or adding formulas to your spreadsheet. This action calculates all tables (spreadsheets) in your document.

DATA FILL To quickly fill the cells in your spreadsheet with the contents of a single cell, you can use the Data Fill button. To fill a range of cells, highlight the range with the upper-left cell being the reference cell. Click Data Fill and the numbers will copy to all the highlighted cells in the spreadsheet.

COPY FORMULA Rather than entering the same formula multiple times, you can quickly copy a formula. To copy a formula to adjoining cells, position the cursor in the cell where the formula is currently located, choose Table/Copy Formula or click Copy Formula in the formula bar. This accesses the Copy Formula dialog box. The cell you are copying from is already identified as the source. You must specify the destination cell in the To Cell box or, if you are copying a formula to multiple cells, click Down or Right and specify the number of times to copy in that direction. Click OK to copy the formula.

Related Entries

Tables, Creating

Memory

WordPerfect requires a minimum of two megabytes of RAM (random access memory), but it runs most efficiently on four or more megabytes of RAM. Also, the speed of the RAM (often 80 nanoseconds or faster) affects the speed of WordPerfect and other programs. As a general rule, the faster the RAM, the faster WordPerfect runs.

If you are running low on RAM, you may want to limit the number of programs and documents that are in memory at the same time. Graphic images also take up a large amount of printer RAM (distinct from your computer's RAM) and may not print if your printer doesn't have enough RAM in its internal buffer. For more ideas on conserving memory, see your Windows documentation.

Merge

WordPerfect's Merge feature allows you to create mailing lists and then merge them with documents, labels, and envelopes. In a merge operation, information is taken from one document and placed at specific locations in another. The document that contains the lists of information is called the *data file,* and the one that receives that information is referred to as the *form file.*

Related Entries

See Chapter 6, "Merge Applications."

Mouse Scrolling

When you use your mouse to scroll through a document using the vertical scroll bar on the right-hand side of the page, be aware that the insertion point does not scroll with the document. To get the insertion point to catch up with the page you are currently working with, click that page after scrolling.

Mouse Shortcuts

In WordPerfect, there are a number of ways that you can select text or blocks of text with your mouse:

- To select a word plus any space that follows, double-click the word.
- To select a sentence, triple-click the sentence.
- To select a paragraph, quadruple-click the paragraph.

- To select multiple full lines of text, click in the left margin and drag your mouse down the left margin of the text you wish to select.
- To select any block of text, place the insertion point at the beginning of the block, then move your mouse pointer to the end of the block. Hold down SHIFT as you click. The entire block, from the insertion point to your mouse pointer, will be selected.

Move

You can move text in WordPerfect using either the keyboard or the mouse.

Menu Selections

Moving Text Using the Keyboard

To move text using the keyboard, select Edit/Cut or press the shortcut key CTRL+X to place the text in the Clipboard. Move your cursor to the desired destination, then select Edit/Paste or press the shortcut key CTRL+V to place it.

Moving Text Using the Mouse

WordPerfect lets you click, drag, and drop text blocks within a document. To move text in this way, highlight the text and click and hold the mouse button on the text selection. The cursor turns into a pointer with pages below it. This indicates that the text can be moved to another location. As you continue to hold the mouse button, drag the pointer to the destination and release the button.

Related Entries

Block

Multiple Copies, Printing

WordPerfect makes it easy for you to print multiple copies of a document.

Menu Selections

To print multiple copies of a document, choose File/Print or click the Print icon on the power bar to display the Print dialog box. In the Copies section of the dialog box, click the up arrow to the right of the Number of Copies text box to increment the number of copies to print.

You can then choose to have the multiple copies created by WordPerfect or, if your printer is configured to print multiple copies of anything sent to it, have the printer generate the copies itself. The default is to have WordPerfect create the copies, but you can change this by choosing Printer from the Generated by option button.

Multiple Documents

WordPerfect allows you to have multiple documents open in memory at once. You can choose File/New or press the CTRL+N shortcut key to start new, empty documents, or you can choose File/Open or press the CTRL+O shortcut key to open existing documents. You can then use the Window menu to switch between documents. Depending on the amount of memory (RAM) in your computer and the size of your documents, you can have up to nine documents open at once.

Menu Selections

Assuming that you have already opened a number of documents, you can switch between them by choosing Window and selecting one of the numbered documents listed at the bottom of the menu. The document with the check mark beside it is the current document. To switch to another document on the list, just click it with your mouse or press the corresponding number beside the document's name and it will appear on your screen.

Related Entries

Displaying Multiple Windows
Windows, Working with Multiple

Multiple Pages, Printing

See "Printing Multiple Pages" in the Print Document entry.

Network Information

WordPerfect is designed to work in a network environment, sharing the WordPerfect program files while users maintain their own document files.

Related Entries

See Chapter 10, "Using WordPerfect for Windows on a Network."

New Document

Whenever you want to begin a new document in WordPerfect, choose File/New and a clean, empty document will appear on your screen. You can have up to nine documents open at one time, whether they are new or existing files.

Related Entries

Multiple Documents

Newspaper Columns

See Columns, Newspaper.

Numbered List

See Bullets & Numbers, Inserting.

Numbers, Inserting

See Bullets & Numbers, Inserting.

Object, Editing

You can edit any object that is linked by OLE (Object Linking and Embedding) that you insert into your document. The object must be one of those supported by WordPerfect.

Related Entries

Object, Inserting
Paste Special

Object, Inserting

In WordPerfect, you can insert and embed an object into a document, creating a link between two documents. When you create a link, you actually copy the source file into your target document as you create the connection. For example, if you are preparing a sales report in WordPerfect based on information contained in a spreadsheet, you can insert the spreadsheet file as an object into your document rather than manually typing the numbers from the printed spreadsheet. This saves you time and eliminates possible errors that result from manually retyping information into your document.

Then, because your document is permanently linked to this external file, any changes you make to that spreadsheet file will automatically update your WordPerfect document. In Windows applications, this type of link between documents is called Object Linking and Embedding (OLE).

Menu Selections

To insert an object into your WordPerfect document, position your cursor and choose Insert/Object. You will see the Insert Object dialog box similar to Figure 11-78. Depending on the various Windows applications installed on your computer, you may have different objects.

Highlight one of the listed objects and click OK. Selecting a specific object opens that application and allows you to create, edit, and finally update the file as an object in WordPerfect. Generally, when you are finished, you can close the application by double-clicking the control menu icon. When you do, the application asks if you want to update the object in the WordPerfect document. Click Yes to update the object and return to WordPerfect.

For a more detailed discussion of OLE and DDE, refer to Chapter 9, "Spreadsheet and Database Files."

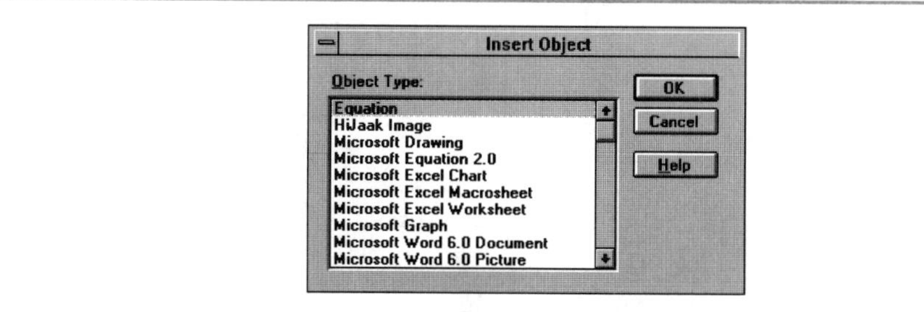

Figure 11-78. *OLE objects supported in WordPerfect*

N

Related Entries

Object, Editing
See Chapter 9, "Spreadsheet and Database Files"

Open

The *Open* command opens a file in its own window. In other words, if you are currently working on one document and open another, WordPerfect opens the second document in another window, and that document becomes the active document. The first document remains in its own window "behind" the current document. Each new document you open overlaps the current one. You can have up to nine documents open at the same time.

You can move and resize these document windows in order to view multiple documents at the same time. You can Cascade or Tile the open documents to view them simultaneously.

Menu Selections

To open a document in its own window, choose File/Open or press the shortcut key CTRL+O. The Open File dialog box, shown in Figure 11-79, contains a Filename text box asking for the name of the file to open, a list of the existing

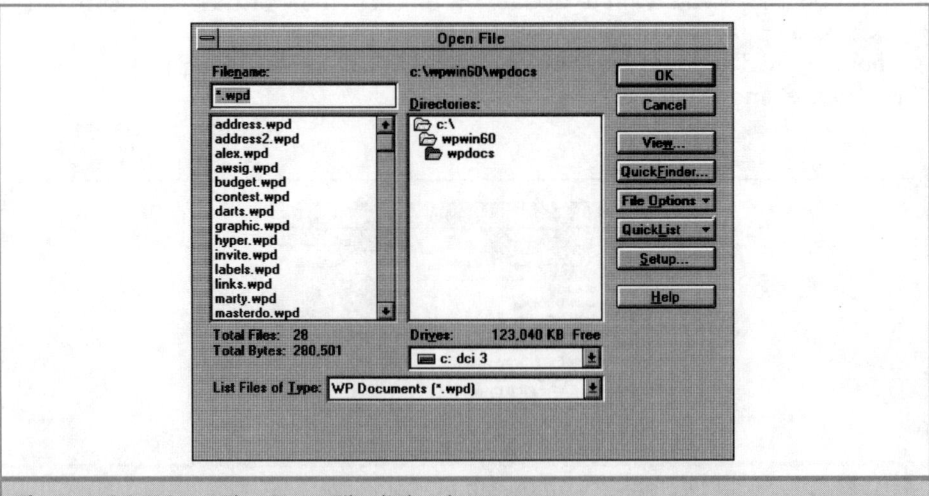

Figure 11-79. *The Open File dialog box*

files in the document directory, a file type text box, a graphical "tree" of the subdirectories on the current disk, and a list of all available disk drives. If QuickList is enabled, the QuickList is displayed either beneath or instead of the graphical tree of subdirectories.

You can open a file from the list by using one of three methods:

- Type the name in the text box and press ENTER or OK.
- Select the file from the list and select OK.
- Double-click the filename.

If the file you want is not listed, you can change directories by selecting one of those listed in the QuickList or Directories box. Select the file and click OK. The drive and directory of the file will be the default the next time you access the Open command.

When you select a filename by clicking just once, file information is displayed in the lower-left corner of the dialog box showing the date and time of the last modification, and the size of the document in bytes. Beneath the Drives list box is the amount of free disk space in KB (kilobytes) on the selected drive. Kilobytes represents about 1,000 bytes, so if you see "Free: 203,024 KB," this really means 203,024,000 bytes or 203 MB (megabytes).

View

If you want a quick preview of the file without really loading it into WordPerfect, you can select View. The highlighted file will be displayed in a special view window.

QuickFinder

QuickFinder lets you perform fast file searches based on criteria that you specify. You type the file type to search for in the File Pattern text box, using alpha-numeric characters and wildcards. Besides just searching for files by file type, you can also search for specific text. If you can't seem to find a document, but you remember a phrase or word from it, you can enter that text in the Search For text box. For further refinement, you can click the left-pointing triangle to the right of the Search For text box. Here you can base the search on logical operators (AND, OR, NOT, and so on); you can specify document components to search (text only, summary only, and so on); you can specify whether the search should be case sensitive or not; and you can specify how far apart the words can be and still qualify as a match.

Normally, WordPerfect searches in the current directory, but you can also choose to search on a different disk or in another directory by using the Search In option button. To filter out all files except for WordPerfect document files (.WPD), enable the WordPerfect Documents Only option.

The QuickFinder includes many more features and many other nuances than can be described in this short section. For more information, refer to Chapter 4, "Managing Files with WordPerfect."

Last Open File List

At the bottom of the File menu, WordPerfect displays the four most recently opened files. If the file you want is one of the four on the list, you can open it by clicking it or by pressing the corresponding file number (1, 2, 3, or 4).

You can turn on and off the list of recent files with the File/Preferences/Environment command. (Disable the Display Last Open Filenames option.)

Opening Files with Other Formats

WordPerfect supports file formats for a variety of word processing programs, including various versions of Ami Pro, WordStar, Microsoft Word, DisplayWrite, XyWrite, MultiMate, WordPerfect for DOS, and ASCII. Any time you attempt to open a file that is not stored in a WordPerfect format, WordPerfect automatically displays the Convert File Format box, which shows the probable file format of the document you are opening. If the format is correct, select OK to convert and open the file. If it is not the correct format, click the down arrow next to the current format name and select the correct format from the alphabetical list. Then select OK to convert and open the file.

When you save the file, WordPerfect displays the Save As dialog box, with the original format of the file displayed in the Format box. If you want to save the file to its original format, click OK. If you want to save it in WordPerfect format instead, click the down arrow next to the current format name, select WordPerfect 6.0 from the list, and then select OK.

Related Entries

Close
Environment
File Conversion
Find Files
Multiple Documents
QuickFinder
QuickList
Retrieve from Clipboard
Save and Save As
Windows

Original Document Backup

See Backup, Original Files.

Other Codes

See Special Codes.

Outline

You can use the WordPerfect Outline feature to number your outline levels automatically as you enter text. WordPerfect uses the standard Roman numeral outline format; however, you can also choose legal numbering, bullets, or paragraph style numbering; or you can create your own numbering format. WordPerfect automatically renumbers your outline topics as you move and delete text from your outline.

Menu Selections

Creating an Outline

To begin using the Outline feature, you must first enter outline mode. When you are ready to return to normal typing, you must turn off outline mode.

To start outline mode, choose Tools/Outline to enter the Outline editor screen (notice the Outline feature bar across the top of the screen). After you choose this, a starting number for the outline appears on the screen. Simply begin typing the contents of your outline. When creating an outline, use the TAB and SHIFT keys extensively to move within the structure of the outline. The following is a list of guidelines for advancing or backtracking levels and entering outline text:

- To start a new sublevel within the current level, press SHIFT+ENTER to advance to the next line and press TAB or click the right arrow on the feature bar to move over to the outline's next sublevel letter or number.
- Press ENTER after each line of text to create the next level.
- To back up one level and begin typing from there, press SHIFT+TAB or click the left arrow button on the feature bar.

- To insert a left indent tab without moving to the next sublevel, press CTRL+TAB.
- To move back without creating previous sublevels, press CTRL+SHIFT+TAB.

As you create the outline, you will notice small numbers to the left of each line in the margin. These numbers correspond to the level and family of the outline. A plus sign following the number indicates that it is the start of a sublevel. When you have completed the outline and are ready to return to normal text style, click Options and choose End/Outine, then choose Close from the feature bar.

Editing an Outline

To insert a new number at the same level, position the cursor at the end of the line just above the line where you want the new number to start, and press ENTER. Press TAB to create a new sublevel or press SHIFT+TAB to move back to a previous level.

If you need to remove a level or sublevel from your outline, highlight that section and delete it. WordPerfect automatically renumbers the outline to adjust for the deleted level.

Moving, Copying, and Deleting Outline Levels

An *outline family* consists of the current level and any sublevels, as shown in Figure 11-80. A family can be moved, copied, or deleted. When you move, copy, or delete an outline family, WordPerfect automatically renumbers the remaining outline as necessary.

To move a family, position the cursor anywhere on the line of the primary level you want to move and click the Hide Family button from the feature bar. This hides all sublevels in that family. Click either the Move Up or Move Down arrow to relocate the family to its new position. Click the Show Family button to expand the family to its original state.

To copy a family, highlight the entire family you want to copy. Select Edit/Copy or press the CTRL+C shortcut key. Move your cursor to the new location and select Edit/Paste or press the CTRL+V shortcut key.

To delete a family, position the cursor at the end of the line immediately preceding the primary level of the family you want to delete and highlight the outline from that point on to encompass the family you want to delete. Any families on the same level below the deletion will move up and be renumbered.

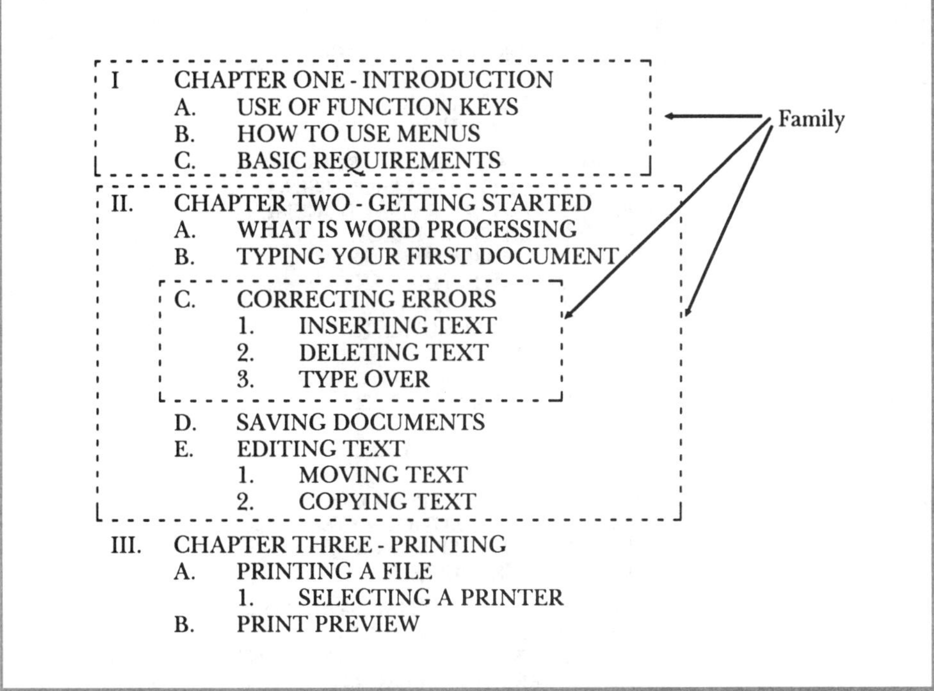

Figure 11-80. *Sample outline families*

Changing Outline Numbering Formats

You can change the outline to a bulleted, heading, legal, numbered, outline, or paragraph numbered format. Examples of these styles are shown in Figure 11-81. You can also define your own format.

To change the numbering format of an existing format, click the pull-down format list and choose the desired format. If the format you want does not exist, you can create it by choosing Define Outline from the Options button on the feature bar. The Outline Define dialog box, shown in Figure 11-82, provides a list of outline formats which you can edit or use as a template.

Highlight the format you want to alter or use as a template for a new format. Click Edit to access the Edit Outline Definition dialog box. From here you can modify the outline format by highlighting the sublevel number or letter. Type in the number you want, or choose from the option menu by clicking the triangle to the right of the text box.

a.

I. CHAPTER ONE - INTRODUCTION
   A. USE OF FUNCTION KEYS
   B. HOW TO USE MENUS
   C. BASIC REQUIREMENTS

II. CHAPTER TWO - GETTING STARTED
   A. WHAT IS WORD PROCESSING
   B. TYPING YOUR FIRST DOCUMENT
   C. CORRECTING ERRORS
      1. INSERTING TEXT
      2. DELETING TEXT
      3. TYPE OVER
   D. SAVING DOCUMENTS
   E. EDITING TEXT
      1. MOVING TEXT
      2. COPYING TEXT

b.

1 CHAPTER ONE - INTRODUCTION
   1.1 USE OF FUNCTION KEYS
   1.2 HOW TO USE MENUS
   1.4 BASIC REQUIREMENTS

2 CHAPTER TWO - GETTING STARTED
   2.1 WHAT IS WORD PROCESSING
   2.2 TYPING YOUR FIRST DOCUMENT
   2.3 CORRECTING ERRORS
      2.3.1 INSERTING TEXT
      2.3.2 DELETING TEXT
      2.3.3 TYPE OVER
   2.4 SAVING DOCUMENTS
   2.5 EDITING TEXT
      2.5.1 MOVING TEXT
      2.5.2 COPYING TEXT

c.

• CHAPTER ONE - INTRODUCTION
   o USE OF FUNCTION KEYS
   o HOW TO USE MENUS
   o BASIC REQUIREMENTS

• CHAPTER TWO - GETTING STARTED
   o WHAT IS WORD PROCESSING
   o TYPING YOUR FIRST DOCUMENT
   o CORRECTING ERRORS
      – INSERTING TEXT
      – DELETING TEXT
      – TYPE OVER
   o SAVING DOCUMENTS
   o EDITING TEXT
      – MOVING TEXT
      – COPYING TEXT

Figure 11-81. *Examples of (a) an outline format, (b) a legal format, and (c) a bullet format*

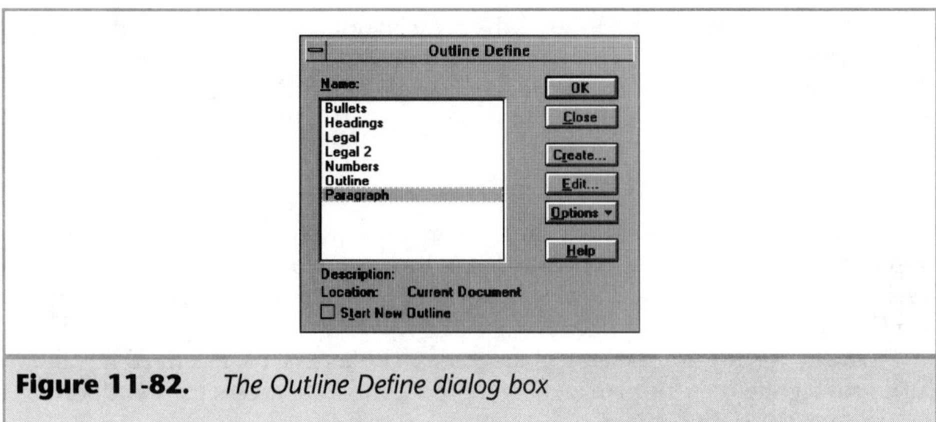

Figure 11-82. *The Outline Define dialog box*

Changing a Level's Style

The Edit Style option in the Edit Outline Definition dialog box allows you to change the style of the outline, including its font, spacing, and other attributes. To change a level's style, highlight the style and click Edit Style. This accesses the Styles Editor dialog box, shown in Figure 11-83.

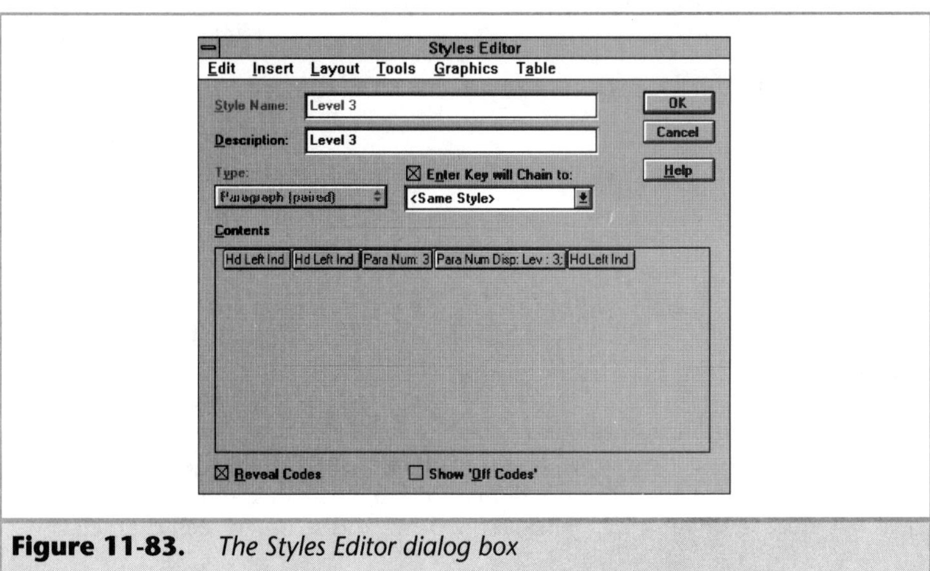

Figure 11-83. *The Styles Editor dialog box*

For example, Figure 11-83 shows the style layout for Level 3 of the Paragraph level format. Notice the two indent codes, followed by other formatting codes. These codes alter the appearance (in the example) of the lowercase roman numeral *i*.

Creating Your Own Format

To define your own format, click Create from the Outline Definition dialog box. Type a name for the style and below that a description of the format. Modify the various outline levels to suit your needs, and click Close to save the new format definition.

You can use any WordPerfect character as a bullet in a user-defined format. To do so, highlight the outline level and press CTRL+W to access the WordPerfect Characters dialog box.

Creating Level Styles

This is useful if you want to include boldface, underlining, or special fonts in your outline. Each level can have its own style definition.

To create a new style, first make sure you have selected the appropriate level in the Edit Outline Definition dialog box. Click Create Style to invoke the Styles Editor dialog box and begin a new style definition. Enter a style name in the first text box, followed by a description in the Description text box. As you apply attributes and spacing for the level, the codes will be displayed in the Contents area of the Styles Editor dialog box. After you complete the dialog box, select OK to return to your document.

Related Entries

Character Sets
Outline
Styles

Overstrike

The Overstrike feature allows you to create special characters by combining two or more characters. For example, if you want to create the not equal sign (≠), you can overstrike the equal with a slash. In addition, you can assign an attribute, such as boldface, underscore, italics, large print, and so on, to each character.

P

NOTE: Remember that many of the characters that you can create with the Overstrike command are available from the WordPerfect Characters dialog box. To access this, select Insert/Character or press the CTRL+W *shortcut key.*

Menu Selections

Position your insertion point where you want the first special character to appear, and choose Layout/Typesetting/Overstrike. The Overstrike dialog box displays a blank text box into which you type the characters you want to overstrike one another.

To assign an attribute to the characters, click the triangle next to the text box and select an attribute from the list. WordPerfect inserts begin and end (paired) codes around your insertion point. Type the characters to which you want to assign the attribute between the begin and end attribute codes. After you have completed the dialog box, select OK to return to your document. WordPerfect inserts an (Ovrstk:) code in front of the first character you typed, inserts any attribute codes you included, and displays the overstriking characters on the screen.

To edit overstrike characters, in Reveal Codes, double-click the (Overstk:) code. Or, place your insertion point in front of the overstruck character, select Layout/Typesetting/Overstrike, and click Next. You can scroll through all of the overstrike characters you have created by clicking Next or Previous.

To cancel an overstrike or cancel any attributes assigned, delete the associated codes.

Page Breaks

There are two types of page breaks: *soft page breaks,* inserted by WordPerfect, and *hard page breaks,* inserted by you. As you type your document, you are not required to insert hard page breaks, because soft page breaks are inserted automatically by WordPerfect at the end of each page. Think of this as a type of floating page break. However, many factors determine where WordPerfect puts a page break. These include the paper size, the top and bottom margins, headers, footers, line spacing and height, widow protection, and so on. Soft page breaks may or may not be aesthetically appealing in the final printout. Therefore, before you print a final copy, you should page through your document and insert your own page breaks, if necessary.

Each time you enter a hard page break, any soft page breaks that follow are automatically adjusted. Hard page breaks that follow are not adjusted, and they can only be removed by you. You should not insert hard page breaks for each draft you print. However, you may want to insert page breaks before you start typing a section that you want to begin on a new page. Soft page breaks are represented in Reveal Codes by (SPg), or by (HRt-SPg) if you insert a hard return that coincides with a soft page break, which WordPerfect inserts as needed. When you enter a hard page break, an (HPg) code is inserted.

Menu Selections

Position the insertion point where you want to begin a new page. Choose Insert/Page Break or press the shortcut key CTRL+ENTER. To remove a hard page break, simply delete the code.

Page Numbering

You can add page numbers to your printout with WordPerfect's Page Numbering feature. You can choose from a number of different positions: left, right, or center at the top or bottom of the page, or at alternating positions for odd and even numbered facing pages. Page numbers at the bottom print on the first line of the bottom margin, and those at the top print on the last line of the top margin. In addition to selecting the position, you can choose a style and beginning number. You can also add text to your page numbers, such as "Page # 1." WordPerfect inserts the codes (Pg Num Fmt: format)(Pg Num Pos: position) where you enter the Page Number command.

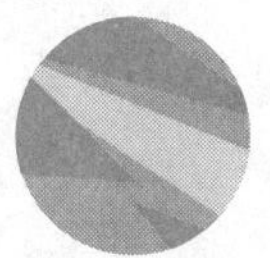

NOTE: *If you add page numbers from this command, be sure to disable page numbering in your headers and footers, or your page numbers will be redundant.*

Menu Selections

Position the insertion point on the page where you want the page numbering to begin. Choose Layout/Page/Numbering to display the Page Numbering dialog box, shown in Figure 11-84.

Click the Position option button and select a position from the list. The sample facing pages will display the approximate character position of your page number, but not the exact line.

If the default positions do not suit your needs, you can insert the page number at your current cursor location by selecting Insert Format and Accompanying Text at Insertion Point from the Page Numbering Option dialog box.

P

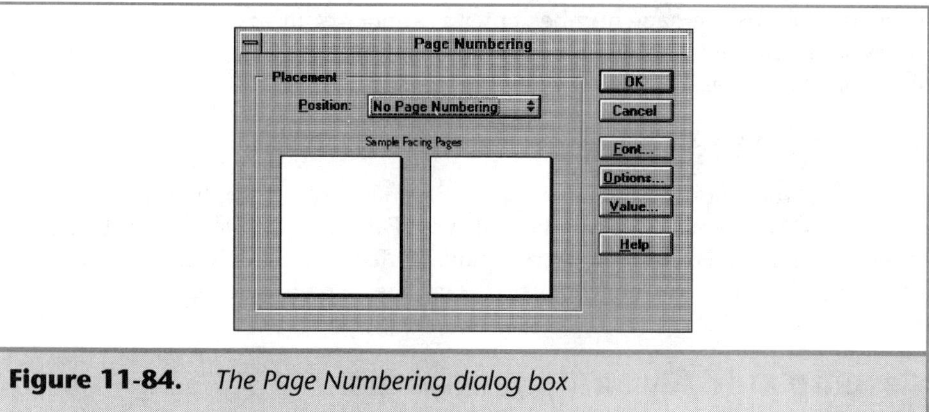

Figure 11-84. *The Page Numbering dialog box*

To discontinue page numbering, move to the page where you want it to stop. Choose Layout/Page/Numbering and select No Page Numbering from the Position option button.

Changing the Font

If you want your page numbers to be displayed differently from the text in your document, you can change the page number to a different font. Click Font in the Page Numbering dialog box and apply the desired font attributes.

Changing the Numbering Style

In addition to traditional (Arabic) numbers, you can print numbers in upper- or lowercase letters, or in Roman numerals. This is useful for such sections of your document as the preface, table of contents, or index. To change the numbering style, click the Page option button in the Page Numbering Options dialog box and select a numbering style from the list.

Changing the Page Number

Page numbering starts on the page where you originally entered the page numbering code and prints the number of the physical page. In other words, if you begin page numbering on page 2, WordPerfect prints the number 2. If you want to change this beginning number, click Value to access the Numbering Value dialog box. In the Page Settings section, change the New Page Number to the desired starting page number and click OK. You can restart your numbering with any number from anywhere in your document. If you want to increase or decrease the existing page number, enter a number from –5 to 5 in the Increase/Decrease Existing Page Number text box, click OK, and the page numbers will increase or decrease by that amount.

Adding Page Number Text

Normally, WordPerfect prints just the page number. However, if you want to include text with your page number, such as "Page #," click Options and enter the desired text in the Format and Accompanying Text box. In this text box, you can commingle text with format codes by typing the text and selecting codes from the Insert option list.

Forcing Odd/Even Page Numbers

Sometimes a particular page, such as the first page in a chapter, has to have an odd or even page number. To force odd or even numbering, move to the page that must be odd or even, choose Layout/Page/Force Page and select the desired option.

Related Entries

Footers, Creating
Headers, Creating

Page View

Page view gives you a different perspective than does draft view in your documents. In Page view, the pages in your document are represented graphically as actual pages. Page breaks actually resemble separate pages, and headers and footers are displayed as they will be on paper, as are endnotes and footnotes. You can work all the time in Page view in WordPerfect. However, the program may seem a bit sluggish, especially if a document contains a lot of layout variations and graphics. This is because the graphics and other enhancements require more complex screen redrawing in Page view.

You can set Page view as the default mode every time you use WordPerfect by selecting File/Preferences/Display and clicking View/Zoom. Change the Default View to Page by clicking the Page button. Click OK. In order for the default to take effect, you must exit and restart WordPerfect.

Menu Selection

View/Page

P

Related Entries

Draft View
Two-Page View

Paper Size

The size of your paper is a determining factor in the layout of your document. For example, in order for WordPerfect to determine where to place page breaks, it must know the size of the paper you are printing on. The default size is 8 1/2 by 11 inches. If you are using different paper, you must change this setting.

WordPerfect includes a number of predefined paper sizes, including standard, bond, letterhead, labels, envelope, transparency, card stock, glossy film, clay based, and other. You can also define your own. When you select a paper size other than the default, WordPerfect inserts a (Paper Sz/Typ:) code at the insertion point. The display of the text may be altered if your change modifies the number of characters that can be displayed on a line. The new paper definition stays in effect until the end of the document or until you change the paper size again. To cancel the paper size change, delete the code.

Menu Selections

Position the cursor at the point in the document where you want to change the paper size. Choose Layout/Page/Paper Size to display the Paper Size dialog box. Highlight the desired paper definition and make sure the information about the paper is correct. If it is correct, click Select to choose the paper.

Creating a Paper Type

If your paper size is not listed, you can design your own paper type and size. Click Create and type a name in the Paper Name text box. Select the paper type you are using from the Type text box and adjust the measurements. Click OK to save the new paper type. Then highlight the paper type you just created from the Paper Definitions list and click Select.

Paper Type

Both the Create Paper Size and Edit Paper Size dialog boxes contain other options that affect how WordPerfect lays out the text. The Paper Type box might tell WordPerfect, for example, that you are printing on envelopes, on legal paper, or on legal paper in landscape mode. To change the paper type, click the down arrow next to the current paper type name and select a type from the pull-down list. If none of the choices describes your paper, select Other and adjust the measurements accordingly.

Text Adjustments

After you print your document, you may decide that the text is too high or low, or too far left or right, despite the margin settings. You can adjust the text from the Text Adjustments area of the Add Paper Size dialog box by selecting Up or Down from the Top option button, or Left or Right from the Side option button.

Orientation

The Paper Orientation group in the Create Paper Size and Edit Paper Size dialog boxes shows how your paper is inserted into your printer: vertically or horizontally. If you are printing on wide paper, click Wide Form.

You can also indicate whether you want the text to be rotated 90 degrees on the page as it comes out of your printer, or printed on wide form paper (commonly termed "wide bar" paper, measuring 8.5" by 14 7/8").

Paper Location

The Paper Location group tells WordPerfect whether you are using (for a dot-matrix printer) manually fed sheets, bin-fed sheets, or continuous forms. For laser printers, the options change to reflect upper tray, default, and manual feed. Because all printers are not the same, your choices may differ. To change this setting, select the type of paper feed from the Location pull-down list.

If you select Bin, enter a bin number in the text box. If this special paper size or type is included in a document that has another size paper as well, you may want to check the Prompt to Load Paper check box (dot-matrix only). If you do, WordPerfect stops printing waits when it encounters this new paper type and prompts you to load the appropriate paper type. Load the paper and click OK to resume printing.

Related Entries

Landscape Printing
See "Document Settings" in Print Document
Printer, Selecting

Paper Type

See Paper Size.

P

Paragraph Numbering

See Outline.

Paragraph Spacing

See Line Height (Leading) Adjustment.

Paragraph Symbol

The paragraph symbol is a visible marker displayed on your screen each time you press ENTER. When you work on a document in WordPerfect, it is often difficult to tell where a paragraph ends, whether a blank area has been created using spaces, tabs, or carriage returns, whether the paragraph is indented, and so on. Along with the paragraph marker there are other nonprinting characters that help you see how your document is formatted, including symbols for spaces, tabs, and alignment.

Menu Selections

To enable the display of the paragraph symbol, select File/Preferences/Display and click Show "¶", as shown here:

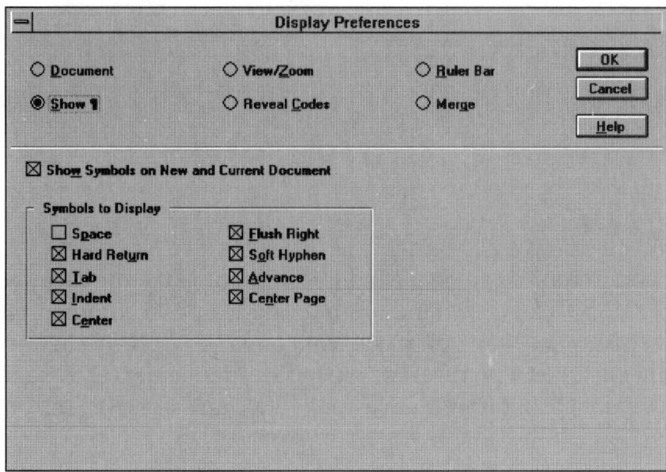

Click Show Symbols on New and Current Document. Make sure Hard Return has a check mark beside it, as do any of the other symbols you want to display on the screen.

NOTE: You may want to disable the Space symbol, because it is displayed erratically in some font styles.

While the extra symbols on the screen may seem distracting at first, you will soon get used to them and actually find that they help improve your productivity. Knowing where stray characters such as spaces and tabs are located will make your formatting much easier and will help you produce more professional looking documents.

Related Entries

Character Sets
Hard Return Character

Parallel Columns

See Columns, Parallel *and* Columns, Parallel with Block Protect.

Password Protection

See Lock Documents.

Paste Special

Text, objects, and graphics can be pasted into a document from a variety of sources. The Paste Special command is similar to the paste command except it allows you to specify the way you paste from another application; the Paste command only pastes as a picture. For example, you may want to paste a real, live chart, linked by OLE, rather than a copy of a chart as a picture.

Menu Selections

To paste using the Paste Special command, you must first copy an image, a cell range from a spreadsheet, a chart, or some other object, and copy it into memory using the Copy command in that application. If you are copying an object from within WordPerfect, you can use Edit/Copy or the shortcut key CTRL+C. Switch to the WordPerfect document where you want to Paste Special and select Edit/Paste Special. The Paste Special dialog box appears, as shown in Figure 11-85.

The example shows the choices available after a chart was copied in Microsoft Excel. You will have different choices, depending on the object you have copied.

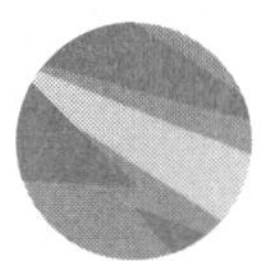

NOTE: When you copy a graphic image within a WordPerfect document that is not from an external source such as a spreadsheet program, it is best not to use the Edit/Paste Special command. If you do, it pastes a degraded "picture" of the graphic rather than a perfect copy you get when you use the Edit/Paste command.

Highlight a data type and click Paste. The object will be placed in the document. If you select Paste Link, then a link is established between the object and its source.

Related Entries

Graphics, Inserting
Linking

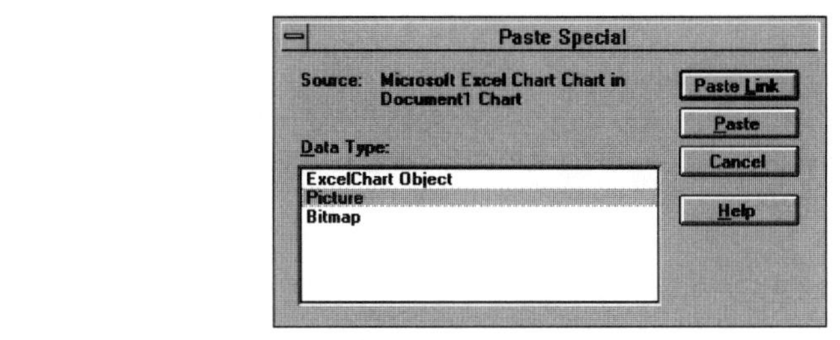

Figure 11-85. *The Paste Special dialog box*

Paste Text

See Move.

PostScript Printing

WordPerfect supports the special features of PostScript printers. A major advantage of using PostScript printers is the ability to scale the fonts to any size up to 200 points. There are 72 points to the inch. Generally 10 points or 12 points produce normal size type, depending on the font. In addition, PostScript printers can produce true shadow or outline fonts as well as white print on a black background. For more information on printing, see Chapter 5, "Working with Your Printer."

Power Bar

The *power bar,* shown here, provides convenient access to the most commonly used commands and features in WordPerfect:

It displays a variety of icons, or small pictures, just beneath the menu bar, which perform specific actions when you click them. For example, you can save a file by clicking the icon resembling a diskette. Or, you can instantly apply columns to your document by clicking the Columns icon.

Menu Selections

To enable the power bar, select View/Power Bar. If you do not want to use the power bar, you can remove it from the display by selecting View/Power Bar again.

You can also customize the power bar to suit your needs by selecting File/Preferences/Power Bar.

Related Entries

Power Bar
See also Chapter 3, "Tools and Techniques."

Preferences

The File/Preferences menu allows you to change WordPerfect defaults for a variety of features, including display preferences, environment settings, file specifications, document summary settings, button and power bars, the status bar, keyboard layouts, menus, writing tools, printing functions, and document importing.

Related Entries

Backup, Original Files
Backup, Timed
Display Fonts
Display Preferences
Document Summary
Environment
Equation Editor
Initial Codes Style, Document
Keyboard Layout
Location of Files
Merge
Print Document
Reveal Codes
Ruler
Table of Authorities
Units of Measure

Print Document

The WordPerfect Print command allows you to select the document or the portion of the document you want to print. It also includes options for setting the print quality and the number of copies and for selecting your printer.

Menu Selections

When you use the Print command, the position of the insertion point makes no difference. If you want to print selected text, first select the text, then choose File/Print or press the F5 shortcut key. The Print dialog box, shown in Figure 11-86, gives you complete control over the printing process.

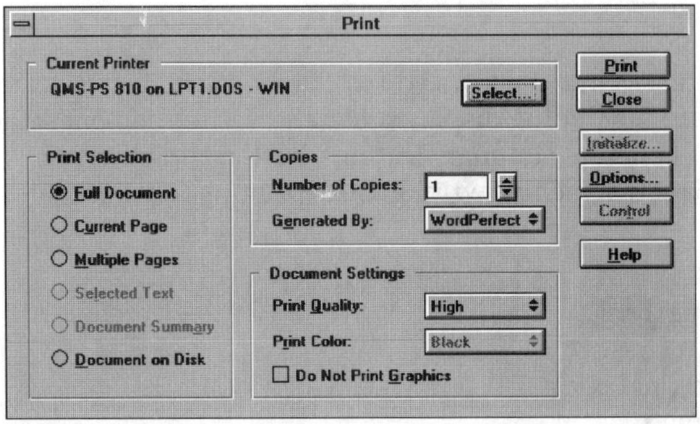

Figure 11-86. *The Print dialog box*

Document Print Options

At the top of the dialog box, the current printer is displayed with a Select command button that allows you to pick another printer. Printers that have been set up in WordPerfect generally offer more choices for printing, such as font control and other printer commands.

In the Print Selection area, you can determine which parts of your document will print: the full document, the current page, multiple pages, selected text, the document summary (if it exists), or a document on disk. Use the Document on Disk option to print a document that has been printed to a disk file by WordPerfect, as it includes all the necessary printer codes. Also, if you have not selected any text prior to choosing the Print command, or if your document does not have a summary, those options will be dimmed in the Print dialog box.

Printing Multiple Copies

The Copies section allows you to select the number of copies of the document that you want to print. You can specify whether WordPerfect controls the number of copies printed or, if your printer can be configured to generate multiple copies by itself, your printer can control the number of copies. For example, if your printer is set up to generate two copies of each page sent to it and you instruct WordPerfect to generate two copies of the document from the Print dialog box, four copies of the pages will be printed.

P

Document Settings

The Document Settings section displays options for print quality, print color, and whether graphics will be printed or not.

The quality of your graphics or text affects the resolution of the characters. The higher the quality, the better the resolution, and the longer it takes to print. For example, high resolution on a dot-matrix printer causes the printer to strike each character twice. High resolution is best for your final printout, but it saves time to print your rough drafts in Draft quality. Another factor in quality is readability. If your printer tends to produce light, hard-to-read print, a higher print quality will improve its legibility.

To change the print quality, click the Print Quality option button and choose High, Medium, or Draft. If your printer supports color printing and you have chosen the appropriate printer driver, the Print Color option button will be accessible, allowing you to print in a color other than black. You can also enable the Do Not Print Graphics option. You might use this option, for instance, when you just want a quick printout, because graphics take longer to print than text.

Downloading WordPerfect Printer Fonts

If you have selected a WordPerfect printer driver and you want to download fonts for the current print job, select the Initialize command button. You only have to download fonts once, unless you turn your printer off or otherwise remove the fonts from printer memory. For information on downloading fonts with a Windows printer driver, consult your Windows documentation.

Printing Multiple Pages

To print only selected pages from the current document, choose Multiple Pages from the Print Selection area. When you select Print, the Multiple Pages dialog box appears, from which you can specify the page numbers, secondary pages, chapters, or volumes to print. Type the individual page numbers you want to print in the appropriate text box with numbers separated by commas and consecutive pages separated by a hyphen, as shown in the following examples:

Example	Result
1,3,8	Prints pages 1, 3, and 8
3-6,9,16-22	Prints pages 3 through 6, prints page 9, and then prints pages 16 through 22

Print Output Options

If you click the Options command button, the Print Output Options dialog box appears, as shown in Figure 11-87. From here you can specify certain print format options, such as printing the document summary, printing in booklet format, printing in reverse order (last page starts printing first), and whether odd, even, or all pages will be printed.

If you choose to print only odd or even page numbers, WordPerfect goes by the numbers assigned in page numbering and prints the corresponding odd or even pages. The Odd option, for example, causes the first, third, fifth, and subsequent odd pages of your document to be printed.

When you have made all the necessary changes, select Print from the Print dialog box to begin printing.

Printing a Document from the Disk

You use the Document on Disk option to print a document that has been printed to a disk file by WordPerfect, because the document includes all the necessary printer codes. To print a document from the disk, choose Document on Disk in the Print Selection area and select Print to access the Document on Disk dialog box. You must specify the drive, path, and filename of the document in the Filename text box. If you are unsure of the location, click the File icon to the right of the text box to browse through the directories on disk. You can also specify which pages of the document to print from this dialog box.

WordPerfect always formats and prints a document using the currently selected printer driver. If the document you want to print from the disk was formatted for another printer, you may end up with strange results. If you are

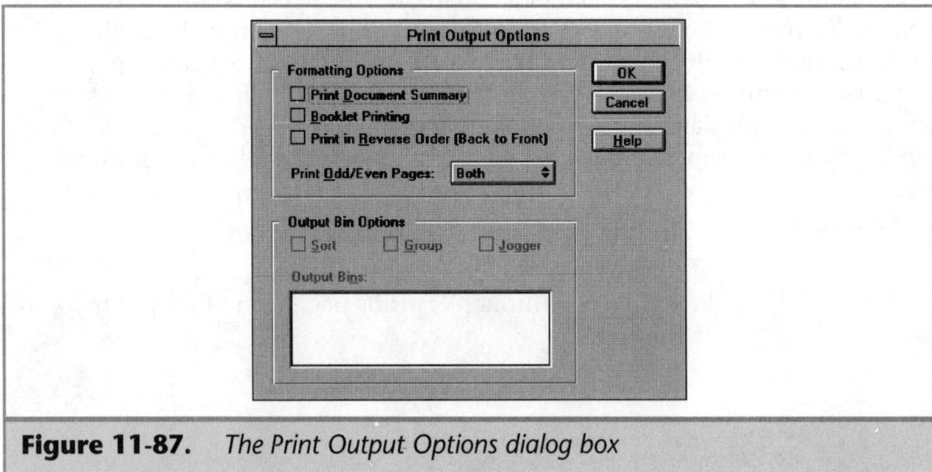

Figure 11-87. *The Print Output Options dialog box*

not sure which printer the document was originally formatted for, open it, before printing, to format it for the current printer.

Printing the Document or Canceling the Print Job

When you have set all the necessary options in the Print dialog box, click the Print button. The WordPerfect Print Job box appears and displays information about the status of the print job, including the current page and copy being printed and the percent of completion:

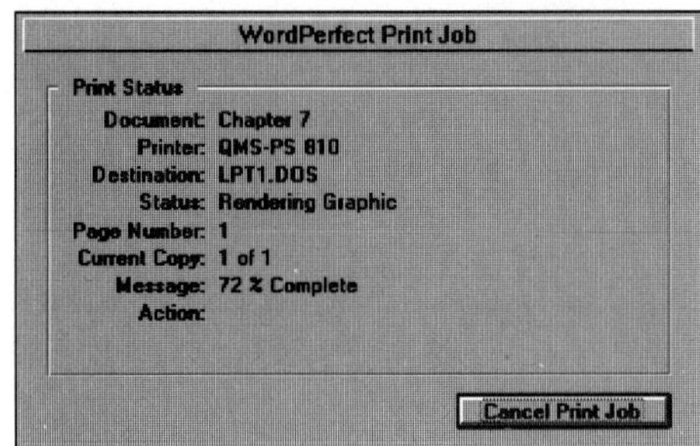

If you want to interrupt the print process, click Cancel Print Job.

Related Entries

Fonts
Open
See "Menu Selections" in the Paper Size entry
Print to Disk
Printer, Selecting

Print Job, Canceling

See the section "Printing the Document or Canceling the Print Job" in the Print Document entry.

Print Manager

When you print a document using a Windows printer driver, it is sent to the Windows Print Manager, a queueing program that manages all print processes.

Because it acts as an electronic print buffer in RAM (memory), the Print Manager frees up your computer to continue working in WordPerfect.

For information on using the Print Manager, consult your Windows documentation.

Related Entries

Printer, Selecting

Print Options

See "Document Print Options" section in the Print Document entry.

Print Page

See "Document Print Options" in the Print Document entry.

Print Quality

See "Document Settings" in the Print Document entry.

Print to Disk

If you do not have a printer available and will be printing your document later or on another computer that uses WordPerfect, you can create a *print file* on the disk. This is a WordPerfect file that incorporates all the printer codes in your document that are recognized by the selected printer. This file can later be printed from DOS, the Windows File Manager, or with the Print Document on Disk feature in WordPerfect. For information about printing from DOS or Windows, see your DOS or Windows documentation.

NOTE: The Print to Disk feature does not create a pure ASCII file on the disk, as do some other programs. For information on creating ASCII files, see the Save and Save As entry.

The procedure for actually printing to a file on disk is the same as printing any document on your printer.

P

Menu Selections

Choose File/Select Printer and choose a WordPerfect printer driver. You may have several printers listed, some with the Windows logo preceding them and others with the WordPerfect logo, as shown in Figure 11-88.

When you highlight a WordPerfect printer, the Setup button accesses different options than are normally available under a Windows driver. This is because the WordPerfect driver is more versatile for WordPerfect than is the Windows driver. The Printer Setup dialog box, shown in Figure 11-89, displays information about your printer. Click the Port option button and select File from the list. Next, type a filename that you will save the file under, or enable on Prompt for Filename to force WordPerfect to ask you to type a filename before saving the file to disk. Click OK when finished.

NOTE: If you have defined a printer so it prints to a file in the Printers option of the Control Panel in Windows, you can print to disk by selecting it. Often, however, it is simpler to use the printing features within WordPerfect.

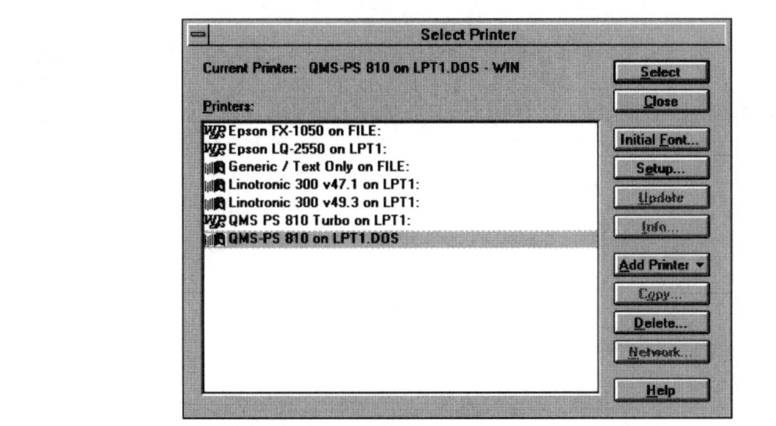

Figure 11-88. *The Select Printer dialog box*

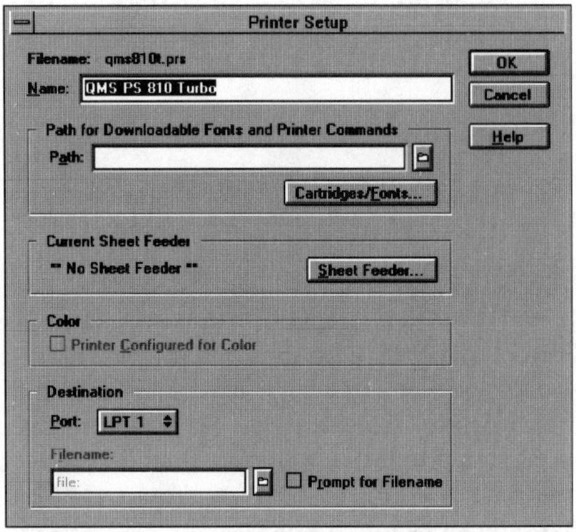

Printer Setup

Filename: qms810t.prs
Name: QMS PS 810 Turbo
OK
Cancel
Help
Path for Downloadable Fonts and Printer Commands
Path:
Cartridges/Fonts...
Current Sheet Feeder
** No Sheet Feeder **
Sheet Feeder...
Color
Printer Configured for Color
Destination
Port: LPT 1
Filename:
file:
Prompt for Filename

Figure 11-89. *The Printer Setup dialog box*

Printer Commands

WordPerfect supports all the features commonly available on today's printers, including italics, boldface, underscore, and landscape mode. However, if your printer supports a feature not available in one of WordPerfect's commands, you need to send what is called a *control* or *setup string* to your printer through WordPerfect.

First, you need to select a WordPerfect printer driver. (This discussion is not applicable to Windows printer drivers.) Second, you need to refer to your printer manual and find the decimal format of the printer code that activates the feature you want. When you specify the code, a (Ptr Cmnd - *code*) is placed at the insertion point and affects the text until WordPerfect encounters another code or until the document ends. To discontinue this printer command, follow the preceding steps and enter the code that cancels it. For example, to discontinue a command for a special print attribute, you could enter the command for normal text. To cancel the command entirely, delete the code.

Menu Selections

After you have selected your WordPerfect printer driver and found the correct printer code, choose Layout/Typesetting/Printer Command. From the Printer Command dialog box, as shown in Figure 11-90, type the decimal code as shown

P

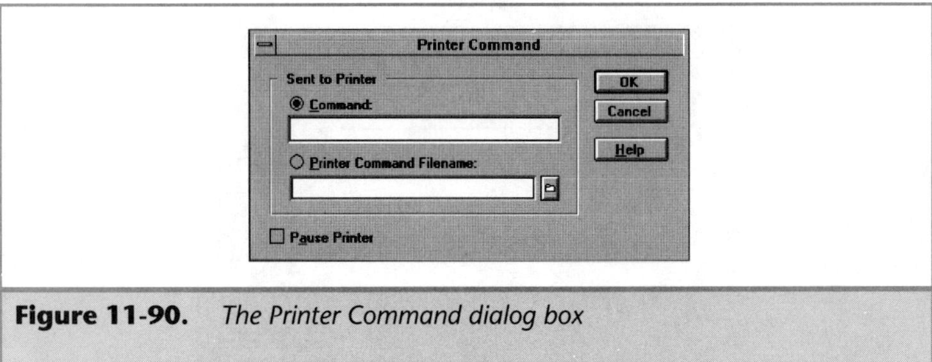

Figure 11-90. *The Printer Command dialog box*

in your printer manual. If you want to save this decimal code in a file, you can select Printer Command Filename and type a filename to which the code can be saved. This saves you from entering the code each time you use the printer.

Otherwise, type the control code in the Command text box. Click OK when you are finished.

Related Entries

Open
Printer, Selecting

Printer, Selecting

A printer driver is a definition file. It gives WordPerfect information that it needs in order to communicate with the printer. WordPerfect provides a printer driver for virtually every printer on the market. Windows also provides its own printer drivers. In WordPerfect you can use both Windows and WordPerfect printer drivers interchangeably. (See "Printer Drivers, Windows Versus WordPerfect" later in this entry.)

Before you print, WordPerfect must know which type of driver you are using, and which printer. Once you make this selection, WordPerfect stores it and you need not repeat the process unless you want to change drivers or printers.

Menu Selections

Choose File/Select Printer. The Select Printer dialog box shown in Figure 11-91 shows a list of available printers that you have installed either from Windows or WordPerfect. The driver type, either Windows or WordPerfect, is indicated by the

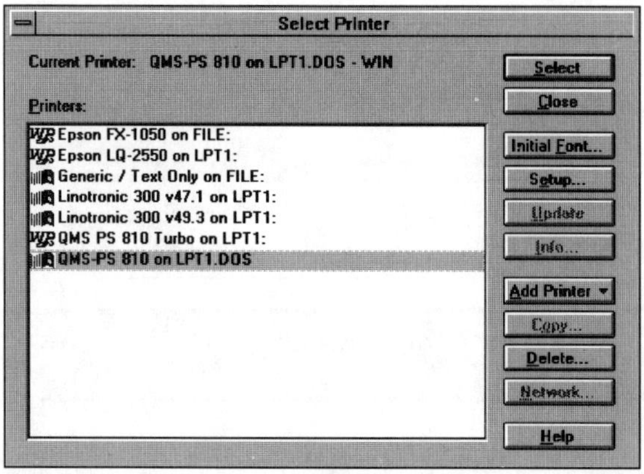

Figure 11-91. *The Select Printer dialog box*

logo to the left of the printer name. If you have installed a driver for your printer that was also installed in Windows, then you will have two drivers for the same printer. This is not a mistake—it just gives you an alternative.

A variety of options are available from this dialog box which affect the way WordPerfect prints to your printer.

Select Printer Options

The active printer is highlighted in the Printers list. Notice that the port for which the printer is configured is displayed in the list. To select another printer, click its name in the list and choose Select. This makes that printer active and closes the dialog box.

Changing the Initial Font

You can change the default font for this driver by clicking the Initial Font button. The Printer Initial Font dialog box displays the available system fonts and the name of the current font. You specify a default font and point size for each WordPerfect printer driver you install. Each time you create a new document using a WordPerfect printer driver, it will automatically start with font and point size. Select the desired font face, style, and size from the dialog box and click OK.

P

Printer Setup

Most of the changes you make to your printer driver can be done through Setup. If you have selected a Windows printer driver, clicking Setup invokes the Windows printer setup dialog box. However, if you have selected a WordPerfect printer driver, you invoke a different dialog box, shown in Figure 11-92, where you can rename the driver, configure your fonts, select a sheet feeder, enable color printing (if the printer supports color printing), and select the destination port.

Usually, you will never need to rename the printer driver, unless, for instance, it is configured for a special purpose. To avoid constantly modifying the same printer driver, you could have two similar printer drivers with different names; one, for example, might print to the printer while the other prints to a file.

CARTRIDGES AND FONTS You can specify a location for various third party "downloadable" fonts in the Path text box. Often, these are termed *soft fonts,* because they are not stored on a physical, or hard, cartridge installed in your printer. WordPerfect will download the font information to your printer, so that you can have access to many more fonts than are offered by the printer manufacturer or by WordPerfect. Once you download fonts to your printer, they remain in the printer's memory until you turn off its power. You must type the

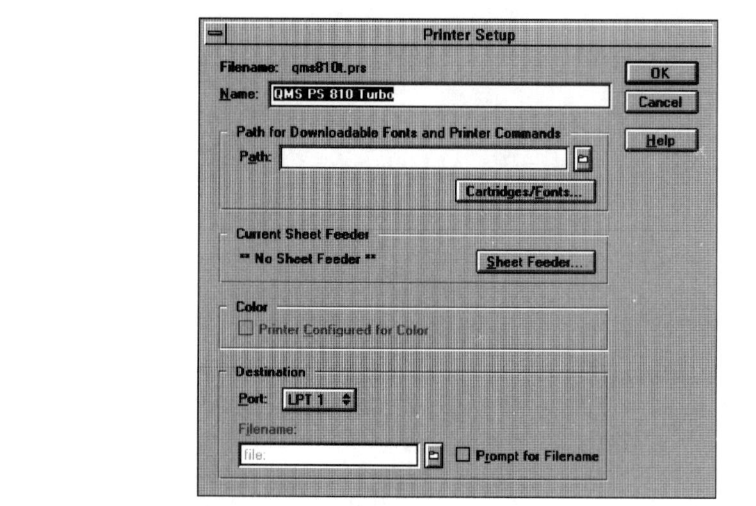

Figure 11-92. *The Printer Setup dialog box*

drive and path where the fonts are located, or browse for them by clicking the File icon to the right of the text box. Select Initialize from the Print dialog box to add the new fonts to those built in to the printer.

Below the text box is the Cartridges/Fonts command button. Click this to invoke the Select Fonts dialog box. Choose the fonts you want to use with this printer. The number of fonts you can have depends on the memory available in your printer.

For more detailed information about working with your printer, refer to Chapter 5, "Working with Your Printer."

SELECTING A DESTINATION The Destination section should display the port or device to which the printer is currently assigned. You can change this setting by clicking the Port option button and selecting the destination from the list. If your printer is a parallel printer, you would select one of the LPT settings. If your printer is a serial printer, you would select one of the COM settings.

Update

WordPerfect keeps printer driver files in .PRS files, usually located in the \WPC20 directory. These files contain the information for each printer driver installed on your system. If you update or customize a printer .ALL file using the Printer Definition Program, you can select Update to automatically add the new information to the .PRS file and update the fonts.

If you have received a new .ALL file from WordPerfect, you should copy it to the appropriate location on your computer and select Update for each of the listed printer drivers so that their .PRS files have the most current information.

Info

Use Info to access the Printer Information dialog box. Here you can view information about a printer, such as its .ALL file date. Sometimes, more technical information is presented for DIP switch settings and how to properly configure the paper location (see Paper Size earlier in this chapter). If you have a sheet feeder assigned in Setup, you can view information about it here as well.

Add Printer

You can quickly add a WordPerfect or Windows printer through this option. Click Add Printer and select either WordPerfect or Windows to install the printer driver. If you add a WordPerfect printer, the Add Printer dialog box appears, from which you can choose to install new drivers (.ALL) or just printer files (.PRS). To install new drivers, click Additional Printers (*.all) and select the desired printer definition from the Printers list. Or, to install just printer files, click Printer Files (*.prs) and click any of the listed printer files to create duplicate printer files. If you want to place the new files in a location other than the default (usually \WPC20), click Change and provide the new drive and directory. Select OK to add the printer files.

Copy

You can copy WordPerfect printer files quickly by highlighting the printer in the Printers list and clicking Copy. When you do, a Copy Printer dialog box appears where you can type in a new printer name or accept the name WordPerfect provides and click OK.

Delete

To remove a printer that you no longer use or that is incorrectly set up, highlight that printer in the Printers list and click Delete. WordPerfect confirms whether you want to delete the printer. If it is the only remaining printer using this .PRS file, place a check mark beside Delete the associated .PRS to remove the .PRS file from the hard disk. Click OK to delete the printer.

Choosing a Network Printer

This option allows you to select a printer from those connected to your network. The Printer Connections list box shows the port and print queue to which you are currently attached. The Available Queues group box lists all the available queues detected by WordPerfect for the current file server.

Printer Drivers, Windows Versus WordPerfect

WordPerfect is one of the few programs that offer you the use of printer drivers separate from the Windows printer drivers. There are several advantages in using WordPerfect drivers over Windows:

- When you specify a WordPerfect driver, you can include multiple paper sizes and types in the same document, as long as they are supported by your printer. When you use a Windows driver, you must specify the paper type, size, and orientation for that driver, and it cannot be changed from within the document.
- WordPerfect drivers allow you to specify individually the quality of print for your text and graphics. You can print each in high, medium, or draft quality to save time.
- WordPerfect offers a greater variety of printer drivers.

Windows drivers also offer advantages:

- You can print graphics in color, assuming your printer supports color. WordPerfect drivers support color only on color PostScript printers.
- Some third-party screen fonts can be used only with Windows printer drivers.
- Certain printers are currently supported only with Windows drivers, such as the *Linotronic 300.*

Related Entries

Paper Size
See "Document Settings" in Print Document
Print to Disk

Printing Control

See Print Document.

Printing Sideways

See Landscape Printing.

Program Files

Program files are the files that control the operation of a program. Program files generally have a file extension of .EXE or .COM, and in Windows, program files often use the extension .PIF. For example, the main program file for WordPerfect is WPWIN.EXE. The WordPerfect icon in Windows is "attached" to, or associated with, the WPWIN.EXE file. Therefore, when you select the WordPerfect icon from Windows to start WordPerfect, Windows loads the WPWIN.EXE program. WordPerfect also requires other .EXE files to run. INSTALL.EXE is used to install the WordPerfect program.

You should not assign the .EXE or .COM extension to your document files.

Program Icon Name

When you install WordPerfect for Windows, it automatically creates a group window called WPWin 6.0, which includes the WordPerfect program, as well as the Speller, Thesaurus, QuickFinder File Indexer, Kickoff, and Installation programs, as shown here:

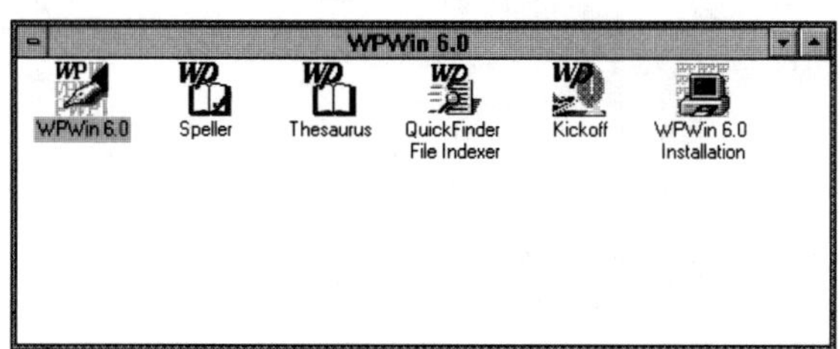

Each program is represented by a special graphic called an *icon,* and WordPerfect assigns each item a name that is displayed below the icon. You can change this name and the associated icon with the Windows File/Properties command. For more information about program groups and items, consult your Windows documentation.

Pull-Down Menus

Pull-down menus are so called because when you select the menu, a list of commands in that category is "pulled down." When the menu is not selected, only the menu name is displayed. The menu bar at the top of the WordPerfect window contains the names of the primary pull-down menus. Figure 11-93 shows the menu bar with an example of a pull-down menu.

Another type of pull-down menu or list is used in dialog boxes. This type of menu usually contains a list of options from which you can make one selection. The menu usually displays the current selection before you pull it down.

Related Entries

Dialog Boxes

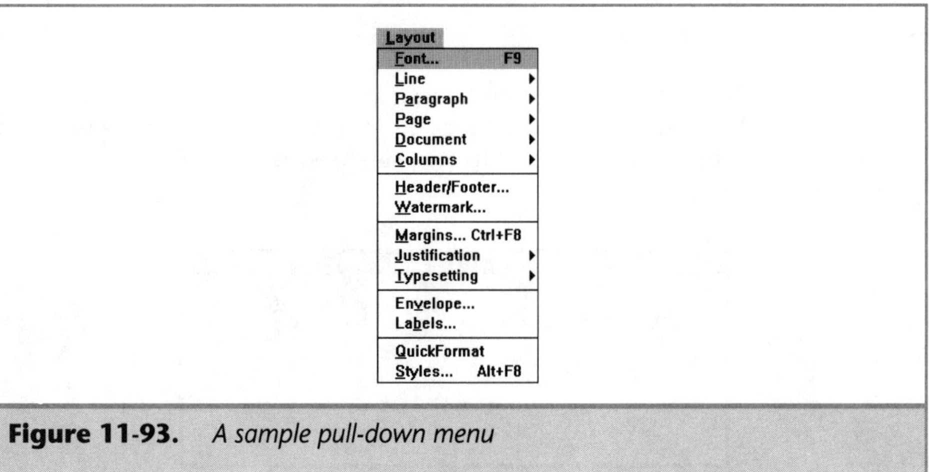

Figure 11-93. *A sample pull-down menu*

QuickFinder

QuickFinder is a very comprehensive file finding utility adapted especially to WordPerfect. Using QuickFinder, you can find files anywhere on your system by specifying the file type, where to search, the date range of the file, and so on.

For detailed information on how to use QuickFinder, refer to Chapter 4, "Managing Files with WordPerfect."

QuickFormat

If you want to copy fonts, attributes, or paragraph styles from one area of your document to another, you can do so with the QuickFormat feature. This lets you ensure that the fonts and attributes in one paragraph match identically with those in another.

Menu Selections

To copy the format of an entire paragraph, position your cursor in the paragraph that contains the desired attributes and select Layout/QuickFormat to enable the QuickFormat feature. You will see the following dialog box:

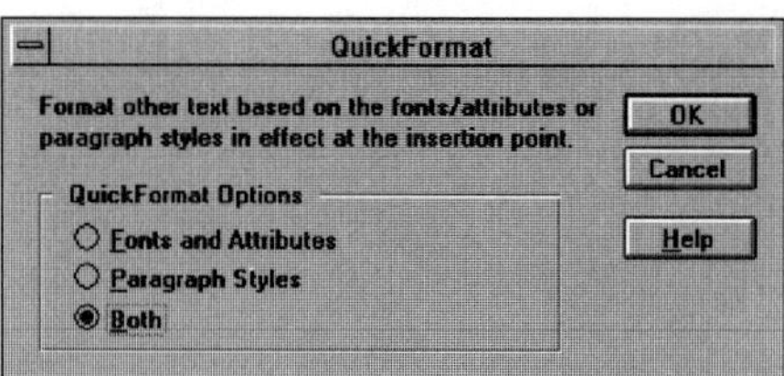

Choose whether you want to QuickFormat with just the Fonts and Attributes, the Paragraph Styles, or Both. Click OK. Once you do, you will notice that your mouse pointer changes to this:

Place the pointer at the desired location and click. The attributes are copied to that point in your document. If you highlight text while QuickFormat is enabled, you will QuickFormat only the selected text.

You can also copy just the attributes of selected text by first highlighting the text that contains the desired attributes and then selecting Layout/QuickFormat. Immediately, your mouse pointer changes to the I-beam and paint roller. Place the pointer at the desired location and click.

If you want to apply the attributes from one area of your document to specific text, you can do so using either method explained previously and then, while your mouse pointer displays as an I-beam and paint roller, select the text you want to QuickFormat.

QuickList

WordPerfect allows you to save and open files from specific directories using the QuickList feature. For example, suppose you want to save a file to the C:\WPWIN60\WPDOCS\ALLEN subdirectory. Rather than find it by navigating through the directory system, you can give it a descriptive name, or alias, like "Allen's Letters," then use QuickList to change to that directory immediately.

For your convenience, WordPerfect includes several predefined QuickLists.

Menu Selections

You first create the directory by using the Windows File Manager, the DOS *mkdir* command, or another utility. Once the directory exists, you can define a name for it by choosing File/Open and clicking the QuickList option button.

Creating and Editing a QuickList

In the Open File dialog box, you have the options of displaying the QuickList box, the Directories box, or Both.

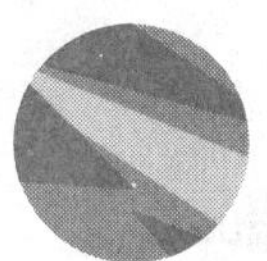

NOTE: You must display the QuickList in order to add, edit, or delete any QuickList.

To display the QuickList box, click QuickList and choose Show QuickList to display only the QuickList box, Show Directories to display only the Directories box, or Show Both to display both boxes simultaneously.

To create a new QuickList, click QuickList and select Add Item. In the Add QuickList Item dialog box, type the drive, directory, and filename (if the QuickList is accessing a file) that this QuickList will reference. If you are unsure of the directory and its location, click the File icon to the right of the text box and browse through the directories. Enter a descriptive name for this directory in the Description text box; this is the name that will appear in the QuickList box. Click OK when you are finished.

To edit a QuickList, first highlight a QuickList in the QuickList box, click QuickList, and choose Edit Item. To remove a QuickList definition from the QuickList box, click QuickList and choose Delete Item.

Then, whenever you want to find or save a specific file in a complex path, just click one of the available entries in the QuickList box.

QuickMark

See the section "Set QuickMark on Save" in the Environment entry.

Redline

The Redline feature is used to point out text that has been added to a document since a previous version. Whenever you use the Document Compare feature, WordPerfect automatically places redline markings over text that has been inserted into the document. However, you can also place redline markings over text manually. Redline text will appear, as its name implies, in red.

Menu Selections

To place redline markings over text, block the text to be redlined and choose Layout/Font and click the Redline option.

Redline Settings

You can change the way redline text will appear on the printed page. On color printers it will be red; on most non-color printers it will appear with a ten percent grey shading over it. You can also opt to have a vertical line or other symbol placed on the left margin, or alternately on the left and right margins, to indicate that text has been added to the document. To change the way redline text prints, choose Layout/Document/Redline Method and choose the desired redline method. The default is Printer Dependent, meaning that redline text will print according to the way your printer handles redline.

You can also choose Mark Left Margin or Mark Alternating Margins, either of which will place a symbol you specify in the margin to indicate that text has been redlined. You can specify any WordPerfect character to display in the margin by using the Redline Character option and selecting from the WordPerfect Characters dialog box, which you can access by pressing CTRL+W. Note that the default redline margin character is the vertical line (|).

Removing Redline Markings

Once you have redline markings on your text, you may want to take them off before the final version of the document is printed. To do this, you use the Remove Markings feature.

To remove redline markings from your document, choose File/Compare Document/Remove Markings. WordPerfect will display a dialog box asking you to confirm that you want the redline markings deleted. When you confirm, WordPerfect will automatically search the document for redline codes and delete them. Note that this does not actually remove the redlined text; only the markings are removed.

Related Entries

Compare Documents

Repeat

You can repeat a keystroke or macro any number of times with the Repeat command.

Menu Selections

To repeat an action, position your cursor where you want the repeat to occur and select Edit/Repeat. This invokes the Repeat dialog box, shown here, in which you can specify the number of times the action will be repeated:

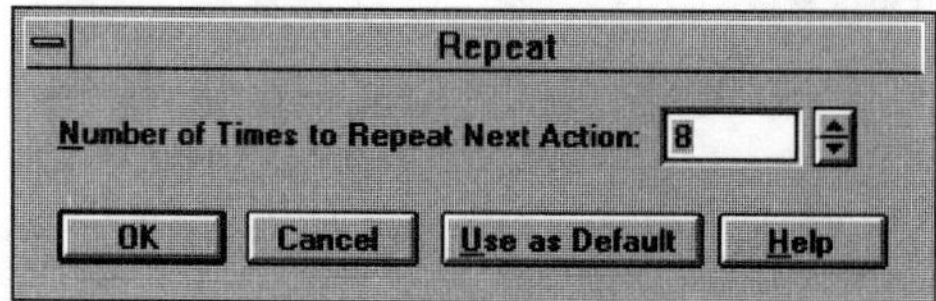

The default number of repetitions is eight, but you can set a new default number by typing it in the text box and clicking Use as Default.

Click OK set the repeat value. Then select a macro, command, or keystroke to repeat the action the specified number of times.

Replace

WordPerfect's Replace feature allows you to scan a document for text that you specify and to replace it with new text. A common use for the Replace feature is to put the characters "XXX" each place that a long text string would occur (like your company's name). You could then replace each occurrence of "XXX" with the name of your company when you finish typing the document.

You might also use this feature if, for example, you have typed a long draft of promotional literature for an upcoming professional meeting to be held in Milwaukee. Just before you are to send the document to the printers, you discover that the meeting is being moved to New Orleans. You can have WordPerfect replace every occurrence of "Milwaukee" with "New Orleans." Of course, you have complete control over which occurrence is replaced and which is not.

Menu Selections

To replace text, choose Edit/Replace, and the Find and Replace dialog box shown here will appear on your screen:

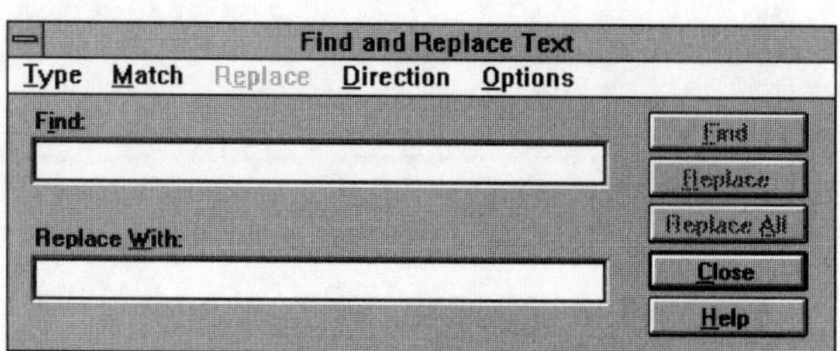

R

Simple Find and Replace

In the Find text box, type the text you want WordPerfect to find. Then press TAB and, in the Replace With text box, type the text with which you want to replace the text found in the document.

Normally, WordPerfect does not pay attention to whether the text it finds is uppercase or lowercase. If you want to match text with the case used in the Find text box, select Match/Case to enable case-sensitivity.

Also, as WordPerfect searches for an occurrence of the word, it may find a "word within a word" unless you enable the Whole Word option. For example, if you type "the" in the Find text box, WordPerfect will also find words such as "gather" and "there," because "the" is a segment of those words. If you enable Match/Whole Word, WordPerfect will find only the word "the."

WordPerfect ordinarily searches in the text of the document and ignores any text in headers, footers, endnotes, footnotes, and so on. If you choose Options/Include Headers, Footers, etc. in Find, WordPerfect looks for a match in the headers, footers, endnotes, footnotes, and so on, as well as the text.

The default is to search forward, but you can also have WordPerfect search the document backward from the current position of the insertion point. Choose the direction of the search by selecting Direction/Backward.

Normally, the Find command begins searching from your cursor's location until it reaches the end of the document. You can direct WordPerfect to start searching from the very beginning of the document, or you can have the search go to the end of the document and then start again at the beginning until it reaches the point where it began the search. To enable either of these options, select Options and choose the corresponding search method.

To replace every occurrence of the text string with the new text without verification, click the Replace All button. Keep in mind that you run the risk of replacing text that you didn't want to replace by using this option.

A more conservative approach is to click the Find button. WordPerfect will search for the desired text and highlight it on your screen. If you want to replace the text, click the Replace button; if you want WordPerfect to ignore this particular text, then click the Find button again to continue the search.

Advanced Find and Replace

You can find and replace codes such as TAB (Hd Left Tab) and line spacing (Ln Spacing) codes by typing them in the Find text box. Of course, you can type them in yourself, but it's much simpler to select the codes in WordPerfect's Codes dialog box and then insert the codes into the text box. To replace codes in your document, select Match/Codes and scroll through the available codes. Highlight the desired code and click Insert. If you want to display only the Merge codes in the Find Codes list, click Display Merge Codes Only.

WordPerfect can also perform a find and replace by font. For example, if you used a combination of New Times Roman and ITC Bookman intermittently throughout a 30 page document, finding all occurrences of the Bookman font manually would be tedious. You can select Match/Font and choose the font type and size for which you want to search. Then in the Replace With text box select Replace/Font and designate the font that will replace the match.

You can limit your find and replace process by first highlighting the text, perhaps several pages of a long document, and then specifying the text to find and replace. Doing this automatically enables the Limit Find Within Selection option in the Options menu.

Related Entries

Codes, Finding and Replacing

Replace Codes

See Codes, Finding and Replacing.

Retrieve from Clipboard

The *Clipboard* is a memory buffer program that runs in the Windows environment whenever you copy or cut text or graphics. Because Windows allows for universal transfer of text or graphics from one Windows program, you can easily transfer text and graphics from other Windows applications into WordPerfect through the Clipboard. Keep in mind that you generally don't see the Clipboard itself during this process; it runs "behind the scenes" while you use WordPerfect.

Menu Selections

Assuming that you have already copied or cut text or a graphic from another location in WordPerfect or from another Windows application, you can retrieve that information from the Clipboard by choosing Edit/Paste or by using the shortcut key CTRL+V. The text or graphic will appear at the location of the insertion point.

Related Entries

Move
Paste Special

Reveal Codes

The Reveal Codes feature allows you to view a document with the formatting codes visible. These formatting codes generally fall into one of two categories. Some codes tell your printer how to format your document, such as bold and type size. Other codes identify unique types of text in your document, such as text to be included in an index or table of contents.

Whenever you add anything other than text to the screen, WordPerfect inserts a code at the cursor location that tells the printer how to format the document. Until you place a code into a document, WordPerfect assumes that all the default codes are in effect, and the document will be formatted and printed accordingly. There are two standard types of codes, *open* and *paired,* which differ from one another in the way they are displayed. An open code is displayed only once, while a paired code appears on either side of the text or area to which it is applied.

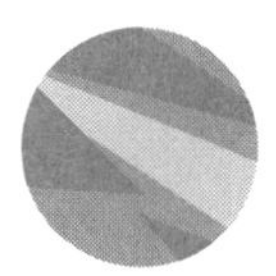

NOTE: If you are working on a lengthy document with a particularly large quantity of attributes and styles, you might inadvertently insert multiple codes or forget to delete some codes. You may want to browse through the document with the reveal codes window open to remove any stray and unnecessary codes, because stray and unnecessary codes consume more disk space and require more print time.

Once an open code is placed into a document, it remains in effect until another similar code is inserted. For example, if you change your line spacing from the default single spacing to double spacing, WordPerfect continues to double space the text from the location where the code is placed until you insert another line spacing code. A double spacing code is an example of an open code and looks like this in Reveal Codes:

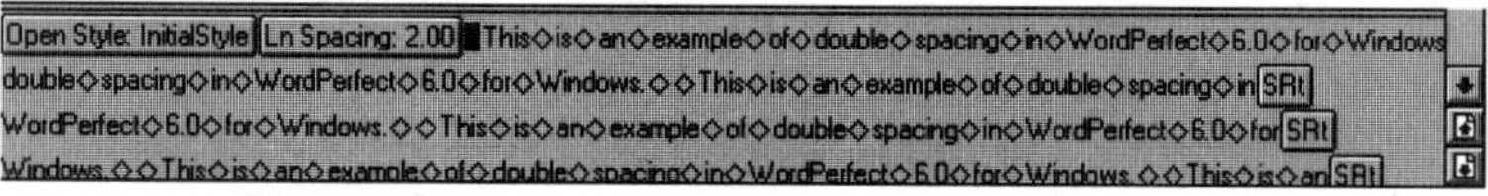

Open Style: InitialStyle
Ln Spacing: 2.00
This◇is◇an◇example◇of◇double◇spacing◇in◇WordPerfect◇6.0◇for◇Windows
double◇spacing◇in◇WordPerfect◇6.0◇for◇Windows.◇◇This◇is◇an◇example◇of◇double◇spacing◇in SRt
WordPerfect◇6.0◇for◇Windows.◇◇This◇is◇an◇example◇of◇double◇spacing◇in◇WordPerfect◇6.0◇for SRt

A paired code precedes and follows the text that it affects; that is, it has both an on and an off code that appear on either side of the text. Most formatting options like bold, underline, and font changes are displayed as paired codes. For example, a bold code looks like this in Reveal Codes:

Menu Selections

To view codes, you must *reveal* the codes on your screen. You can reveal codes by choosing View/Reveal Codes from the menu bar, or by pressing the shortcut key ALT+F3. The document screen will split horizontally with the standard document window on top and the Reveal Codes window below. Codes will appear in raised, typeset boxes. To turn off Reveal Codes, choose View/Reveal Codes again. This option is a toggle switch: select it once to turn it on and select it again to turn it off.

It is usually a good idea to turn off the Reveal Codes feature after editing the codes, because it is somewhat confusing to be typing on two screens at once. Besides, it tends to slow down the screen rewrites.

Editing Reveal Codes

You can use Reveal Codes to delete codes you no longer want in the document. For example, if you have text that is underlined and bold and you want it to be only bold, you can use Reveal Codes to remove the underline code.

To edit a specific code in your document, position the insertion point near the location where you believe the code is located and choose View/Reveal Codes. At this point, you should ignore the upper half of the screen and concentrate on the lower portion.

Position the insertion point on the code you want to remove and press the DELETE key. The code will disappear and the document will readjust, if necessary.

Changing the Size of the Reveal Codes Window

If you want the Reveal Codes window to appear larger or smaller than the default, you can adjust it in two ways. To temporarily adjust the window size, click on the Reveal Codes border and drag it up or down to the size you want. If you want to permanently set the size, select File/Preferences/Display and click on Reveal Codes. This accesses the preferences for the Reveal Codes window.

Click Window Size in the Options section and adjust the percentage of the window size you want Reveal Codes to fill.

NOTE: Another way you can temporarily resize the Reveal Codes window is to click and drag the small black bar that appears above and below the scroll bar on the right side of the WordPerfect window.

In addition to adjusting the window size, you can have WordPerfect display the Reveal Codes window as the default by clicking on Show Reveal Codes on New and Current Document.

Ruler

The WordPerfect Ruler allows you to alter the format of a document without having to go through a number of menu selections. Using the Ruler, you can set and adjust tabs, modify the paragraph format, alter the margins, adjust columns, and create tables. The ruler bar is divided into three areas: the margin slide bar, the ruler measurement area, and the tab markers area, as shown in Figure 11-94.

Menu Selections

To display Ruler on the screen, choose View/Ruler Bar or press the shortcut key ALT+SHIFT+F3. At the top of the ruler bar (just below the menu bar) is a white slide bar that contains double triangles representing the current margin settings (see Figure 11-94). By clicking and dragging these triangles, you can instantly adjust your left and right margins.

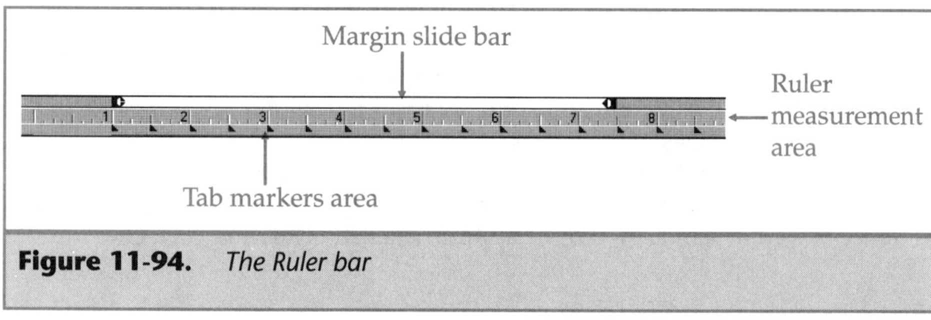

Figure 11-94. *The Ruler bar*

Every half inch under the Ruler bar are triangles that represent left-aligned tabs. The alignment of the tab is indicated by the orientation of the triangle. You can double-click any of these triangular tab markers to bring up the Tab Set dialog box or right-click and choose Tab Set from the shortcut menu. Click Clear All to delete the default tabs from the Ruler bar.

In the Settings section of the Tab Set dialog box is a Type option button. Click this to change the tab style. Notice that each tab setting uses a different triangular marker. Click OK to accept the new tab style. The tab marker of the type you select will be placed in the Ruler bar. To remove an unwanted tab, simply click it and drag it down away from the Ruler bar.

You can modify the appearance of your paragraphs by changing the paragraph format. Right-click anywhere on the Ruler bar, except the tab marker area, and choose Paragraph Format from the shortcut menu. You can adjust the First Line Indent to create an indent on the first line of each paragraph. To increase the amount of space between your paragraphs, change Spacing Between Paragraphs to a larger number. You can also fine-tune the left and right paragraph margins (which are different from the page margins) by changing their settings. The sample box shows an example of the settings you have chosen. Click OK when finished.

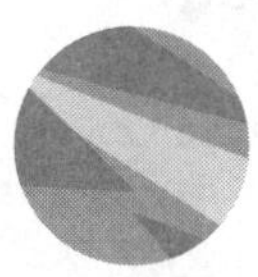

NOTE: *You can improve the appearance of your document on-screen by increasing the amount of spacing between paragraphs. This reduces the need to press* ENTER *more than once between paragraphs. Normally there is one line between paragraphs, but a space of 1.5 or 2 enhances the readability of the document.*

Although you can adjust the margins by moving the markers on the slide bar, this does not permit exact margin settings. To set the margins precisely in inches, right-click anywhere on the Ruler bar except the tab marker area and select Margins from the shortcut menu. In the Margins dialog box, adjust the settings to suit your needs. An example of the margin changes appears in the sample box. Click OK when finished.

To add columns to your document, position the insertion point where you want the columns to begin and click the Columns button. Choose the number and type of columns you want, click OK, and WordPerfect sets up columns in your document. You now have margin slide bars for each column in the document. This allows you to adjust the width of the columns by dragging the corresponding triangles in the margin slide bars.

To insert a table into the document, right-click anywhere on the Ruler bar except the tab marker area and select Tables from the shortcut menu. Specify the number of columns and rows in the appropriate text boxes and click OK.

Related Entries

See Columns entries
Margins
See Tables entries
Tabs, Setting
See also Chapter 3, "Tools and Techniques."

S

Save and Save As

Saving your document copies it from your computer's temporary memory, called random-access memory or RAM, onto your computer disk. It is important to save frequently, so that you don't lose any of your work as the result of a power failure or some other unfortunate event.

Whenever you begin a new file, WordPerfect opens a new window and displays a generic name followed by a number in the format [Document#]. Each new document is numbered consecutively, starting with 1, that is [Document1], [Document2], and so on. Each time you start WordPerfect, the numbering starts over again from 1. These names are not used to save the files on the disk; they only keep track of new documents you have not yet named. The first time you save a document with the File/Save command, WordPerfect asks you for a name. After that, whenever you use the File/Save command, WordPerfect automatically saves the document under the name you last gave it and replaces the old file on the disk. If you want to assign a new name to the current file, use File/Save As. This displays a dialog box in which you can specify the new filename.

Menu Selections

To save the current document, choose File/Save, use the CTRL+S shortcut keys, or click the Save button on the powerbar. The first time you save a document, WordPerfect will display the Save As dialog box, shown in Figure 11-95. At the top of the box is the Filename text box, in which you can type a name up to eight characters long followed by a period and an optional three-character extension. Unless you specify a path, the file will be saved in the current directory. After you type the name, select OK to save the file and close the document.

The Save As dialog box will be displayed any time you choose the File/Save As command or press the F3 shortcut key. After a file has first been saved, you typically use this command to save it under a different name without modifying the original file.

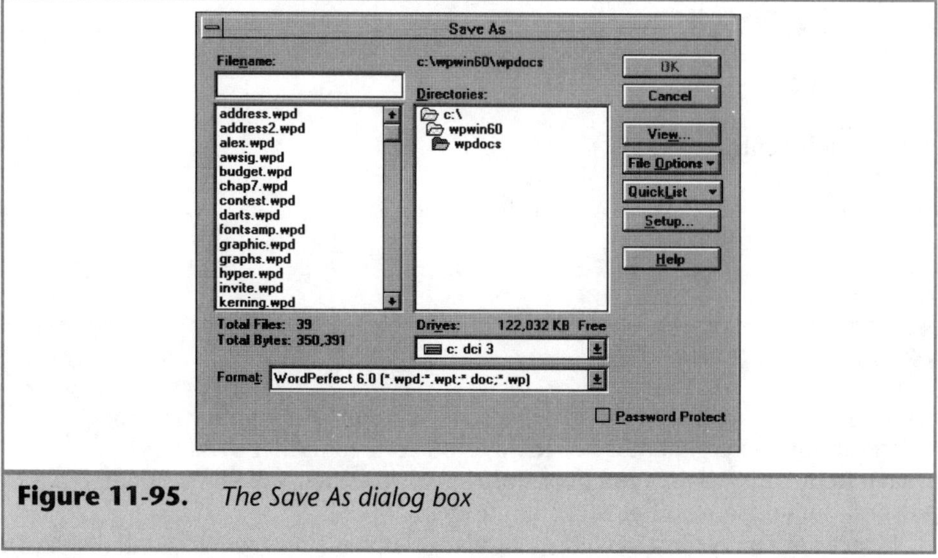

Figure 11-95. *The Save As dialog box*

As soon as you open or save a document, the word "- unmodified" appears after the filename on the title bar to indicate that you have not made any changes since the last save. After entering text or making a correction, the word "- unmodified" disappears. The absence of this word in the title bar lets you know that the file has been modified but not saved. The word "- unmodified" also appears in the Window menu list next to any open documents that remain unchanged. Subsequently, when you choose File/Save, the document will be saved with the same filename, without prompting.

Saving Selected Text

If you highlight text and then use the File/Save or File/Save As commands, the Save dialog box is displayed:

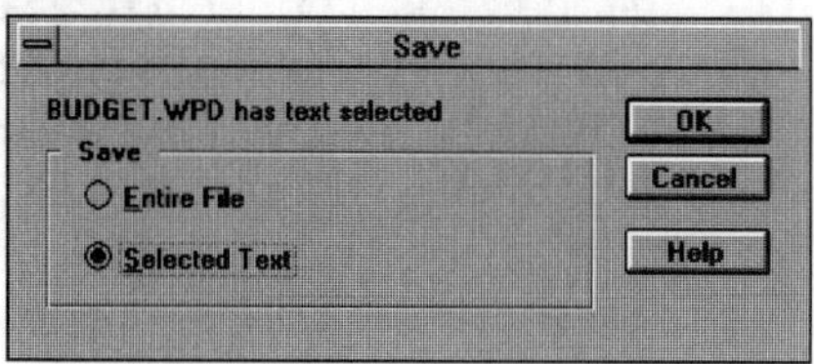

WordPerfect displays this dialog box any time you attempt to save a document in which text is highlighted. If you want to save the entire file, click on the Entire File option; otherwise, choose Selected Text. If you choose to save Selected Text, you are prompted for the name of the file in which you want the selected text saved.

Changing Directories

Below the Save As text box there is a list box with the names of files in the current directory. To the right there is another list box that shows the directory structure on the current drive. Below that there is a control for changing the current drive.

You can save the document in another directory by one of two methods. First, you can supply the full path and filename in the Filename text box. If you don't want to do this, you can change the current disk drive by using the Drives field and choose a directory in the Directories field. When you select OK, the file is saved in the drive, directory, and file you have specified.

NOTE: *If you enter the name of a file that already exists in the current directory, WordPerfect displays a message box asking you if you want to replace the file. If you select Yes, the file on disk will be replaced with your document. If you select No, the Save As dialog box will be displayed again, asking you for another filename.*

Saving in Another Format

Normally, WordPerfect saves files in its own file format. However, WordPerfect supports a variety of other file formats, including various versions of Ami Pro, WordStar, Office Writer, DisplayWrite, MultiMate, Microsoft Word, ASCII, and WordPerfect 4.2, 5.0, and 5.1.

If you want to use a WordPerfect file with another word processing program, you can use the Format list in the Save As dialog box. The default format is, of course, WordPerfect. If you click the down arrow next to the current format, you can select from the list of available file formats. If you don't see the format you want, select ASCII Generic Word Processor (DOS). Most word processing programs can read ASCII files, but formatting enhancements will be lost.

Related Entries

ASCII Text Files
New Document
QuickList

S

Save to Clipboard

See Block *and* Clipboard.

Screen Colors

If you have a color monitor, you can use a color palette to enhance the appearance of your screen. The colors of your window text, background, menu bar, and title bar are determined by Windows, using the Control Panel program. However, you can use WordPerfect to change colors for codes displayed in the Reveal Codes screen.

For the Reveal Codes screen, WordPerfect has chosen default colors for the text and background. If you do not like the current color settings, you can change them.

Menu Selections

Choose File/Preferences/Display to access the Display Preferences dialog box.

Changing Reveal Code Colors

To change the colors displayed in the Reveal Codes screen, select the Reveal Codes button in the Display Preferences dialog box. The Display Preferences dialog box will change, appearing as shown in Figure 11-96.

In the lower-right corner of the dialog box, you can change the text and background colors used in the Reveal Codes window. Select the Text or Background button, and then choose one of the colors offered.

Select OK to save your changes, or select Cancel if you change your mind.

Related Entries

Colors, Screen
Display Preferences

Scroll Bars

Scroll bars appear in all WordPerfect document windows and in other active windows when the information displayed does not fit in the window. *Horizontal scroll bars* allow you to scroll the display to the right and left; *vertical scroll bars* allow you to scroll the display up and down. When you use a scroll bar, the insertion point does not move as it does when you use the arrow keys.

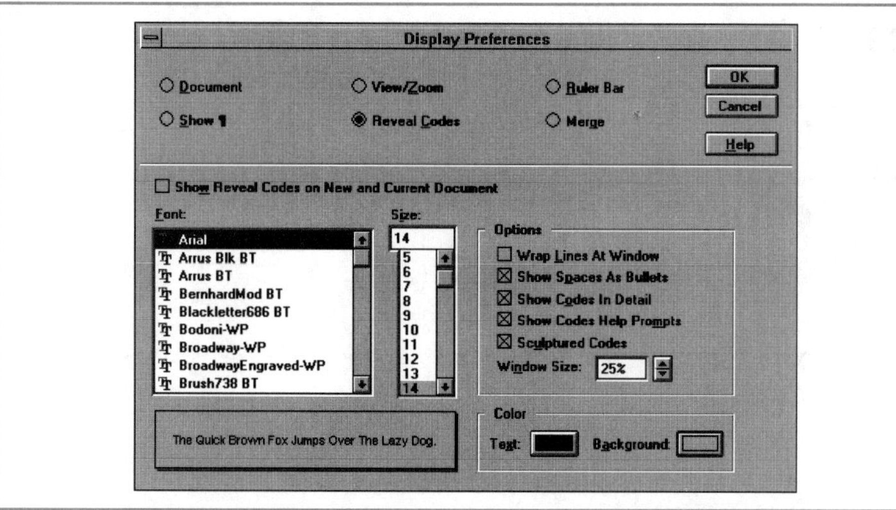

Figure 11-96. *The Display Preferences dialog box for the Reveal Codes window*

Using Scroll Bars

Each time you click the down arrow at the bottom of the vertical scroll bar, the text rolls forward one line; click the up arrow, and the text scrolls back one line. If you hold down the left mouse button, the screen scrolls rapidly until you release the button. Each time you click the horizontal scroll bar arrow, the text moves in the direction of the arrow.

The *scroll box* is a gray box on your scroll bars. You can use your mouse to drag the scroll box up and down (or left and right) to move more rapidly through the document. The screen does not reposition itself until you release the mouse button.

When you move text with the scroll bars, the insertion point may disappear. Click the mouse button in the document and it will reappear.

You can control the display of scroll bars in the File/Preferences/Display dialog box.

Related Entries

Display Preferences

Search

See Finding Text.

Select Printer

See Printer, Selecting.

Select Records

See the "Selecting Records" section in the Sort entry.

Select Text

See the "Techniques for Blocking Text" section in the Block entry.

Shortcut Keys

WordPerfect supplies a number of keystroke shortcuts that allow you to access commonly used menu selections. These are accessed by pressing either a function key, the CTRL key plus a letter, or the ALT key plus a letter. For example, if you want to access the sorting capabilities of WordPerfect, you can press ALT+F9. There are numerous keyboard combinations you can use with WordPerfect; they are documented throughout this book.

If you desire, you can create your own keyboard shortcuts by modifying the keyboard layout. For instance, you can assign macros to specific keyboard combinations.

Related Entries

Macros
See also Appendix B, "WordPerfect Keyboards."

Shortcut Menus

A shortcut menu is a handy feature in WordPerfect that allows you to see a context-sensitive menu of features. Shortcut menus are displayed by pointing to an area of the WordPerfect screen and clicking the right mouse button. For instance, if you point to the ruler and click the right mouse button, you will see the following menu:

Tab Set...
Paragraph Format...
Margins...
Columns...
Tables...
Hide Ruler Bar
Preferences...

Soft Return

Wordperfect inserts a soft return code (SRt) at the end of a line of text where a word wrap has taken place. These soft returns are adjusted as paragraphs are edited. Soft return character codes differ from hard return character codes, which are inserted whenever you press ENTER.

Related Entries

Hard Return
Hard Return Character

Sort

WordPerfect can sort five different types of text: lines, paragraphs, merge records, and table rows or columns. Each of these items is treated as a separate record. In a line sort, each record ends with a hard or soft return; in a paragraph sort, a record ends with two or more hard carriage returns; in a merge sort, a record ends with an (End Record) code; and in a table, each table row or column is a record.

Records can be further divided into fields which are sorted within each record. The following combinations are possible:

- You can sort a line record by tabular columns and by words within each column. For example, field 2, word 2 would sort by last name if the names were stored in first name/last name order in the second column. If there are no tabular columns, lines are sorted by the first characters in the line.
- You can sort a paragraph record by a particular line and, within each line, by a particular word. For example, line 1, word 1 would sort on the first word of a numbered paragraph.

- You can sort a merge record by a field, a line within a field, and a word within a line. For example, field 3, line 1, word 3 might sort by ZIP code in an address record, assuming field three was the City, State, ZIP field.
- You can sort a table record by cell, lines within cells, and words within lines.

Line fields (in a paragraph, merge, or table sort) are separated (delimited) by soft or hard returns. Tabular fields are separated by a single or equal number of tab characters. Word fields are separated by spaces.

NOTE: Tabular fields in the same column must be separated by an equal number of tab codes. Additional tab codes are treated as part of the following fields and are considered the first character in the field.

You can choose ascending (A-Z or 1-10) or descending (Z-A or 10-1) sorts. However, for this to work properly, you must identify the sort correctly as alpha (letters) or numeric (numbers). If you define the sort inaccurately—for example, as an alpha sort on numbers—you can have the following type of error occur in an ascending sort:

20
500
70

As you can see, these numbers were sorted by the first character, from left to right.

You can sort on up to nine keys. You choose additional keys only if the primary key contains duplicate values. For example, in a merge sort in which you had multiple records for each state, you might want to sort by state (first key), within state by city (second key), and perhaps within city by ZIP code (third key).

You can sort an entire document or selected text. Your sorted output can be directed to the current document, or to a different document.

Menu Selections

If necessary, select the text you want to sort. Choose Tools/Sort or press the shortcut keys ALT+F9 to display the Sort dialog box, shown in Figure 11-97.

Select the record type and sort order. The Table row and Column options will be greyed out unless you are in a table area.

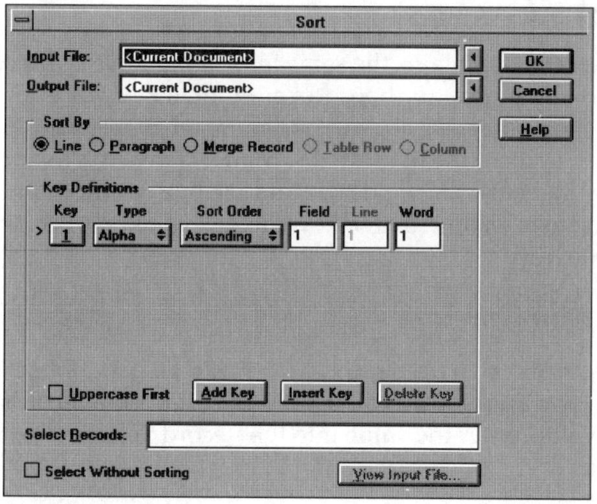

Figure 11-97. *The Sort dialog box*

Defining Keys

Before you conduct the sort, you must define your keys. Keys are the entries on which you want the information sorted. Initially, only the definition for a single key is displayed. Select Alpha or Numeric as the type. Then specify the number of the field, line, or word you want to sort by.

If you select a line sort, you can specify the tabular field (column) and the word within the tabular field. If you make no changes, WordPerfect will sort by only the first word (or tabular field) in the line (field 1, word 1).

If you select a paragraph sort, you can select the line, tabular field within each line, and word within each column. If you make no changes, WordPerfect sorts by the first word of the first line of the paragraph.

If you select a merge sort, you can select the field, line within each field, and word within each line. If you make no changes, WordPerfect sorts by the first word of the first line of the first field.

If you select a table sort, you can specify the cell, line within each cell, and word within each line. If you make no changes, WordPerfect sorts by the first word in the first line of the first cell.

Additional Keys

If more than one record contains the same information in the selected key field, line, or word, you may want to choose an additional key. For example, if you select "state" as the primary key to sort and there are a number of records from California, you may want the list sorted secondarily by city. To add a second key, select Insert Key and enter the field type and the line, word, or field numbers. You can continue to insert up to nine keys. To delete a key, select the key and then select Delete Key.

Selecting Records

You can select records on the basis of the key field. For example, if you are sorting by state, you might want to select all the California records. To select records by key value, enter the value into the Record Selection text box, using the following format:

```
key#=value
```

For example, to select records with "CA" in the state field, if state is the first key, enter

```
key1=CA
```

The key value can be entered in any combination of upper- or lowercase letters. Matches are found regardless of case.

You can use the additional symbols shown in Table 11-4 when selecting fields. (The examples assume that key1 is "state," key2 is "city," and key3 is "salary.")

WordPerfect evaluates the selected statement from left to right, unless parentheses are included. Portions of search statements in parentheses are evaluated first, from left to right.

Selecting Global Keys

Occasionally you might want to select records that contain a certain value anywhere in the entire record. For example, you might want to select paragraphs in a contract that include a reference to a specific product, such as disk drives. In that case you would enter

```
keyg=disk drives
```

in the Record Selection text box. "Keyg" is a WordPerfect code for a global key.

Key	Description	Code Example	Code Effect
+	Matches either key	key1=CA+key2= Denver	Either CA or Denver records will be selected
*	Matches both keys	key1=CA*key2= San Francisco	Selects only records in San Francisco, CA
<>	Does not match key	key1<>CA	Selects records not in CA
>	Greater-than key	key1>CA	Selects records where the state value comes after CA alphabetically, such as CT, CO, or OH
		key3>20000	Selects records with salaries greater than 20,000
<	Less-than key	key1<CA	Selects records where the state value falls before CA alphabetically, such as AK or AL
		key3<20000	Selects records with salaries less than 20,000
<=	Less-than or equal to key	key1<=CA	Selects CA records as well as those that come before it alphabetically
		key3<=20000	Selects records with salaries 20,000 or less
>=	Greater-than or equal to key	key1>=CA	Selects CA as well as records that follow it alphabetically
		key3>=20000	Selects records with salaries of 20,000 or more

Table 11-4. *Additional Symbols for Selecting Records*

For best results, use only the = symbol with the keyg selection. This will select all records that contain the global key. If you were to use, for example, keyg>d, WordPerfect would select all records that contain *any* word beginning with a letter after *d*.

If you want to select records without sorting, select the Select Without Sorting checkbox in the lower-left corner of the Sort dialog box.

Performing the Sort

When you select OK, WordPerfect begins the sort. As it is sorting, WordPerfect displays a Sort Status dialog box, showing how many records are being sorted and/or selected. After the sort is complete, the destination document contains the newly sorted and selected records.

Sound

WordPerfect allows you to add sound clips to your documents, provided that you have the proper sound hardware necessary to reproduce the sounds. WordPerfect supports the more popular sound boards, including the Sound Blaster.

Menu Selections

To insert or delete sounds, use the Insert/Sound menu option. You will see the Sound Clips dialog box, shown in Figure 11-98.

To insert a sound, choose Insert and supply a name for the clip, as well as a filename for the actual audio file. When you click OK, the sound clip is added to the list of sound clips in the document. This list is visible in the Sound Clips dialog box.

Other controls on this dialog box allow you to record sounds, save them to disk, and delete sounds from the document file.

Once a sound clip is inserted in your document, you can play it by clicking the sound clip icon, which is on the left margin of your document.

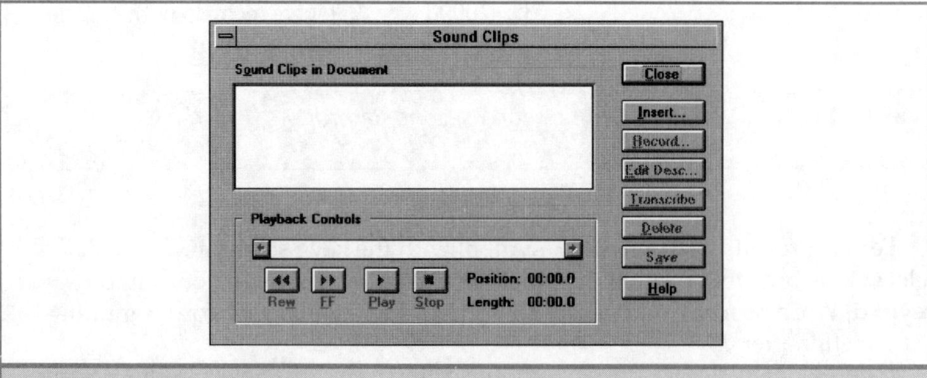

Figure 11-98. *The Sound Clips dialog box*

Special Codes

Special codes are unique forms of commonly used characters that WordPerfect treats in a special way. These codes affect the way certain tabs behave and the way hyphens and spaces are treated when text falls at the end of the line.

Menu Selections

To create a special code, first place the insertion point where you want to insert the code and choose Layout/Line/Other Codes. The Other Codes dialog box, shown in Figure 11-99, is divided into four groups: Hard Tab Codes, Hard Tab Codes with Dot Leaders, Hyphenation Codes, and Other Codes.

Hard Tabs

Hard tab codes change the type of tab at a particular location for that line only. For example, suppose you have a left tab which you would like to be a center tab in one line only. Instead of changing the current tab setting just for that tab and then changing it back again, you can insert a hard center tab. The tabs at that location in other lines will remain left-justified.

To insert a hard tab code, select Left, Center, Right, or Decimal from the dialog box. If you want to insert a dot leader tab, select Left, Center, Right, or Decimal from the Hard Tab Codes with Dot Leaders group. Use Reveal Codes to view the code.

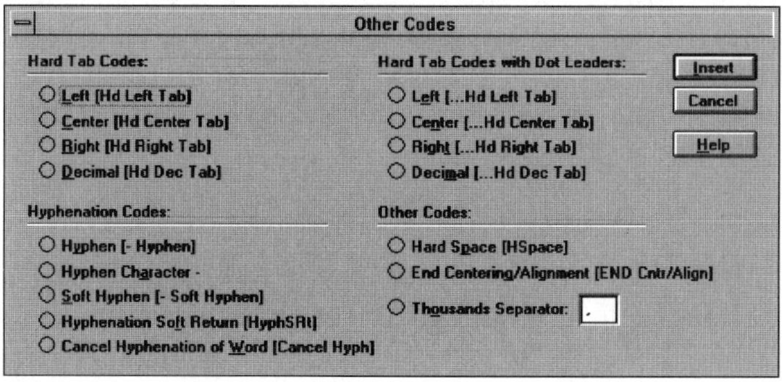

Figure 11-99. *The Other Codes dialog box*

Hyphenation Codes

Hyphenation codes tell WordPerfect how to handle words during hyphenation. These codes are placed at the insertion point when you make your selections.

Select Hyphen from the Hyphenation Codes group when you want a hyphen to be displayed and printed, and when it is acceptable to break up words at the hyphen when they fall at the end of a line. This is equivalent to simply typing the - key.

Select Hyphen Character if you want to insert a hard hyphen between two words that must be treated as one word and which should not be broken up at the hyphen when they fall at the end of a line. An example might be a hyphenated name such as Smythe-Jones. You can also enter the hyphen from the keyboard by pressing CTRL+-.

Select Soft Hyphen when you want to show WordPerfect where to break up a word when it is hyphenated at the end of a line. This soft hyphen will appear in the Reveal Codes window, but it will not be displayed or printed unless the word is broken up at the end of the line. You can also use the shortcut keys CTRL+SHIFT+- to insert a soft hyphen.

Hyphenation Soft Return also tells WordPerfect where to break words should they fall at the end of a line, but without inserting a hyphen. Although its name suggests hyphenation usage only, Hyphenation Soft Return is also useful for words separated by a slash (/) character, such as "and/or" that fall at the end of a line.

Select Cancel Hyphenation of Word if hyphenation is on and you don't want to hyphenate the word. Place the insertion point in front of the word you don't want hyphenated before selecting this code.

Hard Spaces

Normally, WordPerfect wraps entire words to the next line when it runs out of room on the right margin, and it considers any string of characters that ends in a space to be a word. Use the *hard space code* when you don't want word wrap to break two or more consecutive words separated by spaces, such as dates, phone numbers, or names. To do this, select Hard Space from the Other Codes dialog box instead of entering a normal space. You can also enter it from the keyboard as you type by pressing CTRL+SPACEBAR.

End Centering

When you are using center justification for text, you can discontinue the centering temporarily by selecting End Centering/Alignment. This discontinues centering for that line only and continues centering on the next line.

Related Entries

Center Text
Hyphenation
Tabs, Setting

Speller

The WordPerfect Speller program checks your spelling against a 115,000 word dictionary supplied with WordPerfect. You can check all or a portion of the current document. You can correct misspelled words, add words to the dictionary, or skip them entirely. The Speller program includes a main and supplemental dictionary. Words are always added to the supplemental dictionary.

The main dictionary is based on United States English. However, you can purchase dictionaries for other languages. You can also purchase other dictionaries for use with special documents, such as legal and scientific.

In addition, you can create your own dictionary, add or delete groups of words in the dictionary, and perform other utility functions by using the WordPerfect Speller feature.

Menu Selections

To check the entire document, choose Tools/Speller from the menus, or use the Speller button on the power bar. The Speller dialog box appears, as shown here:

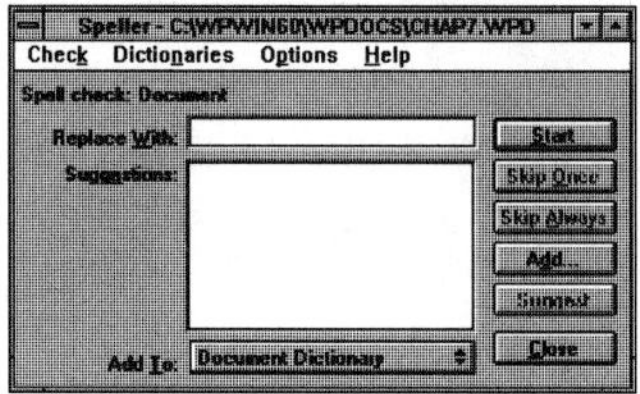

The name of the current document is displayed in the title bar of the box. The choices under the Check menu allow you to specify what portion of your document should be checked. You can instruct WordPerfect to check the current word, sentence, paragraph, page, document, selected text, text entry/box, to check to the end of the document, or to check a specific number of pages. By default, WordPerfect checks the entire document; you will need to explicitly make a change if this is not what you want the program to do.

Select Start to begin the Speller. When WordPerfect encounters a word not found in either the main or supplemental dictionary, it displays the message "Not found:", followed by the word. The word is highlighted in the document, as well. In the Suggestions box, WordPerfect displays what it determines to be the words most similar to the misspelled word.

You have the following choices at this point:

- Select the correct spelling from the Suggestions box and select Replace to replace the incorrect word. For more suggestions, select Suggest.
- If the word is just mistyped, you can correct it in the Replace With text box and select Replace to replace the incorrect word with your edited version.
- If the word is spelled correctly and will be used again, you can select Add to add the word to the supplemental dictionary.
- Select Skip Once to skip just this occurrence of the word or Skip Always to skip all occurrences of this word in this document.

Looking up a Word or Pattern

You can enter any word or word pattern in the Word text box and ask for suggested spellings. Simply type the word and select Suggest. If you are not certain of the spelling, you can create a word pattern by typing the characters you do know and including wildcards to represent unknown characters. The * represents multiple characters; the ? represents a single character. Enter the pattern and then select Suggest. For example:

w*r Causes WordPerfect to suggest options including water, wackier, wastepaper, watercolor, wonder, and whatsoever—that is, all words beginning with *w* and ending with *r*.

w??r Causes WordPerfect to suggest wear, weir, and whir—that is, the only words in its dictionary beginning with *w* followed by exactly two letters and ending with *r*.

Selecting a Dictionary

If you need to choose another main or supplemental dictionary, select the Dictionaries menu, and then choose either Main or Supplementary, depending on which dictionary you want to specify. WordPerfect will display either the Main Dictionaries or the Supplementary Dictionaries dialog box (the latter is shown in Figure 11-100). Both of these dialog boxes display a list of dictionaries in the order in which they are searched by the Speller.

The buttons to the right of the dictionary list allow you to add (Insert) or remove (Delete) dictionaries from the list. You can also use the Edit button to make changes to a specific dictionary. When you are happy with the dictionary search list, click Close.

Speller Options

Choose Options from the Speller menu to turn on and off the settings that cause WordPerfect to query words with numbers, duplicate words, or irregular capitalization.

Interactive Spell Check While Editing

The fact that the Speller dialog box remains open until you close it can work to your advantage. With the dialog box open, you can scroll through your document as you edit, checking selected text. Click your document window to activate it and select Start from the Speller dialog box when you want to spell-check selected text. Even if you are in the middle of checking your text, you can return to your document by clicking the document window. If you catch an error that has gone undetected by the Speller, you can stop and fix the mistake. Then select Resume (which temporarily replaces the Replace button) from the Speller dialog box to return to the spell check.

Related Entries

Language
Windows, Working with Multiple

Spreadsheet Linking and Importing

See Chapter 9, "Spreadsheet and Database Files."

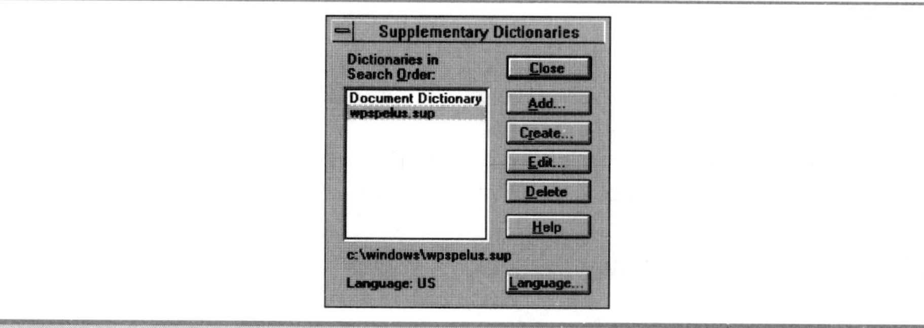

Figure 11-100. *The Supplemental Dictionaries dialog box*

Start a New Page

See Page Breaks.

Startup Options

Ordinarily, when you want to use WordPerfect for Windows, you first run the Windows program from DOS by typing **win**, wait for it to load, and then select the WordPerfect icon from its group window. However, you can load both Windows and WordPerfect with one command line from DOS. In addition, you can specify a file to open or a macro to run when WordPerfect starts. The following is a list of the startup options and a brief description of each one.

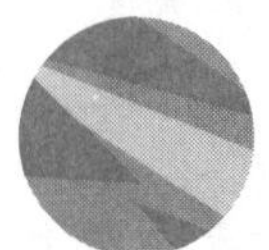

NOTE: *You can specify the startup options either from the DOS command line or, when running WordPerfect from Windows, by using the Windows File/Run command. From DOS, you must type* ***WIN*** *at the beginning of each command to launch Windows. For brevity, all but the first of the following startup options do not show the WIN part of the command.*

WIN WPWIN The WIN WPWIN command loads Windows from DOS and then loads WordPerfect. The directory for WPWIN must be in your path.

WPWIN/D-(DRIVE/DIRECTORY) WordPerfect creates temporary buffer files on the disk to hold extra data while it is processing. Normally, these files are stored in the directory where your WPWIN.EXE file is located. To store these files in another drive or directory, use this option. For example:

```
WPWIN/D-C:\TEMP
```

stores the buffer files in a directory called \TEMP on drive C. This option is useful if you want to use a RAM drive instead of disk space.

WPWIN FILENAME This option loads WordPerfect and opens the specified file. You must include a path if the file is not stored in the current directory. For example:

```
WPWIN D:\ARCHIVE\DATA\SMITH.LET
```

opens a file called SMITH.LET from the \ARCHIVE\DATA directory on drive D.

WPWIN/M (MACRO NAME) This option loads WordPerfect and also runs the specified macro. Remember to include a path if the macro is not in the current directory.

WPWIN/NB If you use the Original Document Backup option, WordPerfect automatically saves a backup of the previously edited version of the current document (called *filename*.BK!). This means that for each document you create, you have two on the disk—the current one and the previous version. This option overrides the Original Backup setting and overwrites the original file each time, saving disk space.

WPWIN/X This option tells WordPerfect to use the original default preference settings for this session. As soon as you exit, the previous preference settings are restored.

Related Entries

Backup, Timed
Preferences
See also Chapter 10, "Using WordPerfect for Windows on a Network."

Status Bar

The status bar, shown at the very bottom of the screen, looks like this:

Times New Roman Regular 14 pt | Insert | Select | Pg 1 Ln 1" Pos 1"

It displays information about the current document and menu selection. The left side of the status bar is used to display the font type of the text at the insertion point.

Elsewhere on the status bar is the word Select. This is dimmed unless you have made a text selection, in which case it is black.

The far right of the status bar displays the page, line, and column position of the insertion point. The position is displayed in the current unit of measure. This is usually in inches ("); however, you can choose to measure distance in other units of measure. If you are in column mode, the current column number is also displayed.

You can change the appearance of the status bar shown by moving, adding, and deleting labels.

Menu Selections

Choose File/Preferences/Status Bar to access the Status Bar Preferences dialog box. In the Status Bar Items list there are 19 choices which affect the appearance of the status bar. The default items are marked with an *X* already. To add an item to the status bar, simply click it to place an *X* in the check box. To remove an item, click it to remove the X. As you add or remove items, you can see the changes take place immediately on the status bar.

If you cannot seem to place the items exactly where you want, try deleting all the items and then adding each in the order you want it to appear on the status bar. Other factors also affect the layout of items on the status bar, such as the font, spacing, and so forth. To change these attributes, click Options. From this Status Bar Options dialog box you can apply the desired font and size attributes to the labels. Click Bold Font and all labels will appear in bold type. If you want to space all items evenly on the status bar, enable Evenly Spaced Items. Since some labels are wider than others, this ensures a "best fit" look for the labels. Choose the graphical appearance of the labels on the status bar by clicking Flat, Inset, or Raised. When you are finished, click OK.

To return the status bar to its original, or default, state, click Default from the Status Bar Preferences dialog box.

Related Entries

Display Preferences
INSERT Key
Pull-Down Menus
Save and Save As
Tables, Creating
Units of Measure

Strikeout Text

You generally use the strikeout attribute to indicate text that has been deleted. It is a technique for drawing attention to edited text. A line is drawn through the text selected for strikeout:

~~change~~

Menu Selections

First select the text that you want to strike out. Choose Layout/Font, and then choose the Strikeout attribute. The line is added to the text and the appropriate codes are inserted at the beginning and end of the selected text.

WordPerfect uses the redline character to indicate text that has been added to a document. The Document Compare feature compares two versions of the same document and automatically adds the appropriate markings to inserted or deleted text.

Related Text

Compare Documents
Redline

Styles

The Styles feature allows you to store multiple formatting codes under a single name. You can then use these styles to format all or a portion of your document. There are two general types of styles: paired and open.

Paired styles can be turned on and off. When a paired style is selected, WordPerfect automatically inserts (Style On: *name*) and (Style off: *name*) codes around your insertion point. Paired styles are practical for section headings, special quotes, and other uniquely formatted text that requires several special attributes such as font and size changes, boldface, and so on.

Open styles can be turned on but not off and are usually designed for formatting an entire document. These codes remain in effect until another of the same open code is encountered. Open styles are useful if your documents use common headers, footers, margin and tab settings, line spacing, and so on. You can also create styles for outlines and paragraph numbering.

Any code can be included in a style, with the exception of those that must be generated, such as tables of contents, endnotes, and indexes.

Styles are generally stored with the current document. They can also be stored separately in a special file called a *style library,* which is stored on the disk with a .STY extension. WordPerfect includes a default library file called LIBRARY.STY. If this file is present, the styles in the file are available for any document. You can also create your own style library files, and the styles stored in these files can also be copied into any document.

Menu Selections

To create a new style, choose Layout/Styles from the menus or use the ALT+F8 shortcut keys to display the Style List dialog box shown in Figure 11-101.

The dialog box displays a list of style names stored with the current template. To create the new style, select Create to display the Styles Editor, displayed in Figure 11-102.

Enter a unique name of up to 12 characters in the Style Name text box. Enter a description of up to 54 characters in the Description text box. The description is optional, but you must enter a name.

The default style type is Paragraph (paired). Click the triangles next to the current type to change the style type. To the right of the Type field you can specify what will happen when this style is active and you press ENTER. Basically, you can specify what you want the following style to be. For instance, let's assume you have defined a heading style, and you know that when you press ENTER at the end of the heading, the next paragraph will always be a regular text paragraph. All you need to do is specify the name of the style you want to follow the heading. If used properly, this is a very powerful feature.

Finally, you can enter, in the Contents box, the codes and text that define the style. This is the heart of the Styles feature: it determines exactly what will happen when you apply the style. When you have finished entering your codes, select OK to save the codes and return to the Styles box. The newly created style is displayed and selected.

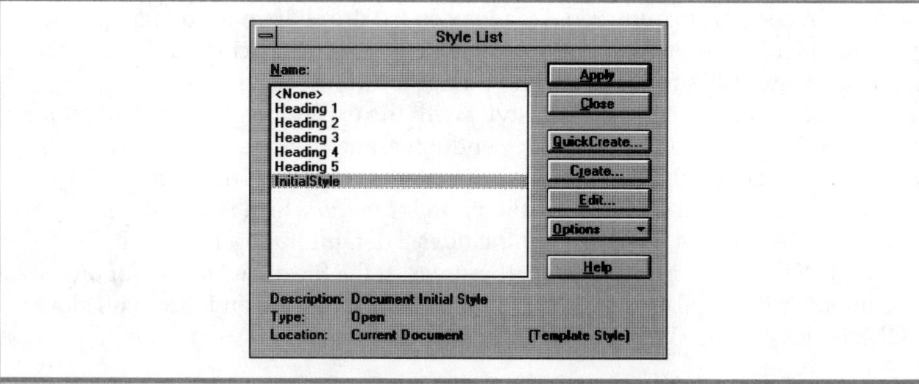

Figure 11-101. *The Style List dialog box*

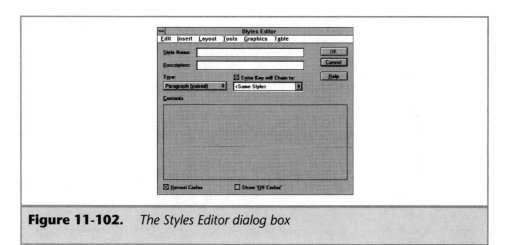

Figure 11-102. *The Styles Editor dialog box*

Applying Styles

To apply a style, position the insertion point where you want the style to take effect. Choose Layout/Styles from the menu or press the ALT+F8 shortcut key. Select the style name and select Apply.

Editing Styles

To edit a style, choose Layout/Styles from the menu or press the ALT+F8 shortcut key. Select the style name and select Edit. The Styles Editor is displayed. From here you can make any corrections or changes desired. Select OK when you are finished.

Deleting Styles

From the Style List dialog box, select the style you want to delete, than select Options/Delete to display the Delete Styles dialog box shown here:

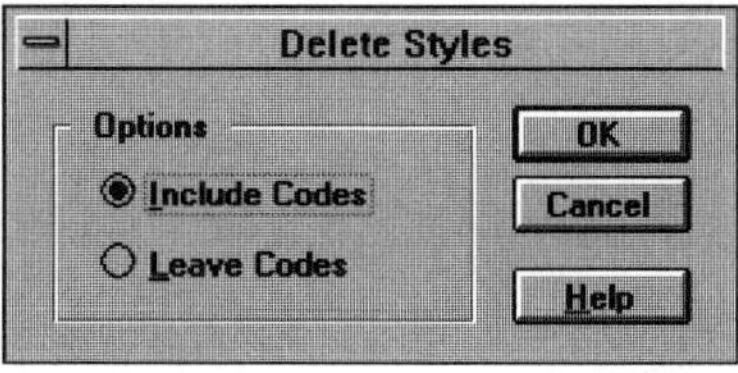

In this box you have two options:

- Select Include Codes if you want to delete the style and the codes from the document. You will no longer be able to use the deleted style in this or any other document unless you previously saved it.

- Select Leave Codes to delete the style but not the codes. WordPerfect will remove the name from the Styles box and delete all references to the name in the document. However it will replace the style codes with the actual codes defined by the style.

Saving Styles

When you save your document, all the styles you created are saved with it. If you want to use these styles in another document, you must save them in a style library file.

To save the styles, choose Layout/Styles or use the ALT+F8 shortcut key to display the Style List dialog box. Select Options/Save As to display the Save Styles To dialog box shown in Figure 11-103. In the Filename field, enter a name for the file that will contain the styles. An extension is not added automatically, so you should provide an appropriate extension, such as .STY. The style library will be saved in the default TEMPLATE directory.

You can also specify what WordPerfect saves in the file. You can specify either User Styles, System Styles, or Both. Select OK to save the style library and return to the Styles dialog box. All of the selected styles will be saved in this library.

Retrieving Styles

If you want to use a style that you created in another document, you must first open the document that contains the style and save the style in a library. Once the style is saved in a library, you can copy the library into another document.

To retrieve a style library, select Layout/Styles or press ALT+F8. Select Options/Retrieve from the Style List dialog box to display the Retrieve Styles From dialog box, shown in Figure 11-104. This box displays a list of the library files stored in the default LIBRARY directory.

Enter the name of the library file to retrieve, or click the file folder to the right of the Filename text box in order to select a library file from disk. Once you have specified a name, click OK. If the style library you are retrieving contains any styles with the same name as those in your current document, WordPerfect displays a dialog box saying that the styles already exist and asks if you want to

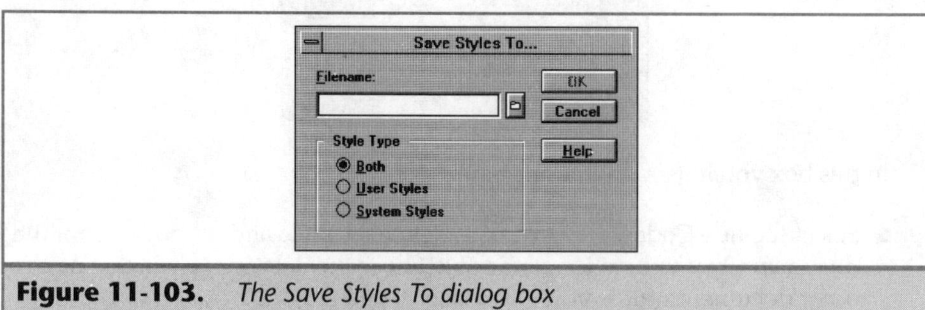

Figure 11-103. *The Save Styles To dialog box*

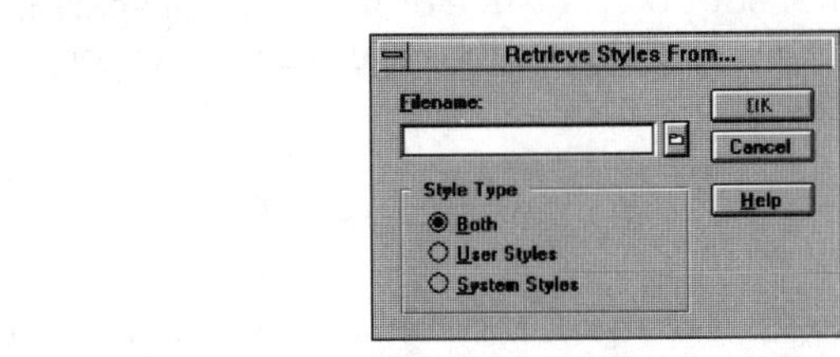

Figure 11-104. *The Retrieve Styles From dialog box*

replace them. If you select Yes, the definitions for those styles with the same name are replaced by those in the retrieved library. If you select No, only styles with no matching names are copied. Most likely, the styles with the same names are identical, but if you are not sure, you are better off selecting No.

Related Entries

Location of Files
Open
Outline

Subdocument

A *subdocument* is a regular WordPerfect document that can also be part of a larger master document. The subdocument is connected to the master by a link and can be printed as part of the master document. A subdocument is identified by the icon in the left margin of the master document.

Related Entries

Master Documents

Subscript

Subscript text is printed below the baseline, as in H_2O. The text will appear subscript on the screen (by about 1/2 line, depending on your printer driver). When the document is printed, the subscript characters will be printed in a smaller size so as not to interfere with the line spacing. Your printer must support half-line or incremental line spacing in order to take advantage of this feature. If your printer does not support half-line or incremental spacing, the subscript text may appear on the same line as the other text; however, it will be printed in smaller type.

Menu Selections

To subscript text, choose Layout/Font to see the Font dialog box. In the Position field, select Subscript.

Related Entries

Fonts
Superscript

Summary

You can create a Document Summary for every file you create. The Document Summary dialog box shown in Figure 11-105 contains Reference and Information groups that allow you to enter descriptive information about your document, as described here. All of these entries are optional.

- In the Descriptive Name text box, you can enter up to 256 characters to briefly describe the document. This is not the same thing as the name of the file on disk.
- In the Descriptive Type text box, you can enter up to 256 characters categorizing the type of document. For example, you may want to use the terms "Memo," "Letter," "Manuscript," and "Contract" to organize your files by type.
- The Creation Date option defaults to the system date and is never changed by WordPerfect once it is first set. You can, however, change the date to reflect the time when the document was actually created.
- Revision Date is modified automatically by WordPerfect each time you revise the document. You cannot change this entry manually.
- In the Author text box, type the name of the author.
- In the Typist text box, type the name of the original typist.
- In the Subject text box, enter the subject of the document. This information can be copied from a portion of the document.

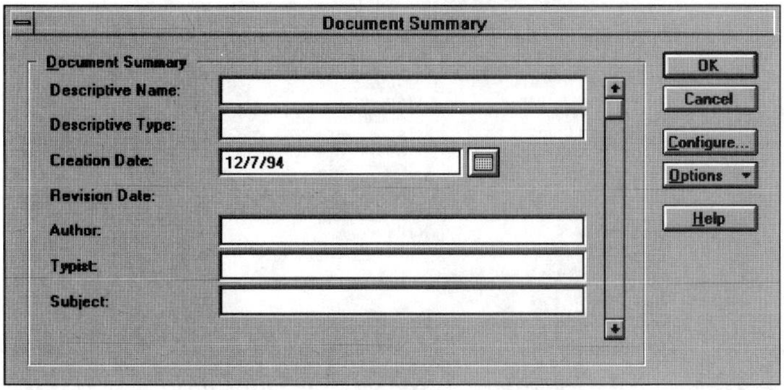

Figure 11-105. *The Document Summary dialog box*

These fields provide all of the information that most people need for summary purposes. However, WordPerfect allows you to change the configuration, as described later in this section.

Menu Selections

To create, view, edit, or print a summary of the current document, choose File/Document Summary. Enter the appropriate information into the text boxes. You can fill in some or all of them, except for the Revision Date box.

The document summary information is stored with the document when you click the OK button.

Changing the Document Summary Configuration

WordPerfect for Windows allows you to modify what information is tracked in the summary fields. This is done by selecting the Configure button at the right side of the Document Summary dialog box. When you do, you will see the Document Summary Configuration dialog box, shown in Figure 11-106.

The right side of this dialog box shows the possible fields you can track in the document summary. WordPerfect provides 51 different fields, covering virtually everything you can think of. The selected fields (the ones that have the checkboxes selected) also appear in the left side of the dialog box. You can then rearrange these fields by moving them with the mouse.

If you click the Use as Default button, your new configuration will be used for all new documents you create. When you are happy with the document summary information, you can click the OK button and your configuration will be saved.

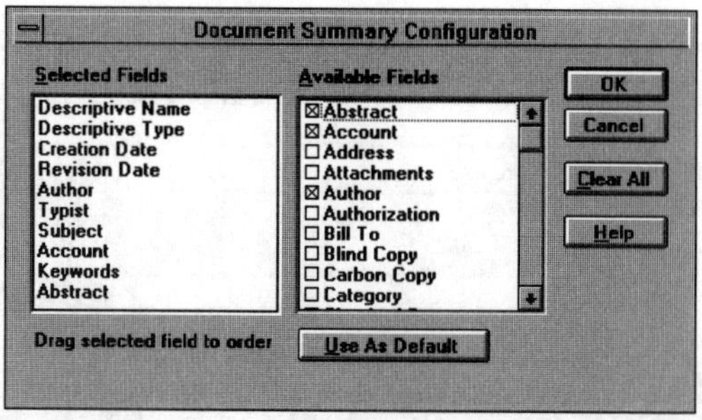

Figure 11-106. *The Document Summary Configuration dialog box*

Related Entries

Document Summary
File Manager
Preferences

Superscript

Superscript text is printed above the baseline, as in $e=mc^2$. The text will appear as superscript on the screen (by about 1/2 line, depending on your printer driver). When the document is printed, the superscript characters will be printed in a smaller size so as not to interfere with the line spacing. Your printer must support half-line or incremental line spacing in order to take advantage of this feature. If your printer does not support half-line or incremental spacing, the superscript text may appear on the same line as the other text; however, it will be printed in smaller type.

Menu Selections

To superscript text, choose Layout/Font to see the Font dialog box. Click the Position option button, and select Superscript.

Related Entries

Fonts
Subscript

Supplemental Dictionary

See Speller.

Suppress

When you include a special page in your document and don't want to print the header, footer, watermark, or page number on that page, you can suppress one or all of these items. The page number sequence will not be affected.

S

Menu Selections

To suppress page formatting, position the insertion point at the beginning of the page. Choose Layout/Page/Suppress to display the Suppress dialog box shown here:

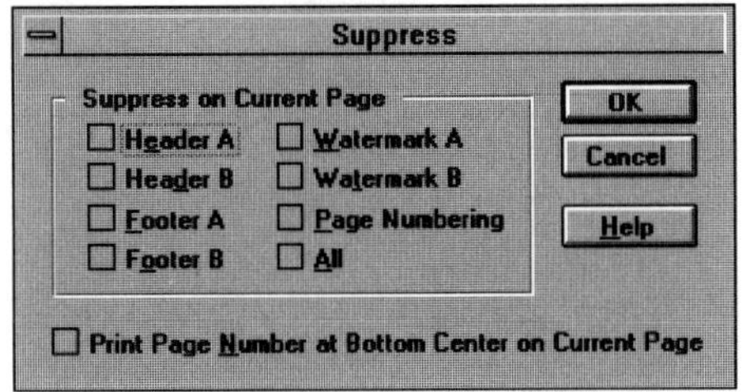

Select one or more page formatting attributes from the list. If you want to print the page number at the bottom center for that page only, select Print Page Number at Bottom Center on Current Page.

Swap Files, Windows

When you are using Windows to work with multiple applications, Windows creates temporary files on the disk to free up memory as you move between applications. These are known as *application swap files*. You can create instruct Windows to create a permanent swap file on your hard disk by allocating a specific amount of disk space to a hidden file named 386SPART.PAR. This disk space will not be available for saving files, but it speeds up the Windows operation and allows you to have more applications open and running.

Consult your Windows documentation for more information on creating swap files.

Switch to Another Document

See Windows, Working with Multiple

Switch to Another Program

When you work under Windows, you can have multiple application programs open simultaneously. These programs might be displayed in another window or minimized into an icon. The Windows program uses a Task List to display all the currently open programs, and you use this Task List to switch programs, tile or cascade all open application windows, or close an application.

Menu Selections

Choose the WordPerfect application control menu and choose Switch To or press the CTRL+ESC shortcut keys to display the Task List shown here:

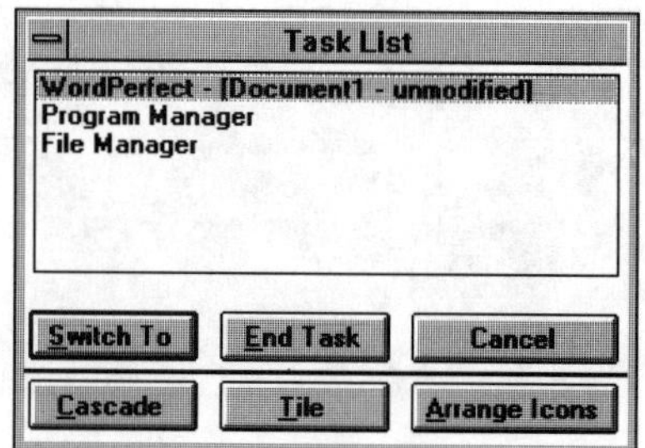

Select the program you want and select Switch To to make it the active program, End Task to close the application, or Tile or Cascade to display all the open application windows. The Program Manager is always displayed in the Task List, because it is always open. If you want to begin another application that is not currently open, switch to the Program Manager.

You can also toggle between open applications by pressing ALT+ESC.

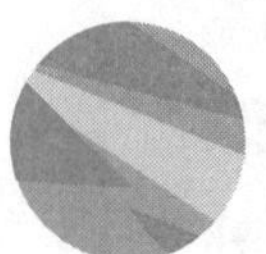

NOTE: If you should accidently minimize the WordPerfect program and can't see the icon, or if you just don't know how to get back into WordPerfect, press CTRL+ESC *to display the Task List, and select WordPerfect from the list. If WordPerfect is not listed, then you exited from program. You must select the icon from the WordPerfect group window to open it again.*

Related Entries

Displaying Multiple Windows

Tab Key

To advance to the tab stops on your ruler, press the TAB key. The key is located at the upper-left corner of your keyboard and is usually labeled with the word "Tab" and left and right arrows.

Table Boxes

See Graphics entries.

Table Lines and Fill

You can choose to format the lines that surround the cells of the table to any number of different options, including to have the table print out with no lines at all. The default is to have a double line around the border of the table and to have single lines surround the cells in the table.

Menu Selections

To change the way the lines in your table print, first select the cells to be adjusted. Then choose Tables/Lines/Fill, and the Table Lines/Fill dialog box appears on your screen, as shown in Figure 11-107.

You can adjust the lines on all sides of the table cells, the selected table area, or the entire table. By clicking the arrows to the right of each of these items, you can have the lines changed to any of 33 different line types.

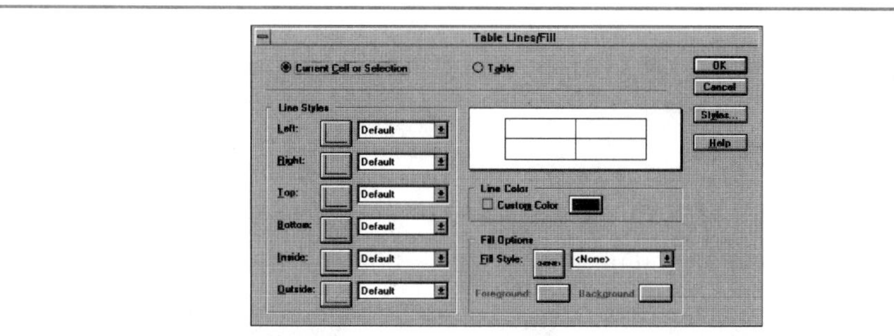

Figure 11-107. *The Table Lines/Fill dialog box*

You can also, if desired, change the way WordPerfect fills the selected table area. In the Fill Options portion of the dialog box, you can select any of 30 different fill types for your table area.

Notice that as you change line and fill settings, the sample in the dialog box changes as well. When you are satisfied with the appearance of the table area, click the OK button.

Table Math

See Math.

Table of Authorities

A *table of authorities* is similar to an index, except that is used primarily in legal documents for citing references to cases, constitutional provisions, statutory provisions, and so on. These citations are referred to as *authorities* and are listed in a table showing the page numbers of each occurrence. Each type of citation or authority can be categorized as a separate section, and you can have up to 16 sections in a document. Before you begin, you should organize information about your table and determine the following:

- The number of different sections, their order, and what type of citations (authorities) they will contain.
- The formal text for each item in a section, as it will appear in the table of authorities.
- A short name or abbreviation for each citation in a section. If a citation is referenced on more than one page, this speeds up the process of marking each occurrence of the citation.

Once you have made these decisions, take the following steps to create the table of authorities:

1. Mark each occurrence of the citation. These marks tell WordPerfect in which section and under what citation to put each occurrence.
2. Define the location and numbering format for each section.
3. If you place your tables of authorities at the beginning of your document, insert a new page number code on the first page of your main document

so that it will start with page 1; otherwise, WordPerfect will begin page numbering with the tables.

4. Generate the tables of authorities.

Menu Selections

Virtually all work with a table of authorities is done using the Table of Authorities feature bar. This feature bar is displayed when you select Tools/Table of Authorities:

The following sections describe how to use the feature bar to perform each step in creating a table of authorities.

Marking Text for the Table of Authorities

It doesn't matter in what order you mark your sections or your citations. However, you might find it easier to start with the first citation of the first section and mark all citations for section 1 before proceeding to the next section. Assign the first occurrence a section number and a short name, then enter the text as you want it to appear in the table. This is referred to as a *full form mark.* For each occurrence of the marked citation after that, you need only refer to the section and short name. This is referred to as a *short form mark.*

Select the first occurrence of the citation in a given section. Select Create Full Form from the feature bar, and you will see the Create Full Form dialog box:

Enter a section name, or select from the available section names. Enter a brief reference name in the Short Form box. If you have selected text, it will be displayed here, and you can use some or all of that text. However, if the selected text has any character attributes, such as bold or underscore, don't include them. You are better off retyping the text without attributes. When you select OK, your document will clear, the feature bar will change, and you can enter the text to be used for the full form, as shown in Figure 11-108.

The selected text will appear at the top of the screen. You can edit this text or replace it with the citation text as you want it to appear in the table. You don't

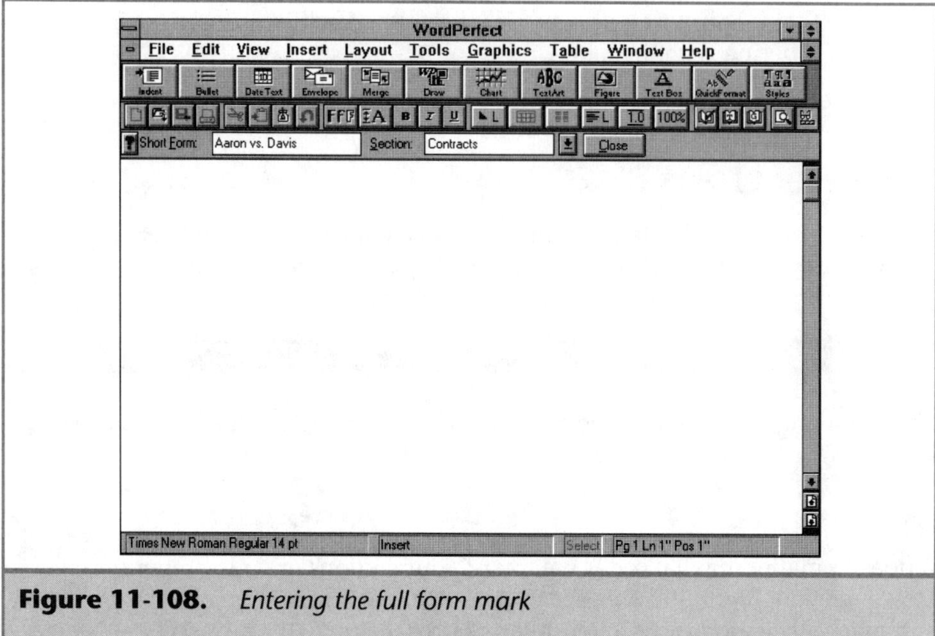

Figure 11-108. *Entering the full form mark*

need to be concerned about page number format. That will be taken care of when you define the table. Your citation text can be up to 30 lines long and can include WordPerfect formatting or character attributes such as hanging indents, boldface, special fonts, and so on.

When you have completed this screen, select Close to return to your document.

Next, locate the next occurrence of this citation and select it as well. This time, choose Mark from the feature bar. This marks the selected text with the citation represented by the short form. Continue selecting and marking each occurrence of the citation. Be sure to enter the correct short name reference; otherwise the citation occurrence will be listed separately in your table preceded by an asterisk, indicating a short form name without a matching full form reference.

Editing a Full Form

You can edit a full form reference by placing the insertion point to the right of the code for the reference you want to edit, and choosing Edit Full Form from the feature bar. This displays the full form text you previously entered for this reference. You can also select Edit Full Form to change the section number or short name. However, a word of caution: if you change the short name reference in your full form, you will also have to remark any subsequent occurrences of this citation and change the short name references that no longer match.

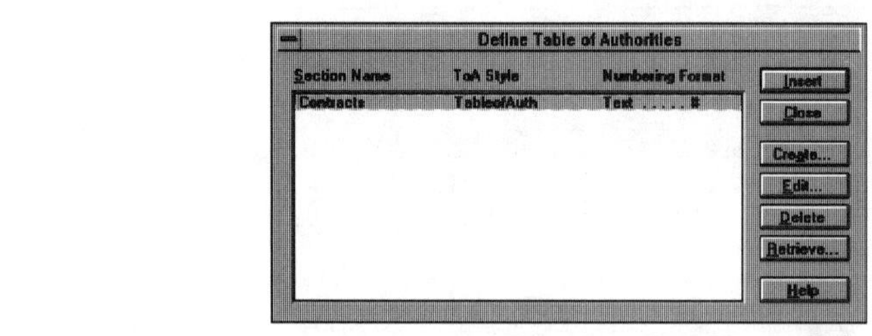

Figure 11-109. *The Define Table of Authorities dialog box*

Defining a Table of Authorities

The next step is to define your table of authorities. Each section is defined separately and in the order and place in which you want it to appear in your document.

Start by placing the insertion point where you want the first section to be located. You may want to place your table of authorities on a page by itself by inserting a hard page break and an appropriate section title or heading. Next, select Define from the feature bar to display the Define Table of Authorities dialog box shown in Figure 11-109.

Choose the section number you are defining, then choose Edit. Figure 11-110 shows the Edit Table of Authorities dialog box.

Make whatever changes you like to the appearance of the section. When you have completed the definition, select OK to return to the previous dialog box. Then choose Insert to mark the place where the table of authorities for this section is to be inserted into your document.

You can repeat the same steps for each section you have defined. Remember to precede each section with a hard page break and a title, if necessary.

Generating a Table of Authorities

After you have marked your citations, defined your table sections, and indicated where they are to be inserted in your document, you are ready to generate your table of authorities. Choose Generate from the feature bar to create the actual table of authorities. The Generate dialog box is displayed, as shown here:

Generate

Generate Table of Contents, Table of Authorities, Indexes, Cross-References and Lists.

OK | Cancel | Options... | Help

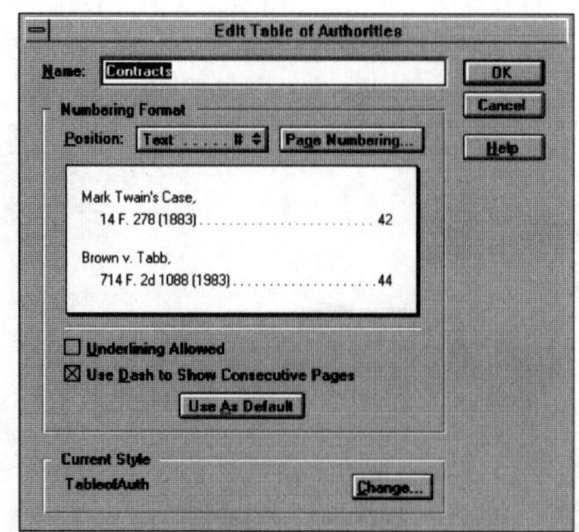

Figure 11-110. *The Edit Table of Authorities dialog box*

Select OK to continue. A series of messages is displayed as WordPerfect makes passes through the document, organizing the table of authorities. If you have not included a new page code at the top of the document, WordPerfect displays a message indicating that no new page number was found. Select OK or press ENTER and your table of authorities will be completed.

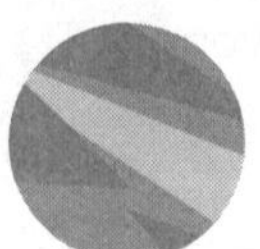

NOTE: *Any short names without full form references will be displayed at the top of the table, preceded by an asterisk. This means you either marked text for a short form and entered a nonexistent short name, or you changed the short name in one or more of your full forms and did not change the associated marked occurrences.*

Remember, each time you make a change to your document, you should regenerate your tables of authorities in case any relevant page numbers or text has changed.

Related Entries

Generate
Page Numbering

Table of Contents

WordPerfect allows you to generate a table of contents from the document. To do so, mark the text that will be used in the table of contents, define the table of contents, and then let WordPerfect generate the table of contents for you.

Menu Selections

All your actions for defining a table of contents are done using the table of contents feature bar. This feature bar appears when you select Tools/Table of Contents from the menu:

To mark an item for inclusion in the table of contents, select the item and click the button that indicates what head level the item represents. For instance, if the text belongs to a level 1 heading, click Mark 1; if it belongs to a level 3 heading, click Mark 3. Keep selecting and marking text until you have marked every item that you wish to include in the table of contents.

Next, position the insertion point where you want the table of contents to be placed. Press CTRL+ENTER to put a page break at that location, then move the insertion point so that it is on the new table of contents page. If you wish, type **Table of Contents** (usually centered at the top of the page), then position the insertion point where you want the table of contents to begin.

Before you can generate the table of contents, you need to define its appearance. Choose Define from the feature bar and the Define Table of Contents dialog box, shown in Figure 11-111, appears.

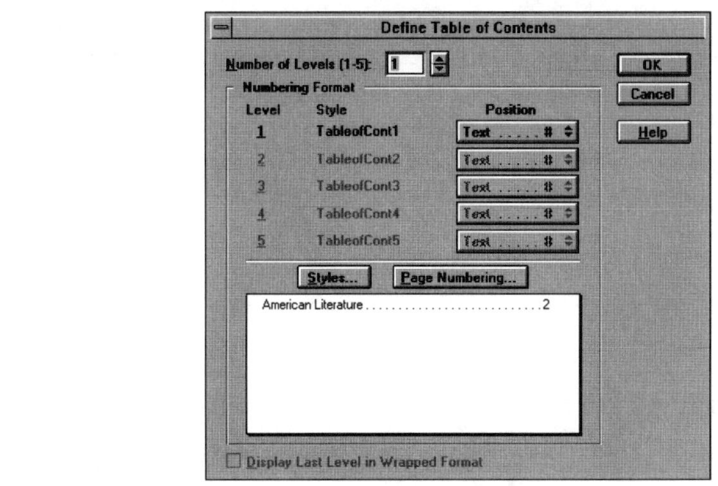

Figure 11-111. *The Define Table of Contents dialog box*

T

You first need to tell WordPerfect how many levels you have marked text for. Click the arrows to the right of the Number of Levels option until you reach the number of levels used. Up to five levels can be defined. If you define three levels, for example, the first three levels under the Numbering Format option become available.

You can further define each level by clicking the arrows to the right of that level, under the Position column. Possible definitions for the levels include:

Option	Meaning
No Numbering	No numbers appear
Text#	Page number right next to text
Text [#]	Page number next to text and in square brackets
Text #	Page number at the right-hand side of the page, with blank space between the text and page number
Text...#	Text on the left, page number on the right, and dot leaders separating the text from the page number

If you check Display Last Level in Wrapped Format (at the bottom of the dialog box), then the text of the lowest level head (greatest number) will wrap if it is too long to fit on the line. Otherwise, text will scroll off screen.

WordPerfect also allows you to define styles for your table of contents (click the Styles button) and to change the appearance of page numbers (click Page Numbering). When you have defined the table of contents the way you want it, click OK.

Now you are ready to generate the table of contents. Choose Generate from the feature bar and click OK when WordPerfect asks if you want to continue. If items in the table of contents change during subsequent edits, you will need to regenerate the table of contents.

Related Entries

Generate
Styles

Tables, Calculating

WordPerfect allows you to set up tables in simple spreadsheet format. This means that you can insert formulas and create dynamic figures in your documents. In order to make this process more automatic, you can instruct WordPerfect to calculate the formulas in your tables automatically.

Menu Selections

To set the calculation mode for WordPerfect tables, choose Table/Calculate from the menu. You will then see the Calculate dialog box, shown in Figure 11-112.

To instruct WordPerfect to calculate either your table or your document automatically, make choices in the Automatic Calculation Mode area. You can also use the buttons on the right side of the dialog box to manually calculate your table or document.

Related Entries

Math

Tables, Creating

WordPerfect allows you to create tables of any size and shape on your screen. Tables are used for creating specialized forms, lists, and parallel columns.

Menu Selections

There are two ways to create a table. The easiest method is to use the Create Table button on the power bar. When you click this button, you will see a grid that represents a table. Hold down the mouse button and move the pointer through the grid to specify the size of the table you want to create. When you release the mouse button, WordPerfect inserts a table at the location of your insertion point.

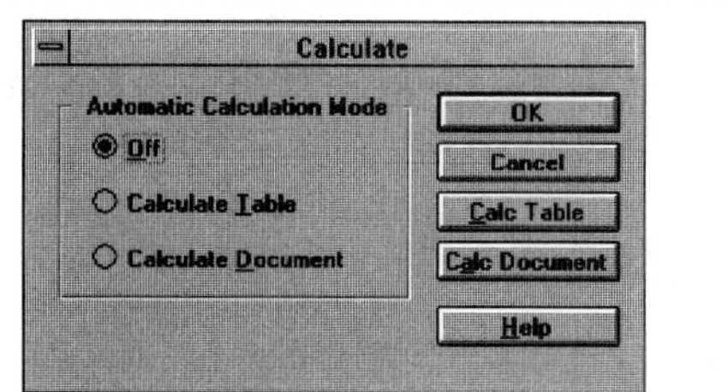

Figure 11-112. *The Calculate dialog box*

The other method of creating a table involves using the menu choices. You can choose Table/Create, and the Create Table dialog box appears on your screen:

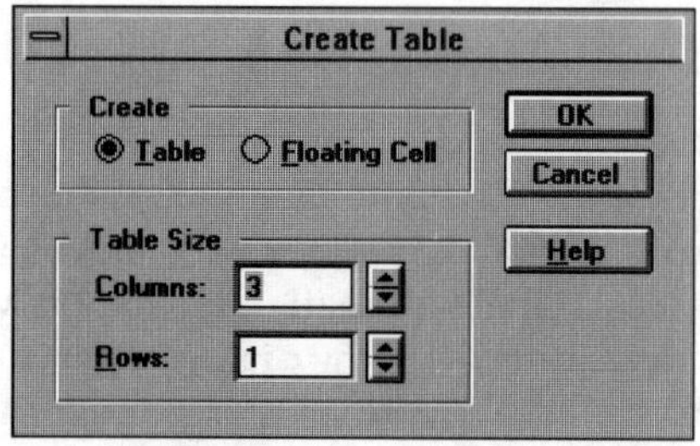

In the Columns box, type the number of columns you want in the table, and then tab to the Rows box and type the number of rows. Click OK, and the table appears on your screen.

To move from cell to cell, you can press TAB or your cursor arrows. When you print your table, it will look just the way it does on the screen.

Related Entries

Power Bar
Tables, Editing

Tables, Data Fill

See Math.

Tables, Editing

Once your table is on the screen, there are a number of editing options available for you to use. Among the more common editing tasks are joining and splitting cells and inserting and deleting columns and rows.

Menu Selections

To join two or more cells, select the cells to be joined with your mouse and choose Table/Join/Cell. The lines between the cells will disappear.

To split a cell into smaller units, select the cell to be split and choose Table/Split/Cell. The Split Cell dialog box will appear. Click Column or Row (depending on how you want the cell split) and type the number of subcells you want to create. If you type **2**, for example, the cell splits into two cells.

To insert columns or rows, choose Table/Insert, and the Insert Columns/Rows dialog box appears, as shown in Figure 11-113. Click Columns or Rows and then type the number of columns or rows you would like to add to the table. Click OK, and, depending on the Placement option chosen, WordPerfect inserts the rows beneath the location of the insertion point and the columns to the right of the insertion point.

To delete columns or rows, select the columns or rows to be deleted, and then choose Table/Delete. Click Columns or Rows, specify the number of columns or rows to delete, and then click OK. The selected columns or rows are deleted.

Tables, Formatting Cells

WordPerfect allows you to change any number of aspects of each cell in a table, including the appearance, size, justification, and alignment of text in the cell, as well as the cell attributes themselves.

Menu Selections

To format the cells in your table, you first select the cells you wish to change, then choose Table/Format. You will see the Format dialog box, as shown in Figure 11-114. Make sure the Cell button is selected at the top of the screen.

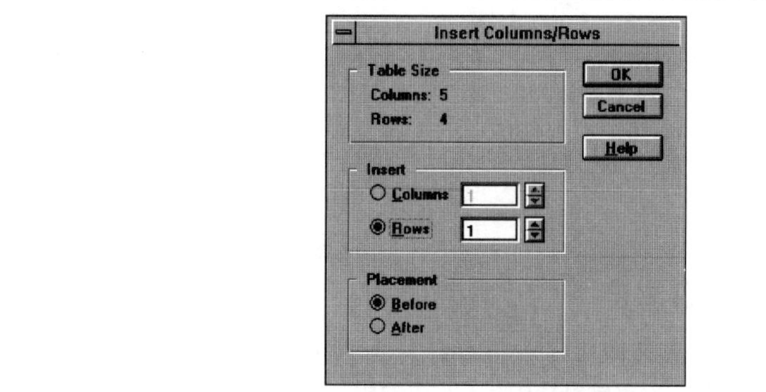

Figure 11-113. *The Insert Columns/Rows dialog box*

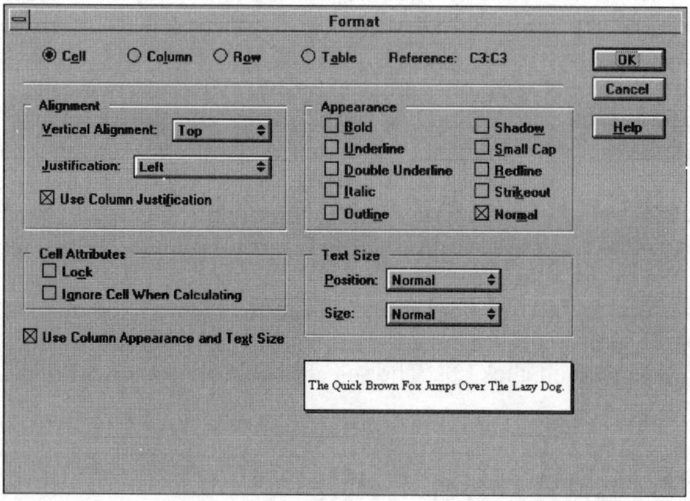

Figure 11-114. *The Format dialog box for cells*

You can select items in the Alignment, Appearance, and Text Size groups as usual. If you click Bold, for example, then text will be in bold in the selected cells.

By clicking the arrows by the Justification box, you can choose to have the text left, full, center, right, or decimal aligned. The Vertical Alignment option allows you to control the vertical alignment of text in the cell. Text can be placed at the top, bottom, or center of the cell. The Mixed option, located in both options, indicates that various justifications are used in the selected cells.

If you click Use Column Justification or Use Column Appearance and Text Size, the settings from the column formatting are transferred to this dialog box.

The Cell Attributes area controls miscellaneous attributes of the selected cells. If you click Lock, you can't edit the information in the selected cells. The last item, Ignore Cell When Calculating, stops the information in the selected cell from being included in the total for the column or row.

Tables, Formatting Columns

The Format dialog box affects the way columns in the table are formatted. In this dialog box you can change the appearance, justification, and size of the text in the columns. You also can adjust the column widths and the number of digits that are displayed when you are calculating columns and rows.

Menu Selections

To format the columns in your table, you first select the columns you wish to change, then choose Table/Format. You will see the Format dialog box, as shown in Figure 11-115. Make sure the Column button is selected at the top of the screen.

You can select items in the Alignment, Appearance, and Text Size groups in the usual way. If you click Bold, for example, then text will be bold in the selected column. To adjust the width of the selected column, click the Width option and type the desired width.

Tables, Formatting Rows

The Format Row dialog box affects the way your rows are displayed in the table. You can adjust both the lines per row and the row height with this feature.

Menu Selections

To format the rows in your table, you first select the rows you wish to change, then choose Table/Format. You will see the Format dialog box, shown in Figure 11-116. Make sure the Row button is selected at the top of the screen.

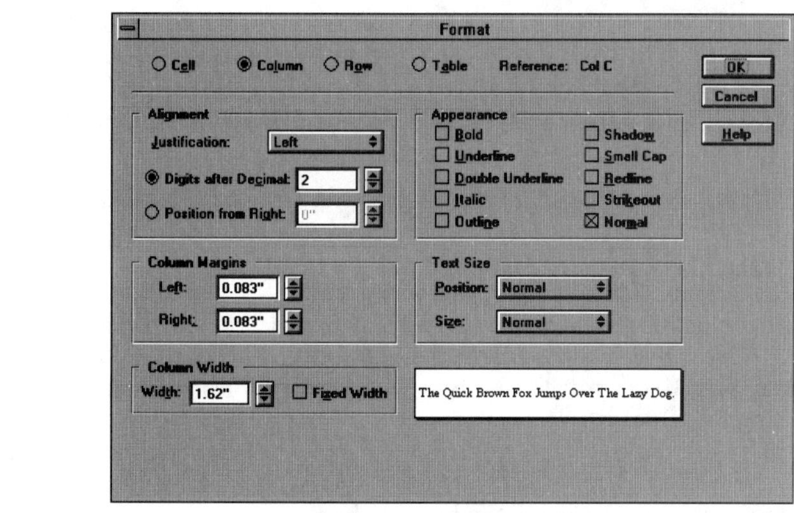

Figure 11-115. *The Format dialog box for columns*

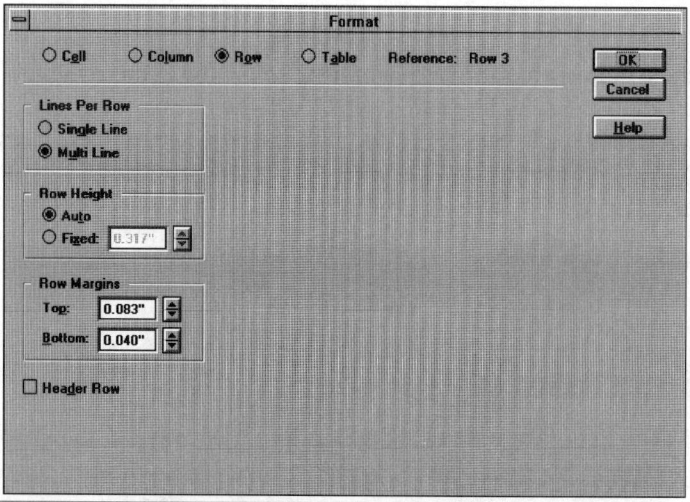

Figure 11-116. *The Format dialog box for rows*

To stop WordPerfect from wrapping text in a cell, click Single Line in the Lines Per Row area. Note that the default under this area is for WordPerfect to allow for multiline cells.

The row height is usually best kept at the default Auto setting, but if you need to change the row height, you can click Fixed and type a set row height. This feature locks a cell to a specific height, which prevents you from entering text once the cell reaches that height.

You can also adjust the margins used between rows by changing the values in the Row Margins area.

Tables, Naming

It is sometimes better to refer to tables and cells by a name, rather than as "Table A" or "cell E3." This is because you might forget the intended result of a formula, its intended use, and so on. You can easily label cells and tables in WordPerfect by first selecting the table, cell, or cell range, then clicking Names in the formula bar. This displays the Table Names in Current Document dialog box, as shown in Figure 11-117. To define a name, click Create and type a name in the text box in the Create Name dialog box. Click OK when finished.

You can also use the Names feature to go to a specific table or cell. To do so, highlight the desired table or cell name and click Goto.

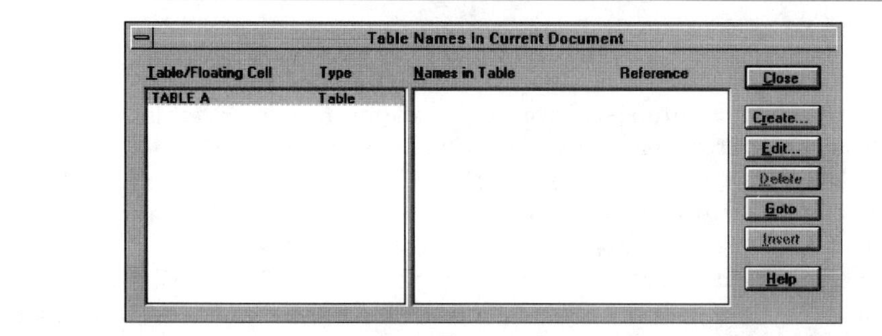

Figure 11-117. *The Table Names in Current Document dialog box*

Tabs, Hard

See Hard Tabs.

Tabs, Setting

You can create four different types of tabs in WordPerfect: left, center, right, and decimal. Each of these tabs can be further defined as dot leader tabs. The tabs themselves actually appear on the ruler. Note each of the types of tabs, as shown in Figure 11-118.

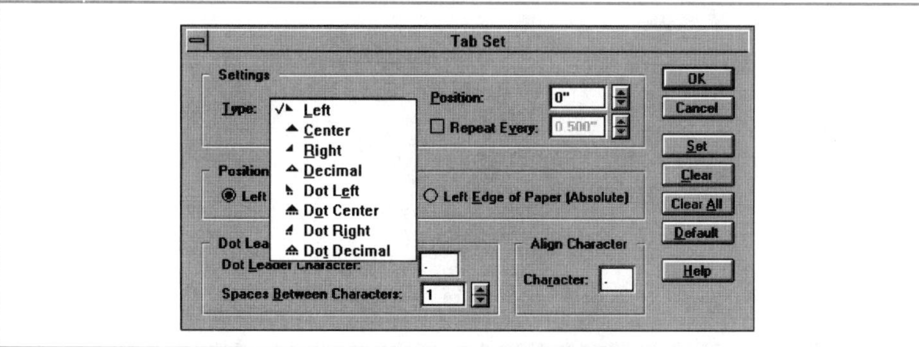

Figure 11-118. *The different types of WordPerfect tabs*

Menu Selections

To set tabs for your document, choose Layout/Line/Tab Set, and the Tab Set dialog box shown in Figure 11-119 appears on your screen. Notice, also, that the ruler appears on your screen (if it was not already visible). At this point, you may want to delete all of the default tabs (left aligned, every half inch) from the Ruler. To do this, click Clear All, and all of the tabs on the ruler bar will disappear.

To set a tab, first select a tab Type. In the Position field, enter the measurement that indicates where you want the tab located. Then click Set to set the tab on the Ruler. This process can be repeated to set as many tabs as necessary.

If you decide you want the same type of tab spaced evenly across the Ruler, first set the type of tab you want, and then enter a value in the Repeat Every field. The tab will be repeated across the entire Ruler.

To delete tabs selectively from the Ruler, select the tab you want to delete, and then click Clear. Once tabs are set where you want them, click OK.

Related Entries

Ruler

Tabular Columns

See Tabs, Setting.

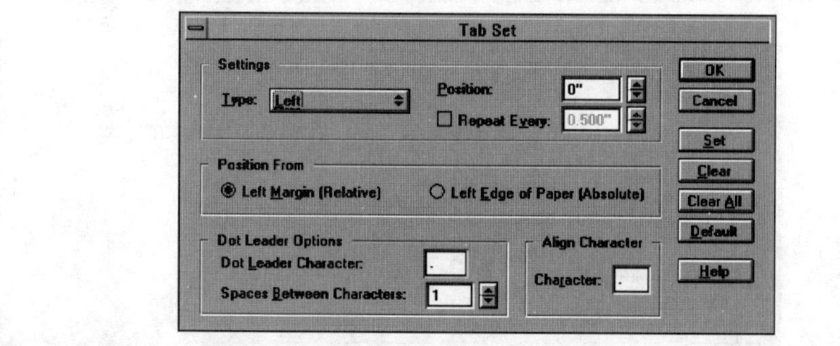

Figure 11-119. *The Tab Set dialog box*

Targets and References

See Cross-Reference.

Templates

WordPerfect 6.0 for Windows has implemented the concept of *templates.* These are nothing more than patterns for how a document should look. Templates can contain anything a regular document can—text, graphics, styles, macros, button bars, and keyboards. Primarily, however, they will contain only formatting. A template, in this sense, is an initial definition of the appearance of a document.

Every document you create in WordPerfect uses a template, even if you don't realize it. WordPerfect allows you to change the name of the template used as the default, however, and you can even create your own templates to define how you want documents to appear.

T

Menu Selections

Templates can be affected through several different menu commands, depending on what you wish to do with them.

Changing the Default Template

To change the default template, select File/Preferences/File from the menu. You will see the File Preferences dialog box. Make sure you select the Templates option at the top of the dialog box, as shown in Figure 11-120.

In the text boxes at the bottom of the dialog box, you can specify the default directory where you want the templates saved, as well as the default file that WordPerfect will use as a template. When you are through making changes, click OK.

Selecting a Template

To select a template, choose File/Template from the menus. You will see the Templates dialog box, shown in Figure 11-121.

Select the name of the template you wish to use, and then click OK.

Creating a Template

A template is created using the File/Template menu choice, which invokes the Templates dialog box, shown in Figure 11-121. If you click the Options button, you can choose Create Template. You will then see the Create Document Template dialog box, shown in Figure 11-122.

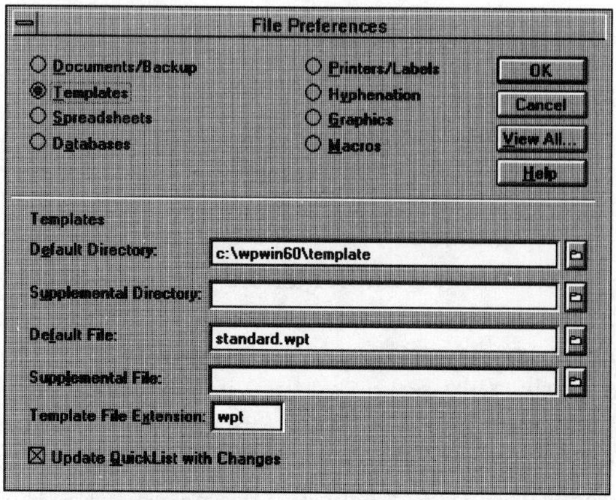

Figure 11-120. *The File Preferences dialog box*

In the Name text box, enter the name of the template you want to create. You can add an optional description of the template in the Description box. In the Name text box in the Template to Base On area, you can supply the name of an existing template you want to use as a starting point for this template.

When you are done providing a name, description, and basis for your new template, you can click OK. You will then see the Template Editor, which looks

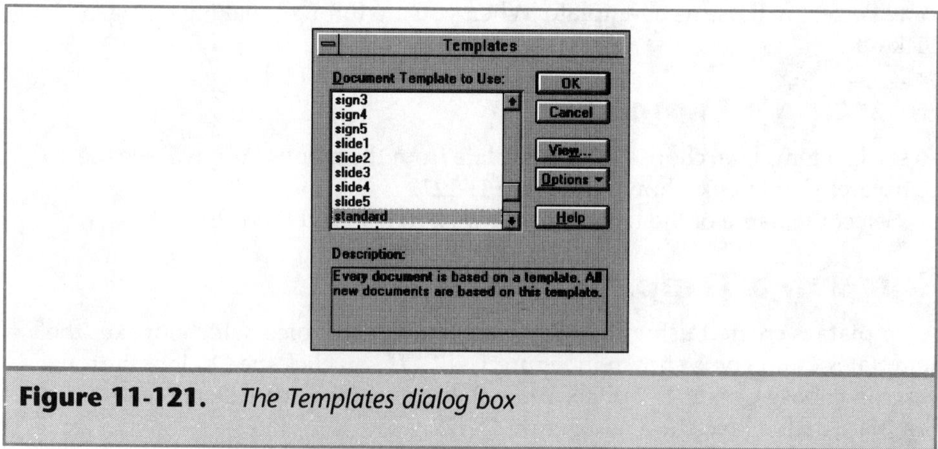

Figure 11-121. *The Templates dialog box*

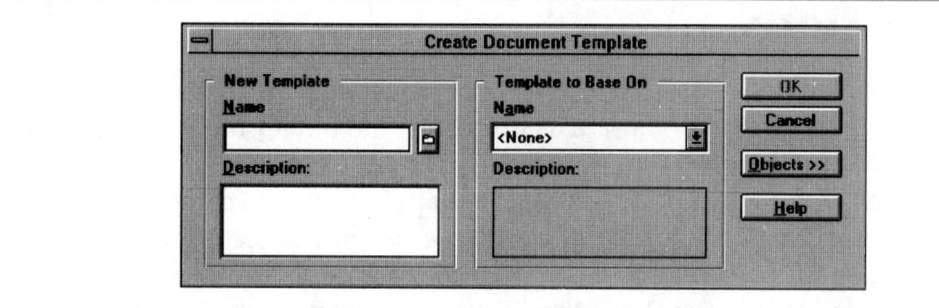

Figure 11-122. *The Create Document Template dialog box*

very much like a regular WordPerfect document, except that a special feature bar appears at the top of the document window. Enter any information or changes you want to include in the template. When you are through, click Exit Template, and the template will be saved to disk.

Text Attributes and Sizes

See Fonts.

Text Boxes

See Graphics entries.

Text Colors

See Colors, Text.

Thesaurus

The Thesaurus is a handy utility program that can suggest alternatives for a selected word. It is indispensable when you need to find just the right connotation or when you wish to avoid needless repetition.

Menu Selections

To use the Thesaurus, select the word you want to change and then choose Tools/Thesaurus or click the Thesaurus button on the power bar. The Thesaurus dialog box, shown in Figure 11-123, appears on your screen.

Alternatives to the word you have selected appear on the screen in the left-hand column. You can scroll up or down the column to see more words; if you would like to find words that are similar to one on the list, click the word and then click the Look Up button. WordPerfect will find alternatives to the selected word. You can also double-click a word to display more words in the columns to the right of the first one. A hand icon will appear to the right of the word that you double-clicked, as shown in Figure 11-124.

Once you have found the word you want to use in the document, select the word and then click the Replace button. WordPerfect replaces the word in the document with the one that you selected.

If you click the Dictionary menu selection, you can access other dictionaries that have been installed in WordPerfect. This option allows you to use the dictionaries of many countries.

The Edit menu selection lets you copy and cut text between the Thesaurus and the Clipboard. The Select All option lets you select whatever is to the right of the Word option for copying or cutting.

The History menu selection remembers each of your selections and allows you to go back to them. Choose History and then click the word to which you wish to return.

Related Entries

Speller

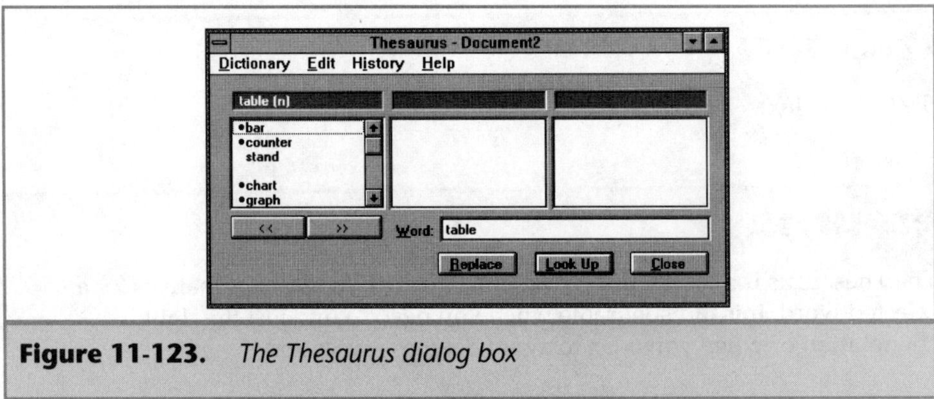

Figure 11-123. *The Thesaurus dialog box*

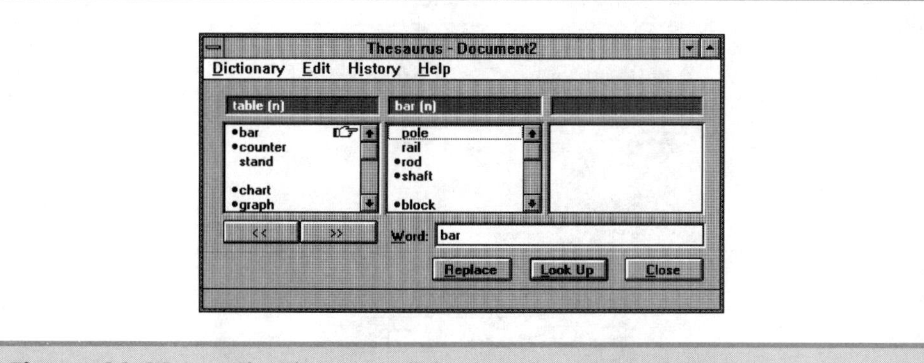

Figure 11-124. *The Thesaurus dialog box showing the hand icon*

T

Tile Windows

See Windows, Working with Multiple.

Timed Backup

The Timed Backup feature can be a lifesaver when the power unexpectedly goes out or if you inadvertently close a document without saving it. WordPerfect, at preset intervals, will save your document. There is a minor lag when the file is being saved, but otherwise this feature hardly interferes with your typing.

Menu Selections

To turn on the Timed Backup feature, choose File/Preferences/File, and the File Preferences dialog box appears on your screen, as shown in Figure 11-125. Make sure that the Documents/Backup button is selected at the top of the dialog box.

You can adjust the Timed Backup to any interval you desire by checking the Timed Document Backup box and then selecting an interval. The backup files are placed in the directory specified in the Backup Directory text box.

You also can click Original Document Backup so that each time you save a document, WordPerfect will make a copy of it and save it in a file with the same first name and .BK! extension. This file will be saved to the same location as the original document.

Figure 11-125. *The File Preferences dialog box*

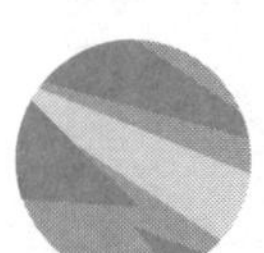

NOTE: *You will want to go in and delete the Original Document (.BK!) files periodically, because they can take up a great deal of disk space.*

Two-Page View

One of the viewing modes supported in WordPerfect 6.0 for Windows is View/Two Page. This mode allows you to see two side-by-side pages in your document, as shown in Figure 11-126.

This viewing mode is good for looking at page layout and balance, but not for actually reading the text.

Related Entries

Draft View
Page View

Typeover

See INSERT Key.

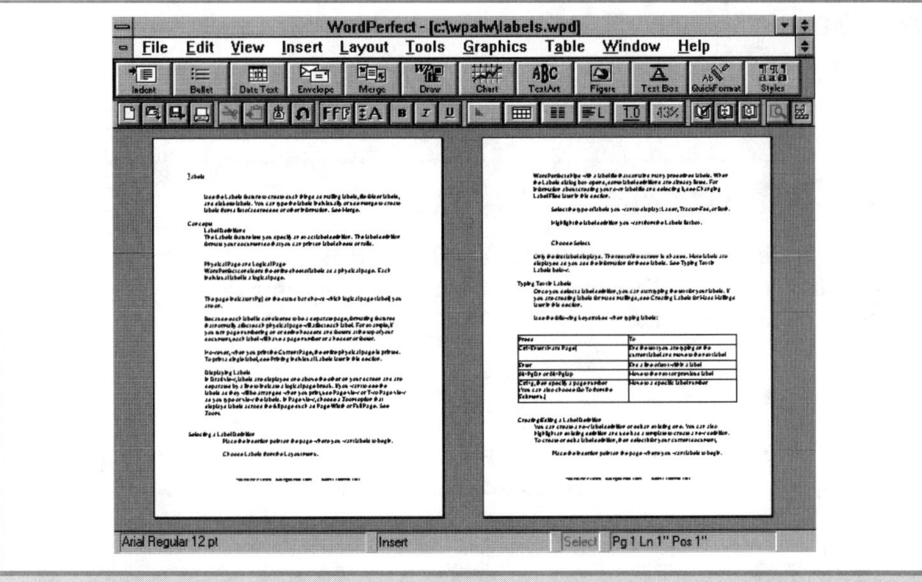

Figure 11-126. *An example of two-page viewing mode*

Typesetting Functions

See Chapter 7, "Desktop Publishing with WordPerfect for Windows."

Undelete

The Undelete command allows you to resurrect text you may have accidentally deleted. After you delete text, select Edit/Undelete; the text you deleted will be inserted in your document, and you will see the Undelete dialog box:

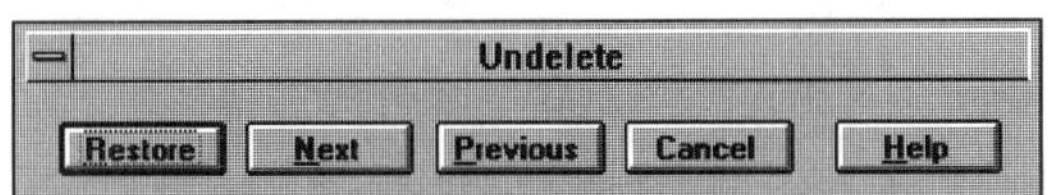

If you select Restore, your deleted text will be placed back into your document. If you select Previous, you will see the block of text you deleted prior to the last one. WordPerfect "remembers" the last three blocks of text you deleted, and you can cycle through these using the Previous and Next buttons.

Menu Selections

To use the Undelete feature, you choose Edit/Undelete from the menu.

Underline Text

Text is underlined for emphasis or to set off a particular word or phrase from surrounding text. If, for instance, you are citing a magazine article, you may wish to underline the magazine title.

Menu Selections

To underline text, choose Layout/Font to invoke the Font dialog box. Select Underline to underline your text and click the OK button.

Undo

In most cases, you can use the Undo feature to reverse the last change you made. For example, if you underline selected text and then press Edit/Undo, the underlining is removed. If you select Edit/Paste to paste text from the Clipboard, selecting Edit/Undo removes the pasted text.

You can also use Undo to bring back text or graphics that have been deleted from the screen. Undo always brings back the last item you deleted and should be used immediately; if you wait, you may inadvertently lose the text or graphic by deleting something else.

Menu Selections

Select Edit/Undo or press CTRL+Z.

Units of Measure

WordPerfect lets you use several different units of measure. The default unit of measure is inch, but you can change it to centimeters, millimeters, points, or 1200ths of an inch.

Menu Selections

To change the unit of measure, choose File/Preferences/Display. You will see the Display Settings dialog box, shown in Figure 11-127. Locate the Measurement area in the lower-right corner of the dialog box. You can change units for either of two settings, Units of Measure or Status/Ruler Bar Display. Units of Measure changes the way numbers appear and the way they are entered in dialog boxes. Status/Ruler Bar Display changes the unit of measure for the status bar and the ruler. You change these settings by clicking the triangles on the appropriate button and selecting the unit of measure you want from the pull-down menu.

Uppercase Text

The Convert Case feature allows you to convert lowercase characters to uppercase.

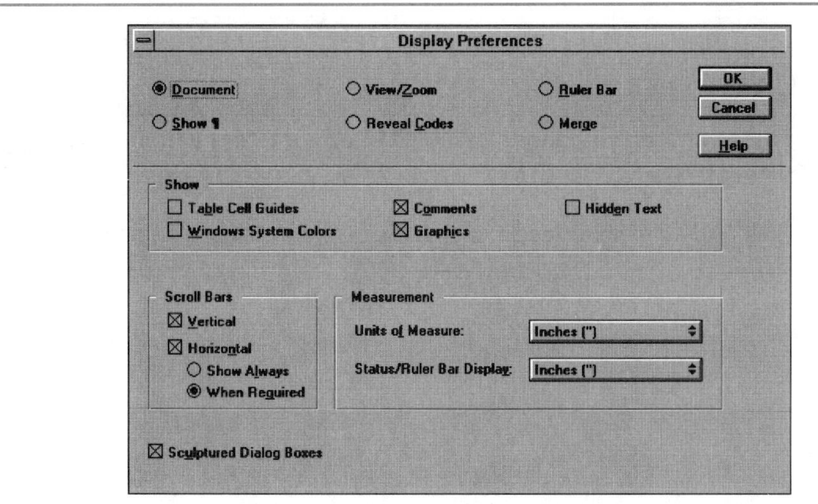

Figure 11-127. *The Display Preferences dialog box*

Menu Selections

To change your text to uppercase, select the text to be changed and then choose Edit/Convert Case. Select Uppercase, and the text adjusts accordingly.

User Boxes

See Graphics entries.

Vertical Lines

See Graphics Lines.

Watermark

Watermarks are faint images that appear in the background of your document. These can be text or graphics, and serve to enhance the design or security of your documents. WordPerfect allows you to have up to two watermarks per document.

Menu Selections

To insert or edit a watermark, choose Layout/Watermark. You will then see the Watermark dialog box:

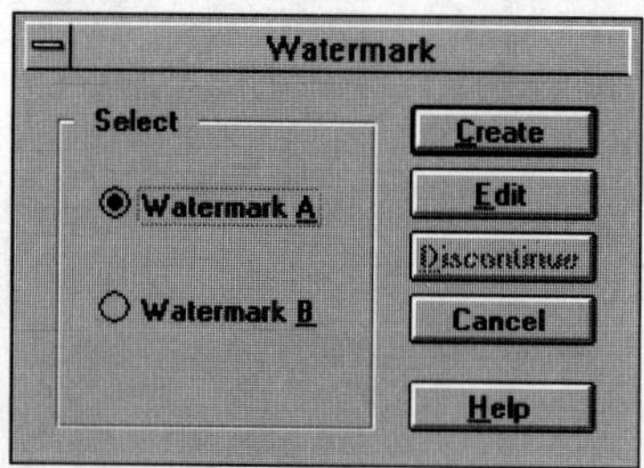

You can then click Create or Edit to invoke the Watermark Editor, which looks like a regular WordPerfect document, except it includes the Watermark feature bar. All you need to do is enter the information you want included in the watermark, and then click Close. Anything you enter in the watermark editor will appear in the background of your document.

Widow/Orphan Protection

Many people consider it bad form to break a paragraph between pages so that a single line remains on one page. The term *widow* refers to the first line of a paragraph left at the bottom of the previous page. The term *orphan* refers to the solitary last line of a paragraph left at the top of the next page. If your word processing requirements restrict you to an exact number of lines per page, as in many legal documents, widows and orphans cannot be avoided. In other cases, however, you may wish to use a WordPerfect feature that prevents widows and orphans from occurring.

Menu Selections

Choose Layout/Page/Keep Text Together. You will see the Keep Text Together dialog box, shown in Figure 11-128. In the top portion of the dialog box, select the checkbox to enable widow/orphan control beginning at the position of the insertion point.

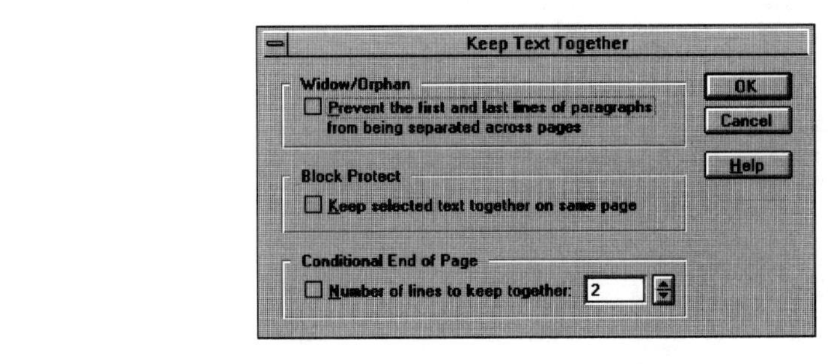

Figure 11-128. *The Keep Text Together dialog box*

Windows

The Windows program is named for its ability to have multiple programs and documents open at the same time, each in a separate window. There are three types of windows:

- Group windows hold icons representing a group of related programs or files.
- Application windows hold programs (WordPerfect, Lotus 1-2-3, Paradox, Excel, and so on).
- Document windows contain documents (letters, spreadsheets, databases, and so on).

An application window displays the program's menu bar; a document window has no menu. However, each open window does have several elements in common: a title bar, which displays the name of the program or document; a maximize or restore button; a minimize button; and a control menu button. You can use these features to move and size each window. In addition, document windows may also display scroll bars for moving through the text.

When you are working with WordPerfect for Windows, you always have at least two windows open: the application window, which holds WordPerfect, and the document window, which holds the document you are working on. By using the File/Open command, you can have up to nine documents open on the screen at one time. Each window has its own maximize and minimize (or restore) buttons, as well as its own control menu button.

Windows Printing

See Printer, Selecting.

Windows, Maximizing, Minimizing, Restoring

See the "Sizing the Windows" section in the Windows, Working with Multiple entry.

Windows, Moving

See the "Moving Windows" section in the Windows, Working with Multiple entry.

Windows, Resizing

See the "Sizing the Windows" section in the Windows, Working with Multiple entry.

Windows, Tiled and Cascading

See the "Displaying Multiple Windows" section in the Windows, Working with Multiple entry.

Windows, Working with Multiple

WordPerfect for Windows allows you to work with multiple windows at one time.

Menu Selections

You can use the File/Open command to open multiple document windows. Once you have several windows open, it is easy to move between documents as well to view multiple documents at the same time.

Moving Between Documents

Only one document window can be active, or current. The title bar of the current window is highlighted; title bars for inactive windows are dimmed. If you have a color monitor, the title bar is displayed in the color assigned to the active window title bar in the Windows Control Panel Color dialog box.

You can move between windows by using the menus, the mouse, or the function keys. If you can see even a corner of a window, you can activate it by clicking in the visible area. Or you can use CTRL+F6 or CTRL+SHIFT+F6 to move to the next or previous document window. These function keys provide an easy way to switch between a number of open documents.

To move to another window using the menus, choose Window. The Window menu displays a numbered list of currently open documents. Select the document from the list, and that document moves to the top of the list and becomes current.

Displaying Multiple Windows

To see all your open documents at the same time, you can use either the Tile feature or the Cascade feature. When tiled, all open document windows are reduced in size so that each window is entirely visible. If you have three or fewer documents open, they appear stacked from the top to the bottom of the screen, with the active window at the top. If you have more than three windows open, some may appear side by side, as shown in Figure 11-129.

When cascaded, document windows appear layered, with the current window on top and only the title bars of the other windows visible behind the current window, as shown in Figure 11-130.

To tile your windows, choose Windows/Tile. To cascade your open document windows, choose Windows/Cascade.

Sizing the Windows

When you first start WordPerfect, its window is *maximized*, that is, the window fills up the screen. When you open a document or start a new one, its window is

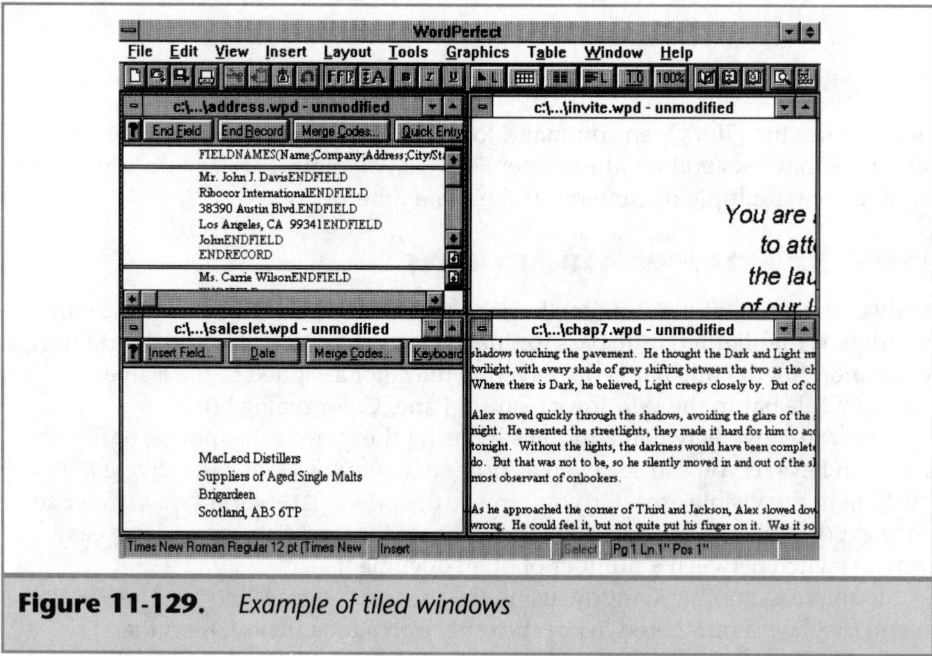

Figure 11-129. *Example of tiled windows*

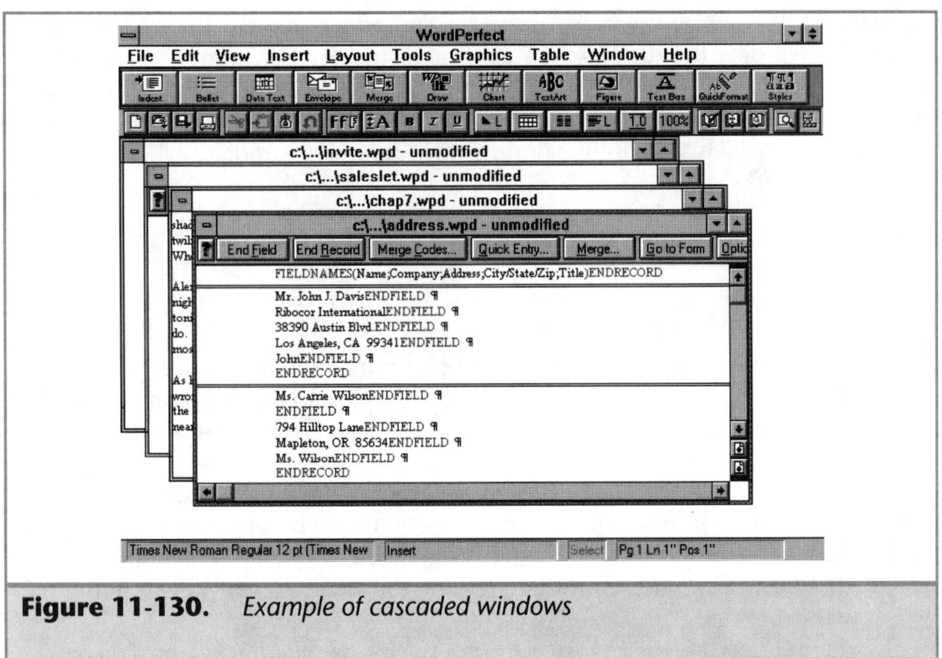

Figure 11-130. *Example of cascaded windows*

also maximized. When you are working with a single document, this is preferable because it allows you to see more text. However, when you are working with multiple documents, you may want each window smaller so you can see each one. You can use the Tile and Cascade features to automatically change the size of all open windows, but you can also change the size of each window individually.

When a window is maximized, the Restore button is displayed. You can reduce the size of the current window automatically by using Restore, which returns the window to its previous size, before it was last maximized.

If the sizes offered by Restore, Cascade, or Tile are not convenient for viewing your documents, you can customize the size of each window individually.

To restore a document window to its previous size, press ALT+- (or click the document control menu icon) to display the document window's control menu. Choose Restore. You can do this only if the window is maximized; if the window is not maximized, the Restore option is dimmed (not available). If the Restore button is displayed, you can click it to restore the previous size of the window instead of using the menu option. To maximize the window, press ALT+- and choose Maximize, or click the maximize button. (If Maximize is greyed out or the Restore icon is shown, the window is already maximized.)

Each open document window can be sized independently. To size a single document window manually, you must first restore it. (You cannot resize a maximized window.) Then press ALT+- to display the control menu and choose Size. A four-sided arrow is displayed in the middle of the window, waiting for you to choose which side of the window you want to expand:

To expand the window from the bottom, press the down arrow; to expand it from the top, press the up arrow, and so on. Continue to press the directional arrow keys until the window is expanded to the desired size. Press ENTER when you are finished.

To size a window diagonally (from the corners), press two directional arrow keys sequentially. For example, to expand the window by the lower-right corner, choose Size from the control menu and press the DOWN ARROW key followed by the RIGHT ARROW key. Then continue pressing the RIGHT ARROW key until the window is expanded.

If you prefer to use the mouse, position the mouse pointer on the side or corner of the window. When the pointer becomes a bidirectional arrow, drag the mouse to expand the window.

You can also restore, size, and maximize the WordPerfect window, using either the buttons or the control menu. To display the application control menu, press ALT+SPACEBAR or click the control menu button.

Moving Windows

When you are working with multiple documents, sizing them is often not enough. You sometimes need to reposition your document windows, if, for example, you want to see them side by side instead of above and below one another. You can move windows by using either the control menu or the mouse; however, you cannot move a maximized window.

To move a window, first make it the current window, and restore it if it is maximized. Next, point your mouse at the title bar area, hold down the left button, and drag the window by its title bar to move it in any direction.

If you are using the keyboard, press ALT+- to display the control menu, and choose Move. The pointer becomes a four-sided arrow. Then you can use your directional arrow keys to move the window in any direction.

Minimizing Windows

Next to the maximize or restore button is the minimize button. (The control menu also contains a Minimize command.) When you *minimize* a window, you reduce it to an icon. This does not close the file. It shrinks it in size only temporarily, to get it out of the way. This is handy if you want to tile or cascade all but one or two windows but you don't want to close the documents in those windows. An icon representing a minimized document window is shown in the lower-left corner of the screen, as shown in Figure 11-131. As you can see, the document name is displayed below the icon.

Press ALT+- to display the control menu, and select Minimize. The window is reduced to an icon, with the filename under the icon. If the other windows are cascaded, the icon will be visible, and you can restore it by double-clicking it. (A single click displays its document control menu, and you can use that to restore or maximize it.) If the other open windows are maximized or tiled, the icon will not be visible. However, even minimized documents are displayed in the Window list, and you can always restore a document by choosing Window and selecting the document name from the list.

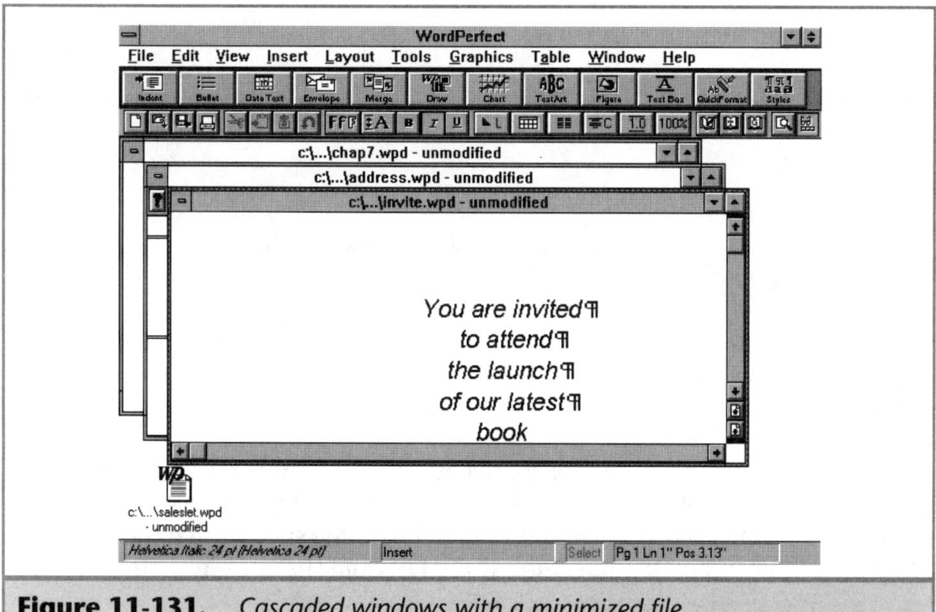

Figure 11-131. *Cascaded windows with a minimized file*

You can also minimize a window by clicking the Minimize icon. However, this icon will not appear if the document window is maximized; you must restore the window first.

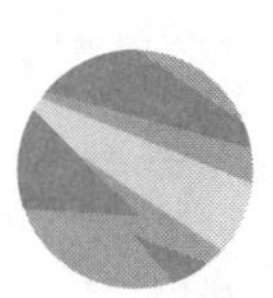

NOTE: *Be careful! The WordPerfect application window also has a minimize button, and if the current document window is maximized, the minimize button is displayed only in the WordPerfect window. If you select the minimize button or choose Minimize from the WordPerfect control menu, you will minimize the WordPerfect application. If this happens, you will in most cases return to the Program Manager. You won't lose anything, but this can be confusing. If you do inadvertently minimize WordPerfect, don't run the WordPerfect program again! It is still in memory. Double-click the WordPerfect icon or restore it from the Windows Task List.*

Related Entries

Open
Switch to Another Document
Windows, Tiled and Cascading
See also Chapter 1, "Windows and WordPerfect."

Word Search

See Finding Text.

Word Spacing

Word spacing is the amount of space WordPerfect inserts between words, and it is commonly a consideration if your text is fully justified. If your printer supports incremental spacing, you can adjust spaces between letters. Otherwise, space is inserted between words only.

For best results, the amount of space between words is generally based on the size, type, and pitch of the font. WordPerfect offers you three different ways to determine spacing between words. You can choose the spacing that is considered optimal by your printer manufacturer (called normal spacing). You can also select optimal spacing determined by WordPerfect. Finally, you can choose the spacing yourself.

Normal and WordPerfect word spacing differ only when you are using proportionally spaced fonts. With a proportional font, WordPerfect automatically calculates a space as one-third the point size of the font. With monospace (that is, nonproportional) fonts, the spacing is determined by the pitch setting. The Normal and WordPerfect settings save you time and trouble by calculating the appropriate spacing based on current font settings.

Menu Selections

To change word spacing, first position the insertion point where you want the change to begin, or select the text in which you want to change the word spacing. Then choose Layout/Typesetting/Word/Letterspacing to display the Word Spacing and Letterspacing dialog box, shown in Figure 11-132.

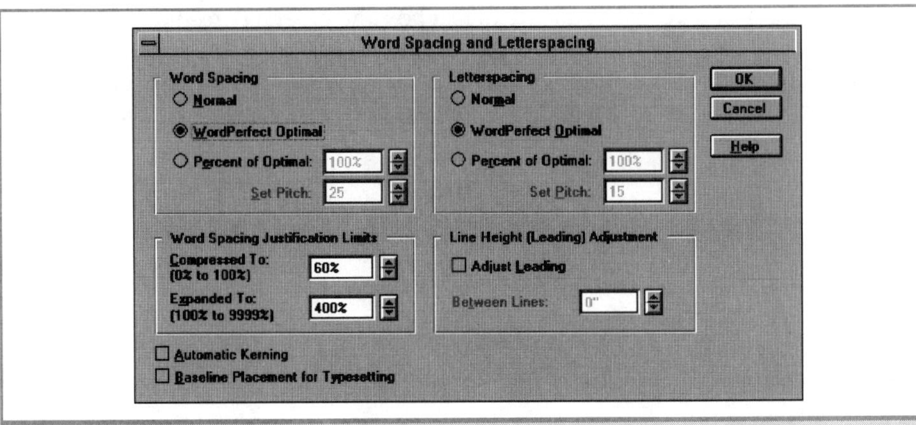

Figure 11-132. *The Word Spacing and Letterspacing dialog box*

This box contains six groups. From the Word Spacing group at the top-left corner, select Normal for spacing considered optimal by your printer manufacturer. Select WordPerfect Optimal for spacing considered optimal by WordPerfect.

To choose your own spacing, select Percent of Optimal in the Word Spacing area and enter a percentage in the text box. For example, if you enter **120%**, the amount of space between words will increase by 20 percent. It might be simpler for you to let WordPerfect determine the increase or decrease based on the pitch (characters per inch) you enter in the Set Pitch text box. The pitch currently displayed is always that of the current font. You can increase the spaces between words by entering a smaller number in the box and decrease the spacing by entering a larger number (more characters per inch).

To determine letter spacing on your own, select Percent of Optimal in the Letterspacing area and enter either a pitch on which to adjust the letter spacing or your own percent of spacing based on the current pitch. This procedure is the same as the one for adjusting word spacing, described previously.

You can increase letter spacing up to 250 percent and decrease it to 50 percent. If the upper limit is reached, WordPerfect will insert spaces between characters. If your printer does not support incremental spacing, you may not notice any change to your text, and no spacing adjustment will take place between letters.

If you feel that the spacing limits do not meet your needs, you can change them. To change the limitations from the Word Spacing and Letterspacing dialog box, select the Compressed To or Expanded To text box and enter a percentage figure.

When you are finished, select OK to close the window and return to your document. To return to the default word spacing, invoke the Word Spacing and Letterspacing dialog box and select the Normal button. To cancel the word spacing, delete the code.

Related Entries

Justification
Kerning, Automatic
Kerning, Manual
Letter Spacing

WordPerfect Characters

See Character Sets.

Zooming

WordPerfect for Windows allows you to use *zooming* to adjust the apparent size of your document. Figures 11-133 and 11-134 show the same screen, one at 100% zooming, and the other at 200% zooming.

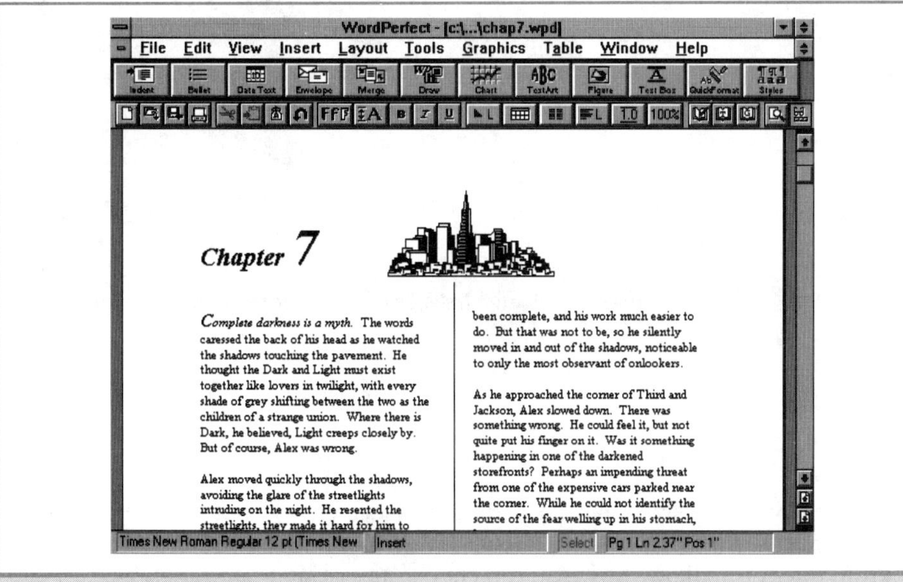

Figure 11-133. *A WordPerfect document at 100% zooming*

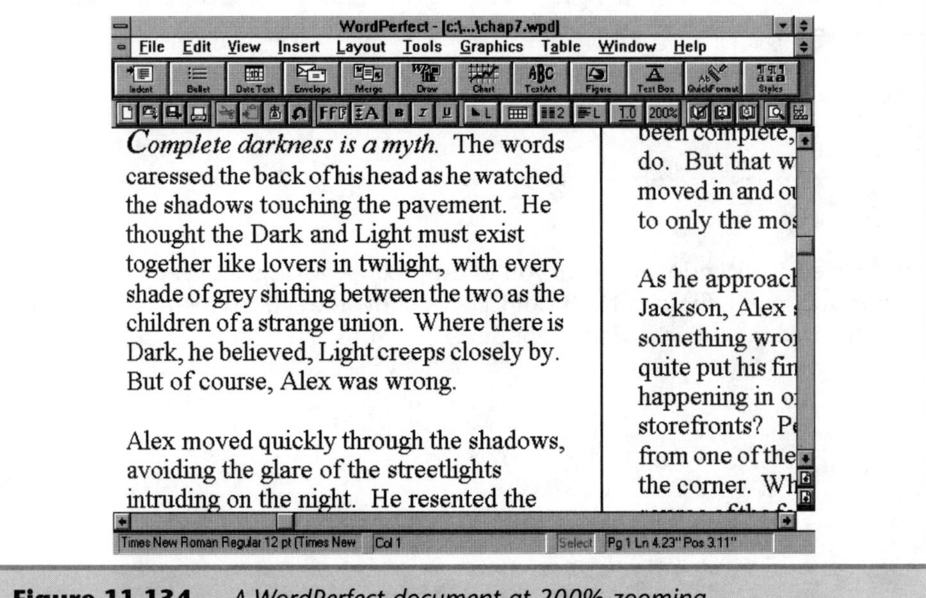

Figure 11-134. *A WordPerfect document at 200% zooming*

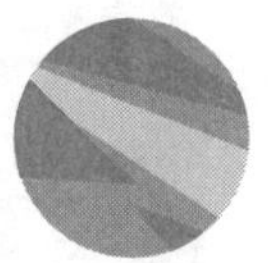

NOTE: *Zooming does not change the size of the document when it is printed; it only changes the viewing size.*

Menu Selections

To adjust the viewing size of your document, select View/Zoom from the menus. You will see the Zoom dialog box, shown in Figure 11-135.

From the Zoom dialog box, you can choose any of several predefined magnification levels. In addition, you can choose a custom level. If you choose Other, you can set any magnification level between 25 percent and 400 percent.

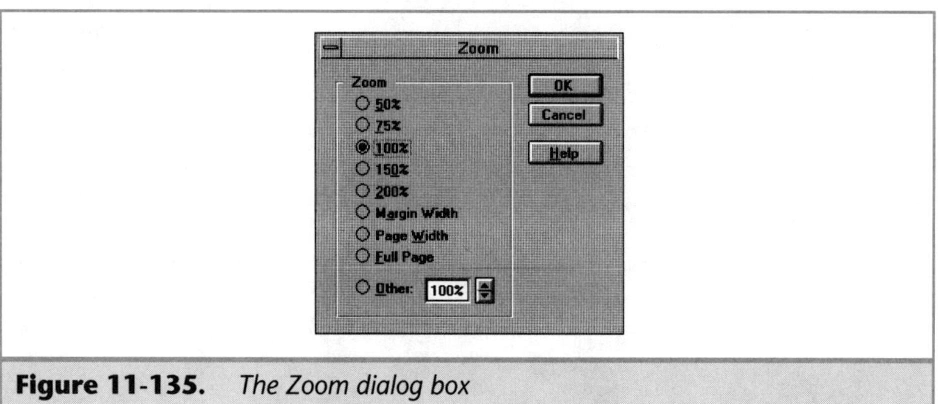

Figure 11-135. *The Zoom dialog box*

PART FOUR

Appendixes

APPENDIX A

Installing Windows and WordPerfect

Before you start WordPerfect for Windows, you must install the Microsoft Windows program and then install the WordPerfect for Windows program files. Both Windows and WordPerfect include installation programs that copy the correct files to your computer's hard disk. Once the installation process is complete for both programs, you can get started with WordPerfect.

System Requirements

There are minimum and recommended hardware requirements for Microsoft Windows and WordPerfect for Windows. The basic recommended system is:

- An IBM or compatible computer with an 80386 or higher processor.
- 4MB or more of computer memory.
- A VGA or better monitor.
- One 3 1/2-inch (720K or 1.44MB) disk drive *and* one 5 1/4-inch high-density (1.2MB) disk drive.
- A hard disk with 55MB or more of free disk space, if you are installing both Windows and WordPerfect for Windows. If you already have Windows installed, and you only need to install WordPerfect, then you only need 31MB of free disk space.

Installing Microsoft Windows

Before you install WordPerfect, you must install the Microsoft Windows program files. Microsoft Windows is sold separately by Microsoft Corporation and is not included in the WordPerfect for Windows package. Once you obtain the Microsoft Windows software, insert disk #1 (Setup) into drive A (or B) of your computer. Then, at the DOS prompt, type **a:setup** (or **b:setup**).

The Windows Setup program asks you to verify your system configuration. Follow the instructions on your screen and the setup program will proceed to copy the Windows program files to your computer's hard disk. The program creates a directory called \WINDOWS and sets up your computer so you can run the Windows software. Follow the messages that appear on your screen for information about the installation process. Occasionally, you will be prompted to replace the disk in the drive with the next numbered disk for the Microsoft Windows program. When the Windows program installation is completed, you can install WordPerfect for Windows.

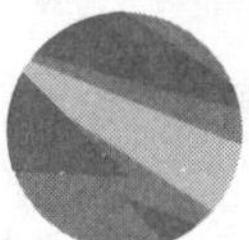

NOTE: *If you have problems with the installation of Windows, consult your Microsoft Windows User's Guide or contact the Microsoft Technical Support group; the phone number and address are listed in your Microsoft Windows manual.*

Installing WordPerfect for Windows

Included in your WordPerfect for Windows package is a set of disks that contains the WordPerfect program files. You must use the WordPerfect Installation program to install these files from the disks. To use this program, you must follow these steps:

1. Start Windows.
2. From the Program Manager (what you see when you first start Windows; see Chapter 1, "Windows and WordPerfect"), choose File/Run.
3. Insert your WordPerfect for Windows Install disk #1 into either drive A or B.
4. Type **a:install** or **b:install**, depending on whether your Install disk is in drive A or B.
5. Choose OK, or press ENTER.

This starts the WordPerfect for Windows installation process. During the process you will be asked many questions, and from time to time you will be prompted to switch disks. You should answer the questions as they are asked, and switch disks when prompted.

The first screen you see will ask you to enter your name and program serial number. When completed, click on the Continue button or press ENTER. You will then see a screen asking what type of installation you wish to perform. At this point, you have the following options.

Standard

If you have never installed WordPerfect for Windows before, choose the Standard option to make sure all necessary files are copied. Note, however, that this option requires the greatest amount of hard disk space, since all WordPerfect files are being installed. The Standard installation automatically copies all necessary files to the necessary directories on your hard drive. If the directories do not already exist, then the installation program creates them.

Also, the Standard installation automatically modifies your AUTOEXEC.BAT and CONFIG.SYS files, if necessary. Changes are made to update your PATH statement and to update other system information. The actual changes made will vary depending on your computer equipment and software. When the Standard installation option is finished, you are ready to start WordPerfect for Windows.

Custom

The Custom option is similar to the Standard installation, except that it prompts you at every step and gives you the chance to specify your own drive locations and path names where the WordPerfect program files are copied. This option also gives you the opportunity to choose which WordPerfect files you want to install. You can, for example, install the WordPerfect program files but skip installation for the Speller, graphics files, or learning files.

Network

If you are installing WordPerfect for Windows to be used from a network, choose the Network option for network installation. Only system managers should choose this option because it requires information about the network environment in which WordPerfect will be running. You do not need to buy a special network version of the software to install on a network. Each WordPerfect for Windows software package can be installed on a single PC or on a network, provided you have purchased a software license for each of the computers on which you plan to use WordPerfect. See Chapter 10 for more information on using WordPerfect for Windows on a network.

Minimum

If you don't have enough hard disk space available to perform a Standard installation, and you are not installing on a network, then choose this type of installation. The only difference between this and the Standard installation is that many of the "optional" files that enrich your use of WordPerfect for Windows are not installed. For instance, the graphics files and other samples are not copied to your system. Whereas the Standard installation requires over 31MB of disk space, this one requires only 14MB.

Options

This choice is used to install optional WordPerfect programs and drivers. Since you can run the install program at any time (even after WordPerfect has been installed for a while), this choice can be used at any later time in order to install additional WordPerfect components. The following sections describe the choices available once you select Options.

Printers

Choose the Printers option when you want to install a new printer driver for use with WordPerfect. Generally, you do not need to choose this option when you first install the program files because WordPerfect can install the printer drivers when you choose any of the regular installation options (Standard, Custom, Network, or Minimum).

The Printer option is most useful when you want to copy additional printer drivers for WordPerfect after you have already installed and used the WordPerfect for Windows program. When you choose this option, you can select the printer driver you want to install from a list of all supported printers. The installation program will prompt you to insert the WordPerfect Printer 1 disk as needed so information for the selected printer can be copied into the WordPerfect directory.

Utilities

WordPerfect Corporation offers a utility disk, separate from WordPerfect for Windows. This disk provides programs which you can use to enhance the operation of your WordPerfect software. If you purchase this option, then this choice is used to install that disk. Before you do this, you should have already installed WordPerfect for Windows on your system.

Language

WordPerfect software is translated into over a dozen different languages. The Language Module disk in your WordPerfect package contains the language files that are needed for the country where you purchased WordPerfect. These files determine how text is hyphenated and also provide language information for the Speller and Thesaurus utility programs. If you write in other languages, such as Spanish, French, or Russian, you can purchase additional language modules for these languages. Then you use the Language option on the Installation Options menu to copy the correct files from the disk to your WordPerfect directory. See the Language entry in Chapter 11, "Commands and Features," for more information about choosing a new language for WordPerfect.

README

Each release of WordPerfect contains README files—that is, text files that provide information about the program that was not printed in the WordPerfect manual. Choose this option to view the README files for the current WordPerfect software.

Starting the WordPerfect Program

When you finish installing WordPerfect for Windows, you are returned to the Program Manager, but you will notice that a new program group has been added for WordPerfect. Open the WordPerfect group window and choose the WordPerfect program icon. This starts the WordPerfect program and opens a new document window, where you can create your first document. For detailed information on starting WordPerfect, and other programs, from the Windows Program Manager, see Chapter 1, "Windows and WordPerfect."

APPENDIX B

Word-Perfect Keyboards

WordPerfect for Windows includes support for various keyboard layouts. The standard layout is called the *WPWin 6.0 Keyboard,* which has keystroke assignments that are common to other programs running under Microsoft Windows, such as CTRL+C to copy and CTRL+V to paste. The WPWin 6.0 Keyboard also has keystroke assignments that are unique to the WordPerfect program.

WordPerfect for Windows also includes a keyboard layout for users of WordPerfect 5.1 for DOS. This keyboard is called the *WPDOS Compatible Keyboard*. The WPDOS Compatible Keyboard layout is designed to let you use WordPerfect for Windows with the keystrokes you know from

WordPerfect 5.1 for DOS. Although this keyboard layout is very similar to the WordPerfect 5.1 for DOS keystroke assignments, not all keys will work as you might expect.

This appendix covers the keystroke assignments for the keyboards supported by the WordPerfect for Windows program. In addition to the WPWin 6.0 and WPDOS Compatible Keyboard layouts, WordPerfect also includes other keyboard layouts that are designed for creating equations and performing common editing tasks. For more information about creating your own keyboard layouts, see the Keyboard Layout entry in Chapter 11, "Commands and Features."

WordPerfect WPWin 6.0 Keyboard

WordPerfect for Windows uses a standard CUA (common user access) keyboard layout that conforms to the standard for other programs running under Windows. With WordPerfect's Keyboard feature, you can alter the keystroke assignments in your copy of WordPerfect and even create your own keyboard layouts.

If you have altered the keyboard layout, you can change back to the standard WordPerfect WPWin 6.0 Keyboard. From WordPerfect, choose File/Preferences/Keyboard to display a list of available keyboard definitions.

Highlight <WPWin 6.0 Keyboard> from the Keyboards list and then choose Select; WordPerfect closes the Keyboard Preferences dialog box and reverts back to the standard WPWin 6.0 Keyboard layout.

Table B-1 lists the keystroke assignments for the WPWin 6.0 Keyboard layout, arranged alphabetically according to the feature names you know or the action you want to perform in the program. In the WordPerfect manual, you will find a similar table with the assignments indexed by keystroke.

Definition	Keystroke
Abbreviation Expand	CTRL+A
Bold Attribute	CTRL+B
Bullet, Insert	CTRL+SHIFT+B
Case Toggle	CTRL+K

Table B-1. *The WordPerfect for Windows (WPWin 6.0) Keyboard Layout*

Definition	Keystroke
Center Justification	CTRL+E
Center Line	SHIFT+F7
Close	CTRL+F4
Close without Saving	CTRL+SHIFT+F4
Column, Select Next	ALT+SHIFT+RIGHT ARROW
Column, Select Previous	ALT+SHIFT+LEFT ARROW
Column, Select to Bottom of	ALT+SHIFT+END
Convert Case	CTRL+K
Copy	CTRL+C
Create New Document	CTRL+N or SHIFT+F4
Create Table	F12
Cut	CTRL+X
Data Fill	CTRL+SHIFT+F12
Date Code	CTRL+SHIFT+D
Date Text	CTRL+D
Decimal Tab	ALT+SHIFT+F7
Decrease Column	CTRL+, or CTRL+SHIFT+,
Define Outline Style...	CTRL+SHIFT+O
Double Indent	CTRL+SHIFT+F7
Down	DOWN ARROW
Draft View	CTRL+F5
Edit Graphic Box	SHIFT+F11
Exit	ALT+F4
Expand Abbreviation	CTRL+A
Feature Bar	ALT+SHIFT+F10
Figure	F11
Find	F2
Find Next	SHIFT+F2
Find Previous	ALT+F2
Flush Right	ALT+F7
Font...	F9
Format...	CTRL+F12
Formatted Page Number	CTRL+SHIFT+P
Full Justification	CTRL+J

Table B-1. *The WordPerfect for Windows (WPWin 6.0) Keyboard Layout* (cont.)

Definition	Keystroke
Generate...	CTRL+F9
Go To...	CTRL+G
Grammatik	ALT+SHIFT+F1
Hanging Indent	CTRL+F7
Help Contents	F1
Hide All Bars	ALT+SHIFT+F5
Horizontal Line	CTRL+F11
Hyphen Character	-
Hyphen Code	CTRL+-
Hyphen Soft	CTRL+SHIFT+-
Ignore Hyphenation	CTRL+/
Increase Column	CTRL+. or CTRL+SHIFT+.
Indent	F7
Indent, Double	CTRL+SHIFT+F7
Indent, Hanging	CTRL+F7
Insert Bullet	CTRL+SHIFT+B
Insert Figure	F11
Insert Formatted Page Number	CTRL+SHIFT+P
Italic Attribute	CTRL+I
Justify Center	CTRL+E
Justify Full	CTRL+J
Justify Left	CTRL+L
Justify Right	CTRL+R
Left	LEFT ARROW
Left Justification	CTRL+L
Line Centering	SHIFT+F7
Line, Horizontal	CTRL+F11
Line, Select Next	SHIFT+DOWN ARROW
Line, Select Previous	SHIFT+UP ARROW
Line, Select to End of	SHIFT+END
Line, Vertical	CTRL+SHIFT+F11
Lines/Fill...	SHIFT+F12
Macro Play...	ALT+F10
Macro Record...	CTRL+F10

Table B-1. *The WordPerfect for Windows (WPWin 6.0) Keyboard Layout* (cont.)

Definition	Keystroke
Margins...	CTRL+F8
Merge...	SHIFT+F9
Move Down One Cell	ALT+DOWN ARROW
Move Down One Screen	PGDN
Move to Bottom of Column	ALT+END
Move to Bottom of Document	CTRL+END
Move to End of Line	END
Move to Next Column	ALT+RIGHT ARROW
Move to Next Page	ALT+PGDN
Move to Next Paragraph	CTRL+DOWN ARROW
Move to Next Word	CTRL+RIGHT ARROW
Move to Previous Column	ALT+LEFT ARROW
Move to Previous Page	ALT+PGUP
Move to Previous Pane	SHIFT+F6
Move to Previous Paragraph	CTRL+UP ARROW
Move to Previous Word	CTRL+LEFT ARROW
Move Up One Cell	ALT+UP ARROW
Move Up One Screen	PGUP
New Document	CTRL+N or SHIFT+F4
Next Open Document	CTRL+F6
Next Pane	F6
Next Window	ALT+F6
Number Type...	ALT+F12
Open File	CTRL+O or F4
Page, Select Next	ALT+SHIFT+PGDN
Page, Select Previous	ALT+SHIFT+PGUP
Page View	ALT+F5
Pane, Move to Next	F6
Pane, Move to Previous	SHIFT+F6
Paragraph, Select Next	CTRL+SHIFT+DOWN ARROW
Paragraph, Select Previous	CTRL+SHIFT+UP ARROW
Paste	CTRL+V
Previous Window	ALT+SHIFT+F6
Print...	F5

Table B-1. *The WordPerfect for Windows (WPWin 6.0) Keyboard Layout* (cont.)

Definition	Keystroke
Print Document	CTRL+P
QuickMark Find	CTRL+Q
QuickMark Set	CTRL+SHIFT+Q
Redisplay Equation Screen	CTRL+F3
Repeat...	SHIFT+F10
Replace	CTRL+F2
Reveal Codes	ALT+F3
Right	RIGHT ARROW
Right Justification	CTRL+R
Ruler Bar	ALT+SHIFT+F3
Save	CTRL+S or SHIFT+F3
Save All	CTRL+SHIFT+S
Save As...	F3
Scroll Left	CTRL+PGUP
Scroll Right	CTRL+PGDN
Select	F8
Select Column Next	ALT+SHIFT+RIGHT ARROW
Select Column Previous	ALT+SHIFT+LEFT ARROW
Select Current Cell	SHIFT+F8
Select Next Cell Down	ALT+SHIFT+DOWN ARROW
Select Next Cell Up	ALT+SHIFT+UP ARROW
Select Next Character	SHIFT+RIGHT ARROW
Select Next Line	SHIFT+DOWN ARROW
Select Next Page	ALT+SHIFT+PGDN
Select Next Paragraph	CTRL+SHIFT+DOWN ARROW
Select Next Word	CTRL+SHIFT+RIGHT ARROW
Select One Screen Down	SHIFT+PGDN
Select One Screen Up	SHIFT+PGUP
Select Previous Character	SHIFT+LEFT ARROW
Select Previous Line	SHIFT+UP ARROW
Select Previous Page	ALT+SHIFT+PGUP
Select Previous Paragraph	CTRL+SHIFT+UP ARROW
Select Previous Word	CTRL+SHIFT+LEFT ARROW
Select to Bottom of Column	ALT+SHIFT+END

Table B-1. *The WordPerfect for Windows (WPWin 6.0) Keyboard Layout (cont.)*

Definition	Keystroke
Select to Bottom of Document	CTRL+SHIFT+END
Select to End of Line	SHIFT+END
Show ¶	CTRL+SHIFT+F3
Sort...	ALT+F9
Speller	CTRL+F1
Styles...	ALT+F8
Sum	CTRL+=
Tab	TAB
Tab, Decimal	ALT+SHIFT+F7
Template...	CTRL+T
Text Box, Create	ALT+F11
Thesaurus	ALT+F1
Undelete...	CTRL+SHIFT+Z
Underline Attribute	CTRL+U
Undo	CTRL+Z
Up	UP ARROW
Vertical Line, Insert	CTRL+SHIFT+F11
View Next Open Document	CTRL+F6
View Previous Open Document	CTRL+SHIFT+F6
What Is...	SHIFT+F1
Window, Next	ALT+F6
Window, Previous	ALT+SHIFT+F6
Word, Select Next	CTRL+SHIFT+RIGHT ARROW
Word, Select Previous	CTRL+SHIFT+LEFT ARROW
WordPerfect Character...	CTRL+W

Table B-1. *The WordPerfect for Windows (WPWin 6.0) Keyboard Layout* (cont.)

WordPerfect 5.1-Compatible Keyboard

WordPerfect for Windows includes a keyboard layout that mimics the keystroke assignments of WordPerfect 5.1 for DOS. If you did not select this keyboard, you can do so at any time from within WordPerfect. First, start WordPerfect for Windows. Then choose File/Preferences/Keyboard from the menu bar; the Keyboard Preferences dialog box appears. Highlight <WPDOS Compatible> and choose Select to make it the active keyboard file and return to the Preferences dialog box. Then choose Close from the Preferences dialog box.

If you are familiar with WordPerfect 5.1, most of the keystrokes you know will work when the WPDOS Compatible Keyboard layout is selected. However, because WordPerfect is running under the Windows environment, some keystrokes will be different from what you would expect. For example, the Copy key (CTRL+C) and the Help key (F1) follow the assignments from the standard Windows layout.

Table B-2 lists the keystroke assignments of the WordPerfect 5.1-compatible keyboard layout. All keystrokes from WordPerfect 5.1 (for DOS) are included, along with the new keystroke assignments. Where possible, feature names from WordPerfect 5.1 are listed in the table with the corresponding feature name from WordPerfect for Windows shown in parentheses.

Feature/Action	Keystroke
Block (Select)	ALT+F4 or F12
Block (Select) Next Character	SHIFT+RIGHT ARROW
Block (Select) Previous Character	SHIFT+LEFT ARROW
Block (Select) Sentence	CTRL+F4
Block (Select) to Beginning of Document	HOME, HOME, SHIFT+UP ARROW
Block (Select) to End of Document	HOME, HOME, SHIFT+DOWN ARROW
Bold Attribute	F6 or CTRL+B
Center Line	SHIFT+F6
Column, Move to Next	ALT+RIGHT ARROW
Column, Move to Previous	ALT+LEFT ARROW
Column, (Select) Next	ALT+SHIFT+RIGHT ARROW
Column, (Select) Previous	ALT+SHIFT+LEFT ARROW
Copy Block	CTRL+C or CTRL+INSERT
Delete Next Character	DELETE
Delete Previous Character	BACKSPACE
Delete to Beginning of Word	HOME+BACKSPACE or HOME+SHIFT+BACKSPACE
Delete to End of Line	CTRL+END or CTRL+SHIFT+END
Delete to End of Page	CTRL+PGDN OR CTRL+SHIFT+PGDN

Table B-2. *The WordPerfect 5.1 for DOS (WPDOS) Keyboard Layout*

Feature/Action	Keystroke
Delete to End of Word	HOME+DELETE
Delete Word	CTRL+BACKSPACE or CTRL+DELETE
Document, Block (Select) to Beginning	HOME, HOME, SHIFT+UP ARROW
Document, Block (Select) to End	HOME, HOME, SHIFT+DOWN ARROW
Document, Display Next Open	F3
Document, Display Previous Open	SHIFT+F3
Document, Move Down One Screen	HOME+DOWN ARROW or PLUS (on the numeric keypad)
Document, Move Screen Left	HOME+LEFT ARROW
Document, Move Screen Right	HOME+RIGHT ARROW
Document, Move to Beginning	HOME, HOME, UP ARROW
Document, Move to Beginning (before codes)	HOME, HOME, HOME, UP ARROW
Document, Move to End	HOME, HOME, DOWN ARROW
Document, Move Up One Screen	HOME+UP ARROW or MINUS (on the numeric keypad)
Exit (Close)	F7
Exit Without Saving (Close)	CTRL+SHIFT+F7
Flush Right	ALT+F6
Font	CTRL+F8
Font, Reset to Normal	CTRL+N
Generate	ALT+SHIFT+F5
Go To	CTRL+HOME or CTRL+G or CTRL+SHIFT+HOME
Hard Center Tab	HOME+SHIFT+F6
Hard Center Tab with dot leaders	HOME, HOME, SHIFT+F6
Hard Decimal Tab	CTRL+F6
Hard Decimal Tab (in outline mode)	HOME+CTRL+F6
Hard Decimal Tab with dot leaders	HOME, HOME, CTRL+F6
Hard Hyphen	HOME+HYPHEN
Hard Page Break	CTRL+ENTER
Hard Right aligned Tab	HOME, ALT+F6
Hard Right Tab with dot leaders	HOME, HOME, ALT+F6
Hard Space	HOME+SPACEBAR or CTRL+SPACEBAR

Table B-2. *The WordPerfect 5.1 for DOS (WPDOS) Keyboard Layout* (cont.)

Feature/Action	Keystroke
Hard Tab	HOME+TAB
Hard Tab with dot leaders	HOME, HOME, TAB
Help, Context Sensitive	F1
Hyphen, Hard	HOME+HYPHEN
Hyphen, Soft	CTRL+HYPHEN or CTRL+SHIFT+HYPHEN
Hyphenation, Cancel for Word	HOME+/
Hyphenation, Special Codes	ALT+SHIFT+F8
Indent, Left and Right Margins	SHIFT+F4
Indent, Left Margin	F4
Invisible Soft Return	HOME+ENTER
Italic Attribute	CTRL+I
Justification, Left	CTRL+L
Line, Block (Select) to Beginning	HOME, HOME, SHIFT+LEFT ARROW
Line, Block (Select) to End	SHIFT+END or HOME, HOME, SHIFT+ RIGHT ARROW
Line, Block (Select) to Next	SHIFT+DOWN ARROW
Line, Block (Select) to Previous	SHIFT+UP ARROW
Line, Block to Beginning (before codes)	HOME, HOME, HOME, SHIFT+ LEFT ARROW
Line, Move to Beginning	HOME, HOME, LEFT ARROW
Line, Move to Beginning (before codes)	HOME, HOME, HOME, LEFT ARROW
Line, Move to End	END or HOME, HOME, RIGHT ARROW
Macro, Play	ALT+F10
Macro, Record	CTRL+F10
Margin Release	SHIFT+TAB
Margin Release (in outline mode)	CTRL+SHIFT+TAB
Merge, End Field Code	F9 or ALT+ENTER
Merge, End Record Code	ALT+SHIFT+ENTER
Move (Cut) Block	CTRL+X or SHIFT+DELETE
Open File	F5
Page, Block (Select) to Next	SHIFT+PGDN
Page, Block (Select) to Previous	SHIFT+PGUP
Page, Move to Top of Next	PGDN
Page, Move to Top of Previous	PGUP
Page Number Display	CTRL+P

Table B-2. *The WordPerfect 5.1 for DOS (WPDOS) Keyboard Layout* (cont.)

Feature/Action	Keystroke
Pane, Next	CTRL+F1
Pane, Previous	CTRL+SHIFT+F1
Paragraph, Block (Select)	CTRL+SHIFT+F4
Paragraph, Block (Select) to Next	CTRL+SHIFT+DOWN ARROW
Paragraph, Block (Select) to Previous	CTRL+SHIFT+UP ARROW
Paragraph, Move to Next	CTRL+DOWN ARROW
Paragraph, Move to Previous	CTRL+UP ARROW
Print	SHIFT+F7
Redisplay	CTRL+F3
Replace	ALT+F2
Retrieve (Open) File	SHIFT+F10
Retrieve (Paste) Block	CTRL+V or SHIFT+INSERT
Reveal Codes On/Off	ALT+F3 or F11
Save File As	F10
Search (Find)	F2
Search (Find) and Replace	ALT+F2
Search (Find) for Next Occurrence	SHIFT+F2
Soft Hyphen	CTRL+HYPHEN or CTRL+SHIFT+HYPHEN
Soft Return, Invisible	HOME+ENTER
Speller	CTRL+F2
Styles	ALT+F8
Switch (Previous Document)	SHIFT+F3
Tab	TAB
Thesaurus	ALT+F1
Typeover Mode	INSERT
Underline Attribute	F8 or CTRL+U
Undo	CTRL+Z or ALT+BACKSPACE
Window, Move to Previous	ALT+SHIFT+F6
Word, Block (Select) Next	CTRL+SHIFT+RIGHT ARROW
Word, Block (Select) Previous	CTRL+SHIFT+LEFT ARROW
Word, Move to Next	CTRL+RIGHT ARROW
Word, Move to Previous	CTRL+LEFT ARROW
WordPerfect Characters	CTRL+W

Table B-2. *The WordPerfect 5.1 for DOS (WPDOS) Keyboard Layout* (cont.)

Additional Keyboard Layouts

In addition to the CUA standard keyboard and the WP 5.1 Compatible keyboard layouts, WordPerfect for Windows includes a keyboard layout with equation characters and commands. The *Equation Editor Keyboard* can help you insert common mathematical characters and commands when you are creating equations with the Graphics/Equation feature. The keystroke assignments for this keyboard are described in the following section.

The Equations Keyboard

To select the Equation Editor Keyboard, choose File/Preferences/Keyboard from the WordPerfect menu bar. Highlight <Equation Editor Keyboard> and choose the Select button. Finally, click on Close to return to the document editing window. For more information about WordPerfect's equation features, see Chapter 11, "Commands and Features."

Keyboard Help

When you have questions about the keystroke assignments, choose Help/Contents and click on the Keystrokes hypertext. A list of keystroke definitions appears on your screen. To view the CUA keyboard template (layout on screen), use the Search function of the Help facility. Locate CUA keyboard template in the search window and click on Go To to view the standard WordPerfect for Windows keystroke assignments. To view the WPDOS Compatible (WP 5.1 for DOS) keyboard layout, locate DOS Keyboard template and click on Go To.

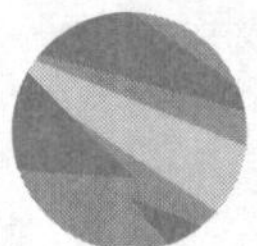

NOTE: On the pull-down menus, keystrokes often appear next to the names of the features they access. The keystrokes displayed on the menus will change to show the assignments from the keyboard layout that is currently selected.

APPENDIX C

WordPerfect Codes

WordPerfect inserts codes into your document text when you choose different formatting commands and other program options. These codes help WordPerfect format your document for the screen and the printer. In the normal document editing window, you will not see the codes embedded in the text, but you can view them with the Reveal Codes window. When your document does not look as it should, the Reveal Codes window will help you locate the codes that are causing the problems.

To display the codes in your document, choose View/Reveal Codes or press the shortcut key ALT+F3. In the Reveal Codes window, codes appear as descriptive words in sculptured graphic boxes. Most of the code names are self-explanatory; however, a few of the codes are somewhat cryptic.

Table C-1 lists all codes that may appear in a WordPerfect for Windows document. Each code is listed as it appears in the Reveal Codes window, except they are not shown graphically. Next to each displayed code is the bracketed search code. Since some codes are paired, there is an On code and an Off code. For search purposes, this allows you to find a code by its property. Next to the search code is an explanation of the code's function, as well as the pull-down menu commands that insert the code. Where applicable, keystrokes are listed from the standard WPWin 6.0 (CUA) keyboard. Codes that are automatically inserted by WordPerfect have no corresponding menu or keystroke commands; these codes are inserted and removed by WordPerfect as needed.

In the table, code names that end with a colon are codes that require a parameter. When Reveal Codes is displayed, these codes show additional information after the colon, such as measurements, that indicate the code settings. Some commands toggle a feature on and off; thus, codes that appear in on/off pairs, like [Bold On] [Bold Off], may have the same menu or command listed next to both codes.

Code	Display & Search Code	Function or Description
*	[* [Many Char]]	Multiple character wildcard
-	[- Hyphen]	Hyphen code
-	[- Hyphen Character]	Normal hyphen
-	[- Soft Hyphen]	Soft hyphen
-	[- Soft Hyphen EOL]	Soft hyphen at end-of-line
	[...Center Tab]	Centered Tab with dot leaders
	[...Dec Tab]	Decimal Tab with dot leaders
	[...Hd Center on Marg]	Hard center on margin with dot leaders
	[...Hd Center Tab]	Hard centered tab with dot leaders
	[...Hd Dec Tab]	Hard decimal-aligned tab with dot leaders
	[...Hd Flush Right]	Hard flush right with dot leaders
	[...Hd Left Tab]	Hard left-aligned tab with dot leaders
	[...Hd Right Tab]	Hard right-aligned tab with dot leaders
	[...Left Tab]	Left tab with dot leaders

Table C-1. *WordPerfect Codes and Menu Selections*

Code	Display & Search Code	Function or Description
	[...Right Tab]	Right tab with dot leaders
	[? (One Char)]	Single character wildcard
	[Auto Hyphen EOL]	Automatically hyphenated end-of-line
	[Bar Code]	Place barcode in document
	[Binding Width]	Set gutter margin (binding width)
Block Pro	[Block Pro Off]	Turn off block protection
Block Pro	[Block Pro On]	Turn on block protection
Bold	[Bold Off]	Turn off bold attribute
Bold	[Bold On]	Turn on bold attribute
	[Bookmark]	Place a bookmark
	[Bot Mar]	Bottom margin definition
	[Box (all)]	Used with Find feature: find next graphic box
	[Box Num Dec]	Decrease box number
	[Box Num Disp]	Display box number at insertion point
	[Box Num Inc]	Increase box number
	[Box Num Meth]	Box numbering method
	[Box Num Set]	Set box number
	[Box: Char Anc.]	Figure box anchored to character
	[Box: Para Anc.]	Figure box anchored to paragraph
	[Box: Pg Anc.]	Figure box anchored to page
	[Calc Col]	Calculate column
	[Cancel Hyph]	Cancel hyphenation of word
	[Cell]	Cell marker
	[Center on Marg (all)]	Used with Find feature: find next center on margin
	[Center Tab]	Center tab
	[Center Tab (all)]	Used with Find feature: find next center tab
	[Change BOL Char]	Change bottom-of-line character
	[Change EOL Char]	Change end-of-line character
	[Chap Num Dec]	Decrease chapter number
	[Chap Num Disp]	Display chapter number
	[Chap Num Inc]	Increase chapter number
	[Chap Num Meth]	Chapter numbering method

Table C-1. *WordPerfect Codes and Menu Selections* (continued)

Code	Display & Search Code	Function or Description
	[Chap Num Set]	Set chapter number
	[Char Shade Change]	Change of character shading
Char Style	[Char Style Off]	Turn off character style
Char Style	[Char Style On]	Turn on character style
	[Cntr Cur Pg]	Center the current page
	[Cntr Pgs]	Center current and subsequent pages
	[Col Border]	Place a defined column border
	[Col Def]	Column definition code
	[Color]	Text color
	[Comment]	Comment
	[Condl EOP]	Conditional end-of-page (line protect)
	[Count Dec]	Decrease counter
	[Count Disp]	Display counter in current
	[Count Inc]	Increase counter
	[Count Meth]	Counting method
	[Count Set]	Set counter
	[Date]	Date code
	[Date Fmt]	Predefined date format
Dbl Und	[Dbl Und Off]	Turn off double underlining
Dbl Und	[Dbl Und On]	Turn on double underlining
	[Dbl-Sided Print]	Enable duplexing (two-sided printing)
DDE Link	[DDE Link Begin]	Begin dynamic data exchange link
DDE Link	[DDE Link End]	End dynamic data exchange link
	[Dec Tab]	Tab to decimal-aligned tab stop
	[Dec Tab (all)]	Used with Find feature: find next decimal tab
	[Dec/Align Char]	User-defined decimal alignment character
	[Def Mark]	Mark text definition
	[Delay]	Delay number of pages
	[Delay On]	Start delayed text/graphic
	[Do Grand Tot]	Used temporarily when converting table/spreadsheet from WordPerfect for DOS

Table C-1. *WordPerfect Codes and Menu Selections* (continued)

Code	Display & Search Code	Function or Description
	[Do Subtot]	Used temporarily when converting table/spreadsheet from WordPerfect for DOS
	[Do Total]	Used temporarily when converting table/spreadsheet from WordPerfect for DOS
	[Dorm HRt]	Dormant hard return
	[Dot Lead Char]	Character to use as dot leader
	[End Cntr/Align]	End of center or alignment code
	[Endnote]	Endnote definition code
	[Endnote Min]	Amount of endnotes to keep together
	[Endnote Num Dec]	Decrease endnote number
	[Endnote Num Disp]	Display endnote number at cursor
	[Endnote Num Inc]	Increase endnote number
	[Endnote Num Meth]	Endnote numbering method
	[Endnote Num Set]	Set endnote number
	[Endnote Placement]	Endnote placement definition
	[Endnote Space]	Spacing between endnotes
Ext Large	[Ext Large Off]	Turn off extra large font attribute
Ext Large	[Ext Large On]	Turn on extra large font attribute
	[Filename]	Insert filename (after saved and named)
Fine	[Fine Off]	Turn off fine font size attribute
Fine	[Fine On]	Turn on fine font size attribute
	[First Ln Ind]	Indent first line definition code
	[Flt Cell Begin]	Begin floating cell
	[Flt Cell End]	End floating cell
	[Font]	Font type/definition
	[Font Size]	Font size definition
	[Footer A]	Footer A definition
	[Footer B]	Footer B definition
	[Footer Sep]	Footer distance from text
	[Footnote]	Footnote definition code
	[Footnote Cont Msg]	Footnote "continued..." message
	[Footnote Min]	Amount of footnotes to keep together

Table C-1. *WordPerfect Codes and Menu Selections* (continued)

Code	Display & Search Code	Function or Description
	[Footnote Num Dec]	Decrease footnote number
	[Footnote Num Disp]	Display footnote number
	[Footnote Num Each Pg]	Footnote numbering on each page
	[Footnote Num Inc]	Increase footnote number
	[Footnote Num Meth]	Footnote numbering method
	[Footnote Num Set]	Set footnote numbering
	[Footnote Sep Ln]	Footnote line separators
	[Footnote Space]	Spacing between footnotes
	[Footnote Txt Pos]	Place notes below text
	[Force]	Force odd/even page
	[Formatted Pg Num]	Insert formatted page number
	[Gen Txt Begin]	Begin generated text
	[Gen Txt End]	End generated text
	[Graph Line]	Graphics line
	[HAdv]	Horizontal advance definition
	[HCol]	Hard column break
	[HCol-SPg]	Hard column break with soft page break
	[Hd Back Tab]	Hard back tab
	[Hd Center on Marg]	Hard center on margin
	[Hd Center on Pos]	Hard center on cursor position
	[Hd Center Tab]	Hard center tab
	[Hd Dec Tab]	Hard decimal tab
	[Hd Flush Right]	Hard flush right
	[Hd Flush Right (all)]	Used with Find feature: find next hard flush right
	[Hd Left Ind]	Hard left indent
	[Hd Left Tab]	Hard left tab
	[Hd Left/Right Indent]	Hard left/right indent definition
	[Hd Right Tab]	Hard right tab
	[Hd Tbl Tab]	Hard table tab
	[Header A]	Header A definition
	[Header B]	Header B definition
	[Header Sep]	Header distance from text
Hidden	[Hidden Off]	End hidden text

Table C-1. *WordPerfect Codes and Menu Selections* (continued)

Code	Display & Search Code	Function or Description
Hidden	[Hidden On]	Begin hidden text
	[Hidden Txt]	Hidden text definition (when hidden text)
	[HPg]	Hard page break
	[HRow-HCol]	Hard row with hard column break
	[HRow-HCol-SPg]	Hard row with hard column and soft page break
	[HRow-HPg]	Hard row with hard page break
	[HRt]	Hard return
	[HRt-SCol]	Hard return with soft column break
	[HRt-SPg]	Hard return with soft page break
	[HSpace]	Hard space
Hypertext	[Hypertext Begin]	Begin hypertext
Hypertext	[Hypertext End]	End hypertext
	[Hyph]	Hyphenation on/off
	[Hyph SRt]	Hyphenate with soft return instead of -
	[Index]	Index definition code
Italic	[Italc Off]	Turn off italic attribute
Italic	[Italc On]	Turn on italic attribute
	[Just]	Justification definition
	[Just Lim]	Word spacing/justification limits definition
	[Kern]	Kerning definition
	[Labels Form]	Type of label currently being used
	[Lang]	Language currently being used
Large	[Large Off]	Turn off large font attribute
Large	[Large On]	Turn on large font attribute
	[Leading Adj]	Leading adjustment definition
	[Left Tab]	Left tab
	[Left Tab (all)]	Used with Find feature: find next left tab
	[Lft HZone]	Left hyphenation zone
	[Lft Mar]	Left margin definition
	[Lft Mar Adj]	Left margin adjustment definition

Table C-1. *WordPerfect Codes and Menu Selections* (continued)

Code	Display & Search Code	Function or Description
	[Link]	Start hypertext link
	[Link End]	End hypertext link
	[Ln Height]	Line height definition code
	[Ln Num]	Line numbering definition
	[Ln Num Meth]	Line numbering method
	[Ln Num Set]	Set line numbering
	[Ln Spacing]	Line spacing definition code
	[Macro Func]	Macro function
	[Math]	Used temporarily when converting table/spreadsheet from WordPerfect for DOS
	[Math Def]	Used temporarily when converting table/spreadsheet from WordPerfect for DOS
	[Math Neg]	Used temporarily when converting table/spreadsheet from WordPerfect for DOS
Mrk Txt ToC	[Mrk ToC Begin]	Mark text for beginning table of contents
	[Mrk Txt List Begin]	Marked beginning of text list
	[Mrk Txt List End]	Marked ending of text list
Mrk Txt ToC	[Mrk Txt ToC End]	Mark text for ending table of contents
	[Open Style]	Use opening style
	[Outline]	Outline mode end marker
Outline	[Outln Off]	Turn off outline text attribute
Outline	[Outln On]	Turn on outline text attribute
	[Ovrstk]	Enable overstrike mode
	[Paper Sz/Typ]	Paper size and type definition code
	[Para Border]	Paragraph border definition
	[Para End (all)]	End of paragraph style
	[Para Num]	Paragraph numbering definition
	[Para Num Dec]	Decrease paragraph number
	[Para Num Disp]	Display paragraph number
	[Para Num Inc]	Increase paragraph number

Table C-1. *WordPerfect Codes and Menu Selections* (continued)

Code	Display & Search Code	Function or Description
	[Para Num Meth]	Paragraph numbering method
	[Para Num Set]	Paragraph numbering set
	[Para Spacing]	Paragraph spacing
	[Para Style]	Outline paragraph style definition
	[Para Style End]	End paragraph style
	[Para Style Txt]	Paragraph style text
	[Pause Ptr]	Pause printer command
	[Pg Border]	Page border definition
	[Pg Num Dec]	Decrease page number
	[Pg Num Disp]	Display page number
	[Pg Num Fmt]	Page numbering format
	[Pg Num Inc]	Increase page number manually
	[Pg Num Meth]	Page numbering method
	[Pg Num Pos]	Position of page number
	[Pg Num Set]	Set page number
	[Ptr Cmnd]	Printer command
Redln	[Redln Off]	Turn off redline attribute
Redln	[Redln On]	Turn on redline attribute
	[Ref Chap]	Cross-reference number for chapter
	[Ref Count]	Cross-reference number for counter
	[Ref Endnote]	Cross-reference number for endnote
	[Ref Footnote]	Cross-reference number for footnote
	[Ref Para]	Cross-reference number for paragraph
	[Ref Pg]	Cross-reference number for page
	[Ref Sec Pg]	Cross-reference number for secondary page
	[Ref Vol]	Cross-reference number for volume
	[Rgt HZone]	Right hyphenation zone
	[Rgt Mar]	Right margin definition
	[Rgt Mar Adj]	Right margin adjust
	[Right Tab (all)]	Used with Find feature: find next right tab
	[Right Tab]	Right tab

Table C-1. *WordPerfect Codes and Menu Selections* (continued)

Code	Display & Search Code	Function or Description
	[Row]	Row label/definition
	[Row-SCol]	Row-soft column break
	[Row-SPg]	Row-soft page break
	[Sec Pg Num Dec]	Decrease secondary page number
	[Sec Pg Num Disp]	Display secondary page number
	[Sec Pg Num Inc]	Increase secondary page number
	[Sec Pg Num Meth]	Secondary page number definition
	[Sec Pg Num Set]	Set secondary page number
Shadw	[Shadw Off]	Turn off shadow attribute
Shadw	[Shadw On]	Turn on shadow attribute
Sm Cap	[Sm Cap Off]	Turn off small capitals
Sm Cap	[Sm Cap On]	Turn on small capitals
Small	[Small Off]	Turn off small font attribute
Small	[Small On]	Turn on small font attribute
	[Sound]	Sound file definition
	[SRt]	Soft return
	[SRt-SCol]	Soft return with soft column break
	[SRt-SPg]	Soft return with soft page break
StkOut	[StkOut Off]	Turn off strikeout mode
StkOut	[StkOut On]	Turn on strikeout mode
	[Style]	Style definition
	[Subdivided Pg]	Subdivided page definition
	[Subdoc]	Subdocument definition
Subdoc	[Subdoc Begin]	Beginning of subdocument
Subdoc	[Subdoc End]	End of subdocument
Subscpt	[Subscpt Off]	Turn off subscript attribute
Subscpt	[Subscpt On]	Turn on subscript attribute
	[Subtot Entry]	Used temporarily when converting table/spreadsheet from WordPerfect for DOS
	[Suppress]	Suppress from appearing on current page
Suprscpt	[Suprscpt Off]	Turn off superscript attribute
Suprscpt	[Suprscpt On]	Turn on superscript attribute

Table C-1. *WordPerfect Codes and Menu Selections* (continued)

Code	Display & Search Code	Function or Description
	[Tab (all)]	Used with Find feature: find next tab
	[Tab Set]	Tab setting definition
	[Target]	Cross-reference target
	[Tbl Dec Tab]	Table decimal tab
	[Tbl Def]	Table definition
	[Tbl Off]	End of table marker
	[Tbl Off-SCol]	End of table-soft column marker
	[Tbl Off-SPg]	End of table-soft page marker
	[THCol]	Temporary hard column marker
	[THCol-SPg]	Temporary hard column-soft page marker
	[Third Party]	Unknown third-party (non-WordPerfect) code
	[Thousands Sep]	User-defined thousands separator
	[THpg]	Temporary hard page
	[THRt]	Temporary hard return
	[THRt-SCol]	Temporary hard return-soft column
	[THRt-SPg]	Temporary hard return-soft page
	[ToA]	Table of authorities definition
	[Top Mar]	Top margin definition
	[Total Entry]	Used temporarily when converting table/spreadsheet from WordPerfect for DOS
	[TSRt]	Temporary soft return
	[TSRt-SCol]	Temporary soft return-soft column
	[TSRt-SPg]	Temporary soft return-soft page
	[Txt Dir]	Used temporarily when converting table/spreadsheet from WordPerfect for DOS
	[Und Off]	Turn off underline attribute
	[Und On]	Turn on underline attribute
	[Undrln Spc]	Enable space underlining
	[Undrln Tab]	Enable tab underlining
	[VAdv]	Vertical advance definition code
	[Very Large Off]	Turn off very large font attribute

Table C-1. *WordPerfect Codes and Menu Selections* (continued)

Code	Display & Search Code	Function or Description
	[Very Large On]	Turn on very large font attribute
	[Vol Num Dec]	Decrease volume number
	[Vol Num Disp]	Display volume number
	[Vol Num Inc]	Increase volume number
	[Vol Num Meth]	Volume numbering method
	[Vol Num Set]	Set volume numbering
	[Watermark A]	Watermark A definition
	[Watermark B]	Watermark B definition
	[Wid/Orph]	Enable Widow/Orphan protection
	[Wrd/Ltr Spacing]	Word/Letterspacing definition
	[Writing Tools]	Writing tools enabled/disabled

Table C-1. *WordPerfect Codes and Menu Selections* (continued)

APPENDIX D

Graphics Programs and Files

This appendix contains information about the types of graphics files you can retrieve into a WordPerfect for Windows graphics box. WordPerfect supports a wide variety of graphics file formats, including many formats that are rarely supported; it is likely that the files created by your graphics software can be used in WordPerfect documents.

Supported Graphics Formats

Table D-1 lists the software programs that can create graphics files accepted by WordPerfect for Windows. Note that the "Accepted Formats" column shows the graphics file format that WordPerfect accepts, but this may not be the standard graphics format of the listed program; in some cases it may be necessary to use the graphics program's Save As (or export) feature to save your graphics images under a different graphics format.

Graphics Program	Accepted Formats
Adobe Illustrator	EPS
Anvil-5000	HPGL
Arts & Letters	CGM
AutoCAD, 9.0, 10.0	DXF, HPGL
AutoSketch, 1.03	DXF, HPGL
Boeing Graph, 4.0	IMG
CCS Designer	HPGL
ChartMaster, 6.21	HPGL
Chemfile 11	HPGL
Chemtext	EPS
CIES (Compuscan)	TIFF
Designer, 1.2 (Micrografx)	HPGL
Designer, 2.0 (Micrografx)	EPS, CGM, PCX, TIFF
DFI Handy Scanner	IMG, TIFF
DiagramMaster, 5.02	HPGL
Diagraph	HPGL
Dr. Halo II, III	DHP
DrawPerfect	CGM, EPS, HPGL, PCX, TIFF, WPG
Easyflow, 4.4	HPGL
Energraphics, 2.1	IMG, TIFF
Freelance Plus, 2.0	CGM

Table D-1. *WordPerfect Codes and Menu Selections*

Graphics Program	Accepted Formats
GEM Draw	GEM
GEM Paint, 2.0	IMG, TIFF
GEM Scan	IMG, TIFF
Generic CAD	HPGL
GeniScan	TIFF
Graph-in-the-Box	HPGL
Graph Plus, 1.3 (Micrografx)	CGM, EPS, HPGL, PCX, TIFF
Graphics Editor 200	HPGL
GraphWriter	CGM
Harvard Graphics, 2.1	CGM, EPS, HPGL
HiJaak	WPG
HOTSHOT Graphics, 1.5	WPG
HP Scanning Gallery, A.01	PCX, TIFF
IBM CADAM	HPGL
IBM CATIA	HPGL
IBM GDDM	HPGL
IBM GPG	HPGL
Lotus 1-2-3, 1a	PIC
Lotus 1-2-3, 3.0	CGM, PCX
Macintosh Paint, 1.5	PNTG
Microsoft Chart	HPGL
Microsoft Excel	HPGL
Mirage	HPGL
Paradox, 3.0	PIC
PC Paint Plus, 1.5	PIC
PC Paintbrush	PCX
PFS: First Publisher	PCX
PicturePak	CGM, PCX, WPG
Pixie	CGM
Pizazz, 1.01	PCX, TIFF
PlanPerfect, 3.0	CGM

Table D-1. *WordPerfect Codes and Menu Selections* (continued)

Graphics Program	Accepted Formats
Reflex, 2.0	PIC
Quattro	EPS, PIC
SAS/Graph	HPGL
ScanMan	TIFF
Schema	HPGL
SignMaster, 5.11	HPGL
SlideWrite Plus, 2.1	HPGL, PCX, TIFF
SuperCalc, 4	PIC
Symphony	PIC
Versacad	HPGL
VGA Paint	PCX, TIFF, WPG
VP Graphics	HPGL
VP Planner	PIC
Windows Draw	HPGL
Windows Paint	MSP
Words & Figures	PIC

Table D-1. *WordPerfect Codes and Menu Selections* (continued)

NOTE: If you use a graphics program that is not listed in this table but that does run under Windows, you can transfer your graphics into WordPerfect through the Windows Clipboard. This is explained in the following section, "Transferring Graphics with the Clipboard."

Transferring Graphics with the Clipboard

If you have problems directly retrieving graphics into WordPerfect, you can transfer graphics images with the Windows Clipboard. It is assumed that the graphics program you are using is designed to run under Microsoft Windows; if not, you may need to convert your graphics files, as described later in this appendix.

To transfer a graphics image through the Windows Clipboard, first start the graphics program that you use. Then open the graphics file that contains the image you want to transfer to WordPerfect. Select the entire image and choose Edit/Copy from the menu bar; this puts a copy of the image into the Windows Clipboard. If you want to capture the entire screen instead, press PRINT SCREEN to copy the displayed screen to the Clipboard.

Once an image is captured to the Clipboard, switch to WordPerfect and choose Edit/Paste (or press CTRL+V). This creates a figure box in WordPerfect with the graphics image stored in the Clipboard. At this point, you can use the graphics features to change the size, location, and appearance of the box. Remember, you cannot edit the graphics image in WordPerfect, but you can switch back to your graphics program and make any changes to the image there. Then copy the edited graphic back to the Clipboard and retrieve it into WordPerfect.

APPENDIX E

Icon Directory

This appendix contains a list of the icons and tools available within WordPerfect for Windows.

Comment Feature Bar

Displayed by selecting Insert/Comment/Create or Insert/Comment/Edit.

	Meaning
1	Displays the feature bar control menu
2	Inserts the user's initials
3	Inserts the user's name
4	Inserts the date
5	Inserts the time
6	Displays next comment
7	Displays previous comment
8	Closes the feature bar

Cross-Reference Feature Bar

Displayed by selecting Tools/Cross Reference, or by clicking on the cross-reference button on the Generate button bar.

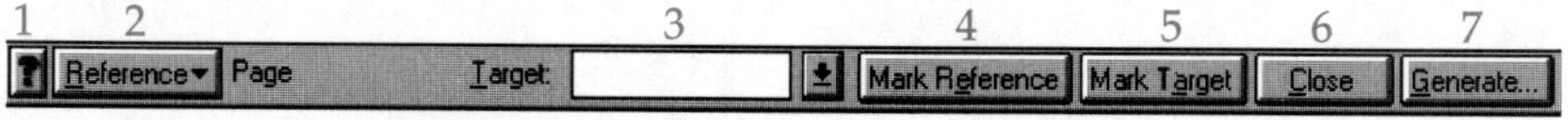

	Meaning
1	Displays the feature bar control menu
2	Allows you to choose which type of cross reference you are creating
3	Shows and allows selection of the cross reference target
4	Inserts codes for the reference
5	Inserts codes for the target
6	Closes the feature bar
7	Generates cross-references, table of authorities, table of contents, indexes, and lists

Delay Codes Feature Bar

Displayed by selecting Layout/Page/Delay Codes, entering a number of pages to delay, and then clicking on OK.

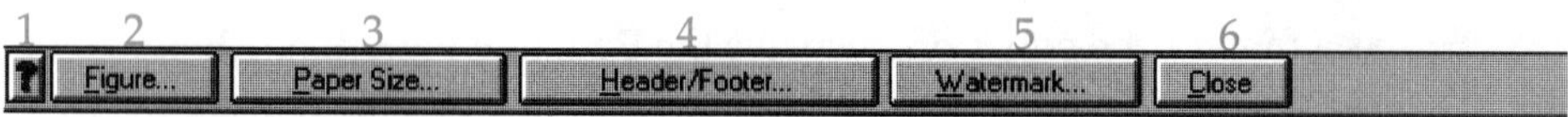

	Meaning
1	Displays the feature bar control menu
2	Inserts a figure
3	Specifies paper size or orientation
4	Defines a header or footer
5	Defines a watermark
6	Closes the feature bar

Equation Editor Button Bar

Displayed in any of the following ways:

- Selecting Graphics/Equation.
- Selecting File/Preferences/Button Bar, choosing Equation Editor, then clicking on Select.
- Clicking on the equation button on the Graphics button bar.

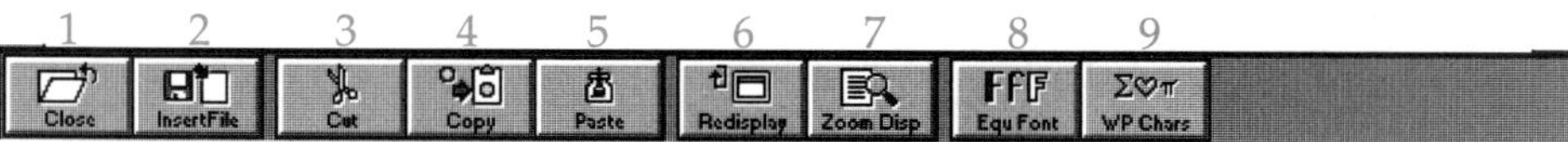

	Meaning
1	Closes the equation editor or current document
2	Allows you to insert a text file; displays the Retrieve Equation Text dialog box
3	Removes the selected text, retaining it in the Clipboard
4	Copies the selected text, placing it in the Clipboard

	Meaning
5	Pastes the contents of the Clipboard at the insertion point
6	Rewrites the equation
7	Zooms equation display in or out; displays the Zoom Equation Display dialog box
8	Selects a font for the equation; displays the Equation Font dialog box
9	Displays the WordPerfect Characters dialog box

Font Button Bar

Displayed by selecting File/Preferences/Button Bar, choosing Font, then clicking on Select.

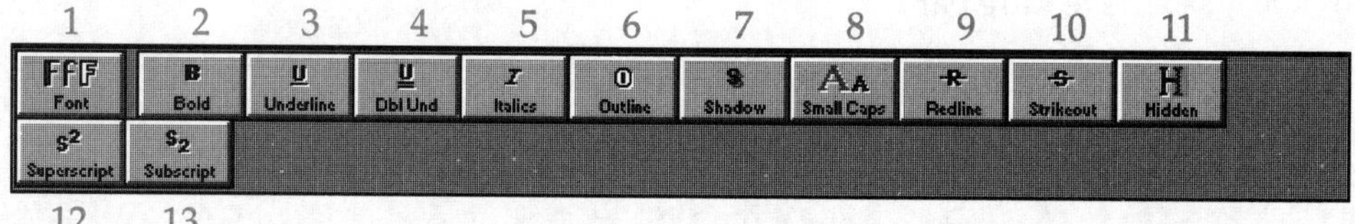

	Meaning
1	Allows you to change font specifications; displays the Font dialog box
2	Turns on or off the bold attribute
3	Turns on or off the underline attribute
4	Turns on or off the double-underline attribute
5	Turns on or off the italics attribute
6	Turns on or off the outline attribute
7	Turns on or off the shadow attribute
8	Turns on or off the small caps attribute
9	Turns on or off the redlining attribute
10	Turns on or off the strikeout attribute
11	Turns on or off the hidden attribute
12	Turns on or off the superscript attribute
13	Turns on or off the subscript attribute

Footnote/Endnote Feature Bar

Displayed by any of the following methods:

- Selecting Insert/Footnote/Create.
- Selecting Insert/Footnote/Edit.
- Selecting Insert/Endnote/Create.
- Selecting Insert/Endnote/Edit.

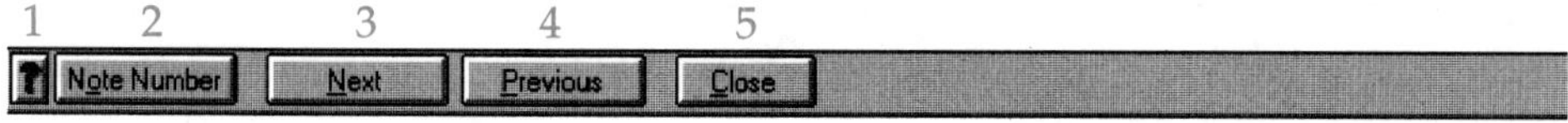

	Meaning
1	Displays the feature bar control menu
2	Inserts note number
3	Displays next footnote or endnote
4	Displays previous footnote or endnote
5	Closes the feature bar

Generate Button Bar

Displayed by selecting File/Preferences/Button Bar, choosing Generate, then clicking on Select.

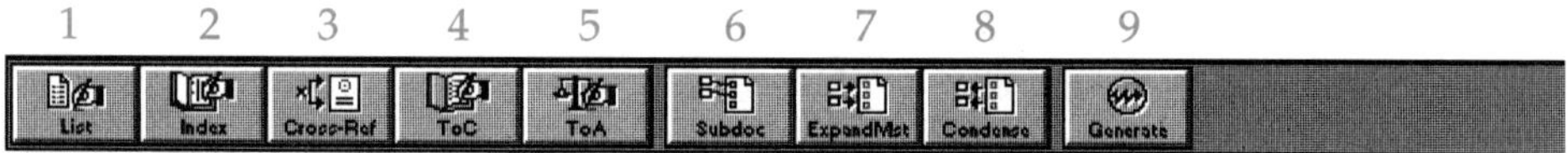

	Meaning
1	Displays the list feature bar
2	Displays the index feature bar
3	Displays the cross-reference feature bar
4	Displays the table of contents feature bar

	Meaning
5	Displays the table of authorities feature bar
6	Creates a subdocument link
7	Expands a master document
8	Condenses a master document
9	Generates cross-references, table of authorities, table of contents, indexes, and lists

Graphics Box Feature Bar

Displayed by any of the following:

- Selecting Graphics/Edit Box.
- Clicking on the Edit Box button on the Graphics button bar.

	Meaning
1	Displays the feature bar control menu
2	Edits the box caption
3	Edits the box content
4	Changes the box position
5	Changes the box size
6	Changes the box border or how it is filled
7	Specifies how text wraps around the box
8	Changes the box style
9	Displays the Image Tools palette
10	Selects the next graphics box
11	Selects the previous graphics box
12	Closes the feature bar

Graphics Button Bar

Displayed after selecting many different functions from the Graphics menu, or by selecting File/Preferences/Button Bar, choosing Graphics, then clicking on Select.

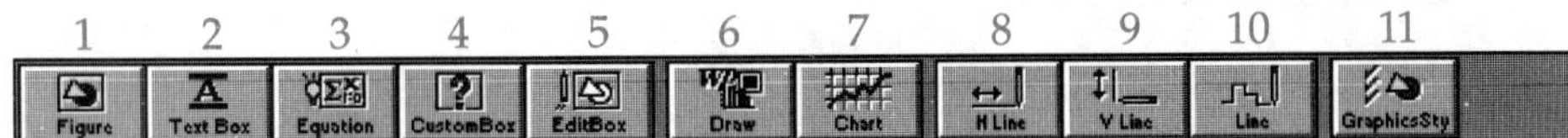

	Meaning
1	Retrieves a figure
2	Creates a text box
3	Creates an equation box; starts the equation editor
4	Creates a custom box
5	Edits a graphics box; displays the Graphics Box feature bar
6	Creates a graphic with WP Draw
7	Creates a chart with WP Draw
8	Creates a horizontal line
9	Creates a vertical line
10	Creates a custom line
11	Creates or edits graphics styles

Header/Footer Feature Bar

Displayed by selecting Layout/Header/Footer/Create (or Edit)

	Meaning
1	Displays the feature bar control menu
2	Inserts numbers (page, section, etc.)
3	Inserts a line

	Meaning
4	Controls placment of the header/footer
5	Sets distance from text
6	Displays next header or footer
7	Displays previous header or footer
8	Closes the feature bar

Hypertext Feature Bar

Displayed after selecting Tools/Hypertext.

	Meaning
1	Displays the feature bar control menu
2	Executes a hypertext jump or associated macro
3	Returns from the previous hypertext jump
4	Displays next hypertext link
5	Displays previous hypertext link
6	Creates a link
7	Edits an existing link
8	Deletes a link
9	Deactivates or activates a link
10	Edits the Hypertext style
11	Closes the feature bar

Image Tools Palette

Displayed by selecting the Tools button from the Graphics Box feature bar.

1 2
3 4
5 6
7 8
9 10
11 12
13 14

	Meaning
1	Rotates the image
2	Moves the image
3	Changes mouse pointer to regular pointer
4	Scales the image
5	Changes to complementary colors
6	Displays image in monochrome only
7	Sets image contrast level
8	Sets image brightness
9	Resets image attributes
10	Specifies how image is filled
11	Mirror image around vertical axis
12	Mirror image around horizontal axis
13	Edits image using WP Draw
14	Changes overall image settings

Index Feature Bar

Displayed by selecting Tools/Index, or by clicking on the index button on the Generate button bar.

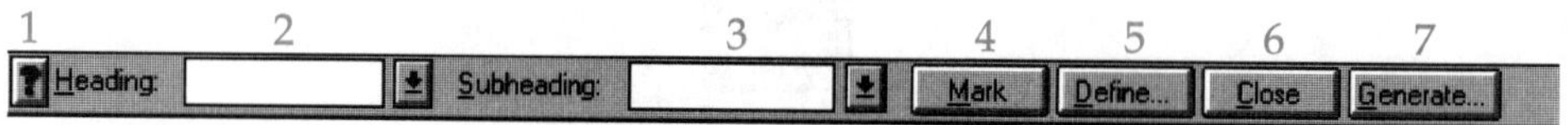

	Meaning
1	Displays the feature bar control menu
2	Shows or selects the index heading
3	Shows or selects the index subheading
4	Marks the selected text for inclusion in the index
5	Defines an index
6	Closes the feature bar
7	Generate cross references, table of authorities, table of contents, indexes, and lists

Layout Button Bar

Displayed by selecting File/Preferences/Button Bar, choosing Layout, then clicking on Select.

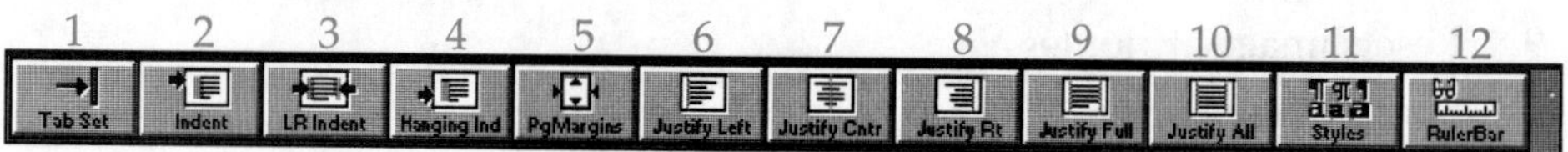

	Meaning
1	Sets tabs
2	Indents left side of paragraph one tab stop
3	Indents left and right side of paragraph one tab stop
4	Creates a hanging indent
5	Sets page margins
6	Aligns text to left margin
7	Centers text between left and right margin
8	Aligns text to right margin
9	Forces text to align to left and right margins, except for last line

	Meaning
10	Forces text to align to left and right margins, including last line
11	Defines or selects styles
12	Displays the ruler

List Feature Bar

Displayed by selecting Tools/List, or by clicking on the list button on the Generate button bar.

	Meaning
1	Displays the feature bar control menu
2	Shows or creates a list name
3	Marks text as belonging to the selected list
4	Defines a list
5	Closes the feature bar
6	Generates cross-references, table of authorities, table of contents, indexes, and lists

Macro Edit Feature Bar

Displayed by selecting Tools/Macro/Macro Bar.

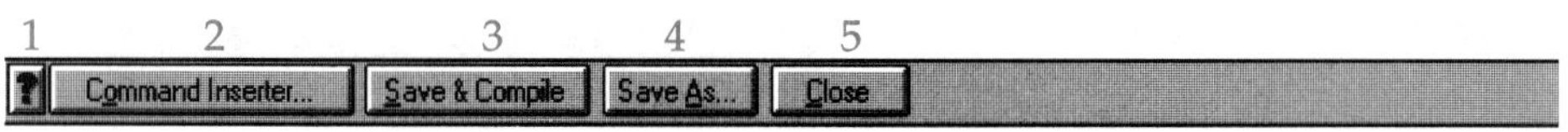

	Meaning
1	Displays the feature bar control menu
2	Inserts macro commands or system variables

	Meaning
3	Saves the macro document and compiles it
4	Saves the macro document using a new filename
5	Closes the feature bar

Macros Button Bar

Displayed by selecting File/Preferences/Button Bar, choosing Macros, then clicking on Select.

	Meaning
1	Saves the current macro document
2	Plays (executes) a macro
3	Turns on the macro recorder
4	Pauses a macro being recorded
5	Edits a macro

Merge Feature Bar (for Data Files)

Displayed by selecting Tools/Merge, choosing to work with a data file, and then clicking on OK.

	Meaning
1	Displays the feature bar control menu
2	Inserts an END FIELD merge code
3	Inserts an END RECORD merge code

	Meaning
4	Inserts a merge code or system variable
5	Allows quick entry of records
6	Merges the data file with a form file
7	Goes to the form file
8	Sets merging options

Merge Feature Bar (for Form Files)

Displayed by selecting Tools/Merge, choosing to work with a form file, and then clicking on OK.

	Meaning
1	Displays the feature bar control menu
2	Inserts a field
3	Inserts the date
4	Inserts a merge code or system variable
5	Inserts a KEYBOARD merge command
6	Merges the form file to a data file
7	Goes to the data file
8	Sets merging options

Outline Button Bar

Displayed by selecting File/Preferences/Button Bar, choosing Outline, then clicking on Select.

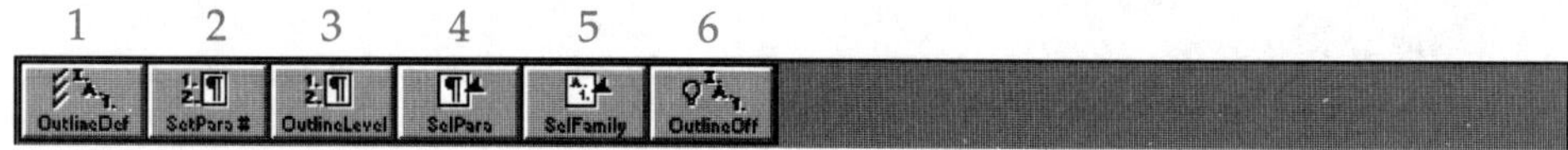

	Meaning
1	Defines an outline
2	Sets the paragraph number
3	Inserts an outline level
4	Selects the paragraph at the insertion point
5	Selects an outline family
6	Turns off outlining; marks end of outline

Outline Feature Bar

Displayed by selecting Tools/Outline.

	Meaning
1	Displays the feature bar control menu
2	Promotes outline level of current paragraph
3	Demotes outline level of current paragraph
4	Moves outline level or family up in the document
5	Moves outline level or family down in the document
6	Changes outline level to text or back
7	Expands all heads under this level
8	Condenses all heads under this level
9	Shows only level 1 heads
10	Shows all heads, level 2 and above
11	Shows all heads, level 3 and above
12	Shows all heads, level 4 and above
13	Shows all heads, level 5 and above

	Meaning
14	Shows all heads, level 6 and above
15	Shows all heads, level 7 and above
16	Shows all heads, level 8 and above
17	Shows all heads
18	Sets outlining options
19	Select a style for the outline level
20	Closes the feature bar

Page Button Bar

Displayed by selecting File/Preferences/Button Bar, choosing Page, then clicking on Select.

1 2 3 4 5 6 7 8 9

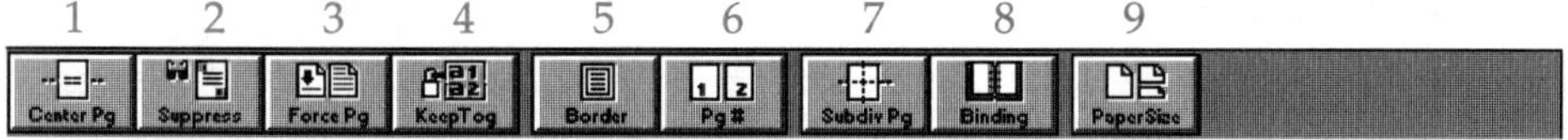

	Meaning
1	Centers page
2	Suppresses headers, footers, watermarks, or page numbers for current page
3	Forces page to have an odd or even number
4	Displays Keep Text Together dialog box
5	Creates or modifies page borders
6	Specifies page numbering
7	Divides a page into sections
8	Specifies binding and duplexing options
9	Specifies paper size and orientation

Power Bar

Displayed by selecting View/Power Bar.

1 2 3 4 5 6 7 8 9 10 11 12 13 14 15 16 17 18 19 20 21 22 23 24

	Meaning
1	Creates a new document
2	Opens an existing document
3	Saves current document
4	Prints current document
5	Removes the selected text, retaining it in the Clipboard
6	Copies the selected text, placing it in the Clipboard
7	Pastes the contents of the Clipboard at the insertion point
8	Undoes selected actions
9	Changes typeface
10	Changes font size
11	Turns on or off the bold attribute
12	Turns on or off the italics attribute
13	Turns on or off the underline attribute
14	Sets tabs
15	Creates a table
16	Defines columns
17	Sets paragraph alignment
18	Sets line spacing
19	Zooms document in or out
20	Spell check
21	Thesaurus
22	Grammar check
23	Zooms out to display full page on screen
24	Hides or displays the button bar

Preferences Button Bar

Displayed by selecting File/Preferences/Button Bar, choosing Preferences, then clicking on Select.

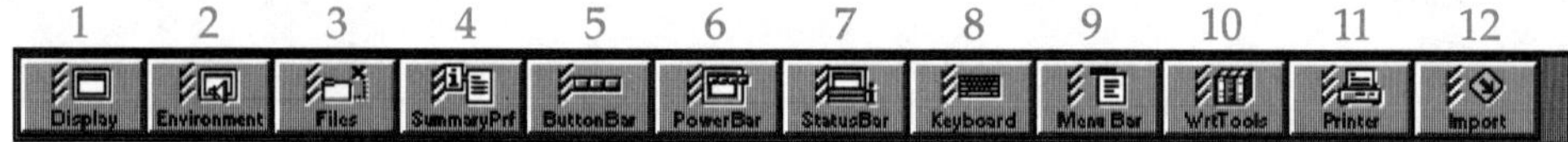

	Meaning
1	Changes display preferences
2	Changes environment preferences
3	Changes files preferences
4	Changes summary preferences
5	Changes button bar preferences
6	Changes power bar preferences
7	Changes status bar preferences
8	Changes keyboard preferences
9	Changes menu bar preferences
10	Changes writing tools preferences
11	Changes printer preferences
12	Changes import preferences

Sound Feature Bar

Displayed by selecting Insert/Sound/Transcribe.

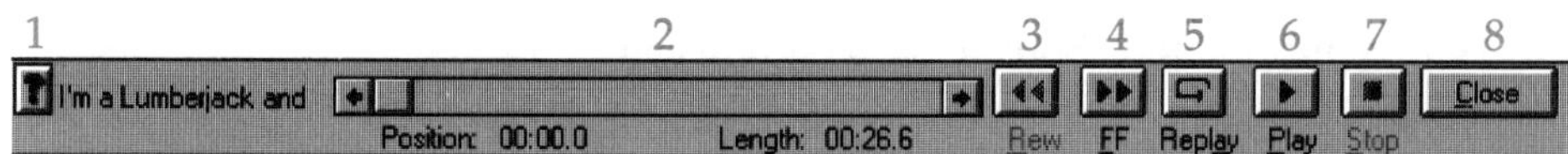

	Meaning
1	Displays the feature bar control menu
2	Sound file scroll bar

	Meaning
3	Rewind
4	Fast Forward
5	Replay sequence
6	Play
7	Stop
8	Closes the feature bar

Table Formula Feature Bar

Displayed by selecting Table/Formula Bar, or by clicking on the TblFormBar button on the Tables button bar.

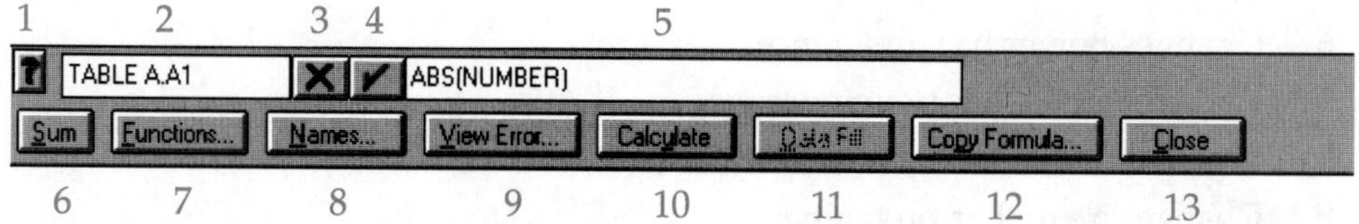

	Meaning
1	Displays the feature bar control menu
2	Shows current table address
3	Cancels formula changes
4	Accepts formula changes
5	Formula entry window
6	Calculates a sum
7	Lists or inserts a function
8	Lists or creates table names
9	Views information about error in current cell
10	Calculates formulas in all document tables
11	Fills a range of cells with data
12	Copies a formula
13	Closes the feature bar

Table of Authorities Feature Bar

Displayed by selecting Tools/Table of Authorities, or by clicking on the ToA button on the Generate button bar.

	Meaning
1	Displays the feature bar control menu
2	Lists or creates short form names
3	Marks the selected text
4	Creates a full form citation; displays ToA Full Form feature bar
5	Edits a full form citation; displays ToA Full Form feature bar
6	Defines a table of authorities
7	Closes the feature bar
8	Generates cross-references, table of authorities, table of contents, indexes, and lists

Table of Contents Feature Bar

Displayed by selecting Tools/Table of Contents, or by clicking on the ToC button on the Generate button bar.

	Meaning
1	Displays the feature bar control menu
2	Marks text for inclusion as a ToC level 1 head
3	Marks text for inclusion as a ToC level 2 head
4	Marks text for inclusion as a ToC level 3 head
5	Marks text for inclusion as a ToC level 4 head

	Meaning
6	Marks text for inclusion as a ToC level 5 head
7	Defines the table of contents
8	Closes the feature bar
9	Generates cross-references, table of authorities, table of contents, indexes, and lists

Tables Button Bar

Displayed by selecting File/Preferences/Button Bar, choosing Tables, then clicking on Select.

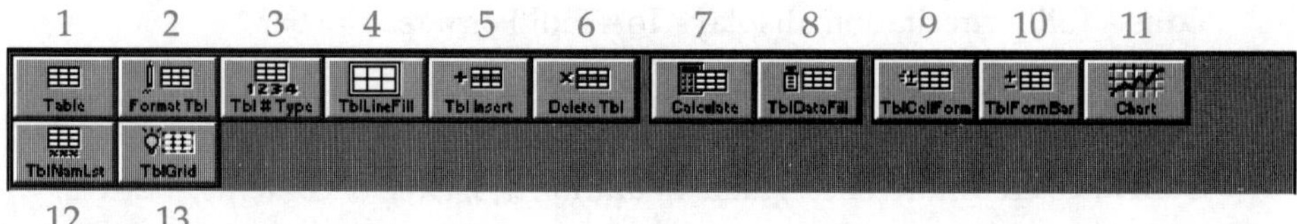

	Meaning
1	Creates a table
2	Formats a table
3	Changes table numbering format
4	Changes table lines and shading
5	Inserts row or column
6	Deletes rows, columns, or data
7	Calculates formulas in all tables in document
8	Fills a range of cells with data
9	Turns cell formula entry on or off
10	Displays the Table Formula feature bar
11	Creates a chart with WP Draw
12	Lists or creates table names
13	Turns table grid on or off

Template Feature Bar

Displayed by selecting File/Template/Options/Create Template or File/Template/Options/Edit Template.

	Meaning
1	Displays the feature bar control menu
2	Creates an object (style, macro, etc.) to be stored with the template
3	Copies or deletes an object
4	Redefines button bars, menus, the keyboard, etc.
5	Creates or edits template description
6	Changes the initial template style codes
7	Closes the feature bar

ToA Full Form Feature Bar

Displayed by clicking on the Create Full Form or Edit Full Form buttons on the Table of Authorities feature bar.

	Meaning
1	Displays the feature bar control menu
2	Lists the short form for this citation
3	Lists or sets the sections for this citation
4	Closes the feature bar

Watermark Feature Bar

Displayed by selecting Layout/Watermark/Create.

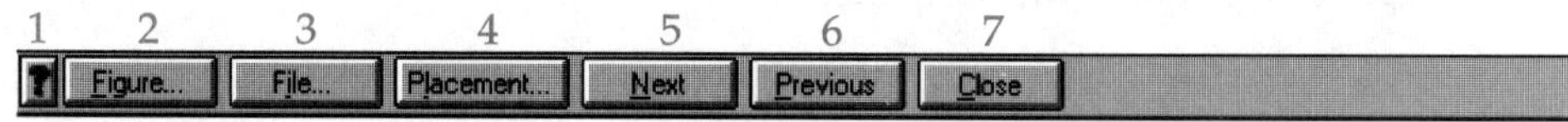

	Meaning
1	Displays the feature bar control menu
2	Inserts an image
3	Inserts a file
4	Controls placement of the watermark
5	Dislpays next watermark
6	Dislpays previous watermark
7	Closes the feature bar

WordPerfect 5.2 Button Bar

Displayed by selecting File/Preferences/Button Bar, choosing WordPerfect 5.2, then clicking on Select.

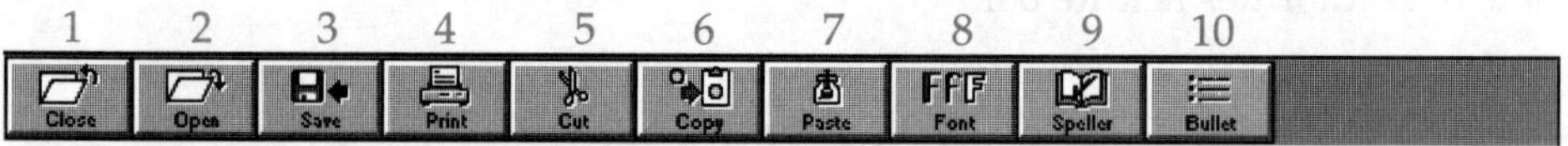

	Meaning
1	Closes a document
2	Opens an existing document
3	Saves current document
4	Prints current document
5	Removes the selected text, retaining it in the Clipboard
6	Copies the selected text, placing it in the Clipboard
7	Pastes the contents of the Clipboard at the insertion point

	Meaning
8	Changes typeface
9	Spell check
10	Inserts bullets and numbering

WordPerfect Button Bar

This is the default button bar displayed when you first install and start WordPerfect. Otherwise, it is displayed by selecting File/Preferences/Button Bar, choosing WordPerfect, then clicking on Select.

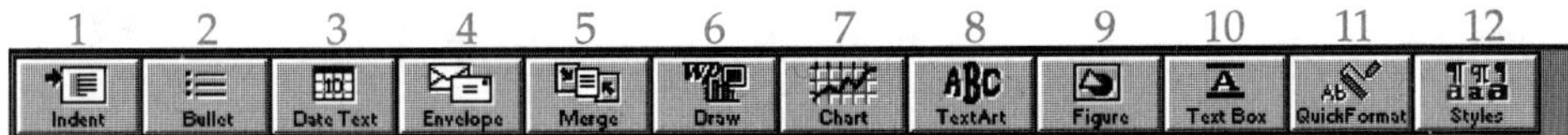

	Meaning
1	Indents left side of paragraph one tab stop
2	Inserts bullets and numbering
3	Inserts the current date
4	Creates an envelope
5	Works with form and data files, or merges them together
6	Creates a graphic with WP Draw
7	Creates a chart with WP Draw
8	Treats text as a graphic, applying special effects
9	Inserts a figure
10	Inserts a text box
11	Copies formatting attributes
12	Defines or selects styles

Miscellaneous Icons

Each of the icons in this section can be viewed by choosing File Preferences, which displays the Preferences dialog box.

Icon	Meaning
	Displays the Display Preferences dialog box
	Displays the Environment dialog box
	Displays the File Preferences dialog box
	Displays the Document Summary Preferences dialog box
	Displays the Button Bar Preferences dialog box
	Displays the Power Bar Preferences dialog box
	Displays the Status Bar Preferences dialog box
	Displays the Keyboard Preferences dialog box
	Displays the Menu Bar Preferences dialog box
	Displays the Writing Tools dialog box
	Displays the Print Preferences dialog box
	Displays the Import Preferences dialog box

Index

C

D

E

G

H

I

L

M

N

Q

R

S

T

Z